❋ FOLK AND FAIRY TALES ❋

D1546493

FOLK & FAIRY TALES

FIFTH EDITION

EDITED BY

MARTIN HALLETT & BARBARA KARASEK

broadview press

BROADVIEW PRESS – www.broadviewpress.com
Peterborough, Ontario, Canada

Founded in 1985, Broadview Press remains a wholly independent publishing house. Broadview's focus is on academic publishing; our titles are accessible to university and college students as well as scholars and general readers. With over 600 titles in print, Broadview has become a leading international publisher in the humanities, with world-wide distribution. Broadview is committed to environmentally responsible publishing and fair business practices.

The interior of this book is printed on 30% recycled paper.

PERMANENT   BIO GAS ENERGY   30%

Library and Archives Canada Cataloguing in Publication

Folk & fairy tales / edited by Martin Hallett & Barbara Karasek. — Fifth edition.

Includes bibliographical references.
ISBN 978-1-55481-365-0 (softcover)

1. Fairy tales. 2. Tales. 3. Folk literature—History and criticism. 4. Fairy tales—History and criticism. I. Hallett, Martin, 1944-, editor II. Karasek, Barbara, 1954-, editor III. Title: Folk and fairy tales.

PZ8.F65 2018   398.2   C2018-901814-3

Broadview Press handles its own distribution in North America:
PO Box 1243, Peterborough, Ontario K9J 7H5, Canada
555 Riverwalk Parkway, Tonawanda, NY 14150, USA
Tel: (705) 743-8990; Fax: (705) 743-8353
email: customerservice@broadviewpress.com

Distribution is handled by Eurospan Group in the UK, Europe, Central Asia, Middle East, Africa, India, Southeast Asia, Central America, South America, and the Caribbean. Distribution is handled by Footprint Books in Australia and New Zealand.

Broadview Press acknowledges the financial support of the Government of Canada through the Canada Book Fund for our publishing activities.

Copy-edited by Martin R. Boyne
Book Design by George Kirkpatrick

PRINTED IN CANADA

CONTENTS

PREFACE • 9
INTRODUCTION • 13

LITTLE RED RIDING HOOD • 25
    The Story of Grandmother, *Paul Delarue* • 28
    The False Grandmother, *Italo Calvino* • 30
    Little Red Riding Hood, *Charles Perrault* • 32
    Little Red Cap, *Jacob and Wilhelm Grimm* • 34
    Lon Po Po: A Red-Riding Hood Story from China, *Ed Young* • 37

CINDERELLA • 40
    Cinderella: or The Little Glass Slipper, *Charles Perrault* • 43
    Ashputtle, *Jacob and Wilhelm Grimm* • 48
    Cap o' Rushes, *Joseph Jacobs* • 53
    Vasilisa the Beautiful, *Aleksandr Afanas'ev* • 57
    Little Gold Star, *Joe Hayes* • 63
    The Little Red Fish and the Clog of Gold, *Inea Bushnaq* • 68
    The Indian Cinderella, *Cyrus Macmillan* • 73

SLEEPING BEAUTY • 76
    Sun, Moon, and Talia (*Sole, Lune, e Talia*), *Giambattista Basile* • 79
    The Sleeping Beauty in the Wood, *Charles Perrault* • 83
    Brier Rose, *Jacob and Wilhelm Grimm* • 89

GROWING UP (IS HARD TO DO) • 92
    Hansel and Gretel, *Jacob and Wilhelm Grimm* • 96
    Snow White, *Jacob and Wilhelm Grimm* • 101
    Rapunzel, *Jacob and Wilhelm Grimm* • 108

The Frog King, or Iron Heinrich, *Jacob and Wilhelm Grimm* • 110
Jack and the Beanstalk, *Joseph Jacobs* • 113
The Ugly Duckling, *Hans Christian Andersen* • 118

THE NATURE OF LOVE • 126
Beauty and the Beast, *Madame Leprince de Beaumont* • 128
East of the Sun and West of the Moon, *Asbjørnsen and Moe* • 138
The Little Mermaid, *Hans Christian Andersen* • 146
The Woman of the Sea, *Helen Waddell* • 162

BRAIN OVER BRAWN (THE TRICKSTER) • 165
The Brave Little Tailor, *Jacob and Wilhelm Grimm* • 168
The Emperor's New Clothes, *Hans Christian Andersen* • 173
Clever Gretel, *Jacob and Wilhelm Grimm* • 177
Flossie and the Fox, *Patricia C. McKissack* • 179
Puss in Boots, *Charles Perrault* • 183
The Story of the Three Little Pigs, *Joseph Jacobs* • 186
The Death of Brer Wolf, *Julius Lester* • 189
From Tiger to Anansi, *Philip M. Sherlock* • 190

VILLAINS • 194
The Juniper Tree, *Jacob and Wilhelm Grimm* • 197
Bluebeard, *Charles Perrault* • 204
Rumpelstiltskin, *Jacob and Wilhelm Grimm* • 208

THE "CAULDRON OF STORY" • 211
The Neapolitan Soldier, *Italo Calvino* • 212
Molly Whuppie, *Joseph Jacobs* • 216
The Young Slave, *Giambattista Basile* • 219
The Robber Bridegroom, *Jacob and Wilhelm Grimm* • 222
The Pig King, *Giovanni Francesco Straparola* • 225
The Frog Maiden, *Maung Htin Aung* • 230

NEW WINE IN OLD BOTTLES • 234
Little Red Riding Hood, *David McPhail* • 238
The Company of Wolves, *Angela Carter* • 240
Wolf, *Francesca Lia Block* • 248
The Sleeping Beauty in the Wood, *Anne Thackeray Ritchie* • 254
When the Clock Strikes, *Tanith Lee* • 266

CONTENTS

The Wicked Stepmother's Lament, *Sara Maitland* • 279

Snow White, *The Merseyside Fairy Story Collective* • 284

Snow, Glass, Apples, *Neil Gaiman* • 290

The Tale of the Rose, *Emma Donoghue* • 300

The Fourth Pig, *Naomi Mitchison* • 305

The Three Little Pigs, *James Finn Garner* • 307

Little Man, *Michael Cunningham* • 308

ILLUSTRATION • 320

Little Red Riding Hood: About a Girl and a Wolf • 322

Sleeping Beauty: From One to Many • 324

Hansel and Gretel: Whether to Laugh or to Cry • 325

Snow White: Shades of Gray • 327

Beauty and the Beast: Getting to Know You • 328

On the Psychiatrist's Couch • 330

Different Worlds: Wouldn't It Be Nice ...? • 331

Once Upon a (Particular) Time • 332

Cauldron of Story—Postmodern Style • 333

Postscript: Some Day My Prince Will Come ... or Not • 335

CRITICISM • 338

On Fairy-Stories, *J.R.R. Tolkien* • 342

The Fairy-Tale Hero: The Image of Man in the Fairy-Tale, *Max Lüthi* • 367

The Struggle for Meaning, *Bruno Bettelheim* • 375

Fairy Tales from a Folkloristic Perspective, *Alan Dundes* • 387

Feminist Fairy-Tale Scholarship, *Donald Haase* • 394

From Traditional Tales, Fairy Stories, and Cautionary Tales to Controversial
   Visual Texts: Do We Need to Be Fearful?, *Sandra L. Beckett* • 408

Did They Live Happily Ever After? Rewriting Fairy Tales for a Contemporary
   Audience, *Laura Tosi* • 432

Disney Revisited, Or, Jiminy Cricket, It's Musty Down Here!,
   Betsy Hearne • 452

Techno-Magic: Cinema and Fairy Tale, *Marina Warner* • 459

The End of Fairy Tales? How Shrek and Friends Have Changed Children's
   Stories, *James Poniewozik* • 466

SELECT BIBLIOGRAPHY • 470

SOURCES • 476

PREFACE

The more things change, the more they remain the same.

WE BEGAN THE PREFACE OF the previous edition of *Folk and Fairy Tales* with the above proverb and see no reason to change it now; as before, we hope that the changes and additions we have made in this new edition result in an anthology that provides a yet more effective and enjoyable introduction to the study of fairy tales.

Once again, we had to keep reminding ourselves that this book is, first and foremost, an *introduction*. From the beginning, we have seen the typical reader of *Folk and Fairy Tales* as a student returning—perhaps somewhat skeptically—to the fairy tale for the first time since elementary school or kindergarten—perhaps even professing to remember nothing about fairy tales that wasn't derived from a Disney movie. Therefore, to revise our selection of tales or criticism purely for the sake of modernity would have been inappropriate; in striving for that elusive happy balance, we have tried to avoid making changes for change's sake. At the same time, the valuable and much appreciated feedback that we have received from those who have used *Folk and Fairy Tales* in the classroom has helped us greatly in adjusting both our selection of tales and the manner in which we present them, both to introduce some lesser-known versions of famous tales and to encourage comparison between versions of one tale or categories of several.

The distinguished American critic Leslie Fiedler (1917–2003) once observed that children's books introduce all the plots used in adult works and that adult responses are frequently based on forgotten or dimly remembered works from childhood. This is particularly true of fairy tales, which, in providing much of our earliest literary and imaginative experience, have surely exerted an enormous influence over us. The goal of this anthology, therefore, is to draw attention not only to the fascination inherent in the tales themselves but also to the insights of some critics who have demonstrated, from a variety of perspectives—folkloric, psychological, feminist, historical, and cultural—that fairy tales have a complexity belied by their humble origins.

Furthermore, fairy tales can have great pedagogical value for teachers and students of literature. The increasing multiculturalism of our society has brought with it many riches; at the same time, however, it presents a problem for the teacher who must endeavor to find some common ground for students from diverse cultural, social, and intellectual backgrounds. In this context, the fairy tale offers a unique opportunity to introduce students to a literary form that is familiar and simple, yet multidimensional. No student can claim to be wholly ignorant of fairy tales, but it is highly unlikely that he or she has ever gone beyond their surface simplicity to discover the surprisingly subtle complexities that lie beneath.

Because the pedagogical technique of challenging expectations has been a major principle influencing our choice and juxtaposition of tales, most of those selected will quickly be recognized as "classics." It must be pointed out, however, that despite their popularity, these well-known tales are not representative of the international body of fairy tales. We did not set out to make our selection comprehensive, since it was our feeling that the greatest advantage could be achieved by guiding students through familiar territory while introducing some new perspectives. It will be the students' task, then, to apply these and other critical approaches more widely, not only to other fairy tales but also to the whole world of literature.

Those familiar with earlier editions of this book will note some changes in our presentation of the tales. We have reorganized our sections to the extent that both comparative and thematic groupings now contain only "classic" tales and some lesser-known variants from other cultures; modern retellings of these and other tales can be found in the "New Wine in Old Bottles" section, which draws attention to the changes that the modern sensibility has seen fit to make to the old tales.

We take a leaf out of the inestimable J.R.R. Tolkien's book (or, more accurately, essay) for the title of a new section, the "Cauldron of Story," which invites the reader to disentangle the various threads that make up many tales. Indeed, we are pleased to reintroduce an excerpt from this seminal essay, written by Tolkien in 1938, which continues to be one of the most definitive pieces ever written on the subject.

Each group of tales is preceded by a critical introduction that begins the process of placing the tale in context. We point out some of the issues that may well have inspired these stories in the first place and outline some of the reactions that they have in turn provoked. One of our objectives has been to show how the creative imagination has worked on and developed the fairy tale, particularly in the sampling of contemporary stories.

We have also expanded the Illustration section, the better to show how modern artists are adopting some radically new perspectives in their interpretation of the tales and also to take note of the evolution of the tale in the comic book and graphic novel.

As with the tales, so with the critical selections, where our goal is to provide the student with a representative sampling of different critical analyses of the fairy tale. As before, our choice has been governed by the fact that this is an introductory anthology; accordingly, we have attempted to make our current selection of essays a judicious balance between old and new that in our view presents wide-ranging and sometimes controversial ideas about the fairy tale.

INTRODUCTION

"FAIRY TALE" IS A PHRASE that is often used rather loosely. A dictionary will probably tell us that it is a story about fairies (which is rarely the case) or else that it is an unbelievable or untrue story (which reflects the rationalistic criticism to which the fairy tale has been subjected). This vagueness of definition has made the term something of a catchall: Lewis Carroll, for instance, described *Through the Looking-Glass* (1871) as a fairy tale, and Andrew Lang saw fit to include an abridged version of Book 1 of Jonathan Swift's *Gulliver's Travels* ("A Voyage to Lilliput") in his *Blue Fairy Book* (1889). So let us clarify the subject a little by introducing two more specific terms: "folk tale" and "literary tale." Once we have established the essential difference between these two terms, we will be in a better position to appreciate the many permutations that have evolved over the years.

"Folk tale" means exactly what it says: it's a tale of the folk. If we resort again to our dictionary, we will learn that "folk" signifies the common people of a nation—and the important point to realize here is that the "common people" were, in the past, generally illiterate. Consequently, their tales were orally transmitted; in other words, they were passed down from generation to generation by word of mouth, until they were eventually recorded and published by such famous individuals as Charles Perrault and Jacob and Wilhelm Grimm. Because we hear so often of "Perrault's Fairy Tales" or of "Tales of the Brothers Grimm," it's natural to assume that these men actually made them up, but that isn't the case; while all three were highly accomplished literary men, none of them were fairy-tale writers. They wrote them *down*, thereby creating what we may term a literary folk tale. The extent of the literary component has become a source of considerable controversy in recent years, in that some fairy-tale researchers[1] have argued that the origins of the fairy tale are

---

1   The most notable advocate for this point of view is Ruth Bottigheimer; see her work *Fairy Tales: A New History* (Albany: SUNY P, 2009).

exclusively literary and that the concept of the tale as a distillation of the wisdom and imagination of the folk is therefore little more than a romantic (and Romantic) illusion.

Consider for a moment what happens when a tale is transposed from oral performance. Even if the collectors of earlier times had had modern recording devices at their disposal, they still could not have published the tales exactly as they had heard them, for the simple reason that the spoken language is very different from the written. In his Foreword to Zora Neale Hurston's collection of Black American tales *Every Tongue Got to Confess*, John Edgar Wideman writes, "All spoken language of course resists exact phonetic inscription" and notes that there are dimensions to verbal art that are necessarily missing: "the immediacy and sensuousness of face-to-face encounter, the spontaneous improvisation of call and response … the voice played as a musical instrument, the kinetics of the speaker."[1]

In most cases, we have no idea how old folk tales are. Once a tale has been told, it is gone; no trace of it remains except in the memories of the teller and the audience. And for the great majority of people today, memory is a fickle instrument—we only have to think back to that examination, or to the last time we lost the shopping list, to realize how quickly (and how thoroughly) we forget. We are thus confronted with the realization that the only authentic version of the folk tale is an oral version—and since one telling will necessarily differ from the next, we must confer authenticity equally on all tellings, or—even more problematic—on the first telling alone, wherever and whenever that may have taken place.

The children's party game "Broken Telephone" provides us with an idea of just how a folk tale may have evolved as it was passed on from generation to generation. The first player begins by whispering a phrase or sentence to his or her neighbor, who must then pass it on to the next, and so on until it reaches the last individual in the chain. Needless to say, in the progress from first to last, the words undergo some startling and often amusing changes, as they are variously misheard, misunderstood, or improved upon. On the simplest level, the game entertains by allowing us to play around with language and intention; on a more sophisticated level, we might see those changes as reflecting the preoccupations (conscious or otherwise) of the players. To put it another way, our moods, desires, and emotions will inevitably affect what is heard; we hear what we want (or expect) to hear. So it is with the folk tale: what we find there is—in part—a fragment of psychic history. An archaeologist unearths a piece of pottery and uses his or her professional experience and knowledge to determine its significance and function in the wider context. In the same way, we

---

1   John Edgar Wideman, "Foreword," in Zora Neale Hurston, *Every Tongue Got to Confess: Negro Folk-Tales from the Gulf States* (New York: HarperCollins, 2001), xv, xvii.

can use our growing familiarity with folk tales to identify some of the psychological elements (the "preoccupations") that give each tale much of its energy and color.

It would be an exaggeration, however, to claim that in a literate culture the oral tale is entirely a thing of the past. Trevor J. Blank quotes the distinguished folklorist Alan Dundes as saying—as early as 1980—that "[t]echnology isn't stamping out folklore; rather, it is becoming a vital factor in the transmission of folklore and it is providing an exciting source of inspiration for the generation of new folklorists."[1] Although the urban legend is much more localized and anecdotal than the folk tale and is characterized by sensationalism and black humor, it too has its origins in aspects of life that provoke anxiety or insecurity, such as our ambivalence toward technology or our suspicion that beneath the veneer of normalcy lurk chaos and madness. As with the folk tale, the "orality" of the Internet is short-lived; Robert Thompson points out that "we have really returned here, in spite of the centralization of technology, to the old-fashioned definition of what folk culture used to be.... We have these jokes and stories that will never see the printed page that exist only as glowing dots of phosphorous. It's not word-of-mouth folk culture but word-of-modem culture."[2] It is intriguing to consider the extent to which the Internet is itself part of the story, a kind of post-literate flux where the word is neither oral nor literate but shares qualities of both.

Today, the status and role of the storyteller are rather different; he or she is more often to be found in the rarefied atmosphere of library or classroom than in the lively informality of market-place or communal festivity. However, there is a difference between what we might term "formal" and "informal" entertainment. "Formal" entertainment is what we consciously seek out for ourselves, generally at some expense. There is a clear and traditional separation between performer and audience, in which the latter plays a passive role as consumer, purchasing the entertainment "product." If we look at "informal" entertainment, however, we find ourselves in surroundings much more congenial to storytelling, because the grouping (as opposed to audience) is likely to be spontaneous and transitory, such as at a cafeteria table or a party. This is not to suggest that there will be an exchange of folk tales in these more intimate settings, but there may well be some storytelling, albeit of a very local and personal nature. Nevertheless, the point can be made that that's probably the way in which many tales originated; the great majority died as quickly as they were born, a few managed a brief existence, and a tiny number contained that mysterious seed of delight, universality, or wisdom that allowed them to beat the odds and survive.

What is emerging, then, is the fact that the fairy tale must be seen as a continuum.

---

1   Alan Dundes, qtd. in Trevor J. Blank, ed., *Folklore and the Internet: Vernacular Expression in a Digital World* (Logan: Utah State UP, 2009), 5.

2   Robert Thompson, qtd. in Blank 7.

At one extreme we find the oral folk tale, which by its very nature cannot be represented in this book. As we have already observed, the oral tale's transformation into literary form requires careful analysis, not only of the tale itself but also of the motives and values of those responsible for its metamorphosis. At the other extreme there is the literary tale, written by a specific person at a specific time, which allows us to readily place the tale in its original context, as we might do in examining any other literary work. In between these two poles, however, we have an almost unlimited number of variations, as tradition blends with invention in the writer's mind. Given this wide range of possibilities, the more general term "fairy tale" is useful in its comprehensiveness.

★ ★ ★

The first two literary collections of fairy tales in the Western tradition are by Italians whose names are relatively unknown outside scholarly circles: Giovanni Francesco Straparola (c. 1480–c. 1557), who published *The Facetious Nights* (1550), and Giambattista Basile (c. 1575–1632), the collector/writer of *The Pentamerone* (1634–36). Unfamiliar though these collections may be, they contain early versions of many tales that would later be made famous by Charles Perrault and the Grimm brothers. Both these men clearly recognized the vitality and appeal of folk tales and brought them to the attention of a literate *adult* audience, adapting and embellishing them as contemporary literary style and social taste demanded. Another similarity shared by these fairy-tale collections is that they are both built around a frame story—a third and celebrated example of which would arrive in the shape of Antoine Galland's translation into French of the *Arabian Nights* (1704).

Even before Perrault published his now-famous collection, the popularity of the fairy tale was growing among the French upper classes, which often gathered in fashionable "salons" to discuss matters of cultural and artistic interest. One outcome of these discussions was an enthusiasm for writing highly stylized literary tales based upon folk-tale models, especially among aristocratic women such as Madame la Comtesse D'Aulnoy (the first author to use the phrase "contes des fées") in 1698, and Madame la Comtesse de Murat. Like Perrault, these aristocratic ladies saw the folk tale as in need of "improvement," and consequently their tales tell us a good deal about eighteenth-century aristocratic manners and present a "feminist" perspective that gives the tales a distinctly contemporary edge. period ‼

However, the most famous name among the French writers/collectors of fairy tales at the beginning of the eighteenth century was Charles Perrault (1628–1703). An influential government bureaucrat in Louis XIV's France, he was involved in a vigorous literary debate of the time known as the Quarrel of the Ancients and the Moderns, in which the "Ancients" were those who asserted the superiority of classical literature and art, while the "Moderns" were of the view that contemporary works were pre-eminent, since they could draw on all the achievements of cultural and social progress. In publishing his collection of fairy tales, *Stories or Tales from Past Times, with Morals* (1697), Perrault made his Modernist credentials clear, since the tales were both French and very un-classical! Yet while this debate is now of interest only to literary historians, his introduction of these tales of the peasants into courtly society showed a little touch of genius. At the same time, we should also assume that Perrault was familiar with the versions of these folk tales written by his predecessors Straparola and Basile, such that Perrault's particular achievement is one of synthesizing literary sophistication with oral simplicity. The daily lives of rural peasant and urban bourgeois (not to mention aristocrat) were literally worlds apart—and Perrault responded to that fact.

One hundred years later, the joint stimuli of nationalism and Romanticism were the driving forces behind the Grimm brothers' fascination with folk tales. At a time of great political and social upheaval, caused first by French occupation and then by the process of unification as the modern Germany was being forged out of a patchwork of tiny states and principalities, there was a growing need to answer a new question: what does it mean to be German? At the same time, they were responding to the contemporary Romantic creed that the true spirit of a people was to be found not in the palaces or even the cities, but in the countryside, far away from urban sophistication. Jacob (1785–1863) and Wilhelm (1786–1859) Grimm might be described as archaeologists of a sort—although contrary to what was once believed, they were rarely if ever involved with any "digs" that first discovered these tales among the unlettered country folk. Such is the pre-eminence of the Grimms' collection *Kinder- und Hausmärchen* (first published 1812–15; published later in English as *Tales for Young and Old*, 1823) that we tend to regard it as being almost as organic and timeless a phenomenon as the tales themselves. It is nevertheless a fact that in more recent times, controversy has swirled around the Grimms' methodology and motivation in assembling their collection. The image of the brothers roaming the German countryside, gathering the tales in remote villages and hamlets, is attractive but false; generally, they were contributed by literate, middle-class friends and relatives, who thus represent yet another intermediary stage between the oral folk tale, on the one hand, and the literary tale on the other. Indeed, the claim made by the Grimms in the Preface to the Second Edition of their tales (1819)—"we have not embellished any detail or feature of the story told itself, but rather rendered its content just as we received it"[1]—appears confusing, given ample evidence to the

---

1   Joyce Crick, *Jacob and Wilhelm Grimm Selected Tales* (London: Oxford UP, 2005), 8. See also Zohar Shavit, *Poetics of Children's Literature* (Athens, GA, and London: U of Georgia P, 1986), 20–27.

contrary. We should not forget, however, that the scholarly brothers were pioneers in revising these tales for an audience radically different from the illiterate country folk among whom they originated. Ralph Manheim, the translator of the Grimm tales in this anthology, asserts that the brothers' genius was in "mak[ing] us hear the voices of the individual storytellers…. In the German text the human voice takes on a wide variety of tones…. But everywhere—or almost—it is a natural human voice, speaking as someone might speak…."[1] And once their popularity among children became apparent, Wilhelm in particular assumed the responsibility of ensuring that the tales were made suitable for the eyes of the child, according to contemporary notions about children's reading.

Yet we should not assume that the Grimms were alone in collecting folktales in the nineteenth century. Even as their tales remain pre-eminent in the public eye, scholars have in recent years brought to our attention several other important collections made later in the century, two of which are from Sicily: Giuseppe Pitrè compiled the encyclopedic *Library of Sicilian Popular Traditions* (1871–1913) in 25 volumes; Laura Gonzenbach published a two-volume collection of Sicilian folktales in 1870. We should note that, like the Grimms in Germany, Pitrè was at least in part inspired by a political movement (known in Italy as the *Risorgimento*) seeking national unification; Franz Xaver von Schönwerth recorded more than 500 folktales from the Upper Palatinate region of Germany where he lived.[2] Erika Eichenseer, who discovered Schönwerth's collection in a German municipal archive, tells us that "[this] enthusiastic nineteenth-century folklorist and collector of tales had recognized that his era was witnessing a rapid decline in oral storytelling traditions. For that reason, he and his friends made the rounds, asking for stories from plainspoken men and women within the confines of their native territory…. This is oral history in the truest sense of the term."[3]

Even when we come to the tales of Hans Christian Andersen (1805–75), the link with folk tale remains strong. We perceive Andersen to be a writer of original fairy tales rather than a collector, and we assume, therefore, that his tales were exclusively of his own invention. What we need to consider is that Andersen came from a

---

1   Ralph Manheim, "Preface," *Grimms' Tales for Young and Old* (Garden City, NY: Anchor P, 1977), 1. Reference to the translator's role alerts us to the presence of yet another intermediary in the fairy tale's journey from its oral origins to the pages of this book; almost all of the traditional tales have been translated into English.

2   Giuseppe Pitrè, *The Collected Sicilian Folk and Fairy Tales of Giuseppe Pitrè*, trans. and ed. Jack Zipes and Joseph Russo (New York: Routledge, 2008); Laura Gonzenbach, collector, *Beautiful Angiola: The Lost Sicilian Folk and Fairy Tales of Laura Gonzenbach*, trans. Jack Zipes (New York: Routledge, 2005); Franz Xaver von Schönwerth, *The Turnip Princess and Other Newly Discovered Fairy Tales*, trans. Maria Tatar (New York: Penguin, 2015).

3   Erika Eichenseer, Foreword, in Schönwerth ix.

poor, working-class background in which the oral folk tale was common currency; consequently, his imagination was well primed before the world of literacy opened up new vistas of fancy to him. So it is hardly surprising to discover that several of Andersen's better-known tales, such as "The Tinderbox" (1835) and "The Emperor's New Clothes" (1837), either allude to or are retellings of traditional stories—some that he heard, and some that he read. We should bear in mind that Andersen was barely a generation younger than the Grimm brothers and was well acquainted with them; ironically, it appears that on at least one occasion the folk tale owed a debt to Andersen: in 1843 the Grimms published a tale that closely resembled "The Princess and the Pea." However, Andersen's literary contribution to the fairy tale differs from that of the Grimms in the sense that, while the latter were concerned primarily with presenting their tales in the most acceptable form to the German people, Andersen had a much more personal involvement with his tales. In his hands, a tale, whatever its source, became yet another opportunity for self-revelation. (It is no coincidence that he entitled one of his autobiographies *The Fairytale of My Life*.) As we have already seen, a knowledge of the historical context of the tales adds an extra dimension to our appreciation of them; in the case of Andersen and the other fairy-tale writers, that aspect becomes more specific, in the sense that we can now place the tales in a personal context as well as a social one.

In the course of the nineteenth century, the fairy tale attracted the attention of a varied group of writers, which suggests that the form retained an energy that survived the transformation from oral tale to literary text. From the mysticism of George MacDonald to the feminism of Anne Ritchie (see p. 254) and the exoticism of Oscar Wilde, the tale offered a flexibility that accommodated some very diverse talents. (Earlier in the century, Charles Dickens was chastising his illustrator George Cruikshank for turning fairy tales into temperance propaganda.[1]) There is no question, however, that many of these writers saw their primary audience as children. Even Charles Perrault, at the end of the seventeenth century, had some awareness of the appeal of fairy tales for children, as is indicated by the frontispiece of the 1697 edition of his tales, with its inscription "Contes de ma Mère L'Oye" ("Tales of Mother Goose") and its depiction of an old woman spinning while she spins her yarn (!) to a group of children. The assumption is extended by his addition of explicit morals to the tales, thus making them overtly cautionary in nature. It is the narrator's ironic tone and occasional comment that betray his interest in appealing to an older, more sophisticated audience.

In England, the presence of the fairy tale in children's literature of the eighteenth century likewise depended on its ability to provide moral instruction. With its fantastic and sometimes violent and amoral content, the fairy tale elicited disapproval

---

1 Charles Dickens, *Household Words: A Weekly Journal*, Vol. VIII, No. 184 (1 Oct. 1853): 97–100.

from both the upholders of Puritan attitudes and the growing advocates of the more rational outlook exemplified in the philosophy and influential educational theories of John Locke. In their efforts to provide children with stories of virtue and piety, both the Rational and the Sunday School Moralists of the late eighteenth and nineteenth centuries also looked upon this popular literature with a consternation verging on horror. In the periodical *The Guardian of Education*, its editor, the influential Sarah Trimmer, warned parents and governesses of the dangers of fairy tales: "A moment's consideration will surely be sufficient to convince people of the least reflection, of the danger, as well as the impropriety, of putting such books as these into the hands of little children, whose minds are susceptible to every impression; and who from the liveliness of their imaginations are apt to convert into realities whatever forcibly strikes their fancy."[1]

Despite this persistent disapproval, however, the tales were made available to eighteenth-century children through a somewhat less "respectable" source of reading material—crudely illustrated chapbooks, in many respects the distant forebears of modern comic books. The purveyors of this popular literature would not have had the scruples of the more reputable publishers, such as John Newbery, who sought to uphold the current educational theories of Locke. Chapbook publishers recognized the attraction of tales of fantasy and imagination and sought to provide them cheaply—generally by means of traveling pedlars—to the folk, child and adult alike. Thus the folk tale had, in a sense, come full circle. In being written down, it had been taken from the illiterate folk; now, as literacy was spreading slowly through the population, the tale could be returned—at a price—to where it came from.

During the early years of the nineteenth century, the Romantics would counter the prevailing criticism of fairy tales and denounce the moralizing and utilitarian books that were being produced for children. In his affirmation of the value of fantasy in his early reading, the poet Samuel Taylor Coleridge reacted against the common disapproval of such literature: "Should children be permitted to read Romances, and Relations of Giants and Magicians and Genii?—I know all that has been said against it; but I have formed my faith in the affirmative—I know no other way of giving the mind a love of 'the great' and 'the Whole.'"[2]

---

1   Sarah Trimmer, "Nursery Tales," *The Guardian of Education* 4 (1805): 74–75, qtd. in *Children and Literature: Views and Reviews*, ed. Virginia Haviland (Glenview, IL: Scott and Foresman, 1973), 7. Trimmer's views persist to this day. In 2011, the UK television channel "W" commissioned a survey of 2,000 adults to mark the launch of the TV series *Grimm* in the United States: along with a general anxiety about the effects of fairy tales upon children were issues such as violence ("Little Red Riding Hood"), child abandonment ("Hansel and Gretel"), and kidnapping ("Rumpelstiltskin").

2   Earl Leslie Griggs, ed., *Collected Letters of Samuel Taylor Coleridge, 1785–1800*, vol. 1 (Oxford: Clarendon P, 1956), 354.

Although resistance to the fairy tale continued throughout the nineteenth century, when the Grimms' fairy tales appeared in England in 1823 they were immediately popular. In the preface to his translation of the tales, Edgar Taylor's one reservation regarding imaginative stories was that they should not interfere with moral education. Despite the success of the Brothers Grimm's work, it would be another twenty years before the fairy tale was fully embraced as literature for children. During the 1840s, the translation into English of Andersen's literary tales gave rise to the publication of a number of fairy-tale collections, which reached its apogee almost fifty years later in Andrew Lang's "color" series, beginning with the *Blue Fairy Book* (1889). After the success of the Grimms' tales, the arrival of Andersen's work represented an important next step in the restitution of the fairy tale, although disapproving voices could still be heard. As Jack Zipes observes, "[Andersen's] unusual tales, which combined fantasy with a moral impulse in line with traditional Christian standards, guaranteed the legitimacy of the literary fairy tale for middle-class audiences."[1] Thus, after centuries of criticism and banishment to the trade of the chapman, fairy tales and fantasy finally achieved the status they have never since lost—that of "approved" literature for children.

The second half of the nineteenth century witnessed the period that is often referred to as the Golden Age of children's literature. It may also have been the time when the lines became blurred as to just what constituted a fairy tale, since many of the works published for children were fantasies, beginning with Lewis Carroll's *Alice's Adventures in Wonderland* (1865)—and as we have already noted, Carroll himself referred to its sequel *Through the Looking-Glass* (1871) as a fairy tale. Be that as it may, the fairy tale evolved in several ways: it grew longer (as in the work of writers such as George MacDonald and Andrew Lang), more didactic (Charles Kingsley's *The Water Babies* and the stories of Mary Louisa Molesworth are examples), and more focused upon social issues.[2] Indeed, this last point raises an interesting paradox in the literary tale's evolution from the folk tale. Despite the *collective* nature of the folk tale's composition, its concerns are generally those of the individual, such as growing up, establishing a relationship, and so on. When we turn to the literary tale, it is attributable to a *single* writer but now tends to deal with social (i.e., collective) subjects.

However, in the process of becoming so closely associated with children, fairy tales have all too often been dismissed as literature not worthy of serious attention

---

1   Jack Zipes, "Introduction," *Victorian Fairy Tales: The Revolt of the Fairies and Elves* (New York: Methuen, 1987), xviii.

2   In *The Victorian Press and the Fairy Tale* (Basingstoke: Palgrave Macmillan, 2008), Caroline Sumpter points to the "continual politicisation of the fairy tale," which resulted in an "intersection between Victorian children's literature, working-class culture and socialist educational practices" (88). It is not surprising to find that "Cinderella" was an important tool in the socialist movement.

on the part of adult readers. In his pioneering essay "On Fairy-Stories" (1938), J.R.R. Tolkien, author of the fantasy works *The Hobbit* and *Lord of the Rings*, was among the first to point out that this association of fairy stories with children is a historical accident and that children "neither like fairy stories more, nor understand them better than they like many other things" (p. 343). Tolkien saw fairy stories as a natural branch of literature sharing the same qualities as may be found in many other genres.

It certainly can be argued that the fairy tale has regained an adult audience in recent times, as the modern tales in this anthology demonstrate. The surprise is in the fact that these tales have been out of favor for so long among older readers, since, as Max Lüthi observes in *Once Upon a Time: On the Nature of Fairy Tales* (1970), fairy tales present us with both adult and child triumphing over their (and our) deepest fears and desires. Perhaps we have been the victims of our own rationalistic preconceptions of what a fairy tale actually is and what it has to say to us. Bruno Bettelheim's observation that at each stage of our lives, fairy tales take on new significance and "speak simultaneously to all levels of the human personality, communicating in a manner which reaches the uneducated mind of the child as well as that of the sophisticated adult" (p. 378) was hardly a revelation in itself, but the impact that his book *The Uses of Enchantment: The Meaning and Importance of Fairy Tales* made when it was published in 1976 suggests that the time was ripe for a reappraisal—a project that has produced a substantial body of scholarship.

For the past fifty years, both writers and illustrators have revised and re-imagined virtually the whole canon of classic fairy tales—a development equally apparent in the visual media. The level of sophistication in these texts varies enormously: Jon Scieszka and Lane Smith's *The Stinky Cheese Man and Other Fairly Stupid Fairy Tales* (1992) and David Wiesner's *The Three Pigs* (2001) are veritable deconstructions of the picture-book concept, while Bill Willingham's *Fables* comic-book series (2002–15) and graphic novels such as Shannon Hale's *Rapunzel's Revenge* (2008) and Matt Phelan's *Snow White* (2016) have carried the fairy tale into a radically different visual world.

A similar range of ambition can be found in novella-length retellings intended for the young-adult reader (primarily female) by authors such as Jane Yolen, Robin McKinley, and Donna Jo Napoli, whose work—not surprisingly—tends to focus upon those tales that deal with the challenges of growing up female. The fairy tale has made inroads into adult fiction as well; several well-known novelists (Margaret Atwood, A.S. Byatt, and Gregory Maguire among them) have acknowledged the deep and abiding influence that fairy tales have had on their own writing. And for those who remain unconvinced about how deeply embedded the fairy tale is in our collective unconscious, we offer for your consideration such titles as *From*

Cinderella to CEO: How to Master the 10 Lessons of Fairy Tales to Transform Your Work Life (2005), *Computational Fairy Tales* (2012), and, from the *Fairy Tales Gone Wrong* series, *Blow Your Nose, Big Bad Wolf!: A Story About Spreading Germs* (2014)—or a selection from the "Once Upon a Spell" series of Adult Fairytale Romance (reader discretion is advised). What emerges is that the fairy tale remains as relevant, democratic, and adaptable as it has ever been in its long history. *(Kinda wanna read those though!)*

Without a doubt, however, the most significant development for the fairy tale in the twentieth century and beyond has come in film. The screening of *Snow White and the Seven Dwarfs* in 1937 launched the phenomenal influence that the Walt Disney studios have exerted ever since upon our experience of the fairy tale. Over eighty years and numerous films later, the Disney animation likely remains the first contact with fairy tale that people all over the world have had. No doubt reluctant to relinquish this domination, the Disney Organization has in recent years been reinventing its own classical repertoire in live-action format, whether by adopting the popular strategy of rehabilitating the villain (thus *Sleeping Beauty* becomes *Maleficent*, 2014) or by earnestly paying tribute to the original (as in *Beauty and the Beast*, 2017). Not surprisingly, the long-running television series *Once Upon a Time*, which started in 2011, is to be found on the ABC network, which is also owned by Disney. *(⟶ YES! BEST SHOW EVER! ♡ you Killian Jones ♡)*

For better or for worse, Walt Disney (1901–66)—like all storytellers, collectors, and rewriters—has put his own imprint upon the tales. However, unlike his predecessors, he combined the power of the film medium with the Disney entertainment empire (Disney World and Disneyland, where we can meet and dine with Cinderella and Sleeping Beauty) to both disseminate and commercialize his vision to an unprecedented degree. Although Disney's influence has provoked fierce criticism (see Betsy Hearne's piece on pp. 452–59), it is only recently—through the medium of film, of course—that Disney's twentieth-century hegemony over the fairy tale has been challenged, initially by sophisticated "fractured" fairy tales such as the *Shrek* series (2001, 2004, 2007, and 2010, with more to come) and *Hoodwinked* (2005 and 2011), as James Poniewozik discusses (pp. 466–69). Yet as the impact of Disney and his rivals so clearly demonstrates, film and television have emerged as the dominant media of popular culture, thereby making the fairy tale very much a part of mass culture, just as it once was a part of folk culture; in this respect, the folk tale has once again come full circle.

★ ★ ★

One essential feature that we hope to have established in this introduction, and that will be confirmed in the sections that follow, is that fairy tales can come in a bewildering number of versions. It begins with the infinite variability of the oral folk tale, continues with the differing assumptions or agendas of collectors, translators, and editors as the tale takes on literary form, and then undergoes constant transformation as generations of writers and illustrators are drawn to this mother-lode of story.

In recent years, the importance of the folk or fairy tale as a global common language and cultural reference has grown as war, persecution, and natural disaster have uprooted enormous numbers of people, often with little more than the clothes on their backs. As they set about the formidable task of rebuilding their lives, the realization that their own traditional tales (in which overcoming radical change is a basic theme) are echoed in other cultures provides a reassuring sense of continuity in an uncertain world.

LITTLE RED RIDING HOOD

For what is unquestionably one of the classic fairy tales, "Little Red Riding Hood" is more surprising for what it lacks than for what it contains. There is no royalty, no enchantment, no romance—just a talking wolf with a big appetite. How then has the heroine of this tale become as famous a figure as her more glamorous cousins, Sleeping Beauty, Cinderella, and Snow White? What is so remarkable about this stark little tale that describes the dramatic confrontation between an innocent little girl and a wicked wolf? How has it come about that the line "Grandmother, what big teeth you have!" is one of the most anticipated and familiar moments in all of Western literature, let alone fairy tale?

First of all, this is not a real wolf—and arguably neither child nor adult reader ever takes him as such. The first story in this section actually identifies him as a "bzou" or werewolf ("wer" is Old English for "man"), and, as Jack Zipes points out in his discussion of this version in *The Trials and Tribulations of Little Red Riding Hood*,

> The direct forebears of Perrault's literary tale were not influenced by sun worship or Christian theology, but by the very material conditions of their existence and traditional pagan superstition. Little children were attacked and killed by animals and grownups in the woods and fields. Hunger often drove people to commit atrocious acts. In the 15th and 16th centuries, violence was difficult to explain on rational grounds. There was a strong superstitious belief in werewolves and witches, uncontrollable magical forces of nature, which threatened the lives of the peasant population.... Consequently, the warning tale became part of a stock oral repertoire of storytellers.[1]

---

1 Jack D. Zipes, ed., *The Trials and Tribulations of Little Red Riding Hood*, 2nd ed. (New York: Routledge, 1993), 23.

Although it was recorded only in 1885, scholars are in general agreement that "The Story of Grandmother" is likely very similar to the version that Charles Perrault heard two hundred years earlier. There are several intriguing aspects to this early version of the tale. The representation of the two paths through the forest as being of needles and pins is no doubt a play on the pine needles that carpet the forest floor; it may also be a sly reference to one of the domestic tasks that awaits feminine maturity. This tale also has a crudeness that underlines its folk origins—a conclusion borne out by the fact that variants from other parts of the world contain similar scatological episodes.

Such an observation could also be made of an Italian version, "The False Grandmother,"[1] which contains similar gross-out details, albeit in a lighter vein. In other respects, however, the tale is quite different; for instance, the character of the girl is more fully developed, both in terms of her harmonious relationship with her environment and the sassiness she shows in defying her would-be attacker ("Hairy ogress!"). Indeed, the fact that the villain is female alters the whole impact of the tale, in that the sexual element is missing; now it highlights the risk of falling victim to the wiles of a con artist. Ariel's villain Ursula is also female

What we see in Perrault's version is the adaptation of a crude folk tale to the more sophisticated tastes of high society. Paul Delarue, the editor of the collection from which "The Story of Grandmother" was taken, observes in his notes that "the common elements that are lacking in [Perrault's] story are precisely those which would have shocked the society of his period by their cruelness [sic] ... and their impropriety."[2] Perrault removes all overt human aspects of his antagonist, relying simply on the powerful archetypal image of the wolf as predator and interloper. By way of compensation for his excision of the tale's vulgarities, Perrault appears to be responsible for the artistic touch of the red riding hood; he would doubtless be both shocked and amused to learn how controversial an addition that turned out to be! He tells us that it's a "hood like the ones that fine ladies wear when they go riding," which suggests that he's again trying to link the tale with the world of his audience—but why is it *red*? We are confronted with a color symbolic of sexuality that provides a further hint about Perrault's own assumptions regarding this tale.

The endings of both "The Story of Grandmother" and "The False Grandmother" catch our eye because their happy outcome is attributable to the girl's practical

---

1   It is noteworthy that both titles of what are probably pre-Perrault versions draw our attention to the grandmother rather than to the girl, thereby changing the emphasis of the story. The Chinese title "Lon Po Po" means "Granny Wolf." Is this further evidence that such tales were originally less concerned with the role of the child?

2   Paul Delarue, comp., *Borzoi Book of French Folk Tales*, trans. Austin E. Fife (New York: Knopf, 1956), 383.

quickwittedness—a quality that Perrault denies his heroine, in keeping with his bourgeois assumptions about female naïveté and vulnerability, which make Little Red Riding Hood into the wolf's unwitting accomplice. Perrault's tragic and presumably truncated ending, which catches the modern reader so much by surprise, goes against folk-tale custom, but it is clear that such an ending suited Perrault's purposes admirably, given the Moral that he appended to the tale: "Children, especially pretty, nicely broughtup young ladies, ought never to talk to strangers ..." Just what induced Perrault to add his Morals to the tales is unclear, but it was surely a critical moment in the evolution of the fairy tale as children's literature; to this day, the belief has persisted that the purpose of a tale is to inculcate morals into young minds. We must remember that Perrault was a pioneer in recognizing the potential appeal of these tales and transforming them from an oral into a literary form. As Jack Zipes points out,

> Perrault's tale of "Little Red Riding Hood" had an unusually successful reception in the 18th century. In fact, it was one of the few literary tales in history which, due to its universality, ambivalence, and clever sexual innuendoes, was reabsorbed by the oral folk tradition. That is, as a result of its massive circulation in print in the 18th and 19th centuries and of the corroboration of peasant experience, it took root in oral folklore and eventually led to the creation of the even more popular Grimms' tale, which had the same effect.[1]

When we turn to the Grimms' version, published over a hundred years later, we find a synthesis of the other three, with some intriguing additions. (Despite the Grimms' insistence that they were capturing the essence of the German spirit in their tales, it is surely not coincidental that the family that contributed this tale was of French extraction.) The red garment remains, as does the wolf; like Perrault, the Grimms choose to gloss over the cannibalistic snack that the girl unwittingly makes of her grandmother, and the "happy" ending has been restored—but only through the intervention of the paternalistic hunter, in a scene derived, according to Delarue, from another French tale, "The Goat and Her Kids." Nevertheless, it can be argued that the Grimm version is the most balanced, at least to the contemporary reader. The hunter presents an image of male goodness that counters the male wickedness of the wolf; the mother appears concerned about her daughter's correct behavior, if not her welfare—and the less familiar appended story, describing the defeat of a second wolf through the teamwork of a wiser girl and grandmother, sends a very different message from Perrault's harsh ending.

---

1   Zipes 31.

The story of Little Red Riding Hood has for so long been an inescapable part of growing up in the English language that it is hard enough to contemplate its greater authenticity in French or German. It comes as an even greater shock, therefore, to realize how old and widespread the tale is in Asia; Delarue points out that versions of the tale are widely distributed in China, Japan, and Korea.[1]

The Chinese "Lon Po Po" also reveals significant structural differences, but, on closer examination, we may be surprised to discover just how many of the elements from the previous versions are to be found here: as in "The Story of Grandmother" and "The False Grandmother," the children escape from the wolf's clutches by means of a clever ruse, and his final demise is brought about by much the same strategy as in the conclusion to "Little Red Cap"—that is, the roles are reversed and the would-be victim gains the upper hand by exploiting the greed and self-indulgence that are central to the fairy-tale wolf's character.

In some respects, this Chinese version has a distinctly contemporary feel. The mother is described as a young widow who teaches her children carefully about the nature of the world; yet the time must come when her children will have to fend for themselves—and at that moment of crisis, the girls prove susceptible to the wolf's trickery. Despite their mistake, however, the sisters (led by the formidable Shang) are able to keep their wits about them and finally outsmart the deceitful wolf. The experience may have deprived them of at least some of their trust in those around them; by the same token, they—like Little Red Cap—will be less likely to be fooled a second time.

THE STORY OF GRANDMOTHER[2]

Paul Delarue

THERE WAS ONCE A WOMAN who had some bread, and she said to her daughter: "You are going to carry a hot loaf and a bottle of milk to your grandmother."

The little girl departed. At the crossroads she met the *bzou*,[3] who said to her: "Where are you going?"

"I'm taking a hot loaf and a bottle of milk to my grandmother."

"What road are you taking," said the *bzou*, "the Needles Road or the Pins Road?"

---

1   In Alan Dundes, ed., *Little Red Riding Hood: A Casebook* (Madison: U of Wisconsin P, 1989), 13.

2   First collected in 1885; this text from Delarue, *The Borzoi Book of French Folktales*, trans. Austin E. Fife (New York: Knopf, 1956).

3   I.e., werewolf.

"The Needles Road," said the little girl.

"Well, I shall take the Pins Road."

The little girl enjoyed herself picking up needles. Meanwhile the *bzou* arrived at her grandmother's, killed her, put some of her flesh in the pantry and a bottle of her blood on the shelf. The little girl arrived and knocked at the door.

"Push the door," said the *bzou*, "it's closed with a wet straw."

"Hello, Grandmother; I'm bringing you a hot loaf and a bottle of milk."

"Put them in the pantry. You eat the meat that's in it and drink a bottle of wine that is on the shelf."

As she ate there was a little cat that said: "A slut is she who eats the flesh and drinks the blood of her grandmother!"

"Undress, my child," said the *bzou*, "and come and sleep beside me."

"Where should I put my apron?"

"Throw it in the fire, my child; you don't need it any more."

"Where should I put my bodice?"

"Throw it in the fire, my child; you don't need it any more."

"Where should I put my dress?"

"Throw it in the fire, my child; you don't need it any more."

"Where should I put my skirt?"

"Throw it in the fire, my child; you don't need it any more."

"Where should I put my hose?"

"Throw it in the fire, my child; you don't need it any more."

"Oh, Grandmother, how hairy you are!"

"It's to keep me warmer, my child."

"Oh, Grandmother, those long nails you have!"

"It's to scratch me better, my child!"

"Oh, Grandmother, those big shoulders that you have!"

"All the better to carry kindling from the woods, my child."

"Oh, Grandmother, those big ears that you have!"

"All the better to hear with, my child."

"Oh, Grandmother, that big mouth you have!"

"All the better to eat you with, my child!"

"Oh, Grandmother, I need to go outside to relieve myself."

"Do it in the bed, my child."

"Oh, Grandmother, I want to go outside."

"All right, but don't stay long."

The *bzou* tied a woolen thread to her foot and let her go out, and when the little girl was outside she tied the end of the string to a big plum tree in the yard. The *bzou* got impatient and said:

"Are you making cables?"

When he became aware that no one answered him, he jumped out of bed and saw that the little girl had escaped. He followed her, but he arrived at her house just at the moment she was safely inside.

Welp. That was disturbing.

THE FALSE GRANDMOTHER[1]

Italo Calvino

A MOTHER HAD TO SIFT FLOUR, and told her little girl to go to her grandmother's and borrow the sifter. The child packed a snack—ring-shaped cakes and bread with oil—and set out.

She came to the Jordan River.

"Jordan River, will you let me pass?"

"Yes, if you give me your ring-shaped cakes."

The Jordan River had a weakness for ring-shaped cakes, which he enjoyed twirling in his whirlpools.

The child tossed the ring-shaped cakes into the river, and the river lowered its waters and let her through.

The little girl came to the Rake Gate.

"Rake Gate, will you let me pass?"

"Yes, if you give me your bread with oil."

The Rake Gate had a weakness for bread with oil, since her hinges were rusty, and bread with oil oiled them for her.

The little girl gave the gate her bread with oil, and the gate opened and let her through.

She reached her grandmother's house, but the door was shut tight.

"Grandmother, Grandmother, come let me in."

"I'm in bed sick. Come through the window."

"I can't make it."

"Come through the cat door."

"I can't squeeze through."

"Well, wait a minute," she said, and lowered a rope, by which she pulled the little girl up through the window. The room was dark. In bed was the ogress, not the grandmother, for the ogress had gobbled up Grandmother all in one piece from

---

1   From *Italian Folktales*, retold by Italo Calvino, trans. George Martin (New York: Pantheon, 1980).

head to toe, all except her teeth, which she had put on to stew in a small stew pan, and her ears, which she had put on to fry in a frying pan.

"Grandmother, Mamma wants the sifter."

"It's late now. I'll give it to you tomorrow. Come to bed."

"Grandmother, I'm hungry, I want my supper first."

"Eat the beans boiling in the boiler."

In the pot were the teeth. The child stirred them around and said, "Grandmother, they're too hard." *NHAT IS WITH THE CANNIBALISM? JESUS*

"Well, eat the fritters in the frying pan."

In the frying pan were the ears. The child felt them with the fork and said, "Grandmother, they're not crisp."

"Well, come to bed. You can eat tomorrow."

The little girl got into bed beside Grandmother. She felt one of her hands and said, "Why are your hands so hairy, Grandmother?"

"From wearing too many rings on my fingers."

She felt her chest. "Why is your chest so hairy, Grandmother?"

"From wearing too many necklaces around my neck."

She felt her hips. "Why are your hips so hairy, Grandmother?"

"Because I wore my corset too tight."

This literally makes zero sense

She felt her tail and reasoned that, hairy or not, Grandmother had never had a tail. That had to be the ogress and nobody else. So she said, "Grandmother, I can't go to sleep unless I first go and take care of a little business."

Grandmother replied, "Go do it in the barn below. I'll let you down through the trapdoor and then draw you back up."

She tied a rope around her and lowered her into the barn. The minute the little girl was down she untied the rope and in her place attached a nanny goat. "Are you through?" asked Grandmother. *Poor goat*

"Just a minute." She finished tying the rope around the nanny goat. "There, I've finished. Pull me back up."

The ogress pulled and pulled, and the little girl began yelling, "Hairy ogress! Hairy ogress!" She threw open the barn and fled. The ogress kept pulling, and up came the nanny goat. She jumped out of bed and ran after the little girl.

When the child reached the Rake Gate, the ogress yelled from a distance; "Rake Gate, don't let her pass!"

But the Rake Gate replied, "Of course I'll let her pass; she gave me her bread with oil."

When the child reached the Jordan River, the ogress shouted, "Jordan River, don't you let her pass!"

But the Jordan River answered, "Of course I'll let her pass; she gave me her ring-shaped cakes."

When the ogress tried to get through, the Jordan River did not lower his waters, and the ogress was swept away in the current. From the bank the little girl made faces at her.

LITTLE RED RIDING HOOD[1]

Charles Perrault

ONCE UPON A TIME, DEEP in the heart of the country, there lived a pretty little girl whose mother adored her, and her grandmother adored her even more. This good woman made her a red hood like the ones that fine ladies wear when they go riding. The hood suited the child so much that soon everybody was calling her Little Red Riding Hood.

One day, her mother baked some cakes on the griddle and said to Little Red Riding Hood:

"Your granny is sick; you must go and visit her. Take her one of these cakes and a little pot of butter."

Little Red Riding Hood went off to the next village to visit her grandmother. As she walked through the wood, she met a wolf, who wanted to eat her but did not dare to because there were woodcutters working nearby. He asked her where she was going. The poor child did not know how dangerous it is to chatter away to wolves and replied innocently:

"I'm going to visit my grandmother to take her this cake and this little pot of butter from my mother."

"Does your grandmother live far away?" asked the wolf.

"Oh yes," said Little Red Riding Hood. "She lives beyond the mill you can see over there, in the first house you come to in the village."

"Well, I shall go and visit her, too," said the wolf. "I will take *this* road and you shall take *that* road and let's see who can get there first."

The wolf ran off by the shortest path and Red Riding Hood went off the longest way and she made it still longer because she dawdled along, gathering nuts and chasing butterflies and picking bunches of wayside flowers.

---

1   First published in 1697. This text from *Sleeping Beauty and Other Favourite Fairy Tales*, trans. Angela Carter (London: Gollancz, 1982).

The wolf soon arrived at Grandmother's house. He knocked on the door, rat tat tat.

"Who's there?"

"Your granddaughter, Little Red Riding Hood," said the wolf, disguising his voice. "I've brought you a cake baked on the griddle and a little pot of butter from my mother."

Grandmother was lying in bed because she was poorly. She called out: "Lift up the latch and walk in!"

The wolf lifted the latch and opened the door. He had not eaten for three days. He threw himself on the good woman and gobbled her up. Then he closed the door behind him and lay down in Grandmother's bed to wait for Little Red Riding Hood. At last she came knocking on the door, rat tat tat.

"Who's there?"

Little Red Riding Hood heard the hoarse voice of the wolf and thought that her grandmother must have caught a cold. She answered:

"It's your granddaughter, Little Red Riding Hood. I've brought you a cake baked on the griddle and a little pot of butter from my mother."

The wolf disguised his voice and said:

"Lift up the latch and walk in."

Little Red Riding Hood lifted the latch and opened the door.

When the wolf saw her come in, he hid himself under the bedclothes and said to her:

"Put the cake and the butter down on the bread-bin and come and lie down with me."

Little Red Riding Hood took off her clothes and went to lie down in the bed. She was surprised to see how odd her grandmother looked. She said to her:

"Grandmother, what big arms you have!"

"All the better to hold you with, my dear."

"Grandmother, what big legs you have!"

"All the better to run with, my dear."

"Grandmother, what big ears you have!"

"All the better to hear with, my dear."

"Grandmother, what big eyes you have!"

"All the better to see with, my dear!"

"Grandmother, what big teeth you have!"

"All the better to eat you up!"

At that, the wicked wolf threw himself upon Little Red Riding Hood and gobbled her up, too.

Moral

Children, especially pretty, nicely brought-up young ladies, ought never to talk to strangers; if they are foolish enough to do so, they should not be surprised if some greedy wolf consumes them, elegant red riding hoods and all.

Now, there are real wolves, with hairy pelts and enormous teeth; but also wolves who seem perfectly charming, sweet-natured and obliging, who pursue young girls in the street and pay them the most flattering attentions.

Unfortunately, these smooth-tongued, smooth-pelted wolves are the most dangerous beasts of all.

LITTLE RED CAP[1]

Jacob and Wilhelm Grimm

ONCE THERE WAS A DEAR little girl whom everyone loved. Her grandmother loved her most of all and didn't know what to give the child next. Once she gave her a little red velvet cap, which was so becoming to her that she never wanted to wear anything else, and that was why everyone called her Little Red Cap. One day her mother said: "Look, Little Red Cap, here's a piece of cake and a bottle of wine. Take them to grandmother. She is sick and weak, and they will make her feel better. You'd better start now before it gets too hot; walk properly like a good little girl, and don't leave the path or you'll fall down and break the bottle and there won't be anything for grandmother. And when you get to her house, don't forget to say good morning, and don't go looking in all the corners."

"I'll do everything right," Little Red Cap promised her mother. Her grandmother lived in the wood, half an hour's walk from the village. No sooner had Little Red Cap set foot in the wood than she met the wolf. But Little Red Cap didn't know what a wicked beast he was, so she wasn't afraid of him. "Good morning, Little Red Cap," he said. "Thank you kindly, wolf." "Where are you going so early, Little Red Cap?" "To my grandmother's." "And what's that you've got under your apron?" "Cake and wine. We baked yesterday, and we want my grandmother, who's sick and weak, to have something nice that will make her feel better." "Where does your grandmother live, Little Red Cap?" "In the wood, fifteen or twenty minutes' walk from here, under the three big oak trees. That's where the house is. It has hazel hedges around it. You must

---

1   First published in 1812/15, in the first edition of *Kinder- und Hausmärchen*. This text from the second edition (1819), from *Grimms' Tales for Young and Old*, trans. Ralph Manheim (Garden City, NY: Anchor P, 1977).

know the place." "How young and tender she is!" thought the wolf. "Why, she'll be even tastier than the old woman. Maybe if I'm crafty enough I can get them both." So, after walking along for a short while beside Little Red Cap, he said: "Little Red Cap, open your eyes. What lovely flowers! Why don't you look around you? I don't believe you even hear how sweetly the birds are singing. It's so gay out here in the wood, yet you trudge along as solemnly as if you were going to school."

Little Red Cap looked up, and when she saw the sunbeams dancing this way and that between the trees and the beautiful flowers all around her, she thought: "Grandmother will be pleased if I bring her a bunch of nice fresh flowers. It's so early now that I'm sure to be there in plenty of time." So she left the path and went into the wood to pick flowers. And when she had picked one, she thought there must be a more beautiful one farther on, so she went deeper and deeper into the wood. As for the wolf, he went straight to the grandmother's house and knocked at the door. "Who's there?" "Little Red Cap, bringing cake and wine. Open the door." "Just raise the latch," cried the grandmother, "I'm too weak to get out of bed." The wolf raised the latch and the door swung open. Without saying a single word he went straight to the grandmother's bed and gobbled her up. Then he put on her clothes and her nightcap, lay down in the bed, and drew the curtains.

Meanwhile Little Red Cap had been running about picking flowers, and when she had as many as she could carry she remembered her grandmother and started off again. She was surprised to find the door open, and when she stepped into the house she had such a strange feeling that she said to herself: "My goodness, I'm usually so glad to see grandmother. Why am I frightened today?" "Good morning," she cried out, but there was no answer. Then she went to the bed and opened the curtains. The grandmother had her cap pulled way down over her face, and looked very strange.

"Oh, grandmother, what big ears you have!"

"The better to hear you with."

"Oh, grandmother, what big eyes you have!"

"The better to see you with."

"Oh, grandmother, what big hands you have!"

"The better to grab you with."

"But, grandmother, what a dreadful big mouth you have!"

"The better to eat you with."

And no sooner had the wolf spoken than he bounded out of bed and gobbled up poor Little Red Cap.

When the wolf had stilled his hunger, he got back into bed, fell asleep, and began to snore very very loud. A hunter was just passing, and he thought: "How the old woman is snoring! I'd better go and see what's wrong." So he stepped into the house and went over to the bed and saw the wolf was in it. "You old sinner!" he said, "I've found you at last. It's been a long time." He levelled his musket and was just about to fire when it occurred to him that the wolf might have swallowed the grandmother and that there might still be a chance of saving her. So instead of firing, he took a pair of scissors and started cutting the sleeping wolf's belly open. After two snips, he saw the little red cap, and after another few snips the little girl jumped out, crying: "Oh, I've been so afraid! It was so dark inside the wolf!" And then the old grandmother came out, and she too was still alive, though she could hardly breathe. Little Red Cap ran outside and brought big stones, and they filled the wolf's belly with them. When he woke up, he wanted to run away, but the stones were so heavy that his legs wouldn't carry him and he fell dead.

All three were happy; the hunter skinned the wolf and went home with the skin, the grandmother ate the cake and drank the wine Little Red Cap had brought her and soon got well; and as for Little Red Cap, she said to herself: "Never again will I leave the path and run off into the wood when my mother tells me not to."

Another story they tell is that when Little Red Cap was taking another cake to her old grandmother another wolf spoke to her and tried to make her leave the path. But Little Red Cap was on her guard. She kept on going, and when she got to her grandmother's she told her how she had met a wolf who had bidden her good day but given her such a wicked look that "if it hadn't been on the open road he'd have gobbled me right up." "Well then," said the grandmother, "we'll just lock the door and he won't be able to get in." In a little while the wolf knocked and called out: "Open the door, grandmother, it's Little Red Cap. I've brought you some cake." But they didn't say a word and they didn't open the door. So Grayhead circled the house once or twice and finally jumped on the roof. His plan was to wait until evening when Little Red Cap would go home, and then he'd creep after her and gobble her up in the darkness. But the grandmother guessed what he had in mind. There was a big stone trough in front of the house, and she said to the child: "Here's a bucket, Little Red Cap. I cooked some sausages yesterday. Take the water I cooked them in and empty it into the trough." Little Red Cap carried water until the trough was full. The smell of the sausages rose up to the wolf's nostrils. He sniffed and looked down, and in the end he stuck his neck out so far that he couldn't keep his footing and began to slide. And he slid off the roof and slid straight into the big trough and was drowned. And Little Red Cap went happily home, and no one harmed her.

LON PO PO: A RED-RIDING HOOD STORY FROM CHINA[1]

Ed Young

ONCE, LONG AGO, THERE WAS a woman who lived alone in the country with her three children, Shang, Tao, and Paotze. On the day of their grandmother's birthday, the good mother set off to see her, leaving the three children at home.

Before she left, she said, "Be good while I am away, my heart-loving children; I will not return tonight. Remember to close the door tight at sunset and latch it well."

But an old wolf lived nearby and saw the good mother leave. At dusk, disguised as an old woman, he came up to the house of the children and knocked on the door twice: bang, bang.

Shang, who was the eldest, said through the latched door, "Who is it?"

"My little jewels," said the wolf, "this is your grandmother, your Po Po."

"Po Po!" Shang said, "Our mother has gone to visit you!"

The wolf acted surprised. "To visit me? I have not met her along the way. She must have taken a different route."

"Po Po!" Shang said. "How is it that you come so late?"

The wolf answered, "The journey is long, my children, and the day is short."

Shang listened through the door. "Po Po," she said, "why is your voice so low?"

"Your grandmother has caught a cold, good children, and it is dark and windy out here. Quickly open up, and let your Po Po come in," the cunning wolf said.

Tao and Paotze could not wait. One unlatched the door and the other opened it. They shouted, "Po Po, Po Po, come in!"

At the moment he entered the door, the wolf blew out the candle.

"Po Po," Shang asked, "why did you blow out the candle? The room is now dark."

The wolf did not answer.

Tao and Paotze rushed to their Po Po and wished to be hugged. The old wolf held Tao. "Good child, you are so plump." He embraced Paotze. "Good child, you have grown to be so sweet."

Soon the old wolf pretended to be sleepy. He yawned. "All the chicks are in the coop," he said. "Po Po is sleepy too." When he climbed into the big bed, Paotze climbed in at one end with the wolf, and Shang and Tao climbed in at the other.

But when Shang stretched, she touched the wolf's tail. "Po Po, Po Po, your foot has a bush on it."

"Po Po has brought hemp strings to weave you a basket," the wolf said.

---

1 Published in 1989 (New York: Philomel Books).

Shang touched the grandmother's sharp claws. "Po Po, Po Po, your hand has thorns on it."

"Po Po has brought an awl[1] to make shoes for you," the wolf said.

At once, Shang lit the light and the wolf blew it out again, but Shang had seen the wolf's hairy face.

"Po Po, Po Po," she said, for she was not only the eldest, she was the most clever, "you must be hungry. Have you eaten gingko nuts?"

"What is gingko?" the wolf asked.

"Gingko is soft and tender, like the skin of a baby. One taste and you will live forever," Shang said, "and the nuts grow on the top of the tree just outside the door."

The wolf gave a sigh. "Oh, dear. Po Po is old, her bones have become brittle. No longer can she climb trees."

"Good Po Po, we can pick some for you," Shang said.

The wolf was delighted.

Shang jumped out of bed and Tao and Paotze came with her to the gingko tree. There, Shang told her sisters about the wolf and all three climbed up the tall tree.

The wolf waited and waited. Plump Tao did not come back. Sweet Paotze did not come back, and no one brought any nuts from the gingko tree. At last the wolf shouted, "Where are you, children?"

"Po Po," Shang called out, "we are on the top of the tree eating gingko nuts."

"Good children," the wolf begged, "pluck some for me."

"But Po Po, gingko is magic only when it is plucked directly from the tree. You must come and pluck it from the tree yourself."

The wolf came outside and paced back and forth under the tree where he heard the three children eating the gingko nuts at the top. "Oh, Po Po, these nuts are so tasty! The skin so tender," Shang said. The wolf's mouth began to water for a taste.

Finally, Shang, the eldest and most clever child, said, "Po Po, Po Po, I have a plan. At the door there is a big basket. Behind it is a rope. Tie the rope to the basket, sit in the basket and throw the other end to me. I can pull you up."

The wolf was overjoyed and fetched the basket and the rope, then threw one end of the rope to the top of the tree. Shang caught the rope and began to pull the basket up and up.

Halfway she let go of the rope, and the basket and the wolf fell to the ground.

"I am so small and weak, Po Po," Shang pretended. "I could not hold the rope alone."

"This time I will help," Tao said. "Let us do it again,"

The wolf had only one thought in his mind: to taste a gingko nut. He climbed into

---

1 Pointed tool for piercing wood and leather.

the basket again. Now Shang and Tao pulled the rope on the basket together, higher and higher.

Again, they let go, and again the wolf tumbled down, down, and bumped his head.

The wolf was furious. He growled and cursed. "We could not hold the rope, Po Po," Shang said, "but only one gingko nut and you will be well again."

"I shall give a hand to my sisters this time," Paotze, the youngest, said. "This time we shall not fail."

Now the children pulled the rope with all of their strength. As they pulled they sang. "Hei yo, hei yo," and the basket rose straight up, higher than the first time, higher than the second time, higher and higher and higher until it nearly reached the top of the tree. When the wolf reached out, he could almost touch the highest branch.

But at that moment, Shang coughed and they all let go of the rope, and the basket fell down and down and down. Not only did the wolf bump his head, but he broke his heart to pieces.

"Po Po," Shang shouted, but there was no answer.

"Po Po," Tao shouted, but there was no answer.

"Po Po," Paotze shouted. There was still no answer. The children climbed to the branches just above the wolf and saw that he was truly dead. Then they climbed down, went into the house, closed the door, locked the door with the latch and fell peacefully asleep.

On the next day, their mother returned with baskets of food from their real Po Po, and the three sisters told her the story of the Po Po who had come.

CINDERELLA

"CINDERELLA," ALONG WITH "LITTLE RED RIDING HOOD" and "Sleeping Beauty," might be described as representing the core of the Western fairy-tale canon. As with its two sister tales, the abiding popularity of "Cinderella" raises the inevitable question: what is the explanation behind such success? Part of the answer lies in the phrase that has entered the vernacular: "hers (or his!) is a real Cinderella story." It signifies that the individual has risen from obscurity and oppression to success and celebrity, perhaps with the implication that the good fortune is well deserved. There can be little doubt that the attraction of this tale has a lot to do with its theme of virtue revealed and rewarded: it invites us to recall times when we felt ourselves unappreciated and rejected and then to share Cinderella's satisfaction at being discovered as a true princess. (Hans Andersen taps into much the same feeling in "The Ugly Duckling.")

It would be interesting to know what "raw material" Perrault used as the basis for his "Cinderella," since in a number of respects it is quite unique. In no other version, for example, do we find a fairy godmother transforming a pumpkin into a coach, mice into horses, or lizards into lackeys—and no other version contains that famous glass slipper. And in light of the subordinate position of women in Perrault's bourgeois world, we should not be surprised to discover that his Cinderella is a rather passive young lady, no stranger to self-denial; she goes out of her way to assist her obnoxious stepsisters in preparing for the ball while denying that she has any right to such pleasures. On their departure, Cinderella collapses in tears, provoking the appearance of a fairy-tale *dea ex machina* in the shape of her fairy godmother, who provides her with all the accoutrements necessary for an impressive entry into high society.

The Grimms' Ashputtle responds to the situation rather differently. Instead of playing the helpless martyr, she makes it clear to her stepmother that she too wishes to go to the ball and is prepared to do whatever is necessary to get there. As a rule, Nature plays a more significant role in the Grimms' tales than in those of Perrault, and that is the case here. Ashputtle's virtue is rewarded by the assistance of both the spirit of her dead mother and the birds that complete the impossible tasks set by her stepmother. This version of the tale is clearly less sophisticated than that by Perrault: its repetitive structure is a reminder of its oral origins, and the rather undignified chases to Ashputtle's home strike a more down-to-earth note. Nowhere is the contrast between the Perrault and Grimm versions more apparent than at the conclusion: while Cinderella's forgiveness is evidence of an intriguing ambivalence toward her stepsisters (recall that at the first ball, Perrault tells us that she "went and sat beside her sisters and devoted herself to entertaining them"), the gruesome ritualistic punishment meted out by the doves (!) in "Ashputtle" provides the visceral satisfaction of revenge.[1]

"Cap o' Rushes" is a variant of a less well-known Cinderella story that can be found in many collections, including those of the Grimm Brothers ("All-Fur") and Perrault ("Donkeyskin"), although it differs from these latter versions in omitting the father's incestuous attraction to his daughter. In this case, the tale begins with a father–daughter confrontation, reminiscent of the scene in Shakespeare's *King Lear* in which the king's youngest daughter, Cordelia, offers as honest and plain an answer to her father as Cap o' Rushes—with the same result.[2] The world of "Cap o' Rushes" has an earthy forthrightness that is made more vivid by the use of dialect that characterized Joseph Jacobs's collection *English Fairy Tales* (1890). Here again there is a striking contrast between the bourgeois virtues of forbearance and self-denial displayed by Cinderella and the vigorous practicality of Cap o' Rushes as she deals with the challenges life throws in her path, a fact made more obvious by the absence of a stepmother and by sisters who, after the opening episode, vanish from the story. Cap o' Rushes reacts to her rejection by creating a plan and following it through to a successful conclusion that not only brings her a husband but also reconciles her with her father.

The Russian tale "Vasilisa the Beautiful" offers an intriguing mixture of qualities that we've encountered in the three earlier tales. At the outset, Vasilisa shows a familiar stoical resolve in dealing with the abuse of stepmother and stepsisters—but when confronted with the far greater threat of the Baba Yaga, she displays a courage and resilience that finally overcomes even this most formidable of "bad mothers." ("Get you gone, blessed daughter! I want no blessed ones in my house!") Although Vasilisa is ultimately rewarded with a royal husband, the manner in which she wins

---

1   In the first edition of the Grimms' tales, the ending focuses on the happy couple rather than on the graphic mutilation of the stepsisters.

2   Shakespeare (no stranger to the world of fairy tale) based the story of *King Lear* on the fairy-tale type "Love like Salt."

him may be somewhat disconcerting to a modern reader: through the traditional feminine skills of spinning, weaving, and sewing! (Being beautiful helps, too....)

The resilience that we have noted in Cap o'Rushes and Vasilisa reappears in the heroines of the next two tales: "Little Gold Star" from New Mexico and "The Little Red Fish and the Clog of Gold" from Iraq. Both girls accept the consequences of encouraging their fathers to remarry, and both receive magical assistance from nature, in the shape of a bird and a fish—a reward for the virtues of compassion and humility that are often central to fairy-tale morality. There is also a religious element evident in both tales, manifested on the one hand in the gold star with which Arcia is blessed and which remains the focus of her beauty (in contrast to the splendid gowns and jewels often granted to Cinderella), and on the other, in the interweaving of magic and Islam ("through the will of Allah and with the help of the little red fish ...") that we may recognize as a familiar characteristic in the *Arabian Nights*. The Iraqi tale also demonstrates how important socio-cultural differences are in our understanding of variations between one version and another. Its editor points out that in Arab society the sexes are so strictly segregated before marriage that "a token [in this case, the golden clog] can well be the inspiration to love, when seeing the girl herself is forbidden."[1] She adds that it is natural for the prince to look to his mother for help in tracking down the elusive maiden, "for a girl worth having would not be exposed to the sight of men outside her household and her family. In such circumstances the Cinderella story seems entirely realistic, and it is told in countless versions in the Arab world"[2]

Although some of the familiar elements in "The Indian Cinderella" may well be attributable to European influence, the fact remains that the flavor of this tale is quite different; it serves to remind us that the term "fairy tale" must have a broad definition if it is to include not only the stories from the Western tradition but also those from other continents and cultures. Unlike the familiar European versions, in which the prince must seek out his elusive bride, here the roles are reversed, although now the seeking becomes a test in itself. Deeply embedded in the natural world, this tale has an impressive mythic quality; the girl's discovery that Strong Wind draws his sled with the Rainbow and uses the Milky Way for his bowstring makes for an impressively large-scale climax to the story. Other unusual elements in this story are the symbolic bathing that transforms the young woman and the fact that, once married to Strong Wind, "she helped him to do great deeds."

---

1   Inea Bushnaq, *Arab Folktales* (New York: Pantheon, 1987), 155–56.
2   Bushnaq 156.

CINDERELLA: OR THE LITTLE GLASS SLIPPER[1]

Charles Perrault

THERE ONCE LIVED A MAN who married twice, and his second wife was the haughtiest and most stuck-up woman in the world. She already had two daughters of her own and her children took after her in every way. Her new husband's first wife had given him a daughter of his own before she died, but she was a lovely and sweet-natured girl, very like her own natural mother, who had been a kind and gentle woman.

The second wedding was hardly over before the stepmother showed her true colours. Her new daughter was so lovable that she made her own children seem even more unpleasant by contrast; so she found the girl insufferable. She gave her all the rough work about the house to do, washing the pots and pans, cleaning out Madame's bedroom and those of her stepsisters, too. She slept at the top of the house, in a garret, on a thin, lumpy mattress, while her stepsisters had rooms with fitted carpets, soft beds and mirrors in which they could see themselves from head to foot. The poor girl bore everything patiently and dared not complain to her father because he would have lost his temper with her. His new wife ruled him with a rod of iron.

When the housework was all done, she would tuck herself away in the chimney corner to sit quietly among the cinders, the only place of privacy she could find, and so the family nicknamed her Cinderbritches. But the younger sister, who was less spiteful than the older one, changed her nickname to Cinderella. Yet even in her dirty clothes, Cinderella could not help but be a hundred times more beautiful than her sisters, however magnificently they dressed themselves up.

The king's son decided to hold a ball to which he invited all the aristocracy. Our two young ladies received their invitations, for they were well connected. Busy and happy, they set about choosing the dresses and hairstyles that would suit them best and that made more work for Cinderella, who had to iron her sisters' petticoats and starch their ruffles. They could talk about nothing except what they were going to wear.

"I shall wear my red velvet with the lace trimming," said the eldest. "Well, I shall wear just a simple skirt but put my coat with the golden flowers over it and, of course, there's always my diamond necklace, which is really rather special," said the youngest.

---

1   First published in 1697. This text from *Sleeping Beauty and Other Favourite Fairy Tales*, trans. Angela Carter (London: Gollancz, 1982).

They sent for a good hairdresser to cut and curl their hair and they bought the best cosmetics. They called Cinderella to ask for her advice, because she had excellent taste. Cinderella helped them to look as pretty as they could and they were very glad of her assistance, although they did not show it.

As she was combing their hair, they said to her:

"Cinderella, dear, wouldn't you like to go to the ball yourself?"

"Oh don't make fun of me, my ladies, how could I possibly go to the ball!"

"Quite right, too; everyone would laugh themselves silly to see Cinderbritches at a ball."

Any other girl but Cinderella would have made horrid tangles of their hair after that, out of spite; but she was kind, and resisted the temptation. The stepsisters could not eat for two days, they were so excited. They broke more than a dozen corset-laces because they pulled them in so tightly in order to make themselves look slender and they were always primping in front of the mirror.

At last the great day arrived. When they went off, Cinderella watched them until they were out of sight and then began to cry. Her godmother saw how she was crying and asked her what the matter was.

"I want ... I want to ..."

But Cinderella was crying so hard she could not get the words out. Her godmother was a fairy. She said: "I think you're crying because you want to go to the ball."

"Yes," said Cinderella, sighing.

"If you are a good girl, I'll send you there," said her godmother.

She took her into her own room and said:

"Go into the garden and pick me a pumpkin."

Cinderella went out to the garden and picked the finest pumpkin she could find. She took it to her godmother, although she could not imagine how a pumpkin was going to help her get to the ball. Her godmother hollowed out the pumpkin until there was nothing left but the shell, struck it with her ring—and instantly the pumpkin changed into a beautiful golden coach.

Then the godmother went to look in the mousetrap, and found six live mice there. She told Cinderella to lift up the lid of the trap enough to let the mice come out one by one and, as each mouse crept out, she struck it lightly with her ring. At the touch of the ring, each mouse changed into a carriage horse. Soon the coach had six dappled greys to draw it.

Then she asked herself what would do for a coachman.

"I'll go and see if there is a rat in the rat-trap," said Cinderella. "A rat would make a splendid coachman."

"Yes, indeed," said her godmother. "Go and see."

There were three fat rats in the rat-trap that Cinderella brought to her. One had particularly fine whiskers, so the godmother chose that one; when she struck him with her ring, he changed into a plump coachman who had the most imposing moustache you could wish to see.

"If you look behind the watering-can in the garden, you'll find six lizards," the godmother told Cinderella. "Bring them to me."

No sooner had Cinderella brought them to her godmother than the lizards were all changed into footmen, who stepped up behind the carriage in their laced uniforms and hung on as if they had done nothing else all their lives.

The fairy said to Cinderella:

"There you are! Now you can go to the ball. Aren't you pleased?"

"Yes, of course. But how can I possibly go to the ball in these wretched rags?"

The godmother had only to touch her with her ring and Cinderella's workaday overalls and apron changed into a dress of cloth of gold and silver, embroidered with precious stones. Then she gave her the prettiest pair of glass slippers. Now Cinderella was ready, she climbed into the coach; but her godmother told her she must be home by midnight because if she stayed at the ball one moment more, her coach would turn back into a pumpkin, her horses to mice, her footmen to lizards and her clothes back into overalls again.

She promised her godmother that she would be sure to return from the ball before midnight. Then she drove off. The king's son had been told that a great princess, hitherto unknown to anyone present, was about to arrive at the ball and ran to receive her. He himself helped her down from her carriage with his royal hand and led her into the ballroom where all the guests were assembled. As soon as they saw her, an enormous silence descended. The dancing ceased, the fiddlers forgot to ply their bows as the entire company gazed at this unknown lady. The only sound in the entire ballroom was a confused murmur:

"Oh, isn't she beautiful!"

Even the king himself, although he was an old man, could not help gazing at her and remarked to the queen that he had not seen such a lovely young lady for a long time. All the women studied her hair and her ball-gown attentively so that they would be able to copy them the next day, provided they could find such a capable hairdresser, such a skillful dressmaker, such magnificent silk.

The king's son seated her in the most honoured place and then led her on to the dance floor; she danced so gracefully, she was still more admired. Then there was a fine supper but the prince could not eat at all, he was too preoccupied with the young lady. She herself went and sat beside her sisters and devoted herself to entertaining them. She shared the oranges and lemons the prince had given her with them and that surprised them very much, for they did not recognise her.

While they were talking, Cinderella heard the chimes of the clock striking a quarter to twelve. She made a deep curtsey and then ran off as quickly as she could. As soon as she got home, she went to find her godmother and thanked her and told her how much she wanted to go to the ball that was to be given the following day, because the king's son had begged her to. While she was telling her godmother everything that had happened, her stepsisters knocked at the door. Cinderella hurried to let them in.

"What a long time you've been!" she said to them yawning, rubbing her eyes and stretching as if she could scarcely keep awake, although she had not wanted to sleep for a single moment since they had left the house.

"If you had come to the ball, you wouldn't have been sleepy!" said one of the sisters. "The most beautiful princess you ever saw arrived unexpectedly and she was so kind to us, she gave us oranges and lemons."

Cinderella asked the name of the princess but they told her nobody knew it, and the king's son was in great distress and would give anything to find out more about her. Cinderella smiled and said:

"Was she really so very beautiful? Goodness me, how lucky you are. And can I never see her for myself? What a shame! Miss Javotte, lend me that old yellow dress you wear around the house so that I can go to the ball tomorrow and see her for myself."

"What?" exclaimed Javotte. "Lend my dress to such a grubby little Cinderbritches as it is—it must think I've lost my reason!"

Cinderella had expected a refusal; and she would have been exceedingly embarrassed if her sister had relented and agreed to lend her a dress and taken her to the ball in it.

Next day, the sisters went off to the ball again. Cinderella went, too, but this time she was even more beautifully dressed than the first time. The king's son did not leave her side and never stopped paying her compliments so that the young girl was utterly absorbed in him and time passed so quickly that she thought it must still be only eleven o'clock when she heard the chimes of midnight. She sprang to her feet and darted off as lightly as a doe. The prince sprang after her but he could not catch her; in her flight, however, she let fall one of her glass slippers and the prince tenderly picked it up. Cinderella arrived home out of breath, without her carriage, without her footmen, in her dirty old clothes again; nothing remained of all her splendour but one of her little slippers, the pair of the one she had dropped. The prince asked the guards at the palace gate if they had seen a princess go out; they replied they had seen nobody leave the castle last night at midnight but a ragged young girl who looked more like a kitchen-maid than a fine lady.

When her sisters came home from the ball, Cinderella asked them if they had enjoyed themselves again; and had the beautiful princess been there? They said, yes; but she had fled at the very stroke of midnight, and so promptly that she had dropped one of her little glass slippers. The king's son had found it and never took his eyes off it for the rest of the evening, so plainly he was very much in love with the beautiful lady to whom it belonged.

They spoke the truth. A few days later, the king's son publicly announced that he would marry whoever possessed the foot for which the glass slipper had been made. They made a start by trying the slipper on the feet of all the princesses; then moved on to the duchesses, then to the rest of the court, but all in vain. At last they brought the slipper to the two sisters, who did all they could to squeeze their feet into the slipper but could not manage it, no matter how hard they tried. Cinderella watched them; she recognised her own slipper at once. She laughed, and said:

"I'd like to try and see if it might not fit me!"

Her sisters giggled and made fun of her but the gentleman who was in charge of the slipper trial looked at Cinderella carefully and saw how beautiful she was. Yes, he said; of course she could try on the slipper. He had received orders to try the slipper on the feet of every girl in the kingdom. He sat Cinderella down and, as soon as he saw her foot, he knew it would fit the slipper perfectly. The two sisters were very much astonished, but not half so astonished as they were when Cinderella took her own glass slipper from her pocket. At that the godmother appeared; she struck Cinderella's overalls with her ring and at once the old clothes were transformed to garments more magnificent than all her ball-dresses.

Then her sisters knew she had been the beautiful lady they had seen at the ball. They threw themselves at her feet to beg her to forgive them for all the bad treatment she had received from them. Cinderella raised them up and kissed them and said she forgave them with all her heart and wanted them only always to love her. Then, dressed in splendour, she was taken to the prince. He thought she was more beautiful than ever and married her a few days later. Cinderella, who was as good as she was beautiful, took her sisters to live in the palace and arranged for both of them to be married, on the same day, to great lords.

Moral

Beauty is a fine thing in a woman; it will always be admired. But charm is beyond price and worth more, in the long run. When her godmother dressed Cinderella up and told her how to behave at the ball, she instructed her in charm. Lovely ladies, this gift is worth more than a fancy hairdo; to win a heart, to reach a happy ending, charm is the true gift of the fairies. Without it, one can achieve nothing; with it, everything.

Another Moral

It is certainly a great advantage to be intelligent, brave, well-born, sensible and have other similar talents given only by heaven. But however great may be your god-given store, they will never help you to get on in the world unless you have either a godfather or a godmother to put them to work for you.

ASHPUTTLE[1]

Jacob and Wilhelm Grimm

A RICH MAN'S WIFE FELL SICK and, feeling that her end was near, she called her only daughter to her bedside and said: "Dear child, be good and say your prayers; God will help you, and I shall look down on you from heaven and always be with you." With that she closed her eyes and died. Every day the little girl went out to her mother's grave and wept, and she went on being good and saying her prayers. When winter came, the snow spread a white cloth over the grave, and when spring took it off, the man remarried.

His new wife brought two daughters into the house. Their faces were beautiful and lily-white, but their hearts were ugly and black. That was the beginning of a bad time for the poor stepchild. "Why should this silly goose sit in the parlour with us?" they said. "People who want to eat bread must earn it. Get into the kitchen where you belong!" They took away her fine clothes and gave her an old gray dress and wooden shoes to wear. "Look at the haughty princess in her finery!" they cried and, laughing, led her to the kitchen. From then on she had to do all the work, getting up before daybreak, carrying water, lighting fires, cooking and washing. In addition the sisters did everything they could to plague her. They jeered at her and poured peas and lentils into the ashes, so that she had to sit there picking them out. At night, when she was tired out with work, she had no bed to sleep in but had to lie in the ashes by the hearth. And they took to calling her Ashputtle because she always looked dusty and dirty.

One day when her father was going to the fair, he asked his two stepdaughters what he should bring them. "Beautiful dresses," said one. "Diamonds and pearls," said the other. "And you, Ashputtle. What would you like?" "Father," she said, "break off the first branch that brushes against your hat on your way home, and bring it to

---

1   First published in 1812/15, in the first edition of *Kinder- und Hausmärchen*. This text from the second edition (1819), from *Grimms' Tales for Young and Old*, trans. Ralph Manheim (Garden City, NY: Anchor P, 1977).

me." So he bought beautiful dresses, diamonds and pearls for his two stepdaughters, and on the way home, as he was riding through a copse, a hazel branch brushed against him and knocked off his hat. So he broke off the branch and took it home with him. When he got home, he gave the stepdaughters what they had asked for, and gave Ashputtle the branch. After thanking him, she went to her mother's grave and planted the hazel sprig over it and cried so hard that her tears fell on the sprig and watered it. It grew and became a beautiful tree. Three times a day Ashputtle went and sat under it and wept and prayed. Each time a little white bird came and perched on the tree, and when Ashputtle made a wish the little bird threw down what she had wished for.

Now it so happened that the king arranged for a celebration. It was to go on for three days and all the beautiful girls in the kingdom were invited, in order that his son might choose a bride. When the two stepsisters heard that they had been asked, they were delighted. They called Ashputtle and said: "Comb our hair, brush our shoes, and fasten our buckles. We're going to the wedding at the king's palace." Ashputtle obeyed, but she wept, for she too would have liked to go dancing, and she begged her stepmother to let her go. "You little sloven!" said the stepmother. "How can you go to a wedding when you're all dusty and dirty? How can you go dancing when you have neither dress nor shoes?" But when Ashputtle begged and begged, the stepmother finally said: "Here, I've dumped a bowlful of lentils in the ashes. If you can pick them out in two hours, you may go." The girl went out the back door to the garden and cried out: "O tame little doves, O turtledoves, and all the birds under heaven, come and help me put

the good ones in the pot
the bad ones in your crop."

Two little white doves came flying through the kitchen window, and then came the turtledoves, and finally all the birds under heaven came flapping and fluttering and settled down by the ashes. The doves nodded their little heads and started in, peck peck peck peck, and all the others started in, peck peck peck peck, and they sorted out all the good lentils and put them in the bowl. Hardly an hour had passed before they finished and flew away. Then the girl brought the bowl to her stepmother, and she was happy, for she thought she'd be allowed to go to the wedding. But the stepmother said: "No, Ashputtle. You have nothing to wear and you don't know how to dance; the people would only laugh at you." When Ashputtle began to cry, the stepmother said: "If you can pick two bowlfuls of lentils out of the ashes in an hour, you may come." And she thought: "She'll never be able to do it." When she had dumped the two bowlfuls of lentils in the ashes, Ashputtle went out the back door to the garden and cried out: "O tame little doves, O turtledoves, and all the birds under heaven, come and help me put

the good ones in the pot
the bad ones in your crop."

Then two little white doves came flying through the kitchen window, and then came the turtledoves, and finally all the birds under heaven came flapping and fluttering and settled down by the ashes. The doves nodded their little heads and started in, peck peck peck peck, and they sorted out all the good lentils and put them in the bowls. Before half an hour had passed, they had finished and they all flew away. Then the girl brought the bowls to her stepmother, and she was happy, for she thought she'd be allowed to go to the wedding. But her stepmother said, "It's no use. You can't come, because you have nothing to wear and you don't know how to dance. We'd only be ashamed of you." Then she turned her back and hurried away with her two proud daughters.

When they had all gone out, Ashputtle went to her mother's grave. She stood under the hazel tree and cried:

"Shake your branches, little tree,
Throw gold and silver down on me."

Whereupon the bird tossed down a gold and silver dress and slippers embroidered with silk and silver. Ashputtle slipped into the dress as fast as she could and went to the wedding. Her sisters and stepmother didn't recognize her. She was so beautiful in her golden dress that they thought she must be the daughter of some foreign king. They never dreamed it could be Ashputtle, for they thought she was sitting at home in her filthy rags, picking lentils out of the ashes. The king's son came up to her, took her by the hand and danced with her. He wouldn't dance with anyone else and he never let go of her hand. When someone else asked for a dance, he said: "She is my partner."

She danced until evening, and then she wanted to go home. The king's son said: "I'll go with you, I'll see you home," for he wanted to find out whom the beautiful girl belonged to. But she got away from him and slipped into the dovecote. The king's son waited until her father arrived, and told him the strange girl had slipped into the dovecote. The old man thought: "Could it be Ashputtle?" and he sent for an ax and a pick and broke into the dovecote, but there was no one inside. When they went indoors, Ashputtle was lying in the ashes in her filthy clothes and a dim oil lamp was burning on the chimney piece, for Ashputtle had slipped out the back end of the dovecote and run to the hazel tree. There she had taken off her fine clothes and put them on the grave, and the bird had taken them away. Then she had put her gray dress on again, crept into the kitchen and lain down in the ashes.

Next day when the festivities started in again and her parents and stepsisters had gone, Ashputtle went to the hazel tree and said:

"Shake your branches, little tree,
    Throw gold and silver down on me."

Whereupon the bird threw down a dress that was even more dazzling than the first one. And when she appeared at the wedding, everyone marvelled at her beauty. The king's son was waiting for her. He took her by the hand and danced with no one but her. When others came and asked her for a dance, he said: "She is my partner." When evening came, she said she was going home. The king's son followed her, wishing to see which house she went into, but she ran away and disappeared into the garden behind the house, where there was a big beautiful tree with the most wonderful pears growing on it. She climbed among the branches as nimbly as a squirrel and the king's son didn't know what had become of her. He waited until her father arrived and said to him: "The strange girl has got away from me and I think she has climbed up in the pear tree." Her father thought: "Could it be Ashputtle?" He sent for an ax and chopped the tree down, but there was no one in it. When they went into the kitchen, Ashputtle was lying there in the ashes as usual, for she had jumped down on the other side of the tree, and put on her filthy gray dress.

On the third day, after her parents and sisters had gone, Ashputtle went back to her mother's grave and said to the tree:

"Shake your branches, little tree,
    Throw gold and silver down on me."

Whereupon the bird threw down a dress that was more radiant than either of the others, and the slippers were all gold. When she appeared at the wedding, the people were too amazed to speak. The king's son danced with no one but her, and when someone else asked her for a dance, he said: "She is my partner."

When evening came, Ashputtle wanted to go home, and the king's son said he'd go with her, but she slipped away so quickly that he couldn't follow. But he had thought up a trick. He had arranged to have the whole staircase brushed with pitch, and as she was running down it the pitch pulled her left slipper off. The king's son picked it up, and it was tiny and delicate and all gold. Next morning he went to the father and said: "No girl shall be my wife but the one this golden shoe fits." The sisters were overjoyed, for they had beautiful feet. The eldest took the shoe to her room to try it on and her mother went with her. But the shoe was too small and she couldn't get her big toe in. So her mother handed her a knife and said: "Cut your toe off. Once you're queen you won't have to walk any more." The girl cut her toe off, forced her foot into the shoe, gritted her teeth against the pain, and went out to the king's son. He accepted her as his bride-to-be, lifted her up on his horse, and rode away with her. But they had to pass the grave. The two doves were sitting in the hazel tree and they cried out:

> "Roocoo, roocoo,
> There's blood in the shoe.
> The foot's too long, the foot's too wide,
> That's not the proper bride."

He looked down at her foot and saw the blood spurting. At that he turned his horse around and took the false bride home again. "No," he said, "this isn't the right girl; let her sister try the shoe on." The sister went to her room and managed to get her toes into the shoe, but her heel was too big. So her mother handed her a knife and said: "Cut off a chunk of your heel. Once you're queen you won't have to walk any more." The girl cut off a chunk of her heel, forced her foot into the shoe, gritted her teeth against the pain, and went out to the king's son. He accepted her as his bride-to-be, lifted her up on his horse, and rode away with her. As they passed the hazel tree, the two doves were sitting there, and they cried out:

> "Roocoo, roocoo,
> There's blood in the shoe.
> The foot's too long, the foot's too wide,
> That's not the proper bride."

He looked down at her foot and saw that blood was spurting from her shoe and staining her white stocking all red. He turned his horse around and took the false bride home again. "This isn't the right girl, either," he said. "Haven't you got another daughter?" "No," said the man, "there's only a puny little kitchen drudge that my dead wife left me. She couldn't possibly be the bride." "Send her up," said the king's son, but the mother said: "Oh no, she's much too dirty to be seen." But he insisted and they had to call her. First she washed her face and hands, and when they were clean, she went upstairs and curtsied to the king's son. He handed her the golden slipper and sat down on a footstool, took her foot out of her heavy wooden shoe, and put it into the slipper. It fitted perfectly. And when she stood up and the king's son looked into her face, he recognized the beautiful girl he had danced with and cried out: "This is my true bride!" The stepmother and the two sisters went pale with fear and rage. But he lifted Ashputtle up on his horse and rode away with her. As they passed the hazel tree, the two white doves called out:

"Roocoo, roocoo,
No blood in the shoe.
Her foot is neither long nor wide,
This one is the proper bride."

Then they flew down and alighted on Ashputtle's shoulders, one on the right and one on the left, and there they sat.

On the day of Ashputtle's wedding, the two stepsisters came and tried to ingratiate themselves and share in her happiness. On the way to church the elder was on the right side of the bridal couple and the younger on the left. The doves came along and pecked out one of the elder sister's eyes and one of the younger sister's eyes. Afterward, on the way out, the elder was on the left side and the younger on the right, and the doves pecked out both the remaining eyes. So both sisters were punished with blindness to the end of their days for being so wicked and false.

CAP O' RUSHES[1]

Joseph Jacobs

WELL, THERE WAS ONCE A very rich gentleman, and he'd three daughters, and he thought he'd see how fond they were of him. So he says to the first, "How much do you love me, my dear?"

"Why," says she, "as I love my life."

"That's good," says he.

So he says to the second, "How much do *you* love me, my dear?"

"Why," says she, "better nor all the world."

"That's good," says he. So he says to the third, "How much do *you* love me, my dear?"

"Why, I love you as fresh meat loves salt," says she.

Well, but he was angry. "You don't love me at all," says he, "and in my house you stay no more." So he drove her out there and then, and shut the door in her face.

---

1   From *English Fairy Tales*, 1890 (repr. New York: Dover, 1967).

Well, she went away on and on till she came to a fen,[1] and there she gathered a lot of rushes and made them into a kind of a sort of a cloak with a hood, to cover her from head to foot, and to hide her fine clothes. And then she went on and on till she came to a great house.

"Do you want a maid?" says she.

"No, we don't," said they.

"I haven't nowhere to go," says she; "and I ask no wages, and do any sort of work," says she.

"Well," said they, "if you like to wash the pots and scrape the saucepans you may stay," said they.

So she stayed there and washed the pots and scraped the saucepans and did all the dirty work. And because she gave no name they called her "Cap o' Rushes."

Well, one day there was to be a great dance a little way off, and the servants were allowed to go and look on at the grand people. Cap o' Rushes said she was too tired to go, so she stayed at home.

But when they were gone she offed with her cap o' rushes, and cleaned herself, and went to the dance. And no one there was so finely dressed as she.

Well, who should be there but her master's son, and what should he do but fall in love with her the minute he set eyes on her. He wouldn't dance with any one else.

But before the dance was done Cap o' Rushes slipped off, and away she went home. And when the other maids came back she was pretending to be asleep with her cap o' rushes on.

Well, next morning they said to her, "You did miss a sight, Cap o' Rushes!"

"What was that?" says she.

"Why, the beautifullest lady you ever see, dressed right gay and ga.'[2] The young master, he never took his eyes off her." "Well, I should have liked to have seen her," says Cap o' Rushes. "Well, there's to be another dance this evening, and perhaps she'll be there."

But, come the evening, Cap o' Rushes said she was too tired to go with them. Howsoever, when they were gone she offed with her cap o' rushes and cleaned herself, and away she went to the dance.

The master's son had been reckoning on seeing her, and he danced with no one else, and never took his eyes off her. But, before the dance was over, she slipped off, and home she went, and when the maids came back she pretended to be asleep with her cap o' rushes on.

---

1   Bog or marsh.
2   And all (colloquial).

Next day they said to her again, "Well, Cap o' Rushes, you should ha' been there to see the lady. There she was again, gay and ga', and the young master he never took his eyes off her."

"Well, there," says she, "I should ha' liked to ha' seen her."

"Well," says they, "there's a dance again this evening, and you must go with us, for she's sure to be there."

Well, come this evening, Cap o' Rushes said she was too tired to go, and do what they would she stayed at home. But when they were gone she offed with her cap o' rushes and cleaned herself, and away she went to the dance.

The master's son was rarely glad when he saw her. He danced with none but her and never took his eyes off her. When she wouldn't tell him her name, nor where she came from, he gave her a ring and told her if he didn't see her again he should die.

Well, before the dance was over, off she slipped, and home she went, and when the maids came home she was pretending to be asleep with her cap o' rushes on.

Well, next day they says to her, "There, Cap o' Rushes, you didn't come last night, and now you won't see the lady, for there's no more dances."

"Well I should have rarely liked to have seen her," says she.

The master's son he tried every way to find out where the lady was gone, but go where he might, and ask whom he might, he never heard anything about her. And he got worse and worse for the love of her till he had to keep his bed.

"Make some gruel for the young master," they said to the cook. "He's dying for the love of the lady." The cook she set about making it when Cap o' Rushes came in.

"What are you adoing of?" says she.

"I'm going to make some gruel for the young master," says the cook, "for he's dying for love of the lady."

"Let me make it," says Cap o' Rushes.

Well, the cook wouldn't at first, but at last she said yes, and Cap o' Rushes made the gruel. And when she had made it she slipped the ring into it on the sly before the cook took it upstairs.

The young man he drank it and then he saw the ring at the bottom.

"Send for the cook," says he.

So up she comes.

"Who made this gruel here?" says he.

"I did," says the cook, for she was frightened.

And he looked at her.

"No, you didn't," says he. "Say who did it, and you shan't be harmed."

"Well, then, 'twas Cap o' Rushes," says she.

"Send Cap o' Rushes here," says he. So Cap o' Rushes came.

"Did you make my gruel?" says he.

"Yes, I did," says she.

"Where did you get this ring?" says he.

"From him that gave it me," says she.

"Who are you, then?" says the young man.

"I'll show you," says she. And she offed with her cap o' rushes, and there she was in her beautiful clothes.

Well, the master's son he got well very soon, and they were to be married in a little time. It was to be a very grand wedding, and every one was asked far and near. And Cap o' Rushes' father was asked. But she never told anybody who she was.

But before the wedding she went to the cook, and says she:

"I want you to dress every dish without a mite o' salt."

"That'll be rare nasty," says the cook.

"That doesn't signify," says she.

"Very well," says the cook.

Well, the wedding-day came, and they were married. And after they were married all the company sat down to the dinner. When they began to eat the meat, it was so tasteless they couldn't eat it. But Cap o' Rushes' father tried first one dish and then another, and then he burst out crying.

"What is the matter?" said the master's son to him.

"Oh!" says he, "I had a daughter. And I asked her how much she loved me. And she said 'As much as fresh meat loves salt.' And I turned her from my door, for I thought she didn't love me. And now I see she loved me best of all. And she may be dead for aught I know."

"No, father, here she is!" says Cap o' Rushes. And she goes up to him and puts her arms round him. And so they were all happy ever after.

VASILISA THE BEAUTIFUL[1]

Aleksandr Afanas'ev

IN A CERTAIN KINGDOM THERE lived a merchant. Although he had been married for twelve years, he had only one daughter, called Vasilisa the Beautiful. When the girl was eight years old, her mother died. On her deathbed the merchant's wife called her daughter, took a doll from under her coverlet, gave it to the girl, and said: "Listen, Vasilisushka. Remember and heed my last words. I am dying, and together with my maternal blessing I leave you this doll. Always keep it with you and do not show it to anyone; if you get into trouble, give the doll food, and ask its advice. When it has eaten, it will tell you what to do in your trouble." Then the mother kissed her child and died.

After his wife's death the merchant mourned as is proper, and then began to think of marrying again. He was a handsome man and had no difficulty in finding a bride, but he liked best a certain widow. Because she was elderly and had two daughters of her own, of almost the same age as Vasilisa, he thought that she was an experienced housewife and mother. So he married her, but was deceived, for she did not turn out to be a good mother for his Vasilisa. Vasilisa was the most beautiful girl in the village; her stepmother and stepsisters were jealous of her beauty and tormented her by giving her all kinds of work to do, hoping that she would grow thin from toil and tanned from exposure to the wind and sun; in truth, she had a most miserable life. But Vasilisa bore all this without complaint and became lovelier and more buxom, every day, while the stepmother and her daughters grew thin and ugly from spite, although they always sat with folded hands, like ladies.

How did all this come about? Vasilisa was helped by her doll. Without its aid the girl could never have managed all that work. In return, Vasilisa sometimes did not eat, but kept the choicest morsels for her doll. And at night, when everyone was asleep, she would lock herself in the little room in which she lived, and would give the doll a treat, saying: "Now, little doll, eat, and listen to my troubles. I live in my father's house but am deprived of all joy; a wicked stepmother is driving me from the white world. Tell me how I should live and what I should do." The doll would eat, then would give her advice and comfort her in her trouble, and in the morning, she would perform all the chores for Vasilisa, who rested in the shade and picked flowers while the flower beds were weeded, the cabbage sprayed, the water brought in, and the stove fired. The doll even showed Vasilisa an herb that would protect her from sunburn. She led an easy life, thanks to her doll.

---

1   First published in 1855. This text from *Russian Fairy Tales*, trans. Norbert Guterman (New York: Pantheon, 1945).

Several years went by. Vasilisa grew up and reached the marriage age. She was wooed by all the young men in the village, but no one would even look at the stepmother's daughters. The stepmother was more spiteful than ever, and her answer to all the suitors was: "I will not give the youngest in marriage before the elder ones." And each time she sent a suitor away, she vented her anger on Vasilisa in cruel blows.

One day the merchant had to leave home for a long time in order to trade in distant lands. The stepmother moved to another house; near that house was a thick forest, and in a glade of that forest stood a hut, and in the hut lived Baba Yaga. She never allowed anyone to come near her and ate human beings as if they were chickens. Having moved into the new house, the merchant's wife, hating Vasilisa, repeatedly sent the girl to the woods for one thing or another; but each time Vasilisa returned home safe and sound: her doll had shown her the way and kept her far from Baba Yaga's hut.

Autumn came. The stepmother gave evening work to all three maidens: the oldest had to make lace, the second to knit stockings, and Vasilisa had to spin; and each one had to finish her task. The stepmother put out the lights all over the house, leaving only one candle in the room where the girls worked, and went to bed. The girls worked. The candle began to smoke; one of the stepsisters took up a scissor to trim it, but instead, following her mother's order, she snuffed it out, as though inadvertently. "What shall we do now?" said the girls. "There is no light in the house and our tasks are not finished. Someone must run to Baba Yaga and get some light." "The pins on my lace give me light," said the one who was making lace. "I shall not go." "I shall not go either," said the one who was knitting stockings, "my knitting needles give me light." "Then you must go," both of them cried to their stepsister. "Go to Baba Yaga!" And they pushed Vasilisa out of the room. She went into her own little room, put the supper she had prepared before her doll, and said: "Now dolly, eat, and aid me in my need. They are sending me to Baba Yaga for a light, and she will eat me up." The doll ate the supper and its eyes gleamed like two candles. "Fear not, Vasilisushka," it said. "Go where you are sent, only keep me with you all the time. With me in your pocket you will suffer no harm from Baba Yaga." Vasilisa made ready, put her doll in her pocket, and, having made the sign of the cross, went into the deep forest.

She walked in fear and trembling. Suddenly a horseman galloped past her: his face was white, he was dressed in white, his horse was white, and his horse's trappings were white—daybreak came to the woods.

She walked on farther, and a second horseman galloped past her: he was all red, he was dressed in red, and his horse was red—the sun began to rise.

Vasilisa walked the whole night and the whole day, and only on the following evening did she come to the glade where Baba Yaga's hut stood. The fence around the hut was made of human bones, and on the spikes were human skulls with staring eyes; the doors had human legs for doorposts, human hands for bolts, and a mouth with sharp teeth in place of a lock. Vasilisa was numb with horror and stood rooted to the spot. Suddenly another horseman rode by. He was all black, he was dressed in black, and his horse was black. He galloped up to Baba Yaga's door and vanished, as though the earth had swallowed him up—night came. But the darkness did not last long. The eyes of all the skulls on the fence began to gleam and the glade was as bright as day. Vasilisa shuddered with fear, but not knowing where to run, remained on the spot.

Soon a terrible noise resounded through the woods; the trees crackled, the dry leaves rustled; from the woods Baba Yaga drove out in a mortar, prodding it on with a pestle, and sweeping her traces with a broom. She rode up to the gate, stopped, and sniffing the air around her, cried: "Fie, fie! I smell a Russian smell! Who is here?" Vasilisa came up to the old witch and, trembling with fear, bowed low to her and said: "It is I, grandmother. My stepsisters sent me to get some light." "Very well," said Baba Yaga. "I know them, but before I give you the light you must live with me and work for me; if not, I will eat you up." Then she turned to the gate and cried: "Hey, my strong bolts, unlock! Open up, my wide gate!" The gate opened, and Baba Yaga drove in whistling. Vasilisa followed her, and then everything closed again.

Having entered the room, Baba Yaga stretched herself out in her chair and said to Vasilisa: "Serve me what is in the stove; I am hungry." Vasilisa lit a torch from the skulls on the fence and began to serve Yaga the food from the stove—and enough food had been prepared for ten people. She brought kvass,[1] mead, beer, and wine from the cellar. The old witch ate and drank everything, leaving for Vasilisa only a little cabbage soup, a crust of bread, and a piece of pork. Then Baba Yaga made ready to go to bed and said: "Tomorrow after I go, see to it that you sweep the yard, clean the hut, cook the dinner, wash the linen, and go to the cornbin and sort out a bushel of wheat. And let everything be done, or I will eat you up!" Having given these orders, Baba Yaga began to snore. Vasilisa set the remnants of the old witch's supper before her doll, wept bitter tears, and said: "Here dolly, eat, and aid me in my need! Baba Yaga has given me a hard task to do and threatens to eat me up if I do not do it all. Help me!" The doll answered: "Fear not, Vasilisa the Beautiful! Eat your supper, say your prayers, and go to sleep; the morning is wiser than the evening."

Very early next morning Vasilisa awoke, after Baba Yaga had arisen, and looked out of the window. The eyes of the skulls were going out; then the white horseman flashed by, and it was daybreak. Baba Yaga went out into the yard, whistled, and the

---

1 Fermented beverage made from rye bread.

mortar, pestle, and broom appeared before her. The red horseman flashed by, and the sun rose. Baba Yaga sat in the mortar, prodded it on with the pestle, and swept her traces with the broom. Vasilisa remained alone, looked about Baba Yaga's hut, was amazed at the abundance of everything, and stopped wondering which work she should do first. For lo and behold, all the work was done; the doll was picking the last shreds of chaff from the wheat. "Ah my savior," said Vasilisa to her doll, "you have delivered me from death." "All you have to do," answered the doll, creeping into Vasilisa's pocket, "is to cook the dinner; cook it with the help of God and then rest, for your health's sake."

When evening came Vasilisa set the table and waited for Baba Yaga. Dusk began to fall, the black horseman flashed by the gate, and night came; only the skulls' eyes were shining. The trees crackled, the leaves rustled; Baba Yaga was coming. Vasilisa met her. "Is everything done?" asked Baba Yaga. "Please see for yourself, grandmother," said Vasilisa. Baba Yaga looked at everything, was annoyed that there was nothing she could complain about, and said: "Very well, then." Then she cried: "My faithful servants, my dear friends, grind my wheat!" Three pairs of hands appeared, took the wheat, and carried it out of sight. Baba Yaga ate her fill, made ready to go to sleep, and again gave her orders to Vasilisa. "Tomorrow," she commanded, "do the same work you have done today, and in addition take the poppy seed from the bin and get rid of the dust, grain by grain; someone threw dust into the bins out of spite." Having said this, the old witch turned to the wall and began to snore, and Vasilisa set about feeding her doll. The doll ate, and spoke as she had spoken the day before: "Pray to God and go to sleep; the morning is wiser than the evening. Everything will be done, Vasilisushka."

Next morning Baba Yaga again left the yard in her mortar, and Vasilisa and the doll soon had all the work done. The old witch came back, looked at everything, and cried: "My faithful servants, my dear friends, press the oil out of the poppy seed!" Three pairs of hands appeared, took the poppy seed, and carried it out of sight. Baba Yaga sat down to dine; she ate, and Vasilisa stood silent. "Why do you not speak to me?" said Baba Yaga. "You stand there as though you were dumb." "I did not dare to speak," said Vasilisa, "but if you'll give me leave, I'd like to ask you something." "Go ahead. But not every question has a good answer; if you know too much, you will soon grow old." "I want to ask you, grandmother, only about what I have seen. As I was on my way to you, a horseman on a white horse, all white himself and dressed in white, overtook me. Who is he?" "He is my bright day," said Baba Yaga. "Then another horseman overtook me; he had a red horse, was red himself, and was dressed in red. Who is he?" "He is my red sun." "And who is the black horseman whom I met at your very gate, grandmother?" "He is my dark night—and all of them are my faithful servants."

Vasilisa remembered the three pairs of hands, but kept silent. "Why don't you ask me more?" said Baba Yaga. "That will be enough," Vasilisa replied. "You said yourself, grandmother, that one who knows too much will grow old soon." "It is well," said Baba Yaga, "that you ask only about what you have seen outside my house, not inside my house; I do not like to have my dirty linen washed in public, and I eat the over-curious. Now I shall ask you something. How do you manage to do the work I set for you?" "I am helped by the blessing of my mother," said Vasilisa. "So that is what it is," shrieked Baba Yaga. "Get you gone, blessed daughter! I want no blessed ones in my house!" She dragged Vasilisa out of the room and pushed her outside the gate, took a skull with burning eyes from the fence, stuck it on a stick, and gave it to the girl, saying: "Here is your light for your stepsisters. Take it; that is what they sent you for."

Vasilisa ran homeward by the light of the skull, which went out only at daybreak, and by nightfall of the following day she reached the house. As she approached the gate, she was about to throw the skull away, thinking that surely they no longer need-ed a light in the house. But suddenly a dull voice came from the skull, saying "Do not throw me away, take me to your stepmother." She looked at the stepmother's house and, seeing that there was no light in the windows, decided to enter with her skull. For the first time she was received kindly. Her stepmother and stepsisters told her that since she had left they had had no fire in the house; they were unable to strike a flame themselves, and whatever light was brought by the neighbors went out the moment it was brought into the house. "Perhaps your fire will last," said the stepmother. The skull was brought into the room, and its eyes kept staring at the stepmother and her daughters, and burned them. They tried to hide, but wherever they went the eyes followed them. By morning they were all burned to ashes; only Vasilisa remained untouched by the fire.

In the morning Vasilisa buried the skull in the ground, locked up the house, and went to the town. A certain childless old woman gave her shelter, and there she lived, waiting for her father's return. One day she said to the woman: "I am weary of sitting without work, grandmother. Buy me some flax, the best you can get; at least I shall be spinning." The old woman bought good flax and Vasilisa set to work. She spun as fast as lightning and her threads were even and thin as a hair. She spun a great deal of yarn; it was time to start weaving it, but no comb fine enough for Vasilisa's yarn could be found, and no one would undertake to make one. Vasilisa asked her doll for aid. The doll said: "Bring me an old comb, an old shuttle, and a horse's mane; I will make a loom for you." Vasilisa got everything that was required and went to sleep, and during the night the doll made a wonderful loom for her.

By the end of the winter the linen was woven, and it was so fine that it could be passed through a needle like a thread. In the spring the linen was bleached, and Vasilisa said to the old woman: "Grandmother, sell this linen and keep the money for yourself." The old woman looked at the linen and gasped: "No, my child! No one can wear such linen except the tsar; I shall take it to the palace." The old woman went to the tsar's palace and walked back and forth beneath the windows. The tsar saw her and asked: "What do you want, old woman?" "Your Majesty," she answered, "I have brought rare merchandise; I do not want to show it to anyone but you." The tsar ordered her to be brought before him, and when he saw the linen he was amazed. "What do you want for it?" asked the tsar. "It has no price, little father tsar! I have brought it as a gift to you." The tsar thanked her and rewarded her with gifts.

The tsar ordered shirts to be made of the linen. It was cut, but nowhere could they find a seamstress who was willing to sew them. For a long time they tried to find one, but in the end the tsar summoned the old woman and said: "You have known how to spin and weave such linen, you must know how to sew shirts of it." "It was not I that spun and wove this linen, Your Majesty," said the old woman. "This is the work of a maiden to whom I give shelter." "Then let her sew the shirts," ordered the tsar.

The old woman returned home and told everything to Vasilisa. "I knew all the time," said Vasilisa to her, "that I would have to do this work." She locked herself in her room and set to work; she sewed without rest and soon a dozen shirts were ready. The old woman took them to the tsar, and Vasilisa washed herself, combed her hair, dressed in her finest clothes, and sat at the window. She sat there waiting to see what would happen. She saw a servant of the tsar entering the courtyard. The messenger came into the room and said: "The tsar wishes to see the needlewoman who made his shirts, and wishes to reward her with his own hands." Vasilisa appeared before the tsar. When the tsar saw Vasilisa the Beautiful he fell madly in love with her. "No, my beauty," he said, "I will not separate from you; you shall be my wife." He took Vasilisa by her white hands, seated her by his side, and the wedding was celebrated at once. Soon Vasilisa's father returned, was overjoyed at her good fortune, and came to live in his daughter's house. Vasilisa took the old woman into her home too, and carried her doll in her pocket till the end of her life.

LITTLE GOLD STAR[1]

Joe Hayes

LONG, LONG AGO THERE LIVED a man whose wife had died. The only family he had was a daughter whose name was Arcia. The man's neighbor was a woman named Margarita, and her husband had died. Margarita had two daughters.

Every day when Arcia would walk down the street in front of Margarita's house, the neighbor would come out and give her something good to eat. She'd give her *pan dulce*[2] or cookies or little honey cakes.

One day Arcia said to her father, "Papa, why don't you marry our neighbor. She's very good to me. She gives me something sweet to eat almost every day."

Her father didn't want to do it. "You'll see, daughter," he said to Arcia—

Today Margarita is so sweet and kind,
But her sweetness will turn bitter with time.

But Arcia insisted. "No! She's a nice woman, and you should marry her." Finally she got her way, and her father married their neighbor.

At first everything was fine. But when summer came and the man went off to the mountains to take his sheep to the high meadows, the stepsisters started quarreling with Arcia.

Margarita no longer liked Arcia. She was very unkind to her. She bought many beautiful gifts for her own daughters—silken dresses and gold jewelry—but when Arcia's shoes wore out, she didn't even buy her a new pair. Arcia had to go around barefoot.

In time the bedroom was so full of the beautiful things of the stepsisters that there was no room for Arcia to sleep there. She had to move to the kitchen and sleep next to the stove.

When Arcia's father returned from the mountains, he chose three young sheep from the flock. He gave one sheep to each girl. "Tend your sheep carefully," he told them. "When they're full grown, you can sell them and keep the money yourselves. Or, if you wish, I'll shear the sheep and you can spin and weave the wool."

The girls began tending their sheep, and Arcia took the best care of hers. Before long it was the fattest of the three and covered with thick wool.

One day Arcia said to her father, "Papa, I want you to shear my sheep for me.

---

1   Published in 2002 (El Paso, TX: Cinco P).
2   Sweet bread.

I'll spin the wool and weave it into a blanket to keep you warm when you go to the mountains."

So the man sheared his daughter's sheep and Arcia carried the wool to the river to wash it. She was bending over, washing the wool in the water of the stream, when suddenly a big hawk came swooping down from the sky and snatched it away from her.

Arcia called out to the bird, "Señor Hawk, please give my wool back to me."

And the hawk replied to her with human speech: "Lift ... up ... your ... eyes ... Look ... where ... I ... fly-y-y."

So she did what the bird had told her to do. She turned her head and looked up. When she looked up, down from the sky came a little gold star, and it fastened itself to her forehead.

She went running home, and as she ran along, the wool fell into her arms, already washed and spun and woven into fine cloth.

When she got home Margarita said, "Take that piece of tin off your forehead!" And she grabbed her and tried to scrape the star off, but the more she scraped, the more brightly it shone.

Her stepsisters were filled with jealousy. They said, "Why shouldn't we have a star on our foreheads too?" And they went looking for their stepfather to have him shear their sheep.

The first one found him and ordered him to shear her sheep. She went running to the river with the wool. As she was washing it in the water of the stream, the hawk came swooping down again and snatched it away.

"You evil bird!" she screamed. "Bring my wool back to me."

The hawk called down, "Lift ... up ... your ... eyes ... Look ... where ... I ... fly-y-y."

"What?" she said. "Don't tell me where to look. I'll look wherever I want to. Bring my wool back right now."

But finally she had to look up to see where the hawk had gone. When she did look up, down from the sky came a long floppy donkey's ear and fastened itself to her forehead!

The girl ran home crying. When her mother saw her she gasped, "Bring me my scissors!" She took her scissors and snipped off the donkey's ear, but a longer and floppier one grew in its place.

From that day on, everyone in the village called the girl *Donkey Ear*!

But the other sister didn't know what had happened, and she went to the river with the wool from her sheep. She started to wash it in the water, and again the hawk swooped down and snatched it away.

"You rotten hawk," she shouted. "Bring my wool back."

"Lift ... up ... your ... eyes ... Look ... where ... I ... fly-y-y."

"I don't have to obey you. Bring my wool back this instant!"

But she too had to look up to find out where the hawk had gone. When she looked up, down from the sky came a long, green cow horn, and it stuck to her forehead.

She ran home, and when her mother saw her, she said, "Bring me a saw!"

With the saw she tried to cut the cow horn off, but the more she cut, the longer and greener it grew. From that day on, everyone in the village called her *Green Horn*!

But all the villagers called Arcia *Little Gold Star*. And so Margarita wouldn't let Arcia go to town anymore. She made her stay home and do all the work. She had to cook supper and clean the house and wash the clothes. She had to chop firewood and carry water from the well.

And then one day when Arcia was going to the well with her bucket, a messenger from the king's palace came by. He was spreading the word that the prince had decided he would like to get married. Since he couldn't find any girl in his own village to fall in love with, he thought he'd give a big party. Every girl from every village throughout the mountains was invited so that the prince could find a bride.

Arcia told her stepsisters what she had heard, and when the day of the party arrived, she helped them get dressed in their silken gowns. She fixed their hair for them so that it would hide the horrible things on their foreheads. She went to the door and waved goodbye as they went off to the party. She didn't even have a pair of shoes, much less a fancy dress for a party, so she had to stay home.

But that evening, all by herself at home, she began to feel sad. She thought, *It won't do any harm if I just go to the palace and look in the window to see what a fine party is like.*

She went to the palace and crept up to the window and peeked in. When she peeked through the window, the little gold star on her forehead began to shine more brightly than the sun. Everyone turned to look.

The prince called out, "Have the girl with the gold star come in here!" And his servants went running to bring Arcia into the party. But when Arcia saw the servants, she was frightened and ran home.

The next day, the prince and his servants started going from house to house looking for the girl with the gold star. Finally they came to Arcia's house. But Margarita made her hide under the table in the kitchen and ordered her not to come out.

The woman called for her own daughters and presented them to the prince. "Your Majesty, one of these might be the girl you're looking for. Aren't they lovely young women?"

The prince took one look at the girls and gasped. He saw the cow horn and the donkey ear on their foreheads.

"No, señora," the prince said politely. "I don't think either one is the girl I'm looking for." And he started backing toward the door.

But just then the cat got up from her bed by the fireplace and walked toward the prince. The cat rubbed against the prince's ankle and purred, "Meeooow ... meeooow ... Arcia is hiding under the table."

"What was that?" the prince asked. "Did the cat say someone is under the table?"

"Oh, no," the woman said. "The cat's just hungry." She picked up the cat and threw it outside.

But the cat came right back and rubbed against the prince's other ankle. "Meeooow ... meeooow ... Arcia is hiding under the table."

"Yes!" the prince insisted. "The cat said someone is under the table. Who is it?" And he told his servants to find out.

When Arcia saw the servants coming toward her, she stood up. Even in her dirty, ragged old clothes she looked as fine and noble as a princess. The prince fell in love with her at first sight.

The prince asked Arcia to marry him, and she said she would. A few days later, the wedding celebration began. It lasted for nine days and nine nights, and the last day was better than the first. And everyone was invited, even the mean Margarita and her two daughters—*Green Horn* and *Donkey Ear*!

I came on a colt
And I'll leave on its mother.
If you liked this story
Then tell me another!

Note for Readers and Storytellers
This Cinderella *cuento* was extremely popular in the mountain communities of New Mexico. All the traditional versions influenced my treatment of the tale, but I especially relied on that of Aurora Lucero White Lea in *Literary Folklore of the Hispanic Southwest*. It is from her version that I got the name Arcia. The traditional versions are consistent in many details and I've tried to retain what I see as essential to the story. The symbolic reward of a gold star on the forehead appears in almost every version of the Cinderella tale in New Mexico. It appears in other tales as well, but it seems especially central to this tale.

One way in which many traditional tellings differ from mine is that the animal which snatches the object away from the girls is most often a fish, rather than a bird. And in most versions the sheep is slaughtered and the sheep's intestines stolen, but I thought this detail was a bit gruesome [for a fully illustrated picture book]. Another element found in many traditional Hispanic tellings, but not in mine, is the appearance of the Blessed Virgin to advise the girls. Of course, only the heroine heeds her advice. I assume she is the same figure who is identified as the Fairy God-mother in the best-known version of Cinderella. I base my telling on a plot form that doesn't require her intervention.

As in my story, almost all traditional versions of the tale give the father's response to the daughter's request that he marry their neighbor in verse form, most commonly

Si hoy nos da sopitas de miel
(Though she gives us bread pudding with honey today,)

Manana nos dara sopitas de hiel.
(Tomorrow she'll give us bread pudding with gall.)

This is a folk expression once fairly popular in New Mexico. The figurative meaning of *sopitas de miel* is roughly equivalent to the contemporary English expression, *nic-ey-nice*. And of course *sopitas de hiel* means the opposite. I changed the verse to one I learned from a teacher at the elementary school in Taos, New Mexico. The poetic elements of the Spanish make it more fun to say. But even more important to me is the name it provides for the stepmother. By referring to her as Margarita, rather than the stepmother, I was able to avoid something that causes some contemporary read-ers and listeners discomfort: the association of so many negative descriptors with the word stepmother in the old tales.

The little verse on the end of the story is more than decoration. Because the old cuentos date from a time when storytelling was a very important activity, they bear remnants of the rituals and form as that accompanied the telling of tales. It was once customary to end each story with a brief verse, just as many people still end every prayer with the word *amen.*

THE LITTLE RED FISH AND THE CLOG OF GOLD[1]

Inea Bushnaq

NEITHER HERE NOR THERE LIVED a man, a fisherman. His wife had drowned in the great river and left him a pretty little girl not more than two years old. In a house nearby lived a widow and her daughter. The women began to come to the fisherman's house to care for the girl and comb her hair, and every time she said to the child, "Am I not like a mother to you?" She tried to please the fisherman, but he always said, "I shall never marry. Stepmothers hate their husband's children even though their rivals are dead and buried." When his daughter grew old enough to pity him when she saw him washing his own clothes, she began to say, "Why don't you marry our neighbor, Father? There is no evil in her, and she loves me as much as her own daughter."

They say water will wear away stone. In the end the fisherman married the widow, and she came to live in his house. The wedding week was not yet over when sure enough, she began to feel jealous of her husband's daughter. She saw how much her father loved the child and indulged her. And she could not help but see that the child was fair, and quick, while her own daughter was thin and sallow, and so clumsy she did not know how to sew the seam of her gown.

No sooner did the woman feel that she was mistress of the house than she began to leave all the work for the girl to do. She would not give her stepchild soap to wash her hair and feet, and she fed her nothing but crusts and crumbs. All this the girl bore patiently, saying not a word. For she did not wish to grieve her father, and she thought, "I picked up the scorpion with my own hand; I'll save myself with my own mind."

Besides her other errands, the fisherman's daughter had to go down to the river each day to bring home her father's catch, the fish they ate and sold. One day from beneath a basket load of three catfish, suddenly one little red fish spoke to her:

Child with such patience to endure,
I beg you now, my life secure.
Throw me back into the water,
And now and always be my daughter.

The girl stopped to listen, half in wonder and half in fear. Then retracing her steps, she flung the fish into the river and said, "Go! People say, 'Do a good deed for, even if

---

1   From *Arab Folktales* (New York: Pantheon Books, 1986).

it is like throwing gold into the sea, in God's sight it is not lost.'" And lifting itself on the face of the water, the little fish replied:

Your kindness is not in vain—
A new mother do you gain.
Come to me when you are sad,
And I shall help to make you glad.

The girl went back to the house and gave the three catfish to her stepmother. When the fisherman returned and asked about the fourth, she told him, "Father, the red fish dropped from my basket. It may have fallen into the river, for I couldn't find it again." "Never mind," he said, "it was a very small fish." But her stepmother began to scold. "You never told me there were four fishes. You never said that you lost one. Go now and look for it, before I curse you!"

It was past sunset and the girl had to walk back to the river in the dark. Her eyes swollen with tears, she stood on the water's edge and called out,

Red fish, my mother and nurse,
Come quickly, and ward off a curse.

And there at her feet appeared the little red fish to comfort her and say, "Though patience is bitter, its fruit is very sweet. Now bend down and take this gold piece from my mouth. Give it to your stepmother, and she will say nothing to you." Which is exactly what happened.

The years came and the years went, and in the fisherman's house life continued as before. Nothing changed except that the two little girls were now young women.

One day a great man, the master of the merchants' guild, announced that his daughter was to be married. It was the custom for the women to gather at the bride's house on the "day of the bride's henna" to celebrate and sing as they watched the girl's feet, palms, and arms being decorated for the wedding with red henna stain. Then every mother brought her unwed daughters to be seen by the mothers of sons. Many a girl's destiny was decided on such a day.

The fisherman's wife rubbed and scrubbed her daughter and dressed her in her finest gown and hurried her off to the master merchant's house with the rest. The fisherman's daughter was left at home to fill the water jar and sweep the floor while they were gone.

But as soon as the two women were out of sight, the fisherman's daughter gathered up her gown and ran down to the river to tell the little red fish her sorrow. "You shall go to the bride's henna and sit on the cushions in the center of the hall," said the little red fish. She gave the girl a small bundle and said, "Here is everything you need to wear, with a comb of pearl for your hair and clogs of gold for your feet. But one thing you must remember: be sure to leave before your stepmother rises to go."

When the girl loosened the cloth that was knotted round the clothes, out fell a gown of silk as green as clover. It was stitched with threads and sequins of gold, and from its folds rose a sweet smell like the essence of roses. Quickly she washed herself and decked herself and tucked the comb of pearl behind her braid and slipped the golden clogs onto her feet and went tripping off to the feast.

The women from every house in the town were there. They paused in their talk to admire her face and her grace, and they thought, "This must be the governor's daughter!" They brought her sherbet and cakes made with almonds and honey and they sat her in the place of honor in the middle of them all. She looked for her stepmother with her daughter and saw them far off, near the door where the peasants were sitting, and the wives of weavers and peddlers.

Her stepmother stared at her and said to herself, "O Allah Whom we praise, how much this lady resembles my husband's daughter! But then, don't they say, 'Every seven men were made from one clod of clay?'" And the stepmother never knew that it was her very own husband's daughter and none other!

Not to spin out our tale, before the rest of the women stood up, the fisherman's daughter went to the mother of the bride to say, "May it be with God's blessings and bounty, O my aunt!" and hurried out. The sun had set and darkness was falling. On her way the girl had to cross a bridge over the stream that flowed into the king's garden. And by fate and divine decree, it happened that as she ran over the bridge one of her golden clogs fell off her foot and into the river below. It was too far to climb down to the water and search in the dusk; what if her stepmother should return home before her? So the girl took off her other shoe, and pulling her cloak around her head, dashed on her way.

When she reached the house she shucked her fine clothes, rolled the pearly comb and golden clog inside them, and hid them under the woodpile. She rubbed her head and hands and feet with earth to make them dirty, and she was standing with her broom when her stepmother found her. The wife looked into her face and examined her hands and feet and said, "Still sweeping after sunset? Or are you hoping to sweep our lives away?"

What of the golden clog? Well, the current carried it into the king's garden and rolled it and rolled it until it came to rest in the pool where the king's son led his stallion to drink. Next day the prince was watering the horse. He saw that every time it lowered its head to drink, something made it shy and step back. What could there be at the bottom of the pool to frighten his stallion? He called the groom, and from the mud the man brought him the shining clog of gold.

When the prince held the beautiful little thing in his hand, he began to imagine the beautiful little foot that had worn it. He walked back to the palace with his heart busy and his mind full of the girl who owned so precious a shoe. The queen saw him lost in thought and said, "May Allah send us good news; why so careworn, my son?" "Yammah, Mother, I want you to find me a wife!" said the prince. "So much thought over one wife and no more?" said the queen. "I'll find you a thousand if you wish! I'll bring every girl in the kingdom to be your wife if you want! But tell me, my son, who is the girl who has stolen your reason?" "I want to marry the girl who owns this clog," replied the prince, and he told his mother how he had found it. "You shall have her, my son," said the queen. "I shall begin my search tomorrow as soon as it is light, and I shall not stop till I find her."

The very next day the prince's mother went to work, in at one house and out at the next with the golden clog tucked under her arm. Wherever she saw a young woman, she measured the shoe against the sole of the maiden's foot. Meanwhile the prince sat in the palace gate waiting for her return. "What news, Mother?" he asked. And she said, "Nothing yet, my son. Be patient, child, put snow on your breast and cool your passion. I'll find her yet."

And so the search continued. Entering at one gate and leaving at the next, the queen visited the houses of the nobles and the merchants and the goldsmiths. She saw the daughters of the craftsmen and the tradesmen. She went into the huts of the water carriers and the weavers, and stopped at each house until only the fishermen's hovels on the bank of the river were left. Every evening when the prince asked for news, she said, "I'll find her, I'll find her."

When the fisherfolk were told that the queen was coming to visit their houses, that wily fisherman's wife got busy. She bathed her daughter and dressed her in her best, she rinsed her hair with henna and rimmed her eyes with *kohl* and rubbed her cheeks till they glowed red. But still when the girl stood beside the fisherman's daughter, it was like a candle in the sun. Much as the stepchild had been ill-treated and starved, through the will of Allah and with the help of the little red fish, she had grown in beauty from day to day. Now her stepmother dragged her out of the house and into the yard. She pushed her into the bakehouse and covered its mouth with the round clay tray on which she spread her dough. This she held down with the stone of her handmill. "Don't dare move until I come for you!" said the stepmother. What could the poor girl do but crouch in the ashes and trust in Allah to save her?

When the queen arrived the stepmother pushed her daughter forward, saying, "Kiss the hands of the prince's mother, ignorant child!" As she had done in the other houses, the queen set the girl beside her and held up her foot and measured the golden clog against it. Just at that moment the neighbor's rooster flew into the yard and began to crow,

Ki-ki-ki-kow!
Let the king's wife know
They put the ugly one on show
And hid the beauty down below!
Ki-ki-ki-kow!

He began again with his piercing cry, and the stepmother raced out and flapped her arms to chase him away. But the queen had heard the words, and she sent her servants to search both high and low. When they pushed aside the cover off the mouth of the oven, they found the girl—fair as the moon in the midst of the ashes. They brought her to the queen, and the golden clog fit as if it had been the mold from which her foot was cast.

The queen was satisfied. She said, "From this hour that daughter of yours is betrothed to my son. Make ready for the wedding. God willing, the procession shall come for her on Friday." And she gave the stepmother a purse filled with gold.

When the woman realized that her plans had failed, that her husband's daughter was to marry the prince while her own remained in the house, she was filled with anger and rage. "I'll see that he sends her back before the night is out," she said.

She took the purse of gold, ran to the perfumer's bazaar, and asked for a purge so strong that it would shred the bowels to tatters. At the sight of the gold the perfumer began to mix the powders in his tray. Then she asked for arsenic and lime, which weaken hair and make it fall, and an ointment that smelled like carrion.

Now the stepmother prepared the bride for her wedding. She washed her hair with henna mixed with arsenic and lime, and spread the foul ointment over her hair. Then she held the girl by her ear and poured the purge down her throat. Soon the wedding procession arrived, with horses and drums, fluttering bright clothes, and the sounds of jollity. They lifted the bride onto the litter and took her away. She came to the palace preceded by music and followed by singing and chanting and clapping of hands. She entered the chamber, the prince lifted the veil off her face, and she shone like a fourteen-day moon. A scent of amber and roses made the prince press his face to her hair. He ran his fingers over her locks, and it was like a man playing with cloth of gold. Now the bride began to feel a heaviness in her belly, but from under the hem of her gown there fell gold pieces in thousands till the carpet and the cushions were covered with gold.

Meanwhile the stepmother waited in her doorway, saying, "Now they'll bring her back in disgrace. Now she'll come home all filthy and bald." But though she stood in the doorway till dawn, from the palace no one came.

The news of the prince's fair wife began to fill the town, and the master merchant's son said to his mother, "They say that the prince's bride has a sister. I want her for my bride." Going to the fisherman's hut, his mother gave the fisherman's wife a purse full of gold and said, "Prepare the bride, for we shall come for her on Friday if God wills." And the fisherman's wife said to herself, "If what I did for my husband's daughter turned her hair to threads of gold and her belly to a fountain of coins, shall I not do the same for my own child?" She hastened to the perfumer and asked for the same powders and drugs, but stronger than before. Then she prepared her child, and the wedding procession came. When the merchant's son lifted her veil, it was like lifting the cover off a grave. The stink was so strong that it choked him, and her hair came away in his hands. So they wrapped the poor bride in her own filth and carried her back to her mother.

As for the prince, he lived with the fisherman's daughter in great happiness and joy, and God blessed them with seven children like seven golden birds.

Mulberry, mulberry,
So ends my story.
If my house were not so far
I'd bring you figs and raisins in a jar.

THE INDIAN CINDERELLA[1]

Cyrus Macmillan

ON THE SHORES OF A wide bay on the Atlantic coast there dwelt in old times a great Indian warrior. It was said that he had been one of Glooskap's[2] best helpers and friends, and that he had done for him many wonderful deeds. But that, no man knows. He had, however, a very wonderful and strange power; he could make himself invisible; he could thus mingle unseen with his enemies and listen to their plots. He was known among the people as Strong Wind, the Invisible. He dwelt with his sister in a tent near the sea, and his sister helped him greatly in his work. Many maidens would have been glad to marry him, and he was much sought after because of his mighty deeds; and it was known that Strong Wind would marry the first maiden who could see him as he came home at night. Many made the trial, but it was a long time before one succeeded.

Strong Wind used a clever trick to test the truthfulness of all who sought to win

---

1 From *Canadian Wonder Tales* (London: John Lane, the Bodley Head, 1918).
2 A legendary figure of the Mi'kmaq First Nations people.

him. Each evening as the day went down, his sister walked on the beach with any girl who wished to make the trial. His sister could always see him, but no one else could see him. And as he came home from work in the twilight, his sister as she saw him drawing near would ask the girl who sought him, "Do you see him?" And each girl would falsely answer, "Yes." And his sister would ask, "With what does he draw his sled?" And each girl would answer, "With the hide of a moose," or "With a pole," or "With a great cord." And then his sister would know that they all had lied, for their answers were mere guesses. And many tried and lied and failed, for Strong Wind would not marry any who were untruthful.

There lived in the village a great chief who had three daughters. Their mother had been long dead. One of these was much younger than the others. She was very beautiful and gentle and well beloved by all, and for that reason her older sisters were very jealous of her charms and treated her very cruelly. They clothed her in rags that she might be ugly; and they cut off her long black hair; and they burned her face with coals from the fire that she might be scarred and disfigured. And they lied to their father, telling him that she had done these things herself. But the young girl was patient and kept her gentle heart and went gladly about her work.

Like other girls, the chief's two eldest daughters tried to win Strong Wind. One evening, as the day went down, they walked on the shore with Strong Wind's sister and waited for his coming. Soon he came home from his day's work, drawing his sled. And his sister asked as usual, "Do you see him?" And each one, lying, answered, "Yes." And she asked, "Of what is his shoulder strap made?" And each, guessing, said, "Of rawhide." Then they entered the tent where they hoped to see Strong Wind eating his supper; and when he took off his coat and his moccasins they could see them, but more than these they saw nothing. And Strong Wind knew that they had lied, and he kept himself from their sight, and they went home dismayed.

One day the chief's youngest daughter with her rags and her burnt face resolved to seek Strong Wind. She patched her clothes with bits of birch bark from the trees, and put on the few little ornaments she possessed, and went forth to try to see the Invisible One as all the other girls of the village had done before. And her sisters laughed at her and called her "Fool"; and as she passed along the road all the people laughed at her because of her tattered frock and her burnt face, but silently she went her way.

Strong Wind's sister received the little girl kindly, and at twilight she took her to the beach. Soon Strong Wind came home drawing his sled. And his sister asked, "Do you see him?" And the girl answered, "No," and his sister wondered greatly because she spoke the truth. And again she asked, "Do you see him now?" And the girl answered, "Yes, and he is very wonderful." And she asked, "With what does he draw his sled?" And the girl answered, "With the Rainbow," and she was much afraid. And she asked further, "Of what is his bowstring?" And the girl answered, "His bowstring is the Milky Way."

Then Strong Wind's sister knew that because the girl had spoken the truth at first her brother had made himself visible to her. And she said, "Truly, you have seen him." And she took her home and bathed her, and all the scars disappeared from her face and body; and her hair grew long and black again like the raven's wing; and she gave her fine clothes to wear and many rich ornaments. Then she bade her take the wife's seat in the tent. Soon Strong Wind entered and sat beside her, and called her his bride. The very next day she became his wife, and ever afterwards she helped him to do great deeds. The girl's two elder sisters were very cross, and they wondered greatly at what had taken place. But Strong Wind, who knew of their cruelty, resolved to punish them. Using his great power, he changed them both into aspen trees and rooted them in the earth. And since that day the leaves of the aspen have always trembled, and they shiver in fear at the approach of Strong Wind, it matters not how softly he comes, for they are still mindful of his great power and anger because of their lies and their cruelty to their sister long ago.

SLEEPING BEAUTY

WE CONCLUDE THE COMPARATIVE SECTIONS with versions of "Sleeping Beauty"—a tale that has achieved popularity and provoked controversy in equal measure. The central character's hundred-year enchanted sleep is at the same time a memorable narrative ploy and a vivid symbol of feminine passivity; it is no wonder, then, that feminist critics have seen a darker aspect to the tale's continued success.

As in the previous sections, there can be little doubt that the earlier version (or versions) had a definite influence upon its successors, but in this case the result of that influence is clearly different. In the versions of "Little Red Riding Hood," we can see the process of literary refinement in the tale's elaboration; now that same process takes the opposite tack, as the tale undergoes significant shrinkage (particularly between Charles Perrault and the Grimms).

Despite the obvious differences between these versions, the central image of the enchanted sleep remains constant and is arguably the key to the popularity of the tale. So the question arises: how could an image of extended inactivity be so crucial to the tale's success? One answer, as P.L. Travers points out,[1] is that the central image of a sleeping princess awaiting the prince who will bring her (and her whole

---

1   P.L. Travers, *About the Sleeping Beauty* (New York: McGraw-Hill, 1975). Travers takes pains to remind us of the multi-faceted nature of the symbol, which she illustrates most effectively in a list of famous sleepers whose concerns often have little to do with growing up: "The idea of the sleeper, of somebody hidden from mortal eye, waiting until the time shall ripen has always been dear to the folkly mind—Snow White asleep in her glass coffin, Brynhild behind her wall of fire, Charlemagne in the heart of France, King Arthur in the Isle of Avalon, Frederick Barbarossa under his mountain in Thuringia. Muchukunda, the Hindu King, slept through eons till he was awakened by the Lord Krishna; Oisin of Ireland dreamed in Tir n'an Og for over three hundred years. Psyche in her magic sleep is a type of Sleeping Beauty, Sumerian Ishtar in the underworld may be said to be another. Holga the Dane is sleeping and waiting, and so, they say, is Sir Francis Drake. Quetzalcoatl of Mexico and Virochocha of Peru are both sleepers. Morgan le Fay of France and England and Dame Holle of Germany are sleeping in raths and cairns" (51).

world) back to life has powerful mythic overtones of death and resurrection. On a more human level, the image is a metaphor of growing up: in each case the heroine falls asleep as a naïve girl and awakens as a mature young woman on the threshold of marriage and adult responsibility. For cultural reasons, the metaphor is generally seen as gender-specific, in that sleep denotes the decorous passivity expected of the virtuous young female—a characteristic that for the most part attracted nineteenth-century approval of this tale, although even in those paternalistic times, a contrary vision was asserting itself, as Anne Ritchie's version of this tale (1874) demonstrates (see p. 254ff). By contrast, the young male must demonstrate his maturity through deeds of action and daring, manifested most effectively in Perrault's version of the tale.

Giambattista Basile was a minor Neapolitan courtier and soldier who was among the first in the Western world to commit the folk tale to paper. It becomes quickly apparent, however, that Basile's tales in *The Pentamerone* (1634) are a good deal more sophisticated than we expect a fairy tale to be; their content, tone, and overall structure hearken back to Giovanni Boccaccio's *The Decameron* (1353) and Geoffrey Chaucer's *The Canterbury Tales* (1387–1400) rather than anticipate the fairy-tale collections that would follow. This quality is well illustrated by Basile's version of "Sleeping Beauty," which is a story of rape, adultery, sexual rivalry, and attempted cannibalism—a far cry from what we have come to expect in this famous tale!

Comparing Basile's tale with Perrault's "The Sleeping Beauty in the Wood" (1697) provides a fascinating glimpse into the evolution of a tale in its literary form, as the Frenchman sets about revising it to match *his* assumptions about what a fairy tale is and who will read (or hear) it. In a nutshell, it might be said that Perrault's approach is rather more subtle than that of his Neapolitan predecessor. Clearly, Perrault wants no part of Basile's evident delight in the salacious aspects of his story. While as a royal courtier he was doubtless no stranger to confrontations between jealous wives and beautiful mistresses, his tale suggests that discretion and a sophisticated cynicism are now the rule in dealing with such matters; social diplomat that he is, Perrault favors the oblique comment, the aside that demonstrates the wit of the writer and makes an accomplice of the reader. Thus, Perrault's prince refrains—at least at the moment of discovery—from all physical contact with the sleeping princess (he is simply present when the enchantment reaches full term, whereas the spell-breaking kiss bestowed by the Grimms' prince implies an arousal that is sexual in nature). We may detect more than a trace of archness, however, when Perrault tells us that the young couple "did not sleep much, that night; the princess did not feel in the least drowsy." Likewise, through his use of symbolism, Perrault finds a way to sublimate the sexual rivalry that gives Basile's more realistic tale much of its impact. In Perrault's version, the king's tigerish wife becomes the prince's ogress mother, which allows the retention of several significant elements (such as the cannibalism motif), while further deflecting the violence of the tale with another touch of sly humor: her intention to eat one of Sleeping Beauty's children is horrific, of course, but there is a certain Gallic *savoir faire* in the instruction to her steward to "serve her up with sauce Robert."

Whatever induced Perrault to add this unexpected sequel, it undeniably gives the tale a modern aspect by confirming our doubts about the customary "happily-ever-after" assurances. Indeed, his addition to the tale clearly invites a Freudian interpretation, as the prince's mother wages her ruthless campaign to destroy all rivals for her son's affections. As suggested above, the lesser-known sequel contains an intriguing insight into *male* maturation, counterpointing Sleeping Beauty's transformation by sleep. The crisis of this episode is brought on by the prince's assumption that becoming king is the external confirmation of his personal maturity; he therefore chooses this moment to reveal the existence of his wife and children to his mother. "Some time afterwards," we are told, in an apparent *non sequitur* that speaks volumes, "the king decided to declare war on his neighbour, the Emperor Cantalabutte"! Given the prince's awareness of his mother's appetites, how are we to explain such a decision? Is his departure an indication of his naïveté, in that he has no inkling of the rivalry that he leaves behind him—or is he in fact so aware of it that he reckons there's more peace to be found in the middle of a battlefield?

After all the excitement of the two earlier versions, it comes as something of a surprise to realize that the much shorter, blander version (1819) by the Brothers Grimm is by far the best known—perhaps for the very reason that the Grimms chose not to darken the blue sky of romance with the storm clouds of jealousy and sexual rivalry that may loom up in human relationships (although, as we noted above, theirs is the version in which Sleeping Beauty's awakening has the clearest sexual connotation). Perrault's claims notwithstanding, it was only with the Grimms that the fairy tale unequivocally entered the child's domain. No trace of Basile's hand remains, and little enough of Perrault's either: a comparison of the gifts presented to Sleeping Beauty by the fairies in the Perrault and Grimm versions offers an intriguing insight into the different worlds from which these tales come. At the same time, it might be said that in Grimm we see the tale stripped down to its narrative core, revealing most clearly its oral origins.

SUN, MOON, AND TALIA (*SOLE, LUNE, E TALIA*)[1]

Giambattista Basile

THERE WAS ONCE A GREAT king who, on the birth of his daughter—to whom he gave the name of Talia—commanded all the wise men and seers in the kingdom to come and tell him what her future would be. These wise men, after many consultations, came to the conclusion that she would be exposed to great danger from a small splinter in some flax. Thereupon the King, to prevent any unfortunate accident, commanded that no flax or hemp or any other similar material should ever come into his house.

One day when Talia was grown up she was standing by the window, and saw an old woman pass who was spinning. Talia had never seen a distaff and spindle, and was therefore delighted with the dancing of the spindle. Prompted by curiosity, she had the old woman brought up to her, and taking the distaff in her hand, began to draw out the thread; but unfortunately a splinter in the hemp got under her fingernail, and she immediately fell dead upon the ground. At this terrible catastrophe the old woman fled from the room, rushing precipitously down the stairs. The stricken father, after having paid for this bucketful of sour wine with a barrelful of tears, left the dead Talia seated on a velvet chair under an embroidered canopy in the palace, which was in the middle of a wood. Then he locked the door and left forever the house which had brought him such evil fortune, so that he might entirely obliterate the memory of his sorrow and suffering.

It happened some time after that a falcon of a king who was out hunting in these parts flew in at the window of this house. As the bird did not return when called back, the King sent someone to knock at the door, thinking the house was inhabited. When they had knocked a long time in vain, the King sent for a vine-dresser's ladder, so that he might climb up himself and see what was inside. He climbed up and went in, and was astonished at not finding a living being anywhere. Finally he came to the room in which sat Talia as if under a spell.

The King called to her, thinking she was asleep; but since nothing he did or said brought her back to her senses, and being on fire with love, he carried her to a couch and, having gathered the fruits of love, left her lying there. Then he returned to his own kingdom and for a long time entirely forgot the affair.

Nine months later, Talia gave birth to two children, a boy and a girl, two splendid pearls. They were looked after by two fairies, who had appeared in the palace, and

---

1   First published in 1634–36. This text from *The Pentamerone*, trans. Benedetto Croce, ed. N.M. Penzer (London: John Lane, the Bodley Head, 1932).

who put the babies to their mother's breast. Once, when one of the babies wanted to suck, it could not find the breast, but got into its mouth instead the finger that had been pricked. This the baby sucked so hard that it drew out the splinter, and Talia was roused as if from a deep sleep. When she saw the two jewels at her side, she clasped them to her breast and held them as dear as life; but she could not understand what had happened, and how she came to be alone in the palace with two children, having everything she required to eat brought to her without seeing anyone.

One day the King bethought himself of the adventure of the fair sleeper and took the opportunity of another hunting expedition to go and see her. Finding her awake and with two prodigies of beauty, he was overpowered with joy. He told Talia what had happened and they made a great compact of friendship, and he remained several days in her company. Then he left her, promising to come again and take her back with him to his kingdom. When he reached his home he was forever talking of Talia and her children. At meals the names of Talia, Sun, and Moon (these were the children's names) were always on his lips; when he went to bed he was always calling one or the other.

The Queen had already had some glimmering of suspicion on account of her husband's long absence when hunting; and hearing his continued calling on Talia, Sun, and Moon, burned with a heat very different from the sun's heat, and calling the King's secretary, said to him: "Listen, my son, you are between Scylla and Charybdis,[1] between the doorpost and the door, between the poker and the grate. If you tell me with whom it is that my husband is in love, I will make you rich; if you hide the truth from me, you shall never be found again, dead or alive." The man, on the one hand moved by fear, and on the other egged on by interest, which is a bandage over the eyes of honour, a blinding of justice and a cast horseshoe to faith, told the Queen all, calling bread bread and wine wine.

Then she sent the same secretary in the King's name to tell Talia that he wished to see his children. Talia was delighted and sent the children. But the Queen, as soon as she had possession of them, with the heart of a Medea,[2] ordered the cook to cut their throats and to make them into hashes and sauces and give them to their unfortunate father to eat.

The cook, who was tender-hearted, was filled with pity on seeing these two golden apples of beauty, and gave them to his wife to hide and prepared two kids,[3] making a hundred different dishes of them. When the hour for dinner arrived, the Queen had the dishes brought in, and whilst the King was eating and enjoying them,

---

1   Two monsters of Greek mythology who lived on opposite sides of a narrow channel of water. The phrase "between Scylla and Charybdis" means having to choose between two undesirable situations.

2   One of the great sorceresses in Greek mythology; when her husband left her, she killed their children.

3   I.e., young goats.

exclaiming: "How good this is, by the life of Lanfusa! How tasty this is, by the soul of my grandmother!" she kept encouraging him, saying: "Eat away, you are eating what is your own." The first two or three times the King paid no attention to these words, but as she kept up the same strain of music, he answered: "I know very well I am eating what is my own; you never brought anything into the house." And getting up in a rage, he went off to a villa not far away to cool his anger down.

The Queen, not satisfied with what she thought she had already done, called the secretary again, and sent him to fetch Talia herself, pretending that the King was expecting her. Talia came at once, longing to see the light of her eyes and little guessing that it was fire that awaited her. She was brought before the Queen, who, with the face of a Nero[1] all inflamed with rage, said to her: "Welcome, Madame Troccola![2] So you are the fine piece of goods, the fine flower my husband is enjoying! You are the cursed bitch that makes my head go round! Now you have got into purgatory, and I will make you pay for all the harm you have done me!"

Talia began to excuse herself, saying it was not her fault and that the King had taken possession of her territory whilst she was sleeping. But the Queen would not listen to her, and commanded that a great fire should be lit in the courtyard of the palace and that Talia should be thrown into it.

The unfortunate Talia, seeing herself lost, threw herself on her knees before the Queen, and begged that at least she should be given time to take off the clothes she was wearing. The Queen, not out of pity for her, but because she wanted to save the clothes, which were embroidered with gold and pearls, said: "Undress—that I agree to."

Talia began to undress, and for each garment that she took off she uttered a shriek. She had taken off her dress, her skirt, and bodice and was about to take off her petticoat, and to utter her last cry, and they were just going to drag her away to reduce her to lye ashes, which they would throw into boiling water to wash Charon's[3] breeches with, when the King saw the spectacle and rushed up to learn what was happening. He asked for his children, and heard from his wife, who reproached him for his betrayal of her, how she had made him eat them himself.

The King abandoned himself to despair. "What!" he cried, "am I the wolf of my own sheep? Alas, why did my veins not recognise the fountain of their own blood? You renegade Turk, this barbarous deed is the work of your hands? Go, you shall get what you deserve; there will be no need to send such a tyrant-faced one to the Colosseum to do penance!"

So saying, he ordered that the Queen should be thrown into the fire lighted for

---

1 A Roman emperor infamous for his cruelty.
2 I.e., busybody.
3 The ferryman in Greek mythology who rowed the souls of the dead across the river Styx to Hades.

Talia, and that the secretary should be thrown in, too, for he had been her handle in this cruel game and the weaver of this wicked web. He would have had the same done to the cook who, as he thought, had cut up his children; but the cook threw himself at the King's feet, saying: "Indeed, my lord, for such a service there should be no other reward than a burning furnace; no pension but a spike-thrust from behind; no entertainment but that of being twisted and shrivelled in the fire; neither could there be any greater honour than for me, a cook, to have my ashes mingle with those of a queen. But this is not the thanks I expect for having saved your children from that spiteful dog who wished to kill them and return to your body what came from it."

The King was beside himself when he heard these words; it seemed to him as if he must be dreaming and that he could not believe his ears. Turning to the cook, he said: "If it is true that you have saved my children, you may be sure I will not leave you turning spits in the kitchen. You shall be in the kitchen of my heart, turning my will just as you please, and you shall have such rewards that you will account yourself the luckiest man in the world."

Whilst the King was speaking, the cook's wife, seeing her husband's difficulties, brought Sun and Moon up to their father, who, playing at the game of three with his wife and children, made a ring of kisses, kissing first one and then the other. He gave a handsome reward to the cook and made him Gentleman of the Bed-chamber. Talia became his wife, and enjoyed a long life with her husband and children, finding it to be true that:

Lucky people, so 'tis said,
Are blessed by Fortune whilst in bed.

THE SLEEPING BEAUTY IN THE WOOD[1]

Charles Perrault

[handwritten: okay but seriously, who gave this dude a pen? f***ed in the head.]

ONCE UPON A TIME, THERE lived a king and a queen who were bitterly unhappy because they did not have any children. They visited all the clinics, all the specialists, made holy vows, went on pilgrimages and said their prayers regularly but with so little success that when, at long last, the queen finally did conceive and, in due course, gave birth to a daughter, they were both wild with joy. Obviously, this baby's christening must be the grandest of all possible christenings; for her godmothers, she would have as many fairies as they could find in the entire kingdom. According to the custom of those times, each fairy would make the child a magic present, so that the princess could acquire every possible perfection. After a long search, they managed to trace seven suitable fairies.

After the ceremony at the church, the guests went back to the royal palace for a party in honour of the fairy godmothers. Each of these important guests found her place was specially laid with a great dish of gold and a golden knife, fork and spoon studded with diamonds and rubies. But as the fairies took their seats, an uninvited guest came storming into the palace, deeply affronted because she had been forgotten—though it was no wonder she'd been overlooked; this old fairy had hidden herself away in her tower for fifteen years and, since nobody had set eyes on her all that time, they thought she was dead, or had been bewitched. The king ordered a place to be laid for her at once but he could not give her a great gold dish and gold cutlery like the other fairies had because only seven sets had been made. The old fairy was very annoyed at that and muttered threats between her teeth. The fairy who sat beside her overheard her and suspected she planned to revenge herself by giving the little princess a very unpleasant present when the time for present giving came. She slipped away behind the tapestry so that she could have the last word, if necessary, and put right any harm the old witch might do the baby.

Now the fairies presented their gifts. The youngest fairy said the princess would grow up to be the loveliest woman in the world. The next said she would have the disposition of an angel, the third that she would be graceful as a gazelle, the fourth gave her the gift of dancing, the fifth of singing like a nightingale, and the sixth said she would be able to play any kind of musical instrument that she wanted to.

But when it came to the old fairy's turn, she shook with spite and announced that, in spite of her beauty and accomplishments, the princess was going to prick her

---

1 First published in 1697. This text from *Sleeping Beauty and Other Favourite Fairy Tales*, trans. Angela Carter (London: Gollancz, 1982).

finger with a spindle and die of it.

All the guests trembled and wept. But the youngest fairy stepped out from behind the tapestry and cried out:

"Don't despair, King and Queen; your daughter will not die—although, alas, I cannot undo entirely the magic of a senior-ranking fairy. The princess *will* prick her finger with a spindle but, instead of dying, she will fall into a deep sleep that will last for a hundred years. And at the end of a hundred years, the son of a king will come to wake her."

In spite of this comfort, the king did all he could to escape the curse; he forbade the use of a spindle, or even the possession of one, on pain of death, in all the lands he governed.

Fifteen or sixteen years went by. The king and queen were spending the summer at a castle in the country and one day the princess decided to explore, prowling through room after room until at last she climbed up a spiral staircase in a tower and came to an attic in which an old lady was sitting, along with her distaff, spinning, for this old lady had not heard how the king had banned the use of a spindle.

"Whatever are you doing, my good woman?" asked the princess.

"I'm spinning, my dear," answered the old lady.

"Oh, how clever!" said the princess. "How do you do it? Give it to me so that I can see if I can do it, too!"

She was very lively and just a little careless; but besides, and most importantly, the fairies had ordained it. No sooner had she picked up the spindle than she pierced her hand with it and fell down in a faint.

The old lady cried for help and the servants came running from all directions. They threw water over her, unlaced her corsets, slapped her hands, rubbed her temples with *eau-de-cologne*—but nothing would wake her.

The king climbed to the attic to see the cause of the clamour and, sad at heart, knew the fairy's curse had come true. He knew the princess' time had come, just as the fairies said it would, and ordered her to be carried to the finest room in the palace and laid there on a bed covered with gold and silver embroidery. She was as beautiful as an angel. Her trance had not yet taken the colour from her face; her cheeks were rosy and her lips like coral. Her eyes were closed but you could hear her breathing very, very softly and, if you saw the slow movement of her breast, you knew she was not dead.

The king ordered she should be left in peace until the time came when she would wake up. At the moment the princess had pricked her finger, the good fairy who saved her life was in the realm of Mataquin, twelve thousand leagues away, but she heard the news immediately from a dwarf who sped to her in a pair of seven-league boots. The fairy left Mataquin at once in a fiery chariot drawn by dragons and arrived at the grieving court an hour later. The king went out to help her down; she approved of all his arrangements but she was very sensitive, and she thought how sad the princess would be when she woke up all alone in that great castle.

So she touched everything in the house, except for the king and queen, with her magic ring—the housekeepers, the maids of honour, the chambermaids, the gentlemen-in-waiting, the court officials, the cooks, the scullions, the errand-boys, the nightwatchmen, the Swiss guards, the page-boys, the footmen; she touched all the horses in the stable, and the stable-boys, too, and even Puff, the princess' little lapdog, who was curled up on her bed beside her. As soon as she touched them with her magic ring, they all fell fast asleep and would not wake up until their mistress woke, ready to look after her when she needed them. Even the spits on the fire, loaded with partridges and pheasants, drowsed off to sleep, and the flames died down and slept, too. All this took only a moment; fairies are fast workers.

The king and queen kissed their darling child but she did not stir. Then they left the palace forever and issued proclamations forbidding anyone to approach it. Within a quarter of an hour, a great number of trees, some large, some small, interlaced with brambles and thorns, sprang up around the park and formed a hedge so thick that neither man nor beast could penetrate it. This hedge grew so tall that you could see only the topmost turrets of the castle, for the fairy had made a safe, magic place where the princess could sleep her sleep out free from prying eyes.

At the end of a hundred years, the son of the king who now ruled over the country went out hunting in that region. He asked the local people what those turrets he could see above the great wood might mean. They replied, each one, as he had heard tell—how it was an old ruin, full of ghosts; or, that all the witches of the country went there to hold their sabbaths. But the most popular story was, that it was the home of an ogre who carried all the children he caught there, to eat them at his leisure, knowing nobody else could follow him through the wood. The prince did not know what to believe. Then an old man said to him:

"My lord, fifty years ago I heard my father say that the most beautiful princess in all the world was sleeping in that castle, and her sleep was going to last for a hundred years, until the prince who is meant to have her comes to wake her up."

When he heard that, the young prince was tremendously excited; he had never heard of such a marvelous adventure and, fired with thoughts of love and glory, he made up his mind there and then to go through the wood. No sooner had he stepped among the trees than the great trunks and branches, the thorns and brambles parted, to let him pass. He saw the castle at the end of a great avenue and walked towards it, though he was surprised to see that none of his attendants could follow him because the trees sprang together again as soon as he had gone between them. But he did not abandon his quest. A young prince in love is always brave. Then he arrived at a courtyard that seemed like a place where only fear lived.

An awful silence filled it and the look of death was on everything. Man and beast stretched on the ground, like corpses; but the pimples on the red noses of the Swiss guards soon showed him they were not dead at all, but sleeping, and the glasses beside them, with the dregs of wine still at the bottoms, showed how they had dozed off after a spree.

He went through a marble courtyard; he climbed a staircase; he went into a guardroom, where the guards were lined up in two ranks, each with a gun on his shoulder, and snoring with all their might. He found several rooms full of gentlemen-in-waiting and fine ladies; some stood, some sat, all slept. At last he arrived in a room that was entirely covered in gilding and, there on a bed with the curtains drawn back so that he could see her clearly, lay a princess about fifteen or sixteen years old and she was so lovely that she seemed, almost, to shine. The prince approached her trembling, and fell on his knees before her.

The enchantment was over; the princess woke. She gazed at him so tenderly you would not have thought it was the first time she had ever seen him.

"Is it you, my prince?" she said. "You have kept me waiting for a long time."

The prince was beside himself with joy when he heard that and the tenderness in her voice overwhelmed him so that he hardly knew how to reply. He told her he loved her better than he loved himself and though he stumbled over the words, that made her very happy, because he showed so much feeling. He was more tongue-tied than she, because she had had plenty of time to dream of what she would say to him; her good fairy had made sure she had sweet dreams during her long sleep. They talked for hours and still had not said half the things they wanted to say to one another.

But the entire palace had woken up with the princess and everyone was going about his business again. Since none of them were in love, they were all dying of hunger. The chief lady-in-waiting, just as ravenous as the rest, lost patience after a while and told the princess loud and clear that dinner was ready. The prince helped the princess up from the bed and she dressed herself with the greatest magnificence; but when she put on her ruff, the prince remembered how his grandmother had worn one just like it. All the princess' clothes were a hundred years out of fashion, but she was no less beautiful because of that.

Supper was served in the hall of mirrors, while the court orchestra played old tunes on violins and oboes they had not touched for a hundred years. After supper, the chaplain married them in the castle chapel and the chief lady-in-waiting drew the curtains round their bed for them. They did not sleep much, that night; the princess did not feel in the least drowsy. The prince left her in the morning, to return to his father's palace.

The king was anxious because his son had been away so long. The prince told him that he had lost himself in the forest while he was out hunting and had spent the night in a charcoal burner's hut, where his host had given him black bread and cheese to eat. The king believed the story but the queen, the prince's mother, was not so easily hoodwinked when she saw that now the young man spent most of his time out hunting in the forest. Though he always arrived back with an excellent excuse when he had spent two or three nights away from home, his mother soon guessed he was in love.

He lived with the princess for more than two years and he gave her two children. They named the eldest, a daughter, Dawn, because she was so beautiful, but they called their son Day because he came after Dawn and was even more beautiful still.

The queen tried to persuade her son to tell her his secret but he dared not confide in her. Although he loved her, he feared her, because she came from a family of ogres and his father had married her only because she was very, very rich. The court whispered that the queen still had ogrish tastes and could hardly keep her hands off little children, so the prince thought it best to say nothing about his own babies.

But when the king died and the prince himself became king, he felt confident enough to publicly announce his marriage and install the new queen, his wife, in his royal palace with a great deal of ceremony. And soon after that, the new king decided to declare war on his neighbour, the Emperor Cantalabutte.

He left the governing of his kingdom in his mother's hands and he trusted her to look after his wife and children for him, too, because he would be away at war for the whole summer.

As soon as he was gone, the queen mother sent her daughter-in-law and her grandchildren away to the country, to a house deep in the woods, so that she could satisfy her hideous appetites with the greatest of ease. She herself arrived at the house a few days later and said to the butler:

"I want to eat little Dawn for my dinner tomorrow."

"Oh my lady!" exclaimed the butler.

"She's just the very thing I fancy," said the queen mother in the voice of an ogress famished for fresh meat. "And I want you to serve her up with sauce Robert."[1]

The poor man saw he could not argue with a hungry ogress, picked up a carving knife and went to little Dawn's room. She was just four years old. When she saw her dear friend, the butler, she ran up to him, laughing, threw her arms around his neck and asked him where her sweeties were. He burst into tears and the knife fell from his hands. He went down to the farmyard and slaughtered a little lamb instead. He served the lamb up in such a delicious sauce the queen mother said she had never eaten so well in her life and he spirited little Dawn away from harm; he handed her over to his wife, who hid her in a cellar, in the servants' quarters.

---

1   French sauce based on mustard and meat juices.

Eight days passed. Then the ogress said to the butler:

"I want to eat little Day for my supper."

The butler was determined to outwit her again. He found little Day playing at fencing with his pet monkey; the child was only three. He took him to his wife, who hid him away with his sister, and served up a tender young kid in his place. The queen mother smacked her lips over the dish, so all went well until the night the wicked ogress said to the butler:

"I want to eat the queen with the same sauce you made for her children."

This time, the poor butler did not know what to do. The queen was twenty, now, if you did not count the hundred years she had been asleep; her skin was white and lovely but it was a little tough, and where in all the farmyard was he to find a beast with skin just like it? There was nothing for it; he must kill the queen to save himself and he went to her room, determined he would not have to enter it a second time. He rushed in with a dagger in his hand and told her her mother-in-law had ordered her to die.

"Be quick about it," she said calmly. "Do as she told you. When I am dead, I shall be with my poor children again, my children whom I love so much."

Because they had been taken away from her without a word of explanation, she thought they were dead.

The butler's heart melted.

"No, no, my lady, you don't need to die so that you can be with your children. I've hidden them away from the queen mother's hunger and I will trick her again, I will give her a young deer for supper instead of you."

He took her to the cellar, where he left her kissing her children and weeping over them, and went to kill a young doe that the queen mother ate for supper with as much relish as if it had been her daughter-in-law. She was very pleased with her own cruelty and practiced telling her son how the wolves had eaten his wife and children while he had been away at the wars.

One night as she prowled about as usual, sniffing for the spoor of fresh meat, she heard a voice coming from the servants' quarters. It was little Day's voice; he was crying because he had been naughty and his mother wanted to whip him. Then the queen mother heard Dawn begging her mother to forgive the little boy. The ogress recognised the voices of her grandchildren and she was furious. She ordered a huge vat to be brought into the middle of the courtyard. She had the vat filled with toads, vipers, snakes and serpents and then the queen, her children, the butler, his wife and his maid were brought in front of her with their hands tied behind their backs. She was going to have them thrown into the vat.

The executioners were just on the point of carrying out their dreadful instructions when the king galloped into the courtyard. Nobody had expected him back so soon. He was astonished at what he saw and asked who had commanded the vat and the bonds. The ogress was so angry to see her plans go awry that she jumped head-first into the vat and the vile beasts inside devoured her in an instant. The king could not help grieving a little; after all, she was his mother. But his beautiful wife and children soon made him happy again.

Moral
A brave, rich, handsome husband is a prize well worth waiting for; but no modern woman would think it was worth waiting for a hundred years. The tale of the Sleeping Beauty shows how long engagements make for happy marriages, but young girls these days want so much to be married I do not have the heart to press the moral.

BRIER ROSE[1]
Jacob and Wilhelm Grimm

LONG, LONG AGO THERE LIVED a king and a queen, who said day after day: "Ah, if only we had a child!" but none ever came. Then one day when the queen was sitting in her bath a frog crawled out of the water and said to her: "You will get your wish; before a year goes by, you will bring a daughter into the world." The frog's prediction came true. The queen gave birth to a baby girl who was so beautiful that the king couldn't get over his joy and decided to give a great feast. He invited not only his relatives, friends, and acquaintances, but also the Wise Women, for he wanted them to feel friendly toward his child. There were thirteen Wise Women in his kingdom, but he only had twelve golden plates for them to eat from, so one of them had to stay home. The feast was celebrated in great splendour and when it was over the Wise Women gave the child their magic gifts; one gave virtue, the second beauty, the third wealth, and so on, until they had given everything a person could wish for in this world. When the eleventh had spoken, the thirteenth suddenly stepped in. She had come to avenge herself for not having been invited, and without a word of greeting, without so much as looking at anyone, she cried out in a loud voice: "When she is fifteen, the princess will prick her finger on a spinning wheel and fall down dead." Then without another word she turned around and left the hall. Everyone was horror-stricken. But the twelfth Wise Woman, who still had her wish to make, stepped

---

1   First published in 1812/15, in the first edition of *Kinder- und Hausmärchen*. This text from the second edition (1819), from *Grimms' Tales for Young and Old*, trans. Ralph Manheim (Garden City, NY: Anchor P, 1977).

forward, and since she couldn't undo the evil spell but only soften it, she said: "The princess will not die, but only fall into a deep hundred-year sleep."

The king, who wanted to guard his beloved child against such a calamity, sent out an order that every spindle in the whole kingdom should be destroyed. All the Wise Women's wishes for the child came true: she grew to be so beautiful, so modest, so sweet-tempered and wise that no one who saw her could help loving her. The day she turned fifteen the king and the queen happened to be away from home and she was left alone. She went all over the castle, examining room after room, and finally she came to an old tower. She climbed a narrow winding staircase, which led to a little door with a rusty key in the lock. She turned the key, the door sprang open, and there in a small room sat an old woman with a spindle, busily spinning her flax. "Good day, old woman," said the princess. "What are you doing?" "I'm spinning," said the old woman, nodding her head. "And what's the thing that twirls around so gaily?" the princess asked. With that she took hold of the spindle and tried to spin, but no sooner had she touched it than the magic spell took effect and she pricked her finger.

The moment she felt the prick she fell down on the bed that was in the room and a deep sleep came over her. And her sleep spread to the entire palace. The king and queen had just come home, and when they entered the great hall they fell asleep and the whole court with them. The horses fell asleep in the stables, the dogs in the courtyard, the pigeons on the roof, and the flies on the wall. Even the fire on the hearth stopped flaming and fell asleep, and the roast stopped crackling, and the cook, who was about to pull the kitchen boy's hair because he had done something wrong, let go and fell asleep. And the wind died down, and not a leaf stirred on the trees outside the castle.

All around the castle a brier hedge began to grow. Each year it grew higher until in the end it surrounded and covered the whole castle and there was no trace of a castle to be seen, not even the flag on the roof. The story of Brier Rose, as people called the beautiful sleeping princess, came to be told far and wide, and from time to time a prince tried to pass through the hedge into the castle. But none succeeded, for the brier bushes clung together as though they had hands, so the young men were caught and couldn't break loose and died a pitiful death. After many years another prince came to the country and heard an old man telling about the brier hedge that was said to conceal a castle, where a beautiful princess named Brier Rose had been sleeping for a hundred years, along with the king and the queen and their whole court. The old man had also heard from his grandfather that a number of princes had tried to pass through the brier hedge and had got caught in it and died a pitiful death. Then the young man said: "I'm not afraid. I will go and see the beautiful Brier Rose." The good man did his best to dissuade him, but the prince wouldn't listen.

It so happened that the hundred years had passed and the day had come for Brier Rose to wake up. As the king's son approached the brier hedge, the briers turned into big beautiful flowers, which opened of their own accord and let him through, then closed behind him to form a hedge again. In the courtyard he saw the horses and mottled hounds lying asleep, and on the roof pigeons were roosting with their heads under their wings. When he went into the castle, the flies were asleep on the wall, the cook in the kitchen was still holding out his hand as though to grab the kitchen boy, and the maid was sitting at the table with a black hen in front of her that needed plucking. Going farther, he saw the whole court asleep in the great hall, and on the dais beside the throne lay the king and the queen. On he went, and everything was so still that he could hear himself breathe. At last he came to the tower and opened the door to the little room where Brier Rose was sleeping. There she lay, so beautiful that he couldn't stop looking at her, and he bent down and kissed her. No sooner had his lips touched hers than Brier Rose opened her eyes, woke up, and smiled sweetly. They went downstairs together, and then the king and the queen and the whole court woke up, and they all looked at each other in amazement. The horses in the courtyard stood up and shook themselves; the hounds jumped to their feet and wagged their tails; the pigeons on the roof took their heads from under their wings, looked around and flew off into the fields; the flies on the wall started crawling, the fire in the kitchen flamed up and cooked the meal; the roast began to crackle again, the cook boxed the kitchen boy's ear so hard that he howled, and the maid plucked the chicken. The prince and Brier Rose were married in splendour, and they lived happily to the end of their lives.

GROWING UP (IS HARD TO DO)

As we have seen, the fairy tale did not begin life as the exclusive property of children, for the simple reason that it was originally told by and for adults—which explains what many would now consider its occasionally unsuitable subject matter. We must remember that the concept of childhood has emerged only over the last three to four hundred years; in earlier times, it was simply not perceived as being a distinct entity. The explanation for this is partly economic and partly psychological in nature. Among the peasantry, children represented a natural resource, but of a kind that required years of nurturing before any return could be expected, years during which the child was actually a drain on scarce resources, with no guarantee that he or she would live long enough to repay such an investment. The child was obliged to grow up quickly and fend for him or herself, so in a world where mere survival was so constant a challenge, it is reasonable to speculate that the emotional attachment between parent and child was sometimes less intense than in our own world of relative affluence and leisure. Their social and psychological insignificance makes it all the more surprising that children are as well represented in the fairy tale as they are. However, the point must be made that although many of the tales we have read so far *begin* with childhood, their major emphasis is upon the transition to adulthood. The tales in this section are distinguished by the fact that their focus is specifically upon childhood with little or no reference to later life.

There is a deep-seated ambivalence toward children reflected in fairy tales. These tales are about children not so much because they are perceived as interesting or entertaining characters (as is generally the assumption today) but rather as representatives of the upcoming generation, prospective claimants of adult privilege and status. On the one hand, there are tales in which love and protectiveness toward offspring are expressed—more often, it may be added, in tales about the rich than about the poor—although the over-protectiveness found in such tales as "Little Red Riding Hood," "Sleeping Beauty," and now "Rapunzel" can be seen as leading to unhappy consequences. On the other hand, there is fear and resentment of the child as a potential burden or rival, memorably depicted in "Hansel and Gretel" and "Snow White."

But why is it that so many of these tales focus upon the girl? The answer, at least in part, is that it has long been more of a challenge to grow up female than to grow up male. The inequality of the sexes runs as a central thread through tale after tale, although there is sometimes an intriguing contrast between the conventional role and the actual behavior of some heroines. One distinction is worthy of note: while the princesses we have encountered thus far all manifest differing degrees of passivity, the peasant girls, such as Gretel, Molly Whuppie, or the unnamed girls in "The Story of Grandmother" and "The False Grandmother," seem to be much more willing and able to seize the initiative. Is this another indication of how important class is in determining patterns of behavior? Yet given the centuries of changing social attitudes through which these stories have been filtered, these patterns should not surprise us too much. We were well into the second half of the twentieth century, in fact, before serious efforts were made (in the form of the feminist fairy tale) to challenge the assumptions that are firmly entrenched in many traditional tales. Quite apart from the innate originality and inventiveness of the narratives themselves, the popular success of such tales as "Sleeping Beauty," "Cinderella," and "Snow White" have been equally attributable to the preconceptions and values of nineteenth-century readers and fairy-tale collectors.

Curiously enough, the few male children who have gained an equivalent renown are either disadvantaged by their small size or else delinquent ne'er-do-wells, such as Jack (of beanstalk fame) or even Aladdin from *The Arabian Nights*. The point here, of course, is that out of such unpromising beginnings comes a winner, through the exercise of such "masculine" qualities as courage, cunning, determination, and a measure of ruthlessness.

The presence and power of the mother is very much an issue in five of the six tales in this section; in both "Hansel and Gretel" and "Snow White," the Grimms chose in later editions to turn mother into stepmother, no doubt because they did not wish to confront their child-readers with such unnatural maternal behavior. (Although the witch in "Rapunzel" has no biological connection with the girl, she nevertheless represents another example of the "bad mother.") By contrast, the father is either entirely absent or a subservient figure.

Several of these tales begin with a depiction of physical hardship—and that is surely based in historical fact. Poverty and famine are experiences that few of us have suffered first hand, so we have little conception of the profound effects they have on those afflicted. So while we may brand the (step)mother of Hansel and Gretel as coldhearted and cruel, we cannot deny that she is responding to a harsh reality in a pragmatic fashion. Is it possible that the roots of these tales reach back to a time when children were, in such extreme circumstances, seen as expendable? In "Jack and the Beanstalk," the situation is reversed, with the widowed mother at the mercy of her immature, good-for-nothing son; while there is certainly no evil intent here, the prospect is nevertheless the same—imminent starvation.

The similarity of structure continues into the second phase of the tales, where the realistic gives way to the fantastic, and the child-characters must learn to fend for themselves or perish in the attempt. That they succeed in overcoming the adult characters that oppose them should be seen as a practical acknowledgment of how the world works rather than as a glorification of intrepid youth. Any notion of the child as natural adventurer and hero was simply incompatible with the attitudes toward childhood that prevailed in earlier times.

Not surprisingly, Freudian critics such as Bruno Bettelheim have much to say about these visceral conflicts between child and adult which, by virtue of being played out in the realm of the imaginary, sublimate anxiety-creating aggression and rivalry into a form that the listener/reader can accept and resolve. Hansel and Gretel return home (escaping the fantasy world via an obviously symbolic body of water) to discover that their (step)mother has died in their absence. The link between (step)mother and witch seems obvious, and although the children choose to return home, one senses that they are now more likely to look after their father rather than the reverse. Thanks in part to the intervention of the dwarves, Snow White survives repeated attempts on her life by her rival (step)mother and, after a Sleeping Beauty–style period of growth, emerges as a woman from her coffin-cocoon. It is Rapunzel who arguably suffers the most in the transition from childhood to adulthood, perhaps because her experience is explicitly sexual.

A striking aspect of "The Frog King" is the rapid development of the central character—she goes from child to married woman in less than three pages. This "accelerated childhood" is in fact not an uncommon occurrence in fairy tale (we see something similar in "Snow White" and "Rapunzel," for instance); we are reminded that this is a world in which children are obliged to grow up fast. Certainly the princess's behavior at the beginning of the tale is childlike, as is her obedience to her father. The ending of the tale is noteworthy, since several well-known alternatives exist that invite quite distinct interpretations. The ending that you will read in this anthology is that preferred by the Grimms. A variant in which the princess permits the frog to sleep on her pillow for three nights and thus break his enchantment was made popular by Edgar Taylor's first English translation of the Grimms' tales in 1823; no doubt he saw such a display of forbearance and resignation as more befitting a well-brought-up young lady.[1] Also not to be forgotten is the ending, where the princess is induced to kiss the frog in order to break his enchantment. Although scholars have had difficulty in tracing the origins of this particular climax to the story, it is nevertheless firmly entrenched in popular culture, where it has provided considerable scope for those adopting a more irreverent approach to the tale.

For his part, Jack comes back to earth the same way he left, but as a dramatically different person: the Jack who kills the giant and bestows wealth and security upon his mother is no longer an aimless, impulsive boy. We must, however, confront the moral question that arises from Jack's thefts from the giant, the last of which seems particularly gratuitous, in that his wealth is assured by his possession of the hen that lays the golden eggs. Some versions of this tale present it as a matter of revenge: Jack's father is absent from the story because he has been killed by the giant, so Jack is simply reclaiming his own. In the case of *this* version, the explanation must be that we judge motive according to the folk tale's simple—even primitive—moral code: the giant is by nature wicked (as his earlier behavior has amply revealed), so his possessions must be ill-gotten. If Jack has the youthful audacity to make the attempt, then to the victor go the spoils. The new generation has passed the test and takes its rightful place, until it in turn finds itself cast in the role of giant or witch, and the struggle begins anew.

The final tale in this section stands apart from the others but is unquestionably about growing up to the extent that its title has entered the language as a description of childhood experience. "The Ugly Duckling," a paradigm of autobiographical fantasy, is arguably Hans Christian Andersen's most famous tale, recounting his struggle to extract himself from the poverty-stricken obscurity of his early years and to make his mark in the artistic world. It is as personal a statement as the others are generalized, reflecting an important difference between the anonymous folk tale and the literary tale. Part of Andersen's genius lay in his ability to express everyone's experience in his own: all those feelings of inadequacy, rejection, and loneliness that we suffered (or *imagine* that we suffered) are captured in that single unforgettable image of the duckling.

---

1   The importance of being aware that a specific tale may have many variants is made clear by Alan Dundes; see pp. 387–94.

HANSEL AND GRETEL[1]

Jacob and Wilhelm Grimm

AT THE EDGE OF A large forest there lived a poor woodcutter with his wife and two children. The little boy's name was Hansel, and the little girl's was Gretel. There was never much to eat in the house, and once, in time of famine, there wasn't even enough bread to go around. One night the woodcutter lay in bed thinking, tossing and turning with worry. All at once he sighed and said to his wife: "What's to become of us? How can we feed our poor children when we haven't even got enough for ourselves?" His wife answered: "Husband, listen to me. Tomorrow at daybreak we'll take the children out to the thickest part of the forest and make a fire for them and give them each a piece of bread. Then we'll leave them and go about our work. They'll never find the way home again and that way we'll be rid of them." "No, Wife," said the man. "I won't do it. How can I bring myself to leave my children alone in the woods? The wild beasts will come and tear them to pieces." "You fool!" she said. "Then all four of us will starve. You may as well start planing the boards for our coffins." And she gave him no peace until he consented. "But I still feel badly about the poor children," he said.

The children were too hungry to sleep, and they heard what their stepmother[2] said to their father. Gretel wept bitter tears and said: "Oh, Hansel, we're lost." "Hush, Gretel," said Hansel. "Don't worry. I'll find a way." When the old people had fallen asleep, he got up, put on his little jacket, opened the bottom half of the Dutch door, and crept outside. The moon was shining bright, and the pebbles around the house glittered like silver coins. Hansel crouched down and stuffed his pocket full of them. Then he went back and said to Gretel: "Don't worry, little sister. Just go to sleep, God won't forsake us," and went back to bed.

At daybreak, before the sun had risen, the woman came and woke the two children. "Get up, you lazybones. We're going to the forest for wood." Then she gave each a piece of bread and said: "This is for your noonday meal. Don't eat it too soon, because there won't be any more." Gretel put the bread under her apron, because Hansel had pebbles in his pocket. Then they all started out for the forest together. When they had gone a little way, Hansel stopped still and looked back in the direction of their house, and every so often he did it again. His father said: "Hansel, why

---

1   First published in 1812/15, in the first edition of *Kinder- und Hausmärchen*. This text from the second edition (1819), from *Grimms' Tales for Young and Old*, trans. Ralph Manheim (Garden City, NY: Anchor P, 1977).

2   The Grimms were concerned that mothers in folk tale were often depicted as villains, so they made the editorial decision to transform them into stepmothers.

do you keep looking back and lagging behind? Wake up and don't forget what your legs are for." "Oh, father," said Hansel, "I'm looking for my white kitten; he's sitting on the roof, trying to bid me good-bye." The woman said: "You fool, that's not your white kitten. It's the morning sun shining on the chimney." But Hansel hadn't been looking at his kitten. Each time, he had taken a shiny pebble from his pocket and dropped it on the ground.

When they came to the middle of the forest, the father said: "Start gathering wood, children, and I'll make a fire to keep you warm." Hansel and Gretel gathered brushwood till they had a little pile of it. The brushwood was kindled and when the flames were high enough the woman said: "Now, children, lie down by the fire and rest. We're going into the forest to cut wood. When we're done, we'll come back and get you."

Hansel and Gretel sat by the fire, and at midday they both ate their pieces of bread. They heard the strokes of an ax and thought their father was nearby. But it wasn't an ax, it was a branch he had tied to a withered tree, and the wind was shaking it to and fro. After sitting there for some time, they became so tired that their eyes closed and they fell into a deep sleep. When at last they awoke, it was dark night. Gretel began to cry and said: "How will we ever get out of this forest?" But Hansel comforted her: "Just wait a little while. As soon as the moon rises, we'll find the way." And when the full moon had risen, Hansel took his little sister by the hand and followed the pebbles, which glistened like newly minted silver pieces and showed them the way. They walked all night and reached their father's house just as day was breaking. They knocked at the door, and when the woman opened it and saw Hansel and Gretel, she said: "Wicked children! Why did you sleep so long in the forest? We thought you'd never get home." But their father was glad, for he had been very unhappy about deserting them.

A while later the whole country was again stricken with famine, and the children heard their mother talking to their father in bed at night: "Everything has been eaten up. We still have half a loaf of bread, and when that's gone there will be no more. The children must go. We'll take them still deeper into the forest, and this time they won't find their way home; it's our only hope." The husband was heavy-hearted, and he thought: "It would be better if I shared the last bite with my children." But the woman wouldn't listen to anything he said; she only scolded and found fault. Once you've said yes, it's hard to say no, and so it was that the woodcutter gave in again.

But the children were awake; they had heard the conversation. When the old people had fallen asleep, Hansel got up again. He wanted to pick up some more pebbles, but the woman had locked the door and he couldn't get out. But he comforted his little sister and said: "Don't cry, Gretel. Just go to sleep, God will help us."

Early in the morning the woman came and got the children out of bed. She gave them their pieces of bread, but they were smaller than the last time. On the way to the forest, Hansel crumbled his bread in his pocket. From time to time he stopped and dropped a few crumbs on the ground. "Hansel," said his father, "why are you always stopping and looking back? Keep moving." "I'm looking at my little pigeon," said Hansel. "He's sitting on the roof, trying to bid me good-bye." "Fool," said the woman. "That's not your little pigeon, it's the morning sun shining on the chimney." But little by little Hansel strewed all his bread on the ground.

The woman led the children still deeper into the forest, to a place where they had never been in all their lives. Again a big fire was made, and the mother said: "Just sit here, children. If you get tired, you can sleep awhile. We're going into the forest to cut wood, and this evening when we've finished we'll come and get you." At midday Gretel shared her bread with Hansel, who had strewn his on the ground. Then they fell asleep and the afternoon passed, but no one came for the poor children. It was dark night when they woke up, and Hansel comforted his little sister. "Gretel," he said, "just wait till the moon rises; then we'll see the breadcrumbs I strewed and they'll show us the way home." When the moon rose, they started out, but they didn't find any breadcrumbs, because the thousands of birds that fly around in the forests and fields had eaten them all up. Hansel said to Gretel: "Don't worry, we'll find the way," but they didn't find it. They walked all night and then all day from morning to night, but they were still in the forest, and they were very hungry, for they had nothing to eat but the few berries they could pick from the bushes. And when they were so tired their legs could carry them no farther, they lay down under a tree and fell asleep.

It was already the third morning since they had left their father's house. They started out again, but they were getting deeper and deeper into the forest, and unless help came soon, they were sure to die of hunger and weariness. At midday, they saw a lovely snowbird sitting on a branch. It sang so beautifully that they stood still and listened. When it had done singing, it flapped its wings and flew on ahead, and they followed until the bird came to a little house and perched on the roof. When they came closer, they saw that the house was made of bread, and the roof was made of cake and the windows of sparkling sugar. "Let's eat," said Hansel, "and the Lord bless our food. I'll take a piece of the roof. You, Gretel, had better take some of the window; it's sweet." Hansel reached up and broke off a bit of the roof to see how it tasted, and Gretel pressed against the windowpanes and nibbled at them. And then a soft voice called from inside:

"Nibble nibble, little mouse,
  Who's that nibbling at my house?"

The children answered:

"The wind so wild,
The heavenly child,"

and went right on eating. Hansel liked the taste of the roof, so he tore off a big chunk, and Gretel broke out a whole round windowpane and sat down on the ground to enjoy it. All at once the door opened, and an old, old woman with a crutch came hobbling out. Hansel and Gretel were so frightened they dropped what they were eating. But the old woman wagged her head and said: "Oh, what dear children! However did you get here? Don't be afraid, come in and stay with me. You will come to no harm." She took them by the hand and led them into her house. A fine meal of milk and pancakes, sugar, apples, and nuts was set before them. And then two little beds were made up clean and white, and Hansel and Gretel got into them and thought they were in heaven.

But the old woman had only pretended to be so kind. Actually she was a wicked witch, who waylaid children and had built her house out of bread to entice them. She killed, cooked, and ate any child who fell into her hands, and that to her was a feast day. Witches have red eyes and can't see very far, but they have a keen sense of smell like animals, so they know when humans are coming. As Hansel and Gretel approached, she laughed her wicked laugh and said with a jeer: "Here come two who will never get away from me." Early in the morning, when the children were still asleep, she got up, and when she saw them resting so sweetly with their plump red cheeks, she muttered to herself: "What tasty morsels they will be!" She grabbed Hansel with her scrawny hand, carried him to a little shed, and closed the iron-barred door behind him. He screamed for all he was worth, but much good it did him. Then she went back to Gretel, shook her awake, and cried: "Get up, lazybones. You must draw water and cook something nice for your brother. He's out in the shed and we've got to fatten him up. When he's nice and fat, I'm going to eat him." Gretel wept bitterly, but in vain; she had to do what the wicked witch told her.

The best of food was cooked for poor Hansel, but Gretel got nothing but crayfish shells. Every morning the old witch crept to the shed and said: "Hansel, hold out your finger. I want to see if you're getting fat." But Hansel held out a bone. The old woman had weak eyes and couldn't see it; she thought it was Hansel's finger and wondered why he wasn't getting fat. When four weeks had gone by and Hansel was as skinny as ever, her impatience got the better of her and she decided not to wait any longer. "Ho there, Gretel," she cried out. "Go and draw water and don't dawdle. Skinny or fat, I'm going to butcher Hansel tomorrow and cook him." Oh, how the little girl wailed at having to carry the water, and how the tears flowed down her cheeks! "Dear God," she cried, "oh, won't you help us? If only the wild beasts had eaten us in the forest, at least we'd have died together." "Stop that blubbering," said the witch. "It won't do you a bit of good."

Early in the morning Gretel had to fill the kettle with water and light the fire. "First we'll bake," said the old witch. "I've heated the oven and kneaded the dough." And she drove poor Gretel out to the oven, which by now was spitting flames. "Crawl in," said the witch, "and see if it's hot enough for the bread." Once Gretel was inside, she meant to close the door and roast her, so as to eat her too. But Gretel saw what she had in mind and said: "I don't know how. How do I get in?" "Silly goose," said the old woman. "The opening is big enough. Look. Even I can get in." She crept to the opening and stuck her head in, whereupon Gretel gave her a push that sent her sprawling, closed the iron door and fastened the bolt. Eek! How horribly she screeched! But Gretel ran away and the wicked witch burned miserably to death.

Gretel ran straight to Hansel, opened the door of the shed, and cried: "Hansel, we're saved! The old witch is dead." Hansel hopped out like a bird when someone opens the door of its cage. How happy they were! They hugged and kissed each other and danced around. And now that there was nothing to be afraid of, they went into the witch's house and in every corner there were boxes full of pearls and precious stones. Hansel stuffed his pockets full of them and said: "These will be much better than pebbles," and Gretel said: "I'll take some home too," and filled her apron with them. "We'd better leave now," said Hansel, "and get out of this bewitched forest." When they had walked a few hours, they came to a big body of water. "How will we ever get across" said Hansel. "I don't see any bridge." "And there's no boat, either," said Gretel, "but over there I see a white duck. She'll help us across if I ask her." And she cried out:

"Duckling, duckling, here is Gretel,
Duckling, duckling, here is Hansel,
No bridge or ferry far and wide—
Duckling, come and give us a ride."

Sure enough, the duck came over to them and Hansel sat down on her back and told his sister to sit beside him. "No," said Gretel, "that would be too much for the poor thing; let her carry us one at a time." And that's just what the good little duck did. And when they were safely across and had walked a little while, the forest began to look more and more familiar, and finally they saw their father's house in the distance. They began to run, and they flew into the house and threw themselves into their father's arms. The poor man hadn't had a happy hour since he had left the children in the forest, and in the meantime his wife had died. Gretel opened out her little apron, the pearls and precious stones went bouncing around the room, and Hansel reached into his pockets and tossed out handful after handful. All their worries were over, and they lived together in pure happiness. My story is done, see the mouse run; if you catch it, you may make yourself a great big fur cap out of it.

SNOW WHITE[1]

Jacob and Wilhelm Grimm

ONCE IN MIDWINTER WHEN THE snowflakes were falling from the sky like feathers, a queen sat sewing at the window, with an ebony frame. And as she was sewing and looking out at the snowflakes, she pricked her finger with her needle and three drops of blood fell on the snow. The red looked so beautiful on the white snow that she thought to herself: "If only I had a child as white as snow and as red as blood and as black as the wood of my window frame." A little while later she gave birth to a daughter, who was as white as snow and as red as blood, and her hair was as black as ebony. They called her Snow White, and when she was born, the queen died.

A year later the king took a second wife. She was beautiful, but she was proud and overbearing, and she couldn't bear the thought that anyone might be more beautiful than she. She had a magic mirror, and when she went up to it and looked at herself, she said:

"Mirror, Mirror, here I stand.
Who is the fairest in the land?"

and the mirror answered:

"You, O Queen, are the fairest in the land."

That set her mind at rest, for she knew the mirror told the truth.

But as Snow White grew, she became more and more beautiful, and by the time she was seven years old she was as beautiful as the day and more beautiful than the queen herself. One day when the queen said to her mirror:

"Mirror, Mirror, here I stand.
Who is the fairest in the land?"

---

[1] First published in 1812/15, in the first edition of *Kinder- und Hausmärchen.* This text from the second edition (1819), from *Grimms' Tales for Young and Old,* trans. Ralph Manheim (Garden City, NY: Anchor P, 1977).

the mirror replied:

"You, O Queen, are the fairest here,
But Snow White is a thousand times more fair."

The Queen gasped, and turned yellow and green with envy. Every time she laid eyes on Snow White after that she hated her so much that her heart turned over in her bosom. Envy and pride grew like weeds in her heart, until she knew no peace by day or by night. Finally she sent for a huntsman and said: "Get that child out of my sight. Take her into the forest and kill her and bring me her lungs and her liver to prove you've done it." The huntsman obeyed. He took the child out into the forest, but when he drew his hunting knife and prepared to pierce Snow White's innocent heart, she began to cry and said: "Oh, dear huntsman, let me live. I'll run off through the wild woods and never come home again." Because of her beauty the hunts-man took pity on her and said: "All right, you poor child. Run away." To himself, he thought: "The wild beasts will soon eat her," but not having to kill her was a great weight off his mind all the same. Just then a young boar came bounding out of the thicket. The huntsman thrust his knife into it, took the lungs and liver and brought them to the queen as proof that he had done her bidding. The cook was ordered to salt and stew them, and the godless woman ate them, thinking she was eating Snow White's lungs and liver.

Meanwhile the poor child was all alone in the great forest. She was so afraid that she looked at all the leaves on the trees and didn't know what to do. She began to run, she ran over sharp stones and through brambles, and the wild beasts passed by with-out harming her. She ran as long as her legs would carry her and then, just before nightfall, she saw a little house and went in to rest. Inside the house everything was tiny, but wonderfully neat and clean. There was a table spread with a white cloth, and on the table there were seven little plates, each with its own knife, fork, and spoon, and seven little cups. Over against the wall there were seven little beds all in a row, covered with spotless white sheets. Snow White was very hungry and thirsty, but she didn't want to eat up anyone's entire meal, so she ate a bit of bread and vegetables from each plate and drank a sip of wine from each cup. Then she was so tired that she lay down on one of the beds, but none of the beds quite suited her; some were too long and some were too short, but the seventh was just right. There she stayed and when she had said her prayers she fell asleep.

When it was quite dark, the owners of the little house came home. They were seven dwarfs who went off to the mountains every day with their picks and shov-els, to mine silver. They lit their seven little candles, and when the light went up they saw someone had been there, because certain things had been moved. The first said: "Who has been sitting in my chair?" The second: "Who has been eating off my plate?" The third: "Who has taken a bite of my bread?" The fourth: "Who has been eating some of my vegetables?" The fifth: "Who has been using my fork?" The sixth: "Who has been cutting with my knife?" And the seventh: "Who has been drinking out of my cup?" Then the first looked around, saw a little hollow in his bed and said: "Who has been lying in my bed?" The others came running, and cried out: "Somebody has been lying in my bed too." But when the seventh looked at his bed, he saw Snow White lying there asleep. He called the others, who came running. They cried out in amazement, went to get their seven little candles, and held them over Snow White: "Heavens above!" they cried. "Heavens above! What a beautiful child!" They were so delighted they didn't wake her but let her go on sleeping in the little bed. The seventh dwarf slept with his comrades, an hour with each one, and then the night was over.

Next morning Snow White woke up, and when she saw the seven dwarfs she was frightened. But they were friendly and asked: "What's your name?" "My name is Snow White," she said. "How did you get to our house?" the dwarfs asked. And she told them how her stepmother had wanted to kill her, how the huntsman had spared her life, and how she had walked all day until at last she found their little house. The dwarfs said: "If you will keep house for us, and do the cooking and make the beds and wash and sew and knit, and keep everything neat and clean, you can stay with us and you'll want for nothing." "Oh, yes," said Snow White. "I'd love to." So she stayed and kept the house in order, and in the morning they went off to the mountains to look for silver and gold, and in the evening they came home again and dinner had to be ready. But all day Snow White was alone, and the kindly dwarfs warned her, saying: "Watch out for your stepmother. She'll soon find out you're here. Don't let anyone in."

After eating Snow White's lungs and liver, the queen felt sure she was again the most beautiful of all. She went to her mirror and said:

"Mirror, Mirror, here I stand.
  Who is the fairest in the land?"

And the mirror replied:

"You, O Queen, are the fairest here,
  But Snow White, who has gone to stay
  With the seven dwarfs far, far away,
  Is a thousand times more fair."

The queen gasped. She knew the mirror told no lies and she realized that the huntsman had deceived her and that Snow White was still alive. She racked her brains for a way to kill her, because she simply had to be the fairest in the land, or envy would leave her no peace. At last she thought up a plan. She stained her face and dressed like an old peddler woman, so that no one could have recognized her. In this disguise she made her way across the seven mountains to the house of the seven dwarfs, knocked at the door and cried out: "Pretty things for sale! For sale!" Snow White looked out of the window and said: "Good day, old woman, what have you got to sell?" "Nice things, nice things!" she replied. "Laces, all colors," and she took out a lace woven of bright-colored silk. "This woman looks so honest," thought Snow White. "It must be all right to let her in." So she unbolted the door and bought the pretty lace. "Child!" said the old woman, "you look a fright. Come, let me lace you up properly." Suspecting nothing, Snow White stepped up and let the old woman put in the new lace.[1] But she did it so quickly and pulled the lace so tight that Snow White's breath was cut off and she fell down as though dead. "Well, well," said the queen, "you're not the fairest in the land now." And she hurried away.

A little while later, at nightfall, the seven dwarfs came home. How horrified they were to see their beloved Snow White lying on the floor! She lay so still they thought she was dead. They lifted her up, and when they saw she was laced too tightly, they cut the lace. She breathed just a little, and then little by little she came to life. When the dwarfs heard what had happened, they said: "That old peddler woman was the wicked queen and no one else. You've got to be careful and never let anyone in when we're away."

When the wicked woman got home, she went to her mirror and asked:

"Mirror, Mirror, here I stand.
Who is the fairest in the land?"

And the mirror answered as usual:

"You, O Queen, are the fairest here,
But Snow White, who has gone to stay
With the seven dwarfs far, far away,
Is a thousand times more fair."

When she heard that, it gave her such a pang that the blood rushed to her heart, for she realized that Snow White had revived. "Never mind," she said. "I'll think

---

1   A ribbon or cord used to tighten a corset.

up something now that will really destroy you," and with the help of some magic spells she knew she made a poisoned comb. Then she disguised herself and took the form of another old woman. And again she made her way over the seven mountains to the house of the seven dwarfs, knocked at the door and said: "Pretty things for sale! For sale!" Snow White looked out and said: "Go away. I can't let anyone in." "You can look, can't you?" said the old woman, taking out the poisoned comb and holding it up. The child liked it so well that she forgot everything else and opened the door. When they had agreed on the price, the old woman said: "Now I'll give your hair a proper combing." Suspecting nothing, poor Snow White stood still for the old woman, but no sooner had the comb touched her hair than the poison took effect and she fell into a dead faint. "There, my beauty," said the wicked woman. "It's all up with you now." And she went away. But luckily it wasn't long till nightfall. When the seven dwarfs came home and found Snow White lying on the floor as though dead, they immediately suspected the stepmother. They examined Snow White and found the poisoned comb, and no sooner had they pulled it out than she woke up and told them what had happened. Again they warned her to be on her guard and not to open the door to anyone. When the queen got home she went to her mirror and said,

"Mirror, Mirror, here I stand.
   Who is the fairest in the land?"

And the mirror answered as before:

"You, O Queen, are the fairest here,
   But Snow White, who has gone to stay
   With the seven dwarfs far, far away,
   Is a thousand times more fair."

When she heard the mirror say that, she trembled and shook with rage. "Snow White must die!" she cried out. "Even if it costs me my own life." Then she went to a secret room that no one else knew about and made a very poisonous apple. It looked so nice on the outside, white with red cheeks, that anyone who saw it would want it; but anyone who ate even the tiniest bit of it would die. When the apple was ready, she stained her face and disguised herself as a peasant woman. And again she made her way across the seven mountains to the house of the seven dwarfs. She knocked at the door and Snow White put her head out of the window. "I can't let anyone in," she said. "The seven dwarfs won't let me." "It doesn't matter," said the peasant woman. "I only want to get rid of these apples. Here, I'll make you a present of one." "No," said Snow White. "I'm not allowed to take anything." "Are you afraid of poison?" said the old woman. "Look, I'm cutting it in half. You eat the red cheek and I'll eat the white cheek." But the apple had been so cleverly made that only the red cheek was poisoned. Snow White longed for the lovely apple, and when she saw the peasant woman taking a bite out of it she couldn't resist. She held out her hand and took the poisonous half. And no sooner had she taken a bite than she fell to the floor dead. The queen gave her a cruel look, laughed a terrible laugh, and said: "White as snow, red as blood, black as ebony. The dwarfs won't revive you this time." And when she got home and questioned the mirror:

"Mirror, Mirror, here I stand.
Who is the fairest in the land?"

The mirror answered at last:

"You, O Queen, are the fairest in the land."

Then her envious heart was at peace, insofar as an envious heart can be at peace.

When the dwarfs came home at nightfall, they found Snow White lying on the floor. No breath came out of her mouth and she was really dead. They lifted her up, looked to see if they could find anything poisonous, unlaced her, combed her hair, washed her in water and wine, but nothing helped; the dear child was dead, and dead she remained. They laid her on a bier, and all seven sat down beside it and mourned, and they wept for three whole days. Then they were going to bury her, but she still looked fresh and alive, and she still had her beautiful red cheeks. "We can't lower her into the black earth," they said, and they had a coffin made out of glass, so that she could be seen from all sides, and they put her into it and wrote her name in gold letters on the coffin, adding that she was a king's daughter. Then they put the coffin on the hilltop, and one of them always stayed there to guard it. And the birds came and wept for Snow White, first an owl, then a raven, and then a dove.

Snow White lay in her coffin for years and years. She didn't rot, but continued to look as if she were asleep, for she was still as white as snow, as red as blood, and as black as ebony. Then one day a prince came to that forest and stopped for the night at the dwarfs' house. He saw the coffin on the hilltop, he saw lovely Snow White inside it, and he read the gold letters on the coffin. He said to the dwarfs: "Let me have the coffin, I'll pay you as much as you like for it." But the dwarfs replied: "We wouldn't part with it for all the money in the world." "Then give it to me," he said, "for I can't go on living unless I look at Snow White. I will honor and cherish her forever." Then the dwarfs took pity on him and gave him the coffin.

The prince's servants hoisted it up on their shoulders and as they were carrying it away they stumbled over a root. The jolt shook the poisoned core, which Snow White had bitten off, out of her throat, and soon she opened her eyes, lifted the coffin lid, sat up, and was alive again. "Oh!" she cried. "Where am I?" "With me!" the prince answered joyfully. Then he told her what had happened and said: "I love you more than anything in the world; come with me to my father's castle and be my wife." Snow White loved him and went with him, and arrangements were made for a splendid wedding feast.

Snow White's wicked stepmother was among those invited to the wedding. When she had put on her fine clothes, she went to her mirror and said:

"Mirror, Mirror, here I stand.
Who is the fairest in the land?"

And the mirror answered:

"You, O Queen, are the fairest here.
But the young queen is a thousand times more fair."

At that the wicked woman spat out a curse. She was so horror-stricken she didn't know what to do. At first she didn't want to go to the wedding, but then she couldn't resist; she just had to go and see the young queen. The moment she entered the hall she recognized Snow White, and she was so terrified that she just stood there and couldn't move. But two iron slippers had already been put into glowing coals. Someone took them out with a pair of tongs and set them down in front of her. She was forced to step into the red-hot shoes and dance till she fell to the floor dead.

RAPUNZEL[1]

Jacob and Wilhelm Grimm

ONCE AFTER A MAN AND wife had long wished in vain for a child, the wife had reason to hope that God would grant them their wish. In the back of their house there was a little window that looked out over a wonderful garden, full of beautiful flowers and vegetables. But there was a high wall around the garden, and no one dared enter it because it belonged to a witch, who was very powerful and everyone was afraid of her. One day the wife stood at this window, looking down into the garden, and her eyes lit on a bed of the finest rapunzel, which is a kind of lettuce. And it looked so fresh and green that she longed for it and her mouth watered. Her craving for it grew from day to day, and she began to waste away because she knew she would never get any. Seeing her so pale and wretched, her husband took fright and asked: "What's the matter with you, dear wife?" "Oh," she said, "I shall die unless I get some rapunzel to eat from the garden behind our house." Her husband, who loved her, thought: "Sooner than let my wife die, I shall get her some of that rapunzel, cost what it may." As night was falling, he climbed the wall into the witch's garden, took a handful of rapunzel, and brought it to his wife. She made it into a salad right away and ate it hungrily. But it tasted so good, so very good, that the next day her craving for it was three times as great. Her husband could see she would know no peace unless he paid another visit to the garden. So at nightfall he climbed the wall again, but when he came down on the other side he had an awful fright, for there was the witch right in front of him. "How dare you!" she said with an angry look. "How dare you sneak into my garden like a thief and steal my rapunzel! I'll make you pay dearly for this." "Oh, please," he said, "please temper justice with mercy. I only did it because I had to. My wife was looking out of the window, and when she saw your rapunzel she felt such a craving for it that she would have died if I hadn't got her some." At that the witch's anger died down and she said: "If that's how it is, you may take as much rapunzel as you wish, but on one condition: that you give me the child your wife will bear. It will have a good life and I shall care for it like a mother." In his fright, the man agreed to everything, and the moment his wife was delivered, the witch appeared, gave the child the name of Rapunzel, and took her away.

Rapunzel grew to be the loveliest child under the sun. When she was twelve years old, the witch took her to the middle of the forest and shut her up in a tower that had neither stairs nor door, but only a little window at the very top. When the witch wanted to come in, she stood down below and called out: "Rapunzel, Rapunzel, Let

1 First published in 1812/15, in the first edition of *Kinder- und Hausmärchen.* This text from the second edition (1819), from *Grimms' Tales for Young and Old*, trans. Ralph Manheim (Garden City, NY: Anchor P, 1977).

down your hair for me." Rapunzel had beautiful long hair, as fine as spun gold. When she heard the witch's voice, she undid her braids and fastened them to the window latch. They fell to the ground twenty ells down, and the witch climbed up on them.

A few years later it so happened that the king's son was passing through the forest. When he came to the tower, he heard someone singing, and the singing was so lovely that he stopped and listened. It was Rapunzel, who in her loneliness was singing to pass the time. The prince wanted to go up to her and he looked for a door but found none. He rode away home, but the singing had so touched his heart that he went out into the forest every day and listened. Once as he was standing behind a tree, he saw a witch come to the foot of the tower and heard her call out:

"Rapunzel, Rapunzel,
Let down your hair."

Whereupon Rapunzel let down her braids, and the witch climbed up to her. "Aha," he thought, "if that's the ladder that goes up to her, then I'll try my luck too." And next day, when it was beginning to get dark, he went to the tower and called out:

"Rapunzel, Rapunzel,
Let down your hair."

A moment later her hair fell to the ground and the prince climbed up.

At first Rapunzel was dreadfully frightened, for she had never seen a man before, but the prince spoke gently to her and told her how he had been so moved by her singing that he couldn't rest easy until he had seen her. At that Rapunzel lost her fear, and when he asked if she would have him as her husband and she saw he was young and handsome, she thought: "He will love me better than my old godmother." So she said yes and put her hand in his. "I'd gladly go with you," she said, "but how will I ever get down? Every time you come, bring a skein of silk and I'll make a ladder with it. When it's finished, I'll climb down, and you will carry me home on your horse." They agreed that in the meantime he would come every evening, because the old witch came during the day. The witch noticed nothing until one day Rapunzel said to her: "Tell me, Godmother, how is it that you're so much harder to pull up than the young prince? With him it hardly takes a minute." "Wicked child!" cried the witch. "What did you say? I thought I had shut you away from the world, but you've deceived me." In her fury she seized Rapunzel's beautiful hair, wound it several times around her left hand and picked up a pair of scissors in her right hand. Snippety-snap went the scissors, and the lovely braids fell to the floor. Then the heartless witch sent poor Rapunzel to a desert place, where she lived in misery and want.

At dusk on the day she had sent Rapunzel away, she fastened the severed braids to the window latch, and when the prince came and called: "Rapunzel, Rapunzel, Let down your hair." she let the hair down. The prince climbed up, but instead of his dearest Rapunzel, the witch was waiting for him with angry, poisonous looks. "Aha!" she cried. "You've come to take your darling wife away, but the bird is gone from the nest, she won't be singing any more; the cat has taken her away and before she's done she'll scratch your eyes out too. You've lost Rapunzel, you'll never see her again." The prince was beside himself with grief, and in his despair he jumped from the tower. It didn't kill him, but the brambles he fell into scratched his eyes out and he was blind. He wandered through the forest, living on roots and berries and weeping and wailing over the loss of his dearest wife. For several years he wandered wretchedly, until at last he came to the desert place where Rapunzel was living in misery with the twins she had borne—a boy and a girl. He heard a voice that seemed familiar, and when he approached Rapunzel recognized him, fell on his neck and wept. Two of her tears dropped on his eyes, which were made clear again, so that he could see as well as ever. He took her to his kingdom, where she was welcomed with rejoicing, and they lived happy and contented for many years to come.

THE FROG KING, OR IRON HEINRICH[1]

Jacob and Wilhelm Grimm

IN OLDEN TIMES, WHEN WISHING still helped, there lived a king, whose daughters were all beautiful, but the youngest was so beautiful that even the sun, who had seen many things, was filled with wonder every time he shone upon her face. Not far from the king's palace there was a great, dark forest, and under an old lime tree in the forest there was a spring. When the weather was very hot, the princess went out to the forest and sat near the edge of the cool spring. And when the time hung heavy on her hands, she took a golden ball, threw it into the air and caught it. It was her favorite plaything.

One day it so happened that when she held out her little hand to catch the golden ball, the ball passed it by, fell to the ground, and rolled straight into the water. The princess followed the ball with her eyes, but it disappeared, and the spring was deep, so deep that you couldn't see the bottom. She began to cry; she cried louder

---

1 First published in 1812/15, in the first edition of *Kinder- und Hausmärchen*. This text from the second edition (1819), from *Grimms' Tales for Young and Old*, trans. Ralph Manheim (Garden City, NY: Anchor P, 1977).

and louder, she was inconsolable. As she was lamenting, someone called out to her: "What's the matter, princess? Why, to hear you wailing, a stone would take pity." She looked to see where the voice came from and saw a frog sticking his big ugly head out of the water. "Oh, it's you, you old splasher," she said. "I'm crying because my ball has fallen into the spring." "Stop crying," said the frog. "I believe I can help you, but what will you give me if I bring you your plaything?" "Anything you like, dear frog," she said. "My clothes, my beads, my jewels, even the golden crown I'm wearing." The frog replied: "I don't want your clothes, your beads and jewels, or your golden crown. But if you will love me, if you will let me be your companion and playmate, and sit at your table and eat from your golden plate and drink from your golden cup and sleep in your bed, if you promise me that, I'll go down and fetch you your golden ball." "Oh yes," she said, "I promise you anything you want, if only you'll bring me my ball." But she thought: "What nonsense that silly frog talks; he lives in the water with other frogs and croaks; how can he be a companion to anybody?"

Once the frog had her promise, he put his head down and dived, and in a little while he came swimming back to the surface. He had her golden ball in his mouth and he tossed it onto the grass. When she saw her beautiful plaything, the princess was very happy. She picked it up and ran off with it. "Wait, wait," cried the frog. "Take me with you, I can't run like you." He croaked and he croaked at the top of his lungs, but it did him no good. The princess didn't listen. She hurried home and soon forgot the poor frog. There was nothing he could do but go back down into his spring.

The next day, when she had sat down to table with the king and all his courtiers and was eating from her golden plate, something came hopping *plip plop, plip plop*, up the marble steps. When it reached the top, it knocked at the door and cried out: "Princess, youngest princess, let me in." She ran to see who was there, and when she opened the door, she saw the frog. She closed the door as fast as she could and went back to the table. She was frightened to death. The king saw that her heart was going pit-a-pat and said: "What are you afraid of, my child? Is there a giant outside come to take you away?" "Oh no," she said. "It's not a giant, but only a nasty frog." "What does a frog want of you?" "O father dear, yesterday when I was playing beside the spring in the forest, my golden ball fell in the water. And because I was crying so, the frog got it for me, and because he insisted, I promised he could be my companion. I never thought he'd get out of his spring. And now he's outside and he wants to come in after me." Then the frog knocked a second time and cried out:

"Princess, youngest princess,
  Let me in.
  Don't you remember what

You promised yesterday
By the cool spring?
Princess, youngest princess,
Let me in."

Then the king said: "When you make a promise, you must keep it; just go and let him in." She went and opened the door; the frog hopped in and followed close at her heels. There he sat and cried out: "Lift me up beside you." She didn't know what to do, but the king ordered her to obey. Once the frog was on the chair, he wanted to be on the table, and once he was on the table, he said: "Now push your golden plate up closer to me, so we can eat together." She did as he asked, but anyone could see she wasn't happy about it. The frog enjoyed his meal, but almost every bite stuck in the princess's throat. Finally he said: "I've had enough to eat and now I'm tired, so carry me to your room and prepare your silken bed. Then we'll lie down and sleep." The princess began to cry. She was afraid of the cold frog; she didn't dare touch him and now he wanted to sleep in her lovely clean bed. But the king grew angry and said: "He helped you when you were in trouble and you mustn't despise him now." Then she picked him up between thumb and forefinger, carried him upstairs, and put him down in a corner. But when she lay down in the bed, he came crawling over and said: "I'm tired. I want to sleep as much as you do; pick me up or I'll tell your father." At that she grew very angry, picked him up and dashed him against the wall with all her might. "Now you'll get your rest, you nasty frog."

But when he fell to the floor, he wasn't a frog any longer; he was a king's son with beautiful smiling eyes. At her father's bidding, he became her dear companion and husband. He told her that a wicked witch had put a spell on him and that no one but she alone could have freed him from the spring, and that they would go to his kingdom together the next day. Then they fell asleep and in the morning when the sun woke them a carriage drove up, drawn by eight white horses in golden harness, with white ostrich plumes on their heads, and behind it stood the young king's servant, the faithful Heinrich. Faithful Heinrich had been so sad when his master was turned into a frog that he had had three iron bands forged around his heart, to keep it from bursting with grief and sadness. The carriage had come to take the young king back to his kingdom. Faithful Heinrich lifted the two of them in and sat down again in back, overjoyed that his master had been set free. When they had gone a bit of the way, the prince heard a cracking sound behind him, as though something had broken. He turned around and cried out: "Heinrich, the carriage is falling apart."

"No, master, it's only an iron ring.
I had it forged around my heart

For fear that it would break in two
When, struck by cruel magic, you
Were turned to a frog in a forest spring."

Once again and yet once again, the cracking was heard, and each time the king's son thought the carriage was falling to pieces, but it was only the bands snapping and falling away from faithful Heinrich's heart, because his master had been set free and was happy.

JACK AND THE BEANSTALK[1]

Joseph Jacobs

THERE WAS ONCE UPON A time a poor widow who had an only son named Jack, and a cow named Milky-white. And all they had to live on was the milk the cow gave every morning, which they carried to the market and sold. But one morning Milky-white gave no milk, and they didn't know what to do.

"What shall we do, what shall we do?" said the widow, wringing her hands.

"Cheer up, mother, I'll go and get work somewhere," said Jack.

"We've tried that before, and nobody would take you," said his mother; "we must sell Milky-white and with the money start shop, or something."

"All right, mother," says Jack; "it's market-day today, and I'll soon sell Milky-white, and then we'll see what we can do."

So he took the cow's halter in his hand, and off he started. He hadn't gone far when he met a funny-looking old man, who said to him: "Good morning, Jack."

"Good morning to you," said Jack, and wondered how he knew his name.

"Well, Jack, and where are you off to?" said the man.

"I'm going to market to sell our cow here."

"Oh, you look the proper sort of chap to sell cows," said the man; "I wonder if you know how many beans make five."

"Two in each hand and one in your mouth," says Jack, as sharp as a needle.

"Right you are," says the man, "and here they are, the very beans themselves," he went on, pulling out of his pocket a number of strange-looking beans. "As you are so sharp," says he, "I don't mind doing a swap with you—your cow for these beans."

"Go along," says Jack; "wouldn't you like it?"

---

1   From *English Fairy Tales*, 1890 (repr. New York: Dover, 1967).

"Ah! you don't know what these beans are," said the man; "if you plant them over-night, by morning they grow right up to the sky."

"Really?" said Jack; "you don't say so."

"Yes, that is so, and if it doesn't turn out to be true you can have your cow back."

"Right," says Jack, and hands him over Milky-white's halter and pockets the beans.

Back goes Jack home, and as he hadn't gone very far it wasn't dusk by the time he got to his door.

"Back already, Jack?" said his mother; "I see you haven't got Milky-white, so you've sold her. How much did you get for her?"

"You'll never guess, mother," says Jack.

"No, you don't say so. Good boy! Five pounds, ten, fifteen, no, it can't be twenty."

"I told you you couldn't guess. What do you say to these beans; they're magical, plant them overnight and—"

"What!" says Jack's mother, "have you been such a fool, such a dolt, such an idiot, as to give away my Milky-white, the best milker in the parish, and prime beef to boot, for a set of paltry beans? Take that! Take that! Take that! And as for your precious beans here they go out of the window. And now off with you to bed. Not a sup shall you drink, and not a bit shall you swallow this very night."

So Jack went upstairs to his little room in the attic, and sad and sorry he was, to be sure, as much for his mother's sake, as for the loss of his supper.

At last he dropped off to sleep.

When he woke up, the room looked so funny. The sun was shining into part of it, and yet all the rest was quite dark and shady. So Jack jumped up and dressed himself and went to the window. And what do you think he saw? Why, the beans his mother had thrown out of the window into the garden had sprung up into a big beanstalk which went up and up and up till it reached the sky. So the man spoke truth after all.

The beanstalk grew up quite close past Jack's window, so all he had to do was to open it and give a jump on to the beanstalk which ran up just like a big ladder. So Jack climbed, and he climbed and he climbed and he climbed and he climbed and he climbed and he climbed till at last he reached the sky. And when he got there he found a long broad road going as straight as a dart. So he walked along and he walked along and he walked along till he came to a great big tall house, and on the doorstep there was a great big tall woman.

"Good morning, mum," says Jack, quite polite-like. "Could you be so kind as to give me some breakfast?" For he hadn't had anything to eat, you know, the night before and was as hungry as a hunter.

"It's breakfast you want, is it?" says the great big tall woman, "It's breakfast you'll be if you don't move off from here. My man is an ogre and there's nothing he likes better than boys broiled on toast. You'd better be moving on or he'll soon be coming."

"Oh! please mum, do give me something to eat, mum. I've had nothing to eat since yesterday morning, really and truly, mum," says Jack. "I may as well be broiled as die of hunger."

Well, the ogre's wife was not half so bad after all. So she took Jack into the kitchen, and gave him a hunk of bread and cheese and a jug of milk. But Jack hadn't half finished these when thump! thump! thump! the whole house began to tremble with the noise of some one coming.

"Goodness gracious me! It's my old man," said the ogre's wife, "what on earth shall I do? Come along quick and jump in here." And she bundled Jack into the oven just as the ogre came in.

He was a big one, to be sure. At his belt he had three calves strung up by the heels, and he unhooked them and threw them down on the table and said: "Here, wife, broil me a couple of these for breakfast. Ah! what's this I smell?

Fee-fi-fo-fum,
I smell the blood of an Englishman,
Be he alive, or be he dead
I'll have his bones to grind my bread."

"Nonsense dear," said his wife, "you're dreaming. Or perhaps you smell the scraps of that little boy you liked so much for yesterday's dinner. Here, you go and have a wash and tidy up, and by the time you come back your breakfast'll be ready for you."

So off the ogre went, and Jack was just going to jump out of the oven and run away when the woman told him not. "Wait till he's asleep," says she; "he always has a doze after breakfast."

Well, the ogre had his breakfast, and after that he goes to a big chest and takes out of it a couple of bags of gold, and down he sits and counts till at last his head began to nod and he began to snore till the whole house shook again.

Then Jack crept out on tiptoe from his oven, and as he was passing the ogre he took one of the bags of gold under his arm, and off he pelters till he came to the beanstalk, and then he threw down the bag of gold, which of course fell into his mother's garden, and then he climbed down and climbed down till at last he got home and told his mother and showed her the gold and said: "Well, mother, wasn't I right about the beans? They are really magical, you see."

So they lived on the bag of gold for some time, but at last they came to the end of it, and Jack made up his mind to try his luck once more up at the top of the beanstalk. So one fine morning he rose up early, and got on to the beanstalk, and he climbed and he climbed and he climbed and he climbed and he climbed and he climbed till at last he came out on to the road again and up to the great big tall house he had been to before. There, sure enough, was the great big tall woman standing on the doorstep.

"Good morning, mum," says Jack, as bold as brass, "could you be so good as to give me something to eat?"

"Go away, my boy," said the big tall woman, "or else my man will eat you for breakfast. But aren't you the youngster who came here once before? Do you know, that very day, my man missed one of his bags of gold."

"That's strange, mum," said Jack, "I dare say I could tell you something about that, but I'm so hungry I can't speak till I've had something to eat."

Well the big tall woman was so curious that she took him in and gave him something to eat. But he had scarcely begun munching it as slowly as he could when thump! thump! thump! they heard the giant's footstep, and his wife hid Jack away in the oven.

All happened as it did before. In came the ogre as he did before, said: "Fee-fi-fo-fum," and had his breakfast of three broiled oxen. Then he said: "Wife, bring me the hen that lays the golden eggs." So she brought it, and the ogre said: "Lay," and it laid an egg all of gold. And then the ogre began to nod his head, and to snore till the house shook.

Then Jack crept out of the oven on tiptoe and caught hold of the golden hen, and was off before you could say "Jack Robinson." But this time the hen gave a cackle which woke the ogre, and just as Jack got out of the house he heard him calling: "Wife, wife, what have you done with my golden hen?"

And the wife said: "Why, my dear?"

But that was all Jack heard, for he rushed off to the beanstalk and climbed down like a house on fire. And when he got home he showed his mother the wonderful hen, and said "Lay" to it; and it laid a golden egg every time he said "Lay."

Well, Jack was not content, and it wasn't very long before he determined to have another try at his luck up there at the top of the beanstalk. So one fine morning, he rose up early, and got on to the beanstalk, and he climbed and he climbed and he climbed and he climbed till he got to the top. But this time he knew better than to go straight to the ogre's house. And when he got near it, he waited behind a bush till he saw the ogre's wife come out with a pail to get some water, and then he crept into the house and got into the copper.[1] He hadn't been there long when he heard thump! thump! thump! as before, and in come the ogre and his wife.

"Fee-fi-fo-fum, I smell the blood of an Englishman," cried out the ogre. "I smell him, wife, I smell him."

"Do you, my dearie?" says the ogre's wife. "Then, if it's that little rogue that stole your gold and the hen that laid the golden eggs he's sure to have got into the oven."

---

1 A large metal pot for boiling laundry.

And they both rushed to the oven. But Jack wasn't there, luckily, and the ogre's wife said: "There you are again with your fee-fi-fo-fum. Why of course it's the boy you caught last night that I've just broiled for your breakfast. How forgetful I am, and how careless you are not to know the difference between live and dead after all these years."

So the ogre sat down to the breakfast and ate it, but every now and then he would mutter: "Well, I could have sworn—" and he'd get up and search the larder and the cupboards and everything, only, luckily, he didn't think of the copper.

After breakfast was over, the ogre called out: "Wife, wife, bring me my golden harp." So she brought it and put it on the table before him. Then he said: "Sing!" and the golden harp sang most beautifully. And it went on singing till the ogre fell asleep, and commenced to snore like thunder.

Then Jack lifted up the copperlid very quietly and got down like a mouse and crept on hands and knees till he came to the table, when up he crawled, caught hold of the golden harp and dashed with it towards the door. But the harp called out quite loud: "Master! Master!" and the ogre woke up just in time to see Jack running off with his harp.

Jack ran as fast as he could, and the ogre came rushing after, and would soon have caught him only Jack had a start and dodged him a bit and knew where he was going. When he got to the beanstalk the ogre was not more than twenty yards away when suddenly he saw Jack disappear like, and when he came to the end of the road he saw Jack underneath climbing down for dear life. Well, the ogre didn't like trusting himself to such a ladder, and he stood and waited, so Jack got another start. But just then the harp cried out: "Master! Master!" and the ogre swung himself down on to the beanstalk, which shook with his weight. Down climbs Jack, and after him climbed the ogre. By this time Jack had climbed down and climbed down and climbed down till he was very nearly home. So he called out: "Mother! Mother! bring me an axe, bring me an axe." And his mother came rushing out with the axe in her hand, but when she came to the beanstalk she stood stock still with fright for there she saw the ogre with his legs just through the clouds.

But Jack jumped down and got hold of the axe and gave a chop at the beanstalk which cut it half in two. The ogre felt the beanstalk shake and quiver so he stopped to see what was the matter. Then Jack gave another chop with the axe, and the beanstalk was cut in two and began to topple over. Then the ogre fell down and broke his crown, and the beanstalk came toppling after.

Then Jack showed his mother his golden harp, and what with showing that and selling the golden eggs, Jack and his mother became very rich, and he married a great princess, and they lived happy ever after.

THE UGLY DUCKLING[1]

Hans Christian Andersen

IT WAS SO BEAUTIFUL OUT in the country. It was summer. The oats were still green, but the wheat was turning yellow. Down in the meadow the grass had been cut and made into haystacks; and there the storks walked on their long red legs talking Egyptian, because that was the language they had been taught by their mothers. The fields were enclosed by woods, and hidden among them were little lakes and pools. Yes, it certainly was lovely out there in the country!

The old castle, with its deep moat surrounding it, lay bathed in sunshine. Between the heavy walls and the edge of the moat there was a narrow strip of land covered by a whole forest of burdock plants. Their leaves were large and some of the stalks were so tall that a child could stand upright under them and imagine that he was in the middle of the wild and lonely woods. Here a duck had built her nest. While she sat waiting for the eggs to hatch, she felt a little sorry for herself because it was taking so long and hardly anybody came to visit her. The other ducks preferred swimming in the moat to sitting under a dock leaf and gossiping.

Finally the eggs began to crack. "Peep ... Peep," they said one after another. The egg yolks had become alive and were sticking out their heads.

"Quack ... Quack ..." said their mother. "Look around you." And the ducklings did; they glanced at the green world about them, and that was what their mother wanted them to do, for green was good for their eyes.

"How big the world is!" piped the little ones, for they had much more space to move around in now than they had had inside the egg.

"Do you think that this is the whole world?" quacked their mother. "The world is much larger than this. It stretches as far as the minister's wheat fields, though I have not been there.... Are you all here?" The duck got up and turned around to look at her nest. "Oh no, the biggest egg hasn't hatched yet; and I'm so tired of sitting here! I wonder how long it will take?" she wailed, and sat down again.

"What's new?" asked an old duck who had come visiting.

"One of the eggs is taking so long," complained the mother duck. "It won't crack. But take a look at the others. They are the sweetest little ducklings you have ever seen; and every one of them looks exactly like their father. That scoundrel hasn't come to visit me once."

"Let me look at the egg that won't hatch," demanded the old duck. "I am sure that

---

1 First published in 1843. This text from *Hans Christian Andersen: His Classic Fairy Tales*, trans. Erik Haugaard (New York: Doubleday, 1974).

it's a turkey egg! I was fooled that way once. You can't imagine what it's like. Turkeys are afraid of the water. I couldn't get them to go into it. I quacked and I nipped them, but nothing helped. Let me see that egg! … Yes, it's a turkey egg. Just let it lie there. You go and teach your young ones how to swim, that's my advice."

"I have sat on it so long that I suppose I can sit a little longer, at least until they get the hay in," replied the mother duck.

"Suit yourself," said the older duck, and went on.

At last the big egg cracked too. "Peep … Peep," said the young one, and tumbled out. He was big and very ugly.

The mother duck looked at him. "He's awfully big for his age," she said. "He doesn't look like any of the others. I wonder if he could be a turkey? Well, we shall soon see. Into the water he will go, even if I have to kick him to make him do it."

The next day the weather was gloriously beautiful. The sun shone on the forest of burdock plants. The mother duck took her whole brood to the moat. "Quack … Quack …" she ordered.

One after another, the little ducklings plunged into the water. For a moment their heads disappeared, but then they popped up again and the little ones floated like so many corks. Their legs knew what to do without being told. All of the new brood swam very nicely, even the ugly one.

"He is no turkey," mumbled the mother. "See how beautifully he uses his legs and how straight he holds his neck. He is my own child and, when you look closely at him, he's quite handsome…. Quack! Quack! Follow me and I'll take you to the henyard and introduce you to everyone. But stay close to me, so that no one steps on you, and look out for the cat."

They heard an awful noise when they arrived at the henyard. Two families of ducks had got into a fight over the head of an eel. Neither of them got it, for it was swiped by the cat.

"That is the way of the world," said the mother duck, and licked her bill. She would have liked to have had the eel's head herself. "Walk nicely," she admonished them. "And remember to bow to the old duck over there. She has Spanish blood in her veins and is the most aristocratic fowl here. That is why she is so fat and has a red rag tied around one of her legs. That is the highest mark of distinction a duck can be given. It means so much that she will never be done away with; and all the other fowl and the human beings know who she is. Quack! Quack! … Don't walk, waddle like well-brought-up ducklings. Keep your legs far apart, just as your mother and father have always done. Bow your heads and say, 'Quack'!" And that was what the little ducklings did.

Other ducks gathered about them and said loudly, "What do we want that gang here for? Aren't there enough of us already? Pooh! Look how ugly one of them is!

[119]

He's the last straw!" And one of the ducks flew over and bit the ugly duckling on the neck.

"Leave him alone!" shouted the mother. "He hasn't done anyone any harm."

"He's big and he doesn't look like everybody else!" replied the duck who had bitten him. "And that's reason enough to beat him."

"Very good-looking children you have," remarked the duck with the red rag around one of her legs. "All of them are beautiful except one. He didn't turn out very well. I wish you could make him over again."

"That's not possible, Your Grace," answered the mother duck. "He may not be handsome, but he has a good character and swims as well as the others, if not a little better. Perhaps he will grow handsomer as he grows older and becomes a bit smaller. He was in the egg too long, and that is why he doesn't have the right shape." She smoothed his neck for a moment and then added, "Besides, he's a drake; and it doesn't matter so much what he looks like. He is strong and I am sure he will be able to take care of himself."

"Well, the others are nice," said the old duck. "Make yourself at home, and if you should find an eel's head, you may bring it to me."

And they were "at home."

The poor little duckling, who had been the last to hatch and was so ugly, was bitten and pushed and made fun of both by the hens and by the other ducks. The turkey cock (who had been born with spurs on, and therefore thought he was an emperor) rustled his feathers as if he were a full-rigged ship under sail, and strutted up to the duckling. He gobbled so loudly at him that his own face got all red.

The poor little duckling did not know where to turn. How he grieved over his own ugliness, and how sad he was! The poor creature was mocked and laughed at by the whole henyard.

That was the first day; and each day that followed was worse than the one before. The poor duckling was chased and mistreated by everyone, even his own sisters and brothers, who quacked again and again, "If only the cat would get you, you ugly thing!"

Even his mother said, "I wish you were far away." The other ducks bit him and the hens pecked at him. The little girl who came to feed the fowls kicked him.

At last the duckling ran away. He flew over the tops of the bushes, frightening all the little birds so that they flew up into the air. "They, too, think I am ugly," thought the duckling, and closed his eyes—but he kept on running.

Finally he came to a great swamp where wild ducks lived; and here he stayed for the night, for he was too tired to go any farther.

In the morning he was discovered by the wild ducks. They looked at him and one of them asked, "What kind of bird are you?"

The ugly duckling bowed in all directions, for he was trying to be as polite as he knew how.

"You are ugly," said the wild ducks, "but that is no concern of ours, as long as you don't try to marry into our family."

The poor duckling wasn't thinking of marriage. All he wanted was to be allowed to swim among the reeds and drink a little water when he was thirsty.

He spent two days in the swamp; then two wild geese came—or rather, two wild ganders, for they were males. They had been hatched not long ago; therefore they were both frank and bold.

"Listen, comrade," they said. "You are so ugly that we like you. Do you want to migrate with us? Not far from here there is a marsh where some beautiful wild geese live. They are all lovely maidens, and you are so ugly that you may seek your fortune among them. Come along."

"Bang! Bang!" Two shots were heard and both ganders fell down dead among the reeds, and the water turned red from their blood.

"Bang! Bang!" Again came the sound of shots, and a flock of wild geese flew up.

The whole swamp was surrounded by hunters; from every direction came the awful noise. Some of the hunters had hidden behind bushes or among the reeds but others, screened from sight by the leaves, sat on the long, low branches of the trees that stretched out over the swamp. The blue smoke from the guns lay like a fog over the water and along the trees. Dogs came splashing through the marsh, and they bent and broke the reeds.

The poor little duckling was terrified. He was about to tuck his head under his wing, in order to hide, when he saw a big dog peering at him through the reeds. The dog's tongue hung out of its mouth and its eyes glistened evilly. It bared its teeth. Splash! It turned away without touching the duckling.

"Oh, thank God!" he sighed. "I am so ugly that even the dog doesn't want to bite me."

The little duckling lay as still as he could while the shots whistled through the reeds. Not until the middle of the afternoon did the shooting stop; but the poor little duckling was still so frightened that he waited several hours longer before taking his head out from under his wing. Then he ran as quickly as he could out of the swamp. Across the fields and the meadows he went, but a wind had come up and he found it hard to make his way against it.

Towards evening he came upon a poor little hut. It was so wretchedly crooked that it looked as if it couldn't make up its mind which way to fall and that was why it was still standing. The wind was blowing so hard that the poor little duckling had to sit down in order not to be blown away. Suddenly he noticed that the door was off its hinges, making a crack; and he squeezed himself through it and was inside.

An old woman lived in the hut with her cat and her hen. The cat was called Sonny and could both arch his back and purr. Oh yes, it could also make sparks if you rubbed its fur the wrong way. The hen had very short legs and that was why she was called Cluck Lowlegs. But she was good at laying eggs, and the old woman loved her as if she were her own child.

In the morning the hen and the cat discovered the duckling. The cat meowed and the hen clucked.

"What is going on?" asked the old woman, and looked around. She couldn't see very well, and when she found the duckling she thought it was a fat, full-grown duck. "What a fine catch!" she exclaimed. "Now we shall have duck eggs, unless it's a drake. We'll give it a try."

So the duckling was allowed to stay for three weeks on probation, but he laid no eggs. The cat was the master of the house and the hen the mistress. They always referred to themselves as "we and the world," for they thought that they were half the world—and the better half at that. The duckling thought that he should be allowed to have a different opinion, but the hen did not agree.

"Can you lay eggs?" she demanded.

"No," answered the duckling.

"Then keep your mouth shut."

And the cat asked, "Can you arch your back? Can you purr? Can you make sparks?"

"No."

"Well, in that case, you have no right to have an opinion when sensible people are talking."

The duckling was sitting in a corner and was in a bad mood. Suddenly he recalled how lovely it could be outside in the fresh air when the sun shone: a great longing to be floating in the water came over the duckling, and he could not help talking about it.

"What is the matter with you?" asked the hen as soon as she had heard what he had to say. "You have nothing to do, that's why you get ideas like that. Lay eggs or purr, and such notions will disappear."

"You have no idea how delightful it is to float in the water, and to dive down to the bottom of a lake and get your head wet," said the duckling.

"Yes, that certainly does sound amusing," said the hen. "You must have gone mad. Ask the cat—he is the most intelligent being I know—ask him whether he likes to swim or dive down to the bottom of a lake. Don't take my word for anything.... Ask the old woman, who is the cleverest person in the world; ask her whether she likes to float and to get her head all wet."

"You don't understand me!" wailed the duckling.

"And if I don't understand you, who will? I hope you don't think that you are wiser than the cat or the old woman—not to mention myself. Don't give yourself airs! Thank your Creator for all He has done for you. Aren't you sitting in a warm room, where you can hear intelligent conversation that you could learn something from? While you, yourself, do nothing but say a lot of nonsense and aren't the least bit amusing! Believe me, that's the truth, and I am only telling it to you for your own good. That's how you recognize a true friend: it's someone who is willing to tell you the truth, no matter how unpleasant it is. Now get to work: lay some eggs, or learn to purr and arch your back."

"I think I'll go out into the wide world," replied the duckling.

"Go right ahead!" said the hen.

And the duckling left. He found a lake where he could float in the water and dive to the bottom. There were other ducks, but they ignored him because he was so ugly.

Autumn came and the leaves turned yellow and brown, then they fell from the trees. The wind caught them and made them dance. The clouds were heavy with hail and snow. A raven sat on a fence and screeched, "Ach! Ach!" because it was so cold. When just thinking of how cold it was is enough to make one shiver, what a terrible time the duckling must have had.

One evening just as the sun was setting gloriously, a flock of beautiful birds came out from among the rushes. Their feathers were so white that they glistened; and they had long, graceful necks. They were swans. They made a very loud cry, then they spread their powerful wings. They were flying south to a warmer climate, where the lakes were not frozen in the winter. Higher and higher they circled. The ugly duckling turned round and round in the water like a wheel and stretched his neck up toward the sky; he felt a strange longing. He screeched so piercingly that he frightened himself.

Oh, he would never forget those beautiful birds, those happy birds. When they were out of sight the duckling dived down under the water to the bottom of the lake; and when he came up again he was beside himself. He did not know the name of those birds or where they were going, and yet he felt he loved them as he had never loved any other creatures. He did not envy them. It did not even occur to him to wish that he were so handsome himself. He would have been happy if the other ducks had let him stay in the henyard: that poor, ugly bird!

The weather grew colder and colder. The duckling had to swim round and round in the water, to keep just a little space for himself that wasn't frozen. Each night his hole became smaller and smaller. On all sides of him the ice creaked and groaned. The little duckling had to keep his feet constantly in motion so that the last bit of open water wouldn't become ice. At last he was too tired to swim any more. He sat still. The ice closed in around him and he was frozen fast.

Early the next morning a farmer saw him and with his clogs broke the ice to free the duckling. The man put the bird under his arm and took it home to his wife, who brought the duckling back to life.

The children wanted to play with him. But the duckling was afraid that they were going to hurt him, so he flapped his wings and flew right into the milk pail. From there he flew into a big bowl of butter and then into a barrel of flour. What a sight he was!

The farmer's wife yelled and chased him with a poker. The children laughed and almost fell on top of each other, trying to catch him; and how they screamed! Luckily for the duckling, the door was open. He got out of the house and found a hiding place beneath some bushes, in the newly fallen snow; and there he lay so still, as though there was hardly any life left in him.

It would be too horrible to tell of all the hardship and suffering the duckling experienced that long winter. It is enough to know that he did survive. When again the sun shone warmly and the larks began to sing, the duckling was lying among the reeds in the swamp. Spring had come!

He spread out his wings to fly. How strong and powerful they were! Before he knew it, he was far from the swamp and flying above a beautiful garden. The apple trees were blooming and the lilac bushes stretched their flower-covered branches over the water of a winding canal. Everything was so beautiful: so fresh and green. Out of a forest of rushes came three swans. They ruffled their feathers and floated so lightly on the water. The ugly duckling recognized the birds and felt again that strange sadness come over him.

"I shall fly over to them, those royal birds! And they can hack me to death because I, who am so ugly, dare to approach them! What difference does it make? It is better to be killed by them than to be bitten by the other ducks, and pecked by the hens, and kicked by the girl who tends the henyard; or to suffer through the winter."

And he lighted on the water and swam towards the magnificent swans. When they saw him they ruffled their feathers and started to swim in his direction. They were coming to meet him.

"Kill me," whispered the poor creature, and bent his head humbly while he waited for death. But what was that he saw in the water? It was his own reflection; and he was no longer an awkward, clumsy, grey bird, so ungainly and so ugly. He was a swan!

It does not matter that one has been born in the henyard as long as one has lain in a swan's egg.

He was thankful that he had known so much want, and gone through so much suffering, for it made him appreciate his present happiness and the loveliness of everything about him all the more. The swans made a circle around him and caressed him with their beaks.

Some children came out into the garden. They had brought bread with them to feed the swans. The youngest child shouted, "Look, there's a new one!" All the children joyfully clapped their hands, and they ran to tell their parents.

Cake and bread were cast on the water for the swans. Everyone agreed that the new swan was the most beautiful of them all. The older swans bowed towards him.

He felt so shy that he hid his head beneath his wing. He was too happy, but not proud, for a kind heart can never be proud. He thought of the time when he had been mocked and persecuted. And now everyone said that he was the most beautiful of the most beautiful birds. And the lilac bushes stretched their branches right down to the water for him. The sun shone so warm and brightly. He ruffled his feathers and raised his slender neck, while out of the joy in his heart, he thought, "Such happiness I did not dream of when I was the ugly duckling."

THE NATURE OF LOVE

LOVE IS ONE OF THE core elements of the fairy tale, to the extent that we take it for granted that however unpromising the circumstances at the outset, the ending will involve—both literally and figuratively—a fairy-tale wedding. And yet it might be argued that the wedding is generally the least interesting part of the story: the excitement is in the journey, not the arrival.

One point of similarity in all four tales in this section is that they all contain non-human characters. We have already considered (see "Little Red Riding Hood") the possibility that the animal (real or mythical) is often the symbolic representation of a particular aspect of the human character, since the fairy tale is first and foremost about people. The essential quality of an animal is its *otherness*; the ability to communicate notwithstanding, the animal represents the unknown, a representation of the shadowy world of instinct. For the inexperienced young woman depicted in many fairy tales, love (and by extension, marriage) represents a challenge. Indeed, for most young women, the concept of love was, if not unknown, then in practical terms irrelevant. We must remember that the husband was rarely of the young woman's choosing, so the prospect was very different from what we take as the norm today. Whether the betrothal was the outcome of economic realities (as in "East of the Sun and West of the Moon") or of suitable bloodlines (which amounted to much the same thing), the fact remains that the young bride-to-be was still the helpless bystander to the negotiations. To say the least, the notion of personal and sexual union with a male stranger was a step into the disturbing unknown, which explains why, in this type of fairy tale, the male often takes the form of an animal. While marriage represents elevation into womanhood, it brings with it also all the anxieties and even revulsion often associated with initiation into sexuality. "Beauty and the Beast," for example, deals with the gradual maturation of a young woman's love to embrace both father and husband;[1] the girl in "East of the Sun and West of the Moon" is the victim of her mother's jealous suspicions about the White Bear and, in consequence, faces—literally—a long and hard road to achieve reconciliation with her lover.

While it may be the common assumption that the fairy-tale romance invariably ends "happily-ever-after," that is often not the case with more recent literary tales. There is plenty of evidence to indicate that we enjoy a sad love story as much as a happy one, and that fact is reflected as much in fairy tale as in other branches of literature.

It is well known that Hans Christian Andersen used his tales to tell his own life story, distilling the frustration, loneliness, and yearning that suffused his own life into a series of memorable fairy-tale characters. If "The Ugly Duckling" recounts his escape from the misery and abuse of his early life, then his longing for love and recognition as an adult surely provides the inspiration for "The Little Mermaid." She faces a cruel—some might say perverse—choice: to seek the prince's love, she must deny her own identity, and when her gamble fails, there can only be one outcome, which Andersen recognizes but cannot accept. In certain respects, this tale can be seen as a parable for our times, as we watch the mermaid literally cut her ties with her own world and struggle with the pain and confusion of being a stranger in a strange land. Andersen's most memorable stories are about *difference*, and nowhere is that fact more evident than in "The Little Mermaid." She is silenced, misunderstood, rejected—one cannot even describe her as a "lost soul" because she has none. While Andersen himself backed away from the inevitability of the mermaid's fate, we have to see Disney's assertion of a happy ending as revealing more about our worldview than Andersen's.

"The Woman of the Sea" (sometimes known as "The Selkie Bride") can be seen as the virtual mirror-image of Andersen's tale. Here too the sea-people have a fascination with the land, but now it is the fisherman who is enamored with the beautiful sea-woman and captures her by hiding her sealskin. In this case, however, difference is a gentler concept; in contrast to the emotional overload of Andersen's tale, the tone is set by the sea-woman's quiet acquiescence to the fisherman's passionate love. When Fate intervenes, however, a choice must be made—and we are left in no doubt about the pain and sorrow involved.

---

1   We should note that the familiar version of this tale, published in 1756 by Jeanne-Marie Leprince de Beaumont (1711–80), is in fact an abridged version of a considerably longer original tale by Gabrielle-Suzanne de Villeneuve (1685–1755).

BEAUTY AND THE BEAST[1]

Madame Leprince de Beaumont

ONCE UPON A TIME THERE lived a merchant who was exceedingly rich. He had six children—three boys and three girls—and being a sensible man he spared no expense upon their education, but engaged tutors of every kind for them. All his daughters were pretty, but the youngest especially was admired by everybody. When she was small she was known simply as "the little beauty," and this name stuck to her, causing a great deal of jealousy on the part of her sisters.

This youngest girl was not only prettier than her sisters, but very much nicer. The two elder girls were very arrogant as a result of their wealth; they pretended to be great ladies, declining to receive the daughters of other merchants, and associating only with people of quality. Every day they went off to balls and theatres, and for walks in the park, with many a gibe at their little sister, who spent much of her time in reading good books.

Now these girls were known to be very rich, and in consequence were sought in marriage by many prominent merchants. The two eldest said they would never marry unless they could find a duke, or at least a count. But Beauty—this, as I have mentioned, was the name by which the youngest was known—very politely thanked all who proposed marriage to her, and said that she was too young at present, and that she wished to keep her father company for several years yet.

Suddenly the merchant lost his fortune, the sole property which remained to him being a small house in the country, a long way from the capital. With tears he broke it to his children that they would have to move to this house, where by working like peasants they might just be able to live.

The two elder girls replied that they did not wish to leave the town, and that they had several admirers who would be only too happy to marry them, notwithstanding their loss of fortune. But the simple maidens were mistaken: their admirers would no longer look at them, now that they were poor. Everybody disliked them on account of their arrogance, and folks declared that they did not deserve pity: in fact, that it was a good thing their pride had had a fall—a turn at minding sheep would teach them how to play the fine lady! "But we are very sorry for Beauty's misfortune," everybody added; "she is such a dear girl, and was always so considerate to poor people: so gentle, and with such charming manners!"

There were even several worthy men who would have married her, despite the fact that she was now penniless; but she told them she could not make up her mind

---

1   First published in 1756. This text from *Sleeping Beauty and Other Favourite Fairy Tales*, trans. Angela Carter (London: Gollancz, 1982).

to leave her poor father in his misfortune, and that she intended to go with him to the country, to comfort him and help him to work. Poor Beauty had been very grieved at first over the loss of her fortune, but she said to herself:

"However much I cry, I shall not recover my wealth, so I must try to be happy without it."

When they were established in the country the merchant and his family started working on the land. Beauty used to rise at four o'clock in the morning, and was busy all day looking after the house, and preparing dinner for the family. At first she found it very hard, for she was not accustomed to work like a servant, but at the end of a couple of months she grew stronger, and her health was improved by the work. When she had leisure she read, or played the harpsichord, or sang at her spinning-wheel.

Her two sisters, on the other hand, were bored to death; they did not get up till ten o'clock in the morning, and they idled about all day. Their only diversion was to bemoan the beautiful clothes they used to wear and the company they used to keep. "Look at our little sister," they would say to each other; "her tastes are so low and her mind so stupid that she is quite content with this miserable state of affairs."

The good merchant did not share the opinion of his two daughters, for he knew that Beauty was more fitted to shine in company than her sisters. He was greatly impressed by the girl's good qualities, and especially by her patience—for her sisters, not content with leaving her all the work of the house, never missed an opportunity of insulting her.

They had been living for a year in this seclusion when the merchant received a letter informing him that a ship on which he had some merchandise had just come safely home. The news nearly turned the heads of the two elder girls, for they thought that at last they would be able to quit their dull life in the country. When they saw their father ready to set out they begged him to bring them back dresses, furs, caps, and finery of every kind. Beauty asked for nothing, thinking to herself that all the money which the merchandise might yield would not be enough to satisfy her sisters' demands.

"You have not asked me for anything," said her father.

"As you are so kind as to think of me," she replied, "please bring me a rose, for there are none here."

Beauty had no real craving for a rose, but she was anxious not to seem to disparage the conduct of her sisters. The latter would have declared that she purposely asked for nothing in order to be different from them.

The merchant duly set forth; but when he reached his destination there was a law-suit over his merchandise, and after much trouble he returned poorer than he had been before. With only thirty miles to go before reaching home, he was already looking forward to the pleasure of seeing his children again, when he found he had to pass through a large wood. Here he lost himself. It was snowing horribly; the wind was so strong that twice he was thrown from his horse, and when night came on he made up his mind he must either die of hunger and cold or be eaten by the wolves that he could hear howling all about him.

Suddenly he saw, at the end of a long avenue of trees, a strong light. It seemed to be some distance away, but he walked towards it, and presently discovered that it came from a large palace, which was all lit up.

The merchant thanked heaven for sending him this help, and hastened to the castle. To his surprise, however, he found no one about in the courtyards. His horse, which had followed him, saw a large stable open and went in; and on finding hay and oats in readiness the poor animal, which was dying of hunger, set to with a will. The merchant tied him up in the stable, and approached the house, where he found not a soul. He entered a large room; here there was a good fire, and a table laden with food, but with a place laid for one only. The rain and snow had soaked him to the skin, so he drew near the fire to dry himself. "I am sure," he remarked to himself, "that the master of this house or his servants will forgive the liberty I am taking; doubtless they will be here soon."

He waited some considerable time; but eleven o'clock struck and still he had seen nobody. Being no longer able to resist his hunger he took a chicken and devoured it in two mouthfuls, trembling. Then he drank several glasses of wine, and becoming bolder ventured out of the room. He went through several magnificently furnished apartments, and finally found a room with a very good bed. It was now past midnight, and as he was very tired he decided to shut the door and go to bed.

It was ten o'clock the next morning when he rose, and he was greatly astonished to find a new suit in place of his own, which had been spoilt. "This palace," he said to himself, "must surely belong to some good fairy, who has taken pity on my plight."

He looked out of the window. The snow had vanished, and his eyes rested instead upon arbours of flowers—a charming spectacle. He went back to the room where he had supped the night before, and found there a little table with a cup of chocolate on it. "I thank you, Madam Fairy," he said aloud, "for being so kind as to think of my breakfast."

Having drunk his chocolate the good man went forth to look for his horse. As he passed under a bower of roses he remembered that Beauty had asked for one, and he plucked a spray from a mass of blooms. The very same moment he heard a terrible noise, and saw a beast coming towards him which was so hideous that he came near to fainting.

"Ungrateful wretch!" said the Beast, in a dreadful voice; "I have saved your life by receiving you into my castle, and in return you steal that which I love better than anything in the world—my roses. You shall pay for this with your life! I give you fifteen minutes to make your peace with Heaven."

The merchant threw himself on his knees and wrung his hands. "Pardon, my lord!" he cried; "one of my daughters had asked for a rose, and I did not dream I should be giving offence by picking one."

"I am not called 'my lord,'" answered the monster, "but 'The Beast.' I have no liking for compliments, but prefer people to say what they think. Do not hope therefore to soften me by flattery. You have daughters, you say; well, I am willing to pardon you if one of your daughters will come, of her own choice, to die in your place. Do not argue with me—go! And swear that if your daughters refuse to die in your place, you will come back again in three months."

The good man had no intention of sacrificing one of his daughters to this hideous monster, but he thought that at least he might have the pleasure of kissing them once again. He therefore swore to return, and the Beast told him he could go when he wished. "I do not wish you to go empty-handed," he added; "return to the room where you slept; you will find there a large empty box. Fill it with what you will; I will have it sent home for you."

With these words the Beast withdrew, leaving the merchant to reflect that if he must indeed die, at all events he would have the consolation of providing for his poor children.

He went back to the room where he had slept. He found there a large number of gold pieces, and with these he filled the box the Beast had mentioned. Having closed the latter, he took his horse, which was still in the stable, and set forth from the palace, as melancholy now as he had been joyous when he entered it.

The horse of its own accord took one of the forest roads, and in a few hours the good man reached his own little house. His children crowded round him, but at sight of them, instead of welcoming their caresses, he burst into tears. In his hand was the bunch of roses which he had brought for Beauty, and he gave it to her with these words:

"Take these roses, Beauty; it is dearly that your poor father will have to pay for them."

Thereupon he told his family of the dire adventure which had befallen him. On hearing the tale the two elder girls were in a great commotion, and began to upbraid Beauty for not weeping as they did. "See to what her smugness has brought this young chit," they said; "surely she might strive to find some way out of this trouble, as we do! But oh, dear me, no; her ladyship is so determined to be different that she can speak of her father's death without a tear!"

"It would be quite useless to weep," said Beauty. "Why should I lament my father's death? He is not going to die. Since the monster agrees to accept a daughter instead, I intend to offer myself to appease his fury. It will be a happiness to do so, for in dying I shall have the joy of saving my father, and of proving to him my devotion."

"No, sister," said her three brothers; "you shall not die; we will go in quest of this monster, and will perish under his blows if we cannot kill him."

"Do not entertain any such hopes, my children," said the merchant; "the power of this Beast is so great that I have not the slightest expectation of escaping him. I am touched by the goodness of Beauty's heart, but I will not expose her to death. I am old and have not much longer to live; and I shall merely lose a few years that will be regretted only on account of you, my dear children."

"I can assure you, father," said Beauty, "that you will not go to this palace without me. You cannot prevent me from following you. Although I am young I am not so very deeply in love with life, and I would rather be devoured by this monster than die of the grief which your loss would cause me." Words were useless. Beauty was quite determined to go to this wonderful palace, and her sisters were not sorry, for they regarded her good qualities with deep jealousy.

The merchant was so taken up with the sorrow of losing his daughter that he forgot all about the box which he had filled with gold. To his astonishment, when he had shut the door of his room and was about to retire for the night, there it was at the side of his bed! He decided not to tell his children that he had become so rich, for his elder daughters would have wanted to go back to town, and he had resolved to die in the country. He did confide his secret to Beauty, however, and the latter told him that during his absence they had entertained some visitors, amongst whom were two admirers of her sisters. She begged her father to let them marry; for she was of such a sweet nature that she loved them, and forgave them with all her heart the evil they had done her.

When Beauty set off with her father the two heartless girls rubbed their eyes with an onion, so as to seem tearful; but her brothers wept in reality, as did also the merchant. Beauty alone did not cry, because she did not want to add to their sorrow.

The horse took the road to the palace, and by evening they espied it, all lit up as before. An empty stable awaited the nag, and when the good merchant and his daughter entered the great hall, they found there a table magnificently laid for two people. The merchant had not the heart to eat, but Beauty, forcing herself to appear calm, sat down and served him. Since the Beast had provided such splendid fare, she thought to herself, he must presumably be anxious to fatten her up before eating her.

When they had finished supper, they heard a terrible noise. With tears the merchant bade farewell to his daughter, for he knew it was the Beast. Beauty herself could not help trembling at the awful apparition, but she did her best to compose herself. The Beast asked her if she had come of her own free will, and she timidly answered that such was the case.

"You are indeed kind," said the Beast, "and I am much obliged to you. You, my good man, will depart tomorrow morning, and you must not think of coming back again. Good-bye, Beauty!"

"Good-bye, Beast!" she answered.

Thereupon the monster suddenly disappeared.

"Daughter," said the merchant, embracing Beauty, "I am nearly dead with fright. Let me be the one to stay here!"

"No, father," said Beauty, firmly, "you must go tomorrow morning, and leave me to the mercy of Heaven. Perhaps pity will be taken on me."

They retired to rest, thinking they would not sleep at all during the night, but they were hardly in bed before their eyes were closed in sleep. In her dreams there appeared to Beauty a lady, who said to her:

"Your virtuous character pleases me, Beauty. In thus undertaking to give your life to save your father you have performed an act of goodness which shall not go unrewarded."

When she woke up Beauty related this dream to her father. He was somewhat consoled by it, but could not refrain from loudly giving vent to his grief when the time came to tear himself away from his beloved child.

As soon as he had gone Beauty sat down in the great hall and began to cry. But she had plenty of courage, and after imploring divine protection she determined to grieve no more during the short time she had yet to live.

She was convinced that the Beast would devour her that night, but made up her mind that in the interval she would walk about and have a look at this beautiful castle, the splendour of which she could not but admire.

Imagine her surprise when she came upon a door on which were the words "Beauty's Room"! She quickly opened this door, and was dazzled by the magnificence of the appointments within. "They are evidently anxious that I should not be dull," she murmured, as she caught sight of a large bookcase, a harpsichord, and several volumes of music. A moment later another thought crossed her mind. "If I had only a day to spend here," she reflected, "such provision would surely not have been made for me."

This notion gave her fresh courage. She opened the bookcase, and found a book in which was written, in letters of gold:

"Ask for anything you wish: you are mistress of all here."

"Alas!" she said with a sigh, "my only wish is to see my poor father, and to know what he is doing."

As she said this to herself she glanced at a large mirror. Imagine her astonishment when she perceived her home reflected in it, and saw her father just approaching. Sorrow was written on his face; but when her sisters came to meet him it was impossible not to detect, despite the grimaces with which they tried to simulate grief, the satisfaction they felt at the loss of their sister. In a moment the vision faded away, yet Beauty could not but think that the Beast was very kind, and that she had nothing much to fear from him.

At midday she found the table laid, and during her meal she enjoyed an excellent concert, though the performers were invisible. But in the evening, as she was about to sit down at the table, she heard the noise made by the Beast, and quaked in spite of herself.

"Beauty," said the monster to her, "may I watch you have your supper?"

"You are master here," said the trembling Beauty.

"Not so," replied the Beast; "it is you who are mistress; you have only to tell me to go, if my presence annoys you, and I will go immediately. Tell me, now, do you not consider me very ugly?"

"I do," said Beauty, "since I must speak the truth; but I think you are also very kind."

"It is as you say," said the monster; "and in addition to being ugly, I lack intelligence. As I am well aware, I am a mere beast."

"It is not the way with stupid people," answered Beauty, "to admit a lack of intelligence. Fools never realise it."

"Sup well, Beauty," said the monster, "and try to banish dullness from your home—for all about you is yours, and I should be sorry to think you were not happy."

"You are indeed kind," said Beauty. "With one thing, I must own, I am well pleased, and that is your kind heart. When I think of that you no longer seem to be ugly."

"Oh yes," answered the Beast, "I have a good heart, right enough, but I am a monster."

"There are many men," said Beauty, "who make worse monsters than you, and I prefer you, notwithstanding your looks, to those who under the semblance of men hide false, corrupt, and ungrateful hearts."

The Beast replied that if only he had a grain of wit he would compliment her in the grand style by way of thanks; but that being so stupid he could only say he was much obliged.

Beauty ate with a good appetite, for she now had scarcely any fear of the Beast. But she nearly died of fright when he put this question to her:

"Beauty, will you be my wife?"

For some time she did not answer, fearing lest she might anger the monster by her refusal. She summoned up courage at last to say, rather fearfully, "No, Beast!"

The poor monster gave forth so terrible a sigh that the noise of it went whistling through the whole palace. But to Beauty's speedy relief the Beast sadly took his leave and left the room, turning several times as he did so to look once more at her. Left alone, Beauty was moved by great compassion for this poor Beast. "What a pity he is so ugly," she said, "for he is so good."

Beauty passed three months in the palace quietly enough. Every evening the Beast paid her a visit, and entertained her at supper by a display of much good sense, if not with what the world calls wit. And every day Beauty was made aware of fresh kindnesses on the part of the monster. Through seeing him often she had become accustomed to his ugliness, and far from dreading the moment of his visit, she frequently looked at her watch to see if it was nine o'clock, the hour when the Beast always appeared.

One thing alone troubled Beauty; every evening, before retiring to bed, the monster asked her if she would be his wife, and seemed overwhelmed with grief when she refused. One day she said to him:

"You distress me, Beast. I wish I could marry you, but I cannot deceive you by allowing you to believe that that can ever be. I will always be your friend—be content with that."

"Needs must," said the Beast. "But let me make the position plain. I know I am very terrible, but I love you very much, and I shall be very happy if you will only remain here. Promise that you will never leave me."

Beauty blushed at these words. She had seen in her mirror that her father was stricken down by the sorrow of having lost her, and she wished very much to see him again. "I would willingly promise to remain with you always," she said to the Beast, "but I have so great a desire to see my father again that I shall die of grief if you refuse me this boon."

"I would rather die myself than cause you grief," said the monster. "I will send you back to your father. You shall stay with him, and your Beast shall die of sorrow at your departure."

"No, no," said Beauty, crying; "I like you too much to wish to cause your death. I promise you I will return in eight days. You have shown me that my sisters are married, and that my brothers have joined the army. My father is all alone; let me stay with him one week."

"You shall be with him tomorrow morning," said the Beast. "But remember your promise. All you have to do when you want to return is to put your ring on a table when you are going to bed. Good-bye, Beauty!"

As usual, the Beast sighed when he said these last words, and Beauty went to bed quite down-hearted at having grieved him.

When she awoke the next morning she found she was in her father's house. She rang a little bell which stood by the side of her bed, and it was answered by their servant, who gave a great cry at sight of her. The good man came running at the noise, and was overwhelmed with joy at the sight of his dear daughter. Their embraces lasted for more than a quarter of an hour. When their transports had subsided, it occurred to Beauty that she had no clothes to put on; but the servant told her that she had just discovered in the next room a chest full of dresses trimmed with gold and studded with diamonds. Beauty felt grateful to the Beast for this attention, and having selected the simplest of the gowns she bade the servant pack up the others, as she wished to send them as presents to her sisters. The words were hardly out of her mouth when the chest disappeared. Her father expressed the opinion that the Beast wished her to keep them all for herself, and in a trice dresses and chest were back again where they were before.

When Beauty had dressed she learned that her sisters, with their husbands, had arrived. Both were very unhappy. The eldest had wedded an exceedingly handsome man, but the latter was so taken up with his own looks that he studied them from morning to night, and despised his wife's beauty. The second had married a man with plenty of brains, but he only used them to pay insults to everybody—his wife first and foremost.

The sisters were greatly mortified when they saw Beauty dressed like a princess, and more beautiful than the dawn. Her caresses were ignored, and the jealousy which they could not stifle only grew worse when she told them how happy she was. Out into the garden went the envious pair, there to vent their spleen[1] to the full.

"Why should this chit be happier than we are?" each demanded of the other; "are we not much nicer than she is?"

"Sister," said the elder, "I have an idea. Let us try to persuade her to stay here longer than the eight days. Her stupid Beast will fly into a rage when he finds she has broken her word, and will very likely devour her."

"You are right, sister," said the other; "but we must make a great fuss of her if we are to make the plan successful."

With this plot decided upon they went upstairs again, and paid such attention to their little sister that Beauty wept for joy. When the eight days had passed the two sisters tore their hair, and showed such grief over her departure that she promised to remain another eight days.

Beauty reproached herself, nevertheless, with the grief she was causing to the poor Beast; moreover, she greatly missed not seeing him. On the tenth night of her stay in her father's house she dreamed that she was in the palace garden, where she saw the Beast lying on the grass nearly dead, and that he upbraided her for her ingratitude. Beauty woke up with a start, and burst into tears.

"I am indeed very wicked," she said, "to cause so much grief to a Beast who has

---

1   I.e., express their anger.

shown me nothing but kindness. Is it his fault that he is so ugly, and has so few wits? He is good, and that makes up for all the rest. Why did I not wish to marry him? I should have been a good deal happier with him than my sisters are with their husbands. It is neither good looks nor brains in a husband that make a woman happy; it is beauty of character, virtue, kindness. All these qualities the Beast has. I admit I have no love for him, but he has my esteem, friendship, and gratitude. At all events I must not make him miserable, or I shall reproach myself all my life."

With these words Beauty rose and placed her ring on the table.

Hardly had she returned to her bed than she was asleep, and when she woke the next morning she saw with joy that she was in the Beast's palace. She dressed in her very best on purpose to please him, and nearly died of impatience all day, waiting for nine o'clock in the evening. But the clock struck in vain: no Beast appeared. Beauty now thought she must have caused his death, and rushed about the palace with loud despairing cries. She looked everywhere, and at last, recalling her dream, dashed into the garden by the canal, where she had seen him in her sleep. There she found the poor Beast lying unconscious, and thought he must be dead. She threw herself on his body, all her horror of his looks forgotten, and feeling his heart still beat, fetched water from the canal and threw it on his face.

The Beast opened his eyes and said to Beauty:

"You forgot your promise. The grief I felt at having lost you made me resolve to die of hunger; but I die content since I have the pleasure of seeing you once more."

"Dear Beast, you shall not die," said Beauty; "you shall live and become my husband. Here and now I offer you my hand, and swear that I will marry none but you. Alas, I fancied I felt only friendship for you, but the sorrow I have experienced clearly proves to me that I cannot live without you."

Beauty had scarce uttered these words when the castle became ablaze with lights before her eyes: fireworks, music—all proclaimed a feast. But these splendours were lost on her: she turned to her dear Beast, still trembling for his danger.

Judge of her surprise now! At her feet she saw no longer the Beast, who had disappeared, but a prince, more beautiful than Love himself, who thanked her for having put an end to his enchantment. With good reason were her eyes riveted upon the prince, but she asked him nevertheless where the Beast had gone.

"You see him at your feet," answered the prince. "A wicked fairy condemned me to retain that form until some beautiful girl should consent to marry me, and she forbade me to betray any sign of intelligence. You alone in all the world could show yourself susceptible to the kindness of my character, and in offering you my crown I do but discharge the obligation that I owe you."

In agreeable surprise Beauty offered her hand to the handsome prince, and assisted him to rise. Together they repaired to the castle, and Beauty was overcome with joy to find, assembled in the hall, her father and her entire family. The lady who had appeared to her in her dream had had them transported to the castle.

"Beauty," said this lady (who was a celebrated fairy), "come and receive the reward of your noble choice. You preferred merit to either beauty or wit, and you certainly deserve to find these qualities combined in one person. It is your destiny to become a great queen, but I hope that the pomp of royalty will not destroy your virtues. As for you, ladies," she continued, turning to Beauty's two sisters, "I know your hearts and the malice they harbour. Your doom is to become statues, and under the stone that wraps you round to retain all your feelings. You will stand at the door of your sister's palace, and I can visit no greater punishment upon you than that you shall be witnesses of her happiness. Only when you recognise your faults can you return to your present shape, and I am very much afraid that you will be statues for ever. Pride, ill-temper, greed, and laziness can all be corrected, but nothing short of a miracle will turn a wicked and envious heart."

In a trice, with a tap of her hand, the fairy transported them all to the prince's realm, where his subjects were delighted to see him again. He married Beauty, and they lived together for a long time in happiness the more perfect because it was founded on virtue.

EAST OF THE SUN AND WEST OF THE MOON[1]

Asbjørnsen and Moe

ONCE UPON A TIME THERE was a poor husbandman who had many children and little to give them in the way either of food or clothing. They were all pretty, but the prettiest of all was the youngest daughter, who was so beautiful that there were no bounds to her beauty.

So once—it was late on a Thursday evening in autumn, and wild weather outside, terribly dark, and raining so heavily and blowing so hard that the walls of the cottage shook again—they were all sitting together by the fireside, each of them busy with something or other, when suddenly someone rapped three times against the window-pane. The man went out to see what could be the matter, and when he got out there stood a great big white bear.

---

1   First published in 1852. This text from *Popular Tales from the Norse*, trans. George Webbe Dasent (New York: D. Appleton, 1859).

"Good-evening to you," said the White Bear.

"Good-evening," said the man.

"Will you give me your youngest daughter?" said the White Bear; "if you will, you shall be as rich as you are now poor."

Truly the man would have had no objection to being rich, but he thought to himself: "I must first ask my daughter about this," so he went in and told them that there was a great white bear outside who had faithfully promised to make them all rich if he might but have the youngest daughter.

She said no, and would not hear of it; so the man went out again, and settled with the White Bear that he should come again next Thursday evening, and get her answer. Then the man persuaded her, and talked so much to her about the wealth that they would have, and what a good thing it would be for herself, that at last she made up her mind to go, and washed and mended all her rags, made herself as smart as she could, and held herself in readiness to set out. Little enough had she to take away with her.

Next Thursday evening the White Bear came to fetch her. She seated herself on his back with her bundle, and thus they departed. When they had gone a great part of the way, the White Bear said: "Are you afraid?"

"No, that I am not," said she.

"Keep tight hold of my fur, and then there is no danger," said he.

And thus she rode far, far away, until they came to a great mountain. Then the White Bear knocked on it, and a door opened, and they went into a castle where there were many brilliantly lighted rooms which shone with gold and silver, likewise a large hall in which there was a well-spread table, and it was so magnificent that it would be hard to make anyone understand how splendid it was. The White Bear gave her a silver bell, and told her that when she needed anything she had but to ring this bell, and what she wanted would appear. So after she had eaten, and night was drawing near, she grew sleepy after her journey, and thought she would like to go to bed. She rang the bell, and scarcely had she touched it before she found herself in a chamber where a bed stood ready made for her, which was as pretty as anyone could wish to sleep in. It had pillows of silk, and curtains of silk fringed with gold, and everything that was in the room was of gold or silver; but when she had lain down and put out the light, a man came and lay down beside her, and behold it was the White Bear, who cast off the form of a beast during the night. She never saw him, however, for he always came after she had put out her light, and went away before daylight appeared.

So all went well and happily for a time, but then she began to be very sad and sorrowful, for all day long she had to go about alone; and she did so wish to go home to her father and mother and brothers and sisters. Then the White Bear asked what it was that she wanted, and she told him that it was so dull there in the mountain, and that she had to go about all alone, and that in her parents' house at home there were all her brothers and sisters, and it was because she could not go to them that she was so sorrowful.

"There might be a cure for that," said the White Bear, "if you would but promise me never to talk with your mother alone, but only when the others are there too; for she will take hold of your hand," he said, "and will want to lead you into a room to talk with you alone; but that you must by no means do, or you will bring great misery on both of us."

So one Sunday the White Bear came and said that they could now set out to see her father and mother, and they journeyed thither, she sitting on his back, and they went a long, long way, and it took a long, long time; but at last they came to a large white farmhouse, and her brothers and sisters were running outside it, playing, and it was so pretty that it was a pleasure to look at it.

"Your parents dwell here now," said the White Bear; "but do not forget what I said to you, or you will do much harm both to yourself and me."

"No, indeed," said she, "I shall never forget"; and as soon as she was at home the White Bear turned round and went back again.

There were such rejoicings when she went in to her parents that it seemed as if they would never come to an end. Everyone thought that he could never be sufficiently grateful to her for all she had done for them all. Now they had everything that they wanted, and everything was as good as it could be. They all asked her how she was getting on where she was. All was well with her too, she said; and she had everything that she could want. What other answers she gave I cannot say, but I am pretty sure that they did not learn much from her. But in the afternoon, after they had dined at mid-day, all happened just as the White Bear had said. Her mother wanted to talk with her alone in her own chamber. But she remembered what the White Bear had said, and would on no account go. "What we have to say can be said at any time," she answered. But somehow or other her mother at last persuaded her, and she was forced to tell the whole story. So she told how every night a man came and lay down beside her when the lights were all put out, and how she never saw him, because he always went away before it grew light in the morning, and how she continually went about in sadness, thinking how happy she would be if she could but see him, and how all day long she had to go about alone, and it was so dull and solitary. "Oh!" cried the mother, in horror, "you are very likely sleeping with a troll! But I will teach you a way to see him. You shall have a bit of one of my candles, which you can take away with you hidden in your breast. Look at him with that when he is asleep, but take care not to let any tallow drop upon him."

So she took the candle, and hid it in her breast, and when evening drew near the White Bear came to fetch her away. When they had gone some distance on their way, the White Bear asked her if everything had not happened just as he had foretold, and she could not own but that it had. "Then, if you have done what your mother wished," said he, "you have brought great misery on both of us." "No," she said, "I have not done anything at all." So when she had reached home and had gone to bed, it was just the same as it had been before, and a man came and lay down beside her, and late at night, when she could hear that he was sleeping, she got up and kindled a light, lit her candle, let her light shine on him, and saw him, and he was the handsomest prince that eyes had ever beheld, and she loved him so much that it seemed to her that she must die if she did not kiss him that very moment. So she did kiss him; but while she was doing it she let three drops of hot tallow fall upon his shirt, and he awoke. "What have you done now?" said he; "you have brought misery on both of us. If you had but held out for the space of one year I should have been free. I have a stepmother who has bewitched me so that I am a white bear by day and a man by night; but now all is at an end between you and me, and I must leave you, and go to her. She lives in a castle which lies east of the sun and west of the moon, and there too is a princess with a nose which is three ells long, and she now is the one whom I must marry."

She wept and lamented, but all in vain, for go he must. Then she asked him if she could not go with him. But no, that could not be. "Can you tell me the way then, and I will seek you—that I may surely be allowed to do!"

"Yes, you may do that," said he; "but there is no way thither. It lies east of the sun and west of the moon, and never would you find your way there."

When she awoke in the morning both the Prince and the castle were gone, and she was lying on a small green patch in the midst of a dark, thick wood. By her side lay the self-same bundle of rags which she had brought with her from her own home. So when she had rubbed the sleep out of her eyes, and wept till she was weary, she set out on her way, and thus she walked for many and many a long day, until at last she came to a great mountain. Outside it an aged woman was sitting, playing with a golden apple. The girl asked her if she knew the way to the Prince who lived with his stepmother in the castle which lay east of the sun and west of the moon, and who was to marry a princess with a nose which was three ells long. "How do you happen to know about him?" enquired the old woman; "maybe you are she who ought to have had him." "Yes, indeed, I am," she said. "So it is you, then?" said the old woman; "I know nothing about him but that he dwells in a castle which is east of the sun and west of the moon. You will be a long time in getting to it, if ever you get to it at all; but you shall have the loan of my horse, and then you can ride on it to an old woman who is a neighbor of mine: perhaps she can tell you about him. When you have got there you must just strike the horse beneath the left ear and bid it go home again; but you may take the golden apple with you."

So the girl seated herself on the horse, and rode for a long, long way, and at last she came to the mountain, where an aged woman was sitting outside with a gold carding-comb.[1] The girl asked her if she knew the way to the castle which lay east of the sun and west of the moon; but she said what the first old woman had said: "I know nothing about it, but that it is east of the sun and west of the moon, and that you will be a long time in getting to it, if ever you get there at all; but you may have the loan of my horse, and then you can ride on it to an old woman who lives the nearest to me: perhaps she may know where the castle is, and when you have got to her you may just strike the horse beneath the left ear and bid it go home again." Then she gave her the gold carding-comb, for it might, perhaps, be of use to her, she said.

So the girl seated herself on the horse, and rode a wearisome long way onwards again, and after a very long time she came to a great mountain, where an aged woman was sitting, spinning at a golden spinning-wheel. Of this woman, too, she enquired if she knew the way to the Prince, and where to find the castle which lay east of the sun and west of the moon. But it was only the same thing once again. "Maybe it was you who should have had the Prince," said the old woman. "Yes, indeed, I should have been the one," said the girl. But this old crone knew the way no better than the others—it was east of the sun and west of the moon, she knew that, "and you will be a long time in getting to it, if ever you get to it at all," she said; "but you may have the loan of my horse, and I think you had better ride to the East Wind, and ask him: perhaps he may know where the castle is, and will blow you thither. But when you have got to him you must just strike the horse beneath the left ear, and he will come home again." And then she gave her the golden spinning-wheel, saying: "Perhaps you may find that you have a use for it."

The girl had to ride for a great many days, and for a long and wearisome time, before she got there; but at last she did arrive, and then she asked the East Wind if he could tell her the way to the Prince who dwelt east of the sun and west of the moon. "Well," said the East Wind, "I have heard tell of the Prince, and of his castle, but I do not know the way to it, for I have never blown so far; but, if you like, I will go with you to my brother the West Wind: he may know that, for he is much stronger than I am. You may sit on my back, and then I can carry you there." So she seated herself on his back, and they did go so swiftly! When they got there, the East Wind went in and said that the girl whom he had brought was the one who ought to have had the Prince up at the castle which lay east of the sun and west of the moon, and that now she was travelling about to find him again, so he had come there with her, and would like to hear if the West Wind knew whereabouts the castle was. "No," said the West Wind; "so far as that have I never blown: but if you like I will go with you to

---

1 A comb used to pull tangles out of wool.

the South Wind, for he is much stronger than either of us, and he has roamed far and wide, and perhaps he can tell you what you want to know. You may seat yourself on my back, and then I will carry you to him."

So she did this, and journeyed to the South Wind, neither was she very long on the way. When they had got there, the West Wind asked him if he could tell her the way to the castle that lay east of the sun and west of the moon, for she was the girl who ought to marry the Prince who lived there. "Oh, indeed!" said the South Wind, "is that she? Well," said he, "I have wandered about a great deal in my time, and in all kinds of places, but I have never blown so far as that. If you like, however, I will go with you to my brother the North Wind; he is the oldest and strongest of all of us, and if he does not know where it is, no one in the whole world will be able to tell you. You may sit upon my back, and then I will carry you there." So she seated herself on his back, and off he went from his house in great haste, and they were not long on the way. When they came near the North Wind's dwelling, he was so wild and frantic that they felt cold gusts a long while before they got there. "What do you want?" he roared out from afar, and they froze as they heard. Said the South Wind: "It is I, and this is she who should have had the Prince who lives in the castle which lies east of the sun and west of the moon. And now she wishes to ask you if you have ever been there, and can tell her the way, for she would gladly find him again."

"Yes," said the North Wind, "I know where it is. I once blew an aspen leaf there, but I was so tired that for many days afterwards I was not able to blow at all. However, if you really are anxious to go there, and are not afraid to go with me, I will take you on my back, and try if I can blow you there."

"Get there I must," said she; "and if there is any way of going I will; and I have no fear, no matter how fast you go."

"Very well then," said the North Wind; "but you must sleep here tonight, for if we are ever to get there we must have the day before us."

The North Wind woke her betimes next morning, and puffed himself up, and made himself so big and so strong that it was frightful to see him, and away they went, high up through the air, as if they would not stop until they had reached the very end of the world. Down below there was such a storm! It blew down woods and houses, and when they were above the sea the ships were wrecked by hundreds. And thus they tore on and on, and a long time went by, and then yet more time passed, and still they were above the sea, and the North Wind grew tired, and more tired, and at last so utterly weary that he was scarcely able to blow any longer, and he sank and sank, lower and lower, until at last he went so low that the crests of the waves dashed against the heels of the poor girl he was carrying. "Art thou afraid?" said the North Wind. "I have no fear," said she; and it was true. But they were not very, very far from land, and there was just enough strength left in the North Wind to enable him to throw her on to the shore, immediately under the windows of a castle which lay east of the sun and west of the moon; but then he was so weary and worn out that he was forced to rest for several days before he could go to his own home again.

Next morning she sat down beneath the walls of the castle to play with the golden apple, and the first person she saw was the maiden with the long nose, who was to have the Prince. "How much do you want for that gold apple of yours, girl?" said she, opening the window. "It can't be bought either for gold or money," answered the girl. "If it cannot be bought either for gold or money, what will buy it? You may say what you please," said the Princess.

"Well, if I may go to the Prince who is here, and be with him tonight, you shall have it," said the girl who had come with the North Wind. "You may do that," said the Princess, for she had made up her mind what she would do. So the Princess got the golden apple, but when the girl went up to the Prince's apartment that night he was asleep, for the Princess had so contrived it. The poor girl called to him, and shook him, and between whiles she wept; but she could not wake him. In the morning, as soon as day dawned, in came the Princess with the long nose, and drove her out again. In the daytime she sat down once more beneath the windows of the castle, and began to card with her golden carding-comb; and then all happened as it had happened before. The princess asked her what she wanted for it, and she replied that it was not for sale, either for gold or money, but that if she could get leave to go to the Prince, and be with him during the night, she should have it. But when she went up to the Prince's room he was again asleep, and, let her call him, or shake him, or weep as she would, he still slept on, and she could not put any life in him. When daylight came in the morning, the Princess with the long nose came too, and once more drove her away. When day had quite come, the girl seated herself under the castle windows, to spin with her golden spinning-wheel, and the Princess with the long nose wanted to have that also. So she opened the window, and asked what she would take for it. The girl said what she had said on each of the former occasions—that it was not for sale either for gold or for money, but if she could get leave to go to the Prince who lived there, and be with him during the night, she should have it.

"Yes," said the Princess, "I will gladly consent to that."

But in that place there were some Christian folk who had been carried off, and they had been sitting in the chamber which was next to that of the Prince, and had heard how a woman had been in there who had wept and called on him two nights running, and they told the Prince of this. So that evening, when the Princess came once more with her sleeping-drink, he pretended to drink, but threw it away behind him, for he suspected that it was a sleeping-drink. So, when the girl went into the Prince's room this time he was awake, and she had to tell him how she had come there. "You have come just in time," said the Prince, "for I should have been married tomorrow; but I will not have the long-nosed Princess, and you alone can save me. I will say that I want to see what my bride can do, and bid her wash the shirt which has the three drops of tallow on it. This she will consent to do, for she does not know that it is you who let them fall on it; but no one can wash them out but one born of Christian folk: it cannot be done by one of a pack of trolls; and then I will say that no one shall ever be my bride but the woman who can do this, and I know that you can." There was great joy and gladness between them all that night, but the next day, when the wedding was to take place, the Prince said, "I must see what my bride can do." "That you may do," said the stepmother.

"I have a fine shirt which I want to wear as my wedding shirt, but three drops of tallow have got upon it which I want to have washed off, and I have vowed to marry no one but the woman who is able to do it. If she cannot do that, she is not worth having."

Well, that was a very small matter, they thought, and agreed to do it. The Princess with the long nose began to wash as well as she could, but the more she washed and rubbed, the larger the spots grew. "Ah! you can't wash at all," said the old troll-hag, who was her mother. "Give it to me." But she too had not had the shirt very long in her hands before it looked worse still, and the more she washed it and rubbed it, the larger and blacker grew the spots.

So the other trolls had to come and wash, but, the more they did, the blacker and uglier grew the shirt, until at length it was as black as if it had been up the chimney. "Oh," cried the Prince, "not one of you is good for anything at all! There is a beggar-girl sitting outside the window, and I'll be bound that she can wash better than any of you! Come in, you girl there!" he cried. So she came in. "Can you wash this shirt clean?" he cried. "Oh! I don't know," she said; "but I will try." And no sooner had she taken the shirt and dipped it in the water than it was white as driven snow, and even whiter than that. "I will marry you," said the Prince.

Then the old troll-hag flew into such a rage that she burst, and the Princess with the long nose and all the little trolls must have burst too, for they have never been heard of since. The Prince and his bride set free all the Christian folk who were imprisoned there, and took away with them all the gold and silver that they could carry, and moved far away from the castle which lay east of the sun and west of the moon.

THE LITTLE MERMAID[1]

Hans Christian Andersen

FAR, FAR FROM LAND, WHERE the waters are as blue as the petals of the corn-flower and as clear as glass, there, where no anchor can reach the bottom, live the mer-people. So deep is this part of the sea that you would have to pile many church towers on top of each other before one of them emerged above the surface.

Now you must not think that at the bottom of the sea there is only white sand. No, here grow the strangest plants and trees; their stems and leaves are so subtle that the slightest current in the water makes them move, as if they were alive. Big and small fishes flit in and out among their branches, just as the birds do up on earth. At the very deepest place, the mer-king has built his castle. Its walls are made of coral and its long pointed windows of amber. The roof is oyster shells that are continually opening and closing. It looks very beautiful, for in each shell lies a pearl, so lustrous that it would be fit for a queen's crown.

The mer-king had been a widower for many years; his mother kept house for him. She was a very intelligent woman but a little too proud of her rank: she wore twelve oysters on her tail; the nobility were only allowed six. Otherwise, she was a most praiseworthy woman, and she took excellent care of her grandchildren, the little princesses. They were six lovely mermaids; the youngest was the most beautiful. Her complexion was as fine as the petal of a rose and her eyes as blue as the deepest lake but, just like everyone else down there, she had no feet; her body ended in a fishtail.

The mermaids were allowed to play all day in the great hall of the castle, where flowers grew on the walls. The big amber windows were kept open and the fishes swam in and out, just as the swallows up on earth fly in through our windows if they are open. But unlike the birds of the air, the fishes were not frightened, they swam right up to the little princesses and ate out of their hands and let themselves be petted.

Around the castle was a great park where there grew fiery-red and deep-blue trees. Their fruits shone as though they were the purest gold, their flowers were like flames, and their branches and leaves were ever in motion. The earth was the finest sand, not white but blue, the color of burning sulphur. There was a blue tinge to everything, down on the bottom of the sea. You could almost believe that you were suspended in mid-air and had the blue sky both above and below you. When the sea was calm, the sun appeared like a crimson flower, from which all light flowed.

Each little princess had her own garden, where she could plant the flowers she liked. One of them had shaped her flower bed so it resembled a whale; and another,

---

1   First published in 1843. This text from *Hans Christian Andersen: His Classic Fairy Tales*, trans. Erik Haugaard (New York: Doubleday, 1974).

as a mermaid. The youngest had planted red flowers in hers; she wanted it to look like the sun; it was round and the crimson flowers did glow as though they were so many little suns. She was a strange little child; quiet and thoughtful. Her sisters' gardens were filled with all sorts of things that they had collected from shipwrecks, but she had only a marble statue of a boy in hers. It had been cut out of stone that was almost transparently clear and had sunk to the bottom of the sea when the ship that had carried it was lost. Close to the statue she had planted a pink tree; it looked like a weeping willow. The tree was taller than the sculpture. Its long soft branches bent towards the sand; it looked as if the top of the tree and its roots wanted to kiss each other.

The princesses liked nothing better than to listen to their old grandmother tell about the world above. She had to recount countless times all she knew about ships, towns, human beings, and the animals that lived up on land. The youngest of the mermaids thought it particularly wonderful that the flowers up there had fragrance, for that they did not have on the bottom of the sea. She also liked to hear about the green forest, where the fishes that swam among the branches could sing most beautifully. Grandmother called the birds "fishes"; otherwise, her little grandchildren would not have understood her, since they had never seen a bird.

"But when you are fifteen, then you will be allowed to swim to the surface," she promised. "Then you can climb up on a rock and sit and watch the big ships sail by. If you dare, you can swim close enough to the shore to see the towns and the forest."

The following year, the oldest of the princesses would be fifteen. From one sister to the next, there was a difference in age of about a year, which meant that the youngest would have to wait more than five whole years before she would be allowed to swim up from the bottom of the sea and take a look at us. But each promised the others that she would return after her first day above, and tell about the things she had seen and describe what she thought was loveliest of all. For the old grandmother could not satisfy their curiosity.

None of the sisters longed so much to see the world above as the youngest, the one who had to wait the longest before she could leave her home. Many a night this quiet, thoughtful little mermaid would stand by the open window, looking up through the dark blue waters where the fishes swam. She could see the moon and the stars; they looked paler but larger down here under the sea. Sometimes a great shadow passed by like a cloud and then she knew that it was either a whale or a ship, with its crew and passengers, that was sailing high above her. None on board could have imagined that a little beautiful mermaid stood in the depths below them and stretched her little white hands up towards the keel of their ship.

The oldest of the sisters had her fifteenth birthday and swam up to the surface of the sea. When she returned she had hundreds of things to tell. But of everything that had happened to her, the loveliest experience by far, she claimed, had been to lie on a sandbank, when the sea was calm and the moon was out, and look at a great city. The lights from the windows and streets had shone like hundreds of stars; and she had been able to hear the rumbling of the carriages and the voices of human beings and, best of all, the sound of music. She had seen all the church towers and steeples and heard their bells ring. And just because she would never be able to enter the city, she longed to do that more than anything else.

How carefully her youngest sister listened to every word and remembered everything that she had been told. When, late in the evening, the little mermaid would stand dreaming by the window and look up through the blue water, then she imagined that she could see the city and hear the bells of the churches ringing.

The next year the second of the sisters was allowed to swim away from home. Her little head had emerged above the water just at the moment when the sun was setting. This sight had been so beautiful that she could hardly describe it. The whole heaven had been covered in gold and the clouds that had sailed above her had been purple and crimson. A flight of wild swans, like a white veil just above the water, had flown by. She had swum toward the sun, but it had set, taking the colors of the clouds, sea, and sky with it.

The third of the sisters, who came of age the following year, was the most daring among them. She had swum way up a broad river! There she had seen green hills covered with vineyards, castles, and farms that peeped out through the great forests. She had heard the birds sing and the sun had been so hot that she had had to swim under the water, some of the time, just to cool off. In a little bay, she had come upon some naked children who were playing and splashing in the water. She had wanted to join them, but when they saw her they got frightened and ran away. A little black animal had come: it was a dog. But she had never seen one before. It had barked so loudly and fiercely that she became terrified and swam right back to the sea. What she never would forget as long as she lived were the beautiful forest, the green hills, and the sweet little children who had been able to swim even though they had no fishtails as she had.

The fourth of the sisters was timid. She stayed far away from shore, out in the middle of the ocean. But that was the most beautiful place of all, she asserted. You could see ever so far and the sky above was like a clear glass bell. The ships she had seen had been so far away that they had looked no bigger than gulls. But the little dolphins had turned somersaults for her and the great whales had sprayed water high up into the air, so that it looked as though there were more than a hundred fountains.

The fifth sister's birthday was in the winter and, therefore, she saw something none of her sisters had seen. The ocean had been green, and huge icebergs had been floating on it. Each of them had been as lovely as a pearl and yet larger than the church towers that human beings built. They had the most fantastic shapes and their surface glittered like diamonds. She had climbed up on the largest one of them all; the wind had played with her long hair, and all the ships had fearfully kept away. Toward evening a storm had begun to blow; dark clouds had gathered and bolts of lightning had flashed while the thunder rolled. The waves had lifted the iceberg high up on their shoulders, and the lightning had colored the ice red. The ships had taken down their sails; and on board, fear and terror had reigned. But the mermaid had just sat on her iceberg and watched the bolts of lightning zigzag across the sky.

The first time that any of the sisters had been allowed to swim to the surface, each had been delighted with her freedom and all she had seen. But now that they were grownups and could swim anywhere they wished, they lost interest in wandering far away; after a month or two the world above lost its attraction. When they were away, they longed for their father's castle, declaring it the most beautiful place of all and the only spot where one really felt at home.

Still, many evenings the five sisters would take each other's hands and rise up through the waters. They had voices far lovelier than any human being. When a storm began to rage and a ship was in danger of being wrecked, then the five sisters would swim in front of it and sing about how beautiful it was down at the bottom of the sea. They begged the sailors not to be frightened but to come down to them. The men could not understand the mermaids' songs; they thought it was the wind that was singing. Besides, they would never see the beauty of the world below them, for if a ship sinks the seamen drown, and when they arrive at the mer-king's castle they are dead.

On such evenings, while her sisters swam, hand in hand, up through the water, the youngest princess had to stay below. She would look sadly up after them and feel like crying; but mermaids can't weep and that makes their suffering even deeper and greater.

"Oh, if only I were fifteen," she would sigh. "I know that I shall love the world above, and the human beings who live up there!"

At last she, too, was fifteen!

"Now you are off our hands," said the old dowager queen.[1] "Let me dress you, just as I dressed your sisters." She put a wreath of white lilies around her hair; each of the petals of every flower was half a pearl. She let eight oysters clip themselves onto the little mermaid's tail, so that everyone could see that she was a princess.

"It hurts," said the little mermaid.

---

1   I.e., queen mother.

"One has to suffer for position," said her old grandmother. The little mermaid would gladly have exchanged her heavy pearl wreath for one of the red flowers from her garden (she thought they suited her much better) but she didn't dare.

"Farewell," she said and rose, light as a bubble, up through the water.

The sun had just set when she lifted her head above the surface. The clouds still had the color of roses and in the horizon was a fine line of gold; in the pale pink sky the first star of evening sparkled, clearly and beautifully. The air was warm and the sea was calm. She saw a three-masted ship; only one of its sails was unfurled, and it hung motionless in the still air. Up on the yards the sailors sat, looking down upon the deck from which music could be heard. As the evening grew darker, hundreds of little colored lamps were hung from the rigging; they looked like the flags of all the nations of the world. The little mermaid swam close to a porthole and the swells lifted her gently so that she could look in through it. The great cabin was filled with gaily dressed people; the handsomest among them was a young prince with large, dark eyes. He looked no older than sixteen, and that was, in truth, his age; that very day was his birthday. All the festivities were for him. The sailors danced on the deck, and as the young prince came up to watch them, a hundred rockets flew into the sky.

The night became as bright as day and the little mermaid got so frightened that she ducked down under the water. But she soon stuck her head up again; and then it looked as if all the stars of the heavens were falling down on top of her. She had never seen fireworks before. Pinwheels turned; rockets shot into the air, and their lights reflected in the dark mirror of the sea. The deck of the ship was so illuminated that every rope could clearly be seen. Oh, how handsome the young prince was! He laughed and smiled and shook hands with everyone, while music was played in the still night.

It grew late, but the little mermaid could not turn her eyes away from the ship and the handsome prince. The colored lamps were put out. No more rockets shot into the air and no more cannons were fired. From the depth of the ocean came a rumbling noise. The little mermaid let the waves be her rocking horse, and they lifted her so that she could look in through the porthole. The ship started to sail faster and faster, as one sail after another was unfurled. Now the waves grew in size and black clouds could be seen on the horizon and far away lightning flashed.

A storm was brewing. The sailors took down the sails. The great ship tossed and rolled in the huge waves that rose as though they were mountains that wanted to bury the ship and break its proud mast. But the ship, like a swan, rode on top of the waves and let them lift her high into the sky. The little mermaid thought it was very amusing to watch the ship sailing so fast, but the sailors didn't. The ship creaked and groaned; the great planks seemed to bulge as the waves hit them. Suddenly the mast snapped as if it were a reed. It tumbled into the water. The ship heeled over, and the sea broke over it.

Only now did the little mermaid understand that the ship was in danger. She had to be careful herself and keep away from the spars and broken pieces of timber that were being flung by the waves. For a moment it grew so dark that she could see nothing, then a bolt of lightning illuminated the sinking ship. She looked for the young prince among the terrified men on board who were trying to save themselves, but not until that very moment, when the ship finally sank, did she see him.

At first, she thought joyfully, "Now he will come down to me!" But then she remembered that man could not live in the sea and the young prince would be dead when he came to her father's castle.

"He must not die," she thought, and dived in among the wreckage, forgetting the danger that she herself was in, for any one of the great beams that were floating in the turbulent sea could have crushed her.

She found him! He was too tired to swim any farther; he had no more strength in his arms and legs to fight the storm-whipped waves. He closed his eyes, waiting for death, and he would have drowned, had the little mermaid not saved him. She held his head above water and let the waves carry them where they would.

By morning the storm was over. Of the wrecked ship not a splinter was to be found. The sun rose, glowing red, and its rays gave color to the young prince's cheeks but his eyes remained closed. The little mermaid kissed his forehead and stroked his wet hair. She thought that he looked like the statue in her garden. She kissed him again and wished passionately that he would live.

In the far distance she saw land; the mountains rose blue in the morning air. The snow on their peaks was as glittering white as swan's feathers. At the shore there was a green forest, and in its midst lay a cloister or a church, the little mermaid did not know which. Lemon and orange trees grew in the garden, and by the entrance gate stood a tall palm tree. There was a little bay nearby, where the water was calm and deep. The mermaid swam with her prince toward the beach. She laid him in the fine white sand, taking care to place his head in the warm sunshine far from the water.

In the big white buildings bells were ringing and a group of young girls was coming out to walk in the garden. The little mermaid swam out to some rocks and hid behind them. She covered her head with seaweed so that she could not be seen and then peeped toward land, to see who would find the poor prince.

Soon one of the young girls discovered him. At first she seemed frightened, and she called the others. A lot of people came. The prince opened his eyes and smiled up at those who stood around him—not out at the sea, where the little mermaid was hiding. But then he could not possibly have known that she was there and that it was she who had saved him. The little mermaid felt so terribly sad; the prince was carried into the big white building, and the little mermaid dived sorrowfully down into the sea and swam home to her father's castle.

She had always been quiet and thoughtful. Now she grew even more silent. Her sisters asked her what she had seen on her first visit up above, but she did not answer.

Many mornings and evenings she would swim back to the place where she had last seen the prince. She watched the fruits in the orchard ripen and be picked, and saw the snow on the high mountains melt, but she never saw the prince. She would return from each of these visits a little sadder. She would seek comfort by embracing the statue in her garden, which looked like the prince. She no longer tended her flowers, and they grew into a wilderness, covering the paths and weaving their long stalks and leaves into the branches of the trees, so that it became quite dark down in her garden.

At last she could bear her sorrow no longer and told one of her sisters about it; and almost at once the others knew as well. But no one else was told; that is, except for a couple of other mermaids, but they didn't tell it to anyone except their nearest and dearest friends. It was one of these friends who knew who the prince was. She, too, had seen the birthday party on the ship, and she could tell where he came from and where his kingdom was.

"Come, little sister," the other princesses called, and with their arms around each other's shoulders they swam.

All in a row they rose to the surface when they came to the shore where the prince's castle stood. It was built of glazed yellow stones and had many flights of marble stairs leading up to it. The steps of one of them went all the way down to the sea. Golden domes rose above the roofs, and pillars bore an arcade that went all the way around the palace. Between the pillars stood marble statues; they looked almost as if they were alive. Through the clear glass of the tall windows, one could look into the most beautiful chambers and halls, where silken curtains and tapestries hung on the walls; and there were large paintings that were a real pleasure to look at. In the largest hall was a fountain. The water shot high up toward the glass cupola in the roof, through which the sunbeams fell on the water and the beautiful flowers that grew in the basin of the fountain.

Now that she knew where the prince lived, the little mermaid spent many evenings and nights looking at the splendid palace. She swam nearer to the land than any of her sisters had ever dared. There was a marble balcony that cast its shadow across a narrow canal, and beneath it she hid and watched the young prince, who thought that he was all alone in the moonlight.

Many an evening she saw the prince sail with his musicians in his beautiful boat. She peeped from behind the tall reeds; and if someone noticed her silver-white veil, they probably thought that they had only seen a swan stretching its wings.

Many a night she heard the fishermen talking to each other and telling about how kind and good the prince was; and she was so glad that she had saved his life when she had found him, half dead, drifting on the waves. She remembered how his head had rested on her chest and with what passion she had kissed him. But he knew nothing about his rescue; he could not even dream about her.

More and more she grew to love human beings and wished that she could leave the sea and live among them. It seemed to her that their world was far larger than hers; on ships, they could sail across the oceans and they could climb the mountains high up above the clouds. Their countries seemed ever so large, covered with fields and forests; she knew that they stretched much farther than she could see. There was so much that she wanted to know; there were many questions that her sisters could not answer. Therefore she asked her old grandmother, since she knew much about the "higher world," as she called the lands above the sea.

"If men are not so unlucky as to drown," asked the little mermaid, "then do they live forever? Don't they die as we do, down here in the sea?"

"Yes, they do," answered her grandmother. "Men must also die and their life span is shorter than ours. We can live until we are three hundred years old; but when we die, we become the foam on the ocean. We cannot even bury our loved ones. We do not have immortal souls. When we die, we shall never rise again. We are like the green reeds: once they are cut they will never be green again. But men have souls that live eternally, even after their bodies have become dust. They rise high up into the clear sky where the stars are. As we rise up through the water to look at the world of man, they rise up to the unknown, the beautiful world, that we shall never see."

"Why do I not have an immortal soul!" sighed the little mermaid unhappily. "I would give all my three hundred years of life for only one day as a human being if, afterward, I should be allowed to live in the heavenly world."

"You shouldn't think about things like that," said her old grandmother. "We live far happier down here than man does up there."

"I am going to die, become foam on the ocean, and never again hear the music of the waves or see the flowers and the burning red sun. Can't I do anything to win an immortal soul?"

"No," said the old merwoman. "Only if a man should fall so much in love with you that you were dearer to him than his mother and father; and he cared so much for you that all his thoughts were of his love for you; and he let a priest take his right hand and put it in yours, while he promised to be eternally true to you, then his soul would flow into your body and you would be able to partake of human happiness. He can give you a soul and yet keep his own. But it will never happen. For that which we consider beautiful down here in the ocean, your fishtail, they find ugly up above, on earth. They have no sense; up there, you have to have two clumsy props, which they call legs, in order to be called beautiful."

The little mermaid sighed and glanced sadly down at her fishtail.

"Let us be happy," said her old grandmother. "We can swim and jump through the waves for three hundred years, that is time enough. Tonight we are going to give a court ball in the castle."

Such a splendor did not exist up above on the earth. The walls and the ceilings of the great hall were made of clear glass; four hundred giant green and pink oyster shells stood in rows along the walls. Blue flames rose from them and not only lighted the hall but also illuminated the sea outside. Numberless fishes—both big and small—swam close to the glass walls; some of them had purple scales, others seemed to be of silver and gold. Through the great hall flowed a swiftly moving current, and on that the mermen and mermaids danced, while they sang their own beautiful songs. Such lovely voices are never heard up on earth; and the little mermaid sang most beautifully of them all. The others clapped their hands when she had finished, and for a moment she felt happy, knowing that she had the most beautiful voice both on earth and in the sea.

But soon she started thinking again of the world above. She could not forget the handsome prince, and mourned because she did not have an immortal soul like his. She sneaked out of her father's palace, away from the ball, from the gaiety, down into her little garden.

From afar the sound of music, of horns being played, came down to her through the water; and she thought: "Now he is sailing up there, the prince whom I love more than I love my father and mother: he who is ever in my thoughts and in whose hands I would gladly place all my hope of happiness. I would dare to do anything to win him and an immortal soul! While my sisters are dancing in the palace, I will go to the sea witch, though I have always feared her, and ask her to help me."

The little mermaid swam toward the turbulent maelstrom; beyond it the sea witch lived. In this part of the great ocean the little mermaid had never been before; here no flowers or seaweeds grew, only the gray naked sea bed stretched toward the center of the maelstrom, that great whirlpool where the water, as if it had been set in motion by gigantic mill wheels, twisted and turned: grinding, tearing, and sucking anything that came within its reach down into its depths. Through this turbulence the little mermaid had to swim, for beyond it lay the bubbling mud flats that the sea witch called her bog and that had to be crossed to come to the place where she lived.

The sea witch's house was in the midst of the strangest forest. The bushes and trees were gigantic polyps that were half plant and half animal. They looked like snakes with hundreds of heads, but they grew out of the ground. Their branches were long slimy arms, and they had fingers as supple as worms; every limb was in constant motion from the root to the utmost point. Everything they could reach they grasped, and never let go of it again. With dread the little mermaid stood at the entrance to the forest; her heart was beating with fear, she almost turned back. But then she remembered her prince and the soul she wanted to gain and her courage returned.

She braided her long hair and bound it around her head, so the polyps could not catch her by it. She held her arms folded tightly across her breast and then she flew through the water as fast as the swiftest fish. The ugly polyps stretched out their arms and their fingers tried to grasp her. She noticed that every one of them was holding, as tightly as iron bands, onto something it had caught. Drowned human beings peeped out as white skeletons among the polyps' arms. There were sea chests, rudders of ships, skeletons of land animals; and then she saw a poor little mermaid who had been caught and strangled; and this sight was to her the most horrible.

At last she came to a great, slimy, open place in the middle of the forest. Big fat eels played in the mud, showing their ugly yellow stomachs. Here the witch had built her house out of the bones of drowned sailors, and there she sat letting a big ugly toad eat out of her mouth, as human beings sometimes let a canary eat sugar candy out of theirs. The ugly eels she called her little chickens, and held them close to her spongy chest.

"I know what you want," she cackled. "And it is stupid of you. But you shall have your wish, for it will bring you misery, little princess. You want to get rid of your fishtail, and instead have two stumps to walk on as human beings have, so that the prince will fall in love with you; and you will gain both him and an immortal soul." The witch laughed so loudly and evilly that the toad and eels she had had on her lap jumped down into the mud.

"You came at the right time," she said. "Tomorrow I could not have helped you; you would have had to wait a year. I will mix you a potion. Drink it tomorrow morning before the sun rises, while you are sitting on the beach. Your tail will divide and shrink, until it becomes what human beings call 'pretty legs.' It will hurt; it will feel as if a sword were going through your body. All who see you will say that you are the most beautiful human child they have ever seen. You will walk more gracefully than any dancer; but every time your foot touches the ground it will feel as though you were walking on knives so sharp that your blood must flow. If you are willing to suffer all this, then I can help you."

"I will," whispered the little mermaid, and thought of her prince and how she would win an immortal soul.

"But remember," screeched the witch, "that once you have a human body you can never become a mermaid again. Never again shall you swim through the waters with your sisters to your father's castle. If you cannot make the prince fall so much in love with you that he forgets both his father and mother, because his every thought concerns only you, and he orders the priest to take his right hand and place it in yours, so that you become man and wife; then, the first morning after he has married another, your heart will break and you will become foam on the ocean."

"I still want to try," said the little mermaid, and her face was as white as a corpse.

"But you will have to pay me, too," grinned the witch. "And I want no small payment. You have the most beautiful voice of all those who live in the ocean. I suppose you have thought of using that to charm your prince; but that voice you will have to give to me. I want the most precious thing you have to pay for my potion. It contains my own blood, so that it can be as sharp as a double-edged sword."

"But if you take my voice," said the little mermaid, "what will I have left?"

"Your beautiful body," said the witch. "Your graceful walk and your lovely eyes. Speak with them and you will be able to capture a human heart. Have you lost your courage? Stick out your little tongue, and let me cut it off in payment, and you shall have the potion."

"Let it happen," whispered the little mermaid.

The witch took out a caldron in which to make the magic potion. "Cleanliness is a virtue," she said. And before she put the pot over the fire, she scrubbed it with eels, which she had made into a whisk.

She cut her chest and let her blood drip into the vessel. The steam that rose became strange figures that were terrifying to see. Every minute, the witch put something different into the caldron. When the brew reached a rolling boil, it sounded as though a crocodile were crying. At last the potion was finished. It looked as clear and pure as water.

"Here it is," said the witch, and cut out the little mermaid's tongue. Now she was mute, she could neither speak nor sing.

"If any of the polyps should try to grab you, on your way back through my forest," said the witch, "you need only spill one drop of the potion on it and its arms and fingers will splinter into a thousand pieces."

But the little mermaid didn't have to do that. Fearfully, the polyps drew away when they saw what she was carrying in her hands; the potion sparkled as though it were a star. Safely, she returned through the forest, the bog, and the maelstrom.

She could see her father's palace. The lights were extinguished in the great hall. Everyone was asleep; and yet she did not dare to seek out her sisters; now that she was mute and was going away from them forever. She felt as if her heart would break with sorrow. She sneaked down into the garden and picked a flower from each of her sisters' gardens; then she threw a thousand finger kisses toward the palace and swam upward through the deep blue sea.

The sun had not yet risen when she reached the prince's castle and sat down on the lowest step of the great marble stairs. The moon was still shining clearly. The little mermaid drank the potion and it felt as if a sword were piercing her little body. She fainted and lay as though she were dead.

When the sun's rays touched the sea she woke and felt a burning pain; but the young prince stood in front of her and looked at her with his coal-black eyes. She looked downward and saw then that she no longer had a fishtail but the most beautiful, little, slender legs that any girl could wish for. She was naked; and therefore she took her long hair and covered herself with it.

The prince asked her who she was and how she had got there. She looked gently and yet ever so sadly up at him with her deep blue eyes, for she could not speak. He took her by the hand and led her up to his castle. And just as the witch had warned, every step felt as though she were walking on sharp knives. But she suffered it gladly. Gracefully as a bubble rising in the water, she walked beside the prince; and everyone who saw her wondered how she could walk so lightly.

In the castle, she was clad in royal clothes of silk and muslin. She was the most beautiful of all, but she was mute and could neither sing nor speak. Beautiful slave girls, clad in silken clothes embroidered with gold, sang for the prince and his royal parents. One sang more beautifully than the rest, and the prince clapped his hands and smiled to her; then the little mermaid was filled with sorrow, for she knew that she had once sung far more beautifully. And she thought, "Oh, if he only knew that to be with him I have given away my voice for all eternity."

Now the slave girls danced, gracefully they moved to the beautiful music. Suddenly the little mermaid lifted her hands and rose on the tips of her toes. She floated more than danced across the floor. No one had ever seen anyone dance as she did. Her every movement revealed her loveliness and her eyes spoke far more eloquently than the slave's song.

Everyone was delighted, especially the prince. He called her his little foundling. She danced again and again, even though each time her little foot touched the floor she felt as if she had stepped on a knife. The prince declared that she should never leave him, and she was given permission to sleep in front of his door on a velvet pillow.

The prince had men's clothes made for her, so that she could accompany him when he went horseback riding. Through the sweet-smelling forest they rode, where green branches touched their shoulders and little birds sang among the leaves. Together they climbed the high mountains and her feet bled so much that others noticed it; but she smiled and followed her prince up ever higher until they could see the clouds sail below them, like flocks of birds migrating to foreign lands.

At night in the castle, while the others slept, she would walk down the broad marble stairs to the sea and cool her poor burning feet in the cold water. Then she would think of her sisters, down in the deep sea.

One night they came; arm in arm they rose above the surface of the water, sing-ing ever so sadly. She waved to them, and they recognized her, and they told her how much sorrow she had brought them. After that they visited her every night; and once she saw, far out to sea, her old grandmother. It had been years since she had stuck her head up into the air; and there, too, was her father the mer-king with his crown on his head. They stretched their hands toward her but did not dare come as near to the land as her sisters.

Day by day the prince grew fonder and fonder of her; but he loved her as he would have loved a good child, and had no thought of making her his queen. And she had to become his wife or she would never have an immortal soul, but on the morning after his marriage would become foam on the great ocean.

"Don't you love me more than you do all others?" was the message in the little mermaid's eyes when the prince kissed her lovely forehead.

"Yes, you are the dearest to me," said the prince, "for you have the kindest heart of them all. You are devoted to me and you look like a young girl I once saw, and will probably never see again. I was in a shipwreck. The waves carried me ashore, where a holy temple lay. Many young girls were in service there; one of them, the youngest of them all, found me on the beach and saved my life. I saw her only twice, but she is the only one I can love in this world; and you look like her. You almost make her picture disappear from my soul. She belongs to the holy temple and, therefore, good fortune has sent you to me instead, and we shall never part."

"Oh, he does not know that it was I who saved his life," thought the little mer-maid. "I carried him across the sea to the forest where the temple stood. I hid behind the rocks and watched over him until he was found. I saw that beautiful girl whom he loves more than me!" And the little mermaid sighed deeply, for cry she couldn't. "He has said that the girl belongs to the holy temple and will never come out into the world, and they will never meet again. But I am with him and see him every day. I will take care of him, love him, and devote my life to him."

Everyone said that the young prince was to be married; he was to have the neigh-boring king's daughter, a beautiful princess. A magnificent ship was built and made ready. It was announced that the prince was traveling to see the neighboring king-dom, but that no one believed. "It is not the country but the princess he is to in-spect," they all agreed.

The little mermaid shook her head and smiled; she knew what the prince thought, and they didn't.

"I must go," he had told her, "I must look at the beautiful princess, my parents demand it. But they won't force me to carry her home as my bride. I can't love her. She does not look like the girl from the temple as you do. If I ever marry, I shall most likely choose you, my little foundling with the eloquent eyes." And he kissed her on her red lips and played with her long hair, and let his head rest so near her heart that it dreamed of human happiness and an immortal soul.

"Are you afraid of the ocean, my little silent child?" asked the prince as they stood on the deck of the splendid ship that was to sail them to the neighboring kingdom. He told the little mermaid how the sea can be still or stormy, and about the fishes that live in it, and what the divers had seen underneath the water. She smiled as he talked, for who knew better than she about the world on the bottom of the ocean?

In the moonlit night, when everyone slept but the sailor at the rudder and the lookout in the bow, she sat on the bulwark and looked down into the clear water. She thought she saw her father's palace; and on the top of its tower her old grandmother was standing with her silver crown on her head, looking up through the currents of the sea, toward the keel of the ship. Her sisters came; they looked at her so sorrowfully and wrung their white hands in despair; she waved to them and smiled. She wanted them to know that she was happy, but just at that moment the little cabin boy came and her sisters dived down under the water; he saw nothing but some white foam on the ocean.

The next morning the ship sailed into the harbor of the great town that belonged to the neighboring king. All the church bells were ringing, and from the tall towers trumpets blew, while the soldiers stood at attention, with banners flying and bayonets on their rifles.

Every day another banquet was held, and balls and parties followed one after the other. But the princess attended none of them, for she did not live in the palace; she was being educated in the holy temple, where she was to learn all the royal virtues. But at last she came.

The little mermaid wanted ever so much to see her; and when she finally did, she had to admit that a more beautiful girl she had never seen before. Her skin was so delicate and fine, and beneath her long dark lashes smiled a pair of faithful, dark blue eyes.

"It is you!" exclaimed the prince. "You are the one who saved me, when I lay half dead on the beach!" And he embraced his blushing bride.

"Oh, now I am too happy," he said to the little mermaid. "That which I never dared hope has now happened! You will share my joy, for I know that you love me more than any of the others do."

The little mermaid kissed his hand; she felt as if her heart were breaking. His wedding morning would bring her death and she would be changed into foam of the ocean.

All the churchbells rang and heralds rode through the streets and announced the wedding to the people. On all the altars costly silver lamps burned with fragrant oils. The priests swung censers with burning incense in them, while the prince and the princess gave each other their hands, and the bishop blessed them. The little mermaid, dressed in silk and gold, held the train of the bride's dress, but her ears did not hear the music, nor did her eyes see the holy ceremony, for this night would bring her death, and she was thinking of all she had lost in this world.

The bride and bridegroom embarked upon the prince's ship; cannons saluted and banners flew. On the main deck, a tent of gold and scarlet cloth had been raised; there on the softest of pillows the bridal couple would sleep.

The sails were unfurled, and they swelled in the wind and the ship glided across the transparent sea.

When it darkened and evening came, colored lamps were lit and the sailors danced on the deck. The little mermaid could not help remembering the first time she had emerged above the waves, when she had seen the almost identical sight. She whirled in the dance, glided as the swallow does in the air when it is pursued. Everyone cheered and applauded her. Never had she danced so beautifully; the sharp knives cut her feet, but she did not feel it, for the pain in her heart was far greater. She knew that this was the last evening that she would see him for whose sake she had given away her lovely voice and left her home and her family; and he would never know of her sacrifice. It was the last night that she would breathe the same air as he, or look out over the deep sea and up into the star-blue heaven. A dreamless, eternal night awaited her, for she had no soul and had not been able to win one.

Until midnight all was gaiety aboard the ship, and the mermaid danced and laughed with the thought of death in her heart. Then the prince kissed his bride and she fondled his long black hair and, arm in arm, they walked into their splendorous tent, to sleep.

The ship grew quiet. Only the sailor at the helm and the little mermaid were awake. She stood with her white arms resting on the railing and looked toward the east. She searched the horizon for the pink of dawn; she knew that the first sunbeams would kill her.

Out of the sea rose her sisters, but the wind could no longer play with their long beautiful hair, for their heads had been shorn.

"We have given our hair to the sea witch, so that she would help you and you would not have to die this night. Here is a knife that the witch has given us. Look how sharp it is! Before the sun rises, you must plunge it into the heart of the prince; when his warm blood sprays on your feet, they will turn into a fishtail and you will be a mermaid again. You will be able to live your three hundred years down in the sea with us, before you die and become foam on the ocean. Hurry! He or you must die before the sun rises. Our grandmother mourns; she, too, has no hair; hers has fallen out from grief. Kill the prince and come back to us! Hurry! See, there is a pink haze on the horizon. Soon the sun will rise and you will die."

The little mermaid heard the sound of her sisters' deep and strange sighing before they disappeared beneath the waves.

She pulled aside the crimson cloth of the tent and saw the beautiful bride sleeping peacefully, with her head resting on the prince's chest. The little mermaid bent down and kissed his handsome forehead. She turned and looked at the sky; more and more, it was turning red. She glanced at the sharp knife; and once more she looked down at the prince. He moved a little in his sleep and whispered the name of his bride. Only she was in his thoughts, in his dreams! The little mermaid's hand trembled as it squeezed the handle of the knife, then she threw the weapon out into the sea. The waves turned red where it fell, as if drops of blood were seeping up through the water.

Again she looked at the prince; her eyes were already glazed in death. She threw herself into the sea and felt her body changing into foam.

The sun rose out of the sea, its rays felt warm and soft on the deathly cold foam. But the little mermaid did not feel death, she saw the sun, and up above her floated hundreds of airy, transparent forms. She could see right through them, see the sails of the ship and the blood-red clouds. Their voices were melodious, so spiritual and tender that no human ear could hear them, just as their forms were so fragile and fine that no human eye could see them. So light were they that they glided through the air, though they had no wings. The little mermaid looked down and saw that she had an ethereal body like theirs.

"Where am I?" she asked; and her voice sounded like theirs—so lovely and so melodious that no human music could reproduce it.

"We are the daughters of the air," they answered. "Mermaids have no immortal soul and can never have one, unless they can obtain the love of a human being. Their chance of obtaining eternal life depends upon others. We, daughters of the air, have not received an eternal soul either; but we can win one by good deeds. We fly to the warm countries, where the heavy air of the plague rests, and blow cool winds to spread it. We carry the smell of flowers that refresh and heal the sick. If for three hundred years we earnestly try to do what is good, we obtain an immortal soul and can take part in the eternal happiness of man. You, little mermaid, have tried with all your heart to do the same. You have suffered and borne your suffering bravely; and that is why you are now among us, the spirits of the air. Do your good deeds and in three hundred years an immortal soul will be yours."

The little mermaid lifted her arms up toward God's sun, and for the first time she felt a tear.

She heard noise coming from the ship. She saw the prince and the princess searching for her. Sadly they looked at the sea, as if they knew that she had thrown herself into the waves. Without being seen, she kissed the bride's forehead and smiled at the prince; then she rose together with the other children of the air, up into a pink cloud that was sailing by.

"In three hundred years I shall rise like this into God's kingdom," she said.

"You may be able to go there before that," whispered one of the others to her. "Invisibly, we fly through the homes of human beings. They can't see us, so they don't know when we are there; but if we find a good child, who makes his parents happy and deserves their love, we smile and God takes a year away from the time of our trial. But if there is a naughty and mean child in the house we come to, we cry; and for every tear we shed, God adds a day to the three hundred years we already must serve."

THE WOMAN OF THE SEA[1]

Helen Waddell

ONE CLEAR SUMMER NIGHT, A young man was walking on the sand by the sea on the Isle of Unst.[2] He had been all day in the hayfields and was come down to the shore to cool himself, for it was the full moon and the wind blowing fresh off the water.

As he came to the shore he saw the sand shining white in the moonlight and on it the sea-people dancing. He had never seen them before, for they show themselves like seals by day, but on this night, because it was midsummer and a full moon, they were dancing for joy. Here and there he saw dark patches where they had flung down their sealskins, but they themselves were as clear as the moon itself, and they cast no shadow.

He crept a little nearer, and his own shadow moved before him, and of a sudden one of the sea-people danced upon it. The dance was broken. They looked about and saw him and with a cry they fled to their sealskins and dived into the waves. The air was full of their soft crying and splashing.

But one of the fairy people ran hither and thither on the sands, wringing her hands as if she had lost something. The young man looked and saw a patch of darkness in his own shadow. It was a seal's skin. Quickly he threw it behind a rock and watched to see what the sea-fairy would do.

She ran down to the edge of the sea and stood with her feet in the foam, crying to

---

1   From *The Princess Splendour and Other Stories* (Harmondsworth: Puffin, 1972).
2   The northernmost of the inhabited British Isles, part of the Shetland Islands.

her people to wait for her, but they had gone too far to hear. The moon shone on her and the young man thought she was the loveliest creature he had ever seen. Then she began to weep softly to herself and the sound of it was so pitiful that he could bear it no longer. He stood upright and went down to her.

"What have you lost, woman of the sea?" he asked her.

She turned at the sound of his voice and looked at him, terrified. For a moment he thought she was going to dive into the sea. Then she came a step nearer and held up her two hands to him.

"Sir," she said, "give it back to me and I and my people will give you the treasure of the sea." Her voice was like the waves singing in a shell.

"I would rather have you than the treasure of the sea," said the young man. Although she hid her face in her hands and fell again to crying, more hopeless than ever, he was not moved.

"It is my wife you shall be," he said. "Come with me now to the priest, and we will go home to our own house, and it is yourself shall be mistress of all I have. It is warm you will be in the long winter nights, sitting at your own hearth stone and the peat burning red, instead of swimming in the cold green sea."

She tried to tell him of the bottom of the sea where there comes neither snow nor darkness of night and the waves are as warm as a river in summer, but he would not listen. Then he threw his cloak around her and lifted her in his arms and they were married in the priest's house.

He brought her home to his little thatched cottage and into the kitchen with its earthen floor, and set her down before the hearth in the red glow of the peat. She cried out when she saw the fire, for she thought it was a strange crimson jewel.

"Have you anything as bonny as that in the sea?" he asked her, kneeling down beside her and she said, so faintly that he could scarcely hear her, "No."

"I know not what there is in the sea," he said, "but there is nothing on land as bonny as you." For the first time she ceased her crying and sat looking into the heart of the fire. It was the first thing that made her forget, even for a moment, the sea which was her home.

All the days she was in the young man's house, she never lost the wonder of the fire and it was the first thing she brought her children to see. For she had three children in the twice seven years she lived with him. She was a good wife to him. She baked his bread and she spun the wool from the fleece of his Shetland sheep.

He never named the seal's skin to her, nor she to him, and he thought she was content, for he loved her dearly and she was happy with her children. Once, when he was ploughing on the headland above the bay, he looked down and saw her standing on the rocks and crying in a mournful voice to a great seal in the water. He said nothing when he came home, for he thought to himself it was not to wonder at if she were lonely for the sight of her own people. As for the seal's skin, he had hidden it well.

There came a September evening and she was busy in the house, and the children playing hide-and-seek in the stacks in the gloaming.[1] She heard them shouting and went out to them.

"What have you found?" she said.

The children came running to her. "It is like a big cat," they said, "but it is softer than a cat. Look!" She looked and saw her seal's skin that was hidden under last year's hay.

She gazed at it, and for a long time she stood still. It was warm dusk and the air was yellow with the afterglow of the sunset. The children had run away again, and their voices among the stacks sounded like the voices of birds. The hens were on the roost already and now and then one of them clucked in its sleep. The air was full of little friendly noises from the sleepy talking of the swallows under the thatch. The door was open and the warm smell of the baking of bread came out to her.

She turned to go in, but a small breath of wind rustled over the stacks and she stopped again. It brought a sound that she had heard so long she never seemed to hear it at all. It was the sea whispering down on the sand. Far out on the rocks the great waves broke in a boom, and close in on the sand the little waves slipped racing back. She took up the seal's skin and went swiftly down the track that led to the sands. The children saw her and cried to her to wait for them, but she did not hear them. She was just out of sight when their father came in from the byre and they ran to tell him.

"Which road did she take?" said he.

"The low road to the sea," they answered, but already their father was running to the shore. The children tried to follow him, but their voices died away behind him, so fast did he run.

As he ran across the hard sands, he saw her dive to join the big seal who was waiting for her, and he gave a loud cry to stop her. For a moment she rested on the surface of the sea, then she cried with her voice that was like the waves singing in a shell, "Fare ye well, and all good befall you, for you were a good man to me."

Then she dived to the fairy places that lie at the bottom of the sea and the big seal with her.

For a long time her husband watched for her to come back to him and the children; but she came no more.

---

1   Haystacks in the twilight.

BRAIN OVER BRAWN
(THE TRICKSTER)

Of all the different motifs to be found in fairy tale, few are older or more widespread than trickster tales. Ancient though the tradition may be, it continues to prosper today in such popular figures as Captain Jack Sparrow and Bart Simpson—presumably because the notions of thumbing our nose at authority, of beating the odds, of spicing up life with a bit of mischief, are as appealing now as they were a thousand years ago. Although in the Western tradition the trickster has acquired a degree of social acceptance as a sort of Robin Hood figure (robbing the rich to help the poor), we should note that in earlier times, he—the role was more or less exclusively male—was a much more amoral character, seeking to indulge his appetites with little regard for others. There is a narcissistic aspect to his behavior that disturbs us even as we are amused by his audacity and quick-wittedness.

But why is it that these tales have retained such popularity? One explanation is to be found in the fact that they come from the folk: stories in which superior size and power are rendered impotent by superior cunning must hold an immediate appeal to people who live with constant reminders of their own political and economic powerlessness. To express discontent with their lot in any direct manner would be to invite swift retribution, so frustrations have to be released imaginatively rather than actively. In this respect, the tales in this section surely provide a kind of socio-political therapy; the exuberant manner in which the underdog/protagonist sets about the task of exploiting the stupidity of his opponent must offer a very pointed satisfaction.

One character that matches this profile to a tee is the Grimms' brave little tailor. His profession puts him close to the bottom of the social heap, but what he lacks in status he more than makes up for in chutzpah. The story illustrates very effectively the enormous psychological advantage to be gained from a combination of unshakable self-confidence and cunning; the declaration on his belt tells no less than the truth, but then as now, the devil is in the details. The note of animosity that creeps into the narrative when the tailor pits his wits against the king is predictable, for reasons discussed above; likewise, his marriage to the princess is clearly not one made in heaven, but this story is more about getting even than about living happily ever after.

As we have seen, the previous Andersen tales in this anthology acquire much of their impact from their author's obsessive need to tell his own story, but that is not the case with "The Emperor's New Clothes," which is a memorable satire of social conformity and gullibility, as resonant today as it was in 1837, when it was first published. The weavers are cut from the same non-existent cloth (pun intended!) as the Grimms' tailor; their skill in exploiting the insecurities and vanity of the royal court has us assuring ourselves that *we* would never be fooled in this way. Once again, Andersen demonstrates his remarkable talent for seizing upon an incisive metaphor for what he wants to say.

Lest one is tempted to draw the conclusion that "female trickster" is an oxymoron, we offer "Clever Gretel," also from the Grimms' collection. At the outset, we learn that she "wore shoes with red heels, and when she went out in them she wiggled and waggled happily" (p. 177), which makes us suspect that there's more than a touch of narcissism in her nature. As Cristina Bacchilega points out, "[m]ore than a survivor, Gretel is an artist of enjoyment."[1] Thus much classist and sexist fun is had as she pulls the wool over the eyes of her ineffectual master, while doing considerable damage to his wine cellar at the same time. Then there is Flossie, descendant of the victim-turned-trickster line that emerged in "The Story of Grandmother," "The False Grandmother," and "Lon Po Po." Not surprisingly, this tale too is close to the oral tradition, as McKissack explains in her Author's Note. Indeed, the setting of the rural American South may remind us of a considerably more notorious mischief-maker in the shape of Brer Rabbit. The fact that Flossie has the situation fully under control signifies a complete reversal of the message of female helplessness in Charles Perrault's "Little Red Riding Hood," a conceptual shift that Angela Carter will bring to triumphant conclusion in "The Company of Wolves," as we shall see.

In Perrault's "Puss in Boots," we are confronted with a mutually beneficial partnership, although it's significant that the roles of servant and master are reversed. The presence of animals in fairy tale is obviously complex and multi-faceted; suffice it to say here that this can be explained partly by the same sense of inferiority that was noted above: if Man is ostensibly the master, then subordinate Animal must find the means to assert his sense of his own self-worth. We should also recall here the

---

1 Cristina Bacchilega, "What's a 'Clever' Woman to Do in the Grimms' Collection?," *Transgressive Tales: Queering the Grimms*, ed. Kay Turner and Pauline Greenhill (Detroit: Wayne State UP, 2012), 32.

point made earlier about the Wolf in "Little Red Riding Hood"—that the animal can be seen as a metaphor for some specific aspect of human nature, such as ferocity or mischief. That "human" element is particularly apparent here in the cat's insistence upon a pair of boots that play no role in the story beyond reminding us that this is no ordinary feline! Thus in "Puss in Boots" we meet a miller's youngest son (as socially disadvantaged, therefore, as any tailor), who acquires fame and fortune entirely through the quick wits of his helpful animal/servant, his contribution being to recognize the potential of Puss's "cunning tricks."

It's no coincidence that many tales of this type feature small animals. The explanation is surely not hard to find: the vulnerability of such creatures must have been quite meaningful to people who saw an obvious parallel with their own lives. With these last two tales, we find ourselves in that branch of folk tale known as beast-fable; yet even in this almost exclusively animal world, what we may term the "power structure" remains as clear as ever, since here too the issue is that of an apparently powerless individual having to find ways to outsmart those who supposedly control his destiny. "The Story of the Three Little Pigs" is another story about confrontation with a wolf—or, to be more exact, *three* encounters. However, the mood could hardly be more different from the rising tension and impending violence of "Little Red Riding Hood," for here the story skips along, caught up in its own repetitive silliness, while underlining the good sense behind the Boy Scout motto of "Be Prepared!" So irresistible is the back-and-forth movement of the tale—one has a strong sense of the narrative voice—that it's easy to forget that two pigs and a wolf get eaten (but all in good fun). The echoes of "Little Red Riding Hood" and "The Three Little Pigs" in "The Death of Brer Wolf," from what is popularly known as the Brer Rabbit group of tales, also leave no doubt as to its membership in the worldwide web of fairy tales. Originating on the West Coast of Africa (where Brer Rabbit is known as *Wakaima*), these tales came to America with the slave trade—and thus the human relevance of these stories is immediately apparent: there is at least a taste of freedom in laughter.

Also aboard those slave-ships that plied their ugly trade between West Africa, the West Indies, and the southern United States was Anansi the spider, another trickster hero who, in some respects, is a larger figure than his compatriot Brer Rabbit. In earlier times, Anansi was believed to be a god, the creator of the world, the possessor of all stories (as our selection reveals!). Like so many of the animals in European folk tale, Anansi (and Brer Rabbit likewise) is a creature with many human attributes; enjoyment of these tales requires us to ignore the distinction. And as Aesop demonstrated, it's very instructive.

The nature of the protagonists in this section deserves some consideration, in that none of them can accurately be described as good, at least in the conventional sense. There is an ambiguous quality in these tales that can be traced in part to the strong hint of amorality shown by their central characters as they pursue their various goals. Yet we should not be surprised by the tales' implicit assumption that cunning is a virtue. The people among whom these tales evolved had little reason to expect any material change for the better in their lives; for them, prosperity and success could be no more than dreams when simple survival was more often the issue. Therefore, it is easy to understand how the character who has the wit and audacity to seize the main chance when it comes along is not to be censored for a lack of honesty or sensitivity.

THE BRAVE LITTLE TAILOR[1]

Jacob and Wilhelm Grimm

ONE SUMMER MORNING A LITTLE tailor was sitting on his table near the window. He was in high good humor and sewed with all his might. A peasant woman came down the street, crying out: "Good jam—cheap!" That sounded sweet to the tailor's ears. He stuck his shapely little head out of the window and cried: "Up here, my good woman, you'll find a buyer." The woman hauled her heavy baskets up the three flights of stairs to the tailor's and he made her unpack every single pot. He examined them all, lifted them up, sniffed at them, and finally said: "This looks like good jam to me; weigh me out three ounces, my good woman, and if it comes to a quarter of a pound you won't find me complaining." The woman, who had hoped to make a good sale, gave him what he asked for, and went away grumbling and very much out of sorts. "God bless this jam and give me health and strength," cried the little tailor. Whereupon he took bread from the cupboard, cut a slice straight across the loaf, and spread it with jam. "I bet this won't taste bitter," he said, "but before biting into it, I'm going to finish my jacket." He put the bread down beside him and went on with his sewing, taking bigger and bigger stitches in his joy. Meanwhile, the flies that had been sitting on the wall, enticed by the sweet smell, came swarming down on the jam. "Hey, who invited you?" cried the little tailor and shooed the unbidden guests away. But the flies, who didn't understand his language, refused to be dismissed and kept coming in greater and greater numbers. Finally, at the end of his patience, the tailor took a rag from the catchall under his table. "Just wait! I'll show

---

1 First published in 1812/15, in the first edition of *Kinder- und Hausmärchen*. This text from the second edition (1819), from *Grimms' Tales for Young and Old*, trans. Ralph Manheim (Garden City, NY: Anchor P, 1977).

you!" he cried, and struck out at them unmercifully. When he stopped and counted, no less than seven flies lay dead with their legs in the air. He couldn't help admiring his bravery. "What a man I am!" he cried. "The whole town must hear of this." And one two three, he cut out a belt for himself, stitched it up, and embroidered on it in big letters: "Seven at one blow!" Then he said: "Town, my foot! The whole world must hear of it!" And for joy his heart wagged like a lamb's tail.

The tailor put on his belt and decided to go out into the world, for clearly his shop was too small for such valor. Before leaving, he ransacked the house for something to take with him, but all he could find was an old cheese, so he put that in his pocket. Just outside the door, he caught sight of a bird that had got itself caught in the bushes, and the bird joined the cheese in his pocket. Ever so bravely he took to the road, and because he was light and nimble, he never seemed to get tired. Up into the mountains he went, and when he reached the highest peak he found an enormous giant sitting there taking it easy and enjoying the view. The little tailor went right up to him; he wasn't the least bit afraid. "Greetings, friend," he said. "Looking out at the great world, are you? Well, that's just where I'm headed for, to try my luck. Would you care to go with me?" The giant looked at the tailor contemptuously and said: "You little pipsqueak! You miserable nobody!" "Is that so?" said the little tailor, unbuttoning his coat and showing the giant his belt. "Read that! That'll show you what kind of man I am!" When he had read what was written—"Seven at one blow!"—the giant thought somewhat better of the little man. All the same, he decided to put him to the test, so he picked up a stone and squeezed it until drops of water appeared. "Do that," he said, "if you've got the strength." "That?" said the tailor. "Why, that's child's play for a man like me." Whereupon he reached into his pocket, took out the soft cheese, and squeezed it until the whey ran out. "What do you think of that?" he cried. "Not so bad, eh?" The giant didn't know what to say; he couldn't believe the little man was so strong. So he picked up a stone and threw it so high that the eye could hardly keep up with it: "All right, you little runt, let's see you do that." "Nice throw," said the tailor, "but it fell to the ground in the end. Watch me throw one that won't ever come back." Whereupon he reached into his pocket, took out the bird, and tossed it into the air. Glad to be free, the bird flew up and away and didn't come back. "Well," said the tailor. "What do you think of that?" "I've got to admit you can throw," said the giant, "but now let's see what you can carry." Pointing at a big oak tree that lay felled on the ground, he said: "If you're strong enough, help me carry this tree out of the forest." "Glad to," said the little man. "You take the trunk over your shoulder, and I'll carry the branches; they're the heaviest part." The giant took the trunk over his shoulder, and the tailor sat down on a branch, so that the giant, who couldn't look around, had to carry the whole tree and the tailor to boot. The tailor felt so chipper in his comfortable back seat that he began to whistle "Three Tailors Went a-Riding," as though hauling trees were child's play to a man of his strength. After carrying the heavy load for quite some distance, the giant was exhausted. "Hey!" he cried out, "I've got to drop it." The tailor jumped nimbly down, put his arms around the tree as if he'd been carrying it, and said to the giant: "I wouldn't have thought a tiny tree would be too much for a big man like you."

They went on together until they came to a cherry tree. The giant grabbed the crown where the cherries ripen soonest, pulled it down, handed it to the tailor, and bade him eat. But the tailor was much too light to hold the tree down. When the giant let go, the crown snapped back into place and the tailor was whisked high into the air. When he had fallen to the ground without hurting himself, the giant cried out: "What's the matter? You mean you're not strong enough to hold that bit of a sapling?" "Not strong enough? How can you say such a thing about a man who did for seven at one blow? I jumped over that tree because the hunters down there were shooting into the thicket. Now you try. See if you can do it." The giant tried, but he couldn't get over the tree and got stuck in the upper branches. Once again the little tailor had won out.

"All right," said the giant. "If you're so brave, let me take you to our cave to spend the night with us." The little tailor was willing and went along with him. When they got to the cave, the other giants were sitting around the fire. Each one was holding a roasted sheep in his hands and eating it. The little tailor looked around and thought: "This place is a good deal roomier than my workshop." The giant showed him a bed and told him to lie down and sleep. But the bed was too big for the little tailor, so instead of getting into it, he crept into a corner. At midnight, when the giant thought the tailor must be sound asleep, he got up, took a big iron bar and split the bed in two with one stroke. That will settle the little runt's hash, he thought. At the crack of dawn the giants started into the forest. They had forgotten all about the little tailor. All at once he came striding along as chipper and bold as you please. The giants were terrified. They thought he would kill them all, and ran away as fast as their legs would carry them.

The little tailor went his way. After following his nose for many days he came to the grounds of a king's palace. Feeling tired, he lay down in the grass and went to sleep, and while he was sleeping some courtiers came along. They examined him from all sides and read the inscription on his belt: "Seven at one blow!" "Goodness," they said, "what can a great war hero like this be doing here in peacetime? He must be some great lord." They went and told the king. "If war should break out," they said, "a man like that would come in very handy. Don't let him leave on any account." This struck the king as good advice, and he sent one of his courtiers to offer the tailor a post in his army. The courtier went back to the sleeper, waited until he stretched his limbs and opened his eyes, and made his offer. "That's just what I came here for," said the tailor. "I'll be glad to enter the king's service." So he was received with honor and given apartments of his own.

But the soldiers, who were taken in by the little tailor, wished him a thousand miles away. "What will become of us?" they asked. "If we quarrel with him and he strikes, seven of us will fall at one blow. We won't last long at that rate." So they took counsel together, went to the king and asked to be released from his service. Because, they said, "we can't hope to keep up with a man who does for seven at one blow." The king was sad to be losing all his faithful servants because of one and wished he had never laid eyes on him. He'd have been glad to get rid of him, but he didn't dare dismiss him for fear the great hero might strike him and all his people dead and seize the throne for himself. He thought and thought, and at last he hit on an idea. He sent word to the little tailor that since he was such a great hero he wanted to make him an offer. There were two giants living in a certain forest, and they were murdering, looting, burning, and laying the country waste. No one dared go near them for fear of his life. If the hero should conquer and kill these two giants, the king would give him his only daughter to wife, with half his kingdom as her dowry. And, moreover, the king would send a hundred knights to back him up. "Sounds like just the thing for me," thought the little tailor. "It's not every day that somebody offers you a beautiful princess and half a kingdom." "It's a deal," he replied. "I'll take care of those giants, and I won't need the hundred knights. You can't expect a man who does for seven at one blow to be afraid of two."

The little tailor started out with the hundred knights at his heels. When they got to the edge of the forest, he said to his companions: "Stay here. I'll attend to the giants by myself." Then he bounded into the woods, peering to the right and to the left. After a while he caught sight of the two giants, who were lying under a tree asleep, snoring so hard that the branches rose and fell. Quick as a flash the little tailor picked up stones, filled both his pockets with them, and climbed the tree. Halfway up, he slid along a branch until he was right over the sleeping giants. Then he picked out one of the giants and dropped stone after stone on his chest. For a long while the giant didn't notice, but in the end he woke up, gave his companion a poke, and said: "Why are you hitting me?" "You're dreaming," said the other. "I'm not hitting you." When they had lain down to sleep again, the tailor dropped a stone on the second giant. "What is this?" he cried. "Why are you pelting me?" "I'm not pelting you!" the first grumbled. They argued awhile, but they were too tired to keep it up and finally their eyes closed again. Then the little tailor took his biggest stone and threw it with all his might at the first giant's chest. "This is too much!" cried the giant, and jumping up like a madman he pushed his companion so hard against the tree that it shook. The other repaid him in kind and they both flew into such a rage that they started pulling up trees and belaboring each other until they both lay dead on the ground.

The little tailor jumped down. "Lucky they didn't pull up the tree I was sitting in," he said to himself. "I'd have had to jump into another like a squirrel. But then we tailors are quick." He drew his sword, gave them both good thrusts in the chest, and went back to the knights. "The job is done," he said. "I've settled their hash. But it was a hard fight. They were so desperate they pulled up trees to fight with, but how could that help them against a man who does for seven at one blow!" "Aren't you even wounded?" the knights asked. "I should say not!" said the tailor. "Not so much as a scratch." The knights wouldn't believe him, so they rode into the forest, where they found the giants lying in pools of blood, with uprooted trees all around them.

The little tailor went to the king and demanded the promised reward, but the king regretted his promise and thought up another way to get rid of the hero. "Before I give you my daughter and half my kingdom," he said, "you will have to perform one more task. There's a unicorn loose in the forest and he's doing a good deal of damage. You will have to catch him first." "If the two giants didn't scare me, why would I worry about a unicorn? Seven at one blow is my meat." Taking a rope and an ax, he went into the forest, and again told the knights who had been sent with him to wait on the fringe. He didn't have long to look. In a short while the unicorn came along and rushed at the tailor, meaning to run him straight through with his horn. "Not so fast!" said the tailor. "It's not as easy as all that." He stood still, waited until the unicorn was quite near him, and then jumped nimbly behind a tree. The unicorn charged full force and rammed into the tree. His horn went in and stuck so fast that he hadn't the strength to pull it out. He was caught. "I've got him," said the tailor. He came out from behind the tree, put the rope around the unicorn's neck and, taking his ax, chopped the wood away from the horn. When that was done, he led the beast to the king.

But the king was still unwilling to grant him the promised reward and made a third demand. Before the wedding he wanted the tailor to capture a wild boar which had been ravaging the forest, and said the royal huntsmen would help him. "Gladly," said the little tailor. "It's child's play." He didn't take the huntsmen into the forest with him, and they were just as pleased, for several times the boar had given them such a reception that they had no desire to seek him out. When the boar caught sight of the tailor, he gnashed his teeth, foamed at the mouth, made a dash at him, and would have lain him out flat if the nimble hero hadn't escaped into a nearby chapel. The boar ran in after him, but the tailor jumped out of the window, ran around the chapel and slammed the door. The infuriated beast was much too heavy and clumsy to jump out of the window, and so he was caught. The little tailor ran back to the huntsmen and told them to go and see the captive with their own eyes. He himself went to the king, who had to keep his promise this time, like it or not, and give him his daughter and half the kingdom. If he had known that, far from being a war hero, the bridegroom was only a little tailor, he would have been even unhappier than he was. And so the wedding was celebrated with great splendor and little joy, and a tailor became a king.

One night the young queen heard her husband talking in his sleep. "Boy," he said, "hurry up with that jerkin you're making and get those breeches mended or I'll break my yardstick over your head." Then she knew how he had got his start in life. Next morning she went to her father, told him her tale of woe, and begged him to help her get rid of a husband who had turned out to be a common tailor. The king bade her take comfort and said: "Leave the door of your bedroom unlocked tonight. My servants will be waiting outside. Once he's asleep they'll go in, tie him up, and put him aboard a ship bound for the end of the world." The young queen was pleased, but the armor-bearer, who was devoted to the hero, heard the whole conversation and told him all about the plot. "They won't get away with that!" said the little tailor. That night he went to bed with his wife at the usual hour. When she thought he was asleep, she got up, opened the door, and lay down again. The little tailor, who was only pretending to be asleep, cried out in a loud voice: "Boy, hurry up with that jerkin you're making and get those breeches mended or I'll break my yardstick over your head. I've done for seven at one blow, killed two giants, brought home a unicorn, and captured a wild boar. And now I'm expected to be afraid of these scoundrels at my door." When they heard that, the servants were terrified. Not one of them dared lay hands on him and they ran as if the hosts of hell had been chasing them. And so the little tailor went on being king for the rest of his days.

THE EMPEROR'S NEW CLOTHES[1]

Hans Christian Andersen

MANY, MANY YEARS AGO THERE was an emperor who was so terribly fond of beautiful new clothes that he spent all his money on his attire. He did not care about his soldiers, or attending the theatre, or even going for a drive in the park, unless it was to show off his new clothes. He had an outfit for every hour of the day. And just as we say, "The king is in his council chamber," his subjects used to say, "The emperor is in his clothes closet."

In the large town where the emperor's palace was, life was gay and happy; and every day new visitors arrived. One day two swindlers came. They told everybody that

---

1   First published in 1837. This text from *Hans Christian Andersen: His Classic Fairy Tales*, trans. Erik Haugaard (New York: Doubleday, 1974).

they were weavers and that they could weave the most marvellous cloth. Not only were the colours and the patterns of their material extraordinarily beautiful, but the cloth had the strange quality of being invisible to anyone who was unfit for his office or unforgivably stupid.

"This is truly marvellous," thought the emperor. "Now if I had robes cut from that material, I should know which of my councillors was unfit for his office, and I would be able to pick out my clever subjects myself. They must weave some material for me!" And he gave the swindlers a lot of money so they could start working at once.

They set up a loom and acted as if they were weaving, but the loom was empty. The fine silk and gold threads they demanded from the emperor they never used, but hid them in their own knapsacks. Late into the night they would sit before their empty loom, pretending to weave.

"I would like to know how far they've come," thought the emperor; but his heart beat strangely when he remembered that those who were stupid or unfit for their office would not be able to see the material. Not that he was really worried that this would happen to him. Still, it might be better to send someone else the first time and see how he fared. Everybody in town had heard about the cloth's magic quality and most of them could hardly wait to find out how stupid or unworthy their neighbours were.

"I shall send my faithful prime minister to see the weaver," thought the emperor. "He will know how to judge the material, for he is both clever and fit for his office, if any man is."

The good-natured old man stepped into the room where the weavers were working and saw the empty loom. He closed his eyes, and opened them again. "God preserve me!" he thought. "I cannot see a thing!" But he didn't say it out loud.

The swindlers asked him to step a little closer so that he could admire the intricate patterns and marvellous colours of the material they were weaving. They both pointed to the empty loom, and the poor old prime minister opened his eyes as wide as he could; but it didn't help, he still couldn't see anything.

"Am I stupid?" he thought. "I can't believe it, but if it is so, it is best no one finds out about it. But maybe I am not fit for my office. No, that is worse, I'd better not admit that I can't see what they are weaving."

"Tell us what you think of it," demanded one of the swindlers.

"It is beautiful. It is very lovely," mumbled the old prime minister, adjusting his glasses. "What patterns! What colours! I shall tell the emperor that I am greatly pleased."

"And that pleases us," the weavers said; and now they described the patterns and told which shades of colour they had used. The prime minister listened attentively, so that he could repeat their words to the emperor, and that is exactly what he did.

The two swindlers demanded more money, and more silk and gold thread. They said they had to use it for their weaving, but their loom remained as empty as ever.

Soon the emperor sent another of his trusted councillors to see how the work was progressing. He looked and looked just as the prime minister had, but since there was nothing to be seen, he didn't see anything.

"Isn't it a marvellous piece of material?" asked one of the swindlers; and they both began to describe the beauty of their cloth again.

"I am not stupid," thought the emperor's councillor. "I must be unfit for my office. That is strange; but I'd better not admit it to anyone." And he started to praise the material, which he could not see, for the loveliness of its patterns and colours.

"I think it is the most charming piece of material I have ever seen," declared the councillor to the emperor.

Everyone in town was talking about the marvellous cloth that the swindlers were weaving.

At last the emperor himself decided to see it before it was removed from the loom. Attended by the most important people in the empire, among them the prime minister and the councillor who had been there before, the emperor entered the room where the weavers were weaving furiously on their empty loom.

"Isn't it *magnifique*?" asked the prime minister.

"Your Majesty, look at the colours and patterns," said the councillor. And the two old gentlemen pointed to the empty loom, believing that all the rest of the company could see the cloth.

"What!" thought the emperor. "I can't see a thing! Why, this is a disaster! Am I stupid? Am I unfit to be emperor? Oh, it is too horrible!" Aloud he said, "It is very lovely. It has my approval," while he nodded his head and looked at the empty loom.

All the councillors, ministers, and men of great importance who had come with him stared and stared; but they saw no more than the emperor had seen, and they said the same thing that he had said, "It is lovely." And they advised him to have clothes cut and sewn, so that he could wear them in the procession at the next great celebration.

"It is magnificent! Beautiful! Excellent!" All of their mouths agreed, though none of their eyes had seen anything. The two swindlers were decorated and given the title "Royal Knight of the Loom."

The night before the procession, the two swindlers didn't sleep at all. They had sixteen candles lighting up the room where they worked. Everyone could see how busy they were, getting the emperor's new clothes finished. They pretended to take cloth from the loom; they cut the air with their big scissors and sewed with needles without thread. At last they announced: "The emperor's new clothes are ready!"

Together with his courtiers, the emperor came. The swindlers lifted their arms as if they were holding something in their hands, and said, "These are the trousers. This is the robe, and here is the train. They are all as light as if they were made of spider webs! It will be as if Your Majesty had almost nothing on, but that is their special virtue."

"Oh yes," breathed all the courtiers; but they saw nothing, for there was nothing to be seen.

"Will Your Imperial Majesty be so gracious as to take off your clothes?" asked the swindlers. "Over there by the big mirror, we shall help you put your new ones on."

The emperor did as he was told; and the swindlers acted as if they were dressing him in the clothes they should have made. Finally they tied around his waist the long train which two of his most noble courtiers were to carry.

The emperor stood in front of the mirror admiring the clothes he couldn't see.

"Oh, how they suit you! A perfect fit!" everyone exclaimed. "What colours! What patterns! The new clothes are magnificent!"

"The crimson canopy, under which Your Imperial Majesty is to walk, is waiting outside," said the imperial master of court ceremony.

"Well, I am dressed. Aren't my clothes becoming?" The emperor turned around once more in front of the mirror, pretending to study his finery.

The two gentlemen of the imperial bedchamber fumbled on the floor trying to find the train which they were supposed to carry. They didn't dare admit that they didn't see anything, so they pretended to pick up the train and held their hands as if they were carrying it.

The emperor walked in the procession under his crimson canopy. And all the people of the town, who had lined the streets or were looking down from the windows, said that the emperor's new clothes were beautiful. "What a magnificent robe! And the train! How well the emperor's clothes suit him!"

None of them were willing to admit that they hadn't seen a thing; for if anyone did, then he was either stupid or unfit for the job he held. Never before had the emperor's clothes been such a success.

"But he doesn't have anything on!" cried a little child.

"Listen to the innocent one," said the proud father. And the people whispered among each other and repeated what the child had said.

"He doesn't have anything on. There's a little child who says that he has nothing on."

"He has nothing on!" shouted all the people at last.

The emperor shivered, for he was certain that they were right; but he thought, "I must bear it until the procession is over." And he walked even more proudly, and the two gentlemen of the imperial bedchamber went on carrying the train that wasn't there.

CLEVER GRETEL[1]

Jacob and Wilhelm Grimm

THERE WAS ONCE A COOK by the name of Gretel, who wore shoes with red heels, and when she went out in them she wiggled and waggled happily, and said to herself: "My, what a pretty girl I am." And when she got home again, she'd be in such a good humor that she'd take a drink of wine, and then, as wine whets the appetite, she'd taste all the best parts of what she was cooking until she was full, and say: "A cook has to know how her cooking tastes."

One day her master said to her: "Gretel, I'm having a guest for dinner. I want you to make us two nice roast chickens." "Yes, master, I'll be glad to," said Gretel. She slit the chickens' throats, scalded, plucked, and spitted them, and toward evening put them over the fire to roast. The chickens began to brown and were almost done, but the guest hadn't arrived. Gretel called in to her master: "If your guest doesn't come soon, I'll have to take the chickens off the fire, but it would be a crying shame not to eat them now, while they're at their juiciest best." "In that case," said the master, "I'll go and get him myself." The moment his back was turned, she put the spit with the chickens on it to one side. "Standing over the fire so long makes a body sweat," she thought, "and sweating makes a body thirsty. How do I know when they'll get here? In the meantime I'll hop down to the cellar and have a little drink." Down she ran, filled a jug from the barrel, said: "God bless it to your use, Gretel," and took a healthy swig. "Wine goes with wine," she said, "and never should they part," and took a healthier swig. Then she went upstairs, put the chickens back on the fire, brushed them with butter, and gave the spit a few lively turns. But the chickens smelled so good that she thought: "Maybe they're not seasoned quite right, I'd better taste them." She touched her fingers to one, licked them, and cried out: "Oh, how delicious these chickens are! It's a crying shame not to eat them this minute!" She went to the window to see if the master and his guest were coming, but there was no one in sight. She went back to the chickens and thought: "That wing is burning. There's only one way to stop it." So she cut the wing off and ate it. It hit the spot, and when she had finished she thought: "I'll have to take the other one off too, or the master will see that something's missing." After doing away with the two wings, she went back to the window to look for her master. No master in sight, so then she had an idea. "How do I know? Maybe they're not coming. Maybe they've stopped at a tavern." She gave herself a poke: "Come on,

---

1 First published in 1812/15, in the first edition of *Kinder- und Hausmärchen*. This text from the second edition (1819), from *Grimms' Tales for Young and Old*, trans. Ralph Manheim (Garden City, NY: Anchor P, 1977).

Gretel. Don't be a spoilsport. One has been cut into; have another drink and finish it up. Once it's gone, you won't have anything to worry about. Why waste God's blessings?" Again she hopped down to the cellar, took a good stiff drink, and polished off the one chicken with joy in her heart. When one chicken was gone and there was still no sign of the master, Gretel looked at the other and said: "Where the one is, there the other should be. Chickens go in pairs, and what's good enough for one is good enough for the other. And besides, another drink won't hurt me any." Whereupon she took an enormous drink and started the second chicken on its way to rejoin the first.

She was still eating lustily when her master came along and called out: "Quick, Gretel. Our guest will be here in a minute." "Oh, yes, sir," said Gretel. "I'll serve you in a jiffy." The master looked in to make sure the table was properly set, took his big carving knife, and began to sharpen it in the pantry. The guest was a well-bred man. When he got to the house, he knocked softly. Gretel hurried to the door and looked out. When she saw the guest, she put her finger to her lips and said: "Sh-sh! Quick, go away! If my master catches you, you're done for. Do you know why he invited you to dinner? Because he wants to cut your ears off. Listen! That's him sharpening his knife!" The guest heard the master whetting his knife and ran down the steps as fast as his legs could carry him. But Gretel wasn't through yet. She ran screaming to her master: "A fine guest you brought into the house!" she cried. "Why, what's the matter, Gretel? What do you mean?" "I mean," she said, "that just as I was getting ready to serve up the chickens he grabbed them and ran away with them." "That's a fine way to behave," said the master, grieved at the loss of his fine chickens. "If he'd only left me one of them! Then at least I'd have something to eat." "Stop! Stop!" he shouted, but the guest pretended not to hear. So still holding his knife the master ran after him, crying out: "Just one! Just one!" meaning that the guest should leave him one chicken and not take both. But the guest thought the master had decided to content himself with one ear, and seeing that he wanted to take both his ears home with him, he ran as if someone had made a fire under his feet.

FLOSSIE AND THE FOX[1]

Patricia C. McKissack

Author's Note

Long before I became a writer, I was a listener. On hot summer evenings our family sat on the porch and listened to my grandmother dramatize a Dunbar[2] poem. But it was always a special treat when my grandfather took the stage. He was a master storyteller who charmed his audience with humorous stories told in the rich and colorful dialect of the rural South. I never wanted to forget them. So, it is through me that my family's storytelling legacy lives on.

Here is a story from my youth, retold in the same rich and colorful language that was my grandfather's. He began all his yarns with a question. "Did I ever tell you 'bout the time lil' Flossie Finley come out the Piney Woods heeling a fox?" I'd snuggle up beside him in the big porch swing, then he'd begin his tale …

"FLO-O-O-OSSIE!"

The sound of Big Mama's voice floated past the cabins in Sophie's Quarters, round the smokehouse, beyond the chicken coop, all the way down to Flossie Finley. Flossie tucked away her straw doll in a hollow log, then hurried to answer her grandmother's call.

"Here I am, Big Mama," Flossie said after catching her breath. It was hot, hotter than a usual Tennessee August day.

Big Mama stopped sortin' peaches and wiped her hands and face with her apron. "Take these to Miz Viola over at the McCutchin Place," she say reaching behind her and handing Flossie a basket of fresh eggs. "Seem like they been troubled by a fox. Miz Viola's chickens be so scared, they can't even now lay a stone." Big Mama clicked her teeth and shook her head.

"Why come Mr. J.W. can't catch the fox with his dogs?" Flossie asked, putting a peach in her apron pocket to eat later.

"Ever-time they corner that ol' slickster, he gets away. I tell you, that fox is one sly critter."

"How do a fox look?" Flossie asked. "I disremember ever seeing one."

Big Mama had to think a bit. "Chile, a fox be just a fox. But one thing for sure, that rascal loves eggs. He'll do most anything to get at some eggs."

---

1   Published in 1986 (New York: Dial).
2   Paul Laurence Dunbar (1872–1906), Black American poet who often wrote in "Negro dialect."

Flossie tucked the basket under her arm and started on her way. "Don't tarry now," Big Mama called. "And be particular 'bout them eggs."

"Yes'um," Flossie answered.

The way through the woods was shorter and cooler than the road route under the open sun. *What if I come upon a fox?* thought Flossie. *Oh well, a fox be just a fox. That aine so scary.*

Flossie commenced to skip along, when she come upon a critter she couldn't recollect ever seeing. He was sittin' 'side the road like he was expectin' somebody. Flossie skipped right up to him and nodded a greeting the way she'd been taught to do.

"Top of the morning to you, Little Missy," the critter replied. "And what is your name?"

"I be Flossie Finley," she answered with a proper curtsy. "I reckon I don't know who you be either."

Slowly the animal circled round Flossie. "I am a fox," he announced, all the time eyeing the basket of eggs. He stopped in front of Flossie, smiled as best a fox can, and bowed. "At your service."

Flossie rocked back on her heels then up on her toes, back and forward, back and forward ... carefully studying the creature who was claiming to be a fox.

"Nope," she said at last. "I just purely don't believe it."

"You don't believe what?" Fox asked, looking way from the basket of eggs for the first time.

"I don't believe you a fox, that's what."

Fox's eyes flashed anger. Then he chuckled softly. "My dear child," he said, sounding right disgusted, "of course I'm a fox. A little girl like you should be simply terrified of me. Whatever do they teach children these days?"

Flossie tossed her head in the air. "Well, whatever you are, you sho' think a heap of yo'self," she said and skipped away.

Fox looked shocked. "Wait," he called. "You mean ... you're not frightened? Not just a bit?"

Flossie stopped. Then she turned and say, "I aine never seen a fox before. So, why should I be scared of you and I don't even-now know you a real fox for a fact?"

Fox pulled himself tall. He cleared his throat. "Are you saying I must offer proof that I am a fox before you will be frightened of me?"

"That's just what I'm saying."

Lil' Flossie skipped on through the piney woods while that Fox fella rushed away lookin' for whatever he needed to prove he was really who he said he was.

Meanwhile Flossie stopped to rest 'side a tree. Suddenly Fox was beside her. "I have the proof," he said. "See, I have thick, luxurious fur. Feel for yourself."

Fox leaned over for Flossie to rub his back.

"Ummm. Feels like rabbit fur to me," she say to Fox. "Shucks! You aine no fox. You a rabbit, all the time trying to fool me."

"Me! A rabbit!" he shouted. "I have you know my reputation precedes me. I am the third generation of foxes who have out-smarted and out-run Mr. J.W. Mc-Cutchin's fine hunting dogs. I have raided some of the best henhouses from Franklin to Madison. Rabbit, indeed! I am a fox, and you will act accordingly!"

Flossie hopped to her feet. She put her free hand on her hip and patted her foot. "Unless you can show you a fox, I'll not accord you nothing!" And without further ceremony she skipped away.

Down the road apiece, Flossie stopped by a bubbling spring. She knelt to get a drink of water. Fox came up to her and said, "I have a long pointed nose. Now that should be proof enough."

"Don't prove a thing to me." Flossie picked some wild flowers. "Come to think of it," she said matter-of-fact-like, "rats got long pointed noses." She snapped her fingers. "That's it! You a rat trying to pass yo'self off as a fox."

That near 'bout took Fox's breath away. "I beg your pardon," he gasped.

"You can beg all you wanna," Flossie say skipping on down the road. "That still don't make you no fox."

"I'll teach you a thing or two, young lady," Fox called after her. "You just wait and see."

Before long Flossie came to a clearing. A large orange tabby was sunning on a tree stump. "Hi, pretty kitty," the girl say and rubbed the cat behind her ears. Meanwhile Fox slipped from behind a clump of bushes.

"Since you won't believe me when I tell you I am a fox," he said stiffly, "perhaps you will believe that fine feline creature toward whom you seem to have some measure of respect."

Flossie looked at the cat and winked her eye. "He sho' use a heap of words," she whispered.

Fox beckoned for Cat to speak up. Cat jumped to a nearby log and yawned and stretched—then she answered. "This is a fox because he has sharp claws and yellow eyes," she purred.

Fox seemed satisfied. But Flossie looked at the cat. She looked at Fox, then once more at both just to be sure. She say, "All due respect, Miz Cat, but both y'all got sharp claws and yellow eyes. So ... that don't prove nothing, cep'n both y'all be cats."

Fox went to howling and running round in circles. He was plum beside himself. "I am a fox and I know it," he shouted. "This is absurd!"

"No call for you to use that kind of language," Flossie said and she skipped away.

"Wait, wait," Fox followed pleading. "I just remembered something. It may be the solution to this—this horrible situation."

"Good. It's about time."

"I—I—I have a bushy tail." Fox seemed to perk up. "That's right," he said. "All foxes are known for their fluffy, bushy tails. That has got to be adequate proof."

"Aine got to be. You got a bushy tail. So do squirrels." Flossie pointed to one overhead leaping from branch to branch in the tree tops. "Here, have a bite of peach," she said, offering Fox first bite of her treat.

But Fox was crying like a natural born baby. "No, no, no," he sobbed. "If I promise you I'm a fox, won't that do?"

Flossie shook her head no.

"Oh, woe is me," Fox hollered. "I may never recover my confidence."

Flossie didn't stop walking. "That's just what I been saying. You just an ol' confidencer. Come tellin' me you was a fox, then can't prove it. Shame on you!"

Long about that time, Flossie and the fox came out of the woods. Flossie cupped her hands over her eyes and caught sight of McCutchin Quarters and Miz Viola's cabin. Fox didn't notice a thing; he just followed behind Flossie begging to be believed.

"Give me one last chance," he pleaded.

Flossie turned on her heels. "Okay. But just this once more."

Fox tried not to whimper, but his voice was real unsteady-like. "I—I have sharp teeth and I can run exceedingly fast." He waited for Flossie to say something.

Slowly the girl rocked from heel to toe ... back and forward. "You know," she finally said, smiling, "it don't make much difference what I think anymore."

"What?" Fox asked. "Why?"

"Cause there's one of Mr. J.W. McCutchin's hounds behind you. He's got sharp teeth and can run fast too. And, by the way that hound's lookin', it's all over for you!"

With a quick glance back Fox dashed toward the woods. "The hound knows who I am!" he shouted. "But I'm not worried. I sure can out-smart and out-run one of Mr. J.W. McCutchin's miserable mutts any old time of the day, because like I told you, I am a fox!"

"I know," said Flossie. "I know." And she turned toward Miz Viola's with the basket of eggs safely tucked under her arm.

PUSS IN BOOTS[1]

Charles Perrault

A CERTAIN POOR MILLER HAD ONLY his mill, his ass and his cat to bequeath to his three sons when he died. The children shared out their patrimony and did not bother to call in the lawyers; if they had done so, they would have been stripped quite bare of course. The eldest took the mill, the second the ass, and the youngest had to make do with the cat.

He felt himself very ill used.

"My brothers can earn an honest living with their inheritance, but once I've eaten my cat and made a muff with his pelt, I shall have to die of hunger."

The cat overheard him but decided to pretend he had not done so; he addressed his master gravely.

"Master, don't fret; give me a bag and a pair of boots to protect my little feet from the thorny undergrowth and you'll see that your father hasn't provided for you so badly, after all."

Although the cat's master could not really believe his cat would support him, he had seen him play so many cunning tricks when he went to catch rats and mice—he would hang upside down by his feet; or hide himself in the meal and play at being dead—that he felt a faint hope his cat might think up some helpful scheme.

When the cat had got what he asked for, he put on his handsome boots and slung the bag round his neck, keeping hold of the drawstrings with his two front paws. He went to a warren where he knew there were a great many rabbits. He put some bran and a selection of juicy weeds at the bottom of the bag and then stretched out quite still, like a corpse, and waited for some ingenuous young rabbit to come and investigate the bag and its appetizing contents.

No sooner had he lain down than a silly bunny jumped into the bag. Instantly, the cat pulled the drawstrings tight and killed the rabbit without mercy.

Proudly bearing his prey, he went to the king and asked to speak to him. He was taken to his majesty's private apartment. As soon as he got inside the door, he made the king a tremendous bow and said:

"Sire, I present you with a delicious young rabbit that my master, the Marquis of Carabas, ordered me to offer you, with his humblest compliments."

Without his master's knowledge or consent, the cat had decided the miller's son should adopt the name of the Marquis of Carabas.

---

1 First published in 1697. This text from *Sleeping Beauty and Other Favourite Fairy Tales*, trans. Angela Carter (London: Gollancz, 1982).

"Tell your master that I thank him with all my heart," said the king.

The next day, the cat hid himself in a cornfield, with his open bag, and two partridges flew into it. He pulled the strings and caught them both. Then he went to present them to the king, just as he had done with the rabbit. The king accepted the partridges with great glee and rewarded the cat with a handsome tip.

The cat kept on taking his master's game to the king for two or three months. One day, he learned that the king planned to take a drive along the riverside with his beautiful daughter. He said to his master:

"If you take my advice, your fortune is made. You just go for a swim in the river at a spot I'll show to you and leave the rest to me."

The Marquis of Carabas obediently went off to swim, although he could not think why the cat should want him to. While he was bathing, the king drove by and the cat cried out with all its might:

"Help! Help! The Marquis of Carabas is drowning!"

The king put his head out of his carriage window when he heard this commotion and recognised the cat who had brought him so much game. He ordered his servants to hurry and save the Marquis of Carabas.

While they were pulling the marquis out of the river, the cat went to the king's carriage and told him how robbers had stolen his master's clothes while he swam in the river even though he'd shouted "Stop thief!" at the top of his voice. In fact, the cunning cat had hidden the miller's son's wretched clothes under a stone.

The king ordered the master of his wardrobe to hurry back to the palace and bring a selection of his own finest garments for the Marquis of Carabas to wear. When the young man put them on, he looked very handsome and the king's daughter thought: "What an attractive young man!" The Marquis of Carabas treated her with respect mingled with tenderness and she fell madly in love.

The king invited the Marquis of Carabas to join him in his carriage and continue the drive in style. The cat was delighted to see his scheme begin to succeed and busily ran ahead of the procession. He came to a band of peasants who were mowing a meadow and said:

"Good people, if you don't tell the king that this meadow belongs to the Marquis of Carabas, I'll make mincemeat of every one of you."

As soon as he saw the mowers, the king asked them who owned the hayfield. They had been so intimidated by the cat that they dutifully chorused:

"It belongs to the Marquis of Carabas."

"You have a fine estate," remarked the king to the marquis.

"The field crops abundantly every year," improvised the marquis.

The cat was still racing ahead of the party and came to a band of harvesters. He said to them:

"Good harvesters, if you don't say that all these cornfields belong to the Marquis of Carabas, I'll make mincemeat of every one of you."

The king passed by a little later and wanted to know who owned the rolling cornfield.

"The Marquis of Carabas possesses them all," said the harvesters.

The king expressed his increasing admiration of the marquis' estates. The cat ran before the carriage and made the same threats to everyone he met on the way; the king was perfectly astonished at the young man's great possessions.

At last the cat arrived at a castle. In this castle lived an ogre. This ogre was extraordinarily rich; he was the true owner of all the land through which the king had travelled. The cat had taken good care to find out all he could about this ogre, and now he asked the servant who answered the door if he could speak to him; he said he couldn't pass so close by the castle without paying his respects to such an important man as its owner.

The ogre made him as welcome as an ogre can.

"I'm told you can transform yourself into all sorts of animals," said the cat. "That you can change yourself into a lion, for example, or even an elephant."

"Quite right," replied the ogre. "Just to show you, I'll turn myself into a lion."

When he found himself face to face with a lion, even our cat was so scared that he jumped up on to the roof and balanced there precariously because his boots weren't made for walking on tiles.

As soon as the ogre had become himself again, the cat clambered down and confessed how terrified he had been.

"But gossip also has it—though I can scarcely believe it—that you also have the power to take the shapes of the very smallest animals. They say you can even shrink down as small as a rat or a mouse. But I must admit, even if it seems rude, that I think that's quite impossible."

"Impossible?" said the ogre. "Just you see!" He changed into a mouse and began to scamper around on the floor. The cat no sooner saw him than he jumped on him and gobbled him up.

Meanwhile, the king saw the ogre's fine castle as he drove by and decided to pay it a visit. The cat heard the sound of carriage wheels on the drawbridge, ran outside and greeted the king.

"Welcome, your majesty, to the castle of the Marquis of Carabas."

"What sir? Does this fine castle also belong to you? I've never seen anything more splendid than this courtyard and the battlements that surround it; may we be permitted to view the interior?"

The marquis gave his hand to the young princess and followed the king. They entered a grand room where they found a banquet ready prepared; the ogre had invited all his friends to a dinner party, but none of the guests dared enter the castle when they saw the king had arrived. The king was delighted with the good qualities of the Marquis of Carabas and his daughter was beside herself about them. There was also the young man's immense wealth to be taken into account. After his fifth or sixth glass of wine, the king said:

"Say the word, my fine fellow, and you shall become my son-in-law."

The marquis bowed very low, immediately accepted the honour the king bestowed on him and married the princess that very day. The cat was made a great lord and gave up hunting mice, except for pleasure.

Moral

A great inheritance may be a fine thing, but hard work and ingenuity will take a young man further than his father's money.

Another Moral

If a miller's son can so quickly win the heart of a princess, that is because clothes, bearing and youth speedily inspire affection; and the means to achieve them are not always entirely commendable.

THE STORY OF THE THREE LITTLE PIGS[1]

Joseph Jacobs

> *Once upon a time when pigs spoke rhyme*
> *And monkeys chewed tobacco,*
> *And hens took snuff to make them tough,*
> *And ducks went quack, quack, quack, O!*

THERE WAS AN OLD SOW with three little pigs, and as she had not enough to keep them, she sent them out to seek their fortune. The first that went off met a man with a bundle of straw, and said to him:

"Please, man, give me that straw to build me a house."

Which the man did, and the little pig built a house with it. Presently came along a wolf, and knocked at the door, and said:

"Little pig, little pig, let me come in."

---

1   From *English Fairy Tales*, 1890 (repr. New York: Dover, 1967).

To which the pig answered:

"No, no, by the hair of my chinny chin chin."

The wolf then answered to that:

"Then I'll huff, and I'll puff, and I'll blow your house in."

So he huffed, and he puffed, and he blew his house in, and ate up the little pig.

The second little pig met a man with a bundle of furze,[1] and said:

"Please, man, give me that furze to build a house."

Which the man did, and the pig built his house. Then along came the wolf, and said:

"Little pig, little pig, let me come in."

"No, no, by the hair of my chinny chin chin."

"Then I'll puff, and I'll huff, and I'll blow your house in."

So he huffed, and he puffed, and he puffed, and he huffed, and at last he blew the house down, and he ate up the little pig.

The third little pig met a man with a load of bricks, and said:

"Please, man, give me those bricks to build a house with."

So the man gave him the bricks, and he built his house with them. So the wolf came, as he did to the other little pigs, and said:

"Little pig, little pig, let me come in."

"No, no, by the hair of my chinny chin chin."

"Then I'll huff, and I'll puff, and I'll blow your house in."

Well, he huffed, and he puffed, and he huffed and he puffed, and he puffed and huffed, but he could *not* get the house down. When he found that he could not, with all his huffing and puffing, blow the house down, he said:

"Little pig, I know where there is a nice field of turnips."

"Where?" said the little pig.

"Oh, in Mr. Smith's Home-field, and if you will be ready tomorrow morning I will call for you, and we will go together, and get some for dinner."

"Very well," said the little pig, "I will be ready. What time do you mean to go?"

"Oh, at six o'clock."

Well, the little pig got up at five, and got the turnips before the wolf came (which he did about six) and who said:

"Little pig, are you ready?"

The little pig said: "Ready! I have been and come back again, and got a nice potful for dinner."

The wolf felt very angry at this, but thought that he would be up to the little pig somehow or other, so he said:

---

1   A flowering shrub.

"Little pig, I know where there is a nice apple-tree."

"Where?" said the pig.

"Down at Merry-garden," replied the wolf, "and if you will not deceive me I will come for you, at five o'clock tomorrow and get some apples."

Well, the little pig bustled up the next morning at four o'clock, and went off for the apples, hoping to get back before the wolf came; but he had further to go, and had to climb the tree, so that just as he was coming down from it, he saw the wolf coming, which, as you may suppose, frightened him very much. When the wolf came up he said:

"Little pig, what! are you here before me? Are they nice apples?"

"Yes, very," said the little pig. "I will throw you down one."

And he threw it so far, that, while the wolf was gone to pick it up, the little pig jumped down and ran home. The next day the wolf came again, and said to the little pig:

"Little pig, there is a fair at Shanklin this afternoon, will you go?"

"Oh yes," said the pig, "I will go; what time shall you be ready?"

"At three," said the wolf. So the little pig went off before the time as usual, and got to the fair, and bought a butter-churn, which he was going home with, when he saw the wolf coming. Then he could not tell what to do. So he got into the churn to hide, and by so doing turned it round, and it rolled down the hill with the pig in it, which frightened the wolf so much, that he ran home without going to the fair. He went to the little pig's house, and told him how frightened he had been by a great round thing which came down the hill past him. Then the little pig said:

"Hah, I frightened you, then. I had been to the fair and bought a butter-churn, and when I saw you, I got into it, and rolled down the hill."

Then the wolf was very angry indeed, and declared he *would* eat up the little pig, and that he would get down the chimney after him. When the little pig saw what he was about, he hung on the pot full of water, and made up a blazing fire, and, just as the wolf was coming down, took off the cover, and in fell the wolf; so the little pig put on the cover again in an instant, boiled him up, and ate him for supper, and lived happy ever afterwards.

THE DEATH OF BRER WOLF[1]

Julius Lester

BRER RABBIT HAD TRICKED BRER Wolf and he was four times seven times eleven mad.

One day Brer Rabbit left his house to go to town, and Brer Wolf tore it down and took off one of his children.

Brer Rabbit built a straw house and Brer Wolf tore that down. Then he made one out of pine tops. Brer Wolf tore that one down. He made one out of bark, and that didn't last too much longer than it takes to drink a milk shake. Finally, Brer Rabbit hired some carpenters and built him a house with a stone foundation, two-car garage, and a picture window. After that, he had a little peace and quiet and wasn't scared to leave home and visit his neighbors every now and then.

One afternoon he was at home when he heard a lot of racket outside. Before he could get up to see what was going on, Brer Wolf bust through the front door. "Save me! Save me! Some hunters with dogs are after me. Hide me somewhere so the dogs won't get me."

"Jump in that chest over there," Brer Rabbit said, pointing toward the fireplace.

Brer Wolf jumped in. He figured that when night came, he'd get out and take care of Brer Rabbit once and for all. He was so busy thinking about what he was going to do, he didn't hear what Brer Rabbit did. Brer Rabbit locked the trunk!

Brer Rabbit sat back down in his rocking chair and stuck a big wad of chewing tobacco in his jaw. This here was rabbit-chewing tobacco. From what I hear, it's supposed to be pretty good. So he sat there just rocking, chewing, and spitting.

"Is the dogs gone yet, Brer Rabbit?" Brer Wolf asked after a while.

"No. I think I hear one sniffing around the chimney."

Brer Rabbit got up and filled a great big pot with water and put it on the fire.

Brer Wolf was listening and said, "What you doing, Brer Rabbit?"

"Just fixing to make you a nice cup of elderberry tea."

Brer Rabbit went to his tool chest, got out a drill, and started boring holes in the chest.

"What you doing now, Brer Rabbit?"

"Just making some holes so you can get some air."

Brer Rabbit put some more wood on the fire.

"Now what you doing?"

"Building the fire up so you won't get cold."

---

1 From *The Tales of Uncle Remus: The Adventures of Brer Rabbit* (New York: Dial, 1987).

The water was boiling now. Brer Rabbit took the kettle off the fire and started pouring it on the chest.

"What's that I hear, Brer Rabbit?"

"Just the wind blowing."

The water started splattering through the holes.

"What's that I feel, Brer Rabbit?"

"Must be fleas biting you."

"They biting mighty hard."

"Turn over," suggested Brer Rabbit.

Brer Wolf turned over and Brer Rabbit kept pouring.

"What's that I feel now, Brer Rabbit?"

"Must be more fleas."

"They eating me up, Brer Rabbit." And them was the last words Brer Wolf said, 'cause that scalding water did what it was supposed to.

Next winter all the neighbors admired the nice wolfskin mittens Brer Rabbit and his family had.

FROM TIGER TO ANANSI[1]

Philip M. Sherlock

ONCE UPON A TIME AND a long long time ago the Tiger was king of the forest.

At evening when all the animals sat together in a circle and talked and laughed together, Snake would ask,

"Who is the strongest of us all?"

"Tiger is strongest," cried the dog. "When Tiger whispers the trees listen. When Tiger is angry and cries out, the trees tremble."

"And who is the weakest of all?" asked Snake.

"Anansi," shouted dog, and they all laughed together. "Anansi the spider is weakest of all. When he whispers no one listens. When he shouts everyone laughs."

Now one day the weakest and strongest came face to face, Anansi and Tiger. They met in a clearing of the forest. The frogs hiding under the cool leaves saw them. The bright green parrots in the branches heard them.

When they met, Anansi bowed so low that his forehead touched the ground. Tiger did not greet him. Tiger just looked at Anansi.

---

1   From *Anansi, the Spiderman: Jamaican Folk Tales* (New York: Crowell, 1954).

"Good morning, Tiger," cried Anansi. "I have a favor to ask."

"And what is it, Anansi?" said Tiger.

"Tiger, we all know that you are strongest of us all. This is why we give your name to many things. We have Tiger lilies, and Tiger stories and Tiger moths and Tiger this and Tiger that. Everyone knows that I am weakest of all. This is why nothing bears my name. Tiger, let something be called after the weakest one so that men may know my name too."

"Well," said Tiger, without so much as a glance toward Anansi, "what would you like to bear your name?"

"The stories," cried Anansi. "The stories that we tell in the forest at evening time when the sun goes down, the stories about Br'er Snake and Br'er Tacumah, Br'er Cow and Br'er Bird and all of us."

Now Tiger liked these stories and he meant to keep them as Tiger stories. He thought to himself, How stupid, how weak this Anansi is. I will play a trick on him so that all the animals will laugh at him. Tiger moved his tail slowly from side to side and said, "Very good, Anansi, very good. I will let the stories be named after you, if you do what I ask."

"Tiger, I will do what you ask."

"Yes, I am sure you will, I am sure you will," said Tiger, moving his tail slowly from side to side. "It is a little thing that I ask. Bring me Mr. Snake alive. Do you know Snake who lives down by the river, Mr. Anansi? Bring him to me alive and you can have the stories."

Tiger stopped speaking. He did not move his tail. He looked at Anansi and waited for him to speak. All the animals in the forest waited. Mr. Frog beneath the cool leaves, Mr. Parrot up in the tree, all watched Anansi. They were all ready to laugh at him.

"Tiger, I will do what you ask," said Anansi. With these words a great wave of laughter burst from the forest. The frogs and parrots laughed. Tiger laughed loudest of all, for how could feeble Anansi catch Snake alive?

Anansi went away. He heard the forest laughing at him from every side.

That was on Monday morning. Anansi sat before his house and thought of plan after plan. At last he hit upon one that could not fail. He would build a Calaban.

On Tuesday morning Anansi built a Calaban. He took a strong vine and made a noose. He hid the vine in the grass. Inside the noose he set some of the berries that Snake loved best. Then he waited. Soon Snake came up the path. He saw the berries and went toward them. He lay across the vine and ate the berries. Anansi pulled at the vine to tighten the noose, but Snake's body was too heavy. Anansi saw that the Calaban had failed.

Wednesday came. Anansi made a deep hole in the ground. He made the sides slippery with grease. In the bottom he put some of the bananas that Snake loved. Then he hid in the bush beside the road and waited.

Snake came crawling down the path toward the river. He was hungry and thirsty. He saw the bananas at the bottom of the hole. He saw that the sides of the hole were slippery. First he wrapped his tail tightly around the trunk of a tree, then he reached down into the hole and ate the bananas. When he was finished he pulled himself up by his tail and crawled away. Anansi had lost his bananas and he had lost Snake, too.

Thursday morning came. Anansi made a Fly Up. Inside the trap he put an egg. Snake came down the path. He was happy this morning, so happy that he lifted his head and a third of his long body from the ground. He just lowered his head, took up the egg in his mouth, and never even touched the trap. The Fly Up could not catch Snake.

What was Anansi to do? Friday morning came. He sat and thought all day. It was no use.

Now it was Saturday morning. This was the last day. Anansi went for a walk down by the river. He passed by the hole where Snake lived. There was Snake, his body hidden in the hole, his head resting on the ground at the entrance to the hole. It was early morning. Snake was watching the sun rise above the mountains.

"Good morning, Anansi," said Snake.

"Good morning, Snake," said Anansi.

"Anansi, I am very angry with you. You have been trying to catch me all week. You set a Fly Up to catch me. The day before you made a Slippery Hole for me. The day before that you made a Calaban. I have a good mind to kill you, Anansi."

"Ah, you are too clever, Snake," said Anansi. "You are much too clever. Yes, what you say is so. I tried to catch you, but I failed. Now I can never prove that you are the longest animal in the world, longer even than the bamboo tree."

"Of course I am the longest of all animals," cried Snake. "I am much longer than the bamboo tree."

"What, longer than that bamboo tree across there?" asked Anansi.

"Of course I am," said Snake. "Look and see." Snake came out of the hole and stretched himself out at full length.

"Yes, you are very, very long," said Anansi, "but the bamboo tree is very long, too. Now that I look at you and at the bamboo tree I must say that the bamboo tree seems longer. But it's hard to say because it is farther away."

"Well, bring it nearer," cried Snake. "Cut it down and put it beside me. You will soon see that I am much longer."

Anansi ran to the bamboo tree and cut it down. He placed it on the ground and cut off all its branches. Bush, bush, bush, bush! There it was, long and straight as a flagstaff.

"Now put it beside me," said Snake.

Anansi put the long bamboo tree down on the ground beside Snake. Then he said:

"Snake, when I go up to see where your head is, you will crawl up. When I go down to see where your tail is, you will crawl down. In that way you will always seem to be longer than the bamboo tree, which really is longer than you are."

"Tie my tail, then!" said Snake. "Tie my tail! I know that I am longer than the bamboo, whatever you say."

Anansi tied Snake's tail to the end of the bamboo. Then he ran up to the other end.

"Stretch, Snake, stretch, and we will see who is longer."

A crowd of animals were gathering round. Here was something better than a race. "Stretch, Snake, stretch," they called.

Snake stretched as hard as he could. Anansi tied him around his middle so that he should not slip back. Now one more try. Snake knew that if he stretched hard enough he would prove to be longer than the bamboo.

Anansi ran up to him. "Rest yourself for a little, Snake, and then stretch again. If you can stretch another six inches you will be longer than the bamboo. Try your hardest. Stretch so that you even have to shut your eyes. Ready?"

"Yes," said Snake. Then Snake made a mighty effort. He stretched so hard that he had to squeeze his eyes shut. "Hooray!" cried the animals. "You are winning, Snake. Just two inches more."

And at that moment Anansi tied Snake's head to the bamboo. There he was. At last he had caught Snake, all by himself.

The animals fell silent. Yes, there Snake was, all tied up, ready to be taken to Tiger. And feeble Anansi had done this. They could laugh at him no more.

And never again did Tiger dare to call these stories by his name. They were Anansi stories forever after, from that day to this.

VILLAINS

In the previous section we encountered a good deal of mischief, which is of course the stock-in-trade of the trickster; generally speaking, the victim suffers little more than embarrassment or a lighter wallet, although it must be acknowledged that some trickster figures show a ruthlessness and amorality that ally them with the darker pathologies in this section.

There is no shortage of villains in the fairy tale, since the black-and-white simplicity of its dramatic structure produces the clearest of distinctions between protagonist and antagonist. We will not find in the fairy tale the kind of psychological analysis typical of the modern omniscient narrator, but once we remind ourselves how concrete the tale often is, we can easily perceive that in many cases the inner self is expressed through action or visual images. In other words, we are very rarely told what a character is thinking, and such editorial comment as Charles Perrault is prone to offer must be seen as extraneous to the tale proper. At the simplest level, then, goodness is equated with beauty and wickedness with ugliness. As we have already observed, however, the equation is often more complex, as in the instance of Snow White's stepmother, whose beauty is all the more disturbing because it is diametrically opposed to her wickedness. Although this externalization reflects a simplistic brand of logic, the tales in this section illustrate very effectively how much subtlety and insight can be conveyed through the use of this "simple" convention.

Practically all the villains that we have met to this point have been female, which raises an interesting question: in a patriarchal society, why is it that the older female is so often depicted not only as malevolent but also as strong and ruthless—qualities that have traditionally been identified with the masculine stereotype? Is this in fact part of the answer: that qualities deemed acceptable, perhaps even desirable, in a male can only be an aberration in a woman? Does the frequent occurrence of the witch in Western fairy tale represent a tacit acknowledgment of a power that has been corrupted by repression and denial? It is reasonable to observe that such women often have a motive for their behavior: Snow White's stepmother fears sexual rivalry, the wicked old fairy in "Sleeping Beauty" resents being passed over, and the witch in "Rapunzel" is just pathologically possessive.

The stepmother's motivation in "The Juniper Tree" is somewhat reminiscent of that of her counterpart in "Cinderella," although the latter's misdeeds pale by comparison.[1] There is no escaping the fact that abuse of (step)children is a recurrent theme in fairy tales: disturbing evidence of a phenomenon with deep roots. The horror at the heart of this tale is intensified by the mesmerizing crescendo of the narrative, as the boy-phoenix goes about exacting a ritual revenge for his stepmother's crime.

It is perhaps not coincidental that the two tales about male villains make them central characters, if only in the sense that their influence (rather than presence) dominates the story. In both cases they eventually get their comeuppance, although not without leaving behind a certain moral murkiness that characterizes these tales and gives them a distinctly modern "feel." That is particularly true of Perrault's "Bluebeard," in part because the central character is a wealthy businessman (not a common fairy-tale profession!) and also because the theme of this tale strikes as raw a nerve today as it ever may have done in the past, constantly reminded as we are of the primitive forces of psychopathic rage. Consequently, this tale has a realism that sets it apart from other tales (including those in this section). Some regard it as having a historical origin, which suggests that the basis of a fairy tale is to be found in the combustible mixture of reality and imagination. Indeed, our ongoing fascination with the mysteries of the aberrant mind is well documented; from Jack the Ripper to Adolf Hitler, from Lady Macbeth to Hannibal Lecter, we find it difficult to avert our eyes from those who would lead us into the moral abyss.

In its dramatic inevitability, "Bluebeard" may usefully be compared to "Little Red Riding Hood": in each tale the central female character falls victim to a rapacious male, and in each there is the same chilling sense of doom as the trap is sprung. One way in which the tales differ, however, is in the level of symbolism: unlike the "human" wolf, Bluebeard appears to be a normal person in every respect except the color of his beard. The story hinges on our readiness to rationalize away what we would prefer not to see, even when the evidence is, so to speak, staring us in the face: "Everything went so well that the youngest daughter began to think that the beard of the master of the house was not so very blue, after all" (p. 204).

---

1   While Cinderella's stepmother is driven by the desire to advance the fortunes of her own daughters, the motivation in "The Juniper Tree" is less apparent, although the references to flame and fire at the climax of the story are surely indicative of the mother's demonic possession (i.e., madness).

Rumpelstiltskin also seems to have his "human" side, despite clearly being of nether-worldly (and thus wicked) origin. We must resist the temptation to interpret his sympathy for the Queen's predicament as evidence of a heart of gold; his name (his English counterpart is called "Spindleshanks") is as clear an indicator as Bluebeard's beard that he is truly a villain. His generosity must be seen in the light of its deceitful and exploitative motive; his "guess-my-name" offer to the Queen is based on the conviction that he is setting her an impossible task.

The ambivalent feelings that both these tales provoke in us suggest that our identification with the characters is more complex than is customary in the fairy tale. In each instance, our sympathies are drawn in different directions at different points in the story. Few of us can, in all honesty, deny the attractiveness of the riches with which Bluebeard seduces his young wife (proof positive of his dastardly scheme) and the irresistibility of the desire to know what lies behind that closet door—she surely acts for us all in opening it. Yet once she has done so, she bears the guilt alone, and we have the luxury of watching in horrified fascination as her disobedience is discovered. Similarly, we can identify with the Queen's acceptance of the bargain offered to her by Rumpelstiltskin since she is left with no alternative; but when the time comes to face the consequences, we again assume the voyeuristic role, torn as we are (an appropriate turn of phrase, considering the story's ending) between the natural desire of the Queen to keep her baby and Rumpelstiltskin's apparent benevolence in granting her another chance.

One other aspect that these two tales have in common is their lack of any "heroic" character; neither Bluebeard's wife nor the Queen in "Rumpelstiltskin" is a very prepossessing figure. The Queen is perhaps more of a victim than the wife, who, the tale implies, is at least partly to blame for her predicament; however, it can be argued how much either character has earned her happy ending. Be that as it may, justice demands that the villains be punished and their victims compensated for the suffering to which they have been subjected. One hopes that their experiences result in a new maturity, although evidence of that can only be seen in Bluebeard's wife, whose generosity toward her family and marriage to a worthy gentleman bespeak a very different frame of mind from that in which she entered her first marriage!

THE JUNIPER TREE[1]

Jacob and Wilhelm Grimm

A LONG TIME AGO, AT LEAST two thousand years, there was a rich man who had a good and beautiful wife, and they loved each other dearly, but much as they longed for children, they had none. Day and night the woman prayed, but no children came. Outside the house there was a garden, and in the garden there was a juniper tree. One winter's day the wife stood under the tree, peeling herself an apple, and as she was peeling the apple she cut her finger and her blood fell on the snow. She looked at the blood and it made her very sad. "Ah!" she sighed. "Ah! If only I had a child as red as blood and as white as snow." When she had said that, she was happy; she had a feeling that something would come of it. Then she went back into the house. A month went by and the snow with it; two months, and the world was green; three months and flowers came out of the ground; four months and the trees of the forest pressed together and the green branches mingled; the woods resounded with the singing of birds and the blossoms fell from the trees. The fifth month passed and she stood under the juniper tree. It smelled so sweet that her heart leaped for joy, and she was so happy she fell down on her knees. When the sixth month had passed, the fruit was big and firm, and she became very still. After the seventh month she snatched at the juniper berries and ate so greedily that she grew sad and sickened. When the eighth month had passed, she called her husband and wept and said: "If I die, bury me under the juniper tree." With that she took comfort and she was happy until the next month had passed. Then she bore a child as white as snow and as red as blood, and when she saw the child she was so happy that she died.

Her husband buried her under the juniper tree and he wept and wept. After a while he felt a little better. Though he still wept now and then, he could bear it, and after another while he took a second wife.

By this second wife he had a daughter, Marleenken. The first wife's child was a little boy, and he was as red as blood and as white as snow. When the woman looked at her daughter, she loved her dearly, but when she looked at the little boy she was sick at heart. It seemed to her that he would always be a thorn in her side, and she kept wondering how she might get the whole fortune for her daughter. The Devil got into her and drove her to hate the little boy and slap him and pinch him and make him stand in the corner. The poor child lived in terror and when he came home from school, there wasn't a quiet nook he could call his own.

---

[1] First published in 1812/15, in the first edition of *Kinder- und Hausmärchen*. This text from the second edition (1819), from *Grimms' Tales for Young and Old*, trans. Ralph Manheim (Garden City, NY: Anchor P, 1977).

One day the woman went up to the pantry. Her little daughter came in and said: "Mother, give me an apple." "Yes, my child," said the woman, and gave her a fine apple out of the chest. Now this chest had a big heavy lid with a big sharp iron lock. "Mother," said the little daughter, "won't you give my brother one too?" That vexed the woman, but she said: "Oh yes, as soon as he gets home from school." When she looked out of the window and saw he was coming, it was as if the Devil had got into her. She snatched the apple away from her daughter and said: "You shan't have one before your brother." Then she threw the apple into the chest and shut the lid. When the little boy came in, the Devil drove her to say as sweetly as could be: "Would you care for an apple, my son?" But her eyes were full of hate. "Mother," said the little boy, "how grisly you look! Yes, give me an apple." Something made her feel she had to press him. "Come with me," she said, and then she raised the lid. "Now pick out a nice apple." When the little boy bent down, the Devil prompted her and bam! she brought the lid down so hard that his head came off and fell in with the red apples. She was overcome with fear and she thought: "If only I could turn away the blame!" She went up to her room and took a white cloth from her drawer. She put the head back on the neck, tied the cloth around it so that nothing could be seen, sat him down in a chair in front of the door, and put an apple in his hand.

Later on Marleenken went to the kitchen. Her mother was standing by the fire, stirring a pot of hot water round and round. "Mother," said Marleenken, "my brother is sitting by the door. He's as white as a sheet and he's holding an apple. I asked him to give me the apple but he didn't answer. It was scary." "Go back," said her mother, "and if he doesn't answer, slap him in the face." So Marleenken went back and said: "Brother, give me the apple." But he didn't say a word, so she slapped him in the face and his head fell off. She was so frightened she began to scream and cry. She ran to her mother and said: "Oh, mother, I've knocked my brother's head off," and she wept and wept and couldn't be comforted. "Marleenken," said her mother, "what a dreadful thing to have done! But don't breathe a word, we won't tell a soul, it can't be undone now. We'll cook him up into stew." The mother took the little boy and chopped him up and put the pieces into the pot and cooked him up into a stew. Marleenken stood there and wept and wept. Her tears fell into the pot and there was no need of salt.

When the father came home, he sat down to table and said: "Where is my son?" The mother served up a big bowl of stew, and Marleenken wept and couldn't stop. The father asked again: "Where is my son?" "Oh," said the mother, "he's gone away to visit his mother's great-uncle; he'll be gone for a little while." "What will he do there? Why, he didn't even say good-bye to me." "Well, he wanted to go, and he asked me if he could stay six weeks. He'll be well taken care of." "It makes me very sad," said the man. "It's not right what he's done, he should have said good-bye to me." Then he began to eat and said: "Marleenken, why are you crying? Your brother will be back soon." And then he said: "Oh, wife, this stew is so good! Give me some more." The more he ate, the more he wanted. "Give me more," he said. "You shan't have any. I have a feeling it all belongs to me." He ate and ate until he had eaten it all up, and he threw all the bones under the table. Marleenken went to her room and got her best silk kerchief. She picked up all the bones from under the table, tied them in the silk kerchief, and took them outside. Weeping bitterly, she put them down in the green grass under the juniper tree. When she had put them down she suddenly felt light at heart and stopped crying. Then the juniper tree moved; its branches parted and came together as though it were clapping its hands for joy. A mist went up from the tree, in the middle of the mist there was a flame, and out of the flame rose a beautiful bird that sang gloriously and flew high into the air. When it was gone, the juniper tree became as it was before, but the kerchief with the bones was gone. And Marleenken felt as light and gay as if her brother were still alive. She went merrily back to the table and ate.

Meanwhile the bird flew off and lighted on the roof of a goldsmith's house and sang:

"My mother killed me,
My father ate me,
My sister Marleenken
Gathered up my bones,
Tied them in a silken kerchief,
And put them under the juniper tree.
Keewitt, keewitt, what a fine bird am I!"

The goldsmith was sitting in his workshop, making a gold chain. He heard the bird singing on his roof and thought: Isn't that beautiful! He stood up and as he was stepping over the threshold one of his slippers fell off. But he went right out into the middle of the street with only one slipper on. He was wearing his apron; in one hand he was holding the gold chain, in the other his pincers, and the sun was shining brightly on the street. He stopped still and looked up at the bird and said: "Bird, you're a wonderful singer! Sing me that song again." "No," said the bird. "I don't sing twice for nothing. Give me that gold chain and I'll sing it again." "Here," said the goldsmith. "Here's the gold chain. Now sing it again." The bird came flying down. Taking the gold chain in his right claw, he settled in front of the goldsmith and sang:

"My mother killed me,
My father ate me,

My sister Marleenken
Gathered up my bones,
Tied them in a silken kerchief,
And put them under the juniper tree.
Keewitt, keewitt, what a fine bird am I!"

Then the bird flew off to a shoemaker's house, lighted on the roof and sang:

"My mother killed me,
My father ate me,
My sister Marleenken
Gathered up my bones,
Tied them in a silken kerchief,
And put them under the juniper tree.
Keewitt, keewitt, what a fine bird am I!"

When the shoemaker heard the song, he ran out in front of his house in his shirt-sleeves and looked up at his roof. He had to shade his eyes with his hand to keep the sun from blinding him. "Bird," he said, "you're a wonderful singer!" And he called in through the door: "Wife! Come out here a minute, there's a bird up there. See him? He's a wonderful singer!" Then he called his daughter and his other children and his apprentices, and his hired man and his maid, and they all came out into the street and looked at the bird, and saw how beautiful he was: he had red and green feathers and a ring like pure gold around his neck, and the eyes in his head glistened like stars. "Bird," said the shoemaker, "sing me that song again." "No," said the bird. "I don't sing twice for nothing. You must give me something." "Wife," said the shoemaker, "go up to the attic. On the top shelf you'll find a pair of red shoes. Bring them down." The woman went and brought the shoes. "There you are, bird," said the man. "Now sing the song again." The bird flew down, took the shoes in his left claw, flew back on the roof, and sang:

"My mother killed me,
My father ate me,
My sister Marleenken
Gathered up my bones,
Tied them in a silken kerchief,
And put them under the juniper tree.
Keewitt, keewitt, what a fine bird am I!"

When he had finished singing he flew away. He had the chain in his right claw and the shoes in his left claw, and he flew far away to a mill, and the mill was turning, clippety clap, clippety clap, clippety clap. And inside the mill sat twenty miller's men, hewing a stone, hick hack hick hack hick hack, and the mill went clippety clap, clippety clap, clippety clap. The bird lighted on a lime tree outside the mill and sang:

"My mother killed me"—

and one stopped working,

"My father ate me"—

and two more stopped working and listened,

"My sister Marleenken"—

and four stopped,

"Gathered up my bones,
Tied them in a silken kerchief"—

and only eight were still hewing,

"And put them under"—

only five

"the juniper tree"—

and only one.

"Keewitt, keewitt, what a fine bird am I!"

The last stopped just in time to hear the end. "Bird," he said, "you're a wonderful singer. I want to hear that too. Sing it again for me." "No," said the bird. "I don't sing twice for nothing. Give me the millstone and I'll sing it again." "If it were only mine," said the miller's man, "I wouldn't hesitate." "It's all right," said the others, "if he sings again he can have it." The bird flew down and the millers, all twenty of them, set to work with a beam and hoisted the stone, heave-ho, heave-ho, heave-ho. The bird stuck his head through the hole and, wearing the stone like a collar, flew back to the tree and sang:

"My mother killed me,
  My father ate me,
  My sister Marleenken
  Gathered up my bones,
  Tied them in a silken kerchief,
  And put them under the juniper tree.
  Keewitt, keewitt, what a fine bird am I!"

When he had finished his song, he spread his wings, and in his right claw he had the chain and in his left claw he had the shoes, and round his neck he had the millstone, and he flew far away to his father's house.

His father and mother and Marleenken were sitting at the table, and the father said: "I suddenly feel so lighthearted, so happy." "I don't," said the mother. "I feel frightened, as if a big storm were coming on." As for Marleenken, she sat there weeping. The bird came flying, and as he lighted on the roof the father said: "Oh, I'm so happy, the sun's shining so bright outside, and I feel as if I were going to see an old friend again." "I don't," said the woman. "I'm so afraid, my teeth are chattering and it's as if I had fire in my veins." And she tore open her bodice. Marleenken sat in her corner and wept. She held her apron up to her eyes and she wept till the apron was sopping wet. Then the bird lighted on the juniper tree and sang:

"My mother killed me"—

At that the mother stopped her ears and closed her eyes; she wanted neither to see nor to hear, but the roaring in her ears was like the loudest storm, and her eyes burned and flashed like lightning.

"My father ate me"—

"Oh, mother," said the man, "there's a beautiful bird out there. He's singing so gloriously, and the sunshine is so warm, the air smells like cinnamon."

"My sister Marleenken"—

Marleenken buried her head in her lap and wept and wept. But the man said: "I'm going out. I've got to see that bird close to." "Oh, don't go," said his wife. "I feel as if the whole house were quaking and going up in flames." But the man went out and looked at the bird.

> "Gathered up my bones,
>   Tied them in a silken kerchief,
>   And put them under the juniper tree.
>   Keewitt, keewitt, what a fine bird am I!"

With that the bird dropped the gold chain, and it fell right around the man's neck and fitted perfectly. He went inside and said: "See what a fine bird that is. He gave me this splendid gold chain, and he's so beautiful." But his wife was so terrified she fell flat on the floor and her cap fell off her head. And the bird sang again:

> "My mother killed me"—

"Oh, if only I were a thousand feet under the ground and couldn't hear it!"

> "My father ate me"—

And again the woman fell down as though dead.

> "My sister Marleenken"—

"I think I'll go out too," said Marleenken, "and see if the bird will give me something." And out she went.

> "Gathered up my bones,
>   Tied them up in a silken kerchief"—

Here he threw down the shoes.

> "And put them under the juniper tree.
>   Keewitt, keewitt, what a fine bird am I!"

All at once she felt light and gay. She put on the new red shoes and danced and bounded into the house. "Oh," she said, "I was so sad when I went out, and now my heart is so light. What a wonderful bird! He gave me a pair of red shoes." The woman jumped to her feet and her hair shot up like tongues of flame. "I feel as if the world were coming to an end. Maybe I'll feel better if I go outside too." As she stepped out of the door, bam! the bird dropped the millstone on her head and squashed it. The father and Marleenken heard the noise and went out. Steam and fire and flame were rising up, and when they were gone little brother was standing there. He took his father and Marleenken by the hand, and they were all very happy, and they went into the house and sat down at the table and ate.

BLUEBEARD[1]

Charles Perrault

THERE ONCE LIVED A MAN who owned fine town houses and fine country houses, dinner services of gold and silver, tapestry chairs and gilded coaches; but, alas, God had also given him a blue beard, which made him look so ghastly that women fled at the sight of him.

A certain neighbor of his was the mother of two beautiful daughters. He decided to marry one or other of them, but he left the girls to decide between themselves which of them should become his wife; whoever would take him could have him. But neither of them wanted him; both felt a profound distaste for a man with a blue beard. They were even more suspicious of him because he had been married several times before and nobody knew what had become of his wives.

In order to make friends with the girls, Bluebeard threw a lavish house-party at one of his country mansions for the sisters, their mother, three or four of their closest friends and several neighbors. The party lasted for eight whole days. Every day there were elaborate parties of pleasure—fishing, hunting, dancing, games, feasting. The guests hardly slept at all but spent the night playing practical jokes on one another. Everything went so well that the youngest daughter began to think that the beard of the master of the house was not so very blue, after all; that he was, all in all, a very fine fellow.

As soon as they returned to town, the marriage took place.

After a month had passed, Bluebeard told his wife he must leave her to her own devices for six weeks or so; he had urgent business in the provinces and must attend to it immediately. But he urged her to enjoy herself while he was away; her friends should visit her and, if she wished, she could take them to the country with her. But, above all, she must keep in good spirits.

---

1   First published in 1697. This text from *Sleeping Beauty and Other Favourite Fairy Tales*, trans. Angela Carter (London: Gollancz, 1982).

"Look!" he said to her. "Here are the keys of my two large attics, where the furniture is stored; this is the key to the cabinet in which I keep the dinner services of gold and silver that are too good to use every day; these are the keys of the strong-boxes in which I keep my money; these are the keys of my chests of precious stones; and this is the pass key that will let you into every one of the rooms in my mansion. Use these keys freely. All is yours. But this little key, here, is the key of the room at the end of the long gallery on the ground floor; open everything, go everywhere, but I absolutely forbid you to go into that little room and, if you so much as open the door, I warn you that nothing will spare you from my wrath."

She promised to do as he told her. He kissed her, got into his carriage and drove away.

Her friends and neighbors did not wait until she sent for them to visit her. They were all eager to see the splendors of her house. None of them had dared to call while the master was at home because his blue beard was so offensive. But now they could explore all the rooms at leisure and each one was more sumptuous than the last. They climbed into the attics and were lost for words with which to admire the number and beauty of the tapestries, the beds, the sofas, the cabinets, the tables, and the long mirrors, some of which had frames of glass, others of silver or gilded vermilion—all more magnificent than anything they had ever seen. They never stopped congratulating their friend on her good luck, but she took no pleasure from the sight of all this luxury because she was utterly consumed with the desire to open the door of the forbidden room.

Her curiosity so tormented her that, at last, without stopping to think how rude it was to leave her friends, she ran down the little staircase so fast she almost tripped and broke her neck. When she reached the door of the forbidden room, she stopped for a moment and remembered that her husband had absolutely forbidden her to go inside. She wondered if he would punish her for being disobedient; but the temptation was so strong she could not resist it. She took the little key, and, trembling, opened the door.

The windows were shuttered and at first she could see nothing; but, after a few moments, her eyes grew accustomed to the gloom and she saw that the floor was covered with clotted blood. In the blood lay the corpses of all the women whom Bluebeard had married and then murdered, one after the other. She thought she was going to die of fright and the key fell from her hand. After she came to her senses, she picked up the key, closed the door and climbed back to her room to recover herself.

She saw the key of this forbidden room was stained with blood and washed it. But the blood would not go away, so she washed it again. Still the bloodstain stayed. She washed it, yet again, more carefully, then scrubbed it with soap and sandstone; but the bloodstain would not budge. It was a magic key and nothing could clean it.

When the blood was scrubbed from one side of the key, the stain immediately reappeared on the other side.

That same night, Bluebeard returned unexpectedly from his journey; a letter had arrived on the way to tell him that his business had already been satisfactorily settled in his absence. His wife did all she could to show him how delighted she was to have him back with her so quickly.

Next day, he asked her for his keys; she gave them to him but her hand was trembling so badly he guessed what had happened.

"How is it that the key of the little room is no longer with the others?" he asked.

"I must have left it upstairs on my dressing-table," she said, flustered.

"Give it to me," said Bluebeard.

She made excuse after excuse but there was no way out; she must go and fetch the key. Bluebeard examined it carefully and said to his wife:

"Why is there blood on this key?"

"I don't know," quavered the poor woman, paler than death.

"You don't know!" said Bluebeard. "But *I* know, very well! You have opened the door of the forbidden room. Well, madame, now you have opened it, you may step straight inside it and take your place beside the ladies whom you have seen there!"

She threw herself at her husband's feet, weeping and begging his forgiveness; she was truly sorry she had been disobedient. She was so beautiful and so distressed that the sight of her would have melted a heart of stone, but Bluebeard's heart was harder than any stone.

"You must die, madame," he said. "And you must die quickly."

She looked at him with eyes full of tears and pleaded:

"Since I must die, give me a little time to pray."

Bluebeard said: "I'll give you a quarter of an hour, but not one moment more."

As soon as she was alone, she called to her sister, Anne, and said:

"Sister Anne, climb to the top of the tower and see if my brothers are coming; they told me they would come to visit me today and if you see them, signal to them to hurry."

Sister Anne climbed to the top of the tower and the poor girl called out to her every minute or so:

"Sister Anne, Sister Anne, do you see anybody coming?"

And Anne, her sister, would reply:

"I see nothing but the sun shining and the grass growing green."

Bluebeard took an enormous cutlass in his hand and shouted to his wife: "Come down at once, or I'll climb up to you!"

"Oh, please, I beg you—just a moment more!" she implored, and called out, in a lower voice: "Sister Anne, Sister Anne, do you see anybody coming?"

Sister Anne replied:

"I see nothing but the sun shining and the grass growing green."

"Come down at once, or I'll climb up to you!" cried Bluebeard.

"I'll be down directly," his wife assured him; but still she whispered: "Sister Anne, Sister Anne, do you see anything coming?"

"I see a great cloud of dust drawing near from the edge of the horizon."

"Is it the dust my brothers make as they ride towards me?"

"Oh, no—it is the dust raised by a flock of sheep!"

"Will you never come down?" thundered Bluebeard.

"Just one moment more!" begged his wife and once again she demanded: "Sister Anne, Sister Anne, do you see anything coming?"

"I see two horsemen in the distance, still far away. Thank God!" she cried a moment later. "They are our brothers; I shall signal to them to hurry."

Bluebeard now shouted so loudly that all the house trembled. His unfortunate wife went down to him and threw herself in tears at his feet, her dishevelled hair tumbling all around her.

"Nothing you can do will save you," said Bluebeard. "You must die." With one hand, he seized her disordered hair and, with the other, raised his cutlass in the air; he meant to chop off her head with it. The poor woman turned her terrified eyes upon him and begged him for a last moment in which to prepare for death.

"No, no!" he said. "Think of your maker." And so he lifted up his cutlass. At that moment came such a loud banging on the door that Bluebeard stopped short. The door opened and in rushed two horsemen with naked blades in their hands.

He recognised his wife's two brothers; one was a dragoon, the other a musketeer. He fled, to save himself, but the two brothers trapped him before he reached the staircase. They thrust their swords through him and left him for dead. Bluebeard's wife was almost as overcome as her husband and did not have enough strength left to get to her feet and kiss her brothers.

Bluebeard left no heirs, so his wife took possession of all his estate. She used part of it to marry her sister Anne to a young man with whom she had been in love for a long time; she used more of it to buy commissions[1] for her two brothers; and she used the rest to marry herself to an honest man who made her forget her sorrows as the wife of Bluebeard.

Moral

Curiosity is a charming passion but may only be satisfied at the price of a thousand regrets; one sees around one a thousand examples of this sad truth every day.

---

1   It was an accepted practice to purchase the rank of officer.

Curiosity is the most fleeting of pleasures; the moment it is satisfied, it ceases to exist and it always proves very, very expensive.

Another Moral
It is easy to see that the events described in this story took place many years ago. No modern husband would dare to be half so terrible, nor to demand of his wife such an impossible thing as to stifle her curiosity. Be he never so quarrelsome or jealous, he'll toe the line as soon as she tells him to. And whatever color his beard might be, it's easy to see which of the two is the master.

RUMPELSTILTSKIN[1]

Jacob and Wilhelm Grimm

ONCE THERE WAS A MILLER who was poor but had a beautiful daughter. One day he happened to be talking with the king, and wanting to impress him he said: "I've got a daughter who can spin straw into gold." The king said to the miller: "That's just the kind of talent that appeals to me. If your daughter is as clever as you say, bring her to my palace tomorrow and I'll see what she can do." When the girl arrived, he took her to a room that was full of straw, gave her a spinning wheel, and said: "Now get to work. You have the whole night ahead of you, but if you haven't spun this straw into gold by tomorrow morning, you will die." Then he locked the room with his own hands and she was left all alone.

The poor miller's daughter sat there, and for the life of her she didn't know what to do. She hadn't the faintest idea how to spin straw into gold, and she was so frightened that in the end she began to cry. Then suddenly the door opened and in stepped a little man. "Good evening, Mistress Miller," he said. "Why are you crying so?" "Oh," she said. "I'm supposed to spin straw into gold, and I don't know how." The little man asked: "What will you give me if I spin it for you?" "My necklace," said the girl. The little man took the necklace, sat down at the spinning wheel, and whirr, whirr, whirr, three turns, and the spool was full. Then he put on another, and whirr, whirr, whirr, three turns, and the second spool was full. All night he spun, and by sun-up all the straw was spun and the spools were full of gold.

First thing in the morning, the king stepped in. He was amazed and delighted

---

1   First published in 1812/15, in the first edition of *Kinder- und Hausmärchen*. This text from the second edition (1819), from *Grimms' Tales for Young and Old*, trans. Ralph Manheim (Garden City, NY: Anchor P, 1977).

when he saw the gold, but the greed for gold grew in his heart. He had the miller's daughter taken to a larger room full of straw and told her to spin this too into gold if she valued her life. She had no idea what to do and she was crying when the door opened. Again the little man appeared and said: "What will you give me if I spin this straw into gold for you?" "The ring off my finger." The little man took the ring and started the wheel whirring again, and by morning he had spun all the straw into glittering gold. The king was overjoyed at the sight, but his appetite for gold wasn't satisfied yet. He had the miller's daughter taken into a still larger room full of straw and said: "You'll have to spin this into gold tonight, but if you succeed, you shall be my wife." "I know she's only a miller's daughter," he said to himself, "but I'll never find a richer woman anywhere."

When the girl was alone, the little man came for the third time and said: "What will you give me if I spin the straw into gold for you this time?" "I have nothing more to give you," said the girl. "Then promise to give me your first child if you get to be queen." "Who knows what the future will bring?" thought the miller's daughter. Besides, she had no choice. She gave the required promise, and again the little man spun the straw into gold. When the king arrived in the morning and found everything as he had wished, he married her, and the beautiful miller's daughter became a queen.

A year later she brought a beautiful child into the world. She had forgotten all about the little man. Suddenly he stepped into her room and said: "Now give me what you promised." The queen was horrified; she promised him all the riches in the kingdom if only he let her keep her child, but the little man said: "No. I'd sooner have a living thing than all the treasures in the world." Then the queen began to weep and wail so heart-rendingly that the little man took pity on her: "I'll give you three days' time," he said. "If by then you know my name, you can keep your child."

The queen racked her brains all night; she went over all the names she had ever heard, and she sent out a messenger to inquire all over the country what other names there might be. When the little man came next day, she started with Caspar, Melchior, and Balthazar, and reeled off all the names she knew, but at each one the little man said: "That is not my name." The second day she sent servants around the district to ask about names, and she tried the strangest and most unusual of them on the little man: "Could your name be Ribcage or Muttonchop or Lacelegs?" But each time he replied: "That is not my name."

The third day the messenger returned and said: "I haven't discovered a single new name, but as I was walking along the edge of the forest, I rounded a bend and found myself at the foot of a high hill, the kind of place where fox and hare bid each other good night. There I saw a hut, and outside the hut a fire was burning, and a ridiculous little man was dancing around the fire and hopping on one foot and bellowing:

'Brew today, tomorrow bake,
 After that the child I'll take,
 And sad the queen will be to lose it.
 Rumpelstiltskin is my name
 But luckily nobody knows it.'

You can imagine how happy the queen was to hear that name. It wasn't long before the little man turned up and asked her: "Well, Your Majesty, what's my name?" She started by asking: "Is it Tom?" "No." "Is it Dick?" "No." "Is it Harry?" "No."

 "Could it be Rumpelstiltskin?"

 "The Devil told you that! The Devil told you that!" the little man screamed, and in his rage he stamped his right foot so hard that it went into the ground up to his waist. Then in his fury he took his left foot in both hands and tore himself in two.

THE "CAULDRON OF STORY"

ONE OF THE MOST IMPORTANT criteria by which we judge modern literature is its originality; however remarkable it may be in other respects, if it can be shown to be too similar to somebody else's work, it is rejected as plagiarism. In the case of the traditional fairy tale, that notion of single ownership is reversed; how can a tale that has been passed on from teller to teller, generation to generation, belong to a single individual? Matters get a little more complicated, to be sure, when that tale is written down, because then issues of ownership and copyright do arise—but that doesn't alter the fundamental fact that borrowing plays a vital role in the world of the oral tale; it is as collective a project as the literary work is personal.

In his pioneering essay "On Fairy-Stories" (1938), J.R.R. Tolkien coined the phrase the "cauldron of story" to describe the stock (!) of material, whole or fragmentary, that has been accumulating ever since human beings first discovered the need to tell stories.[1] We might expand Tolkien's image a little by suggesting that along with the "universal" cauldron that contains all the stories ever told, there is the "personal" cauldron, large or small, that belongs to each storyteller and from which he or she draws the story or combination of story-segments from which a new story is being created. As we grow more familiar with the characteristic structure and ingredients of the fairy tale, we realize that predictability and interchangeability are fundamental to its nature—qualities that enhance the teller's ability to combine the parts of the tale in a way no-one has done before.

The tales in this section illustrate how this principle works in practice. The fact that these "hybrid" tales are to be found in early and disparate collections of fairy tales indicates how much of an accepted practice this has been in the evolution of fairy tale—and how much older and well-known some of the "fragments" must be,

---

1   An Irish storyteller friend of ours expressed this principle of public ownership very succinctly: "You keep the tales by giving them away...."

to find their way into the work of Straparola and Basile. One might compare the experience of reading them to that of listening to a jazz musician improvising on his tune; he shows his skill by weaving in snatches of other tunes, while the audience plays its part by recognizing the allusions. Surely that was—and is—part of the fun of a good storytelling session!

THE NEAPOLITAN SOLDIER[1]

Italo Calvino

THREE SOLDIERS HAD DESERTED THEIR regiment and taken to the open road. One was a Roman, one a Florentine, while the smallest was a Neapolitan. After traveling far and wide, they were overtaken by darkness in a forest. The Roman, who was the oldest of the three, said, "Boys, this is no time for us all three to go to sleep. We must take turns keeping watch an hour at a time."

He volunteered for the first watch, and the other two threw down their knapsacks, unrolled their blankets, and went fast asleep. The watch was almost up, when out of the forest rushed a giant.

"What are you doing here?" he asked the soldier.

"None of your business," replied the soldier, without even bothering to turn around.

The giant lunged at him, but the soldier proved the swifter of the two by drawing his sword and cutting off the giant's head. Then he picked up the head with one hand and the body with the other and threw them into a nearby well. He carefully cleaned his sword, resheathed it, and called his companion who was supposed to keep the next watch. Before awakening him, though, he thought, I'd better say nothing about the giant, or this Florentine will take fright and flee. So when the Florentine was awake and asking, "Did you see anything?" the Roman replied, "Nothing at all, everything was as calm as could be." Then he went to sleep.

The Florentine began his watch, and when it was just about up, here came another giant exactly like the first, who asked, "What are you doing here?"

"That's no business of yours or anybody else's," answered the Florentine.

The giant sprang at him, but in a flash the soldier drew his sword and lopped off his head, which he picked up along with the body and threw into the well. His watch was up, and he thought, I'd better say nothing of this to the lily-livered Neapolitan.

---

1   From *Italian Folktales*, retold by Italo Calvino, trans. George Martin (New York: Pantheon, 1980).

THE "CAULDRON OF STORY"

If he knew that things like this went on around here, he'd take to his heels and we'd never see him again.

So, when the Neapolitan asked, "Did you see any action?" the Florentine replied, "None at all, you've nothing to worry about." Then he went to sleep.

The Neapolitan watched for almost an hour, and the forest was perfectly still. Suddenly the leaves rustled and out ran a giant. "What are you doing here?"

"What business is it of yours?" replied the Neapolitan.

The giant held up a hand that would have squashed the Neapolitan flatter than a pancake, had he not dodged it, brandished his sword, and swept off the giant's head, after which he threw the remains into the well.

It was the Roman's turn once more to keep watch, but the Neapolitan thought, I first want to see where the giant came from. He therefore plunged into the forest, spied a light, hastened toward it, and came to a cottage. Peeping through the keyhole, he saw three old women in conversation before the fireplace.

"It's already past midnight, and our husbands are not yet back," said one.

"Do you suppose something has happened to them?" asked another. "It might not be a bad idea," said the third, "to go after them. What do you say?"

"Let's go right now," said the first. "I'll carry the lantern that enables you to see a hundred miles ahead."

"And I'll bring the sword," said the second, "which in every sweep wipes out an army."

"And I'll bring the shotgun that can kill the she-wolf at the king's palace," said the third.

"Let's be on our way." At that, they threw open the door.

Hiding behind the doorpost with sword in hand, the Neapolitan was all ready for them. Out came the first woman holding the lantern, and swish! her head flew off before she could say a single "Amen." Out came the second, and swish! her soul sped to kingdom come. Out came the third and went the way of her sisters.

The soldier now had the witches' lantern, sword, and shotgun and decided to try them out immediately. "We'll just see if those three dotards were telling the truth." He raised the lantern and saw an army a hundred miles away besieging a castle, and chained on the balcony was a she-wolf with flaming eyes. "Let's just see how the sword works." He picked it up and swung it around, then raised the lantern once more and peered into space: every last warrior lay lifeless on the ground beside his splintered lance and dead horse. Then the Neapolitan picked up the gun and shot the she-wolf.

"Now I'll go and see everything from close up," he said.

He walked and walked and finally reached the castle. His knocks and calls all went unanswered. He went inside and walked through all the rooms, but saw no one until he came to the most beautiful chamber of all, where a lovely maiden sat sleeping in a plush armchair.

The soldier went up to her, but she continued to sleep. One of her slippers had dropped off her foot, and the soldier picked it up and put it in his pocket. Then he kissed her and tiptoed away.

He was no sooner gone than the sleeping maiden awakened. She called her maids of honor, who were also sleeping in the next room. They woke up and ran to the princess, exclaiming, "The spell is broken! The spell is broken! We have awakened! The princess has awakened! Who could the knight be who freed us?"

"Quick," said the princess, "look out the windows and see if you see anyone."

The maids looked out and saw the massacred army and the slain she-wolf. Then the princess said, "Hurry to His Majesty, my father, and tell him a brave knight came and defeated the army that held me prisoner, killed the she-wolf that stood guard over me, and broke the evil spell by kissing me." She glanced at her bare foot and added, "And then he went off with my left slipper."

Overjoyed, the king had notices posted all over town: WHOEVER COMES FORWARD AS MY DAUGHTER'S DELIVERER SHALL HAVE HER IN MARRIAGE, BE HE PRINCE OR PAUPER.

In the meantime the Neapolitan had gone back to his companions in broad daylight. When he awakened them, they asked immediately, "Why didn't you call us earlier? How many hours did you watch?"

But he wasn't about to tell them all that had happened and simply said, "I was so wide-awake I watched the rest of the night."

Time went by without bringing a soul to town to claim the princess as his rightful bride. "What can we do?" wondered the king.

The princess had an idea. "Papa, let's open a country inn and put up a sign that reads: HERE YOU CAN EAT, DRINK, AND SLEEP AT NO CHARGE for three days. That will draw many people, and we'll surely hear something important."

They opened the inn, with the king's daughter acting as innkeeper. Who should then come by but our three soldiers as hungry as bears, and singing as usual, in spite of hard times. They read the sign, and the Neapolitan said, "Boys, here you can eat and sleep for nothing."

"Don't believe a word of it," replied his companions. "They just say that, the better to cheat people."

But the princess-innkeeper came out and invited them in, assuring them of the truth of every word of the sign. They entered the inn, and the princess served them a supper fit for a king. Then she took a seat at their table and said, "Well, what news do you bring from the world outside? Way off in the country like this, I never know what's going on elsewhere."

"We have very little of interest to report, madam," answered the Roman who then smugly told of the time he was keeping watch when suddenly confronted by a giant whose head he cut off.

"Zounds!" exclaimed the Florentine. "I too had something similar happen to me," and he told about his giant.

"And you, sir?" said the princess to the Neapolitan. "Has nothing ever happened to you?"

His companions burst out laughing. "You don't think he would have anything to tell, do you? Our friend here is such a coward he'd run and hide for a whole week if he heard a leaf rustle in the dark."

"Don't belittle the poor boy like that," said the maiden, who insisted that he too tell something.

So the Neapolitan said, "If you really want the truth, I too was confronted by a giant while you two were sleeping and I killed him."

"Ha, ha, ha!" laughed his companions. "You'd die of fright if you so much as saw a giant! That's enough! We don't want to hear any more, we're going to bed." And they went off and left him with the princess.

She served him wine and coaxed him to go on with his story. Thus, little by little, he came out with everything—the three old women, the lantern, the shotgun, the sword, and the lovely maiden he had kissed as she slept, and her slipper he had carried off.

"Do you still have the slipper?"

"Here it is," replied the soldier drawing it from his pocket.

Overjoyed the princess kept filling his glass until he fell asleep, then said to her valet, "Take him to the bedchamber I prepared especially for him, remove his clothes, and put out kingly garb for him on the chair."

When the Neapolitan awakened next morning he was in a room decorated entirely in gold and brocade. He went to put on his clothes and found in their place robes for a king. He pinched himself to make sure he wasn't dreaming and, unable to make heads or tails of a thing, he rang the bell.

Four liveried servants entered and bowed down to him. "At Your Highness's service. Did Your Highness sleep well?"

The Neapolitan blinked. "Have you lost your mind? What highness are you talking about? Give me my things so I can get dressed, and be done with this comedy."

"Calm down, Highness. We are here to shave you and dress your hair."

"Where are my companions? Where did you put my things?"

"They are coming right away, you will have everything immediately, but allow us first to dress you, Highness."

Once he realized there was no getting around them, the soldier let the servants proceed: they shaved him, dressed his hair, and clothed him in a kingly outfit. Then they brought in his chocolate, cake, and sweets. After breakfast he said, "Am I going to see my companions or not?"

"Right away, Highness."

In came the Roman and the Florentine, whose mouths flew open when they saw him dressed in such finery. "What are you doing in that costume?"

"You tell me. Your guess is as good as mine."

"Goodness knows what you've cooked up!" replied his companions. "You must have told the lady some pretty tall tales last night!"

"For your information, I told no tall tales to anyone."

"So how do you account for what's happening now?"

"I'll explain," said the king, coming in just then with the princess in her finest robe. "My daughter was under a spell, and this young man set her free."

By questions and answers, they got the entire story.

"I am therefore making him my daughter's husband," said the king, "and my heir. As for yourselves, have no fears. You will become dukes, since had you not slain the other two giants, my daughter would not be free today."

The wedding was celebrated to the great joy of all, and followed by a grand feast.

On the menu was chicken à la king:
Long live the queen!
Long live the king!

MOLLY WHUPPIE[1]

Joseph Jacobs

ONCE UPON A TIME THERE was a man and a wife who had too many children, and they could not get meat for them, so they took the three youngest and left them in a wood. They travelled and travelled and could see never a house. It began to be dark, and they were hungry. At last they saw a light and made for it; it turned out to be a house. They knocked at the door, and a woman came to it, who said: "What do you want?" They said: "Please let us in and give us something to eat." The woman said: "I can't do that, as my man is a giant, and he would kill you if he comes home." They begged hard. "Let us stop for a little while," said they, "and we will go away

---

1   From *English Fairy Tales*, 1890 (repr. New York: Dover, 1967).

before he comes." So she took them in, and set them down before the fire, and gave them milk and bread; but just as they had begun to eat, a great knock came to the door, and a dreadful voice said:

"Fee, fie, fo, fum,
I smell the blood of some earthly one.

Who have you there wife?" "Eh," said the wife, "it's three poor lassies[1] cold and hungry, and they will go away. Ye won't touch 'em, man." He said nothing, but ate up a big supper, and ordered them to stay all night. Now he had three lassies of his own, and they were to sleep in the same bed with the three strangers. The youngest of the three strange lassies was called Molly Whuppie, and she was very clever. She noticed that before they went to bed the giant put straw ropes round her neck and her sisters', and round his own lassies' necks he put gold chains. So Molly took care and did not fall asleep, but waited till she was sure every one was sleeping sound. Then she slipped out of the bed, and took the straw ropes off her own and her sisters' necks, and took the gold chains off the giant's lassies. She then put the straw ropes on the giant's lassies and the gold on herself and her sisters, and lay down. And in the middle of the night up rose the giant, armed with a great club, and felt for the necks with the straw. It was dark. He took his own lassies out of bed on to the floor, and battered them until they were dead, and then lay down again, thinking he had managed finely. Molly thought it time she and her sisters were off and away, so she wakened them and told them to be quiet, and they slipped out of the house. They all got out safe, and they ran and ran, and never stopped until morning, when they saw a grand house before them. It turned out to be a king's house: so Molly went in, and told her story to the king. He said: "Well, Molly, you are a clever girl, and you have managed well; but, if you would manage better, and go back, and steal the giant's sword that hangs on the back of his bed, I would give your eldest sister my eldest son to marry." Molly said she would try. So she went back, and managed to slip into the giant's house, and crept in below the bed. The giant came home, and ate up a great supper, and went to bed. Molly waited until he was snoring, and she crept out, and reached over the giant and got down the sword; but just as she got it out over the bed, it gave a rattle, and up jumped the giant, and Molly ran out at the door and the sword with her; and she ran, and he ran, till they came to the "Bridge of one hair"; and she got over, but he couldn't, and he says, "Woe worth ye, Molly Whuppie! never ye come again." And she says: "Twice yet, carle,"[2] quoth she, "I'll come to

---

1   Girls (Scottish).

2   Man.

Spain."[1] So Molly took the sword to the king, and her sister was married to his son.

Well, the king he says: "Ye've managed well, Molly; but if ye would manage better, and steal the purse that lies below the giant's pillow, I would marry your second sister to my second son." And Molly said she would try. So she set out for the giant's house, and slipped in, and hid again below the bed, and waited till the giant had eaten his supper, and was snoring sound asleep. She slipped out, and slipped her hand below the pillow, and got out the purse; but just as she was going out the giant wakened, and ran after her; and she ran, and he ran, till they came to the "Bridge of one hair," and she got over, but he couldn't, and he said, "Woe worth ye, Molly Whuppie! never you come again." "Once yet, carle," quoth she, "I'll come to Spain." So Molly took the purse to the king, and her second sister was married to the king's second son.

After that the king says to Molly: "Molly, you are a clever girl, but if you would do better yet, and steal the giant's ring that he wears on his finger, I will give you my youngest son for yourself." Molly said she would try. So back she goes to the giant's house, and hides herself below the bed. The giant wasn't long ere he came home, and, after he had eaten a great big supper, he went to his bed, and shortly was snoring loud. Molly crept out and reached over the bed, and got hold of the giant's hand, and she pulled and she pulled until she got off the ring; but just as she got it off the giant got up, and gripped her by the hand, and he says: "Now I have caught you, Molly Whuppie, and, if I had done as much ill to you as ye have done to me, what would ye do to me?"

Molly says: "I would put you into a sack, and I'd put the cat inside wi' you, and the dog aside you, and a needle and thread and a shears, and I'd hang you up upon the wall, and I'd go to the wood, and choose the thickest stick I could get, and I would come home, and take you down, and bang you till you were dead."

"Well, Molly," says the giant, "I'll just do that to you."

So he gets a sack, and puts Molly into it, and the cat and the dog beside her, and a needle and thread and shears, and hangs her up upon the wall, and goes to the wood to choose a stick.

Molly she sings out: "Oh, if ye saw what I see."

"Oh," says the giant's wife, "what do ye see, Molly?"

But Molly never said a word but, "Oh, if ye saw what I see!"

The giant's wife begged that Molly would take her up into the sack till she would see what Molly saw. So Molly took the shears and cut a hole in the sack, and took out the needle and thread with her, and jumped down and helped the giant's wife up into the sack, and sewed up the hole.

---

1   I.e., I'll venture into enemy territory.

The giant's wife saw nothing, and began to ask to get down again; but Molly never minded, but hid herself at the back of the door. Home came the giant, and a great big tree in his hand, and he took down the sack, and began to batter it. His wife cried, "It's me, man"; but the dog barked and the cat mewed, and he did not know his wife's voice. But Molly came out from the back of the door, and the giant saw her, and he ran after her; and he ran and she ran, till they came to the "Bridge of one hair," and she got over but he couldn't; and he said, "Woe worth you, Molly Whuppie! never you come again." "Never more, carle," quoth she, "will I come again to Spain."

So Molly took the ring to the king, and she was married to his youngest son, and she never saw the giant again.

THE YOUNG SLAVE[1]

Giambattista Basile

THERE WAS ONCE UPON A time a baron of Selvascura who had an unmarried sister. This sister always used to go and play in a garden with other girls of her own age. One day they found a lovely rose in full bloom, so they made a compact that whoever jumped clean over it without even touching a single leaf should win something. But although many of the girls jumped leapfrog over it, they all hit it, and not one of them jumped clean over. But when the turn came to Lilla, the Baron's sister, she stood back a little and took such a run at it that she jumped right over to the other side of the rose. Nevertheless, one leaf fell, but she was so quick and ready that she picked it up from the ground without anyone noticing and swallowed it, thereby winning the prize.

Not less than three days later, Lilla felt herself to be pregnant, and nearly died of grief, for she well knew that she had done nothing compromising or dishonest, and could not therefore understand how it was possible for her belly to have swollen. She at once ran to some fairies who were her friends, and when they heard her story, they told her not to worry, for the cause of it all was the rose-leaf that she had swallowed.

When Lilla understood this, she took precautions to conceal her condition as much as possible, and when the hour of her deliverance came, she gave birth in hiding to a lovely little girl whom she named Lisa. She sent her to the fairies and they each gave her some charm, but the last one slipped and twisted her foot so badly as

---

1 First published in 1634–36. This text from *The Pentamerone*, trans. Benedetto Croce (London: John Lane, the Bodley Head, 1932).

she was running to see the child, that in her acute pain she hurled a curse at her, to the effect that when she was seven years old, her mother, whilst combing out the child's hair, would leave the comb in her tresses, stuck into the head, and from this the child would perish.

At the end of seven years the disaster occurred, and the despairing mother, lamenting bitterly, encased the body in seven caskets of crystal, one within the other, and placed her in a distant room of the palace, keeping the key in her pocket. However, after some time her grief brought her to her grave. When she felt the end to be near, she called her brother and said to him, "My brother, I feel death's hook dragging me away inch by inch. I leave you all my belongings for you to have and dispose of as you like; but you must promise me never to open the last room in this house, and always keep the key safely in the casket." The brother, who loved her above all things, gave her his word; at the same moment she breathed, "Adieu, for the beans are ripe."

At the end of some years this lord (who had in the meantime taken a wife) was invited to a hunting-party. He recommended the care of the house to his wife, and begged her above all not to open the room, the key of which he kept in the casket. However, as soon as he had turned his back, she began to feel suspicious, and impelled by jealousy and consumed by curiosity, which is woman's first attribute, took the key and went to open the room. There she saw the young girl, clearly visible through the crystal caskets, so she opened them one by one and found that she seemed to be asleep. Lisa had grown like any other woman, and the caskets had lengthened with her, keeping pace as she grew.

When she beheld this lovely creature, the jealous woman at once thought, "By my life, this is a fine thing! Keys at one's girdle, yet nature makes horns![1] No wonder he never let anyone open the door and see the devil that he worshipped inside the caskets!" Saying this, she seized the girl by the hair, dragged her out, and in so doing caused the comb to drop out, so that the sleeping Lisa awoke, calling out, "Mother, mother!"

"I'll give you mother, and father too!" cried the Baroness, who was as bitter as a slave, as angry as a bitch with a litter of pups, and as venomous as a snake. She straightaway cut off the girl's hair and thrashed her with the tresses, dressed her in rags, and every day heaped blows on her head and bruises on her face, blacking her eyes and making her mouth look as if she had eaten raw pigeons.

When her husband came back from his hunting-party, and saw this girl being so hardly used, he asked who she was. His wife answered him that she was a slave sent her by her aunt, only fit for the rope's end, and that one had to be forever beating her.

---

1   I.e., even when you think everything's under control, your spouse will find a way to cheat on you.

Now it happened one day, when the Baron had occasion to go to a fair, that he asked everyone in the house, including even the cats, what they would like him to buy for them, and when they had all chosen, one thing and one another, he turned at last to the slave. But his wife flew into a rage and acted unbecomingly to a Christian, saying, "That's right, class her with all the others, this thick-lipped slave, let everyone be brought down to the same level and all use the urinal. Don't pay so much attention to a worthless bitch, let her go to the devil." But the Baron who was kind and courteous insisted that the slave should also ask for something. And she said to him, "I want nothing but a doll, a knife, and a pumice-stone; and if you forget them, may you never be able to cross the first river that you come to on your journey!"

The Baron brought all the other things, but forgot just those for which his niece had asked him; so when he came to a river that carried down stones and trees to the shore to lay foundations of fears and raise walls of wonder, he found it impossible to ford it. Then he remembered the spell put on him by the slave, and turned back and bought the three articles in question. When he arrived home he gave out to each one the thing for which they had asked.

When Lisa had what she wanted, she went into the kitchen, and, putting the doll in front of her, began to weep and lament and recount all the story of her troubles to that bundle of cloth just as if it had been a real person. When it did not reply, she took the knife and sharpened it on the pumice-stone and said, "Mind, if you don't answer me, I will dig this into you, and that will put an end to the game!" And the doll, swelling up like a reed when it has been blown into, answered at last, "All right, I have understood you! I'm not deaf!"

This music had already gone on for a couple of days, when the Baron, who had a little room on the other side of the kitchen, chanced to hear this song, and putting his eye to the keyhole, saw Lisa telling the doll all about her mother's jump over the rose-leaf, how she swallowed it, her own birth, the spell, the curse of the last fairy, the comb left in her hair, her death, how she was shut into the seven caskets and placed in that room, her mother's death, the key entrusted to the brother, his departure for the hunt, the jealousy of his wife, how she opened the room against her husband's commands, how she cut off her hair and treated her like a slave, and the many, many torments she had inflicted on her. And all the while she wept and said, "Answer me, dolly, or I will kill myself with this knife." And sharpening it on the pumice-stone, she would have plunged it into herself had not the Baron kicked down the door and snatched the knife out of her hand.

He made her tell him the story again at greater length and then he embraced his niece and took her away from that house, and left her in the charge of one of his relations in order that she should get better, for the hard usage inflicted on her by that heart of a Medea[1] had made her quite thin and pale. After several months, when she had become as beautiful as a goddess, the Baron brought her home and told everyone that she was his niece. He ordered a great banquet, and when the viands had been cleared away, he asked Lisa to tell the story of the hardships she had undergone and of the cruelty of his wife—a tale which made all the guests weep. Then he drove his wife away, sending her back to her parents, and gave his niece a handsome husband of her own choice. Thus Lisa testified that

Heaven rains favors on us when we least expect it.

THE ROBBER BRIDEGROOM[2]
Jacob and Wilhelm Grimm

THERE WAS ONCE A MILLER who had a beautiful daughter, and when she grew up he wanted to see her well married and provided for. He thought: "If the right kind of suitor comes along and asks for her hand, I'll let him have her." A suitor soon turned up. He seemed to be very rich, and since the miller could see nothing wrong with the man, he promised him his daughter. But the girl didn't love him as a girl should love her betrothed, and she didn't trust him. Whenever she looked at him or thought about him, her heart shrank with horror. Once he said to her: "You're engaged to me, but you never come to see me." The girl replied: "I don't know where you live." Her betrothed said: "My house is in the dark forest." She tried to get out of it by saying she couldn't find the way. The bridegroom said: "I expect you to visit me there next Sunday. I've already invited the guests, and I'll strew ashes in the forest to help you find the way." When Sunday came and the girl was ready to set out, she was terrified, though she herself didn't know why, and she filled both her pockets with peas and lentils to mark the path. At the entrance to the forest she found the trail of ashes and followed it, but at every step she threw a few peas on the ground to the right and left of her. She walked almost all day until she came to the darkest part of the forest. There she saw a house standing all by itself, and she didn't like it because it

---

1   In the Greek myth, Medea married Jason (of Golden Fleece fame), but when he left her, she killed their two children.

2   First published in 1812/15, in the first edition of *Kinder- und Hausmärchen*. This text from the second edition (1819), from *Grimms' Tales for Young and Old*, trans. Ralph Manheim (Garden City, NY: Anchor P, 1977).

looked so dark and forbidding. She went in but there was no one to be seen and the place was deadly silent. Suddenly a voice cried out:

"Go home, young bride, go home,
To a murderer's house you've come."

She looked up and saw that the voice came from a bird in a cage that was hanging on the wall. Again it cried out:

"Go home, young bride, go home,
To a murderer's house you've come."

The girl went from room to room until she had seen the whole house, but all the rooms were empty and there wasn't a living soul to be seen. Finally she went down to the cellar. An old, old woman was sitting there wagging her head. "Can you tell me if my betrothed lives here?" the girl asked. "Oh, you poor child," said the old woman. "What a place you've come to! This is a den of murderers. You expect to be wedded soon, but it's death you're going to wed. Look. They've made me put this big kettle on to boil. If they lay hands on you, they'll chop you to pieces without mercy, and they'll cook you and eat you, because they're ogres. You'd be lost if I didn't take pity on you and save you."

The old woman hid her behind a big barrel, where she couldn't be seen. "Be as still as a mouse," she said. "Don't budge or it will be the end of you. Tonight when the robbers are asleep, we'll run away. I've been waiting a long time for this chance." No sooner had she spoken than the wicked robbers came home, dragging another young girl. They were drunk and paid no attention to her screams and moans. They gave her wine to drink, three glasses full, one white, one red, one yellow, and her heart burst in two. Then they tore off her fine clothes, put her on a table, chopped her beautiful body into pieces, and sprinkled them with salt. The poor bride behind the barrel shuddered and trembled, for now she saw what the robbers had in mind for her. One of them caught sight of a gold ring on the murdered girl's little finger and when it wouldn't come off easily he took an ax and chopped off the finger. But the finger jumped over the barrel and fell straight into the bride's lap. The robber took a candle and went looking for it, but he couldn't find it. Another of the robbers asked him: "Have you looked behind the big barrel?" But the old woman cried: "Come and eat! You can look for it tomorrow. The finger won't run away."

"The old woman is right," said the robbers. They stopped looking and sat down to eat. The old woman poured a sleeping potion in their wine, and it wasn't long before they lay down, fell asleep, and began to snore. When the bride heard them, she came out from behind the barrel. The sleepers were lying on the ground in rows. She had to walk over them, and she was very much afraid of waking one of them, but God guided her steps. The old woman went upstairs with her and opened the door, and they hurried away from the den of murderers as fast as they could go. The wind had carried away the ashes, but the peas and lentils had sprouted and showed the way in the moonlight. They walked all night. In the morning they came to the mill and the girl told her father everything that had happened.

When the wedding day came, the bridegroom appeared, and the miller had invited all his friends and relatives. As they sat down at the table, each guest was asked to tell a story. When the bride sat silent and didn't open her mouth, the bridegroom said to her: "Can't you think of anything, my love? You too must tell us a story." "Very well," she replied. "I will tell you a dream. I was walking through a forest alone. At last I came to a house. When I went in, there wasn't a soul to be seen, but on the wall there was a bird in a cage, and it cried out:

'Go home, young bride, go home,
    To a murderer's house you've come.'

And then it said the same thing again. My darling, it was only a dream. Then I went from room to room, and all the rooms were empty, and everything was strange and forbidding. Finally I went down to the cellar. And there sat an old, old woman, wagging her head. I asked her: 'Does my betrothed live here?' And she answered: 'Oh, you poor child. You've come to a den of murderers. Your betrothed does live here, but he's going to chop you up and kill you, and then he'll cook you and eat you.' My darling, it was only a dream. But the old woman hid me behind a big barrel, and no sooner was I hidden than the robbers came in, dragging a young girl. They gave her three kinds of wine, white, red, and yellow, and her heart burst in two. My darling, it was only a dream. They pulled off her fine clothes, chopped her beautiful body into pieces, and sprinkled them with salt. My darling, it was only a dream. One of the robbers saw there was still a ring on her little finger, and when it didn't come off easily he took an ax and chopped it off, but the finger jumped up and flew over the big barrel and fell in my lap. And here is the finger with the ring on it!" With these words she took it out and showed it to the company.

The robber, who had turned as white as a sheet during her story, jumped up and tried to run away, but the guests held him fast and handed him over to the authorities. And he and his whole band were executed for their crimes.

THE PIG KING[1]

Giovanni Francesco Straparola

FAIR LADIES, IF MAN WERE to spend a thousand years in rendering thanks to his Creator for having made him in the form of a human and not of a brute beast, he could not speak gratitude enough. This reflection calls to mind the story of one who was born as a pig, but afterwards became a comely youth. Nevertheless, to his dying day he was known to the people over whom he ruled as King Pig.

You must know, dear ladies, that Galeotto, King of Anglia, was a man highly blessed in worldly riches, and in his wife Ersilia, the daughter of Matthias, King of Hungary, a princess who, in virtue and beauty, outshone all the other ladies of the time. And Galeotto was a wise king, ruling his land so that no man could hear complaint against him. Though they had been married several years they had no child, wherefore they both were much aggrieved. While Ersilia was walking one day in her garden she felt suddenly weary, and catching sight of a spot covered with fresh green turf, she went up to it and sat down, and, overcome with weariness and soothed by the sweet singing of the birds in the green foliage, she fell asleep.

And it chanced that while she slept there passed by three fairies who held mankind somewhat in scorn, and these, when they beheld the sleeping queen, halted, and gazing upon her beauty, took counsel together how they might protect her and throw a spell upon her. When they were agreed the first cried out, "I will that no man shall be able to harm her, and that, the next time she lie with her husband, she may be with child and bear a son who shall not have his equal in all the world for beauty." Then the second said, "I will that no one shall ever have power to offend her, and that the prince who shall be born of her shall be gifted with every virtue under the sun." And the third said, "And I will that she shall be the wisest among women, but that the son whom she shall conceive shall be born in the skin of a pig, with a pig's ways and manners, and in this state he shall be constrained to abide till he shall have three times taken a woman to wife."

As soon as the three fairies had flown away Ersilia awoke, and straightway arose and went back to the palace, taking with her the flowers she had plucked. Not many days had passed before she knew herself to be with child, and when the time of her delivery was come, she gave birth to a son with members like those of a pig and not of a human being. When tidings of this prodigy came to the ears of the king and queen they were greatly aggrieved, and the king, bearing in mind how good and wise

---

1   First published in 1550. This text from *The Facetious Nights of Straparola*, trans. W.G. Waters (London: Society of Bibliophiles, 1891).

his queen was, often felt moved to put this offspring of hers to death and cast it into the sea, in order that she might be spared the shame of having given birth to him. But when he debated in his mind and considered that this son, let him be what he might, was of his own begetting, he put aside the cruel purpose which he had been harbouring, and, seized with pity and grief, he made up his mind that the son should be brought up and nurtured like a rational being and not as a brute beast. The child, therefore, being nursed with the greatest care, would often be brought to the queen and put his little snout and his little paws in his mother's lap, and she, moved by natural affection, would caress him by stroking his bristly back with her hand, and embracing and kissing him as if he had been of human form. Then he would wag his tail and give other signs to show that he was conscious of his mother's affection.

The pigling, when he grew older, began to talk like a human being, and to wander abroad in the city, but whenever he came near to any mud or dirt he would always wallow therein, after the manner of pigs, and return all covered with filth. Then, when he approached the king and queen, he would rub his sides against their fair garments, defiling them with all manner of dirt, but because he was indeed their own son they bore it all.

One day he came home covered with mud and filth, as was his wont, and lay down on his mother's rich robe, and said in a grunting tone, "Mother, I wish to get married." When the queen heard this, she replied, "Do not talk so foolishly. What maid would ever take you for a husband, and do you think that any noble or knight would give his daughter to one so dirty and ill-savoured as you?" But he kept on grunting that he must have a wife of one sort or another. The queen, not knowing how to manage him in this matter, asked the king what they should do in their trouble: "Our son wishes to marry, but where shall we find anyone who will take him as a husband?" Every day the pig would come back to his mother with the same demand: "I must have a wife, and I will never leave you in peace until you procure for me a certain maiden I have seen to-day, who pleases me greatly."

It happened that this maiden was a daughter of a poor woman who had three daughters, each one of them being very lovely. When the queen heard this, she had brought before her the poor woman and her eldest daughter, and said, "Good mother, you are poor and burdened with children. If you will agree to what I shall say to you, you will be rich. I have this son who is, as you see, in form a pig, and I would like to marry him to your eldest daughter. Do not consider him, but think of the king and of me, and remember that your daughter will inherit this whole kingdom when the king and I shall be dead."

When the young girl listened to the words of the queen she was greatly disturbed in her mind and blushed red for shame, and then said that on no account would she listen to the queen's proposition; but the poor mother pleaded so urgently with her that at last she yielded. When the pig came home one day, all covered with dirt as usual, his mother said to him, "My son, we have found for you the wife you desire." And then she had the bride brought in, who by this time had been robed in sumptuous regal attire, and presented her to the pig prince. When he saw how lovely and desirable she was he was filled with joy, and, all foul and dirty as he was, jumped round about her, endeavouring by his pawing and nuzzling to show some sign of his affection. But she, when she found he was soiling her beautiful dress, thrust him aside; where upon the pig said to her, "Why do you push me thus? Have I not had these garments made for you myself?" Then she answered disdainfully, "No, neither you nor any other of the whole kingdom of hogs has done this thing." And when it was time to go to bed, the young girl said to herself, "What am I to do with this foul beast? This very night, while he lies asleep, I will kill him." The pig prince, who was not far off, heard these words, but said nothing, and when the two retired to their chamber he got into the bed, stinking and dirty as he was, and defiled the sumptuous bed with his filthy paws and snout. He lay down by his spouse, who was not long in falling asleep, and then he struck her with his sharp hoofs and drove them into her breast so that he killed her.

The next morning the queen went to visit her daughter-in-law, and to her great grief found that the pig had killed her; and when he came back from wandering about the city he said, in reply to the queen's bitter reproaches, that he had only dealt with his wife as she intended to deal with him, and then withdrew in an ill humour. Not many days had passed before the pig prince again began to plead with the queen to allow him to marry one of the other sisters, and when the queen at first would not listen to his petition he persisted in his purpose, and threatened to ruin everything in the place if he could not have her as wife. The queen, when she heard this, went to the king and told him everything, and he answered that perhaps it would be wiser to kill their ill-fated offspring before he might work some fatal mischief in the city. But the queen felt all the tenderness of a mother towards him, and loved him very dearly in spite of his brutal person, and could not endure the thought of being parted from him; so she summoned once more to the palace the poor woman, together with her second daughter, and held a long discourse with her, begging her the while to give her daughter in marriage. At last the girl assented to take the pig prince for a husband; but her fate was no happier than her sister's, for the bridegroom killed her, as he had killed his other bride, and then fled headlong from the palace.

When he came back, dirty as usual and smelling so foully that no one could approach him, the king and queen censured him gravely for the outrage he had committed; but again he cried out boldly that if he had not killed her she would have killed him. As it had happened before, the pig in a very short time began to plead with his mother again to let him marry the youngest sister, who was much more beautiful than either of the others; and when this request of his was refused, he became more insistent than ever, and in the end began to threaten the queen's life in violent and bloodthirsty words, unless he should have given to him the young girl for his wife. The queen, when she heard this shameful and unnatural speech, was well-nigh broken-hearted and about to go out of her mind; but, putting all other considerations aside, she called for the poor woman and her third daughter, who was named Meldina, and thus addressed her: "Meldina, my child, I should be greatly pleased if you would take the pig prince for a husband; pay no regard to him, but to his father and to me; then, if you will be prudent and bear patiently with him, you may be the happiest woman in the world." To this speech Meldina answered, with a grateful smile upon her face, that she was quite content to do as the queen asked her, and thanked her humbly for deigning to choose her as a daughter-in-law; for, seeing that she herself had nothing in the world, it was indeed great good fortune that she, a poor girl, should become the daughter-in-law of a potent sovereign. The queen, when she heard this modest and amiable reply, could not keep back her tears for the happiness she felt; but she feared all the time that the same fate might be in store for Meldina as her sisters.

When the new bride had been clothed in rich attire and decked with jewels, and was awaiting the bridegroom, the pig prince came in, filthier and more muddy than ever; but she spread out her rich gown and besought him to lie down by her side. Whereupon the queen told her to thrust him away, but to this she would not consent, and spoke thus to the queen: "There are three wise sayings, gracious lady, which I remember having heard. The first is that it is folly to waste time in searching for that which cannot be found. The second is that we should believe nothing we may hear, except those things which bear the marks of sense and reason. The third is that, when once you have got possession of some rare and precious treasure, prize it well and keep a firm hold upon it."

When the maiden had finished speaking, the pig prince, who had been wide awake and had heard all that she had said, got up, kissed her on the face and neck and bosom and shoulders with his tongue, and she was not backward in returning his caresses; so that he was fired with a warm love for her. As soon as the time for retiring for the night had come, the bride went to bed and awaited her unseemly spouse, and, as soon as he came, she raised the coverlet and bade him lie near to her and put his head upon the pillow, covering him carefully with the bed-clothes and drawing the curtains so that he might feel no cold. When morning came the pig got up and ranged abroad to pasture, as was his wont, and very soon after the queen went to the bride's chamber, expecting to find that she had met with the same fate as her sisters; but when she saw her lying in the bed, all defiled with mud as it was, and looking pleased and contented, she thanked God for this favour, that her son had at last found a spouse according to his liking.

One day, soon after this, when the pig prince was conversing pleasantly with his wife, he said to her: "Meldina, my beloved wife, if I could be fully sure that you could keep a secret, I would now tell you one of mine; something I have kept hidden for many years. I know you to be very prudent and wise, and that you love me truly; so I wish to make you the sharer of my secret." "You may safely tell it to me, if you will," said Meldina, "for I promise never to reveal it to anyone without your consent." Whereupon, being now sure of his wife's discretion and fidelity, he straightaway shook off from his body the foul and dirty skin of the pig, and stood revealed as a handsome and well-shaped young man, and all that night rested closely folded in the arms of his beloved wife. But he charged her solemnly to keep silence about this wonder she had seen, for the time had not yet come for his complete delivery from this misery. So when he left the bed he donned the dirty pig's hide once more. I leave you to imagine for yourselves how great was the joy of Meldina when she discovered that, instead of a pig, she had gained a handsome and gallant young prince for a husband. Not long after this she proved to be with child, and when the time of her delivery came she gave birth to a fair and shapely boy. The joy of the king and queen was unbounded, especially when they found that the newborn child had the form of a human being and not that of a beast.

But the burden of the strange and weighty secret which her husband had confided to her pressed heavily upon Meldina, and one day she went to her mother-in-law and said: "Gracious queen, when first I married your son I believed I was married to a beast, but now I find that you have given me the comeliest, the worthiest, and the most gallant young man ever born into the world to be my husband. For know that when he comes into my chamber to lie by my side, he casts off his dirty hide and leaves it on the ground, and is changed into a graceful handsome youth. No one could believe this marvel unless they saw it with their own eyes." When the queen heard these words she was sure that her daughter-in-law must be jesting with her, but Meldina insisted that what she said was true. And when the queen demanded to know how she might witness with her own eyes the truth of this thing, Meldina replied: "Come to my chamber tonight, when we shall be in our first sleep; the door will be open, and you will find that what I tell you is the truth."

That same night, when the time came, and all were gone to rest, the queen let some torches be kindled and went, accompanied by the king, to the chamber of her son, and when she had entered she saw the pig's skin lying on the floor in the corner of the room, and having gone to the bedside, found a handsome young man in whose arms Meldina was lying. And when they saw this, the delight of the king and queen was very great, and the king gave order that before anyone should leave the chamber the pig's hide should be torn to shreds. So great was their joy over the recovery of their son that they nearly died from it.

And King Galeotto, when he saw that he had so fine a son, and a grandchild as well, laid aside his diadem and his royal robes, and advanced to his place his son, whom he let be crowned with the greatest pomp, and who was ever afterwards known as King Pig. Thus, to the great contentment of all the people, the young king began his reign, and he lived long and happily with Meldina his beloved wife.

THE FROG MAIDEN[1]

Maung Htin Aung

AN OLD COUPLE WAS CHILDLESS, and the husband and the wife longed for a child. So when the wife found that she was with child, they were overjoyed; but to their great disappointment, the wife gave birth not to a human child, but to a little she-frog. However, as the little frog spoke and behaved as a human child, not only the parents but also the neighbours came to love her and called her affectionately "Little Miss Frog."

Some years later the woman died, and the man decided to marry again. The woman he chose was a widow with two ugly daughters and they were very jealous of Little Miss Frog's popularity with the neighbours. All three took a delight in illtreating Little Miss Frog.

One day the youngest of the king's four sons announced that he would perform the hair-washing ceremony[2] on a certain date and he invited all young ladies to join in the ceremony, as he would choose at the end of the ceremony one of them to be his princess.

On the morning of the appointed day the two ugly sisters dressed themselves in fine raiment, and with great hopes of being chosen by the Prince they started for the palace. Little Miss Frog ran after them, and pleaded, "Sisters, please let me come with you."

---

1   From *Burmese Folk-Tales* (London: Oxford UP, 1948).

2   "Typically a part of the Burmese New Year's Water Festival, this ceremony reflects Buddhist belief that, as the noblest part of the body, the head should be clean for the new year. It also marks a time when people strive to obey the Five Precepts of Zen Buddhism, as does the prince when he keeps his word about marrying the one who catches the flowers." Raymond E. Jones and Jon C. Stott, eds., *A World of Stories: Traditional Tales for Children* (Don Mills, ON: Oxford UP Canada, 2006), 331.

The sisters laughed and said mockingly, "What, the little frog wants to come? The invitation is to young ladies and not to young frogs." Little Miss Frog walked along with them towards the palace, pleading for permission to come. But the sisters were adamant, and so at the palace gates she was left behind. However, she spoke so sweetly to the guards that they allowed her to go in. Little Miss Frog found hundreds of young ladies gathered round the pool full of lilies in the palace grounds; and she took her place among them and waited for the Prince.

The Prince now appeared, and washed his hair in the pool. The ladies also let down their hair and joined in the ceremony. At the end of the ceremony, the Prince declared that as the ladies were all beautiful, he did not know whom to choose and so he would throw a posy of jasmines into the air; and the lady on whose head the posy fell would be his princess. The Prince then threw the posy into the air, and all the ladies present looked up expectantly. The posy, however, fell on Little Miss Frog's head, to the great annoyance of the ladies, especially the two stepsisters. The Prince also was disappointed, but he felt that he should keep his word. So little Miss Frog was married to the Prince, and she became Little Princess Frog.

Some time later, the old king called his four sons to him and said, "My sons, I am now too old to rule the country, and I want to retire to the forest and become a hermit. So I must appoint one of you as my successor. As I love you all alike, I will give you a task to perform, and he who performs it successfully shall be king in my place. The task is, bring me a golden deer at sunrise on the seventh day from now."

The Youngest Prince went home to Little Princess Frog and told her about the task. "What, only a golden deer!" exclaimed Princess Frog. "Eat as usual, my Prince, and on the appointed day I will give you the golden deer." So the Youngest Prince stayed at home, while the three elder princes went into the forest in search of the deer. On the seventh day before sunrise, Little Princess Frog woke up her husband and said, "Go to the palace, Prince, and here is your golden deer." The young Prince looked, then rubbed his eyes, and looked again. There was no mistake about it; the deer which Little Princess Frog was holding by a lead was really of pure gold. So he went to the palace, and to the great annoyance of the elder princes who brought ordinary deer, he was declared to be the heir by the king. The elder princes, however, pleaded for a second chance, and the king reluctantly agreed.

"Then perform this second task," said the king. "On the seventh day from now at sunrise, you must bring me the rice that never becomes stale, and the meat that is ever fresh."

The Youngest Prince went home and told Princess Frog about the new task. "Don't you worry, sweet Prince," said Princess Frog. "Eat as usual, sleep as usual, and on the appointed day I will give you the rice and meat." So the youngest Prince stayed at home, while the three elder princes went in search of the rice and meat. On the seventh day at sunrise, Little Princess Frog woke up her husband and said, "My Lord, go to the palace now, and here is your rice and meat." The Youngest Prince took the rice and meat, and went to the palace, and to the great annoyance of the elder princes who brought only well-cooked rice and meat, he was again declared to be the heir. But the three elder princes again pleaded for one more chance, and the king said, "This is positively the last task. On the seventh day from now at sunrise, bring me the most beautiful woman on this earth."

"Ho, ho!" said the three elder princes to themselves in great joy. "Our wives are very beautiful, and we will bring them. One of us is sure to be declared heir, and our good-for-nothing brother will be nowhere this time." The Youngest Prince overheard their remark, and felt sad, for his wife was a frog and ugly. When he reached home, he said to his wife, "Dear Princess, I must go and look for the most beautiful woman on this earth. My brothers will bring their wives, for they are really beautiful, but I will find someone who is more beautiful."

"Don't you fret, my Prince," replied Princess Frog. "Eat as usual, sleep as usual, and you can take me to the palace on the appointed day; surely I shall be declared to be the most beautiful woman."

The Youngest Prince looked at the Princess in surprise; but he did not want to hurt her feelings, and he said gently, "All right, Princess, I will take you with me on the appointed day."

On the seventh day at dawn, Little Princess Frog woke up the Prince and said, "My Lord, I must make myself beautiful. So please wait outside and call me when it is nearly time to go." The Prince left the room as requested. After some moments, the Prince shouted from the outside, "Princess, it is time for us to go."

"Please wait, my Lord," replied the Princess, "I am just powdering my face."

After some moments the Prince shouted, "Princess, we must go now."

"All right, my Lord," replied the Princess, "please open the door for me."

The Prince thought to himself, "Perhaps, just as she was able to obtain the golden deer and the wonderful rice and meat, she is able to make herself beautiful," and he expectantly opened the door, but he was disappointed to see Little Princess Frog still a frog and as ugly as ever. However, so as not to hurt her feelings, the Prince said nothing and took her along to the palace. When the Prince entered the audience-chamber with his Frog Princess the three elder princes with their wives were already there. The king looked at the Prince in surprise and said, "Where is your beautiful maiden?"

"I will answer for the prince, my king," said the Frog Princess. "I am his beautiful maiden." She then took off her frog skin and stood a beautiful maiden dressed in silk and satin. The king declared her to be the most beautiful maiden in the world, and selected the Prince as his successor on the throne. The Prince asked his Princess never to put on the ugly frog skin again, and the Frog Princess, to accede to his request, threw the skin into the fire.

NEW WINE IN OLD BOTTLES

FROM THE BEGINNING, THE ORAL tale has been subject to a version of the Darwinian law of survival of the fittest. The few tales containing that magic seed of memorability were those that were passed down through the generations, to be finally recorded in print. Today, however, the permanence of print has altered the situation in that while modern retellings of well-known fairy tales are abundant, the reader must be ready to distinguish the mediocre from the memorable. Many writers have been seduced by the apparent simplicity and familiarity of the fairy tale to try their hand at the form; surprisingly few have managed better than a pale imitation.

To produce a contemporary version of a "classic" fairy tale is a complex challenge, not least because the "classics" are very familiar—although their popularity likely has more to do with Disney than with the literary versions. As we have seen, the appropriation of the fairy tale as children's literature began with the Grimms in the early nineteenth century, that view largely predominating until the last quarter of the twentieth century, when some writers began to look beyond the "kiddie-lit" designation and rediscover a deeper, more visceral energy in the tales—a reminder that they were for adults before they were for children. In more recent years, that momentum has grown, such that in the visual media as well as the literary, the fairy tale has re-established itself as adult entertainment alongside its "suitable-for-children" predecessor.

The familiarity of the tales also invites an ironic perspective, as the writer imposes a modern self-consciousness upon the one-dimensional nature of fairy-tale characterization. Much imaginative effort has been expended on bringing some psychological depth, both to notorious antagonists such as Cinderella's stepmother or to helpless innocents such as Little Red Riding Hood, no doubt reflecting our society's fascination with the deeper wellsprings of human behavior.

There can be little doubt that the strongest influence on fairy tales in the last fifty years has been feminism, which partly explains why two-thirds of the tales in this section are by women. As they have struggled to assert their position in the social and political worlds, some have identified the fairy tale as an early contributor to sexual inequality, noting that the female is often depicted as passive and subservient, the beautiful appendage to the superior male.

We begin this section with three very different modern treatments of "Little Red Riding Hood," which remains one of the most compelling tales in the Western canon. David McPhail's version continues the work begun by the Grimms to make the fairy tale accord with current expectations for children's literature. While adhering to the traditional non-specific setting, his Little Red Riding Hood (1995) is clever and resourceful,[1] the Wolf is outsmarted in comic fashion with no-one getting hurt, and the moral messages are communicated without a hint of the violence and underlying sexuality that are so much a part of earlier versions of the tale.

At the other end of the literary spectrum is Angela Carter, who in "The Company of Wolves" (1979) is clearly not writing for the child reader: her diction is too sophisticated, her interpretation of the tale too complex and disturbing. It is as if Carter is returning the tale to something resembling its original condition, while recognizing that modern literate adults represent a very different audience from their ancestors who first *heard* the tale in a very different world. It is clearly the *real* world behind the folk tale that particularly fascinated Carter—that potent cocktail of superstition, fear, and primitive religion that together lead the human imagination to strange and disturbing places. Thus, the first part of her tale is devoted to creating a realistic context that is a far cry from the romantic dream-world that has become the customary backdrop to modern retellings of fairy tales. Consequently, this story has a flesh-and-blood materiality that is just one among several reminders of "The Story of Grandmother." Carter's most significant revision of the tale comes at the end, however, when she startles us with what amounts to a radical reversal of sexual stereotypes. If we inject some ferocity into the female and some tenderness into the male, who knows what the outcome might be....

To this point, all the versions of Little Red Riding Hood have been set in rural surroundings, as befits their origins. The modern world, however, is essentially an urban one, and that fact is reflected in Francesca Lia Block's "Wolf" (2000), which takes place, at least in part, in the concrete jungle of Los Angeles. While Carter brings new life to the tale by creating a quasi-historical context, Block finds her perspective in the harsh light of social realism (Sarah Moon uses the medium of photography to much the same effect, see Figure 3). For the first time, the story is told from the girl's point of view (and, like Carter, Block has chosen to add some years to her central character, whose age, the "Little" in her name notwithstanding, has been ambiguous

---

1   Curiously enough, the depiction of her is reminiscent of the girl in the earlier versions of the story.

from the beginning). With this story of abuse, loneliness, and misery, we have come a long way from the fairy-tale world of Little Red Riding Hood, but that same sense of imminent crisis is still in the air; the fact that so many writers have chosen to explore such traumatic experience says something both about us and about the extraordinary resonance of this encounter between a girl and a wolf.

While we suggest above that feminism has been the primary perspective over the past fifty years, the work of one of the women writers represented here goes back considerably further—to 1874, in fact. Anne Thackeray Ritchie adapted a number of classic tales to comment upon various aspects of Victorian social life, producing in "The Sleeping Beauty in the Wood" an incisive critique of bourgeois attitudes. Ritchie's contention that "[f]airy stories are everywhere and every day" (p. 255) makes clear her intention to locate the tale firmly in the here and now.

One innovation that contemporary writers have introduced to the fairy tale is variation of the narrative voice. Customarily, the tale is recounted in the third person by a narrator who rarely intervenes in the story (one well-known exception is the rather cryptic ending to the Grimms' "Hansel and Gretel": "My story is done, see the mouse run; if you catch it, you may make yourself a great big fur cap out of it" [p. 101]). By contrast, many recent retellings have made the fairy tale multi-dimensional by giving the reader some new perspectives. Thus, the mystery of Tanith Lee's tale is enhanced by its enigmatic narrator, whose motivation remains in question to the tale's unsettling end.

In "When the Clock Strikes" (1983), her gothic makeover of "Cinderella," Lee comes close to turning the story inside out. To convince us of the moral darkness of the world that she is describing, Lee introduces the Cinderella theme in relation to Ashella's mother in that she, too, is the object of a search—but for a purpose very different from marriage. As in previous versions, the close relationship between mother and daughter is emphasized, but now it is a bond of hatred and desire for vengeance that passes from one generation to the next. Here again, there is a stepmother and stepsisters, but this time they are well-meaning and inoffensive. Angela Carter produced her startling revision of "Little Red Riding Hood" essentially by reversing the roles of girl and "wolf"; Lee uses much the same tactic here by creating what amounts to an "anti-fairy tale" in which love becomes hate and marriage turns into murder.

Our orthodox assumptions about Cinderella are thrown into quite a different light in "The Wicked Stepmother's Lament" (1996), by Sara Maitland, who fashions a daring synthesis of "once upon a time" and "the here and now" (at one point, the stepmother-narrator comments on her reaction to seeing Disney's Snow White), but at the core of Maitland's tale is an insight applicable to a world of stories beyond "Cinderella": that there is a profound gap between the innocence of childhood and the experience of adulthood, a gap made deeper by conventional assumptions about growing up female.

The Merseyside Fairy Story Collective's version of "Snow White" (1972) takes a stance that is as political as it is feminist—a fact hinted at by its "Collective" origins. The wicked Queen is now a combination of Big Sister and Consumer-in-Chief, opposed by a Snow White who has clear revolutionary propensities ("take only what you need from the people of the kingdom and let them keep the rest so that they will no longer be cold and hungry and miserable" [p. 286]). "Snow White" is first and foremost a story about power and the lengths to which some are prepared to go to achieve and retain it. In the traditional tale, that power is based upon beauty, the equation that explains the lasting notoriety of such women as Cleopatra and Helen of Troy. The Collective's point is that the source of power has changed, and in very deft fashion they capture that shift in the role of the mirror: what was once the arbiter of beauty ("You, O Queen, are the fairest in the land ...") is now a computer monitor—the magic mirror of the Information Age.

By making Snow White's stepmother his narrator in "Snow, Glass, Apples" (1998), Neil Gaiman transforms the story in as startling a fashion as Maitland reconfigures "Cinderella." Gaiman's tactic is indicative of an important trend in modern retellings: the black-and-white morality of the traditional tale has been moderated to shades of grey, reflecting our awareness of human complexity and motivation. In addition, it is Gaiman's intention to complicate matters further by turning the familiar inside out: now Snow White is the villain of the piece, as demonically driven and literally heartless as her stepmother ever was; the dwarves have become "people in the forest" whom Gaiman characterizes as "greedy, feral, [and] dangerous"—and then there's the prince, with his taste for extreme passivity in women.[1]

One feature of the fairy tale that sets it apart from other literary forms is what might be termed the archetypal anonymity of its characters. While the plot commands one's attention, the characters leave everything to the imagination, as if they are silhouettes against a minimal background. In "The Tale of the Rose" (1997), Emma Donoghue focusses her attention on the abstractions of "Beauty" and "Beast" and creates a new tale; she changes virtually nothing in Madame de Beaumont's plot, apart from the villagers' curious comment about the young queen, which is resolved only by the challenging conclusion. In the introduction to "The Nature of

---

1   One need look no further than *The Sleeping Beauty Trilogy* (1983–85), by Anne Rice, to appreciate how effectively the sexual element in the fairy tale can be exploited. As is the custom with recent adaptations, Rice's extended erotic narrative, which caters to specialized tastes collectively referred to as BDSM (bondage, discipline, sadomasochism), owes little beyond the name of the central character to any version of the fairy tale. That did not prevent the books from becoming best-sellers; in fact, in light of the runaway success of the *Fifty Shades* trilogy (2011), itself born out of fan-fiction response to the *Twilight* series, Rice's books were reprinted (2012).

Love" (see p. 126), we suggested that "the essential quality of an animal [or a beast] is its 'otherness,'" and it is this concept that Donoghue uses to broaden the definition not of love but of sexuality.

The two modern versions of "The Story of the Three Little Pigs" in this section illustrate the fairy tale's capacity to illuminate dramatically different perspectives and provoke equally different responses. Published in 1936 as the threat of Fascism was growing in Europe, "The Fourth Pig" by Naomi Mitchison uses the simple structure of the original tale to communicate the helplessness and panic of those in the path of this implacable Beast. In contrast to Mitchison's apocalyptic vision, James Finn Garner suffuses his 1994 version with the evanescent language and concepts of pop psychology, thus transforming fantasy into parody.

Michael Cunningham's "Little Man" (2015) provides a fitting conclusion to this section in that it takes some of the characteristics we have noted in other contemporary tales one step further. In our experience as teachers, we have observed that students often feel that Rumpelstiltskin is hard done by; after all, despite his sinister intentions, he does give the queen a chance to escape her bargain, does he not? Cunningham builds on this feeling by making him tell his own story, although with an unusual degree of detachment. Like other writers in this section, Cunningham is adept at creating a sense of continuity between our reality and the world of the fairy tale: his "little man" is quite aware how absurd it would be to "Apply to adopt an infant as a two-hundred-year-old gnome" (p. 309).

LITTLE RED RIDING HOOD[1]

David McPhail

ONCE THERE WAS A GIRL called Little Red Riding Hood because, whenever she went out, she wore a pretty red cape.

One day her mother baked some cookies and asked Little Red Riding Hood to take them to Grandmother, who was ill and could not leave her bed.

"Stay on the path and don't dawdle," instructed Little Red Riding Hood's mother. And the girl started off.

Little Red Riding Hood was about halfway to Grandmother's house when she met a wolf, but as she didn't know what a bad sort of animal he was, she did not feel afraid.

---

1   Published in 1995 (New York: Scholastic).

"Where are you off to so early this fine day?" inquired the wolf.

"I'm taking some cookies to my grandmother," answered Little Red Riding Hood.

"And where does your grandmother live?" the wolf persisted.

"Her house stands beneath the three oak trees," said Little Red Riding Hood.

As she was innocently explaining all this, the wolf was thinking, *If I can get there before her, I'll eat the grandmother for my main course and this tender young morsel for my dessert.*

"Your grandmother would surely love a bouquet of flowers," the wolf said to Little Red Riding Hood.

And that set Little Red Riding Hood to thinking about it.

So Little Red Riding Hood ventured farther and farther off the path to pick flowers, while the wolf went hastily to Grandmother's house and knocked on the door.

"Who's there?" called the grandmother in a very weak voice.

"It's your dear granddaughter," lied the wolf. "Please open the door."

"Come in," said the grandmother. "The door is not locked."

As soon as the door opened, the grandmother realized her mistake.

For instead of the darling Little Red Riding Hood, a wicked wolf stepped into the room. And though the grandmother's body was weak, she ran into the wardrobe and locked the door.

The wolf would have torn the door right off its hinges, but through the window, he saw Little Red Riding Hood walking down the path.

So the wolf put on the grandmother's cap and glasses, which had fallen to the floor, climbed into the bed, and pulled the covers up to his chin.

When she got to her grandmother's house, Little Red Riding Hood was surprised to see an open door. Nevertheless, she stepped inside.

"Good morning, Grandmother," she called. But there was no answer. Little Red Riding Hood stepped closer to the bed.

As the curtain had been drawn around the bed, Little Red Riding Hood could not see clearly in the dim light. "Oh, Grandmother," she exclaimed, "what big *ears* you have!"

"All the better to *hear* you with," said the wolf.

"Oh, Grandmother," said Little Red Riding Hood, "what big *eyes* you have!"

"All the better to *see* you with," said the wolf.

"Oh, Grandmother," said Little Red Riding Hood, "what big *teeth* you have!"

"All the better to *eat* you with!" said the wolf and he threw back the covers.

But Little Red Riding Hood was too quick for the wolf, and before he could catch her, she crawled under the bed.

The angry wolf went after her, but as he was much bigger than Little Red Riding Hood, he got stuck.

Little Red Riding Hood came out from under the bed and jumped on top of it. She jumped up and down, and shouted at the top of her voice, "Help! Help! There's a big bad wolf in here, and I fear he has eaten my grandmother!"

Little Red Riding Hood's grandmother, on hearing this, came out of the wardrobe.

Meanwhile, everyone who happened to be in the forest that day, including a woodcutter with a mighty sharp ax, heard Little Red Riding Hood's cries and ran to help.

They had nearly reached the cottage when the wolf finally managed to squeeze out from under the bed and stagger through the door.

The last time Little Red Riding Hood saw the wolf, he was running down the path, followed closely by a hostile crowd.

And Little Red Riding Hood never saw or heard from him again.

THE COMPANY OF WOLVES[1]

Angela Carter

ONE BEAST AND ONLY ONE howls in the woods by night.

The wolf is carnivore incarnate and he's as cunning as he is ferocious; once he's had a taste of flesh, then nothing else will do.

At night, the eyes of wolves shine like candle flames, yellowish, reddish, but that is because the pupils of their eyes fatten on darkness and catch the light from your lantern to flash it back to you—red for danger; if a wolf's eyes reflect only moonlight, then they gleam a cold and unnatural green, a mineral, a piercing color. If the benighted traveler spies those luminous, terrible sequins stitched suddenly on the black thickets, then he knows he must run, if fear has not struck him stock-still.

But those eyes are all you will be able to glimpse of the forest assassins as they cluster invisibly round your smell of meat as you go through the wood unwisely late. They will be like shadows, they will be like wraiths, gray members of a congregation of nightmare. Hark! his long, wavering howl … an aria of fear made audible.

The wolfsong is the sound of the rendering you will suffer, in itself a murdering.

It is winter and cold weather. In this region of mountain and forest, there is now nothing for the wolves to eat. Goats and sheep are locked up in the byre, the deer departed for the remaining pasturage on the southern slopes—wolves grow lean and famished. There is so little flesh on them that you could count the starveling ribs

---

1   From *The Bloody Chamber and Other Stories* (London: Gollancz, 1979).

through their pelts, if they gave you time before they pounced. Those slavering jaws; the lolling tongue; the rime of saliva on the grizzled chops—of all the teeming perils of the night and the forest, ghosts, hobgoblins, ogres that grill babies upon gridirons, witches that fatten their captives in cages for cannibal tables, the wolf is worst, for he cannot listen to reason.

You are always in danger in the forest, where no people are. Step between the portals of the great pines where the shaggy branches tangle about you, trapping the unwary traveler in nets as if the vegetation itself were in a plot with the wolves who live there, as though the wicked trees go fishing on behalf of their friends—step between the gateposts of the forest with the greatest trepidation and infinite precautions, for if you stray from the path for one instant, the wolves will eat you. They are gray as famine, they are as unkind as plague.

The grave-eyed children of the sparse villages always carry knives with them when they go out to tend the little flocks of goats that provide the homesteads with acrid milk and rank, maggoty cheeses. Their knives are half as big as they are; the blades are sharpened daily.

But the wolves have ways of arriving at your own hearthside. We try and try but sometimes we cannot keep them out. There is no winter's night the cottager does not fear to see a lean, gray, famished snout questing under the door, and there was a woman once bitten in her own kitchen as she was straining the macaroni.

Fear and flee the wolf; for worst of all, the wolf may be more than he seems.

There was a hunter once, near here, that trapped a wolf in a pit. This wolf had massacred the sheep and goats; eaten up a mad old man who used to live by himself in a hut halfway up the mountain and sing to Jesus all day; pounced on a girl looking after the sheep, but she made such a commotion that men came with rifles and scared him away and tried to track him into the forest but he was cunning and easily gave them the slip. So this hunter dug a pit and put a duck in it, for bait, all alive-oh; and he covered the pit with straw smeared with wolf dung. Quack, quack! went the duck, and a wolf came slinking out of the forest, a big one, a heavy one, he weighed as much as a grown man and the straw gave way beneath him—into the pit he tumbled. The hunter jumped down after him, slit his throat, cut off all his paws for a trophy.

And then no wolf at all lay in front of the hunter, but the bloody trunk of a man, headless, footless, dying, dead.

A witch from up the valley once turned an entire wedding party into wolves because the groom had settled on another girl. She used to order them to visit her, at night, from spite, and they would sit and howl around her cottage for her, serenading her with their misery.

Not so very long ago, a young woman in our village married a man who vanished clean away on her wedding night. The bed was made with new sheets and the bride lay down in it; the groom said he was going out to relieve himself, insisted on it, for the sake of decency, and she drew the coverlet up to her chin and lay there. And she waited and she waited and then she waited again—surely he's been gone a long time? Until she jumps up in bed and shrieks to hear a howling, coming on the wind from the forest.

That long-drawn, wavering howl has, for all its fearful resonance, some inherent sadness in it, as if the beasts would love to be less beastly if only they knew how and never cease to mourn their own condition. There is a vast melancholy in the canticles of the wolves, melancholy infinite as the forest, endless as these long nights of winter, and yet that ghastly sadness, that mourning for their own, irremediable appetites, can never move the heart, for not one phrase in it hints at the possibility of redemption; grace could not come to the wolf from its own despair, only through some external mediator, so that, sometimes, the beast will look as if he half welcomes the knife that dispatches him.

That young woman's brothers searched the outhouses and the haystacks but never found any remains, so the sensible girl dried her eyes and found herself another husband, not too shy to piss in a pot, who spent the nights indoors. She gave him a pair of bonny babies and all went right as a trivet until, one freezing night, the night of the solstice, the hinge of the year when things do not fit together as well as they should, the longest night, her first good man came home again.

A great thump on the door announced him as she was stirring the soup for the father of her children and she knew him the moment she lifted the latch to him although it was years since she's worn black for him and now he was in rags and his hair hung down his back and never saw a comb, alive with lice.

"Here I am again, missis," he said. "Get me my bowl of cabbage and be quick about it."

Then her second husband came in with wood for the fire and when the first one saw she'd slept with another man and, worse, clapped his red eyes on her little children, who'd crept into the kitchen to see what all the din was about, he shouted: "I wish I were a wolf again, to teach this whore a lesson!" So a wolf he instantly became and tore off the eldest boy's left foot before he was chopped up with a hatchet they used for chopping logs. But when the wolf lay bleeding and gasping its last, the pelt peeled off again and he was just as he had been, years ago, when he ran away from his marriage bed, so that she wept and her second husband beat her.

They say there's an ointment the Devil gives you that turns you into a wolf the minute you rub it on. Or that he was born feet first and had a wolf for his father and his torso is a man's but his legs and genitals are a wolf's. And he has a wolf's heart.

Seven years is a werewolf's natural span, but if you burn his human clothing you condemn him to wolfishness for the rest of his life, so old wives hereabouts think it some protection to throw a hat or an apron at the werewolf, as if clothes made the man. Yet by the eyes, those phosphorescent eyes, you know him in all his shapes; the eyes alone unchanged by metamorphosis.

Before he can become a wolf, the lycanthrope[1] strips stark naked. If you spy a naked man among the pines, you must run as if the Devil were after you.

It is midwinter and the robin, friend of man, sits on the handle of the gardener's spade and sings. It is the worst time in all the year for wolves, but this strong-minded child insists she will go off through the wood. She is quite sure the wild beasts cannot harm her although, well-warned, she lays a carving knife in the basket her mother has packed with cheeses. There is a bottle of harsh liquor distilled from brambles; a batch of flat oat cakes baked on the hearthstone; a pot or two of jam. The flaxen-haired girl will take these delicious gifts to a reclusive grandmother so old the burden of her years is crushing her to death. Granny lives two hours' trudge through the winter woods; the child wraps herself up in her thick shawl, draws it over her head. She steps into her stout wooden shoes; she is dressed and ready and it is Christmas Eve. The malign door of the solstice still swings upon its hinges, but she has been too much loved ever to feel scared.

Children do not stay young for long in this savage country. There are no toys for them to play with, so they work hard and grow wise, but this one, so pretty and the youngest of her family, a little latecomer, had been indulged by her mother and the grandmother who'd knitted the red shawl that, today, has the ominous if brilliant look of blood on snow. Her breasts have just begun to swell; her hair is like lint, so fair it hardly makes a shadow on her pale forehead; her cheeks are an emblematic scarlet and white and she has just started her woman's bleeding, the clock inside her that will strike, henceforward, once a month.

She stands and moves within the invisible pentacle of her own virginity. She is an unbroken egg; she is a sealed vessel; she has inside her a magic space the entrance to which is shut tight with a plug of membrane; she is a closed system; she does not know how to shiver. She has her knife and she is afraid of nothing.

Her father might forbid her, if he were home, but he is away in the forest, gathering wood, and her mother cannot deny her.

The forest closed upon her like a pair of jaws.

There is always something to look at in the forest, even in the middle of winter—the huddled mounds of birds, succumbed to the lethargy of the season, heaped on the creaking boughs and too forlorn to sing; the bright frills of the winter fungi on the blotched trunks of the trees; the cuneiform slots of rabbits and deer, the

---

1   Werewolf.

herringbone tracks of the birds, a hare as lean as a rasher of bacon streaking across the path where the thin sunlight dapples the russet brakes[1] of last year's bracken.

When she heard the freezing howl of a distant wolf, her practiced hand sprang to the handle of her knife, but she saw no sign of a wolf at all, nor of a naked man, neither, but then she heard a clattering among the brushwood and there sprang onto the path a fully clothed one, a very handsome young one, in the green coat and wide-awake hat of a hunter, laden with carcasses of game birds. She had her hand on her knife at the first rustle of twigs, but he laughed with a flash of white teeth when he saw her and made her a comic yet flattering little bow; she'd never seen such a fine fellow before, not among the rustic clowns of her native village. So on they went together, through the thickening light of the afternoon.

Soon they were laughing and joking like old friends. When he offered to carry her basket, she gave it to him although her knife was in it because he told her his rifle would protect them. As the day darkened, it began to snow again; she felt the first flakes settle on her eyelashes, but now there was only half a mile to go and there would be a fire, and hot tea, and a welcome, a warm one, surely, for the dashing huntsman as well as for herself.

This young man had a remarkable object in his pocket. It was a compass. She looked at the little round glass face in the palm of his hand and watched the waver-ing needle with a vague wonder. He assured her this compass had taken him safe-ly through the wood on his hunting trip because the needle always told him with perfect accuracy where the north was. She did not believe it; she knew she should never leave the path on the way through the wood or else she would be lost instantly. He laughed at her again; gleaming trails of spittle clung to his teeth. He said if he plunged off the path into the forest that surrounded them, he could guarantee to arrive at her grandmother's house a good quarter of an hour before she did, plotting his way through the undergrowth with his compass, while she trudged the long way, along the winding path.

I don't believe you. Besides, aren't you afraid of the wolves?

He only tapped the gleaming butt of his rifle and grinned.

Is it a bet? he asked her. Shall we make a game of it? What will you give me if I get to your grandmother's house before you?

What would you like? she asked disingenuously.

A kiss.

Commonplaces of a rustic seduction; she lowered her eyes and blushed.

He went through the undergrowth and took her basket with him, but she for-got to be afraid of the beasts, although now the moon was rising, for she wanted

---

1   Undergrowth.

to dawdle on her way to make sure the handsome gentleman would win his wager.

Grandmother's house stood by itself a little way out of the village. The freshly falling snow blew in eddies about the kitchen garden and the young man stepped delicately up the snowy path to the door as if he were reluctant to get his feet wet, swinging his bundle of game and the girl's basket and humming a little tune to himself.

There is a faint trace of blood on his chin; he has been snacking on his catch.

Aged and frail, granny is three-quarters succumbed to the mortality the ache in her bones promises her and almost ready to give in entirely. A boy came out from the village to build up her hearth for the night an hour ago and the kitchen crackles with busy firelight. She has her Bible for company; she is a pious old woman. She is propped up on several pillows in the bed set into the wall peasant fashion, wrapped up in the patchwork quilt she made before she was married, more years ago than she cares to remember. Two china spaniels with liver-colored blotches on their coats and black noses sit on either side of the fireplace. There is a bright rug of woven rags on the pantiles. The grandfather clock ticks away her eroding time.

We keep the wolves out by living well.

He rapped upon the panels with his hairy knuckles.

It is your granddaughter, he mimicked in a high soprano.

Lift up the latch and walk in, my darling.

You can tell them by their eyes, eyes of a beast of prey, nocturnal, devastating eyes as red as a wound; you can hurl your Bible at him and your apron after, granny; you thought that was a sure prophylactic[1] against these infernal vermin … Now call on Christ and his mother and all the angels in heaven to protect you, but it won't do you any good.

His feral muzzle is sharp as a knife; he drops his golden burden of gnawed pheasant on the table and puts down your dear girl's basket, too. Oh, my God, what have you done with her?

Off with his disguise, that coat of forest-colored cloth, the hat with the feather tucked into the ribbon; his matted hair streams down his white shirt and she can see the lice moving in it. The sticks in the hearth shift and hiss; night and the forest has come into the kitchen with darkness tangled in its hair.

He strips off his shirt. His skin is the color and texture of vellum. A crisp stripe of hair runs down his belly, his nipples are ripe and dark as poison fruit, but he's so thin you could count the ribs under his skin if only he gave you the time. He strips off his trousers and she can see how hairy his legs are. His genitals, huge. Ah! huge.

---

1 Protective course of action.

The last thing the old lady saw in all this world was a young man, eyes like cinders, naked as a stone, approaching her bed.

The wolf is carnivore incarnate.

When he had finished with her, he licked his chops and quickly dressed himself again, until he was just as he had been when he came through her door. He burned the inedible hair in the fireplace and wrapped the bones up in a napkin that he hid away under the bed in the wooden chest in which he found a clean pair of sheets. These he carefully put on the bed instead of the telltale stained ones he stowed away in the laundry basket. He plumped up the pillows and shook out the patchwork quilt, he picked up the Bible from the floor, closed it and laid it on the table. All was as it had been before except that grandmother was gone. The sticks twitched in the grate, the clock ticked and the young man sat patiently, deceitfully beside the bed in granny's nightcap.

Rat-a-tap-tap.

Who's there, he quavers in granny's antique falsetto.

Only your granddaughter.

So she came in, bringing with her a flurry of snow that melted in tears on the tiles, and perhaps she was a little disappointed to see only her grandmother sitting beside the fire. But then he flung off the blanket and sprang to the door, pressing his back against it so that she could not get out again.

The girl looked round the room and saw there was not even the indentation of a head on the smooth cheek of the pillow and how, for the first time she's seen it so, the Bible lay closed on the table. The tick of the clock cracked like a whip. She wanted her knife from her basket but she did not dare reach for it because his eyes were fixed upon her—huge eyes that now seemed to shine with a unique, interior light, eyes the size of saucers, saucers full of Greek fire,[1] diabolic phosphorescence.

What big eyes you have.

All the better to see you with.

No trace at all of the old woman except for a tuft of white hair that had caught in the bark of an unburned log. When the girl saw that, she knew she was in danger of death.

Where is my grandmother?

There's nobody here but we two, my darling.

Now a great howling rose up all around them, near, very near, as close as the kitchen garden, the howling of a multitude of wolves; she knew the worst wolves are hairy on the inside and she shivered, in spite of the scarlet shawl she pulled more closely round herself as if it could protect her, although it was as red as the blood she must spill.

---

1   Inflammable mixtures once used in naval warfare.

Who has come to sing us carols? she said.

Those are the voices of my brothers, darling; I love the company of wolves. Look out of the window and you'll see them.

Snow half-caked the lattice and she opened it to look into the garden. It was a white night of moon and snow; the blizzard whirled round the gaunt, gray beasts who squatted on their haunches among the rows of winter cabbage, pointing their sharp snouts to the moon and howling as if their hearts would break. Ten wolves; twenty wolves—so many wolves she could not count them, howling in concert as if demented or deranged. Their eyes reflected the light from the kitchen and shone like a hundred candles.

It is very cold, poor things, she said; no wonder they howl so.

She closed the window on the wolves' threnody[1] and took off her scarlet shawl, the color of poppies, the color of sacrifices, the color of her menses, and since her fear did her no good, she ceased to be afraid.

What shall I do with my shawl?

Throw it on the fire, dear one. You won't need it again.

She bundled up her shawl and threw it on the blaze, which instantly consumed it. Then she drew her blouse over her head; her small breasts gleamed as if the snow had invaded the room.

What shall I do with my blouse?

Into the fire with it, too, my pet.

The thin muslin went flaring up the chimney like a magic bird and now off came her skirt, her woolen stockings, her shoes, and onto the fire they went, too, and were gone for good. The firelight shone through the edges of her skin; now she was clothed only in her untouched integument[2] of flesh. Thus dazzling, naked, she combed out her hair with her fingers; her hair looked white as the snow outside. Then went directly to the man with red eyes in whose unkempt mane the lice moved; she stood up on tiptoe and unbuttoned the collar of his shirt.

What big arms you have.

All the better to hug you with.

Every wolf in the world now howled a prothalamion[3] outside the window as she freely gave the kiss she owed him.

What big teeth you have!

She saw how his jaw began to slaver and the room was full of the clamour of the forest's *Liebestod*,[4] but the wise child never flinched, even when he answered:

---

1   Song of lamentation for the dead.
2   Natural outer covering, such as skin.
3   A song to celebrate a forthcoming wedding.
4   German: "Love death." i.e., the consummation of love in death.

All the better to eat you with.

The girl burst out laughing; she knew she was nobody's meat. She laughed at him full in the face, she ripped off his shirt for him and flung it into the fire, in the fiery wake of her own discarded clothing. The flames danced like dead souls on Walpurgisnacht[1] and the old bones under the bed set up a terrible clattering, but she did not pay them any heed.

Carnivore incarnate, only immaculate flesh appeases him.

She will lay his fearful head on her lap and she will pick out the lice from his pelt and perhaps she will put the lice into her own mouth and eat them, as he will bid her, as she would do in a savage marriage ceremony.

The blizzard will die down.

The blizzard died down, leaving the mountains as randomly covered with snow as if a blind woman had thrown a sheet over them, the upper branches of the forest pines limed, creaking, swollen with the fall.

Snowlight, moonlight, a confusion of pawprints.

All silent, all still.

Midnight; and the clock strikes. It is Christmas Day, the werewolves' birthday; the door of the solstice stands wide open; let them all sink through.

See! Sweet and sound she sleeps in granny's bed, between the paws of the tender wolf.

WOLF[2]

Francesca Lia Block

THEY DON'T BELIEVE ME. THEY think I'm crazy. But let me tell you something, it be a wicked wicked world out there if you didn't already know.

My mom and he were fighting and that was nothing new. And he was drinking, same old thing. But then I heard her mention me, how she knew what he was doing. And no fucking way was she going to sit around and let that happen. She was taking me away and he better not try to stop her. He said, no way, she couldn't leave.

That's when I started getting scared for both of us, my mom and me. How the hell did she know about that? He would think for sure I told her. And then he'd do

---

1   The eve of 1 May, when witches are supposed to meet.
2   From *The Rose and the Beast* (New York: HarperCollins, 2000).

what he had promised he'd do every night he held me under the crush of his putrid skanky body.

I knew I had to get out of there. I put all my stuff together as quick and quiet as possible—just some clothes, and this one stuffed lamb my mom gave me when I was little and my piggy-bank money that I'd been saving—and I climbed out the window of the condo. It was a hot night and I could smell my own sweat but it was different. I smelled the same old fear I'm used to but it was mixed with the night and the air and the moon and the trees and it was like freedom, that's what I smelled on my skin.

Same old boring boring story America can't stop telling itself. What is this sicko fascination? Every book and movie practically has to have a little, right? But why do you think all those runaways are on the streets tearing up their veins with junk and selling themselves so they can sleep in the gutter? What do you think the alternative was at home?

I booked because I am not a victim by nature. I had been planning on leaving, but I didn't want to lose my mom and I knew the only way I could get her to leave him was if I told her what he did. That was out of the question, not only because of what he might do to me but what it would do to her.

I knew I had to go back and help her, but I have to admit to you that at that moment I was scared shitless and it didn't seem like the time to try any heroics. That's when I knew I had to get to the desert because there was only one person I had in the world besides my mom.

I really love my mom. You know we were like best friends and I didn't even really need any other friend. She was so much fun to hang with. We cut each other's hair and shared clothes. Her taste was kind of youngish and cute, but it worked because she looked pretty young. People thought we were sisters. She knew all the song lyrics and we sang along in the car. We both can't carry a tune. Couldn't? What else about her? It's so hard to think of things sometimes, when you're trying to describe somebody so someone else will know. But that's the thing about it—no one can ever know. Basically you're totally alone and the only person in the world who made me feel not completely that way was her because after all we were made of the same stuff. She used to say to me, Baby, I'll always be with you. No matter what happens to me I'm still here. I believed her until he started coming into my room. Maybe she was still with me but I couldn't be with her those times. It was like if I did then she'd hurt so bad I'd lose her forever.

I figured the only place I could go would be to the desert, so I got together all my money and went to the bus station and bought a ticket. On the ride I started getting the shakes real bad thinking that maybe I shouldn't have left my mom alone like that and maybe I should go back but I was chickenshit, I guess. I leaned my head on the glass and it felt cool and when we got out of the city I started feeling a little better like

I could breathe. L.A. isn't really so bad as people think. I guess. I mean there are gangs at my school but they aren't really active or violent except for the isolated incident. I have experienced one big earthquake in my life and it really didn't bother me so much because I'd rather feel out of control at the mercy of nature than other ways, if you know what I mean. I just closed my eyes and let it ride itself out. I kind of wished he'd been on top of me then because it might have scared him and made him feel retribution was at hand, but I seriously doubt that. I don't blame the earth for shaking because she is probably so sick of people fucking with her all the time—building things and poisoning her and that. L.A. is also known for the smog, but my mom said that when she was growing up it was way worse and that they had to have smog alerts all the time where they couldn't do P.E.[1] Now that part I would have liked because P.E. sucks. I'm not very athletic, maybe cause I smoke, and I hate getting undressed in front of some of those stupid bitches who like to see what kind of underwear you have on so they can dis you in yet another ingenious way. Anyway, my smoking is way worse for my lungs than the smog, so I don't care about it too much. My mom hated that I smoke and she tried everything—tears and the patch and Nicorette and homeopathic remedies and trips to an acupuncturist, but finally she gave up.

I was wanting a cigarette bad on that bus and thinking about how it would taste, better than the normal taste in my mouth, which I consider tainted by him, and how I can always weirdly breathe a lot better when I have one. My mom read somewhere that smoker's smoke as a way to breathe more, so yoga is supposed to help, but that is one thing she couldn't get me to try. My grandmother, I knew she wouldn't mind the smoking—what could she say? My mom called her Barb the chimney. There is something so dry and brittle, so sort of flammable about her, you'd think it'd be dangerous for her to light up like that.

I liked the desert from when I visited there. I liked that it was hot and clean-feeling, and the sand and rocks and cactus didn't make you think too much about love and if you had it or not. They kind of made your mind still, whereas L.A.—even the best parts, maybe especially the best parts, like flowering trees and neon signs and different kinds of ethnic food and music—made you feel agitated and like you were never really getting what you needed. Maybe L.A. had some untapped resources and hidden treasures that would make me feel full and happy and that I didn't know about yet but I wasn't dying to find them just then. If I had a choice I'd probably like to go to Bali or someplace like that where people are more natural and believe in art and dreams and color and love. Does any place like that exist? The main reason L.A. was okay was because that is where my mom was and anywhere she was I had decided to make my home.

---

1   Physical education class.

On the bus there was this boy with straight brown hair hanging in his pale freckled face. He looked really sad. I wanted to talk to him so much but of course I didn't. I am freaked that if I get close to a boy he will somehow find out what happened to me—like it's a scar he'll see or a smell or something, a red flag—and he'll hate me and go away. This boy kind of looked like maybe something had happened to him, too, but you can't know for sure. Sometimes I'd think I'd see signs of it in people but then I wondered if I was just trying not to feel so alone. That sounds sick, I guess, trying to almost wish what I went through on someone else for company. But I don't mean it that way. I don't wish it on anyone, believe me, but if they've been there I would like to talk to them about it.

The boy was writing furiously in a notebook, like maybe a journal, which I thought was cool. This journal now is the best thing I've ever done in my whole life. It's the only good thing really that they've given me here.

One of our assignments was to write about your perfect dream day. I wonder what this boy's perfect dream day would be. Probably to get to fuck Pamela Lee or something. Unless he was really as cool as I hoped, in which case it would be to wake up in a bed full of cute kitties and puppies and eat a bowl full of chocolate chip cookies in milk and get on a plane and get to go to a warm, clean, safe place (the cats and dogs would arrive there later, not at all stressed from their journey) where you could swim in blue-crystal water all day naked without being afraid and you could lie in the sun and tell your best friend (who was also there) your funniest stories so that you both laughed so hard you thought you'd pop and at night you got to go to a restaurant full of balloons and candles and stuffed bears, like my birthdays when I was little, and eat mounds of ice cream after removing the circuses of tiny plastic animals from on top.

In my case, the best friend would be my mom, of course, and maybe this boy if he turned out to be real cool and not stupid. I fell asleep for a little while and I had this really bad dream. I can't remember what it was but I woke up feeling like someone had been slugging me. And then I thought about my mom, I waited to feel her there with me, like I did whenever I was scared, but it was like those times when he came into my room—she wasn't anywhere. She was gone then and I think that was when I knew but I wouldn't let myself.

I think when you are born an angel should say to you, hopefully kindly and not in the fake voice of an airline attendant: Here you go on this long, long dream. Don't even try to wake up. Just let it go on until it is over. You will learn many things. Just relax and observe because there just is pain and that's it mostly and you aren't going to be able to escape no matter what. Eventually it will all be over anyway. Good luck.

I had to get off the bus before the boy with the notebook and as I passed him he looked up. I saw in his journal that he hadn't been writing but sketching, and he ripped out a page and handed it to me. I saw it was a picture of a girl's face but that is all that registered because I was thinking about how my stomach had dropped, how I had to keep walking, step by step, and get off the bus and I'd never be able to see him again and somehow it really really mattered.

When I got off the bus and lit up I saw that the picture was me—except way prettier than I think I look, but just as sad as I feel. And then it was too late to do anything because the bus was gone and so was he.

I stopped at the liquor store and bought a bag of pretzels and a Mountain Dew because I hadn't eaten all day and my stomach was talking pretty loud. Everything tasted of bitter smoke. Then after I'd eaten I started walking along the road to my grandma's. She lives off the highway on this dirt road surrounded by cactus and other desert plants. It was pretty dark so you could see the stars really big and bright, and I thought how cold the sky was and not welcoming or magical at all. It just made me feel really lonely. A bat flew past like a sharp shadow and I could hear owls and coyotes. The coyote howls were the sound I would have made if I could have. Deep and sad but scary enough that no one would mess with me, either.

My grandma has a used stuff store so her house is like this crazy warehouse full of junk like those little plaster statuettes from the seventies of these ugly little kids with stupid sayings that are supposed to be funny, and lots of old clothes like army jackets and jeans and ladies' nylon shirts, and cocktail glasses, broken china, old books, trinkets, gadgets, just a lot of stuff that you think no one would want but they do, I guess, because she's been in business a long time. Mostly people come just to talk to her because she is sort of this wise woman of the desert who's been through a lot in her life and then they end up buying something, I think, as a way to pay her back for the free counseling. She's cool, with a desert-lined face and a bandanna over her hair and long skinny legs in jeans. She was always after my mom to drop that guy and move out here with her but my mom wouldn't. My mom still was holding on to her secret dream of being an actress but nothing had panned out yet. She was so pretty, I thought it would, though. Even though she had started to look a little older. But she could have gotten those commercials where they use the women her age to sell household products and aspirin and stuff. She would have been good at that because of her face and her voice, which are kind and honest and you just trust her.

I hadn't told Grandma anything about him, but I think she knew that he was fucked up. She didn't know how much, though, or she wouldn't have let us stay there. Sometimes I wanted to go and tell her, but I was afraid then Mom would have to know and maybe hate me so much that she'd kick me out.

My mom and I used to get dressed up and put makeup on each other and pretend to do commercials. We had this mother-daughter one that was pretty cool. She said I was a natural, but I wouldn't want to be an actor because I didn't like people looking at me that much. Except that boy on the bus, because his drawing wasn't about the outside of my body, but how I felt inside and you could tell by the way he did it, and the way he smiled, that he understood those feelings so I didn't mind that he saw them. My mom felt that I'd be good anyway, because she said that a lot of actors don't like people looking at them and that is how they create these personas to hide behind so people will see that and the really good ones are created to hide a lot of things. I guess for that reason I might be okay but I still hated the idea of going on auditions and having people tell me I wasn't pretty enough or something. My mom said it was interesting and challenging but I saw it start to wear on her.

Grandma wasn't there when I knocked so I went around the back, where she sat sometimes at night to smoke, and it was quiet there, too. That's when I started feeling sick like at night in my bed trying not to breathe or vomit. Because I saw his Buick sitting there in the sand.

Maybe I have read too many fairy tales. Maybe no one will believe me.

I poked around the house and looked through the windows and after a while I heard their voices and I saw them in this cluttered little storage room piled up with the stuff she sells at the store. Everything looked this glazed brown fluorescent color. When I saw his face I knew something really bad had happened. I remembered the dream I had had and thought about my mom. All of a sudden I was inside that room, I don't really remember how I got there, but I was standing next to my grandma and I saw she had her shotgun in her hand.

He was saying, Barb, calm down, now, okay. Just calm down. When he saw me his eyes narrowed like dark slashes and I heard a coyote out in the night.

My grandmother looked at me and at him and her mouth was this little line stitched up with wrinkles. She kept looking at him but she said to me, Babe, are you okay?

I said I had heard him yelling at mom and I left. She asked him what happened with Nance and he said they had a little argument, that was all, put down the gun, please, Barb.

Then I just lost it, I saw my grandma maybe start to back down a little and I went ballistic. I started screaming how he had raped me for years and I wanted to kill him and if we didn't he'd kill us. Maybe my mom was already dead.

I don't know what else I said, but I do know that he started laughing at me, this hideous tooth laugh, and I remembered him above me in that bed with his clammy hand on my mouth and his ugly ugly weight and me trying to keep hanging on because I wouldn't let him take my mom away, that was the one thing he could never do and now he had. Then I had the gun and I pulled the trigger. My grandma had taught me how once, without my mom knowing, in case I ever needed to defend myself, she said.

My grandma says that she did it. She says that he came at us and she said to him, I've killed a lot prettier, sweeter innocents than you with this shotgun, meaning the animals when she used to go out hunting, which is a pretty good line and everything, but she didn't do it. It was me.

I have no regrets about him. I don't care about much anymore, really. Only one thing.

Maybe one night I'll be asleep and I'll feel a hand like a dove on my cheekbone and feel her breath cool like peppermints and when I open my eyes my mom will be there like an angel, saying in the softest voice, When you are born it is like a long, long dream. Don't try to wake up. Just go along until it is over. Don't be afraid. You may not know it all the time but I am with you. I am with you.

THE SLEEPING BEAUTY IN THE WOOD[1]

Anne Thackeray Ritchie

A KIND ENCHANTRESS ONE DAY PUT into my hand a mystic volume prettily lettered and bound in green, saying, "I am so fond of this book. It has all the dear old fairy tales in it; one never tires of them. Do take it."

I carried the little book away with me, and spent a very pleasant, quiet evening at home by the fire, with H. at the opposite corner, and other old friends, whom I felt I had somewhat neglected of late. Jack and the Beanstalk, Puss in Boots, the gallant and quixotic Giant-killer, and dearest Cinderella, whom we every one of us must have loved, I should think, ever since we first knew her in her little brown pinafore: I wondered, as I shut them all up for the night between their green boards, what it was that made these stories so fresh and so vivid. Why did not they fall to pieces, vanish, explode, disappear, like so many of their contemporaries and descendants? And yet, far from being forgotten and passing away, it would seem as if each generation in turn, as it came into the world, looks to be delighted still by the brilliant pageant, and never tires or wearies of it. And on their side princes and princesses never seem to grow any older; the castles and the lovely gardens flourish without need of repair or whitewash, or plumbers or glaziers. The princesses' gowns, too,—sun, moon, and star color,—do not wear out or pass out of fashion or require altering. Even the seven-leagued boots do not appear to be the worse for wear. Numbers of realistic stories for children have passed away. Little Henry and his Bearer, Poor Harry and

---

1   From *Five Old Friends, and a Young Prince* (London: Smith Elder, 1905).

Lucy,[1] have very nearly given up their little artless ghosts and prattle, and ceased making their own beds for the instruction of less excellently brought up little boys and girls; and, notwithstanding a very interesting article in the *Saturday Review*, it must be owned that Harry Sandford and Tommy Merton[2] are not familiar playfellows in our nurseries and school-rooms, and have passed somewhat out of date. But not so all these centenarians,—Prince Riquet,[3] Carabas,[4] Little Red Riding-hood, Bluebeard, and others. They seem as if they would never grow old. They play with the children, they amuse the elders, there seems no end to their fund of spirits and perennial youth.

H., to whom I made this remark, said, from the opposite chimney-corner, "No wonder; the stories are only histories of real, living persons turned into fairy princes and princesses. Fairy stories are everywhere and every day. We are all princes and princesses in disguise, or ogres or wicked dwarfs. All these histories are the histories of human nature, which does not seem to change very much in a thousand years or so, and we don't get tired of the fairies because they are so true to it."

After this little speech of H.'s, we spent an unprofitable half-hour reviewing our acquaintance, and classing them under their real characters and qualities. We had dined with Lord Carabas only the day before, and met Puss in Boots; Beauty and the Beast were also there. We uncharitably counted up, I am ashamed to say, no less than six Bluebeards. Jack and the Beanstalk we had met just starting on his climb. A Red Riding-hood; a girl with toads dropping from her mouth: we knew three or four of each. Cinderellas—alas! who does not know more than one dear, poor, pretty Cinderella; and as for sleeping princesses in the woods, how many one can reckon up! Young, old, ugly, pretty, awakening, sleeping still.

"Do you remember Cecilia Lulworth," said H., "and Dorlicote? Poor Cecilia!"

Some lives are *couleur de rose*, people say; others seem to be, if not *couleur de rose* all through, yet full of bright, beautiful tints, blues, pinks, little bits of harmonious cheerfulness. Other lives, if not so brilliant, and seeming more or less gray at times, are very sweet and gentle in tone, with faint gleams of gold or lilac to brighten them. And then again others, alas! are black and hopeless from the beginning. Besides these, there are some which have always appeared to me as if they were of a dark, dull hue; a dingy, heavy brown, which no happiness, or interest, or bright color

---

1   *Little Henry and his Bearer* (1814), by Mary Martha Sherwood; *Harry and Lucy* (1801), by Maria Edgeworth. Both these women, the former a Sunday-school moralist and the latter a Rational moralist, wrote for the spiritual and moral improvement (rather than the entertainment) of their child-readers.

2   *The History of Sandford and Merton* (1783–89), by Thomas Day. Another classic of the Rational-moralist school of writing.

3   A character in Charles Perrault's fairy tale "Riquet of the Tuft."

4   "Marquis of Carabas" is the title that Puss in Boots invents for his master (see p. 183).

could ever enliven. Blues turn sickly, roses seem faded, and yellow lilacs look red and ugly upon these heavy backgrounds. Poor Cecilia,—as H. called her,—hers had always seemed to me one of these latter existences, unutterably dull, commonplace, respectable, stinted, ugly, and useless.

Lulworth Hall, with the great, dark park bounded by limestone walls, with iron gates here and there, looked like a blot upon the bright and lovely landscape. The place from a distance, compared with the surrounding country, was a blur and a blemish as it were,—sad, silent, solitary.

Travellers passing by sometimes asked if the place was uninhabited, and were told, "No, shure,—fam'ly lives thear all the yeaurr round." Some charitable souls might wonder what life could be like behind those dull gates. One day a young fellow riding by saw rather a sweet woman's face gazing for an instant through the bars, and he went on his way with a momentary thrill of pity. Need I say that it was poor Cecilia who looked out vacantly to see who was passing along the high-road. She was surrounded by hideous moreen,[1] oil-cloth, punctuality, narrow-mindedness, horsehair, and mahogany. Loud bells rang at intervals, regular, monotonous. Surly but devoted attendants waited upon her. She was rarely alone; her mother did not think it right that a girl in Cecilia's position should "race" about the grounds unattended; as for going outside the walls it was not to be thought of. When Cecilia went out with her gloves on, and her goloshes, her mother's companion, Miss Bowley, walked beside her up and down the dark laurel walk at the back of the house,— up and down, down and up, up and down. "I think I am getting tired, Maria," Miss Lulworth would say at last. "If so we had better return to the hall," Maria would reply, "although it is before our time." And then they would walk home in silence, between the iron railings and laurel-bushes.

As Cecilia walked erectly by Miss Bowley's side, the rooks went whirling over their heads, the slugs crept sleepily along the path under the shadow of the grass and the weeds; they heard no sounds except the cawing of the birds, and the distant monotonous, hacking noise of the gardener and his boy digging in the kitchen-garden.

Cecilia, peeping into the long drab drawing-room on her return, might, perhaps, see her mother, erect and dignified, at her open desk, composing, writing, crossing, re-reading, an endless letter to an indifferent cousin in Ireland, with a single candle and a small piece of blotting-paper, and a pen-wiper made of ravellings,[2] all spread out before her.

"You have come home early, Cecil," says the lady, without looking up. "You had

---

1   Ribbed upholstery fabric.
2   A tangle of broken or discarded threads.

better make the most of your time, and practise till the dressing-bell rings. Maria will kindly take up your things."

And then in the chill twilight Cecilia sits down to the jangling instrument, with the worn silk flutings. A faded rack it is upon which her fingers had been distended ever since she can remember. A great many people think, there is nothing in the world so good for children as scoldings, whippings, dark cupboards, and dry bread and water, upon which they expect them to grow up into tall, fat, cheerful, amiable men and women; and a great many people think that for grown-up young people the silence, the chillness, the monotony and sadness of their own fading twilight days is all that is required. Mrs. Lulworth and Maria Bowley, her companion, Cecilia's late governess, were quite of this opinion. They themselves, when they were little girls, had been slapped, snubbed, locked up in closets, thrust into bed at all sorts of hours, flattened out on backboards, set on high stools to play the piano for days together, made to hem frills five or six weeks long, and to learn immense pieces of poetry, so that they had to stop at home all the afternoon. And though Mrs. Lulworth had grown up stupid, suspicious, narrow-minded, soured, and overbearing, and had married for an establishment, and Miss Bowley, her governess's daughter, had turned out nervous, undecided, melancholy, and anxious, and had never married at all, yet they determined to bring up Cecilia as they themselves had been brought up, and sincerely thought they could not do better.

When Mrs. Lulworth married, she said to Maria, "You must come and live with me, and help to educate my children some day, Maria. For the present I shall not have a home of my own; we are going to reside with my husband's aunt, Mrs. Dormer. She is a very wealthy person, far advanced in years. She is greatly annoyed with Mr. and Mrs. John Lulworth's vagaries, and she has asked me and my husband to take their places at Dorlicote Hall." At the end of ten years Mrs. Lulworth wrote again: "We are now permanently established in our aunt's house. I hear you are in want of a situation; pray come and superintend the education of my only child, Cecilia (she is named after her godmother, Mrs. Dormer). She is now nearly three years old, and I feel that she begins to require some discipline."

This letter was written at that same desk twenty-two years before Cecilia began her practising that autumn evening. She was twenty-five years old now, but like a child in inexperience, in ignorance, in placidity; a fortunate stolidity and slowness of temperament had saved her from being crushed and nipped in the bud, as it were. She was not bored because she had never known any other life. It seemed to her only natural that all days should be alike, rung in and out by the jangling breakfast, lunch, dinner, and prayer-bells. Mr. Dormer—a little chip of a man—read prayers suitable for every day in the week; the servants filed in, maids first, then the men. Once Cecilia saw one of the maids blush and look down smiling as she marched out after the others. Miss Dormer wondered a little, and thought she would ask Susan why she looked so strangely; but Susan married the groom soon after, and went away, and Cecilia never had an opportunity of speaking to her.

Night after night Mr. Dormer replaced his spectacles with a click, and pulled up his shirt-collar when the service was ended. Night after night old Mrs. Dormer coughed a little moaning cough. If she spoke, it was generally to make some little, bitter remark. Every night she shook hands with her nephew and niece, kissed Cecilia's blooming cheek, and patted out of the room. She was a little woman with starling eyes. She had never got over her husband's death. She did not always know when she moaned. She dressed in black, and lived alone in her turret, where she had various old-fashioned occupations,—tatting,[1] camphor-boxes to sort, a real old spinning-wheel and distaff among other things, at which Cecilia, when she was a child, had pricked her fingers trying to make it whirr as her aunt did. Spinning-wheels have quite gone out, but I know of one or two old ladies who still use them. Mrs. Dormer would go nowhere, and would see no one. So at least her niece, the master-spirit, declared, and the old lady got to believe it at last. I don't know how much the fear of the obnoxious John and his wife and children may have had to do with this arrangement.

When her great aunt was gone it was Cecilia's turn to gather her work together at a warning sign from her mother, and walk away through the long, chilly passages to her slumbers in the great green four-post bed. And so time passed. Cecilia grew up. She had neither friends nor lovers. She was not happy nor unhappy. She could read, but she never cared to open a book. She was quite contented; for she thought Lulworth Hall the finest place, and its inmates the most important people in the world. She worked a great deal, embroidering interminable quilts and braided toilet-covers and fish-napkins. She never thought of anything but the utterest commonplaces and platitudes. She considered that being respectable and decorous, and a little pompous and overbearing, was the duty of every well-brought-up lady and gentleman. Tonight she banged away very placidly at Rhodes' air,[2] for the twentieth time breaking down in the same passage and making the same mistake, until the dressing-bell rang, and Cecilia, feeling she had done her duty, then extinguished her candle, and went upstairs across the great, chill hall, up the bare oil-cloth gallery, to her room.

Most young women have some pleasure, whatever their troubles may be, in dressing, and pretty trinkets and beads and ribbons and necklaces. An unconscious love of art and intuition leads some of them, even plain ones, to adorn themselves. The colors and ribbon ends brighten bright faces, enliven dull ones, deck what is already

---

1 Making lace by hand.

2 Like Ritchie, Hugh Rhodes was concerned about childhood morality; see his *Boke of Nurture* (1545).

lovable, or, at all events, make the most of what materials there are. Even a May-pole, crowned and flowered and tastily ribboned, is a pleasing object. And, indeed, the art of decoration—seems to me a charming natural instinct, and one which is not nearly enough encouraged, and a gift which every woman should try to acquire. Some girls, like birds, know how to weave, out of ends of rags, of threads and morsels and straws, a beautiful whole, a work of real genius for their habitation. Frivolities, say some; waste of time, say others,—expense, vanity. The strong-minded dowagers shake their heads at it all,—Mrs. Lulworth among them; only why had Nature painted Cecilia's cheeks of brightest pink, instead of bilious orange, like poor Maria Bowley's? why was her hair all crisp and curly? and were her white, even teeth, and her clear, gray eyes, vanity and frivolity too? Cecilia was rather too stout for her age; she had not much expression in her face. And no wonder. There was not much to be expressive about in her poor little stinted life. She could not go into raptures over the mahogany sideboard, the camphene lamp in the drawing-room, the four-post beds indoors, the laurel-bushes without, the Moorish temple with yellow glass windows, or the wigwam summer-house, which were the alternate boundaries of her daily walks.

Cecilia was not allowed a fire to dress herself by; a grim maid, however, attended, and I suppose she was surrounded, as people say, by every comfort. There was a horsehair sofa, everything was large, solid, brown as I have said, grim, and in its place. The rooms at Lulworth Hall did not take the impression of their inmate; the inmate was moulded by the room. There were in Cecilia's no young lady-like trifles lying here and there; upon the chest of drawers there stood a mahogany workbox, square, with a key,—that was the only attempt at feminine elegance,—a little faded chenille, I believe, was to be seen round the clock on the chimney-piece, and a black and white check dressing-gown and an ugly little pair of slippers were set out before the toilet-table. On the bed, Cecilia's dinner-costume was lying,—a sickly green dress, trimmed with black,—and a white flower for her hair. On the toilet-table an old-fashioned jasper serpent-necklace and a set of amethysts were displayed for her to choose from, also mittens and a couple of hair-bracelets. The girl was quite content, and she would go down gravely to dinner, smoothing out her hideous toggery.

Mrs. Dormer never came down before dinner. All day long she stayed up in her room, dozing and trying remedies, and occasionally looking over old journals and letters until it was time to come downstairs. She liked to see Cecilia's pretty face at one side of the table, while her nephew carved, and Mrs. Lulworth recounted any of the stirring events of the day. She was used to the life,—she was sixty when they came to her, she was long past eighty now,—the last twenty years had been like a long sleep, with the dream of what happened when she was alive and in the world continually passing before her.

When the Lulworths first came to her she had been in a low and nervous state, only stipulated for quiet and peace, and that no one was to come to her house of mourning. The John Lulworths, a cheery couple, broke down at the end of a month or two, and preferred giving up all chance of their aunt's great inheritance to living in such utter silence and seclusion. Upon Charles, the younger brother and his wife, the habit had grown, until now anything else would have been toil and misery to them. Except the old rector from the village, the doctor now and then, no other human creature ever crossed the threshold. For Cecilia's sake Miss Bowley once ventured to hint,—

"Cecilia with her expectations has the whole world before her."

"Maria!" said Mrs. Lulworth, severely; and, indeed, to this foolish woman it seemed as if money would add more to her daughter's happiness than the delights, the wonders, the interests, the glamours of youth. Charles Lulworth, shrivelled, selfish, dull, worn-out, did not trouble his head about Cecilia's happiness, and let his wife do as she liked with the girl.

This especial night when Cecilia came down in her ugly green dress, it seemed to her as if something unusual had been going on. The old lady's eyes looked bright and glittering, her father seemed more animated than usual, her mother looked mysterious and put out. It might have been fancy, but Cecilia thought they all stopped talking as she came into the room; but then dinner was announced, and her father offered Mrs. Dormer his arm immediately, and they went into the dining-room.

It must have been fancy. Everything was as usual. "They have put up a few hurdles in Dalron's field, I see," said Mrs. Lulworth. "Charles, you ought to give orders for repairing the lock of the harness-room."

"Have they seen to the pump-handle?" said Mr. Lulworth.

"I think not." And then there was a dead silence.

"Potatoes," said Cecilia, to the footman. "Mamma, we saw ever so many slugs in the laurel walk, Maria and I,—didn't we, Maria? I think there are a great many slugs in our place."

Old Mrs. Dormer looked up while Cecilia was speaking, and suddenly interrupted her in the middle of her sentence. "How old are you, child?" she said; "are you seventeen or eighteen?"

"Eighteen! Aunt Cecilia. I am five-and-twenty," said Cecilia, staring.

"Good gracious! is it possible?" said her father, surprised.

"Cecil is a woman now," said her mother.

"Five-and-twenty!" said the old lady, quite crossly. "I had no idea time went so fast. She ought to have been married long ago; that is, if she means to marry at all."

"Pray, my dear aunt, do not put such ideas—" Mrs. Lulworth began.

"I don't intend to marry," said Cecilia, peeling an orange, and quite unmoved, and she slowly curled the rind of her orange in the air. "I think people are very stupid to marry. Look at poor Jane Simmonds; her husband beats her; Jones saw her."

"So you don't intend to marry?" said the old lady, with an odd inflection in her voice. "Young ladies were not so wisely brought up in my early days," and she gave a great sigh. "I was reading an old letter this morning from your poor father, Charles,— all about happiness, and love in a cot, and two little curly-headed boys,—Jack, you know, and yourself. I should rather like to see John again."

"What, my dear aunt, after his unparalleled audacity? I declare the thought of his impudent letter makes my blood boil," exclaimed Mrs. Lulworth.

"Does it?" said the old lady. "Cecilia, my dear, you must know that your uncle has discovered that the entail was not cut off from a certain property which my father left me, and which I brought to my husband. He has therefore written me a very business-like letter, in which he says he wishes for no alteration at present, but begs that, in the event of my making my will, I should remember this, and not complicate matters by leaving it to yourself, as had been my intention. I see nothing to offend in the request. Your mother thinks differently."

Cecilia was so amazed at being told anything that she only stared again, and, opening a wide mouth, popped into it such a great piece of orange that she could not speak for some minutes.

"Cecilia has certainly attained years of discretion," said her great-aunt; "she does not compromise herself by giving any opinion on matters she does not understand."

Notwithstanding her outward imperturbability, Cecilia was a little stirred and interested by this history, and by the little conversation which had preceded it. Her mother was sitting upright in her chair as usual, netting with vigorous action; her large foot outstretched, her stiff, bony hands working and jerking monotonously. Her father was dozing in his arm-chair. Old Mrs. Dormer, too, was nodding in her corner. The monotonous Maria was stitching in the lamplight. Gray and black shadows loomed all round her. The far end of the room was quite dark; the great curtains swept from their ancient cornices. Cecilia, for the first time in all her life, wondered whether she should ever live all her life in this spot,—ever go away? It seemed impossible, unnatural, that she should ever do so. Silent, dull as it was, she was used to it, and did not know what was amiss ...

Young Frank Lulworth, the lawyer of the family—John Lulworth's eldest son—it was who had found it all out. His father wrote that with Mrs. Dormer's permission he proposed coming down in a day or two to show her the papers, and to explain to her personally how the matter stood. "My son and I," said John Lulworth, "both feel that this would be far more agreeable to our feelings, and perhaps to yours, than having recourse to the usual professional intervention; for we have no desire to press our claims for the present; and we only wish that in the ultimate disposal of your property you should be aware how the matter really stands. We have always been led to suppose that the estate actually in question has been long destined by you for your grand-niece, Cecilia Lulworth. I hear from our old friend, Dr. Hicks, that she is remarkably pretty and very amiable. Perhaps such vague possibilities are best unmentioned; but it has occurred to me that in the event of a mutual understanding springing up between the young folks,—my son and your grand-niece,—the connection might be agreeable to us all, and lead to a renewal of that family intercourse which has been, to my great regret, suspended for some time past."

Old Mrs. Dormer, in her shaky Italian handwriting, answered her nephew's letter by return of post:—

"MY DEAR NEPHEW,—I must acknowledge the receipt of your epistle of the 13th instant. By all means invite your son to pay us his proposed visit. We can then talk over business matters at our leisure, and young Francis can be introduced to his relatives. Although a long time has elapsed since we last met, believe me, my dear nephew, not unmindful of by-gone associations, and yours, very truly, always,

"C. DORMER."

The letter was in the postman's bag when old Mrs. Dormer informed Mrs. Charles of what she had done.

Frank Lulworth thought that in all his life he had never seen anything so dismal, so silent, so neglected, as Dorlicote Park, when he drove up, a few days after, through the iron gates and along the black laurel wilderness which led to the house. The laurel branches, all unpruned, untrained, were twisting savagely in and out, wreathing and interlacing one another, clutching tender shootings, wrestling with the young oak-trees and the limes. He passed by black and sombre avenues leading to mouldy temples, to crumbling summer-houses; he saw what had once been a flower-garden, now all run to seed,—wild, straggling, forlorn; a broken-down bench, a heap of hurdles lying on the ground, a field-mouse darting across the road, a desolate autumn sun shining upon all this mouldering ornament and confusion. It seemed more forlorn and melancholy by contrast, somehow, coming as he did out of the loveliest country and natural sweetness into the dark and tangled wilderness within these limestone walls of Dorlicote.

The parish of Dorlicote-cum-Rockington looks prettier in the autumn than at any other time. A hundred crisp tints, jewelled rays,—grays, browns, purples, glinting golds, and silvers,—rustle and sparkle upon the branches of the nut-trees, of the bushes and thickets. Soft blue mists and purple tints rest upon the distant hills; scarlet berries glow among the brown leaves of the hedges; lovely mists fall and vanish suddenly, revealing bright and sweet autumnal sights; blackberries, stacks of corn, brown leaves crisping upon the turf, great pears hanging sweetening in the sun over the cottage lintels, cows grazing and whisking their tails, blue smoke curling from the tall farm chimneys; all is peaceful, prosperous, golden. You can see the sea on clear days from certain knolls and hillocks ...

Out of all these pleasant sights young Lulworth came into this dreary splendor. He heard no sounds of life,—he saw no one. His coachman had opened the iron gate. "They doan't keep no one to moind the gate," said the driver; "only tradesmen cooms to th'ouse." Even the gardener and his boy were out of the way; and when they got sight of the house at last, many of the blinds were down and shutters shut, and only two chimneys were smoking. There was some one living in the place, however, for a watch-dog who was lying asleep in his kennel woke up and gave a heartrending howl when Frank got out and rang at the bell.

He had to wait an immense time before anybody answered, although a little page in buttons came and stared at him in blank amazement from one of the basement windows, and never moved. Through the same window Frank could see into the kitchen, and he was amused when a sleepy, fat cook came up behind the little page and languidly boxed his ears, and seemed to order him off the premises.

The butler, who at last answered the door, seemed utterly taken aback,—nobody had called for months past, and here was a perfect stranger taking out his card, and asking for Mrs. Dormer, as if it was the most natural thing in the world. The under-butler was half-asleep in his pantry, and had not heard the door-bell. The page—the very same whose ears had been boxed—came wondering to the door, and went to ascertain whether Mrs. Dormer would see the gentleman or not.

"What a vault, what a catacomb, what an ugly old place!" thought Frank, as he waited. He heard steps far, far away; then came a long silence, and then a heavy tread slowly approaching, and the old butler beckoned to him to follow,—through a cob-web-color room, through a brown room, through a gray room, into a great, dim, drab drawing-room, where the old lady was sitting alone. She had come down her back stairs to receive him; it was years since she had left her room before dinner.

Even old ladies look kindly upon a tall, well-built, good-looking, good-humored young man. Frank's nose was a little too long, his mouth a little too straight; but he was a handsome young fellow, with a charming manner. Only, as he came up, he was somewhat shy and undecided,—he did not know exactly how to address the old lady. This was his great-aunt. He knew nothing whatever about her, but she was very rich; she had invited him to come, and she had a kind face, he thought; should he,—ought he to embrace her? Perhaps he ought, and he made the slightest possible movement in this direction. Mrs. Dormer, divining his object, pushed him weakly away. "How do you do? No embraces, thank you. I don't care for kissing at my age.

Sit down,—there, in that chair opposite,—and now tell me about your father, and all the family, and about this ridiculous discovery of yours. I don't believe a word of it."

The interview between them was long and satisfactory on the whole. The unconscious Cecilia and Miss Bowley returned that afternoon from their usual airing, and, as it happened, Cecilia said, "O Maria! I left my mittens in the drawing-room last night. I will go and fetch them." And, little thinking of what was awaiting her, she flung open the door and marched in through the anteroom,—mushroom hat and brown veil, goloshes and dowdy gown, as usual. "What is this?" thought young Lulworth; "why, who would have supposed it was such a pretty girl?" for suddenly the figure stopped short, and a lovely, fresh face looked up in utter amazement out of the hideous disguise.

"There, don't stare, child," said the old lady. "This is Francis Lulworth, a very intelligent young man, who has got hold of your fortune and ruined all your chances, my dear. He wanted to embrace me just now. Francis, you may as well salute your cousin instead: she is much more of an age for such compliments," said Mrs. Dormer, waving her hand.

The impassive Cecilia, perfectly bewildered, and not in the least understanding, only turned her great, sleepy, astonished eyes upon her cousin, and stood perfectly still as if she was one of those beautiful wax-dolls one sees stuck up to be stared at. If she had been surprised before, utter consternation can scarcely convey her state of mind when young Lulworth stepped up and obeyed her aunt's behest. And, indeed, a stronger-minded person than Cecilia might have been taken aback, who had come into the drawing-room to fetch her mittens, and was met in such an astounding fashion. Frank, half laughing, half kindly, seeing that Cecilia stood quite still and stared at him, supposed it was expected, and did as he was told.

The poor girl gave one gasp of horror, and blushed for the first time, I believe, in the course of her whole existence. Bowley, fixed and open-mouthed from the inner room, suddenly fled with a scream, which recalled Cecilia to a sense of outraged propriety; for, blushing and blinking more deeply, she at last gave three little sobs, and then, O horror! burst into tears!

"Highty-tighty! what a much ado about nothing!" said the old lady, losing her temper and feeling not a little guilty, and much alarmed as to what her niece Mrs. Lulworth might say were she to come on the scene.

"I beg your pardon. I am so very, very sorry," said the young man, quite confused and puzzled. "I ought to have known better. I frightened you. I am your cousin, you know, and really,—pray, pray excuse my stupidity," he said, looking anxiously into the fair, placid face along which the tears were coursing in two streams, like a child's.

"Such a thing never happened in all my life before," said Cecilia. "I know it is wrong to cry, but really—really—"

"Leave off crying directly, miss," said her aunt, testily, "and let us have no more of this nonsense." The old lady dreaded the mother's arrival every instant. Frank, half laughing, but quite unhappy at the poor girl's distress, had taken up his hat to go that minute, not knowing what else to do.

"Ah! you're going," says old Mrs. Dormer; "no wonder. Cecilia, you have driven your cousin away by your rudeness."

"I'm not rude," sobbed Cecilia. "I can't help crying."

"The girl is a greater idiot than I took her for," cried the old lady. "She has been kept here locked up until she has not a single idea left in her silly noddle. No man of sense could endure her for five minutes. You wish to leave the place, I see, and no wonder!"

"I really think," said Frank, "that under the circumstances it is the best thing I can do. Miss Lulworth, I am sure, would wish me to go."

"Certainly," said Cecilia. "Go away, pray go away. Oh, how silly I am!"

Here was a catastrophe!

The poor old fairy was all puzzled and bewildered: her arts were powerless in this emergency. The princess had awakened, but in tears. The prince still stood by, distressed and concerned, feeling horribly guilty, and yet scarcely able to help laughing. Poor Cecilia! her aunt's reproaches had only bewildered her more and more; and for the first time in her life she was bewildered, discomposed, forgetful of hours. It was the hour of calisthenics; but Miss Lulworth forgot everything that might have been expected from a young lady of her admirable bringing-up.

Fairy tales are never very long, and this one ought to come to an end. The princess was awake now; her simplicity and beauty touched the young prince, who did not, I think, really intend to go, though he took up his hat.

Certainly the story would not be worth the telling if they had not been married soon after, and lived happily all the rest of their lives.

★ ★ ★

It is not in fairy tales only that things fall out as one could wish, and indeed, H. and T. agreed the other night that fairies, although invisible, had not entirely vanished out of the land.

It is certainly like a fairy transformation to see Cecilia nowadays in her own home with her children and husband about her. Bright, merry, full of sympathy and interest, she seems to grow prettier every minute.

When Frank fell in love with her and proposed, old Mrs. Dormer insisted upon instantly giving up the Dorlicote Farm for the young people to live in. Mr. and Mrs. Frank Lulworth are obliged to live in London, but they go there every summer with their children; and for some years after her marriage, Cecilia's godmother, who took the opportunity of the wedding to break through many of her recluse habits, used to come and see her every day in a magnificent yellow chariot.

Some day I may perhaps tell you more about the fairies and enchanting princesses of my acquaintance.

WHEN THE CLOCK STRIKES[1]

Tanith Lee

YES, THE GREAT BALLROOM IS filled only with dust now. The slender columns of white marble and the slender columns of rose-red marble are woven together by cobwebs. The vivid frescoes, on which the duke's treasury spent so much, are dimmed by the dust; the faces of the painted goddesses look gray. And the velvet curtains—touch them, they will crumble. Two hundred years, now, since anyone danced in this place on the sea-green floor in the candle gleam. Two hundred years since the wonderful clock struck for the very last time.

I thought you might care to examine the clock. It was considered exceptional in its day. The pedestal is ebony and the face fine porcelain. And these figures, which are of silver, would pass slowly about the circlet of the face. Each figure represents, you understand, an hour. And as the appropriate hours came level with this golden bell, they would strike it the correct number of times. All the figures are unique, you see. Beginning at the first hour, they are, in this order, a girl-child, a dwarf, a maiden, a youth, a lady, and a knight. And here, notice, the figures grow older as the day declines: a queen and king for the seventh and eighth hours, and after these, an abbess and a magician and next to last, a hag. But the very last is strangest of all. The twelfth figure: do you recognize him? It is Death. Yes, a most curious clock. It was reckoned a marvelous thing then. But it has not struck for two hundred years. Possibly you have been told the story? No? Oh, but I am certain that you have heard it, in another form, perhaps.

However, as you have some while to wait for your carriage, I will recount the tale, if you wish.

I will start with what is said of the clock. In those years, this city was prosperous, a stronghold—not as you see it today. Much was made in the city that was ornamental and unusual. But the clock, on which the twelfth hour was Death, caused something

---

1   From *Red as Blood, or Tales from the Sisters Grimmer* (New York: Daw, 1983).

of a stir. It was thought unlucky, foolhardy, to have such a clock. It began to be murmured, jokingly by some, by others in earnest, that one night when the clock struck
the twelfth hour, Death would truly strike with it.

Now life has always been a chancy business, and it was more so then. The Great
Plague had come but twenty years before and was not yet forgotten. Besides, in the
duke's court there was much intrigue, while enemies might be supposed to plot beyond the city walls, as happens even in our present age. But there was another thing.

It was rumored that the duke had obtained both his title and the city treacher-
ously. Rumor declared that he had systematically destroyed those who had stood in
line before him, the members of the princely house that formerly ruled here. He had
accomplished the task slyly, hiring assassins talented with poisons and daggers. But
rumor also declared that the duke had not been sufficiently thorough. For though
he had meant to rid himself of all that rival house, a single descendant remained, so
obscure he had not traced her—for it was a woman.

Of course, such matters were not spoken of openly. Like the prophecy of the
clock, it was a subject for the dark.

Nevertheless, I will tell you at once, there was such a descendant he had missed in
his bloody work. And she was a woman. Royal and proud she was, and seething with
bitter spite and a hunger for vengeance, and as bloody as the duke, had he known it,
in her own way.

For her safety and disguise, she had long ago wed a wealthy merchant in the city
and presently bore the man a daughter. The merchant, a dealer in silks, was respect-
ed, a good fellow but not wise. He rejoiced in his handsome and aristocratic wife. He
never dreamed what she might be about when he was not with her. In fact, she had
sworn allegiance to Satanas. In the dead of night she would go up into an old tower
adjoining the merchant's house, and there she would say portions of the Black Mass,
offer sacrifice, and thereafter practice witchcraft against the duke. This witchery took
a common form, the creation of a wax image and the maiming of the image that, by
sympathy, the injuries inflicted on the wax be passed on to the living body of the victim. The woman was capable in what she did. The duke fell sick. He lost the use of his
limbs and was racked by excruciating pains from which he could get no relief. Thinking himself on the brink of death, the duke named his sixteen-year-old son his heir.
This son was dear to the duke, as everyone knew, and be sure the woman knew it too.

She intended sorcerously to murder the young man in his turn, preferably in his
father's sight. Thus she let the duke linger in his agony and commenced planning the
fate of the prince.

Now all this while she had not been toiling alone. She had one helper. It was her
own daughter, a maid of fourteen, that she had recruited to her service nearly as soon
as the infant could walk. At six or seven, the child had been lisping the satanic rite

along with her mother. At fourteen, you may imagine, the girl was well versed in the black arts, though she did not have her mother's natural genius for them.

Perhaps you would like me to describe the daughter at this point. It has a bearing on the story, for the girl was astonishingly beautiful. Her hair was the rich dark red of antique burnished copper, her eyes were the hue of the reddish-golden amber that traders bring from the East. When she walked, you would say she was dancing. But when she danced, a gate seemed to open in the world, and bright fire spangled inside it, but she was the fire.

The girl and her mother were close as gloves in a box. Their games in the old tower bound them closer. No doubt the woman believed herself clever to have got such a helpmate, but it proved her undoing.

It was in this manner. The silk merchant, who had never suspected his wife for an instant of anything, began to mistrust the daughter. She was not like other girls. Despite her great beauty, she professed no interest in marriage and none in clothes or jewels. She preferred to read in the garden at the foot of the tower. Her mother had taught the girl her letters, though the merchant himself could read but poorly. And often the father peered at the books his daughter read, unable to make head nor tail of them, yet somehow not liking them. One night very late, the silk merchant came home from a guild dinner in the city, and he saw a slim pale shadow gliding up the steps of the old tower, and he knew it for his child. On impulse, he followed her, but quietly. He had not considered any evil so far and did not want to alarm her. At an angle of the stair, the lighted room above, he paused to spy and listen. He had something of a shock when he heard his wife's voice rise up in glad welcome. But what came next drained the blood from his heart. He crept away and went to his cellar for wine to stay himself. After the third glass he ran for neighbors and for the watch.

The woman and her daughter heard the shouts below and saw the torches in the garden. It was no use dissembling. The tower was littered with evidence of vile deeds, besides what the woman kept in a chest beneath her unknowing husband's bed. She understood it was all up with her, and she understood, too, how witchcraft was punished hereabouts. She snatched a knife from the altar.

The girl shrieked when she realized what her mother was at. The woman caught the girl by her red hair and shook her.

"Listen to me, my daughter," she cried, "and listen carefully, for the minutes are short. If you do as I tell you, you can escape their wrath and only I need die. And if you live I am satisfied, for you can carry on my labor after me. My vengeance I shall leave you, and my witchcraft to exact it by. Indeed, I promise you stronger powers than mine. I will beg my lord Satanas for it, and he will not deny me, for he is just, in his fashion, and I have served him well. Now will you attend?"

"I will," said the girl.

So the woman advised her and swore her to the fellowship of Hell. And then the woman forced the knife into her own heart and dropped dead on the floor of the tower.

When the men burst in with their swords and staves and their torches and their madness, the girl was ready for them.

She stood blank-faced, blank-eyed, with her arms hanging at her sides. When one touched her, she dropped down at his feet.

"Surely she is innocent," this man said. She was lovely enough that it was hard to accuse her. Then her father went to her and took her hand and lifted her. At that, the girl opened her eyes, and she said, as if terrified: "How did I come here? I was in my chamber and sleeping ..."

"The woman has bewitched her," her father said.

He desired very much that this be so. And when the girl clung to his hand and wept, he was certain of it. They showed her the body with the knife in it. The girl screamed and seemed to lose her senses totally.

She was put to bed. In the morning, a priest came and questioned her. She answered steadfastly. She remembered nothing, not even of the great books she had been observed reading. When they told her what was in them, she screamed again and apparently would have thrown herself from the narrow window, only the priest stopped her.

Finally, they brought her the holy cross in order that she might kiss it and prove herself blameless.

Then she knelt, and whispered softly, that nobody should hear but one: "Lord Satanas, protect thy handmaid." And either that gentleman has more power than he is credited with or else the symbols of God are only as holy as the men who deal in them, for she embraced the cross and it left her unscathed.

At that, the whole household thanked God. The whole household saving, of course, the woman's daughter. She had another to thank.

The woman's body was burned and the ashes put into unconsecrated ground beyond the city gates. Though they had discovered her to be a witch, they had not discovered the direction her witchcraft had selected. Nor did they find the wax image with its limbs all twisted and stuck through with needles. The girl had taken that up and concealed it. The duke continued in his distress, but he did not die. Sometimes, in the dead of night, the girl would unearth the image from under a loose brick by the hearth and gloat over it, but she did nothing else. Not yet. She was fourteen, and the cloud of her mother's acts still hovered over her. She knew what she must do next.

The period of mourning ended.

"Daughter," said the silk merchant to her, "why do you not remove your black? The woman was malign and led you into wickedness. How long will you mourn her, who deserves no mourning?"

"Oh, my father," she said, "never think I regret my wretched mother. It is my own unwitting sin I mourn," and she grasped his hand and spilled her tears on it. "I would rather live in a convent," said she, "than mingle with proper folk. And I would seek a convent too, if it were not that I cannot bear to be parted from you."

Do you suppose she smiled secretly as she said this? One might suppose it. Presently she donned a robe of sackcloth and poured ashes over her red-copper hair. "It is my penance," she said. "I am glad to atone for my sins."

People forgot her beauty. She was at pains to obscure it. She slunk about like an aged woman, a rag pulled over her head, dirt smeared on her cheeks and brow. She elected to sleep in a cold cramped attic and sat all day by a smoky hearth in the kitchens. When someone came to her and begged her to wash her face and put on suitable clothes and sit in the rooms of the house, she smiled modestly, drawing the rag of a piece of hair over her face. "I swear," she said, "I am glad to be humble before God and men."

They reckoned her pious and they reckoned her simple. Two years passed. They mislaid her beauty altogether and reckoned her ugly. They found it hard to call to mind who she was exactly, as she sat in the ashes or shuffled unattended about the streets like a crone.

At the end of the second year, the silk merchant married again. It was inevitable, for he was not a man who liked to live alone.

On this occasion, his choice was a harmless widow. She already had two daughters, pretty in an unremarkable style. Perhaps the merchant hoped they would comfort him for what had gone before, this normal cheery wife and the two sweet, rather silly daughters, whose chief interests were clothes and weddings. Perhaps he hoped also that his deranged daughter might be drawn out by company. But that hope floundered. Not that the new mother did not try to be pleasant to the girl. And the new sisters, their hearts grieved by her condition, went to great lengths to enlist her friendship. They begged her to come from the kitchens or the attic. Failing in that, they sometimes ventured to join her, their fine silk dresses trailing on the greasy floor. They combed her hair, exclaiming, when some of the ash and dirt were removed, on its color. But no sooner had they turned away than the girl gathered up handfuls of soot and ash and rubbed them into her hair again. Now and then, the sisters attempted to interest their bizarre relative in a bracelet or a gown or a current song. They spoke to her of the young men they had seen at the suppers or the balls which were then given regularly by the rich families of the city. The girl ignored it all. If she ever said anything, it was to do with penance and humility. At last, as must happen, the sisters wearied of her and left her alone. They had no cares and did not want to share in hers. They came to resent her moping grayness, as indeed the merchant's second wife had already done.

"Can you do nothing with that girl?" she demanded of her husband. "People will say that I and my daughters are responsible for her condition and that I ill-treat the maid from jealousy of her dead mother."

"Now how could anyone say that," protested the merchant, "when you are famous as the epitome of generosity and kindness?"

Another year passed, and saw no difference in the household.

A difference there was, but not visible.

The girl who slouched in the corner of the hearth was seventeen. Under the filth and grime she was, impossibly, more beautiful, although no one could see it.

And there was one other invisible item: her power (which all this time she had nurtured, saying her prayers to Satanas in the black of midnight), her power rising like a dark moon in her soul.

Three days after her seventeenth birthday, the girl straggled about the streets, as she frequently did. A few noted her and muttered it was the merchant's ugly simple daughter and paid no more attention. Most did not know her at all. She had made herself appear one with the scores of impoverished flotsam which constantly roamed the city, beggars and starvelings. Just outside the city gates, these persons congregated in large numbers, slumped around fires of burning refuse or else wandering to and fro in search of edible seeds, scraps, the miracle of a dropped coin. Here the girl now came and began to wander about as they did. Dusk gathered and the shadows thickened. The girl sank to her knees in a patch of earth as if she had found something. Two or three of the beggars sneaked over to see if it were worth snatching from her—but the girl was only scrabbling in the empty soil. The beggars, making signs to each other that she was touched by God—mad—left her alone. But very far from mad, the girl presently dug up a stoppered urn. In this urn were the ashes and charred bones of her mother. She had got a clue as to the location of the urn by devious questioning here and there. Her occult power had helped her to be sure of it.

In the twilight, padding along through the narrow streets and alleys of the city, the girl brought the urn homeward. In the garden, at the foot of the old tower, gloom-wrapped, unwitnessed, she unstoppered the urn and buried the ashes freshly. She muttered certain unholy magics over the grave. Then she snapped off the sprig of a young hazel tree and planted it in the newly turned ground.

I hazard you have begun to recognize the story by now. I see you suppose I tell it wrongly. Believe me, this is the truth of the matter. But if you would rather I left off the tale … no doubt your carriage will soon be here—No? Very well. I shall continue.

I think I should speak of the duke's son at this juncture. The prince was nineteen, able, intelligent, and of noble bearing. He was of that rather swarthy type of looks one finds here in the north, but tall and slim and clear-eyed. There is an ancient square where you may see a statue of him, but much eroded by two centuries and the elements. After the city was sacked, no care was lavished on it.

The duke treasured his son. He had constant delight in the sight of the young man and what he said and did. It was the only happiness the invalid had.

Then, one night, the duke screamed out in his bed. Servants came running with candles. The duke moaned that a sword was transfixing his heart, an inch at a time. The prince hurried into the chamber, but in that instant the duke spasmed horribly and died. No mark was on his body. There had never been a mark to show what ailed him.

The prince wept. They were genuine tears. He had nothing to reproach his father with, everything to thank him for. Presently, they brought the young man the seal ring of the city, and he put it on.

It was winter, a cold blue-white weather with snow in the streets and country-side and a hard wizened sun that drove thin sharp blades of light through the sky but gave no warmth. The duke's funeral cortege passed slowly across the snow: the broad open chariots, draped with black and silver; the black-plumed horses; the chanting priests with their glittering robes, their jeweled crucifixes and golden censers. Crowds lined the roadways to watch the spectacle. Among the beggar women stood a girl. No one noticed her. They did not glimpse the expression she veiled in her ragged scarf. She gazed at the bier pitilessly. As the young prince rode by in his sables, the seal ring on his hand, the eyes of the girl burned through her ashy hair, like a red fox through grasses.

The duke was buried in the mausoleum you can visit to this day, on the east side of the city. Several months elapsed. The prince put his grief from him and took up the business of the city competently. Wise and courteous he was, but he rarely smiled. At nineteen, his spirit seemed worn. You might think he guessed the destiny that hung over him.

The winter was a hard one too. The snow had come and, having come, was loath to withdraw. When at last the spring returned, flushing the hills with color, it was no longer sensible to be sad.

The prince's name day fell about this time. A great banquet was planned, a ball. There had been neither in the palace for nigh on three years, not since the duke's fatal illness first claimed him. Now the royal doors were to be thrown open to all men of influence and their families. The prince was liberal, charming, and clever even in this. Aristocrat and rich trader were to mingle in the beautiful dining room, and in this very chamber, among the frescoes, the marble, and the candelabra. Even a merchant's daughter, if the merchant was notable in the city, would get to dance on the sea-green floor, under the white eye of the fearful clock.

The clock. There was some renewed controversy about the clock. They did not dare speak to the young prince. He was a skeptic, as his father had been. But had not a death already occurred? Was the clock not a flying in the jaws of fate? For those disturbed by it, there was a dim writing in their minds, in the dust of the street or the pattern of blossoms. *When the clock strikes*—But people do not positively heed these warnings. Man is afraid of his fears. He ignores the shadow of the wolf thrown on the paving before him, saying: It is only a shadow.

The silk merchant received his invitation to the palace, and to be sure, thought nothing of the clock. His house had been thrown into uproar. The most luscious silks of his workshop were carried into the house and laid before the wife and her two daughters, who chirruped and squealed with excitement. "Oh, Father," cried the two sisters, "may I have this one with the gold piping?" "Oh, Father, this one with the design of pineapples?" Later a jeweler arrived and set out his trays. The merchant was generous. He wanted his women to look their best. It might be the night of their lives. Yet all the while, at the back of his mind, a little dark spot, itching, aching. He tried to ignore the spot, not scratch at it. His true daughter, the mad one. Nobody bothered to tell her about the invitation to the palace. They knew how she would react, mumbling in her hair about her sin and her penance, paddling her hands in the greasy ash to smear her face. Even the servants avoided her, as if she were just the cat seated by the fire. Less than the cat, for the cat saw to the mice—just a block of stone. And yet, how fair she might have looked, decked in the pick of the merchant's wares, jewels at her throat. The prince himself could not have been unaware of her. And though marriage was impossible, other, less holy though equally honorable contracts might have been arranged, to the benefit of all concerned. The merchant sighed. He had scratched the darkness after all. He attempted to comfort himself by watching the two sisters exult over their apparel. He refused to admit that the finery would somehow make them seem but more ordinary than they were by contrast.

The evening of the banquet arrived. The family set off. Most of the servants sidled after. The prince had distributed largess in the city; oxen roasted in the squares, and the wine was free by royal order.

The house grew somber. In the deserted kitchen, the fire went out.

By the hearth, a segment of gloom rose up.

The girl glanced around her, and she laughed softly and shook out her filthy hair. Of course, she knew as much as anyone, and more than most. This was to be her night too.

A few minutes later she was in the garden beneath the old tower, standing over the young hazel tree which had thrust up from the earth. It had become strong, the tree, despite the harsh winter. Now the girl nodded to it. She chanted under her breath. At length a pale light began to glow, far down near where the roots of the tree held to the ground. Out of the pale glow flew a thin black bird, which perched on the girl's shoulder. Together, the girl and the bird passed into the old tower. High up, a fire blazed that no one had lit. A tub steamed with scented water that no one had drawn. Shapes that were not real and barely seen flitted about. Rare perfumes, the rustle of garments, the glint of gems as yet invisible, filled and did not fill the restless air.

Need I describe further? No. You will have seen paintings which depict the attendance upon a witch of her familiar demons. How one bathes her, another anoints her, another brings clothes and ornaments. Perhaps you do not credit such things in any case. Never mind that. I will tell you what happened in the courtyard before the palace.

Many carriages and chariots had driven through the square, avoiding the roasting oxen, the barrels of wine, the cheering drunken citizens, and so through the gates into the courtyard. Just before ten o'clock (the hour, if you recall the clock, of the magician), a solitary carriage drove through the square and into the court. The people in the square gawped at the carriage and pressed forward to see who would step out of it, this latecomer. It was a remarkable vehicle that looked to be fashioned of solid gold, all but the domed roof, that was transparent flashing crystal. Six black horses drew it. The coachman and postilions were clad in crimson, and strangely masked as curious beasts and reptiles. One of these beast-men now hopped down and opened the door of the carriage. Out came a woman's figure in a cloak of white fur, and glided up the palace stair and in at the doors.

There was dancing in the ballroom. The whole chamber was bright and clamorous with music and the voices of men and women. There, between those two pillars, the prince sat in his chair, dark, courteous, seldom smiling. Here the musicians played, the deep-throated viol, the lively mandolin. And there the dancers moved up and down on the sea-green floor. But the music and the dancers had just paused. The figures on the clock were themselves in motion. The hour of the magician was about to strike.

As it struck, through the doorway came the figure in the fur cloak. And as if they must, every eye turned to her.

For an instant she stood there, all white, as though she had brought the winter snow back with her. And then she loosed the cloak from her shoulders, it slipped away, and she was all fire.

She wore a gown of apricot brocade embroidered thickly with gold. Her sleeves and the bodice of her gown were slashed over ivory satin sewn with large rosy pearls. Pearls, too, were wound in her hair, that was the shade of antique burnished copper. She was so beautiful that when the clock was still, nobody spoke. She was so beautiful that it was hard to look at her for very long.

The prince got up from his chair. He did not know he had. Now he started out across the floor, between the dancers, who parted silently to let him through. He went toward the girl in the doorway as if she drew him by a chain.

The prince had hardly ever acted without considering first what he did. Now he did not consider. He bowed to the girl.

"Madam," he said. "You are welcome, Madam," he said. "Tell me who you are."

She smiled.

"My rank," she said. "Would you know that, my lord? It is similar to yours, or would be were I now mistress in my dead mother's palace. But, unfortunately, an unscrupulous man caused the downfall of our house."

"Misfortune indeed," said the prince. "Tell me your name. Let me right the wrong done you."

"You shall," said the girl. "Trust me, you shall. For my name, I would rather keep it secret for the present. But you may call me, if you will, a pet name I have given myself—Ashella."

"Ashella ... But I see no ash about you," said the prince, dazzled by her gleam, laughing a little, stiffly, for laughter was not his habit.

"Ash and cinders from a cold and bitter hearth," said she. But she smiled again. "Now everyone is staring at us, my lord, and the musicians are impatient to begin again. Out of all these ladies, can it be you will lead me in the dance?"

"As long as you will dance," he said. "You shall dance with me."

And that is how it was.

There were many dances, slow and fast, whirling measures and gentle ones. And here and there, the prince and the maiden were parted. Always then he looked eagerly after her, sparing no regard for the other girls whose hands lay in his. It was not like him, he was usually so careful. But the other young men who danced on that floor, who clasped her fingers or her narrow waist in the dance, also gazed after her when she was gone. She danced, as she appeared, like fire. Though if you had asked those young men whether they would rather tie her to themselves, as the prince did, they would have been at a loss. For it is not easy to keep pace with fire.

The hour of the hag struck on the clock.

The prince grew weary of dancing with the girl and losing her in the dance to others and refinding her and losing her again.

Behind the curtains there is a tall window in the east wall that opens on the terrace above the garden. He drew her out there, into the spring night. He gave an order, and small tables were brought with delicacies and sweets and wine. He sat by her, watching every gesture she made, as if he would paint her portrait afterward.

In the ballroom, here, under the clock, the people murmured. But it was not quite the murmur you would expect, the scandalous murmur about a woman come from nowhere that the prince had made so much of. At the periphery of the ballroom, the silk merchant sat, pale as a ghost, thinking of a ghost, the living ghost of his true daughter. No one else recognized her. Only he. Some trick of his heart had enabled him to know her. He said nothing of it. As the stepsisters and wife gossiped with other wives and sisters, an awful foreboding weighed him down, sent him cold and dumb.

And now it is almost midnight, the moment when the page of the night turns over into day. Almost midnight, the hour when the figure of Death strikes the golden bell of the clock. And what will happen when the clock strikes? Your face announces that you know. Be patient; let us see if you do.

"I am being foolish," said the prince to Ashella on the terrace. "But perhaps I am entitled to be foolish, just once in my life. What are you saying?" For the girl was speaking low beside him, and he could not catch her words.

"I am saying a spell to bind you to me," she said.

"But I am already bound."

"Be bound, then. Never go free."

"I do not wish it," he said. He kissed her hands, and he said, "I do not know you, but I will wed you. Is that proof your spell has worked? I will wed you, and get back for you the rights you have lost."

"If it were only so simple," said Ashella, smiling, smiling. "But the debt is too cruel. Justice requires a harsher payment."

And then, in the ballroom, Death struck the first note on the golden bell.

The girl smiled and she said:

"I curse you in my mother's name."

The second stroke.

"I curse you in my own name."

The third stroke.

"And in the name of those that your father slew."

The fourth stroke.

"And in the name of my Master, who rules the world."

As the fifth, the sixth, the seventh strokes pealed out, the prince stood nonplussed. At the eighth and ninth strokes, the strength of the malediction seemed to curdle his blood. He shivered and his brain writhed. At the tenth stroke, he saw a change in the loveliness before him. She grew thinner, taller. At the eleventh stroke, he beheld a thing in a ragged black cowl and robe. It grinned at him. It was all grin below a triangle of sockets of nose and eyes. At the twelfth stroke, the prince saw Death and knew him.

In the ballroom, a hideous grinding noise, as the gears of the clock failed. Followed by a hollow booming, as the mechanism stopped entirely.

The conjuration of Death vanished from the terrace.

Only one thing was left behind. A woman's shoe. A shoe no woman could ever have danced in. It was made of glass.

Did you intend to protest about the shoe? Shall I finish the story, or would you rather I did not? It is not the ending you are familiar with. Yes, I perceive you understand that now.

I will go quickly, then, for your carriage must soon be here. And there is not a great deal more to relate.

The prince lost his mind. Partly from what he had seen, partly from the spells the young witch had netted him in. He could think of nothing but the girl who had named herself Ashella. He raved that Death had borne her away but he would recover her from Death. She had left the glass shoe as token of her love. He must discover her with the aid of the shoe. Whomsoever the shoe fitted would be Ashella. For there was this added complication, that Death might hide her actual appearance. None had seen the girl before. She had disappeared like smoke. The one infallible test was the shoe. That was why she had left it for him.

His ministers would have reasoned with the prince, but he was past reason. His intellect had collapsed totally as only a profound intellect can. A lunatic, he rode about the city. He struck out at those who argued with him. On a particular occasion, drawing a dagger, he killed, not apparently noticing what he did. His demand was explicit. Every woman, young or old, maid or married, must come forth from her home, must put her foot into the shoe of glass. They came. They had no choice. Some approached in terror, some weeping. Even the aged beggar women obliged, and they cackled, enjoying the sight of royalty gone mad. One alone did not come.

Now it is not illogical that out of the hundreds of women whose feet were put into the shoe, a single woman might have been found that the shoe fitted. But this did not happen. Nor did the situation alter, despite a lurid fable that some, tickled by the idea of wedding the prince, cut off their toes that the shoe might fit them. And if they did, it was to no avail, for still the shoe did not.

Is it really surprising? The shoe was sorcerous. It constantly changed itself, its shape, its size, in order that no foot, save one, could ever be got into it.

Summer spread across the land. The city took on its golden summer glaze, its fetid summer spell.

What had been a whisper of intrigue swelled into a steady distant thunder. Plots were hatched.

One day the silk merchant was brought, trembling and gray of face, to the prince. The merchant's dumbness had broken. He had unburdened himself of his fear at confession, but the priest had not proved honest. In the dawn, men had knocked on the door of the merchant's house. Now he stumbled to the chair of the prince.

Both looked twice their years, but if anything, the prince looked the elder. He did not lift his eyes. Over and over in his hands he turned the glass shoe.

The merchant, stumbling, too, in his speech, told the tale of his first wife and his daughter. He told everything, leaving out no detail. He did not even omit the end: that since the night of the banquet the girl had been absent from his house, taking nothing with her—save a young hazel from the garden beneath the tower.

The prince leapt from his chair.

His clothes were filthy and unkempt. His face was smeared with sweat and dust ... it resembled, momentarily, another face.

Without guard or attendant, the prince ran through the city toward the merchant's house, and on the road, the intriguers waylaid and slew him. As he fell, the glass shoe dropped from his hands and shattered in a thousand fragments.

There is little else worth mentioning.

Those who usurped the city were villains and not merely that but fools. Within a year, external enemies were at the gates. A year more, and the city had been sacked, half burned out, ruined. The manner in which you find it now is somewhat better than it was then. And it is not now anything for a man to be proud of. As you were quick to note, many here earn a miserable existence by conducting visitors about the streets, the palace, showing them the dregs of the city's past.

Which was not a request, in fact, for you to give me money. Throw some from your carriage window if your conscience bothers you. My own wants are few.

No, I have no further news of the girl Ashella, the witch. A devotee of Satanas, she has doubtless worked plentiful woe in the world. And a witch is long-lived. Even so, she will die eventually. None escapes Death. Then you may pity her, if you like. Those who serve the gentleman below—who can guess what their final lot will be? But I am very sorry the story did not please you. It is not, maybe, a happy choice before a journey.

And there is your carriage at last.

What? Ah, no, I shall stay here in the ballroom, where you came on me. I have often paused here through the years. It is the clock. It has a certain—what shall I call it?—power to draw me back.

I am not trying to unnerve you. Why should you suppose that? Because of my knowledge of the city, of the story? You think that I am implying that I myself am Death? Now you laugh. Yes, it is absurd. Observe the twelfth figure on the clock. Is he not as you always heard Death described? And am I in the least like that twelfth figure?

Although, of course, the story was not as you have heard it, either.

THE WICKED STEPMOTHER'S LAMENT[1]

Sara Maitland

The wife of a rich man fell sick and, as she felt that her end was drawing near, she called her only daughter to her bedside and said, "Dear child, be good and pious, and then the good God will always protect you, and I will look down from heaven and be near you." Thereupon she closed her eyes and departed. Every day the maiden went out to her mother's grave and wept, and she remained pious and good. When winter came the snow spread a white sheet over the grave and by the time the spring sun had drawn it off again the man had taken another wife ...

Now began a bad time for the poor step-child ... They took her pretty clothes away, put an old grey bedgown on her and gave her wooden shoes ... She had to do hard work from morning to night, get up before daybreak, carry water, light fires, cook and wash ... In the evening when she had worked until she was weary she had no bed to go to but had to sleep by the hearth in the cinders. And as on that account she always looked dusty and dirty, they called her Cinderella.

YOU KNOW THE REST I expect. Almost everyone does.

I'm not exactly looking for self-justification. There's this thing going on at the moment where women tell all the old stories again and turn them inside-out and back-to-front—so the characters you always thought were the goodies turn out to be the baddies, and vice versa, and a whole lot of guilt is laid to rest: or that at least is the theory. I'm not sure myself that the guilt isn't just passed on to the next person, *intacta*, so to speak. Certainly I want to carry and cope with my own guilt, because I want to carry and cope with my own virtue and I really don't see that you can have one without the other. Anyway, it would be hard to find a version of this story where I would come out a shiny new-style heroine: no true version, anyway. All I want to say is that it's more complicated, more complex, than it's told, and the reasons why it's told the way it is are complex too.

But I'm not willing to be a victim. I was not innocent, and I have grown out of innocence now and even out of wanting to be thought innocent. Living is a harsh business, as no one warned us when we were young and carefree under the apple bough, and I feel the weight of that ancient harshness and I want to embrace it, and not opt for some washed-out aseptic, hand-wringing, Disneyland garbage. (Though

---

1   From *A Book of Spells* (London: Michael Joseph, 1987).

come to think of it he went none-too-easy on step-mothers, did he? Snow White's scared the socks off me the first time I saw the film—and partly of course because I recognised myself. But I digress.)

Look. It was like this. Or rather it was more like this, or parts of it were like this, or this is one part of it.

She was dead pretty in a Pears soap sort of way, and, honestly, terribly sweet and good. At first all I wanted her to do was concentrate. Concentration is the key to power. You have to concentrate on what is real. Concentration is not good or bad necessarily, but it is powerful. Enough power to change the world, that's all I wanted. (I was younger then, of course; but actually they're starving and killing whales and forests and each other out there; shutting your eyes and pretending they're not doesn't change anything. It does matter.) And what she was not was powerful. She wouldn't look out for herself. She was so sweet and so hopeful; so full of faith and forgiveness and love. You have to touch anger somewhere, rage even; you have to spit and roar and bite and scream and know it before you can be safe. And she never bloody would.

When I first married her father I thought she was so lovely, so good and so sad. And so like her mother. I knew her mother very well, you see; we grew up together. I loved her mother. Really. With so much hope and fondness and awareness of her worth. But—and I don't know how to explain this without sounding like an embittered old bitch which I probably am—she was too good. Too giving. She gave herself away, indiscriminately. She didn't even give herself as a precious gift. She gave herself away as though she wasn't worth hanging on to. Generous to a fault, they said, when she was young, but no one acted as though it were a fault, so she never learned. "Free with Kellogg's cornflakes" was her motto. She equated loving with suffering, I thought at one time, but that wasn't right, it was worse, she equated loving with being; as though she did not exist unless she was denying her existence. I mean, he was not a bad bloke, her husband, indeed I'm married to him myself, and I like him and we have good times together, but he wasn't worth it—no one is—not what she gave him, which was her whole self with no price tag on.

And it was just the same with that child. Yes, yes, one can understand: she had difficulty getting pregnant actually, she had difficulties carrying those babies to term too. Even I can guess how that might hurt. But her little girl was her great reward for suffering, and at the same time was also her handle on a whole new world of self-giving. And yes, of course she looked so lovely, who could have resisted her, propped up in her bed with that tiny lovely child sucking, sucking, sucking? The mother who denied her little one nothing, the good mother, the one we all longed for, pouring herself out into the child. Well, I'll tell you, I've done it too, it is hell caring for a tiny daughter, I know. Everything, everything drags you into hell: the fact that you love and desire her, the fact that she's so needy and vulnerable, the fact that she never leaves you alone until your dreams are smashed in little piles and shabby with neglect, the fact that pleasure and guilt come so precisely together, as so seldom happens, working towards the same end and sucking your very selfhood out of you. It is a perilous time for a woman, that nursing of a daughter, and you can only survive it if you cling to yourself with a fierce and passionate love, *and* you back that up with a trained and militant lust for justice *and* you scream at the people around you to meet your needs and desires *and* you do not let them off, *and* when all is said and done you sit back and laugh at yourself with a well-timed and not unmalicious irony. Well, she could not, of course she could not, so she did not survive. She was never angry, she never asked, she took resignation—that tragic so-called virtue—as a ninth-rate alternative to reality and never even realised she had been short-changed.

So when I first married my husband I only meant to tease her a little, to rile her, to make her fight back. I couldn't bear it, that she was so like her mother and would go the same way. My girls were more like me, less agreeable to have about the house, but tough as old boots and capable of getting what they needed and not worrying too much about what they wanted or oughted, so to speak. I didn't have to worry about them. I just could not believe the sweetness of that little girl and her wide-eyed belief that I would be happy and love her if she would just deny herself and follow me. So of course I exploited her a bit, pushed and tested it, if you understand, because I couldn't believe it. Then I just wanted her to *see*, to see that life is not all sweetness and light, that people are not automatically to be trusted, that fairy godmothers are unreliable and damned thin on the ground, and that even the most silvery of princes soon goes out hunting and fighting and drinking and whoring, and doesn't give one tuppenny-ha'penny curse more for you than you give for yourself. Well, she could have looked at her father and known. He hardly proved himself to be the great romantic lover of all time, even at an age when that would have been appropriate, never mind later. He had after all replaced darling Mummy with me, and pretty damned quick too, and so long as he was getting his end off and his supper on the table he wasn't going to exert himself on her behalf, as I pointed out to her, by no means kindly.

(And, I should like to add, I still don't understand about that. I couldn't believe how little the bastard finally cared when it came to the point. Perhaps he was bored to tears by goodness, perhaps he was too lazy. He was a sentimental old fart about her, of course, his eyes could fill with nostalgic tears every time he looked at her and thought of her dead mother; but he never *did* anything; or even asked me to stop doing anything. She never asked, and he never had eyes to see, or energy or … God knows what went on in his head about her and as far as I'm concerned God's welcome. She loved him and trusted him and served him and he never even bloody noticed. Which sort of makes my point actually because he would never treat me like that, and yet he and I get on very well now; like each other and have good times in bed and out of it. Of course I'd never have let him tell me how to behave, but he might have tried, at least just once.)

Anyway, no, she would not see. She would not blame her father. She would not blame her mother, not even for dying, which is the ultimate outrage from someone you love. And she would not blame me. She just smiled and accepted, smiled and invented castles in the air to which someone, though never herself, would come and take her one day, smiled and loved me. No matter what I did to her, she just smiled.

So, yes, in the end I was cruel. I don't know how to explain it and I do not attempt to justify it. Her *wetness* infuriated me. I could not shake her good will, her hopefulness, her capacity to love and love and love such a pointless and even dangerous object. I could not make her hate me. Not even for a moment. I could not make her hate me. And I cannot explain what that frustration did to me. I hated her insane dog-like devotion where it was so undeserved. She treated me as her mother had treated him. I think I hated her stupidity most of all. I can hear myself almost blaming her for my belly-deep madness; I don't want to do that; I don't want to get into blaming the victim and she was my victim. I was older than her, and stronger than her, and had more power than her; and there was no excuse. No excuse, I thought the first time I ever hit her, but there was an excuse and it was my wild need, and it escalated.

So in the end—and yes I have examined all the motives and reasons why one woman should be cruel to another and I do not find them explanatory—so in the end I was cruel to her. I goaded and humiliated and pushed and bullied her. I used all my powers, my superior strength, my superior age, my superior intelligence, against her. I beat her, in the end, systematically and severely; but more than that I used her and worked her and denied her pleasures and gave her pain. I violated her space, her dignity, her integrity, her privacy, even her humanity and perhaps her physical safety. There was an insane urge in me, not simply to hurt her, but to have her admit that I had hurt her. I would lie awake at night appalled, and scald myself with contempt, with anger and with self-disgust, but I had only to see her in the morning for my temper to rise and I would start again, start again at her with an unreasonable savagery that seemed to upset me more than it upset her. Picking, picking and pecking, endlessly. She tried my patience as no one else had ever done and finally I gave up the struggle and threw it away and entered into the horrible game with all my considerable capacity for concentration.

And nothing worked. I could not make her angry. I could not make her hate me. I could not stop her loving me with a depth and a generosity and a forgivingness that were the final blow. Nothing moved her to more than a simper. Nothing penetrated the fantasies and day dreams with which her head was stuffed so full I'm surprised she didn't slur her consonants. She was locked into perpetual passivity and gratitude and love. Even when she was beaten she covered her bruises to protect me; even when she was hungry she would not take food from my cupboards to feed herself; even when I mocked her she smiled at me tenderly.

All I wanted was for her to grow up, to grow up and realise that life was not a bed of roses and that she had to take some responsibility for her own life, to take some action on her own behalf, instead of waiting and waiting and waiting for something or someone to come shining out of the dark and force safety on her as I forced pain. What Someone? Another like her father who had done nothing, nothing whatever, to help her and never would? Another like him whom she could love generously and hopelessly and serve touchingly and givingly until weariness and pain killed her too. I couldn't understand it. Even when I beat her, even as I beat her, she loved me, she just loved and smiled and hoped and waited, day-dreamed and night-dreamed, and waited and waited and waited. She was untouchable and infantile. I couldn't save her and I couldn't damage her. God knows, I tried.

And now of course it's just an ancient habit. It has lost its sharp edges, lost the passion in both of us to see it out in conflict, between dream and reality, between hope and cynicism. There is a great weariness in me, and I cannot summon up the fire of conviction. I do not concentrate any more, I do not have enough concentration, enough energy, enough power. Perhaps she has won, because she drained that out of me years and years ago. Sometimes I despair, which wastes still more concentration. We plod on together, because we always have. Sweetly she keeps at it, smile, smile, dream, hope, wait, love, forgive, smile, smile, bloody smile. Tiredly, I keep at it too: "Sweep that grate." "Tidy your room." "Do your homework." "What can you see in that nerd?" "Take out those damn ear-phones and pay attention." "Life doesn't come free, you have to work on it." "Wake up, hurry up, stop day-dreaming, no you can't, yes you must, get a move on, don't be so stupid," and "You're not going to the ball, or party, or disco, or over your Nan's, dressed like *that*."

She calls it nagging.

She calls me Mummy.

SNOW WHITE[1]

The Merseyside Fairy Story Collective

HIGH ABOVE A FAR OFF kingdom, carved into the rock of a mountainside, there once stood a mighty castle. It was so high that the people working on the distant plain could look up and see it among the clouds and when they saw it they trembled, for it was the castle of the cruel and powerful Queen of the Mountains.

The Queen of the Mountains had ten thousand soldiers at her command. She sat upon a throne of marble dressed in robes weighed down with glittering jewels, and holding in her hand a magic mirror. This mirror could answer any question the Queen asked it and in it the Queen could see what was happening anywhere in her kingdom. When she looked into the mirror and saw any of her subjects doing things which displeased her she sent soldiers to punish them.

Night and day her soldiers stood guard on the walls of the castle and every day they watched as people from all over the kingdom toiled up the steep pathway carrying heavy loads: iron to shoe the royal horses; weapons to arm the royal soldiers; food to be cooked in the royal kitchens; cloth to clothe the royal servants. The procession wound on and on up the mountainside to the castle. The people were carrying with them all the useful and beautiful things that had been made in the kingdom, for everything they made belonged to the Queen and they were allowed to keep only what was left over or spoiled.

No one could save anything from the Queen of the Mountains for no place was hidden from her magic mirror. Every day the riches of the kingdom were brought to her and every night she asked the mirror:

Mirror, mirror in my hand,
Who is the happiest in the land?

Then in a silvery voice the mirror always replied:

Queen, all bow to your command,
You are the happiest in the land.

And the Queen would smile.

One day, among the procession climbing the steep path to the castle were a pale little girl called Snow White and seven little men, dwarfs, even smaller than she.

---

1   From *Spare Rib* 51 (1976).

Snow White and the dwarfs were carrying between them a heavy chest bound with metal bands. They had travelled all the way from the diamond mines beside the distant sea. There, far underground, often in danger, they and many other men, women and children, worked long and weary hours. Every year they must send a chestful of diamonds to the Queen of the Mountains or they would be cruelly punished.

When the other people in the procession reached the castle gates the lovely things they had been carrying were taken from them and they were sent away, but Snow White and the seven dwarfs were surrounded by soldiers and brought to the throne of the Queen herself.

"Open the chest," ordered the Queen as they bowed before her.

Two dwarfs lifted the lid. The chest was full of glittering diamonds and on top of them lay a necklace shaped like branches of ice. The Queen held the necklace up to the light.

"Did you make this?" she asked Snow White.

"Yes Majesty," said the girl.

"It is well made," said the Queen. "You are to stay in the castle as a jewellery maker."

Snow White's pale cheeks turned red and she opened her mouth to cry "No!" but each of the seven dwarfs put a crooked finger to his lips, warning her to be silent.

"Take her to the workshop!" ordered the Queen.

The soldiers led Snow White and the dwarfs out of the throne room and up a twisting stairway to a small room at the top of a tower. In the room there was a work bench with jeweller's tools laid out on it. All around the walls, stored in tall glass jars, gleamed jewels of many colours: amethysts, emeralds, rubies, sapphires, topaz. Little light came through the one small window but the jewels shone so brightly that when Snow White looked at them her eyes were dazzled and her head began to ache.

Snow White and the seven dwarfs took the diamonds from the chest and put them into empty glass jars. Then, one by one, the seven little men kissed Snow White goodbye. There were tears in their eyes for she was their dearest friend. They shouldered the empty chest and went slowly down the twisting staircase.

"You are very lucky," said one of the soldiers to Snow White. "You will no longer be poor and lead a hard life toiling underground in the mine. Here servants will wait on you. You will sleep in a soft, scented bed and be brought whatever delicious food and drink you want. And, if the Queen is especially pleased with your work she will give you rich rewards."

"But my friends will still be toiling in the mine," said Snow White and her heart felt like a stone with sorrow.

In the long days and weeks which followed Snow White grew more and more skilful at making beautiful pieces of jewellery out of the precious stones and metals in the workshop. The jewellery pleased the Queen of the Mountains. One evening she summoned Snow White to the throne room.

"This brooch pleased me," said the Queen. "You may choose a reward."

"Oh, Majesty," answered Snow White, falling on her knees, "please let me go home."

The Queen was angry. She turned her mirror towards Snow White and in it the little girl could see the dwarfs and all her other friends digging in the mine and dragging heavy loads along its narrow tunnels.

"You could have anything your heart desires and yet you ask to return to that miserable life!" the Queen exclaimed. "Go back to your work and think hard before you enter my presence again."

So, as she deftly twisted the metal and fitted the precious stones, Snow White thought long and hard. She thought of the sufferings she had shared with her friends in the distant mines; of how they and all the people of the land spent their whole lives working to make lovely things for the Queen of the Mountains while they themselves had barely enough to live on. And Snow White knew what she would ask for.

"I will make a jewelled belt so beautiful that the Queen will call me before her again," she thought and at once set to work.

"Well, Snow White," said the Queen as the girl stood before her throne a second time, "you have had time to think. Tell me your heart's desire and I will grant it, for what you have made is more beautiful than anything in my treasure chambers." As she spoke the Queen ran her fingers along the red and purple gems of the jewelled belt.

"Majesty," said Snow White, "I have thought and what I ask for is this: take only what you need from the people of the kingdom and let them keep the rest so that they will no longer be cold and hungry and miserable."

The Queen's eyes glittered with rage and her hand tightened on the jewelled belt, but when she spoke her voice was as sweet as honey.

"Snow White, if anyone but you had spoken such treachery, I would have ordered my soldiers to throw them from the walls of the castle onto the rocks below. But you have a rare skill and are young enough to change your thoughts. Come close and look in my mirror."

Snow White looked into the magic mirror and saw herself reflected there, but strangely. She was wearing working clothes and yet in the mirror she was dressed in a richly embroidered gown, pearls and rubies were entwined in her long hair and on her head was a golden crown.

"You see, Snow White," said the Queen, "you could be a princess. Now go."

Snow White went back to the workshop. She stood gazing out of the tiny window and thinking of how she had looked in the mirror, adorned with jewels and gold. Far below her she could see the daily procession of people carrying up the mountainside all the things they had made and must give to the Queen. Beyond them the green plain stretched out until it reached the distant hills. On the other side of the hills was the sea and Snow White's home. The words of a song which she and her friends used to sing when the long day's work in the mine was over came back to her mind.

Emerald's green but grass is greener
Sapphires pale beside the sea.
No jet as black as the wild night sky,
No ruby red
No ruby red
No ruby red as hearts which cry to be free.

"What my friends long for is my heart's desire too," thought Snow White, "but the Queen of the Mountain will never set us free."

Soon the Queen summoned Snow White before her throne a third time.

"No flower in all my gardens is as delicately shaped as these ear-rings you have made," she said. "What reward do you want?"

"Nothing, Majesty," said Snow White quietly.

"Foolish girl!" cried the Queen, "I know you are unhappy, yet you only have to ask and you can become a princess. Very well, you will continue to make jewellery for me, but from now on soldiers will stand guard at the foot of the tower where you work and unless you choose to be a princess you will never leave the tower again."

The months passed by. Still Snow White remained alone in the tower and did not ask for her reward. Quiet and pale, she sat at her work, thinking and waiting.

When a whole year had passed Snow White looked from her tiny window and saw below, among the people toiling up the pathway to the castle, seven little figures carrying between them a heavy chest. It was her friends the dwarfs at last.

Snow White waited for the dwarfs to bring the chest of diamonds to the workshop but when the chest was brought in it was carried by some of the Queen's soldiers.

"The Queen has given orders that you are not to see your friends from the mine," said one of the soldiers. "She is watching them in her mirror all the time they are here."

"Please go back to the foot of the stairs and leave me alone," said Snow White in a sad voice. "I will fill the glass jars with diamonds and put the empty chest outside the door."

The soldiers did as she asked, for they liked Snow White and secretly admired her for daring to displease the Queen.

An hour later they returned and took the chest away, down the twisting stairway and into the courtyard where the dwarfs were waiting. The little men swung it onto their shoulders and carried it out of the castle gates and down the mountainside.

All that day the Queen of the Mountains sat on her throne and watched in her mirror as the dwarfs went further and further away. By the time that evening came they had crossed the distant hills. The Queen smiled to herself and asked the mirror her usual question:

Mirror, mirror in my hand
Who is happiest in the land?

In its silvery voice, the mirror replied:

Though all bow to your command,
Snow White is happiest in the land.

"Snow White!" hissed the Queen, "Show me Snow White!"

Then, in the mirror, she saw the seven dwarfs lifting the lid off the chest and out of the chest climbed Snow White, her face full of joy.

The Queen's rage was terrible. She ordered that the soldiers who had let Snow White escape were to be thrown from the castle walls. Throughout the night she sat on her throne speaking to no one. Then, as the sun rose, she gave orders to her soldiers.

"Go to the diamond mines," she commanded. "Seal up the entrance while Snow White and her companions are working so that they will all die underground."

Many of the soldiers were filled with horror but they dared not disobey. The Queen watched in her mirror as they sealed up the way out of the mine and when it was done, she laughed.

Word of the terrible thing done at the Queen's command spread quickly through the land. Many people came to where the Queen's soldiers stood guard beside the sealed up entrance to the mine. As the day wore on, more and more people arrived. They stood there quietly at a little distance from the soldiers, as if they were waiting for something to happen. By evening, a great crowd had gathered. They lit fires to keep themselves warm through the night and talked in low voices about all the people trapped underground and the cruelty of the Queen of the Mountains. They knew that by now there must be little air left to breathe down in the mine. Soon Snow White and her friends would be dead as the Queen of the Mountains had commanded.

Suddenly, among some rocks on the outskirts of the crowd, a tapping sound could be heard. As the people looked at each other in bewilderment, one of the rocks began to move and then was pushed aside from behind to reveal a narrow shaft going deep into the earth. Climbing from this passage was one of the dwarfs.

"Just in time," wheezed the dwarf. "I do not think we could have gone on digging much longer. My oldest brother remembered that when he was very young there was another way out of the mine. He led us to the place and we dug in the dark until the way was opened up."

One by one, helping each other, the workers from the diamond mine climbed out into the fresh night air. Some were faint, some were bruised and many had torn and bleeding hands, but every child, woman and man was safe. Among them was Snow White.

The great crowd of people round the fires and the soldiers stared in amazement. Then the people began to cheer. Some of the soldiers joined in the cheering but others drew their weapons. One of these called out to Snow White.

"Snow White," he ordered, "you must come with us at once back to the castle."

"No," answered Snow White, "I will not go back to the castle and we will send no more diamonds to the Queen. Everyone will keep the things they make and send nothing to the Queen of the Mountains."

As she spoke the cheers grew louder and louder.

"Then we will kill you," said the soldier.

"You may kill some of us," said Snow White, "but in the end you will lose for there are far more people than there are soldiers."

The people realised that this was true and they surrounded the soldiers determined to take their weapons from them, whatever the cost.

Far away on her marble throne, the Queen of the Mountains took the jewellery Snow White had made and broke it into pieces. In her magic mirror she could see all that was happening. She knew that the people of the land were rising up against her.

Mirror, mirror in my hand
Make them bow to my command,

she ordered her mirror. But the mirror answered:

Queen who was so rich and grand
The people cast you from the land.

The magic mirror misted over and when the mist had gone, the Queen could see nothing reflected there but her own face.

Still grasping the mirror in her hand, the Queen of the Mountains rose from her throne and climbed the stone steps to the highest battlements of the castle. From there she could look out and see with her own eyes the crowds of people gathering on the distant plain. In fear and fury she lifted the mirror above her head and flung it from the castle wall.

The mirror would not leave her hand. She fell with it and hurtled screaming down and down until she was shattered into fragments on the rocks below.

SNOW, GLASS, APPLES[1]

Neil Gaiman

I DO NOT KNOW WHAT MANNER of thing she is. None of us do. She killed her mother in the birthing, but that's never enough to account for it.

They call me wise, but I am far from wise, for all that I foresaw fragments of it, frozen moments caught in pools of water or in the cold glass of my mirror. If I were wise I would not have tried to change what I saw. If I were wise I would have killed myself before ever I encountered her, before ever I caught him.

Wise, and a witch, or so they said, and I'd seen his face in my dreams and in reflections for all my life: sixteen years of dreaming of him before he reined his horse by the bridge that morning and asked my name. He helped me onto his high horse and we rode together to my little cottage, my face buried in the gold of his hair. He asked for the best of what I had; a king's right, it was.

His beard was red-bronze in the morning light, and I knew him, not as a king, for I knew nothing of kings then, but as my love. He took all he wanted from me, the right of kings, but he returned to me on the following day and on the night after that: his beard so red, his hair so gold, his eyes the blue of a summer sky, his skin tanned the gentle brown of ripe wheat.

His daughter was only a child: no more than five years of age when I came to the palace. A portrait of her dead mother hung in the princess's tower room: a tall woman, hair the color of dark wood, eyes nut-brown. She was of a different blood to her pale daughter.

The girl would not eat with us.

I do not know where in the palace she ate.

I had my own chambers. My husband the king, he had his own rooms also. When he wanted me he would send for me, and I would go to him, and pleasure him, and take my pleasure with him.

---

1   From *Smoke and Mirrors* (New York: Avon Books, 1998).

One night, several months after I was brought to the palace, she came to my rooms. She was six. I was embroidering by lamplight, squinting my eyes against the lamp's smoke and fitful illumination. When I looked up, she was there.

"Princess?"

She said nothing. Her eyes were black as coal, black as her hair; her lips were redder than blood. She looked up at me and smiled. Her teeth seemed sharp, even then, in the lamplight.

"What are you doing away from your room?"

"I'm hungry," she said, like any child.

It was winter, when fresh food is a dream of warmth and sunlight; but I had strings of whole apples, cored and dried, hanging from the beams of my chamber, and I pulled an apple down for her.

"Here."

Autumn is the time of drying, of preserving, a time of picking apples, of rendering the goose fat. Winter is the time of hunger, of snow, and of death; and it is the time of the midwinter feast, when we rub the goose fat into the skin of a whole pig, stuffed with that autumn's apples; then we roast it or spit it, and we prepare to feast upon the crackling.

She took the dried apple from me and began to chew it with her sharp yellow teeth.

"Is it good?"

She nodded. I had always been scared of the little princess, but at that moment I warmed to her and, with my fingers, gently, I stroked her cheek. She looked at me and smiled—she smiled but rarely—then she sank her teeth into the base of my thumb, the Mound of Venus, and she drew blood.

I began to shriek, from pain and from surprise, but she looked at me and I fell silent.

The little princess fastened her mouth to my hand and licked and sucked and drank. When she was finished, she left my chamber. Beneath my gaze the cut that she had made began to close, to scab, and to heal. The next day it was an old scar: I might have cut my hand with a pocketknife in my childhood.

I had been frozen by her, owned and dominated. That scared me, more than the blood she had fed on. After that night I locked my chamber door at dusk, barring it with an oaken pole, and I had the smith forge iron bars, which he placed across my windows.

My husband, my love, my king, sent for me less and less, and when I came to him he was dizzy, listless, confused. He could no longer make love as a man makes love, and he would not permit me to pleasure him with my mouth: the one time I tried, he started violently, and began to weep. I pulled my mouth away and held him tightly until the sobbing had stopped, and he slept, like a child.

I ran my fingers across his skin as he slept. It was covered in a multitude of ancient scars. But I could recall no scars from the days of our courtship, save one, on his side, where a boar had gored him when he was a youth.

Soon he was a shadow of the man I had met and loved by the bridge. His bones showed, blue and white, beneath his skin. I was with him at the last: his hands were cold as stone, his eyes milky blue, his hair and beard faded and lustreless and limp. He died unshriven, his skin nipped and pocked from head to toe with tiny, old scars.

He weighed near to nothing. The ground was frozen hard, and we could dig no grave for him, so we made a cairn of rocks and stones above his body, as a memorial only, for there was little enough of him left to protect from the hunger of the beasts and the birds.

So I was queen.

And I was foolish, and young—eighteen summers had come and gone since first I saw daylight—and I did not do what I would do, now.

If it were today, I would have her heart cut out, true. But then I would have her head and arms and legs cut off. I would have them disembowel her. And then I would watch in the town square as the hangman heated the fire to white-heat with bellows, watch unblinking as he consigned each part of her to the fire. I would have archers around the square, who would shoot any bird or animal that came close to the flames, any raven or dog or hawk or rat. And I would not close my eyes until the princess was ash, and a gentle wind could scatter her like snow.

I did not do this thing, and we pay for our mistakes.

They say I was fooled; that it was not her heart. That it was the heart of an animal—a stag, perhaps, or a boar. They say that, and they are wrong.

And some say (but it is *her* lie, not mine) that I was given the heart, and that I ate it. Lies and half-truths fall like snow, covering the things that I remember, the things I saw. A landscape, unrecognizable after a snowfall; that is what she has made of my life.

There were scars on my love, her father's thighs, and on his ballock-pouch, and on his male member, when he died.

I did not go with them. They took her in the day, while she slept, and was at her weakest. They took her to the heart of the forest, and there they opened her blouse, and they cut out her heart, and they left her dead, in a gully, for the forest to swallow.

The forest is a dark place, the border to many kingdoms; no one would be foolish enough to claim jurisdiction over it. Outlaws live in the forest. Robbers live in the forest, and so do wolves. You can ride through the forest for a dozen days and never see a soul; but there are eyes upon you the entire time.

They brought me her heart. I know it was hers—no sow's heart or doe's would have continued to beat and pulse after it had been cut out, as that one did.

I took it to my chamber.

I did not eat it: I hung it from the beams above my bed, placed it on a length of twine that I strung with rowan berries, orange-red as a robin's breast, and with bulbs of garlic.

Outside the snow fell, covering the footprints of my huntsmen, covering her tiny body in the forest where it lay.

I had the smith remove the iron bars from my windows, and I would spend some time in my room each afternoon through the short winter days, gazing out over the forest, until darkness fell.

There were, as I have already stated, people in the forest. They would come out, some of them, for the Spring Fair: a greedy, feral, dangerous people; some were stunted—dwarfs and midgets and hunchbacks; others had the huge teeth and vacant gazes of idiots; some had fingers like flippers or crab claws. They would creep out of the forest each year for the Spring Fair, held when the snows had melted.

As a young lass I had worked at the fair, and they had scared me then, the forest folk. I told fortunes for the fairgoers, scrying[1] in a pool of still water; and later, when I was older, in a disk of polished glass, its back all silvered—a gift from a merchant whose straying horse I had seen in a pool of ink.

The stallholders at the fair were afraid of the forest folk; they would nail their wares to the bare boards of their stalls—slabs of gingerbread or leather belts were nailed with great iron nails to the wood. If their wares were not nailed, they said, the forest folk would take them and run away, chewing on the stolen gingerbread, flailing about them with the belts.

The forest folk had money, though: a coin here, another there, sometimes stained green by time or the earth, the face on the coin unknown to even the oldest of us. Also they had things to trade, and thus the fair continued, serving the outcasts and the dwarfs, serving the robbers (if they were circumspect) who preyed on the rare travelers from lands beyond the forest, or on gypsies, or on the deer. (This was robbery in the eyes of the law. The deer were the queen's.)

The years passed by slowly, and my people claimed that I ruled them with wisdom. The heart still hung above my bed, pulsing gently in the night. If there were any who mourned the child, I saw no evidence: she was a thing of terror, back then, and they believed themselves well rid of her.

Spring Fair followed Spring Fair: five of them, each sadder, poorer, shoddier than the one before. Fewer of the forest folk came out of the forest to buy. Those who did seemed subdued and listless. The stallholders stopped nailing their wares to the boards of their stalls. And by the fifth year but a handful of folk came from the forest—a fearful huddle of little hairy men, and no one else.

---

1   Predicting the future.

The Lord of the Fair, and his page, came to me when the fair was done. I had known him slightly, before I was queen.

"I do not come to you as my queen," he said.

I said nothing. I listened.

"I come to you because you are wise," he continued. "When you were a child you found a strayed foal by staring into a pool of ink; when you were a maiden you found a lost infant who had wandered far from her mother, by staring into that mirror of yours. You know secrets and you can seek out things hidden. My queen," he asked, "what is taking the forest folk? Next year there will be no Spring Fair. The travelers from other kingdoms have grown scarce and few, the folk of the forest are almost gone. Another year like the last, and we shall all starve."

I commanded my maidservant to bring me my looking glass. It was a simple thing, a silver-backed glass disk, which I kept wrapped in a doeskin, in a chest, in my chamber.

They brought it to me then, and I gazed into it:

She was twelve and she was no longer a little child. Her skin was still pale, her eyes and hair coal-black, her lips blood-red. She wore the clothes she had worn when she left the castle for the last time—the blouse, the skirt—although they were much let-out, much mended. Over them she wore a leather cloak, and instead of boots she had leather bags, tied with thongs, over her tiny feet.

She was standing in the forest, beside a tree.

As I watched, in the eye of my mind, I saw her edge and step and flitter and pad from tree to tree, like an animal: a bat or a wolf. She was following someone.

He was a monk. He wore sackcloth, and his feet were bare and scabbed and hard. His beard and tonsure were of a length, overgrown, unshaven.

She watched him from behind the trees. Eventually he paused for the night and began to make a fire, laying twigs down, breaking up a robin's nest as kindling. He had a tinderbox in his robe, and he knocked the flint against the steel until the sparks caught the tinder and the fire flamed. There had been two eggs in the nest he had found, and these he ate raw. They cannot have been much of a meal for so big a man.

He sat there in the firelight, and she came out from her hiding place. She crouched down on the other side of the fire, and stared at him. He grinned, as if it were a long time since he had seen another human, and beckoned her over to him.

She stood up and walked around the fire, and waited, an arm's length away. He pulled in his robe until he found a coin—a tiny copper penny—and tossed it to her. She caught it, and nodded, and went to him. He pulled at the rope around his waist, and his robe swung open. His body was as hairy as a bear's. She pushed him back onto the moss. One hand crept, spiderlike, through the tangle of hair, until it closed on his manhood; the other hand traced a circle on his left nipple. He closed his eyes and fumbled one huge hand under her skirt. She lowered her mouth to the nipple she had been teasing, her smooth skin white on the furry brown body of him.

She sank her teeth deep into his breast. His eyes opened, then they closed again, and she drank.

She straddled him, and she fed. As she did so, a thin blackish liquid began to dribble from between her legs …

"Do you know what is keeping the travelers from our town? What is happening to the forest people?" asked the Lord of the Fair.

I covered the mirror in doeskin, and told him that I would personally take it upon myself to make the forest safe once more.

I had to, although she terrified me. I was the queen.

A foolish woman would have gone then into the forest and tried to capture the creature; but I had been foolish once and had no wish to be so a second time.

I spent time with old books. I spent time with the gypsy women (who passed through our country across the mountains to the south, rather than cross the forest to the north and the west).

I prepared myself and obtained those things I would need, and when the first snows began to fall, I was ready.

Naked, I was, and alone in the highest tower of the palace, a place open to the sky. The winds chilled my body; goose pimples crept across my arms and thighs and breasts. I carried a silver basin, and a basket in which I had placed a silver knife, a silver pin, some tongs, a gray robe, and three green apples.

I put them down and stood there, unclothed, on the tower, humble before the night sky and the wind. Had any man seen me standing there, I would have had his eyes; but there was no one to spy. Clouds scudded across the sky, hiding and uncovering the waning moon.

I took the silver knife and slashed my left arm—once, twice, three times. The blood dripped into the basin, scarlet seeming black in the moonlight.

I added the powder from the vial that hung around my neck. It was a brown dust, made of dried herbs and the skin of a particular toad, and from certain other things. It thickened the blood, while preventing it from clotting.

I took the three apples, one by one, and pricked their skins gently with my silver pin. Then I placed the apples in the silver bowl and let them sit there while the first tiny flakes of snow of the year fell slowly onto my skin, and onto the apples, and onto the blood.

When dawn began to brighten the sky I covered myself with the gray cloak, and took the red apples from the silver bowl, one by one, lifting each into my basket with silver tongs, taking care not to touch it. There was nothing left of my blood or of the brown powder in the silver bowl, nothing save a black residue, like a verdigris, on the inside.

I buried the bowl in the earth. Then I cast a glamour on the apples (as once, years before, by a bridge, I had cast a glamour on myself), that they were, beyond any doubt, the most wonderful apples in the world, and the crimson blush of their skins was the warm color of fresh blood.

I pulled the hood of my cloak low over my face, and I took ribbons and pretty hair ornaments with me, placed them above the apples in the reed basket, and I walked alone into the forest until I came to her dwelling: a high sandstone cliff, laced with deep caves going back a way into the rock wall.

There were trees and boulders around the cliff face, and I walked quietly and gently from tree to tree without disturbing a twig or a fallen leaf. Eventually I found my place to hide, and I waited, and I watched.

After some hours, a clutch of dwarfs crawled out of the hole in the cave front—ugly, misshapen, hairy little men, the old inhabitants of this country. You saw them seldom now.

They vanished into the wood, and none of them espied me, though one of them stopped to piss against the rock I hid behind.

I waited. No more came out.

I went to the cave entrance and hallooed into it, in a cracked old voice.

The scar on my Mound of Venus throbbed and pulsed as she came toward me, out of the darkness, naked and alone.

She was thirteen years of age, my stepdaughter, and nothing marred the perfect whiteness of her skin, save for the livid scar on her left breast, where her heart had been cut from her long since.

The insides of her thighs were stained with wet black filth.

She peered at me, hidden, as I was, in my cloak. She looked at me hungrily. "Ribbons, goodwife," I croaked. "Pretty ribbons for your hair ..."

She smiled and beckoned to me. A tug; the scar on my hand was pulling me toward her. I did what I had planned to do, but I did it more readily than I had planned: I dropped my basket and screeched like the bloodless old peddler woman I was pretending to be, and I ran.

My gray cloak was the color of the forest, and I was fast; she did not catch me.

I made my way back to the palace.

I did not see it. Let us imagine, though, the girl returning, frustrated and hungry, to her cave, and finding my fallen basket on the ground.

What did she do?

I like to think she played first with the ribbons, twined them into her raven hair, looped them around her pale neck or her tiny waist.

And then, curious, she moved the cloth to see what else was in the basket, and she saw the red, red apples.

They smelled like fresh apples, of course; and they also smelled of blood. And she was hungry. I imagine her picking up an apple, pressing it against her cheek, feeling the cold smoothness of it against her skin.

And she opened her mouth and bit deep into it …

By the time I reached my chambers, the heart that hung from the roof beam, with the apples and hams and the dried sausages, had ceased to beat. It hung there, quietly, without motion or life, and I felt safe once more.

That winter the snows were high and deep, and were late melting. We were all hungry come the spring.

The Spring Fair was slightly improved that year. The forest folk were few, but they were there, and there were travelers from the lands beyond the forest.

I saw the little hairy men of the forest cave buying and bargaining for pieces of glass, and lumps of crystal and of quartz rock. They paid for the glass with silver coins—the spoils of my stepdaughter's depredations, I had no doubt. When it got about what they were buying, townsfolk rushed back to their homes and came back with their lucky crystals, and, in a few cases, with whole sheets of glass.

I thought briefly about having the little men killed, but I did not. As long as the heart hung, silent and immobile and cold, from the beam of my chamber, I was safe, and so were the folk of the forest, and, thus, eventually, the folk of the town.

My twenty-fifth year came, and my stepdaughter had eaten the poisoned fruit two winters back, when the prince came to my palace. He was tall, very tall, with cold green eyes and the swarthy skin of those from beyond the mountains.

He rode with a small retinue: large enough to defend him, small enough that another monarch—myself, for instance—would not view him as a potential threat.

I was practical: I thought of the alliance of our lands, thought of the kingdom running from the forests all the way south to the sea; I thought of my golden-haired bearded love, dead these eight years; and, in the night, I went to the prince's room.

I am no innocent, although my late husband, who was once my king, was truly my first lover, no matter what they say.

At first the prince seemed excited. He bade me remove my shift, and made me stand in front of the opened window, far from the fire, until my skin was chilled stone-cold. Then he asked me to lie upon my back, with my hands folded across my breasts, my eyes wide open—but staring only at the beams above. He told me not to move, and to breathe as little as possible. He implored me to say nothing. He spread my legs apart.

It was then that he entered me.

As he began to thrust inside me, I felt my hips raise, felt myself begin to match him, grind for grind, push for push. I moaned. I could not help myself.

His manhood slid out of me. I reached out and touched it, a tiny, slippery thing.

"Please," he said softly. "You must neither move nor speak. Just lie there on the stones, so cold and so fair."

I tried, but he had lost whatever force it was that had made him virile; and, some short while later, I left the prince's room, his curses and tears still resounding in my ears.

He left early the next morning, with all his men, and they rode off into the forest.

I imagine his loins, now, as he rode, a knot of frustration at the base of his manhood. I imagine his pale lips pressed so tightly together. Then I imagine his little troupe riding through the forest, finally coming upon the glass-and-crystal cairn of my stepdaughter. So pale. So cold. Naked beneath the glass, and little more than a girl, and dead.

In my fancy, I can almost feel the sudden hardness of his manhood inside his britches, envision the lust that took him then, the prayers he muttered beneath his breath in thanks for his good fortune. I imagine him negotiating with the little hairy men—offering them gold and spices for the lovely corpse under the crystal mound.

Did they take his gold willingly? Or did they look up to see his men on their horses, with their sharp swords and their spears, and realize they had no alternative?

I do not know. I was not there; I was not scrying. I can only imagine ...

Hands, pulling off the lumps of glass and quartz from her cold body. Hands, gently caressing her cold cheek, moving her cold arm, rejoicing to find the corpse still fresh and pliable.

Did he take her there, in front of them all? Or did he have her carried to a secluded nook before he mounted her?

I cannot say.

Did he shake the apple from her throat? Or did her eyes slowly open as he pounded into her cold body; did her mouth open, those red lips part, those sharp yellow teeth close on his swarthy neck, as the blood, which is the life, trickled down her throat, washing down and away the lump of apple, my own, my poison?

I imagine; I do not know.

This I do know: I was woken in the night by her heart pulsing and beating once more. Salt blood dripped onto my face from above. I sat up. My hand burned and pounded as if I had hit the base of my thumb with a rock.

There was a hammering on the door. I felt afraid, but I am a queen, and I would not show fear. I opened the door.

First his men walked into my chamber and stood around me, with their sharp swords, and their long spears.

Then he came in; and he spat in my face.

Finally, she walked into my chamber, as she had when I was first a queen and she was a child of six. She had not changed. Not really.

She pulled down the twine on which her heart was hanging. She pulled off the rowan berries, one by one; pulled off the garlic bulb—now a dried thing, after all these years; then she took up her own, her pumping heart—a small thing, no larger than that of a nanny goat or a she-bear—as it brimmed and pumped its blood into her hand.

Her fingernails must have been as sharp as glass: she opened her breast with them, running them over the purple scar. Her chest gaped, suddenly, open and bloodless. She licked her heart, once, as the blood ran over her hands, and she pushed the heart deep into her breast.

I saw her do it. I saw her close the flesh of her breast once more. I saw the purple scar begin to fade.

Her prince looked briefly concerned, but he put his arm around her nonetheless, and they stood, side by side, and they waited.

And she stayed cold, and the bloom of death remained on her lips, and his lust was not diminished in any way.

They told me they would marry, and the kingdoms would indeed be joined. They told me that I would be with them on their wedding day.

It is starting to get hot in here.

They have told the people bad things about me; a little truth to add savor to the dish, but mixed with many lies.

I was bound and kept in a tiny stone cell beneath the palace, and I remained there through the autumn. Today they fetched me out of the cell; they stripped the rags from me, and washed the filth from me, and then they shaved my head and my loins, and they rubbed my skin with goose-grease.

The snow was falling as they carried me—two men at each hand, two men at each leg—utterly exposed, and spread-eagled and cold, through the midwinter crowds, and brought me to this kiln.

My stepdaughter stood there with her prince. She watched me, in my indignity, but she said nothing.

As they thrust me inside, jeering and chaffing as they did so, I saw one snowflake land upon her white cheek, and remain there without melting.

They closed the kiln door behind me. It is getting hotter in here, and outside they are singing and cheering and banging on the sides of the kiln.

She was not laughing, or jeering, or talking. She did not sneer at me or turn away. She looked at me, though; and for a moment I saw myself reflected in her eyes.

I will not scream. I will not give them that satisfaction. They will have my body, but my soul and my story are my own, and will die with me.

[299]

The goose-grease begins to melt and glisten upon my skin. I shall make no sound at all. I shall think no more on this.

I shall think instead of the snowflake on her cheek.

I think of her hair as black as coal, her lips, redder than blood, her skin, snow-white.

THE TALE OF THE ROSE[1]

Emma Donoghue

IN THIS LIFE I HAVE nothing to do but cavort on the wind, but in my last it was my fate to be a woman.

I was beautiful, or so my father told me. My oval mirror showed me a face with nothing written on it. I had suitors aplenty but wanted none of them: their doggish devotion seemed too easily won. I had an appetite for magic, even then. I wanted something improbable and perfect as a red rose just opening.

Then in a spring storm my father's ships were lost at sea, and my suitors wanted none of me. I looked in my mirror, and saw, not myself, but every place I'd never been.

The servants were there one day and gone the next; they seemed to melt into the countryside. Last year's leaves and papers blew across the courtyard as we packed to go. My father lifted heavy trunks till veins embroidered his forehead. He found me a blanket to wrap my mirror in for the journey. My sisters held up their pale sleek fingers and complained to the wind. How could they be expected to toil with their hands?

I tucked up my skirts and got on with it. It gave me a strange pleasure to see what my back could bend to, my arms could bear. It was not that I was better than my sisters, only that I could see further.

Our new home was a cottage; my father showed me how to nail my mirror to the flaking wall. There were weeds and grasses but no roses. Down by the river, where I pounded my father's shirts white on the black rocks, I found a kind of peace. My hands grew numb and my dark hair tangled in the sunshine. I was washing my old self away; by midsummer I was almost ready.

My sisters sat just outside the door, in case a prince should ride by. The warm breeze carried the occasional scornful laugh my way.

---

1   From *Kissing the Witch* (New York: HarperCollins, 1997).

As summer was leaving with the chilly birds, my father got word that one of his ships had come safe to shore after all. His pale eyes stood out like eggs. What he wanted most, he said, was to bring us each home whatever we wanted. My sisters asked for heavy dresses, lined cloaks, fur-topped boots, anything to keep the wind out. I knew that nothing could keep the wind out, so I asked for a red rose just opening.

The first snow had fallen before my father came home, but he did have a rose for me. My sisters waited in the doorway, arms crossed. I ran to greet him, this bent bush who was my father inching across the white ground. I took the rose into my hand before he could drop it. My father fell down. The petals were scarlet behind their skin of frost.

We piled every blanket we possessed on top of him; still his tremors shook the bed. My sisters wept and cursed, but he couldn't hear them. They cried themselves to sleep beside the fire.

That night in his delirium he raved of a blizzard and a castle, a stolen rose and a hooded beast. Then all of a sudden he was wide awake. He gripped my wrist and said, Daughter, I have sold you.

The story came wild and roundabout, in darts and flurries. I listened, fitting together the jagged pieces of my future. For a red rose and his life and a box of gold, my father had promised the beast the first thing he saw when he reached home. He had thought the first thing might be a cat. He had hoped the first thing might be a bird.

My heart pounded on the anvil of my breastbone. Father, I whispered, what does a promise mean when it is made to a monster?

He shut his trembling eyes. It's no use, he said, his tongue dry in his mouth. The beast will find us, track us down, smell us out no matter where we run. And then water ran down his cheeks as if his eyes were dissolving. Daughter, he said in a voice like old wood breaking, can you ever forgive me?

I could only answer his question with one of my own. Putting my hand over his mouth, I whispered, Which of us would not sell all we had to stay alive?

He turned his face to the wall.

Father, I said, I will be ready to leave in the morning.

Now you may tell me that I should have felt betrayed, but I was shaking with excitement. I should have felt like a possession, but for the first time in my life I seemed to own myself. I went as a hostage, but it seemed as if I was riding into battle.

I left the rose drying against my mirror, in case I ever came home. My sisters, onion eyed, watched us leave at dawn. They couldn't understand why my father carried no gun to kill the beast. To them a word was not something to be kept.

The castle was in the middle of a forest where the sun never shone. Every villager we stopped to ask the way spat when they heard our destination. There had been no wedding or christening in that castle for a whole generation. The young queen had been exiled, imprisoned, devoured (here the stories diverged) by a hooded beast who could be seen at sunset walking on the battlements. No one had ever seen the monster's face and lived to describe it.

We stopped to rest when the light was thinning. My father scanned the paths through the trees, trying to remember his way. His eyes swiveled like a lamb's do when the wolves are circling. He took a deep breath and began to speak, but I said, Hush.

Night fell before we reached the castle, but the light spilling from the great doors led us through the trees. The beast was waiting at the top of the steps, back to the light, swaddled in darkness. I strained to see the contours of the mask. I imagined a different deformity for every layer of black cloth.

The voice, when it came, was not cruel but hoarse, as if it had not been much used in twenty years. The beast asked me, Do you come consenting?

I did. I was sick to my stomach, but I did.

My father's mouth opened and shut a few times, as if he was releasing words that the cold air swallowed up. I kissed his papery cheek and watched him ride away. His face was lost in the horse's mane.

Though I explored the castle from top to bottom over the first few days, I found no trace of the missing queen. Instead there was a door with my name on it, and the walls of my room were white satin. There were a hundred dresses cut to my shape. The great mirror showed me whatever I wanted to see. I had keys to every room in the castle except the one where the beast slept. The first book I opened said in gold letters: You are the mistress: ask for whatever you wish.

I didn't know what to ask for. I had a room of my own, and time and treasures at my command. I had everything I could want except the key to the story.

Only at dinner was I not alone. The beast liked to watch me eat. I had never noticed myself eating before; each time I swallowed, I blushed.

At dinner on the seventh night, the beast spoke. I knocked over my glass, and red wine ran the length of the table. I don't remember what the words were. The voice came out muffled and scratchy from behind the mask.

After a fortnight, we were talking like the wind and the roof slates, the rushes and the river, the cat and the mouse. The beast was always courteous; I wondered what scorn this courtesy veiled. The beast was always gentle; I wondered what violence hid behind this gentleness.

I was cold. The wind wormed through the shutters. I was lonely. In all this estate there was no one like me. But I had never felt so beautiful.

I sat in my satin-walled room, before the gold mirror. I looked deep into the pool of my face, and tried to imagine what the beast looked like. The more hideous my imaginings, the more my own face seemed to glow. Because I thought the beast must be everything I was not: dark to my light, rough to my smooth, hoarse to my sweet. When I walked on the battlements under the waning moon, the beast was the grotesque shadow I threw behind me.

One night at dinner the beast said, You have never seen my face. Do you still picture me as a monster?

I did. The beast knew it.

By day I sat by the fire in my white-satin room reading tales of wonder. There were so many books on so many shelves, I knew I could live to be old without coming to the end of them. The sound of the pages turning was the sound of magic. The dry liquid feel of paper under fingertips was what magic felt like.

One night at dinner the beast said, You have never felt my touch. Do you still shrink from it?

I did. The beast knew it.

At sunset I liked to wrap up in furs and walk in the rose garden. The days were stretching, the light was lingering a few minutes longer each evening. The rosebushes held up their spiked fingers against the yellow sky, caging me in.

One night at dinner the beast asked, What if I let you go? Would you stay of your own free will?

I would not. The beast knew it.

And when I looked in the great gold mirror that night, I thought I could make out the shape of my father, lying with his feverish face turned to the ceiling. The book did say I was to ask for whatever I wanted.

I set off in the morning. I promised to return on the eighth day, and I meant it when I said it.

Taking leave on the steps, the beast said, I must tell you before you go: I am not a man.

I knew it. Every tale I had ever heard of trolls, ogres, goblins, rose to my lips.

The beast said, You do not understand.

But I was riding away.

The journey was long, but my blood was jangling bells. It was dark when I reached home. My sisters were whispering over the broth. My father turned his face to me and tears carved their way across it. The rose, stiff against the mirror, was still red.

By the third day he could sit up in my arms. By the fifth day he was eating at table and patting my knee. On the seventh day my sisters told me in whispers that it would surely kill him if I went back to the castle. Now I had paid my ransom, they said, what could possess me to return to a monster? My father's eyes followed me round the cottage.

The days trickled by and it was spring. I pounded shirts on black rocks down by the river. I felt young again, as if nothing had happened, as if there had never been a door with my name on it.

But one night I woke to find myself sitting in front of my mirror. In its dark pool I thought I could see the castle garden, a late frost on the trees, a black shape on the grass. I found the old papery rose clenched in my fist, flaking into nothing.

This time I asked no permission of anyone. I kissed my dozing father and whispered in his ear. I couldn't tell if he heard me. I saddled my horse, and was gone before first light.

It was sunset when I reached the castle, and the doors were swinging wide. I ran through the grounds, searching behind every tree. At last I came to the rose garden, where the first buds were hunched against the night air. There I found the beast, a crumpled bundle eaten by frost.

I pulled and pulled until the padded mask lay uppermost. I breathed my heat on it, and kissed the spot I had warmed. I pulled off the veils one by one. Surely it couldn't matter what I saw now?

I saw hair black as rocks under water. I saw a face white as old linen. I saw lips red as a rose just opening.

I saw that the beast was a woman. And that she was breathing, which seemed to matter more.

This was a strange story, one I would have to learn a new language to read, a language I could not learn except by trying to read the story.

I was a slow learner but a stubborn one. It took me days to learn that there was nothing monstrous about this woman who had lived alone in a castle, setting all her suitors riddles they could make no sense of, refusing to do the things queens are supposed to do, until the day when, knowing no one who could see her true face, she made a mask and from then on showed her face to no one. It took me weeks to understand why the faceless mask and the name of a beast might be chosen over all the great world had to offer. After months of looking, I saw that beauty was infinitely various, and found it behind her white face.

I struggled to guess these riddles and make sense of our story, and before I knew it summer was come again, and the red roses just opening.

And as the years flowed by, some villagers told travelers of a beast and a beauty who lived in the castle and could be seen walking on the battlements, and others told of two beauties, and others, of two beasts.

THE FOURTH PIG[1]

Naomi Mitchison

SOMETIMES THE WOLF IS QUIET. He is not molesting us. It may be that he is away ravaging in far places which we cannot picture, and do not care about, or it may be that he lies up in his den, sated for the time, with half-slumberous, blood-weighted eyes, the torn flesh hot in his belly provoking miasmic evil which will turn, as he grows cold and hungry again, into some new cunning which may, after all, not be capable of frustration by the meek. For we never know. Sometimes the Wolf is stupid and can be frightened away. We may even say to ourselves that we have killed him. But more often, although we try not to think about this, the Wolf is too much for us; he refuses to be hoodwinked by the gentle or subtle. And, in the end, it is he who has the teeth and claws, the strength and the will to evil. And thus it comes, many times, that his slavering jaws crush down through broken arteries of shrieking innocents, death to the weak lamb, the merry rabbits, the jolly pigs, death to Mother Henny-penny with her downy chicks just hatched, death to Father Cocky-locky with his noble songs to the dawn, death sooner or later to Fox the inventor and story-teller, the intelligent one who yet cannot escape always. So they die in jerking agony under the sun, and the Wolf gulps them into his belly, and his juices dissolve their once lively and sentient flesh.

Sometimes the Wolf is quiet. But now the Wolf is loose and ranging and we are aware of him. We have seen in parts of our forest this Spring, how the soft leaves and air-dancing flowers have been crushed to bleeding sap, and among their green deaths come pain signs of fur and feather, of dreadful surprise and hopeless struggle. The Wolf, the Wolf has been there.

He may be hiding behind this tree or that tree. He may be disguised as kindly sheep or helpful horse. He may not be on us yet. It is possible that we shall have a breathing space. But we do not know how to use it. We cannot prepare because the Wolf never attacks the same way twice. Or he may now, at this instant, be about to spring from behind what we thought was safe and familiar. It is terrible for us to know—and not to know.

I have a pain in my head because I am trying to think about the Wolf, and the Wolf is not there to be thought about. And if he were there I could not think—I could only run, squealing. The thought of the Wolf is more than a pig's brain can hold, more than a pig's trembling, round body can be strong against. If only I could be told from which direction the Wolf would come and in what shape. We dare not

---

1 First published in 1936. This text from *The Fourth Pig* (Princeton, NJ: Princeton UP, 2014).

be merry any longer because we are listening for the Wolf. It is too much for us. There—yes, over there—is that my friend whom I know or is it the Wolf disguised? It seems to be my friend, but I dare not trust him to come near because he might be the Wolf. Because I am not sure that he or he or he may not be the Wolf in disguise, I approach fiercely and suspiciously. One movement that reminds me of what I believe the Wolf is like, and I have struck out, I have knocked down, I have injured or killed my friend. And ah then, can I be sure that the Wolf is not in me, that I am not myself the Wolf's finally clever and successful disguise?

My three brothers live in the brick house now, and they are all afraid, even Three who was too clever for the Wolf once. But how can he tell to what hugeness and terror the Wolf may not have grown now? The brick house has been reinforced with steel and concrete, so that windows and chimneys are blocked up, and the door itself is double-barred. They cannot see the sunlight or smell the flowers, but Three has installed a lighting and heating plant in the cellar. He pretends it is better like that. Yet even so, might not Wolf have so practised his huffing and puffing that even this may not be strong enough to stand against him?

I cannot remember how it was in the time of One, in the innocence of the world before thought came and memory and foresight, and knowledge of the Wolf. Nor do I remember the time of Two when one's house had indeed to be of stronger stuff than the original hay, but yet after the building of it there was dancing and singing, Maypoles and Feast-days and the village green at evening. But I can remember a little the time of Three who thought he knew everything and could destroy the Wolf, although by then it should have been apparent that this is beyond our power. Oh, he was clever, was Three! He could make things and alter things; he laughed at the others and told them of the inevitability of the Wolf coming, but proclaimed also that he had a sanctuary.

And so indeed it was for a time, but now he too is afraid and there is no more playing and dancing for the others. And I am full grown now, I am Four, without shelter and without hope. I can sing the song still, the brave song of the pigs, crying out we are not afraid, we have this and that and the other, and we will die waving the Pig banner, and perhaps after we are dead there will be something, the shadow of the rustling of bright straw, the shadow of the taste of crunched acorns, the silver shadow of the way back to the old sty. Something, if only we knew what it was. The song says all that, and I can sing it. I can sing it still, in the time that is left.

It may be better not to be afraid, and it may be that One and Two were truly not afraid. In the time before knowledge, in the time of dancing, none wasted thought or life in being afraid—not until the Wolf was on them, not till his teeth broke sucking into their neck-veins and the song broke into screechings. Three was afraid, but yet he thought he had the cure for fear; he thought the time would come when no pig need fear the Wolf. But I—I know I am afraid, and afraid almost all the time, even when I am singing the song; the noise of ourselves singing it doesn't keep the fear out of the back of my head any longer. I can smell the Wolf's breath above all the sweet smells of Spring and the rich smells of Autumn. I can hear the padding of the Wolf's feet a very long way off in the forest, coming nearer. And I know there is no way of stopping him. Even if I could help being afraid. But I cannot help it. I am afraid now.

THE THREE LITTLE PIGS[1]

James Finn Garner

ONCE THERE WERE THREE LITTLE pigs who lived together in mutual respect and in harmony with their environment. Using materials that were indigenous to the area, they each built a beautiful house. One pig built a house of straw, one a house of sticks, and one a house of dung, clay, and creeper vines shaped into bricks and baked in a small kiln. When they were finished, the pigs were satisfied with their work and settled back to live in peace and self-determination.

But their idyll was soon shattered. One day, along came a big, bad wolf with expansionist ideas. He saw the pigs and grew very hungry, in both a physical and an ideological sense. When the pigs saw the wolf, they ran into the house of straw. The wolf ran up to the house and banged on the door, shouting, "Little pigs, little pigs, let me in!"

The pigs shouted back, "Your gunboat tactics hold no fear for pigs defending their homes and culture."

But the wolf wasn't to be denied what he thought was his manifest destiny. So he huffed and puffed and blew down the house of straw. The frightened pigs ran to the house of sticks, with the wolf in hot pursuit. Where the house of straw had stood, other wolves bought up the land and started a banana plantation.

At the house of sticks, the wolf again banged on the door and shouted, "Little pigs, little pigs, let me in!"

The pigs shouted back, "Go to hell, you carnivorous, imperialistic oppressor!"

At this, the wolf chuckled condescendingly. He thought to himself: "They are so childlike in their ways. It will be a shame to see them go, but progress cannot be stopped."

So the wolf huffed and puffed and blew down the house of sticks. The pigs ran to the house of bricks, with the wolf close at their heels. Where the house of sticks had

---

1   From *Politically Correct Bedtime Stories* (New York: Macmillan, 1994).

stood, other wolves built a time-share condo resort complex for vacationing wolves, with each unit a fiberglass reconstruction of the house of sticks, as well as native curio shops, snorkeling, and dolphin shows.

At the house of bricks, the wolf again banged on the door and shouted, "Little pigs, little pigs, let me in!"

This time in response, the pigs sang songs of solidarity and wrote letters of protest to the United Nations.

By now the wolf was getting angry at the pigs' refusal to see the situation from the carnivore's point of view. So he huffed and puffed, and huffed and puffed, then grabbed his chest and fell over dead from a massive heart attack brought on from eating too many fatty foods.

The three little pigs rejoiced that justice had triumphed and did a little dance around the corpse of the wolf. Their next step was to liberate their homeland. They gathered together a band of other pigs who had been forced off their lands. This new brigade of *porcinistas* attacked the resort complex with machine guns and rocket launchers and slaughtered the cruel wolf oppressors, sending a clear signal to the rest of the hemisphere not to meddle in their internal affairs. Then the pigs set up a model socialist democracy with free education, universal health care, and affordable housing for everyone.

Please note: The wolf in this story was a metaphorical construct. No actual wolves were harmed in the writing of the story.

LITTLE MAN[1]

Michael Cunningham

WHAT IF YOU HAD A child?

If you had a child, your job would be more than getting through the various holiday rushes, and wondering exactly how insane Mrs. Witters in Accounts Payable is going to be on any given day. It'd be about procuring tiny shoes and pull-toys and dental checkups; it'd be about paying into a college fund.

The unextraordinary house to which you return nightly? It'd be someone's future ur-house. It'd be the place—decades hence—someone will remember forever, a seat of comfort and succor, its rooms rendered larger and grander, exalted, by memory. This sofa, those lamps, purchased in a hurry, deemed good enough for now, then

---

1   From *A Wild Swan: and Other Stories* (New York: Farrar, Straus and Giroux, 2015).

(they seem to be here still, years later): they'd be legendary, to someone.

Imagine reaching the point at which you want a child more than you can remember wanting anything else.

Having a child is not, however, anything like ordering a pizza. All the more so if you're a malformed, dwarfish man whose occupation, were you forced to name one, would be … What would you call yourself? A goblin? An imp? Adoption agencies are reluctant about *doctors* and *lawyers*, if they're single and over forty. So go ahead. Apply to adopt an infant as a two-hundred-year-old gnome.

You are driven slightly insane—you try to talk yourself down, it works some nights better than others—by the fact that for so much of the population, children simply … appear. Bing bang boom. A single act of love and, nine months later, this flowering, as mindless and senseless as a crocus bursting out of a bulb.

It's one thing to envy wealth and beauty and other gifts that seem to have been granted to others, but not you, by obscure but inarguable givers. It's another thing entirely to yearn for what's so readily available to any drunk and barmaid who link up for three minutes in one of the darker corners of any dank and scrofulous pub.

You listen carefully, then, when you hear the rumor. Some impoverished miller, a man whose business is going under (the small mill-owners, the ones who grind by hand, are vanishing—their flour and meal cost twice what the corporations can churn out, and the big-brand product is free of the gritty bits that find their way into a sack of flour no matter how careful you are); a man who hasn't got health insurance or investments, who hasn't been putting money into a pension (he's needed every cent just to keep the mill open).

That man has told the king his daughter can spin straw into gold.

The miller must have felt driven to it. He must have thought he needed a claim that outrageous if he was going to attract the attention of the king at all.

You suppose (as an aspiring parent yourself, you prefer to think of other parents as un-deranged) he hopes that if he can get his daughter into the palace, if he can figure out a way for her to meet the king, the king will be so smitten (doesn't every father believe his daughter to be irresistible?) that he'll forget about the absurd straw-into-gold story, after he's seen the pale grace of the girl's neck; after she's aimed that smile at him; after he's heard the sweet clarinet tone of her soft but surprisingly sonorous voice.

The miller apparently was unable to imagine all the pale-necked, shyly smiling girls the king has met already. Like most fathers, it's inconceivable to him that his daughter may not be singular; that she may be lovely and funny and smart, but not so much more so as to obliterate all the other contending girls.

The miller, poor foolish doting father that he is, never expected his daughter to get locked into a room full of straw, and commanded to spin it all into gold by morning, any more than most fathers expect their daughters to be un-sought-after by boys, or rejected by colleges, or abused by the men they eventually marry. Such notions don't appear on the spectrum of paternal possibility.

It gets worse.

The king, who really hates being fooled, announces, from the doorway of the cellar room filled with straw, that if the girl hasn't spun it all into gold by morning, he'll have her executed.

What? Wait a minute ...

The miller starts to confess, to beg forgiveness. He was joking; no, he was sinfully proud, he wanted his daughter to meet the king, he was worried about her future; I mean, your majesty, you can't be thinking of *killing* her ...

The king looks glacially at the miller, has a guard escort him away, and withdraws, locking the door behind him.

Here's where you come in.

You're descended from a long line of minor wizards. Your people have, for generations, been able to summon rain, exorcise poltergeists, find lost wedding rings.

No one in the family, not over the last few centuries at any rate, has thought of making a living at it. It's not ... respectable. It smells of desperation. And—as is the way with spells and conjurings—it's not one hundred percent reliable. It's an art, not a science. Who wants to refund a farmer's money as he stands destitute in his still-parched fields? Who wants to say, *I'm sorry, it works most of the time,* to the elderly couple who still hear cackles of laughter coming from under their mattress, whose cutlery still jumps up from the dinner table and flies around the room?

When you hear the story about the girl who can supposedly spin straw into gold (it's the talk of the kingdom), you don't immediately think, *This might be a way for me to get a child.* That would be too many steps down the line for most people, and you, though you have a potent heart and ferocity of intention, are not a particularly serious thinker. You work more from instinct. It's instinct, then, that tells you, *Help this girl, good might come of it.* Maybe simply because you, and you alone, have something to offer her. You who've never before had much to offer any of the girls who passed by, laughing with their boyfriends, leaving traces of perfume in their wake; perfume and powder and a quickening of the air they so recently occupied.

Spinning straw into gold is beyond your current capabilities, but not necessarily impossible to learn. There are ancient texts. There's your Aunt Farfalee, older than some of the texts but still alive, as far as you know; the only truly gifted member of your ragtag cohort, who are more generally prone to making rats speak in Flemish, or summoning beetles out of other people's Christmas pies.

Castles are easy to penetrate. Most people don't know that; most people think of them as fortified, impregnable. Castles, however, have been remodeled and revised, over and over again, by countless generations. There was the child-king who insisted on secret passageways, with peepholes that opened through the eyes of the ancestral portraits. There was the paranoid king who had escape tunnels dug, miles of them, opening out into woods, country lanes, and graveyards.

The girl, however, is surprised and impressed when you materialize in the chamber full of straw. It has nothing to do with magic. Already, though, you've got credibility.

At first glance you see why the miller thought his gamble might work. She's a true beauty, slightly unorthodox, in the way of most great beauties. Her skin is smooth and poreless as pale pink china, her nose ever so slightly longer than it should be, her brown-black eyes wide-set, sable-lashed, all but quivering with curiosity, with depths.

She stares at you. She doesn't speak. Her life, starting this morning, has become so strange to her (she who yesterday was sewing grain sacks and sweeping stray corn kernels from the floor) that the sudden appearance of a twisted and stub-footed man, just under four feet tall, with a chin as long as a turnip, seems like merely another in the new string of impossibilities.

You tell her you're there to help. She nods her thanks. You get to work.

It doesn't go well, at first. The straw, run through the spinning wheel, comes out simply as straw, shredded and bent.

You refuse to panic, though. You repeat, silently, the spell taught to you by Aunt Farfalee (who is by now no bigger than a badger, with blank white eyes and fingers thin and stiff as icicles). You concentrate—belief is crucial. One of the reasons ordinary people are incapable of magic is simple dearth of conviction.

And, eventually … yes. The first few stalks are only touched with gold, like eroded relics, but the next are more gold than straw, and soon enough the wheel is spitting them out, strand upon strand of pure golden straw, deep in color, not the hard yellow of some gold but a yellow suffused with pink, ever so slightly incandescent in the torchlit room.

You both—you and the girl—watch, enraptured, as the piles of straw dwindle and masses of golden strands skitter onto the limestone floor. It's the closest you've come, yet, to love, to lovemaking—you at the spinning wheel with the girl behind you (she forgetfully puts her hand, gently, on your shoulder), watching in shared astonishment as the straw is spun into gold.

When it's all finished, she says, "My lord."

You're not sure whether she's referring to you or to God.

"Glad to be of service," you answer. "I should go, now."

"Let me give you something."

"No need."

But still, she takes a strand of beads from her neck, and holds them out to you. They're garnets, cheap, probably dyed, though in this room, at this moment, with all that golden straw emanating its faint light, they're as potently red-black as heart's blood.

She says, "My father gave me these for my eighteenth birthday."

She drapes the necklace over your head. An awkward moment occurs, when the beads catch on your chin, but the girl lifts them off, and her fingertips brush against your face. The strand of beads falls onto your chest. Onto the declivity where, were you a normal man, your chest would be.

"Thank you," she says.

You bow and depart. She sees you slipping away through the secret door, devoid of hinges or knob, one of the many commanded by the long-dead paranoid king.

"That's not magic," she laughs.

"No," you answer. "But magic is sometimes all about knowing where the secret door is, and how to open it."

With that, you're gone.

You hear about it the next day, as you walk along the edges of town, wearing the strand of garnets under your stained woolen shirt.

The girl pulled it off. She spun the straw into gold.

The king's response? Do it again tonight, in a bigger room, with twice as much straw.

He's joking. Right?

He's not joking. This, after all, is the king who passed the law about putting trousers on cats and dogs, who made too-loud laughter a punishable crime. According to rumor, he was abused by his father, the last king. But that's the story people always tell, isn't it, when they want to explain inexplicable behavior?

You do it again that night. The spinning is effortless by now. As you spin, you perform little comic flourishes for the girl. You spin for a while one-handed. You spin with your back to the wheel. You spin with your eyes closed.

She laughs and claps her hands. Her laughter is low and sonorous, like the sound of a clarinet.

This time, when you've finished, she gives you a ring. It, too, is cheap—silver, with a speck of diamond sunk into it.

She says, "This was my mother's."

She slips it onto your pinkie. It fits, just barely. You stand for a moment, staring at your own hand, which is not by any standards a pretty sight, with its knobbed knuckles and thick, yellowed nails. But here it is, your hand, with her ring on one of its fingers.

You slip away without speaking. You're afraid that anything you might say would be embarrassingly earnest.

The next day ...

Right. One last roomful of straw, twice the size again. The king promises that this is the last, but insists on this third and final act of alchemy. He believes, it seems, that value resides in threes, which would explain the three garish and unnecessary towers he's had plunked onto the castle walls, the three advisers to whom he never listens, the three annual parades in commemoration of nothing in particular beyond the celebration of the king himself.

And ...

If the girl pulls it off one more time, the king has announced he'll marry her, make her his queen.

That's the reward? Marriage to a man who'd have had you decapitated if you'd failed to produce not just one but three miracles?

Surely the girl will refuse.

You go to the castle one more time and do it again. It seems that it should be routine by now, the sight of the golden straw piling up, the fiery gleam of it, but somehow repetition hasn't rendered it commonplace. It is (or so you imagine) a little like being in love; like wondering anew, every morning, over the outwardly unremarkable fact that your lover is there, in bed beside you, about to open her eyes, and that, every morning, your face will be the first thing she sees.

When you've finished, she says, "I'm afraid I have nothing more to give you."

You pause. You're shocked to realize that you want something more from her. You've told yourself, the past two nights, that the necklace and the ring are marvels, but extraneous acts of gratitude; that you'd have done what you've done for nothing more than the sight of her thankful face.

It's surprising, then, that on this final night, you don't want to leave unrewarded. That you desire, with upsetting urgency, another token, a talisman, a further piece of evidence. Maybe it's because you know you won't see her again.

You say, "You aren't going to marry him, are you?"

She looks down at the floor, which is littered with stray strands of golden straw. She says, "I'd be queen."

"But you'd married to him. That would be the man who was going to kill you if you didn't produce the goods."

She lifts her head and looks at you.

"My father could live in the palace with me."

"And yet. You can't marry a monster."

"My father would live in the castle. The king's physicians would attend to him. He's ill, grain dust gets into your lungs."

You're as surprised as she is when you hear yourself say, "Promise me your first-born child, then."

She merely blinks in astonishment, by way of an answer.

You've said it, though. You might as well forge on.

"Let me raise your first child," you say. "I'll be a good father, I'll teach the child magic, I'll teach the child generosity and forgiveness. The king isn't going to be much along those lines, don't you think?"

"If I refuse," she says, "will you expose me?"

Oh.

You don't want to descend to blackmail. You wish she hadn't posed the question, and you have no idea about how to answer. You'd never expose her. But you're so sure about your ability to rescue the still-unconceived child, who will, without your help, be abused by the father (don't men who've been abused always do the same to their children?), who'll become another punishing and capricious king in his own time, who'll demand meaningless parades and still-gaudier towers and who knows what else.

She interprets your silence as a yes. Yes, you'll turn her in if she doesn't promise the child to you.

She says, "All right, then. I promise to give you my firstborn child."

You could take it back. You could tell her you were kidding, you'd never take a woman's child.

But you find—surprise—that you like this capitulation from her, this helpless acceding, from the most recent embodiment of all the girls over all the years who've given you nothing, not even a curious glance.

Welcome to the darker side of love.

You leave again without speaking. This time, though, it's not from fear of embarrassment. This time it's because you're greedy and ashamed, it's because you want the child, you need the child, and yet you can't bear to be yourself at this moment; you can't stand there any longer, enjoying your mastery over her.

The royal wedding takes place. Suddenly this common girl, this miller's daughter, is a celebrity; suddenly her face emblazons everything from banners to souvenir coffee mugs.

And she looks like a queen. Her glowy pallor, her dark intelligent eyes, are every bit as royal-looking as they need to be.

A year later, when the little boy is born, you go to the palace.

You've thought of letting it pass—of course you have—but after those nights of sleepless wondering over the life ahead, the return to the amplified solitude and hopelessness in which you've lived for the past year (people have tried to sell you key chains and medallions with the girl's face on them, assuming, as well they might, that you're just another customer; you, who wear the string of garnets under your shirts, who wear the silver ring on your finger) ...

You can't let it pass after the bouts of self-torture about the confines of your face and body. Until those nights of spinning, no girl has ever let you get close enough for you to realize that you're possessed of wit and allure and compassion, that you'd be coveted, you'd be sought-after, if you were just ...

Neither Aunt Farfalee nor the oldest and most revered of the texts has anything to say about transforming gnomes into straight-spined, striking men. Aunt Farfalee told you, in the low, rattling sigh that was once her voice, that magic has its limits; that the flesh has proven consistently, over centuries, vulnerable to afflictions but never, not even for the most potent of wizards, subject to improvement.

You go to the palace.

It's not hard to get an audience with the king and queen. One of the traditions, a custom so old and entrenched that even this king dare not abolish it, is the weekly Wednesday audience, at which any citizen who wishes to can appear in the throne room and register a complaint, after the king has taken a wife.

You are not the first in line. You wait as a corpulent young woman reports that a coven of witches in her district is causing the goats to walk on their hind legs, and saunter inside as if they owned the place. You wait as an old man objects to the new tax being levied on every denizen who lives past the age of eighty, which is the king's way of claiming as his own that which would otherwise be passed along to his subjects' heirs.

As you stand in line, you see that the queen sees you.

She looks entirely natural on the throne, every bit as much as does her image on banners and mugs and key chains. She's noticed you, but nothing changes in her expression. She listens with the customary feigned attention to the woman whose goats are sitting down to dinner with the family, to the man who doesn't want his fortune sucked away before he dies. It's widely known that these audiences with king and queen never produce results of any kind. Still, people want to come and be heard.

As you wait, you notice the girl's father, the miller (the former miller), seated among the members of court, in a three-cornered hat and ermine collar. He regards the line of assembled supplicants with a dowager aunt's indignity; with an expression of superiority and sentimental piety—the recently bankrupt man who gambled with his daughter's life, and happens, thanks to you, to have won.

When your turn arrives, you bow to queen and king. The king nods his traditional, absentminded acknowledgment. His head might have been carved from marble.

His eyes are ice-blue under the rim of his gem-encrusted crown. He might already be, in life, the stone version that will top his sarcophagus.

You say, "My queen, I think you know what I've come for."

The king looks disapprovingly at his wife. His face bears no hint of question. He skips over the possibility of innocence. He only wonders what, exactly, it is she must have done.

The queen nods. You can't tell what's going through her mind. She's learned, apparently, during the past year, how to evince an expression of royal opacity, which she did not possess when you were spinning the straw into gold for her.

She says, "Please reconsider."

You're not about to reconsider. You might have considered reconsidering before you found yourself in the presence of these two, this tyrannical and ignorant monarch and the girl who agreed to marry him.

You tell her that a promise was made. You leave it at that. She glances over at the king, and can't conceal a moment of miller's-daughter nervousness.

She turns to you again. She says, "This is awkward, isn't it?"

You waver. You're assaulted by conflicting emotions. You understand the position she's in. You care for her. You're in love with her. It's probably the hopeless ferocity of your love that impels you to stand firm, to refuse her refusal—she who has on one hand succeeded spectacularly and, on the other, consented to what has to be, at best, a cold and brutal marriage. You can't simply relent and walk back out of the room. You can't bring yourself to be so debased.

She doesn't care for you, after all. You're someone who did her a favor, once. She doesn't even know your name.

With that thought, you decide to offer a compromise.

You tell her she has three days to guess your name, in the general spirit of her husband's fixation on threes. If she can accomplish that, if she can guess your name within the next three days, the deal's off.

If she can't ...

You do not of course say this aloud, but if she can't, you'll raise the child in a forest glade. You'll teach him the botanical names of the trees, and the secret names of the animals. You'll instruct him in the arts of mercy and patience. And you'll see, in the boy, certain of her aspects—the great dark pools of her eyes, maybe, or her slightly exaggerated, aristocratic nose.

The queen nods in agreement. The king scowls. He can't, however, ask questions, not here, not with his subjects lined up before him. He can't appear to be baffled, underinformed, misused.

You bow again and, as straight-backed as your torqued spine will allow it, you back out of the throne room.

You'll never know what went on between queen and king once they were alone together. You hope she confessed everything, and insisted that a vow, once made, can't be broken. You even go so far as to imagine she might defend you for your offer of a possible reprieve.

You suspect, though, that she still feels endangered; that she can't be sure her husband will forgive her for allowing him to believe she herself had spun the straw into gold. Having produced a male heir she has now, after all, rendered herself dispensable. And so, when confronted, she probably came up with … some tale of spells and curses, some fabrication in which you, a hobgoblin, are entirely to blame.

You wish you could feel more purely angry about that possibility. You wish you didn't sympathize, not even a little, with her, in the predicament she's created for herself.

This, then, is love. This is the experience from which you've felt exiled for so long. This rage mixed up with empathy; this simultaneous desire for admiration and victory.

You wish you found it more unpleasant. Or, at any rate, you wish you found it as unpleasant as it actually is.

The queen sends messengers out all over the kingdom, in an attempt to track down your name. You know how futile that is. You live in a cottage carved into a tree, so deep in the woods that no hiker or wanderer has ever passed by. You have no friends, and your relatives live not only far away but in residences at least as obscure as your own (consider Aunt Farfalee's tiny grotto, reachable only by swimming fifty feet underwater). You're not registered anywhere. You've never signed anything.

You return to the castle the next day, and the next. The king scowls murderously (what story *has* he been told?) as the queen runs through a gamut of guesses.

Althalos? Borin? Cassius? Cedric? Destrain? Fendrel? Hadrian? Gavin? Gregory? Lief? Merek? Rowan? Rulf? Sadon? Tybalt? Xalvador? Zane?

No no no no no no no no no no no no no no no and no.

It's looking good.

But then, on the night of the second day, you make your fatal mistake. You'll wonder, afterward—why did I build a fire in front of the cottage tree, and do that little song and dance? It seemed harmless at the time, and you were so happy, so sure. You'd found yourself sitting alone in your parlor, thinking of where the cradle should go, wondering who'd teach you to fold a diaper, picturing the child's face as he looks up into yours and says, Father.

It's too much, just sitting inside like that, by yourself. It's too little. You hurry out into the blackness of the forest night, into the chirruping of the insects and the far-off hoots of the owls. You build a fire. You grant yourself a pint of ale, and then you grant yourself another.

And, almost against your own will, it seems that you're dancing around the fire. It seems that you've made up a song.

Tonight I brew, tomorrow I bake,
And then the queen's child I will take.
For little knows the royal dame ...

How likely is it that the youngest of the queen's messengers, the one most desperate for advancement, the one who's been threatened with dismissal (he's too avid and dramatic in his delivery of messages, he bows too low, he's getting on the king's nerves) ... how likely is it that that particular young hustler, knowing every inch of the civilized kingdom to have been scoured already, every door knocked on, thought to go out into the woods that night, wondering if he was wasting precious time but hoping that maybe, maybe, the little man lived off the grid ...

How likely is it that he sees your fire, creeps through the bracken, and listens to the ditty you're singing?

★ ★ ★

You return, triumphant, to the castle on the third and final afternoon. You are for the first time in your life a figure of power, of threat. Finally, you cannot be ignored or dismissed.

The queen appears to be flustered. She says, "Well, then, this is my last chance."

You have the courtesy to refrain from answering.

She says, "Is it Brom?"

No.

"Is it Leofrick?"

No.

"Is it Ulric?"

No.

Then there is a moment—a millimoment, the tiniest imaginable fraction of time—when the queen thinks of giving her baby to you. You see it on her face. There's a moment when she knows she could rescue you as you once rescued her; when she imagines throwing it all away and going off with you and her child. She does not, could not, love you, but she remembers standing in the room on that first night, when the straw started turning to gold; when she understood that an impossible situation had been met with an impossible result; when she thoughtlessly laid her hand on the sackcloth-covered gnarls of your shoulder ... She thinks (*whoosh*, by the time you've read *whoosh*, she's no longer thinking of it) that she could leave her heartless husband, she could live in the woods with you and the child …

Whoosh.

The king shoots her an arctic glare. She looks at you, her dark eyes avid and level, her neck arched and her shoulders flung back.

She speaks your name.

It's not possible.

The king grins a conquering, predatory grin. The queen turns away.

The world, which had been about to transform itself, changes back again. The world reveals itself to be nothing more than you, scuttling out of the throne room, hurrying through town, returning to the empty little house that's always there, that's always been there, waiting for you.

You stamp your right foot. You stamp it so hard, with such enchantment-compelled force, that it goes right through the marble floor, sinks to your ankle.

You stamp your left foot. Same thing. You are standing now, trembling, insane with fury and disappointment, ankle-deep in the royal floor.

The queen keeps her face averted. The king emits a peal of laughter that sounds like disdain itself.

And with that, you split in half.

It's the strangest imaginable sensation. It's as if some strip of invisible tape that's been holding you together, from mid-forehead to crotch, has suddenly been stripped away. It's no more painful than pulling off a bandage. And then you fall onto your knees, and you're looking at yourself, twice, both of you pitched forward, blinking in astonishment at a self who is blinking in astonishment at you, who are blinking in astonishment at him, who is blinking in astonishment at you …

The queen silently summons two of the guards, who lift you in two pieces from the floor in which you've become mired, who carry you, one half apiece, out of the room. They take you all the way back to your place in the woods, and leave you there.

There are two of you now. Neither is sufficient unto itself, but you learn, over time, to join your two halves together, and hobble around. There are limits to what you can do, though you're able to get from place to place. Each half, naturally enough, requires the cooperation of the other, and you find yourself getting snappish with yourself; you find yourself cursing yourself for your clumsiness, your over-eagerness, your lack of consideration for your other half. You feel it doubly. Still, you go on. Still, you step in tandem, make your slow and careful way up and down the stairs, admonishing, warning, each of you urging the other to slow down, or speed up, or wait a second. What else can you do? Each would be helpless without the other. Each would be stranded, laid flat, abandoned, bereft.

ILLUSTRATION

No PUBLISHER NOWADAYS WOULD DREAM of trying to sell a volume of fairy tales that was not accompanied by illustrations; indeed, one might be forgiven for thinking that the illustrator is sometimes of greater importance than the tales, which are chosen primarily as suitable vehicles for his or her artistic prowess. The modern fairy-tale book consists, as often as not, of a single tale told primarily in pictures: the text has become a secondary consideration. It's an intriguing question: does the inclusion of illustrations stifle the reader's imagination by imposing a visual representation upon it, or do the pictures actually enhance the reader's imaginative response to the story? Clearly there are many factors involved, such as the age of the reader, the ability of the artist, and the meanings suggested by the illustrations. Yet even if we were able somehow to calculate relative values for such factors, how could we then compare the quality of the reader's response with and without the presence of illustrations? Calculations aside, there can be no question but that pictures add one more dimension to the various imaginative experiences of reading a tale, being read a tale, and being *told* a tale.

The origin of the fairy tale is oral, which accounts for its unique qualities: the emphasis upon action, the lack of physical detail, and the quick movement from one event to another—all ideally suited to the art of the storyteller. Furthermore, a tale can be told in many different ways, its impact upon the audience deriving from the intention, approach, and abilities of the teller. As we have seen, however, the evolution of the oral tale into printed text has all but obliterated the services of the storyteller, leaving room for the intercession of a new intermediary. Although without a teller there is no story, it can reasonably be argued that without an illustrator, the text is still there on the printed page, and yet, as Perry Nodelman points out in his instructive book *Words about Pictures*,[1] our imaginations can rarely achieve the

---

1   Perry Nodelman, *Words about Pictures: The Narrative Art of Children's Picture Books* (Athens: U of Georgia P, 1988).

vividness and specificity that can be found in a good illustration. To achieve these qualities, both teller and illustrator must give something of themselves to the tale in order to infuse it with new life, since in its "basic" form the tale leaves ample scope for the inventiveness of both contributors as they work within the framework of the story to create something new.

For example, one significant challenge for the artist is the depiction of characters familiar in name but not in image; he or she presumes thus to make explicit what is vague in the tales (we are told no more than that Little Red Riding Hood is "the prettiest [girl] that had ever been seen" or that Rumpelstiltskin is "a little man"). Alternatively, the artist may choose to concentrate upon the setting of the tale, giving a specificity to time and place that is denied by the traditional beginning of "once upon a time." Most important, however, is the interpretation of events an illustration can provide. Indeed, the opportunity to expand and interpret has also been exploited by recorders of the tales for, as we noted earlier, Charles Perrault and the Grimm brothers were quite prepared to leave their mark on the tales in the process of making them more suitable for their respective audiences. There is, of course, no guarantee that the embellishment provided by teller or artist will necessarily enrich the tale: we all know how painful an experience it can be to listen to a flat, indifferent reading of a tale, or how disappointed we feel when confronted by illustrations that do little more than fill space on the page. However, as Nodelman points out, illustrators, like the storytellers before them, have the power to transform the tale into a rich and meaningful tapestry.

We are told that every picture tells a story; an illustration tells at least two, for not only does it provide a visual dimension for the story it accompanies, but it also reveals something of the assumptions and values of the artist and of the culture to which he or she belongs. In this sense, illustrators are no different from the storytellers or the fairy-tale compilers of the past who inevitably kept an eye on their audience, making sure their material was both suitable and satisfying. As a result, the pictures that accompany fairy tales are often as much a mirror as are the tales themselves.

Thus, the encounter between the text and the reader's imagination is made more complex by the contribution of the illustrator, who imposes his or her particular vision and tone upon the narrative. Just how completely the reading of a tale can be influenced by different artists' interpretations will be demonstrated in the following pages: though the words may remain the same, the pictures tell a different story. At the beginning of this chapter we commented that no modern publisher would seriously consider producing a book of fairy tales without illustrations; we might now add that few would publish such a book without illustrations in color. At the same time, the black-and-white originals that are included in our selection

provide evidence that some contemporary illustrators are making the artistic decision to work in monochrome. We have chosen examples of illustrative work that
range from the nineteenth century to the present day. It is admittedly a very partial
selection, since the number of illustrated versions of fairy tales has increased dramatically in recent years. However, it may serve to give some indication of the variety
of approaches that certain artists have adopted over the years—and we hope it may
provide the student with some stimulus to seek out the work of others.

Little Red Riding Hood: About a Girl and a Wolf

As we pointed out in our introduction to this tale, there is more to the story than
a simple warning to children not to speak to strangers, although this is clearly the
critical point in the story that attracts—in one way or another—all the illustrators
in this section.

The fact that the pictures by Gustave Doré are among the earliest examples of
fairy-tale illustration makes his insight into Perrault's tales all the more impressive,
not least because his engravings are of course without the benefit (or is it the dis-
traction?) of color. His version of the meeting between Little Red Riding Hood
and the wolf (Figure 1, 1862) is remarkable for its realistic depiction of the wolf, as
opposed to the anthropomorphic interpretation that many subsequent illustrators
have adopted. Nevertheless, he provides us with a carefully detailed portrait of the
relationship between the two characters, which foreshadows the outcome of their
encounter. As is often the case in Doré's work, the eyes are the focal point of the
picture, in this instance, the fascinated gaze that binds prey to predator. He creates
a claustrophobic atmosphere as the little girl finds herself hemmed in by the wolf,
whose proximity appears at first glance to be protective; the impact is all the more effective because the observer alone knows that deception and evil intent are at work
here. Subtler still is the detail of the girl's unfastened shoe-strap, indicative of her
vulnerability, her unpreparedness for harsh experience. As the little girl gazes up at
the wolf as if hypnotized, her whole body expresses a naïve trust and uncertainty.
Although the wolf is depicted from a highly unusual perspective creating the impression of an upright human stance, Doré still manages to include his penetrating stare.
That, together with the half-protective, half-suggestive movement of his hindquar-
ters toward Little Red Riding Hood, reveals to the discerning eye what is to follow.

Doré's depiction of Grandmother Wolf in bed with Little Red Riding Hood (Figure 2, 1862)—in itself a daring moment in the tale to depict—can only be described
as a masterpiece of psychological insight; the picture's stillness is all the more

riveting as we anticipate the frenzy to come. Once again, our attention is drawn to the eyes, the windows of the soul. We observe the girl's expression of intermingled fear and fascination, but equally striking is the demeanor of the wolf. He lies inert, paying no attention to the girl, the granny cap pulled absurdly over his ears, apparently lost in his own gloomy thoughts. Is Doré not implying a certain "sympathy for the Devil" here, as the wolf considers the base indignities to which his appetites have brought him? He will fulfill his role as a predator, but he will have no illusions about his shame and depravity. Angela Carter expresses a startlingly similar insight in "The Company of Wolves":

> There is a vast melancholy in the canticles of the wolves, melancholy infinite as the forest, endless as these long nights of winter, and yet that ghastly sadness, that mourning for their own, irremediable appetites, can never move the heart, for not one phrase in it hints at the possibility of redemption; grace could not come to the wolf from its own despair, only through some external mediator, so that, sometimes, the beast will look as if he half welcomes the knife that dispatches him. (p. 242)

Thus, the imminent assault is rendered all the more disturbing by the psychological depth and intensity that Doré brings to this image.

Like Doré before her, Sarah Moon focuses on the same fateful moment of meeting (Figure 3, 1983), only this time in very different surroundings. She too captures that sense of isolation that we noted in Doré's image, created over one hundred years earlier. Moon's decision to locate the tale in a modern urban context and use the "truthful" medium of photography to illustrate a story about sexual abuse sends a shock through the reader's system—but once the associative leap is made, the story's impact is irresistible, so striking and apposite is her imagery. The girl is a startled creature caught in the glare of the car's headlights, the darkness of the street creates the same claustrophobic effect as Doré's forest, and the menace implicit in the shiny, cold anonymity of the car—a familiar modern symbol of male status and power—is perhaps more meaningful for a contemporary reader than the sight of the "wolf" himself. As in Doré's illustration, the viewer bears the burden of anticipating Perrault's tragic ending. However, Moon's graphic photo-journalistic treatment of this very familiar story capitalizes on the ever-increasing currency of the visual medium, rendering the text all but extraneous. It also reminds us how familiar we are with the story that these photographs tell, as a brief glance at today's news headlines will confirm.

The intensity that Roberto Innocenti brings to his interpretation of the tale (Figure 4, 2012) is of an entirely different order than that in the two previous, although the accompanying text makes clear that he is well aware of the original. His premise is that the legendary forest is just one small step away from the contemporary urban jungle—and once that fact is established, he sets about depicting a mayhem that all but leaps off the page: you can hear the roar, you can smell the fumes. It is impossible to "read" Innocenti's illustration in the same way as we respond to those of Doré and Moon, both of whom focus our attention on a single crucial moment. Innocenti requires us to absorb the whole frantic scene, in which our heroine is just an insignificant detail—and that is surely his point. The cumulative effect of the pent-up aggression and impatience that confront us at this street-crossing is so overwhelming that we almost miss the wolfish creature in the military-style vehicle that Sophia[1] is about to cross in front of. The devil is in the details....

While Innocenti's intended audience is open to some debate, it is immediately apparent that Mireille Levert is working with the child-reader in mind. The picture (Figure 5, 1995) is not without hints of menace, in the sudden bend in the path, the stance (not to mention the salivation) of the wolf, even the fallen tree that represents an additional obstacle for the little girl. And like many artists before her, Levert cannot resist the temptation to exploit the similarity between a tree root and an animal's claw! Yet these sinister aspects of the scene are mitigated by what we might term the cheerful plumpness of Levert's style, manifested in those same trees, which are somewhat reminiscent of ice-cream cones. Indeed, the picture's emphasis on roundness is concentrated on Little Red Riding Hood herself; she is virtually a series of circles, from nose to basket. As for the wolf, his back may be up, but the suggestion is of playfulness rather than ferocity; even though readers young or old know that mischief is afoot, the happy ending is guaranteed.

Sleeping Beauty: From One to Many

In this section, we meet two artists working at opposite ends of the illustrative spectrum, so to speak. On the one hand, text reigns supreme in the version illustrated by Michael Foreman, who provides just one illustration for the tale (Figure 6, 1978). As a result, his intention is to provide not so much a visual accompaniment to the tale as a definitive interpretation of it. One may therefore assume that he chose his moment carefully, in order to clearly communicate his understanding of the tale as eloquently and succinctly as possible. In the tradition of the finest illustrators, Foreman acknowledges the depth of the fairy tale by, in effect, providing two pictures in

---

1   A curious choice for the girl's name, since "Sophia" is a Greek word meaning "wisdom."

one, since it contains both a narrative and a symbolic level. As with the tale itself, however, the reader sees what he or she is ready to see. There may well be those who object to such an overtly Freudian interpretation, but it is undeniable that such controversy breathes new life into the fairy tale.

By contrast, Trina Schart Hyman tells the tale in pictures (Figure 7, 1977), which have been carefully combined with text in the design of the double-page spread. There is no single climactic picture, since the intention here is to maintain a continuity of illustration, with the result that setting, characterization, and interpretation are given ample consideration. Thus, while Hyman creates an effective quasi-medieval context for the tale through a rich combination of architectural and costume detail, it is not at the expense of the human drama. Although there is a modern, cinematic glamor to the principal characters depicted here, there is no denying the excitement with which Hyman infuses this courtyard scene, where all is intense action and emotion. As we point out in our introduction to "Sleeping Beauty," the fate of the princess has a profound effect on the greater community, a fact that Hyman expresses very effectively in this lively illustration.

Hansel and Gretel: Whether to Laugh or to Cry

The sophistication of the work of some modern illustrators once again raises the issue of audience: to whom are these pictures addressed? Notwithstanding the fact that these tales are commonly perceived as children's literature, the (adult) artist intuitively responds to their symbolism, which, as we have already seen in Michael Foreman's illustration (Figure 6), can result in a startlingly different interpretation.

Like Moon and Innocenti in their versions of "Little Red Riding Hood" (Figures 3 and 4), Anthony Browne takes the step of giving "Hansel and Gretel" a modern setting: this family lives in a brick house containing many of the household items that populate our world also. He too has been careful to evoke a modern setting that is nevertheless distant enough (vaguely mid-twentieth century) not to be exactly identifiable, thereby combining the open-endedness of "once upon a time" with the here and now. In Browne's opening illustration of the parlor (Figure 8, 1981), the familiar look of modern poverty is immediately apparent in the dirty, peeling wallpaper and the threadbare rug, as well as in the father's face and demeanor as he looks in vain through what is clearly the "Classified" section of the newspaper. More arresting, however, is the manner in which Browne manages to underline the crucial aspect of family dynamics and the stepmother's role in the lives of her husband and children. Browne sets her apart from the rest of her family: glamorous and comfortable, she watches a passenger jet take off on television. Through the symbols that permeate the picture—the abandoned "Gretel" doll, the bird mark on the ceiling—Browne paints us a story as meaningful as the words themselves. Illustrators such as Browne, Moon, and Innocenti remind us that fairy tales, like Shakespeare's dramas, are as pertinent today as they ever were.

It takes no more than a glance at the work of Tony Ross to realize that his approach (Figure 9, 1989) is quite different from that of the artists we have examined thus far: the contemporary cartoon style, the bright poster colors, the zany characterization, all add to the slapstick mood that substantially reinvents the tale. Not surprisingly, Ross also rewrites the text, since it's clear that his irreverent style is incompatible with the serious tone of the Grimms' narrative. The previous illustration in this section is noticeably static; we are invited to absorb the moment. With Ross, the moment is fleeting, since the action here is little short of manic; the witch is clearly no stranger to the concept of fast food. In keeping with this frenetic pace, the jokes come thick and fast: the unhappy face on the mug, the tadpole jelly, the animal entourage ready and willing to partake of the feast—all contribute to the atmosphere of heedless self-gratification. If Browne's picture conveys a mood of gloomy withdrawal, here all is noise and good times, as the witch takes wicked pleasure in exploiting the tendency of innocent children to have eyes bigger than their stomachs. Ross's vigorous treatment may lack historical detail and psychological depth, but his sense of the absurd provides ample evidence of the fairy tale's adaptability.

Nothing that we have encountered thus far prepares us for the nightmarish vision of Susanne Janssen (Figure 10, 2007). Color is now a threat rather than a reassurance, not least because it is the witch's bizarrely inappropriate red party-dress that first commands our attention. We are not comforted by her apparent detachment from the children; we know the story too well to be deceived by the serene self-satisfaction on that haggard, mask-like face. Janssen's use of collage is central to the impact of her illustration, in that the raw emotion of this encounter between innocence and evil is countered by the disconnectedness, not only of the characters but also of the imagery as a whole. In an earlier picture, the children stare up at a witch's house that resembles an ornate urban high-rise; now, with the unnerving instability and illogic that characterizes nightmare, the building has shrunk to the size of a doll's house that Hansel appears to be dreamily toying with, even as Gretel registers a degree of surprise. The cumulative effect of all these incongruities forces the reader to hesitate and wonder—it is the sheer unexpectedness of the composition that creates its eerie power. Janssen is surely less interested in what *is* happening than in what is *going* to happen; our familiarity with the tale makes it all too clear that this is the calm before the storm.

In recent times, the task of encouraging children to read has been complicated by competition from television, video games, and the like, that place emphasis on the visual to the detriment of the literary. One strategy adopted by educators and publishers alike to counter this challenge has been to combine the appeal of the fairy tale with the "cool" trends in popular culture. Thus, the influence of the Japanese *manga* comic style is immediately apparent in Sean Dietrich's graphic-novel artwork (Figure 11, 2008). While the innocence and the anxious state of the children may provide psychological justification, the exaggerated eye-size (not to mention the unusual hair color) has more to do with imposing cool *manga* stylistics on the traditional story. At the same time, this excerpt demonstrates how readily the tale can be adapted to the comic-book format: the simple morality, the flatness of character, and the emphasis upon sensational incident supply the graphic artist/writer with features remarkably similar to those of the comic book.

While Dietrich's illustration is part of a "graphic novel" explicitly designed for children—the series of which it is a part is monitored by both a librarian reviewer and a reading consultant—the Zenescope version of the tale (Figure 12, 2005) is clearly intended for a very different readership. This is a series that relies on a steady diet of spectacular bosoms and lurid violence to achieve its moral ends. The back-cover blurb informs us that the volume "explores a much darker side of the infamous fables you heard as a child as these classic tales are retold and re-imagined with a terrifying twist you'll simply love as an adult."

This reincarnation of the fairy tale in comic-book format reveals that its evolution is as much circular as it is linear. Whatever its status among the guardians of culture and education over the centuries, the fairy tale has remained a staple of popular culture. Ignoring the strictures of its critics and any concern for quality, the purveyors of cheap broadsheets and chapbooks of the eighteenth century satisfied a demand for the fairy tale among the common people, many of whom would have been barely literate. The fairy tale's resurgence in the primarily visual medium of the comic book provides evidence to support the view that through its versatility, its adaptability, and its universality, the tale is as healthy—and as relevant—as ever.

Snow White: Shades of Gray

We have already examined several instances of illustrators' growing fascination with the dark currents that flow though fairy tale. It is as if the longstanding assumption that fairy tales belong to children has kept a censorious lid on this bubbling pot of human experience (Tolkien's "Cauldron of Story"!) until the cover is finally blown and the tales are rediscovered and refashioned for an adult audience. It is certainly no coincidence that both these versions of "Snow White" are monochromatic, given the pessimistic view of human behavior they present.

Unlike other fairy-tale graphic novels, Matt Phelan's retelling of "Snow White" (Figure 13, 2016) actually does live up to its billing, since it's 216 pages long. Phelan also updates the story to Depression-era America, telling the story almost entirely in gray tones that create a very different picture to the Technicolor lushness of Disney's version. The street-kids who become the protectors of this American princess inhabit a very different world from that of Sleepy, Happy, and Doc; they have more in common with Fagin's troop of juvenile pickpockets in Charles Dickens's *Oliver Twist* (1837–39). The dark, *film-noir* style of the drawing is evocative of the hard-boiled detective novels of the 1930s—not least because it's Detective *Prince* who brings some joy into Samantha White's life after her trials and tribulations!

While Phelan's New York is a dark and dangerous place, it seems almost wholesome alongside the venality and decadence of Ana Juan's "Snowhite" (Figure 14, 2011). Certainly, Juan's pictures present as cruel and disturbing a vision here as the text of Neil Gaiman in "Snow, Glass, Apples" (see p. 290ff). This is a world driven by exploitation, lust, and self-gratification; Snowhite's comatose state comes from a hypodermic syringe rather than a magic apple, but the terseness of Juan's text leaves no room for a happy ending. The behavior of *Mr.* Prince takes us back, in more ways than one, not only to the Prince in Gaiman's version, but as far back as the King in Basile's "Sun, Moon, and Talia" (see p. 79ff) and even to the wolf in "Little Red Riding Hood." Just how entrenched Juan sees such attitudes as being is revealed in the observation that follows this scene: "By now, Snowhite realized that woodland beasts do not only live outside walls of the house"—which surely echoes Perrault's warning in the Moral he appended to "Little Red Riding Hood" more than three hundred years ago.

Beauty and the Beast: Getting to Know You

It is appealing to think of Walter Crane as something of a revolutionary, in that he defied the drabness of nineteenth-century industrial England by producing a variety of carefully designed and colorful fairy-tale books of which "Beauty and the Beast" is one. He was also much involved—along with such contemporaries as William Morris—in the Arts and Crafts Movement in Britain, which sought to re-assert the role of the craftsman in a world that was quickly succumbing to the new phenomenon of mass production. As he observed, "[Children's books] are attractive to designers of an imaginative tendency, for in a sober and matter-of-fact age they afford perhaps the only outlet for unrestrained flights of fancy open to the modern illustrator, who likes to revolt against the despotism of facts."[1] Crane was a teacher as much as an artist, and he set out to educate the eye as much as to please it, believing that an aesthetic sense was key to a civilized society. Consequently, we may find in his illustration of "Beauty and the Beast" (Figure 15, 1874) a greater concern with style than with the substance of the story: the flatness of the picture is reminiscent of a classical frieze, the Beast's more modern attire notwithstanding. Crane freely acknowledged that the timelessness of fairy tales allowed him an artistic license that he was quite prepared to take advantage of: "I was in the habit of putting in all sorts of subsidiary detail that interested me, and often made them the vehicle for my ideas in furniture and decoration."[2] The preoccupation with decoration and various artistic styles makes this an elegant but at the same time rather detached, even distracting, illustration— there is simply no room for the emotional tension that surely fills this encounter.

In strong contrast to the decorous *sang-froid* of Crane's illustration is the ferocity and passion in Alan Barrett's depiction of the Beast (Figure 16, 1972). Over the years, artists have depicted the Beast in a variety of ways, ranging from leonine to monstrous, yet he generally manifests the kind of savage nobility that we associate with certain large animals. Barrett's intention, on the other hand, is to provoke a more visceral reaction, something closer to the terror inspired by a Beast that on first meeting appears irrational, alien, and cruel. From our voyeuristic position as reader, we turn the page only to be confronted by the open jaws of the enraged Beast and thus find ourselves cast in Beauty's position: for a moment, our identification with the heroine is complete. Curiously enough, Barrett's illustration bears a striking resemblance to the most memorable image from Steven Spielberg's iconic movie *Jaws* (1975), which might itself be regarded as something of an urban legend.

A quite different contrast, this time to all the "subsidiary detail" in Crane's picture, may be found in the work of Barry Moser (Figure 17, 1992), whose minimalist approach produces an illustration as stark as Crane's is elaborate. It is a trademark of Moser's style to look for the key moments in the story and then reduce them to the specific character—or even gesture—that represents the crux of that particular episode. All distractions of color, descriptive detail, and movement are omitted, and out of the darkness an image emerges that arrests our attention: Beauty and the Beast are playing the strategic and intellectual game of chess. Nancy Willard, the author of the text of this version, clearly intends the chess-game as a metaphor for

---

1   Qtd. in Richard Dalby, "Walter Crane," *The Golden Age of Children's Book Illustration* (London: Michael O'Mara Books, 1991), 22.

2   Qtd. in Rodney K. Engen, *Walter Crane as a Book Illustrator* (London: Academy Editions, 1975), 5.

the psychological intricacy and uncertainty of a developing relationship—"She tried not to show her horror as his claws groped for the pieces, and she had to help him make his moves." There may be horror, but Moser's illustration also conveys tenderness and compassion in Beauty's guiding hand.

On the Psychiatrist's Couch

The work of Stasys Eidrigevičius brings us to the post-Freudian world of psychoanalysis. In *Puss in Boots* (Figure 18, 1990), Eidrigevičius represents not so much the events of the story as the visions they might elicit in the dream-world of our unconscious where the facts of daily life mesh with our fears and desires. Such an approach naturally invites controversy, particularly in what is assumed to be a book for children, since the world of dreams is variously perceived as either disturbing or nonsensical. Be that as it may, Eidrigevičius's illustrations obey the rules that govern the workings of the unconscious. Just as our dreams scramble the details of our daily lives, the images are not faithful representations of Perrault's text. For instance, when the ogre transforms himself into a lion, "Puss was so frightened that he leapt onto the roof." The roof, of course, offers some escape, so why is Puss made to perch on a chair that is caught in the jaws of the transformed ogre? The image illustrates the logic of the unconscious, where every character and every situation is an extension of ourselves, our fears and desires, and the boundaries of time and space are not adhered to. It is easier to identify with the frightened Puss perched on a chair; it is where we would seek safety from a rampant mouse—the metamorphosis that Puss intends to invite the ogre to make next. Thus, the image captures the fear inherent in the present moment (although Puss's posture suggests his escape) and also anticipates the next development. Because the transformed ogre bears an unmistakable resemblance to the cat who is in due course planning to devour him, the image represents both moments in the story while, at the same time, suggesting that the ogre is very much Puss's alter ego—which should come as no surprise, given Puss's ruthless behavior elsewhere. Thus, the starkness and simplicity of this illustration belie its intensity and the complexity of its multiple identifications and levels of meaning. We should recall that although Bruno Bettelheim's discussion of fairy tales relates primarily to children, he does make the observation that they speak to internal (and, at times, unconscious) struggles we experience throughout our lives.

Different Worlds: Wouldn't It Be Nice ...?

Arthur Rackham was one of the most eminent artists to emerge from what has become known as the Golden Age of children's book illustration (1860–1930). Rackham's wide and lasting popularity rests largely upon the appeal of his extraordinary fantasy worlds, which are believable because they are so firmly rooted in realistic detail. In this sense, Rackham anticipates, in visual terms, J.R.R. Tolkien's creation of a believable "Secondary World."[1] Rackham's approach is evident in his illustration from "Hansel and Gretel" (Figure 19, 1909), in which the encounter between the children and the witch reveals a Dickensian combination of the realistic and the grotesque. Although Rackham's focus is clearly on the *human* drama, the observer is equally drawn in by the picturesque setting, the soothing quality of the sepia tones, and the intricate delicacy of the details of wood, leaf, and stone. The attraction of the cottage is certainly not in the sweetness of its candy composition (which Rackham all but ignores) as in its romantic quaintness. We, like the children with whom we identify, long to see what lies beyond the antique bottle panes of the open window—surely a kettle on the boil and cookies in a jar—a welcoming home were it not for the witch who stands at the door. Illustrated is a moment of confrontation with the unexpected and forbidding on the one hand and the welcoming and comforting on the other, which Rackham reveals in the reactions and body postures of both witch and children. So attractive is Rackham's mix of fantasy and reality that it imbues his world with an energy that promises a positive outcome to the confrontation.

Unlike Rackham, Daniel Egnéus has followed the more recent practice of fully illustrating the fairy tale; however, he follows Rackham in using the story as inspiration for his own imaginary world. The title provides a hint of what is to come: although "Little Red Riding Hood" refers to Perrault's story, what is being illustrated is the Grimm version (Figure 20, 2011). This element of inconsistency, in fact, seems to be the guiding principle behind Egnéus's approach. At each turn of the page, the reader is confronted with the unexpected, as the logic of time and place are consistently ignored and scrambled. Egnéus begins by situating "Once upon a time" in what looks like classical Rome, only to shift on the next page to what is immediately recognizable as Venice; so what are we to make of the dark woods through which Little Red Riding Hood must now travel, "about a half hour's walk from the village ..."? The elaborate costumes reinforce the classical Italianate setting—the Wolf appears in a ruffled and plumed Venetian nobleman's cloak—yet we find an

---

1   For a recent cinematic equivalent to the sheer convincingness of Rackham's fairy-tale world, one might well nominate Peter Jackson's masterful re-creation of Tolkien's Middle-earth in his *Lord of the Rings* trilogy (2001–03).

impossibly young Grandmother sitting at her Singer sewing-machine, stitching Little Red Riding Hood's cloak or listening to music on her wind-up gramophone! Different double-spreads present a spectrum of colors from light to dark, and even the well-known words of the tale are literally "dressed-up" in constantly changing colors and font-sizes, requiring the reader to decide what interpretation to place on such variation.[1] Not only does Egnéus change time-periods and places from page to page, but his approach to characterization is also unorthodox, as is evident in the wolf's approach to Grandmother's "house," which may strike us as something closer to a *palazzo*. Although we are well aware that this is a tense moment in the story, given the wolf's intentions, Egnéus chooses to inject some humor into the wolf's scampering haste—indicated by use of the freeze-frame technique—through the fanciful, pastel landscape. As if to further distract us from the impending violence, he adds a sly joke that actually sabotages the freeze-frame logic: note one wolf-image helping another to climb the creepers onto the bridge!

Clearly Egnéus has no intention of allowing his readers to simply sit back and let him do all the work; his innovative approach demands careful attention and thought. Although the initial response to his inconsistencies may be frustration, the perceptive reader will be rewarded with a new and exciting vision.

Once Upon a (Particular) Time

"Once upon a time...." There can be no doubt that the all-inclusiveness of the fairy tale's opening lines has ensured its endurance and currency across international time zones; nevertheless, it is precisely this vagueness that invites the creativity of the artist. As we have already seen, an illustrator has the power to create a world that may be beyond our own imaginings. In the following examples, we will take a look at some of the effects that specific settings can produce.

Take for example Paul Zelinsky's depiction of the scene in "Rumpelstiltskin" where the "little man" returns to pursue his claim for the Queen's child (Figure 21, 1986). Zelinsky's work is meticulous in its attention to setting in all its detail, but the story comes first. Our eye is drawn initially to the expressions of the two women, and then to the cause of their distress, as Rumpelstiltskin appears in the door. Once

---

1   It's worth noting that Egnéus has impressive credentials in the world of advertising, where the eye-catching coordination of text, font, and image is the predominant concern; indeed, this edition is published as part of a series entitled Harper Design, evidence that the fairy tale continues to inspire creative responses from many different quarters.

we have absorbed the drama of the moment, there is much to explore in Zelinsky's elaborate creation of this late-medieval scene—which arguably remains a popular choice of setting for the traditional fairy tale, present exceptions notwithstanding. The fact that Zelinsky chose to create his illustration in the form of an oil painting—complete with an Italianate country-scene beyond the balcony—testifies to the unique challenge that the fairy tale offers to the artist to synthesize fantasy and reality in such a way as to create belief in what Tolkien terms a "Secondary World."

Surely part of the pleasure in viewing (and perhaps illustrating) David Roberts's *Rapunzel: A Groovy Fairy Tale* (Figure 22, 2003)[1] is in seeing the story unfold in a time and place with which one may even be personally familiar. Turning the pages is like a trip down Memory Lane—not so much for *what* is happening as for the surroundings *in which* it's happening—in this case, the not-so-distant "hippy era" of the late 1960s and early 1970s. We have already seen the desire to bring the fairy tale into the modern world; now, however, the tendency is for even greater specificity. Zelinsky created a believable quasi-historical world through the realistic and detailed depiction of texture and composition; Roberts amply displays the recognizable memorabilia of the day. Rapunzel's room contains an assortment of all the icons of the period: posters of rock 'n' roll idols, LPs and turntable, rice-paper and lava lamps, white vinyl bed headboard, plants, bell-bottom pants, coffee-house-guitar-playing boyfriend, and, of course, the requisite long hair. We look at these pages and remember our own pasts, or those of our parents or grandparents, with the realization that Rapunzel could have been one of us. In taking us somewhere else, the vision of an artist like Zelinsky enlarges our sense of wonder; the closer-to-home settings of some contemporary artists also elicit surprise by showing us that the fairy tale has an immediacy and a relevance that are very much our own.

Cauldron of Story—Postmodern Style

What should be amply clear by now is that the evolution of the fairy tale, in both text and image, is a dynamic one. We have already seen some evidence, in the shape of James Finn Garner's story from *Politically Correct Bedtime Stories*, to suggest that the fairy tale has entered the postmodern age. If further proof is necessary, it can surely be found in *The Stinky Cheese Man and other Fairly Stupid Tales*, by Jon Scieszka and Lane Smith, from which Figure 23 (1992) is taken. (The cheerful cynicism of these

---

1   Roberts's enthusiasm for "dating" the fairy tale can also be seen in *Cinderella: An Art Deco Love Story* (2001) and *Sleeping Beauty: A Mid-Century Fairy Tale* (2017).

titles tells a story in itself!) The sophistication of both text and illustration is remarkable; "Giant Story" is little short of a deconstruction of the fairy tale, of storytelling, perhaps even of the book itself. It is also an example of the current approach (see Tosi, p. 432ff) that favors mixing up the stories to produce what has been termed a "fairy-tale salad." This "tossed" approach, evident in the text and images of "Giant Story," demands, however, an equal sophistication on the part of the reader-viewer: an extensive familiarity with fairy tales and their illustrations is needed to appreciate the numerous allusions found here. A closer examination reveals references not only to "Puss in Boots," "Snow White," and "Cinderella," but also to some of the "classics" of children's literature such as nursery rhymes and, more specifically, Heinrich Hoffman's "Struwwelpeter" (1848) and Ludwig Bemelmans's "Madeline" (1939), to name just a couple. Smith's chaotic collage provides a visual representation of Tolkien's seminal image of the "Cauldron of Story," suggesting the ever-bubbling, ever-replenished mixture of human experience and imagination that manifests itself in the fairy tale.

Our other example comes from the world of the comic book, a field that has experienced extraordinary growth over the last few years, particularly in the sophistication and originality to be found in the graphic novel. Its success marks an intriguing (some might say inevitable) coming together of word and image that has caught the popular imagination.

The most significant comic-book series based on the fairy tale is Bill Willingham's *Fables*[1] (Figure 24, 2002). His stories are set in the real world—now New York, now the Cascade Mountains—but the central group of characters are a "who's who" of the fairy-tale world: Snow White, Cinderella, Goldilocks, Bluebeard, Prince Charming—and Bigby Wolf (as in Big Bad Wolf), arguably Willingham's most intriguing character, who is surely based on the mythology surrounding the actor Humphrey Bogart, particularly in his role as Dashiel Hammett's chain-smoking private eye Sam Spade, from an era we have encountered already in Matt Phelan's graphic novel of "Snow White."

Given the demanding sequential nature of the comic-book structure, Willingham's choice of the term "fable" as opposed to "fairy tale" is arguably to gain access to draw from a larger frame of reference.[2] While fairy-tale characters remain the core of the adventures, many of the supporting cast are drawn from other classic works of fantasy, such as *Alice's Adventures in Wonderland*, *Pinocchio*, and even *Animal Farm*,

---

1   *Fables* (2002–15) is one of the longest-running comic-book series in the history of the medium and has won numerous awards.

2   A similar range of characters is present in the ABC television series *Once Upon a Time* (first broadcast in 2011), notwithstanding the obvious fairy-tale orientation of its title.

not to mention personifications of Nature (North Wind, Jack Frost) and nursery-rhyme characters (Mary Mary Quite Contrary, Little Boy Blue). It is quickly apparent, however, that the female characters in particular bear little resemblance to their originals—or, more accurately, to their depiction in the nineteenth-century texts that we tend to regard as original—and even less to the Disney versions that were so influential in the last century. The innocent damsels-in-distress of yesteryear have been transformed into sophisticated and sensual women who are as ambitious and often as devious as their male counterparts: Snow White is now a glamorous municipal administrator, while Goldilocks has been transformed into a voluptuous psychopath. The frame-story whereby Willingham binds these elements together is ingenious: the fairy-tale world is threatened by the forces of the mysterious Adversary, which is in essence a version of the age-old struggle between Reason and Imagination. Despite the vigor and inventiveness of the narrative, however, we may feel that the connection with the world of fairy tale is often tenuous. By simply adopting the names of classic fairy-tale characters, Willingham is investing his own creations with a power and mystique that they have not earned, although the ongoing popularity of *Fables* suggests that he has re-energized them in their radically different *milieu*. His views on fairy tales and their adaptation are revealing:

> The thing that moved me toward fairy-tale stories: One, it's a group of characters and stories that we all own. Every single person in the world owns all of these characters and stories outright. We're all born with an inheritance that we can take advantage of. I think those of us who are doing fairy-tale-based stories are the ones who are sort of cashing in on our inheritance…. You do not have to get anyone's permission to do a new version of "Snow White," for example. And we're social people. We get ideas from each other.[1]

Postscript: Some Day My Prince Will Come … or Not

Nowhere is the role of the visual artist more obvious than in the popular medium of film, synonymous in the world of fairy tale with the work of Walt Disney. However, our familiarity with fairy tales today is attributable not only to Disney's pioneering work in the field but also to his numerous successors and rivals who have carved out their own extensions of his Magic Kingdom.

---

1   "Fable Master: Bill Willingham Modernized Fairy Tales before Modernizing Fairy Tales Was Cool," *Willamette Week* 24 April 2013, http://www.wweek.com/portland/article-20556-fable_master.html.

The transfer from book to screen represents an important qualitative leap in the reader-cum-viewer's experience of the tale. Quality and quantity of the illustrations aside, the book still provides the reader (or listener) with the text of the story and, thus, imaginative ownership of the material. The reader still has some scope to decide how much of an influence the visual images will have on his or her experience of the narrative. Nevertheless, the number, if not the quality, of pictures is bound to make a difference, and, as we have seen, the growing tendency to illustrate fairy tales ever more profusely can have the effect of relegating the text to secondary importance. This predominance of the visual image at the expense of the text is made complete in the medium of film. The most obvious contrast, of course, is the *total* reliance on the visual image to recreate the story; without any text, each and every detail must be graphically represented—and many more details have to be *invented*, since the fairy tale leaves much to the imagination.

Not least is the problem of how to make the inherently dark side of fairy tales—their violence and cruelty—visually acceptable to a child audience. In *Snow White* (1937), his first animated tale, Disney had to deal with the stepmother's cannibalism, her three attempts to kill Snow White, and her subsequent horrific death. (Such a gruesome "happy ending" is not untypical of the fairy tale. Much of our satisfaction, in fact, derives from the inexorable working-out of poetic justice in the tales, however harsh it may be.) As with many illustrators confronted with the same issue, Disney's solution was to reduce or eliminate as much of the violent and cruel material as possible. However, the diminution of the stepmother's role and the two-dimensional doll-like portrayal of the characters, the comic characterization of the dwarves, the addition of domestic scenes with cute animal helpers, and the romantic ending—all to the accompaniment of cheerful song and dance—provide a radical departure from the spirit and essence of the original fairy tale. While Disney was quick to recognize and exploit the visually exciting potential of the "scary" scenes he added to the stories—one of the most memorable scenes from *Sleeping Beauty* (1959) is the battle between the Prince and Maleficent during which she transforms herself into a fire-breathing dragon—the effect was to replace the disturbing or complex elements of the tale with the titillation of violence as spectacle, something Hollywood has always excelled at.

As his many critics have pointed out, Disney's shortcomings have less to do with his alteration of the story—the prerogative of every artist—than with his departure from the *spirit* of the fairy tale. As we pointed out at the beginning of this section, in reworking the raw material, the artist's response must be sensitive to its depth of meaning. In the process of translating these stories from book to screen, Disney reduced them to the romantic stereotypes and clichés that have given fairy tales a bad name, especially among feminist critics. More recently, of course, the studio has

Figure 1: In the woods Little Red Riding Hood met old Father Wolf (1867), Gustav Doré

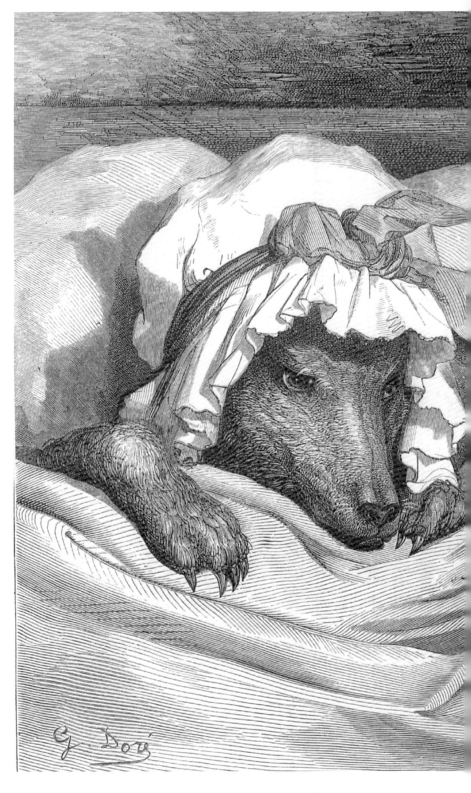

Figure 2: She was astonished to see how her grandmother looked (1867), Gustav Doré

Figure 3: "As she was going through the wood, she met with the Wolf." Little Red Riding Hood (1983), Sarah Moon

Figure 4: "Outside, the forest is big." The Girl in Red, illustrated by Roberto Innocenti, 2012

Figure 5: Little Red Riding Hood (1995), Mireille Levert

Figure 6: Opening a Pathway to Briar Rose (1978), Michael Foreman

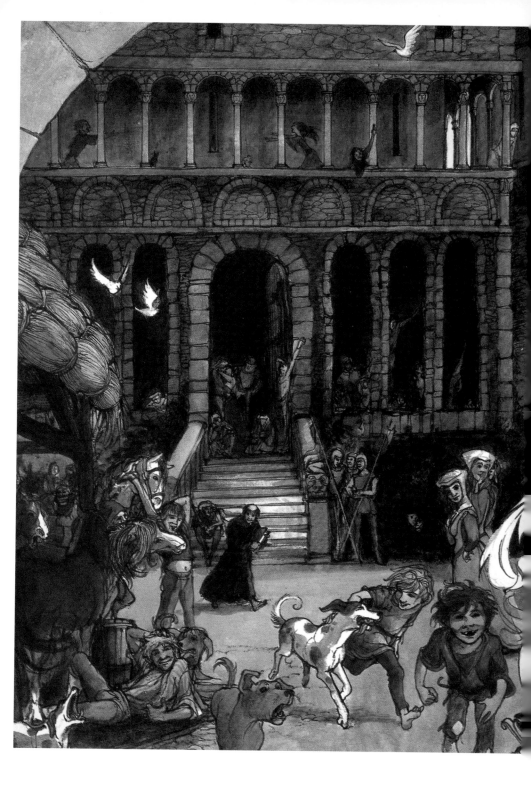

Figure 7: The Sleeping Beauty (1977), Trina Schart Hyman

After a little while, they went down from the tower together, hand in hand. Where one drop of blood drains a castle of life, so one kiss can bring it alive again. Then the King and Queen woke up, and so did all their knights and ladies, and everyone looked at each other with astonishment in their sleepy eyes. The horses in the stable stood up and shook themselves, and the grooms scratched their heads and stretched their legs. The hounds began to leap about, barking at nothing and wagging their tails.

Figure 8: Hansel and Gretel (1981), Anthony Browne

Figure 9: Hansel and Gretel (1989), Tony Ross

(40)

Figure 10: Hansel und Gretel (2007), Susanne Janssen

41

Figure 11: Hansel and Gretel: The Graphic Novel (2008), Sean Dietrich

Figure 12: Grimm Fairy Tales: Hansel and Gretel (2005), Joe Tyler and Ralph Tedesco

Figure 13: Snow White: A Graphic Novel (2016), Matt Phelan

Figure 14: Snowhite, "Inevitably, he had his way with her." (2011), Ana Juan

Figure 15: Beauty and the Beast (1874), Walter Crane

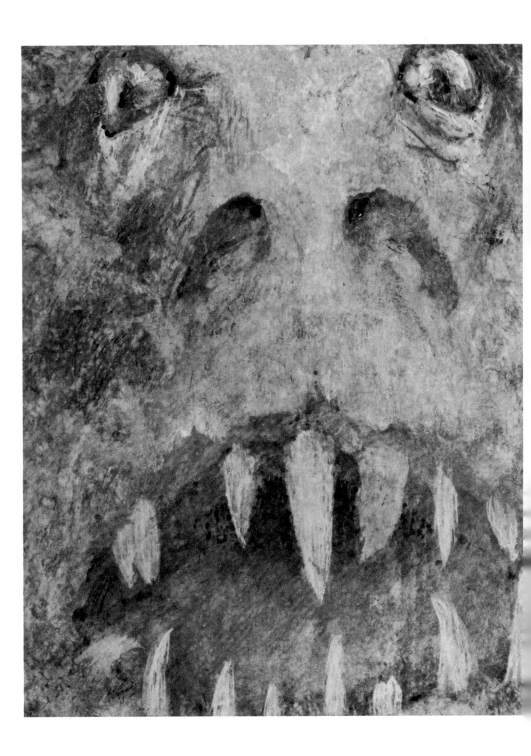

Figure 16: Beauty and the Beast (1972), Alan Barrett

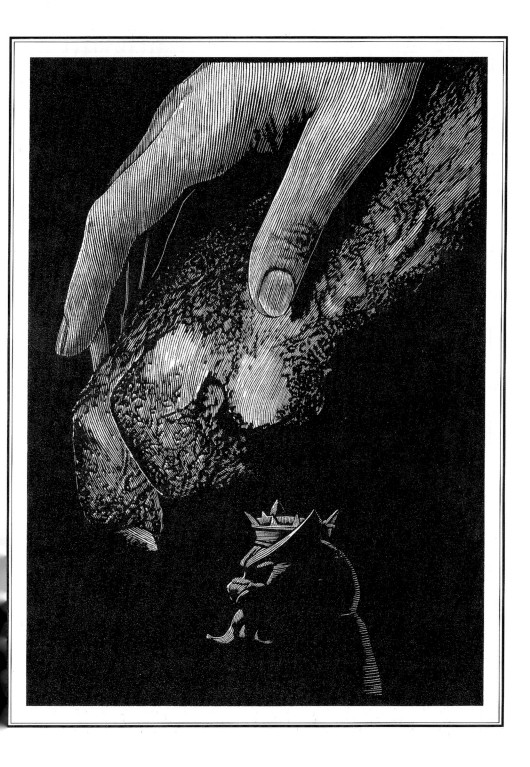

Figure 17: Beauty and the Beast (1992), Barry Moser

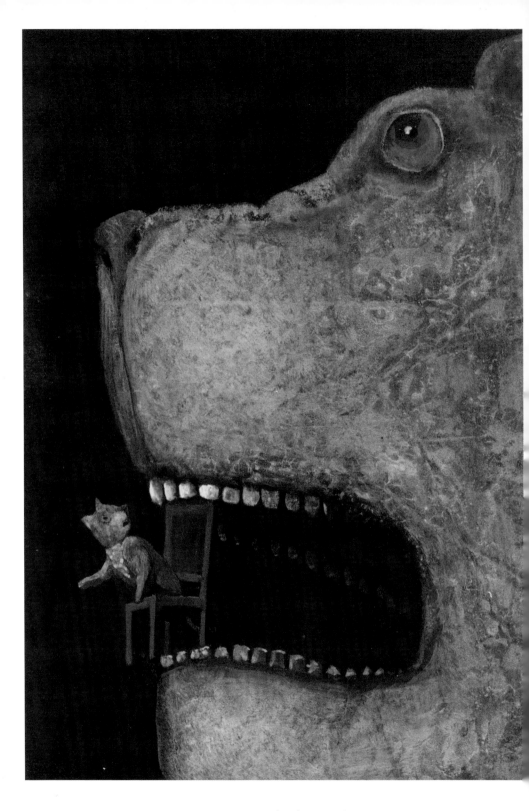

Figure 18: Puss in Boots (1990), Stasys Eidrigevičius

Figure 19: "All at once the door opened and an old, old Woman, supporting herself on a crutch, came hobbling out."

Hansel and Gretel (1909), Arthur Rackham

The
wolf
ran straight
to
GRANDMOTHER'
house

Figure 20: Little Red Riding Hood (2011), Daniel Egnéus

and
knocked
at the
DOOR.

Figure 21: Rumpelstiltskin (1986), Paul Zelinsky

Figure 22: Rapunzel: A Groovy 70s Fairy Tale (2003), David Roberts

THE END

of the evil Stepmother

said "I'll HUFF and SNUFF and give you three wishes."

The beast changed into

SEVEN DWARVES

HAPPILY EVER AFTER

for a spell had been cast by a Wicked Witch

Once upon a time

"That's your story?" said Jack.
"You've got to be kidding. That's not a
Fairly Stupid Tale. That's an Incredibly Stupid Tale.
That's an Unbelievably Stupid Tale. That is
the Most Stupid Tale I Ever— *awwwk!*"
The Giant grabbed Jack and dragged him to the next page.

Figure 23: Giant Story (1992), Jon Scieszka and Lane Smith

AS *SORRY* AS I AM FOR YOUR MARITAL "*DIFFICULTIES*," IT ISN'T ANY OF MY BUSINESS. WE *BARELY* HAVE ENOUGH MONEY AND MANPOWER TO RUN THE MOST *BASIC* OF UNDERGROUND GOVERNMENT SERVICES.

WE CAN'T *AFFORD* TO DO MARITAL COUNSELING, AND TO BE PERFECTLY *CANDID*, I WOULDN'T ALLOW IT IF WE *COULD*.

THE *MUNDANES* MAY LOOK TO THEIR GOVERNMENT TO SOLVE THEIR PROBLEMS, BUT IN THE *FABLE* COMMUNITY, WE *EXPECT* YOU TO BE ABLE TO RUN YOUR *OWN* LIVES.

OUR *ONLY* CONCERN IS THAT YOU'RE CURRENTLY IN VIOLATION OF OUR MOST *VITAL* LAW: NO FABLE SHALL, BY ACTION OR INACTION, CAUSE OUR MAGICAL NATURE TO BECOME KNOWN TO THE MUNDANE WORLD.

SNOW WHITE
DIRECTOR OF OPERATIONS

IF YOU CAN'T *MAINTAIN* A NORMAL *HUMAN* APPEARANCE OR PURCHASE A CONCEALING *GLAMOUR* FROM ONE OF OUR WITCHES--

--OUR RULES MANDATE THAT YOU BE *RELOCATED* UPSTATE TO THE *FARM*, WHERE ALL THE OTHER NONHUMAN FABLES LIVE.

BUT WE DIDN'T *ESCAPE* FROM THE HOMELANDS WITH OUR FORTUNE *INTACT*! WE CAN'T *AFFORD* A GLAMOUR POWERFUL ENOUGH TO HIDE MY HUSBAND'S CURSE. WE *BARELY* MAKE ENOUGH BETWEEN US TO GET *BY*.

UND ITH THOTH THAME MONEY TWUBBLES THAT EXATHERBATHES OWAH MAWITAL PWOBWEMS AND MAKTH THE CURTH COME BACK.

AS *SYMPATHETIC* AS I AM TO YOUR TROUBLES, I CAN'T BE OF ANY *HELP* TO YOU.

MANY OF THE FABLES--I'D EVEN SAY *MOST* OF US--LOST OUR LANDS, TITLES AND FORTUNES WHEN WE WERE FORCED *OUT* OF OUR HOMELANDS BY THE *ADVERSARY*.

WE HAVE TO MAKE DO AS *BEST* WE CAN.

SNOW WHITE
DIRECTOR OF OPERATIONS

Figure 24: Fables: Legends in Exile (2012), Bill Willingham

bowed to changing social attitudes and undertaken a major revision of the Disney heroine, launched (with considerable fanfare) in "Beauty and the Beast" (1991) and consolidated in several subsequent animations, including "Tangled" (2010) and "Frozen" (2013). Other studios have followed suit, showing how carefully these organizations test the public mood. In truth, the continuing appetite for such productions reveals as much about our own attitudes and aspirations as about fairy tale (see Hearne, p. 452ff). The fact is that Disney's animations have become as much a part of the fairy-tale canon as the Grimm Brothers' tales; indeed, it can be argued that Disney was no more or less a man of his time as the Brothers Grimm and Charles Perrault were before him; they too manipulated the fairy tale to suit the tastes and expectations of their readers.

CRITICISM

Serious critical attention to the fairy tale is essentially a phenomenon that began in the twentieth century. As we have noted in our introduction, discussion prior to that tended to be dismissive, even condemnatory, despite the positive testimonials of various literary figures. In the English-speaking world, a breakthrough of sorts came through the intervention of the eminent scholar and writer Andrew Lang, who, through the publication of his twelve-volume "color" series (1889–1910), was responsible for popularizing the fairy tale well beyond what we might term the classical canon of Charles Perrault and the Grimm brothers. As a folklorist, Lang was representative of a new field of study that seized upon the folk tale as a repository of valuable information about traditional beliefs, superstitions, and customs. This field of knowledge was gradually absorbed into the larger discipline of anthropology, culminating in the monumental project, initiated in Finland in 1910 by Antti Aarne and extended by the American Stith Thompson in 1927 and 1961, to produce a comprehensive index of types and motifs found in the entire corpus of fairy tale.

It's now eighty years since a distinguished but relatively unknown professor at Oxford University by the name of J.R.R. Tolkien wrote an essay, "On Fairy-Stories" (1938) at a time when serious interest in fairy tales in England was confined to the very young and a few pioneering academics. Tolkien went on, of course, to become a giant of fantasy literature; there can be few who are unfamiliar with *The Hobbit* and his celebrated trilogy *Lord of the Rings*. What makes "On Fairy-Stories" memorable, however, is that Tolkien was one of the first to look beyond the limitations of fairy-tales-as-children's-stories and take them seriously as literature. The results have influenced and inspired fairy-tale studies ever since.

Fairy-tale scholarship has long prospered in the German-speaking world, in part as the legacy of the Grimm brothers and their Romantic contemporaries. Much of this valuable work remains unavailable in English, but fortunately several works by the Swiss scholar Max Lüthi have been translated, an excerpt from one of which (*Once Upon a Time*, 1970) is included here. Lüthi's major concern is to demonstrate the fairy tale's preoccupation with, and relevance for, humanity; drawing upon his knowledge of the European fairy tale, Lüthi tackles such aspects as the central character's gender, isolation, social position, and personal maturation (in this last respect anticipating ideas that would later be more fully explored by Bruno Bettelheim). He was indeed among the first to counter the nineteenth-century view that fairy tales were of interest only to children; on the contrary, "[t]he ease and calm assurance with which [the fairy tale] stylizes, sublimates, and abstracts makes it the quintessence of the poetic process" (p. 375). Despite the age of this excerpt (first published in English in 1970), its insights into the purpose and focus of the fairy tale remain as illuminating as ever.

In turning to the work of Bruno Bettelheim, we can observe a contrast to the general perspective of critics such as Lüthi in a more narrowly defined interest in the fairy tale. As a well-known child psychologist, Bettelheim came to write his influential work *The Uses of Enchantment* (1976) in the conviction that "more can be learned from [fairy tales] about the inner problems of human beings, and of the right solutions to their predicaments in any society, than from any other type of story within a child's comprehension" (p. 377). It has been argued that in his desire to demonstrate the psychic merits of the fairy tale, Bettelheim is selective not only in the tales he chooses to discuss but even in the versions thereof: what may hold true for version A may well be contradicted by version B.[1] Certainly since his death there have been disturbing accusations aimed at Bettelheim regarding the validity of his work both as a psychologist and as a critic. Be that as it may, there is no denying that the publication of his book renewed interest in and appreciation of the fairy tale; as one critic has acknowledged, "[o]nce one has grasped the Bettelheim method, with its unspoken rules—characters can be doublets or triplets of each other, all objects have symbolic meaning—not only do fairy tales become quite easy to interpret, they also provoke and reward interpretation."[2] While such an open-ended prescription may lead to some analytic over-exuberance, it undeniably brings a living relevance to the tales.

More recently, the critical examination of the fairy tale has proceeded apace, especially in the second half of the last century, and from a variety of different perspectives, as we hope our selection in the following pages illustrates. Given the unique history and evolution of the fairy tale, however, problems can arise if it is subjected

1   See Dundes, p. 387ff.

2   Tom Shippey, "Rewriting the Core: Transformations of the Fairy Tale in Contemporary Writing," *A Companion to the Fairy Tale*, ed. Hilda Davidson and Anna Chaudri (Cambridge: D.S. Brewer, 2003), 258.

to literary criteria that take no account of such matters as multiple national and international variants and inadequate chronological evidence. To clarify this issue more fully, we include the essay "Fairy Tales from a Folkloristic Perspective" (1986) by the distinguished folklorist Alan Dundes, who makes no bones about his concern that many current fairy-tale studies, in favoring the literary approach, tend to build substantial theories upon a single fairy-tale variant or a particular socio-cultural context. From a folkloristic perspective, this is, of course, a flawed methodology.

There can be little doubt, however, that the most vigorous field of fairy-tale criticism over the last fifty years has been the feminist one. As we have seen, the fairy tale firmly established itself as an important part of children's literature in the course of the nineteenth century, so it should come as no surprise that many of the most popular tales just happened to reflect and endorse established gender roles. It is as if growing indignation at this skewed patriarchal perspective finally reached boiling point and spilled over into a wholesale condemnation of the tales' insidious influence upon the young female mindset. In his book *Fairy Tales and Feminism* (2004), some excerpts from which we include here, Donald Haase provides a valuable overview not only of that lively period during which feminist thinkers responded to this deep-seated bias in fairy tales, but also of how the seeds of gender distortion were sown by the Brothers Grimm and earlier; research indicates that this is not a new problem.

Through the course of this anthology, we have seen how, on numerous fronts, the interpretation of fairy tales has taken a darker turn as it has come full circle in once again attracting an older audience. Not surprisingly, this shift has also manifested itself in the picture-book, to the extent that we find ourselves debating its place in contemporary literature; clearly it has become something more than simply a branch of children's literature. As Sandra L. Beckett observes, "Since the 1960s, picturebooks have made great strides in freeing themselves from the rigid moral codes and taboos that long governed children's literature" (p. 429), and in her article she traces the development of this new phenomenon and examines the motivation of illustrators who confront issues and experiences that have hitherto been regarded as inappropriate for young minds.

The desire to write or adapt fairy tales in order to subvert their historically accepted ideology is certainly evident if one examines today's burgeoning juvenile market. Laura Tosi's survey of contemporary fairy-tale publications reveals three particular types: "morally correct," postmodernist, and feminist rewritings. What they all share, however, is a high degree of what has been termed in academic circles "intertextuality"; in other words, their numerous allusions and hybrid composition depend heavily on the reader's familiarity with the fairy-tale canon and narrative structure. However, as Tosi points out, these non-conventional approaches and techniques have revitalized the fairy-tale genre for children.

[340]

One medium that has quite simply revolutionized the fairy tale in the modern world is film—and in that field, the name of Walt Disney has reigned supreme. In the constant ebb and flow of our cultural scene, the Disney product has proved remarkably resilient, although that may be due more to skillful marketing than to fidelity to the fairy tale—there is no clearer instance of what Jack Zipes has called the "commodification" of the fairy tale. While in no way excusing Disney for the liberties that he (or his team) took with his raw material, Betsy Hearne, in her article "Disney Revisited, Or, Jiminy Cricket, It's Musty Down Here!" (1997), is nevertheless concerned that we judge Disney's intervention in the light of what has previously happened in the evolution of the fairy tale. As we have already seen, research has shown conclusively that what such luminaries as Perrault and the Grimms passed on to posterity was sometimes quite different from what they received. Therefore, to condemn Disney for his influence is analogous to shooting the messenger, says Hearne. Disney has been successful, at least in part, because he has given us—children and adults alike—what we want.

In "Techno-Magic: Cinema and Fairy Tale" and "Utopian Dreams/Wishful Thinking" (2014), Marina Warner investigates the close connection between fairy tale and film, made all the more apparent by the wonders of CGI. Yet even as the fairy-tale film revels in its technical wizardry, Warner notes that the story has continued to reflect changing social values, most obviously in the transformation of the young heroine from passive trophy to self-assertive leader: "By far the most striking development in the alliance of fairy tale and cinema as vehicles in family entertainment has been the rise of political sensitivity, and resulting tinkering with stories to show awareness of gender, power relations, and ethnic representation" (see p. 461). Her analysis reveals that the above quotation from Beckett regarding picture-books could equally be applied to film, to the degree that fairy-tale films have split into two camps: those that are intended as "family entertainment" and strive to deliver the status quo with a dash of progressive daring, and those that use these iconic narratives to explore (and sometimes to exploit) the darker corners of human experience.

Over the last fifty years, the production of animated fairy tales has been transformed into a competitive and enormously lucrative business. The technological refinement in the magic of animation has brought about an extraordinary expansion in its appeal. Fantasy rules—and the fairy tale has continued to adapt (or, more accurately, it has *been* adapted) to changing circumstances. All this has not occurred without consequences, however, as James Poniewozik pointed out in a perceptive article in *Time* magazine anticipating the opening of *Shrek the Third* in 2007. In the article, which is reproduced as the final selection below, he makes the point that in our media-dominated world, these sophisticated and elaborate parodies now represent the first exposure that many children have to the world of fairy tale. It is as if amid all the shock and awe of special effects and technological wizardry, the voice (and the companionship) of the storyteller has been all but drowned out; the audience's imagination has been short-circuited by watching the impossible made not just possible but downright easy, with the result that we are in danger of losing our capacity to wonder. Poniewozik finds some cause for optimism in the creative invention that occasionally asserts itself amid all the "riffing on our cartoon patrimony," but there's no denying the strength of the cash-flow current.

ON FAIRY-STORIES[1]

J.R.R. Tolkien

[...]

Children

I WILL NOW TURN TO CHILDREN, and so come to the last and most important of the three questions: what, if any, are the values and functions of fairy-stories *now*? It is usually assumed that children are the natural or the specially appropriate audience for fairy-stories. In describing a fairy-story which they think adults might possibly read for their own entertainment, reviewers frequently indulge in such waggeries as: "this book is for children from the ages of six to sixty." But I have never yet seen the puff of a new motor-model that began thus: "this toy will amuse infants from seventeen to seventy"; though that to my mind would be much more appropriate. Is there any *essential* connection between children and fairy-stories? Is there any call for comment, if an adult reads them for himself? *Reads* them as tales, that is, not *studies* them as curios. Adults are allowed to collect and study anything, even old theatre-programmes or paper bags.

Among those who still have enough wisdom not to think fairy-stories pernicious, the common opinion seems to be that there is a natural connection between the minds of children and fairy-stories, of the same order as the connection between children's bodies and milk. I think this is an error; at best an error of false sentiment, and one that is therefore most often made by those who, for whatever private reason (such as childlessness), tend to think of children as a special kind of creature, almost

---

1   First published in 1938. This text from *Essays Presented to Charles Williams*, ed. C.S. Lewis (Oxford: Oxford UP, 1947). All notes are Tolkien's unless presented in brackets.

a different race, rather than as normal, if immature, members of a particular family, and of the human family at large.

Actually, the association of children and fairy-stories is an accident of our domestic history. Fairy-stories have in the modern lettered world been relegated to the "nursery," as shabby or old-fashioned furniture is relegated to the playroom, primarily because the adults do not want it, and do not mind if it is misused.[1] It is not the choice of the children which decides this. Children as a class—except in a common lack of experience they are not one—neither like fairy-stories more, nor understand them better than adults do; and no more than they like many other things. They are young and growing, and normally have keen appetites, so the fairy-stories as a rule go down well enough. But in fact only some children, and some adults, have any special taste for them; and when they have it, it is not exclusive, nor even necessarily dominant.[2] It is a taste, too, that would not appear, I think, very early in childhood without artificial stimulus; it is certainly one that does not decrease but increases with age, if it is innate.

It is true that in recent times fairy-stories have usually been written or "adapted" for children. But so may music be, or verse, or novels, or history, or scientific manuals. It is a dangerous process, even when it is necessary. It is indeed only saved from disaster by the fact that the arts and sciences are not as a whole relegated to the nursery; the nursery and schoolroom are merely given such tastes and glimpses of the adult thing as seem fit for them in adult opinion (often much mistaken). Any one

---

1 In the case of stories and other nursery lore, there is also another factor. Wealthier families employed women to look after their children, and the stories were provided by these nurses, who were sometimes in touch with rustic and traditional lore forgotten by their "betters." It is long since this source dried up, at any rate in England; but it once had some importance. But again there is no proof of the special fitness of children as the recipients of this vanishing "folk-lore." The nurses might just as well (or better) have been left to choose the pictures and furniture.

2 As far as my knowledge goes, children who have an early bent for writing have no special inclination to attempt the writing of fairy-stories, unless that has been almost the sole form of literature presented to them; and they fail most markedly when they try. It is not an easy form. If children have any special leaning it is to Beast-fable, which adults often confuse with Fairy-story. The best stories by children that I have seen have been either "realistic" (in intent), or have had as their characters animals and birds, who were in the main the zoomorphic human beings usual in Beast-fable. I imagine that this form is so often adopted principally because it allows a large measure of realism: the representation of domestic events and talk that children really know. The form itself is, however, as a rule, suggested or imposed by adults. It has a curious preponderance in the literature, good and bad, that is nowadays commonly presented to young children: I suppose it is felt to go with "Natural History," semi-scientific books about beasts and birds that are also considered to be proper pabulum for the young. And it is reinforced by the bears and rabbits that seem in recent times almost to have ousted human dolls from the play-rooms even of little girls. Children make up sagas, often long and elaborate, about their dolls. If these are shaped like bears, bears will be the characters of the sagas; but they will talk like people.

of these things would, if left altogether in the nursery, become gravely impaired. So would a beautiful table, a good picture, or a useful machine (such as a microscope), be defaced or broken, if it were left long unregarded in a schoolroom. Fairy-stories banished in this way, cut off from a full adult art, would in the end be ruined; indeed in so far as they have been so banished, they have been ruined.

The value of fairy-stories is thus not, in my opinion, to be found by considering children in particular. Collections of fairy-stories are, in fact, by nature attics and lumber-rooms, only by temporary and local custom play-rooms. Their contents are disordered, and often battered, a jumble of different dates, purposes, and tastes; but among them may occasionally be found a thing of permanent virtue: an old work of art, not too much damaged, that only stupidity would ever have stuffed away.

Andrew Lang's *Fairy Books* are not, perhaps, lumber-rooms. They are more like stalls in a rummage-sale. Someone with a duster and a fair eye for things that retain some value has been round the attics and box-rooms. His collections are largely a by-product of his adult study of mythology and folk-lore; but they were made into and presented as books for children.[1] Some of the reasons that Lang gave are worth considering.

The introduction to the first of the series speaks of "children to whom and for whom they are told." "They represent," he says, "the young age of man true to his early loves, and have his unblunted edge of belief, a fresh appetite for marvels." "'Is it true?'" he says, "is the great question children ask."

I suspect that *belief* and *appetite for marvels* are here regarded as identical or as closely related. They are radically different, though the appetite for marvels is not at once or at first differentiated by a growing human mind from its general appetite. It seems fairly clear that Lang was using belief in its ordinary sense: belief that a thing exists or can happen in the real (primary) world. If so, then I fear that Lang's words, stripped of sentiment, can only imply that the teller of marvellous tales to children, must or may, or at any rate does trade on their *credulity*, on the lack of experience which makes it less easy for children to distinguish fact from fiction in particular cases, though the distinction in itself is fundamental to the sane human mind, and to fairy-stories.

Children are capable, of course, of *literary belief*, when the storymaker's art is good enough to produce it. That state of mind has been called "willing suspension of disbelief." But this does not seem to me a good description of what happens. What really happens is that the story-maker proves a successful "sub-creator." He makes a Secondary World which your mind can enter. Inside it, what he relates is "true": it

---

1   By Lang and his helpers. It is not true of the majority of the contents in their original (or oldest surviving) forms.

accords with the laws of that world. You therefore believe it, while you are, as it were, inside. The moment disbelief arises, the spell is broken; the magic, or rather art, has failed. You are then out in the Primary World again, looking at the little abortive Secondary World from outside. If you are obliged, by kindliness or circumstance, to stay, then disbelief must be suspended (or stifled), otherwise listening and looking would become intolerable. But this suspension of disbelief is a substitute for the genuine thing, a subterfuge we use when condescending to games or make-believe, or when trying (more or less willingly) to find what virtue we can in the work of an art that has for us failed.

A real enthusiast for cricket is in the enchanted state: Secondary Belief. I, when I watch a match, am on the lower level. I can achieve (more or less) willing suspension of disbelief, when I am held there and supported by some other motive that will keep away boredom: for instance, a wild, heraldic, preference for dark blue rather than light. This suspension of disbelief may thus be a somewhat tired, shabby, or sentimental state of mind, and so lean to the "adult." I fancy it is often the state of adults in the presence of a fairy-story. They are held there and supported by sentiment (memories of childhood, or notions of what childhood ought to be like); they think they ought to like the tale. But if they really liked it, for itself, they would not have to suspend disbelief: they would believe—in this sense.

Now if Lang had meant anything like this there might have been some truth in his words. It may be argued that it is easier to work the spell with children. Perhaps it is, though I am not sure of this. The appearance that it is so is often, I think, an adult illusion produced by children's humility, their lack of critical experience and vocabulary, and their voracity (proper to their rapid growth). They like to try to like what is given to them: if they do not like it, they cannot well express their dislike or give reasons for it (and so may conceal it); and they like a great mass of different things indiscriminately, without troubling to analyse the planes of their belief. In any case I doubt if this potion—the enchantment of the effective fairy-story—is really one of the kind that becomes "blunted" by use, less potent after repeated draughts.

"'Is it true?' is the great question children ask," Lang said. They do ask that question, I know; and it is not one to be rashly or idly answered.[1] But that question is hardly evidence of "unblunted belief," or even of the desire for it. Most often it proceeds from the child's desire to know which kind of literature he is faced with. Children's knowledge of the world is often so small that they cannot judge, off-hand and without help, between the fantastic, the strange (that is rare or remote facts),

---

1 Far more often they have asked me: "Was he good? Was he wicked?" That is, they were more concerned to get the Right side and the Wrong side clear. For that is a question equally important in History and in Faërie.

the nonsensical, and the merely "grown-up" (that is ordinary things of their parents' world, much of which still remains unexplored). But they recognise the different classes, and may like all of them at times. Of course the borders between them are often fluctuating or confused; but that is not only true for children. We all know the differences in kind, but we are not always sure how to place anything that we hear. A child may well believe a report that there are ogres in the next county; many grown-up persons find it easy to believe of another country; and as for another planet, very few adults seem able to imagine it as peopled, if at all, by anything but monsters of iniquity.

Now I was one of the children whom Andrew Lang was addressing—I was born at about the same time as the *Green Fairy Book*—the children for whom he seemed to think that fairy-stories were the equivalent of the adult novel, and of whom he said: "Their taste remains like the taste of their naked ancestors thousands of years ago; and they seem to like fairy-tales better than history, poetry, geography, or arithmetic."[1] But do we really know much about these "naked ancestors," except that they were certainly not naked? Our fairy-stories, however old certain elements in them may be, are certainly not the same as theirs. Yet if it is assumed that we have fairy-stories because they did, then probably we have history, geography, poetry, and arithmetic because they liked these things too, as far as they could get them, and in so far as they had yet separated the many branches of their general interest in everything.

And as for children of the present day, Lang's description does not fit my own memories, or my experience of children. Lang may have been mistaken about the children he knew, but if he was not, then at any rate children differ considerably, even within the narrow borders of Britain, and such generalizations which treat them as a class (disregarding their individual talents, and the influences of the countryside they live in, and their upbringing) are delusory. I had no special "wish to believe." I wanted to know. Belief depended on the way in which stories were presented to me, by older people, or by the authors, or on the inherent tone and quality of the tale. But at no time can I remember that the enjoyment of a story was dependent upon belief that such things could happen, or had happened, in "real life." Fairy-stories were plainly not primarily concerned with possibility, but with desirability. If they awakened *desire*, satisfying it while often whetting it unbearably, they succeeded. It is not necessary to be more explicit here, for I hope to say something later about this desire, a complex of many ingredients, some universal, some particular to modern men (including modern children), or even to certain kinds of men. I had no desire to have either dreams or adventures like *Alice*, and the account of them merely amused me. I had very little desire to look for buried treasure or fight pirates, and *Treasure*

---

1   Preface to the *Violet Fairy Book*.

Island left me cool. Red Indians were better: there were bows and arrows (I had and have a wholly unsatisfied desire to shoot well with a bow), and strange languages, and glimpses of an archaic mode of life, and, above all, forests in such stories. But the land of Merlin and Arthur was better than these, and best of all the nameless North of Sigurd of the Völsungs,[1] and the prince of all dragons. Such lands were pre-eminently desirable. I never imagined that the dragon was of the same order as the horse. And that was not solely because I saw horses daily, but never even the footprint of a worm.[2] The dragon had the trade-mark *Of Faërie* written plain upon him. In whatever world he had his being it was an Other-world. Fantasy, the making or glimpsing of Other-worlds, was the heart of the desire of Faërie. I desired dragons with a profound desire. Of course, I in my timid body did not wish to have them in the neighbourhood, intruding into my relatively safe world, in which it was, for instance, possible to read stories in peace of mind, free from fear.[3] But the world that contained even the imagination of Fáfnir[4] was richer and more beautiful, at whatever cost of peril. The dweller in the quiet and fertile plains may hear of the tormented hills and the unharvested sea and long for them in his heart. For the heart is hard though the body be soft.

All the same, important as I now perceive the fairy-story element in early reading to have been, speaking for myself as a child, I can only say that a liking for fairy-stories was not a dominant characteristic of early taste. A real taste for them awoke after "nursery" days, and after the years, few but long-seeming, between learning to read and going to school. In that (I nearly wrote "happy" or "golden," it was really a

---

1   [A legendary hero in Norse mythology, a central character of the Völsunga saga.]

2   I was introduced to zoology and paleontology ("for children") quite as early as to Faërie. I saw pictures of living beasts and of true (so I was told) prehistoric animals. I liked the "prehistoric" animals best: they had at least lived long ago, and hypothesis (based on somewhat slender evidence) cannot avoid a gleam of fantasy. But I did not like being told that these creatures were "dragons." I can still re-feel the irritation that I felt in childhood at assertions of instructive relatives (or their gift-books) such as these: "snowflakes are fairy jewels," or "are more beautiful than fairy jewels"; "the marvels of the ocean depths are more wonderful than fairyland." Children expect the differences they feel but cannot analyse to be explained by their elders, or at least recognised, not to be ignored or denied. I was keenly alive to the beauty of "Real things," but it seemed to me quibbling to confuse this with the wonder of "Other things." I was eager to study Nature, actually more eager than I was to read most fairy-stories; but I did not want to be quibbled into Science and cheated out of Faërie by people who seemed to assume that by some kind of original sin I should prefer fairy-tales, but according to some kind of new religion I ought to be induced to like science. Nature is no doubt a life-study, or a study for eternity (for those so gifted); but there is a part of man which is not "Nature," and which therefore is not obliged to study it, and is, in fact, wholly unsatisfied by it.

3   This is, naturally, often enough what children mean when they ask: "Is this true?" They mean: "I like this, but is it contemporary? Am I safe in my bed?" The answer: "There is certainly no dragon in England today," is all that they want to hear.

4   [Son of the dwarf king Hreidmar. Through a curse he was turned into a dragon and killed by Sigurd.]

sad and troublous) time I liked many other things as well, or better: such as history, astronomy, botany, grammar, and etymology. I agreed with Lang's generalised "children" not at all in principle, and only in some points by accident: I was, for instance, insensitive to poetry, and skipped it if it came in tales. Poetry I discovered much later in Latin and Greek, and especially through being made to try and translate English verse into classical verse. A real taste for fairy-stories was wakened by philology on the threshold of manhood, and quickened to full life by war.

I have said, perhaps, more than enough on this point. At least it will be plain that in my opinion fairy-stories should not be *specially* associated with children. They are associated with them: naturally, because children are human and fairy-stories are a natural human taste (though not necessarily a universal one); accidentally, because fairy-stories are a large part of the literary lumber that in latter-day Europe has been stuffed away in attics; unnaturally, because of erroneous sentiment about children, a sentiment that seems to increase with the decline in children.

It is true that the age of childhood-sentiment has produced some delightful books (especially charming, however, to adults) of the fairy kind or near to it; but it has also produced a dreadful undergrowth of stories written or adapted to what was or is conceived to be the measure of children's minds and needs. The old stories are mollified or bowdlerized, instead of being reserved; the imitations are often merely silly, Pig-wiggenry without even the intrigue; or patronizing; or (deadliest of all) covertly sniggering, with an eye on the other grown-ups present. I will not accuse Andrew Lang of sniggering, but certainly he smiled to himself, and certainly too often he had an eye on the faces of other clever people over the heads of his child-audience—to the very grave detriment of the *Chronicles of Pantouflia* (1889).

Dasent replied with vigour and justice to the prudish critics of his translations from Norse popular tales. Yet he committed the astonishing folly of particularly *forbidding* children to read the last two in his collection. That a man could study fairy-stories and not learn better than that seems almost incredible. But neither criticism, rejoinder, nor prohibition would have been necessary if children had not unnecessarily been regarded as the inevitable readers of the book.

I do not deny that there is a truth in Andrew Lang's words (sentimental though they may sound): "He who would enter into the Kingdom of Faerie should have the heart of a little child." For that possession is necessary to all high adventure, into kingdoms, both less and far greater than Faërie. But humility and innocence—these things "the heart of a child" must mean in such a context—do not necessarily imply an uncritical wonder, nor indeed an uncritical tenderness. Chesterton once remarked that the children in whose company he saw Maeterlinck's *Blue Bird* (1908) were dissatisfied "because it did not end with a Day of Judgement, and it was not revealed to the hero and the heroine that the Dog had been faithful and the Cat faithless." "For children," he says, "are innocent and love justice; while most of us are wicked and naturally prefer mercy."

Andrew Lang was confused on this point. He was at pains to defend the slaying of the Yellow Dwarf by Prince Ricardo in one of his own fairy-stories. "I hate cruelty," he said, "... but that was in fair fight, sword in hand, and the dwarf, peace to his ashes! died in harness." Yet it is not clear that "fair fight" is less cruel than "fair judgement"; or that piercing a dwarf with a sword is more just than the execution of wicked kings and evil stepmothers—which Lang abjures: he sends the criminals (as he boasts) to retirement on ample pensions. That is mercy untempered by justice. It is true that this plea was not addressed to children but to parents and guardians, to whom Lang was recommending his own *Prince Prigio* and *Prince Ricardo* as suitable for their charges.[1] It is parents and guardians who have classified fairy-stories as *Juvenilia*. And this is a small sample of the falsification of values that results.

If we use *child* in a good sense (it has also legitimately a bad one) we must not allow that to push us into the sentimentality of only using *adult* or *grown-up* in a bad sense (it has also legitimately a good one). The process of growing older is not necessarily allied to growing wickeder, though the two do often happen together. Children are meant to grow up, and not to become Peter Pans. Not to lose innocence and wonder, but to proceed on the appointed journey: that journey upon which it is certainly not better to travel hopefully than to arrive, though we must travel hopefully if we are to arrive. But it is one of the lessons of fairy-stories (if we can speak of the lessons of things that do not lecture) that on callow, lumpish, and selfish youth peril, sorrow, and the shadow of death can bestow dignity, and even sometimes wisdom.

Let us not divide the human race into Eloi and Morlocks:[2] pretty children— "elves" as the eighteenth century often idiotically called them—with their fairy-tales (carefully pruned), and dark Morlocks tending their machines. If fairy-story as a kind is worth reading at all it is worthy to be written for and read by adults. They will, of course, put more in and get more out than children can. Then, as a branch of a genuine art, children may hope to get fairy-stories fit for them to read and yet within their measure; as they may hope to get suitable introductions to poetry, history, and the sciences. Though it may be better for them to read some things, especially fairy-stories, that are beyond their measure rather than short of it. Their books like their clothes should allow for growth, and their books at any rate should encourage it.

Very well, then. If adults are to read fairy-stories as a natural branch of literature—neither playing at being children, nor pretending to be choosing for children, nor being boys who would not grow up—what are the values and functions of this

---

1   Preface to *The Lilac Fairy Book.*
2   [Species evolved from humanity to opposite extremes in *The Time Machine* (1895) by H.G. Wells.]

kind? That is, I think, the last and most important question. I have already hinted at some of my answers. First of all: if written with art, the prime value of fairy-stories will simply be that value which, as literature, they share with other literary forms. But fairy-stories offer also, in a peculiar degree or mode, these things: Fantasy, Recovery, Escape, Consolation, all things of which children have, as a rule, less need than older people. Most of them are nowadays very commonly considered to be bad for anybody. I will consider them briefly, and will begin with *Fantasy*.

Fantasy

The human mind is capable of forming mental images of things not actually present. The faculty of conceiving the images is (or was) naturally called Imagination. But in recent times, in technical not normal language, Imagination has often been held to be something higher than the mere image-making, ascribed to the operations of Fancy (a reduced and depreciatory form of the older word Fantasy); an attempt is thus made to restrict, I should say misapply, Imagination to "the power of giving to ideal creations the inner consistency of reality."

Ridiculous though it may be for one so ill-instructed to have an opinion on this critical matter, I venture to think the verbal distinction philologically inappropriate, and the analysis inaccurate. The mental power of image-making is one thing, or aspect; and it should appropriately be called Imagination. The perception of the image, the grasp of its implications, and the control, which are necessary to a successful expression, may vary in vividness and strength: but this is a difference of degree in Imagination, not a difference in kind. The achievement of the expression, which gives (or seems to give) "the inner consistency of reality,"[1] is indeed another thing, or aspect, needing another name: Art, the operative link between Imagination and the final result, Sub-creation. For my present purpose I require a word which shall embrace both the Sub-creative Art in itself and a quality of strangeness and wonder in the Expression, derived from the Image: a quality essential to the fairy-story. I propose, therefore, to arrogate to myself the powers of Humpty-Dumpty, and to use Fantasy for this purpose: in a sense, that is, which combines with its older and higher use as an equivalent of Imagination the derived notions of "unreality" (that is, of unlikeness to the Primary World), of freedom from the domination of observed "fact," in short of the fantastic. I am thus not only aware but glad of the etymological and semantic connections of *fantasy* with *fantastic*: with images of things that are not only "not actually present," but which are indeed not to be found in our primary world at all, or are generally believed not to be found there. But while admitting that, I do not assent to the depreciative

---

1   That is: which commands or induces Secondary Belief.

tone. That the images are of things not in the primary world (if that indeed is possible) is a virtue not a vice. Fantasy (in this sense) is, I think, not a lower but a higher form of Art, indeed the most nearly pure form, and so (when achieved) the most potent.

Fantasy, of course, starts out with an advantage: arresting strangeness. But that advantage has been turned against it, and has contributed to its disrepute. Many people dislike being "arrested." They dislike any meddling with the Primary World, or such small glimpses of it as are familiar to them. They, therefore, stupidly and even maliciously confound Fantasy with Dreaming, in which there is no Art;[1] and with mental disorders, in which there is not even control: with delusion and hallucination.

But the error or malice, engendered by disquiet and consequent dislike, is not the only cause of this confusion. Fantasy has also an essential drawback: it is difficult to achieve. Fantasy may be, as I think, not less but more sub-creative; but at any rate it is found in practice that "the inner consistency of reality" is more difficult to produce, the more unlike are the images and the rearrangements of primary material to the actual arrangements of the Primary World. It is easier to produce this kind of "reality" with more "sober" material. Fantasy thus, too often, remains undeveloped; it is and has been used frivolously, or only half-seriously, or merely for decoration: it remains merely "fanciful." Anyone inheriting the fantastic device of human language can say *the green sun*. Many can then imagine or picture it. But that is not enough—though it may already be a more potent thing than many a "thumbnail sketch" or "transcript of life" that receives literary praise.

To make a Secondary World inside which the green sun will be credible, commanding Secondary Belief, will probably require labour and thought, and will certainly demand a special skill, a kind of elvish craft. Few attempt such difficult tasks. But when they are attempted and in any degree accomplished then we have a rare achievement of Art: indeed narrative art, story-making in its primary and most potent mode.

In human art Fantasy is a thing best left to words, to true literature. In painting, for instance, the visible presentation of the fantastic image is technically too easy; the hand tends to outrun the mind, even to overthrow it.[2] Silliness or morbidity are

---

1 This is not true of all dreams. In some Fantasy seems to take a part. But this is exceptional. Fantasy is a rational, not an irrational, activity.

2 There is, for example, in surrealism commonly present a morbidity or unease very rarely found in literary fantasy. The mind that produced the depicted images may often be suspected to have been in fact already morbid; yet this is not a necessary explanation in all cases. A curious disturbance of the mind is often set up by the very act of drawing things of this kind, a state similar in quality and consciousness of morbidity to the sensations in a high fever, when the mind develops a distressing fecundity and facility in figure-making, seeing forms sinister or grotesque in all visible objects about it.

   I am speaking here, of course, of the primary expression of Fantasy in "pictorial" arts, not of "illustrations"; nor of the cinematograph. However good in themselves, illustrations do little good (continued)

frequent results. It is a misfortune that Drama, an art fundamentally distinct from Literature, should so commonly be considered together with it, or as a branch of it. Among these misfortunes we may reckon the depreciation of Fantasy. For in part at least this depreciation is due to the natural desire of critics to cry up the forms of literature or "imagination" that they themselves, innately or by training, prefer. And criticism in a country that has produced so great a Drama, and possesses the works of William Shakespeare, tends to be far too dramatic. But Drama is naturally hostile to Fantasy. Fantasy, even of the simplest kind, hardly ever succeeds in Drama, when that is presented as it should be, visibly and audibly acted. Fantastic forms are not to be counterfeited. Men dressed up as talking animals may achieve buffoonery or mimicry, but they do not achieve Fantasy. This is, I think, well illustrated by the failure of the bastard form, pantomime. The nearer it is to "dramatised fairy-story" the worse it is. It is only tolerable when the plot and its fantasy are reduced to a mere vestigiary framework for farce, and no "belief" of any kind in any part of the performance is required or expected of anybody. This is, of course, partly due to the fact that the producers of drama have to, or try to, work with mechanism to represent either Fantasy or Magic. I once saw a so-called "children's pantomime," the straight story of *Puss-in-Boots*, with even the metamorphosis of the ogre into a mouse. Had this been mechanically successful it would either have terrified the spectators or else have been just a turn of high-class conjuring. As it was, though done with some ingenuity of lighting, disbelief had not so much to be suspended as hung, drawn, and quartered.

In *Macbeth*, when it is read, I find the witches tolerable: they have a narrative function and some hint of dark significance; though they are vulgarised, poor things of their kind. They are almost intolerable in the play. They would be quite intolerable, if I were not fortified by some memory of them as they are in the story as read. I am told that I should feel differently if I had the mind of the period, with its witch-hunts and witch-trials. But that is to say: if I regarded the witches as possible, indeed likely, in the Primary World; in other words, if they ceased to be "Fantasy." That argument concedes the point. To be dissolved, or to be degraded, is the likely fate of

---

to fairy-stories. The radical distinction between all art (including drama) that offers a *visible* presentation and true literature is that it imposes one visible form. Literature works from mind to mind and is thus more progenitive. It is at once more universal and more poignantly particular. If it speaks of *bread* or *wine* or *stone* or *tree*, it appeals to the whole of these things, to their ideas; yet each hearer will give to them a peculiar personal embodiment in his imagination. Should the story say "he ate bread," the dramatic producer or painter can only show "a piece of bread" according to his taste or fancy, but the hearer of the story will think of bread in general and picture it in some form of his own. If a story says "he climbed a hill and saw a river in the valley below," the illustrator may catch, or nearly catch, his own vision of such a scene; but every hearer of the words will have his own picture, and it will be made out of all the hills and rivers and dales he has ever seen, but specially out of The Hill, The River, The Valley which were for him the first embodiment of the word.

Fantasy when a dramatist tries to use it, even such a dramatist as Shakespeare. *Macbeth* is indeed a work by a playwright who ought, at least on this occasion, to have written a story, if he had the skill or patience for that art.

A reason, more important, I think, than the inadequacy of stage-effects, is this: Drama has, of its very nature, already attempted a kind of bogus, or shall I say at least substitute, magic: *the visible and audible presentation of imaginary men in a story.* That is in itself an attempt to counterfeit the magician's wand. To introduce, even with mechanical success, into this quasi-magical secondary world a further fantasy or magic is to demand, as it were, an inner or tertiary world. It is a world too much. To make such a thing may not be impossible. I have never seen it done with success. But at least it cannot be claimed as the proper mode of Drama, in which walking and talking people have been found to be the natural instruments of Art and illusion.[1]

For this precise reason—that the characters, and even the scenes, are in Drama not imagined but actually beheld—Drama is, even though it uses a similar material (words, verse, plot), an art fundamentally different from narrative art. Thus, if you prefer Drama to Literature (as many literary critics plainly do), or form your critical theories primarily from dramatic critics, or even from Drama, you are apt to misunderstand pure story-making, and to constrain it to the limitations of stage-plays. You are, for instance, likely to prefer characters, even the basest and dullest, to things. Very little about trees as trees can be got into a play.

Now "Faërian Drama"—those plays which according to abundant records the elves have often presented to men—can produce Fantasy with a realism and

---

1   I am referring, of course, primarily to fantasy of forms and visible shapes. Drama can be made out of the impact upon human characters of some event of Fantasy, or Faërie, that requires no machinery, or that can be assumed or reported to have happened. But that is not fantasy in dramatic result; the human characters hold the stage and upon them attention is concentrated. Drama of this sort (exemplified by some of [J.M.] Barrie's plays) can be used frivolously, or it can be used for satire, or for conveying such "messages" as the playwright may have in his mind—for men. Drama is anthropocentric. Fairy-story and Fantasy need not be. There are, for instance, many stories telling how men and women have disappeared and spent years among the fairies, without noticing the passage of time, or appearing to grow older. In *Mary Rose* Barrie wrote a play on this theme. No fairy is seen. The cruelly tormented human beings are there all the time. In spite of the sentimental star and the angelic voices at the end (in the printed version) it is a painful play, and can easily be made diabolic: by substituting (as I have seen it done) the elvish call for "angel voices" at the end. The non-dramatic fairy-stories, in so far as they are concerned with human victims, can also be pathetic or horrible. But they need not be. In most of them the fairies are also there, on equal terms. In some stories they are the real interest. Many of the short folk-lore accounts of such incidents purport to be just pieces of "evidence" about fairies, items in an age long accumulation of "lore" concerning them and the modes of their existence. The sufferings of human beings who come into contact with them (often enough, wilfully) are thus seen in quite a different perspective. A drama could be made about the sufferings of a victim of research in radiology, but hardly about radium itself. But it is possible to be primarily interested in radium (not radiologists)—or primarily interested in Faërie, not tortured mortals. One interest will produce a scientific book, the other a fairy-story. Drama cannot well cope with either.

immediacy beyond the compass of any human mechanism. As a result their usual effect (upon a man) is to go beyond Secondary Belief. If you are present at a Faërian drama you yourself are, or think that you are, bodily inside its Secondary World. The experience may be very similar to Dreaming and has (it would seem) sometimes (by men) been confounded with it. But in Faërian drama you are in a dream that some other mind is weaving, and the knowledge of that alarming fact may slip from your grasp. To experience *directly* a Secondary World: the potion is too strong, and you give to it Primary Belief, however marvelous the events. You are deluded—whether that is the intention of the elves (always or at any time) is another question. They at any rate are not themselves deluded. This is for them a form of Art, and distinct from Wizardry or Magic, properly so called. They do not live in it, though they can, perhaps, afford to spend more time at it than human artists can. The Primary World, Reality, of elves and men is the same, if differently valued and perceived.

We need a word for this elvish craft, but all the words that have been applied to it have been blurred and confused with other things. Magic is ready to hand, and I have used it above, but I should not have done so: Magic should be reserved for the operations of the Magician. Art is the human process that produces by the way (it is not its only or ultimate object) Secondary Belief. Art of the same sort, if more skilled and effortless, the elves can also use, or so the reports seem to show; but the more potent and specially elvish craft I will, for lack of a less debatable word, call Enchantment. Enchantment produces a Secondary World into which both designer and spectator can enter, to the satisfaction of their senses while they are inside; but in its purity it is artistic in desire and purpose. Magic produces, or pretends to produce, an alteration in the Primary World. It does not matter by whom it is said to be practised, fay [i.e., fairy] or mortal, it remains distinct from the other two; it is not an art but a technique; its desire is *power* in this world, domination of things and wills.

To the elvish craft, Enchantment, Fantasy aspires, and when it is successful of all forms of human art most nearly approaches. At the heart of many man-made stories of the elves lies, open or concealed, pure or unalloyed, the desire for a living, realised sub-creative art, which (however much it may outwardly resemble it) is inwardly wholly different from the greed for self-centred power which is the mark of the mere Magician. Of this desire the elves, in their better (but still perilous) part, are largely made; and it is from them that we may learn what is the central desire and aspiration of human Fantasy—even if the elves are, all the more in so far as they are, only a product of Fantasy itself. That creative desire is only cheated by counterfeits, whether the innocent but clumsy devices of the human dramatist, or the malevolent frauds of the magicians. In this world it is for men unsatisfiable, and so imperishable. Uncorrupted, it does not seek delusion nor bewitchment and domination; it seeks shared enrichment, partners in making and delight, not slaves.

To many, Fantasy, this sub-creative art which plays strange tricks with the world and all that is in it, combining nouns and redistributing adjectives, has seemed suspect, if not illegitimate. To some it has seemed at least a childish folly, a thing only for peoples or for persons in their youth. As for its legitimacy I will say no more than to quote a brief passage from a letter I once wrote to a man who described myth and fairy-story as "lies"; though to do him justice he was kind enough and confused enough to call fairy-story-making "Breathing a lie through Silver."

Dear Sir, I said—
Although now long estranged,
Man is not wholly lost nor wholly changed.
Disgraced he may be, yet is not de-throned,
and keeps the rags of lordship once he owned:
Man, Sub-creator, the refracted Light
through whom is splintered from a single White
to many hues, and endlessly combined
in living shapes that move from mind to mind.
Though all the crannies of the world we filled
with Elves and Goblins, though we dared to build
Gods and their houses out of dark and light,
and sowed the seed of dragons—'twas our right
(used or misused). That right has not decayed;
we make still by the law in which we're made.

Fantasy is a natural human activity. It certainly does not destroy or even insult Reason; and it does not either blunt the appetite for, nor obscure the perception of, scientific verity. On the contrary. The keener and the clearer is the reason, the better fantasy will it make. If men were ever in a state in which they did not want to know or could not perceive truth (facts or evidence), then Fantasy would languish until they were cured. If they ever get into that state (it would not seem at all impossible), Fantasy will perish, and become Morbid Delusion.

For creative Fantasy is founded upon the hard recognition that things are so in the world as it appears under the sun; on a recognition of fact, but not a slavery to it. So upon logic was founded the nonsense that displays itself in the tales and rhymes of Lewis Carroll. If men really could not distinguish between frogs and men, fairy-stories about frog-kings would not have arisen.

Fantasy can, of course, be carried to excess. It can be ill done. It can be put to evil uses. It may even delude the minds out of which it came. But of what human thing in this fallen world is that not true? Men have conceived not only of elves, but they have imagined gods, and worshipped them, even worshipped those most deformed by their authors' own evil. But they have made false gods out of other materials: their notions, their banners, their monies; even their sciences and their social and economic theories have demanded human sacrifice. *Abusus non tollit usum.*[1] Fantasy remains a human right: we make in our measure and in our derivative mode, because we are made: and not only made, but made in the image and likeness of a Maker.

Recovery, Escape, Consolation

As for old age, whether personal or belonging to the times in which we live, it may be true, as is often supposed, that this imposes disabilities. But it is in the main an idea produced by the mere *study* of fairy-stories. The analytic study of fairy-stories is as bad a preparation for the enjoying or the writing of them as would be the historical study of the drama of all lands and times for the enjoyment or writing of stage-plays. The study may indeed become depressing. It is easy for the student to feel that with all his labour he is collecting only a few leaves, many of them now torn or decayed, from the countless foliage of the Tree of Tales, with which the Forest of Days is carpeted. It seems vain to add to the litter. Who can design a new leaf? The patterns from bud to unfolding, and the colours from spring to autumn were all discovered by men long ago. But that is not true. The seed of the tree can be replanted in almost any soil, even in one so smoke-ridden (as Lang said) as that of England. Spring is, of course, not really less beautiful because we have seen or heard of other like events: like events, never from world's beginning to world's end the same event. Each leaf, of oak and ash and thorn, is a unique embodiment of the pattern, and for some this very year may be *the* embodiment, the first even seen and recognised, though oaks have put forth leaves for countless generations of men.

We do not, or need not, despair of drawing because all lines must be either curved or straight, nor of painting because there are only three "primary" colours. We may indeed be older now, in so far as we are heirs in enjoyment or in practice of many generations of ancestors in the arts. In this inheritance of wealth there may be a danger of boredom or of anxiety to be original, and that may lead to a distaste for fine drawing, delicate pattern, and "pretty" colours, or else to mere manipulation and over-elaboration of old material, clever and heartless. But the true road of escape from such weariness is not to be found in the wilfully awkward, clumsy, or misshapen, not in making all things dark or unremittingly violent; nor in the mixing of colours on through subtlety to drabness, and the fantastical complication of shapes to the point of silliness and on towards delirium. Before we reach such states

---

1   [Latin: abuse does not nullify use, i.e., misuse of something does not disqualify its proper use.]

we need recovery. We should look at green again, and be startled anew (but not blinded) by blue and yellow and red. We should meet the centaur and the dragon, and then perhaps suddenly behold, like the ancient shepherds, sheep, and dogs, and horses—and wolves. This recovery fairy-stories help us to make. In that sense only a taste for them may make us, or keep us, childish.

Recovery (which includes return and renewal of health) is a re-gaining—regaining of a clear view. I do not say "seeing things as they are" and involve myself with the philosophers, though I might venture to say "seeing things as we are (or were) meant to see them"—as things apart from ourselves. We need, in any case, to clean our windows; so that the things seen clearly may be freed from the drab blur of triteness or familiarity—from possessiveness. Of all faces those of our *familiares* are the ones both most difficult to play fantastic tricks with, and most difficult really to see with fresh attention, perceiving their likeness and unlikeness: that they are faces, and yet unique faces. This triteness is really the penalty of "appropriation": the things that are trite, or (in a bad sense) familiar, are the things that we have appropriated, legally or mentally. We say we know them. They have become like the things which once attracted us by their glitter, or their colour, or their shape, and we laid hands on them, and then locked them in our hoard, acquired them, and acquiring ceased to look at them.

Of course, fairy-stories are not the only means of recovery, or prophylactic against loss. Humility is enough. And there is (especially for the humble) *Mooreeffoc*, or Chestertonian Fantasy. *Mooreeffoc* is a fantastic word, but it could be seen written up in every town in this land. It is Coffee-room, viewed from the inside through a glass door, as it was seen by Dickens on a dark London day; and it was used by Chesterton to denote the queerness of things that have become trite, when they are seen suddenly from a new angle. That kind of "fantasy" most people would allow to be wholesome enough; and it can never lack for material. But it has, I think, only a limited power; for the reason that recovery of freshness of vision is its only virtue. The word *Mooreeffoc* may cause you suddenly to realise that England is an utterly alien land, lost either in some remote past age glimpsed by history, or in some strange dim future to be reached only by a time-machine; to see the amazing oddity and interest of its inhabitants and their customs and feeding-habits; but it cannot do more than that: act as a time-telescope focused on one spot. Creative fantasy, because it is mainly trying to do something else (make something new), may open your hoard and let all the locked things fly away like caged birds. The gems all turn into flowers or flames, and you will be warned that all you had (or knew) was dangerous and potent, not really effectively chained, free and wild; no more yours than they were you.

The "fantastic" elements in verse and prose of other kinds, even when only decorative or occasional, help in this release. But not so thoroughly as a fairy-story, a thing built on or about Fantasy, of which Fantasy is the core. Fantasy is made out of the Primary World, but a good craftsman loves his material, and has a knowledge and feeling for clay, stone and wood which only the art of making can give. By the forging of Gram[1] cold iron was revealed; by the making of Pegasus[2] horses were ennobled; in the Trees of the Sun and Moon root and stock, flower and fruit are manifested in glory.

And actually fairy-stories deal largely, or (the better ones) mainly, with simple or fundamental things, untouched by Fantasy, but these simplicities are made all the more luminous by their setting. For the story-maker who allows himself to be "free with" Nature can be her lover not her slave. It was in fairy-stories that I first divined the potency of the words, and the wonder of the things, such as stone, and wood, and iron; tree and grass; house and fire; bread and wine.

I will now conclude by considering Escape and Consolation, which are naturally closely connected. Though fairy-stories are of course by no means the only medium of Escape, they are today one of the most obvious and (to some) outrageous forms of "escapist" literature; and it is thus reasonable to attach to a consideration of them some considerations of this term "escape" in criticism generally.

I have claimed that Escape is one of the main functions of fairy-stories, and since I do not disapprove of them, it is plain that I do not accept the tone of scorn or pity with which "Escape" is now so often used: a tone for which the uses of the word outside literary criticism give no warrant at all. In what the misusers are fond of calling Real Life, Escape is evidently as a rule very practical, and may even be heroic. In real life it is difficult to blame it, unless it fails; in criticism it would seem to be the worse the better it succeeds. Evidently we are faced by a misuse of words, and also by a confusion of thought. Why should a man be scorned, if, finding himself in prison, he tries to get out and go home? Or if, when he cannot do so, he thinks and talks about other topics than jailers and prison walls? The world outside has not become less real because the prisoner cannot see it. In using Escape in this way the critics have chosen the wrong word, and, what is more, they are confusing, not always by sincere error, the Escape of the Prisoner with the Flight of the Deserter. Just so a Party-spokesman might have labelled departure from the misery of the Führer's or any other Reich and even criticism of it as treachery. In the same way these critics, to make confusion worse, and so to bring into contempt their opponents, stick their label of scorn not only on to Desertion, but on to real Escape, and what are often its companions, Disgust, Anger, Condemnation, and Revolt. Not only do they confound the escape of the prisoner with the flight of the deserter; but they would seem

---

1   [Sigurd's sword in the Völsunga saga.]
2   [Mythical winged stallion in Greek mythology.]

to prefer the acquiescence of the "quisling" to the resistance of the patriot. To such thinking you have only to say "the land you loved is doomed" to excuse any treachery, indeed to glorify it.

For a trifling instance: not to mention (indeed not to parade) electric street-lamps of mass-produced pattern in your tale is Escape (in that sense). But it may, almost certainly does, proceed from a considered disgust for so typical a product of the Robot Age, that combines elaboration and ingenuity of means with ugliness, and (often) with inferiority of result. These lamps may be excluded from the tale simply because they are bad lamps; and it is possible that one of the lessons to be learnt from the story is the realization of this fact. But out comes the big stick: "Electric lamps have come to stay," they say. Long ago Chesterton truly remarked that, as soon as he heard that anything "had come to stay," he knew that it would be very soon replaced—indeed regarded as pitiably obsolete and shabby. "The march of Science, its tempo quickened by the needs of war, goes inexorably on ... making some things obsolete, and foreshadowing new developments in the utilization of electricity": an advertisement. This says the same thing only more menacingly. The electric street-lamp may indeed be ignored, simply because it is so insignificant and transient. Fairy-stories, at any rate, have many more permanent and fundamental things to talk about. Lightning, for example. The escapist is not so subservient to the whims of evanescent fashion as these opponents. He does not make things (which it may be quite rational to regard as bad) his masters or his gods by worshipping them as inevitable, even "inexorable." And his opponents, so easily contemptuous, have no guarantee that he will stop there: he might rouse men to pull down the street-lamps. Escapism has another and even wickeder face: Reaction.

Not long ago—incredible though it may seem—I heard a clerk of Oxford declare that he "welcomed" the proximity of mass-production robot factories, and the roar of self-obstructive mechanical traffic, because it brought his university into "contact with real life." He may have meant that the way men were living and working in the twentieth century was increasing in barbarity at an alarming rate, and that the loud demonstration of this in the streets of Oxford might serve as a warning that it is not possible to preserve for long an oasis of sanity in a desert of unreason by mere fences, without actual offensive action (practical and intellectual). I fear he did not. In any case the expression "real life" in this context seems to fall short of academic standards. The notion that motor-cars are more "alive" than, say, centaurs or dragons is curious; that they are more "real" than, say, horses is pathetically absurd. How real, how startlingly alive is a factory chimney compared with an elm tree: poor obsolete thing, insubstantial dream of an escapist!

For my part, I cannot convince myself that the roof of Bletchley station is more "real" than the clouds. And as an artefact I find it less inspiring than the legendary dome of heaven. The bridge to platform 4 is to me less interesting than Bifröst guarded by Heimdall with the Gjallarhorn.[1] From the wildness of my heart I cannot exclude the question whether railway-engineers, if they had been brought up on more fantasy, might not have done better with all their abundant means than they commonly do. Fairy-stories might be, I guess, better Masters of Arts than the academic person I have referred to.

Much that he (I must suppose) and others (certainly) would call "serious" literature is no more than play under a glass roof by the side of a municipal swimming-bath. Fairy-stories may invent monsters that fly in the air or dwell in the deep, but at least they do not try to escape from heaven or the sea.

And if we leave aside for a moment "fantasy," I do not think that the reader or the maker of fairy-stories need even be ashamed of the "escape" of archaism: of preferring not dragons but horses, castles, sailing-ships, bows and arrows; not only elves, but knights and kings and priests. For it is after all possible for a rational man, after reflection (quite unconnected with fairy-story or romance), to arrive at the condemnation, implicit at least in the mere silence of "escapist" literature, of progressive things like factories, or the machine-guns and bombs that appear to be their most natural and inevitable, dare we say "inexorable," products.

"The rawness and ugliness of modern European life"—that real life whose contact we should welcome—"is the sign of a biological inferiority, of an insufficient or false reaction to environment."[2] The maddest castle that ever came out of a giant's bag in a wild Gaelic story is not only much less ugly than a robot-factory, it is also (to use a very modern phrase) "in a very real sense" a great deal more real. Why should we not escape from or condemn the "grim Assyrian" absurdity of top-hats, or the Morlockian horror of factories? They are condemned even by the writers of that most escapist form of all literature, stories of Science fiction. These prophets often foretell (and many seem to yearn for) a world like one big glass-roofed railway-station. But from them it is as a rule very hard to gather what men in such a world-town will *do*. They may abandon the "full Victorian panoply" for loose garments (with zip fasteners), but will use this freedom mainly, it would appear, in order to play with mechanical toys in the soon-cloying game of moving at high speed. To judge by some of these

---

1   [In Norse mythology, Bifrost is a burning rainbow bridge protected by the god Heimdall with his resounding horn.]

2   Christopher Dawson, *Progress and Religion* [1929], pp. 58, 59. Later he adds: "The full Victorian panoply of top-hat and frock-coat undoubtedly expressed something essential in the nineteenth-century culture, and hence it has with that culture spread all over the world, as no fashion of clothing has ever done before. It is possible that our descendants will recognise in it a kind of grim Assyrian beauty, fit emblem of the ruthless and great age that created it; but however that may be, it misses the direct and inevitable beauty that all clothing should have, because like its parent culture it was out of touch with the life of nature and of human nature as well."

tales they will still be as lustful, vengeful, and greedy as ever; and the ideals of their idealists hardly reach farther than the splendid notion of building more towns of the same sort on other planets. It is indeed an age of "improved means to deteriorated ends." It is part of the essential malady of such days—producing the desire to escape, not indeed from life, but from our present time and self-made misery—that we are acutely conscious both of the ugliness of our works, and of their evil. So that to us evil and ugliness seem indissolubly allied. We find it difficult to conceive of evil and beauty together. The fear of the beautiful fay that ran through the elder ages almost eludes our grasp. Even more alarming: goodness is itself bereft of its proper beauty. In Faërie one can indeed conceive of an ogre who possesses a castle hideous as a nightmare (for the evil of the ogre wills it so), but one cannot conceive of a house built with a good purpose—an inn, a hostel for travellers, the hall of a virtuous and noble king—that is yet sickeningly ugly. At the present day it would be rash to hope to see one that was not—unless it was built before our time.

This, however, is the modern and special (or accidental) "escapist" aspect of fairy-stories, which they share with romances and other stories out of or about the past. Many stories out of the past have only become "escapist" in their appeal through surviving from a time when men were as a rule delighted with the work of their hands into our time, when many men feel disgust with man-made things.

But there are also other and more profound "escapisms" that have always appeared in fairy-tale and legend. There are other things more grim and terrible to fly from than the noise, stench, ruthlessness, and extravagance of the internal-combustion engine. There are hunger, thirst, poverty, pain, sorrow, injustice, death. And even when men are not facing hard things such as these, there are ancient limitations from which fairy-stories offer a sort of escape, and old ambitions and desires (touching the very roots of fantasy) to which they offer a kind of satisfaction and consolation. Some are pardonable weaknesses or curiosities: such as the desire to visit, free as a fish, the deep sea; or the longing for the noiseless, gracious, economical flight of a bird, that longing which the aeroplane cheats, except in rare moments, seen high and by wind and distance noiseless, turning in the sun: that is, precisely when imagined and not used. There are profounder wishes: such as the desire to converse with other living things. On this desire, as ancient as the Fall, is largely founded the talking of beasts and creatures in fairy-tales, and especially the magical understanding of their proper speech. This is the root, and not the "confusion" attributed to the minds of men of the unrecorded past, an alleged "absence of the sense of separation of ourselves from beasts."[1] A vivid sense of that separation is very ancient; but also a sense that it was a severance:

---

1   The absence of this sense is a mere hypothesis concerning men of the lost past, whatever wild confusions men of today, degraded or deluded, may suffer. It is just as legitimate an hypothesis, and one more (continued)

a strange fate and a guilt lies on us. Other creatures are like other realms with which Man has broken off relations, and sees now only from the outside at a distance, being at war with them, or on the terms of an uneasy armistice. There are a few men who are privileged to travel abroad a little; others must be content with travellers' tales. Even about frogs. In speaking of that rather odd but widespread fairy-story *The Frog King* Max Müller asked in his prim way: "How came such a story ever to be invented? Human beings were, we may hope, at all times sufficiently enlightened to know that a marriage between a frog and the daughter of a queen was absurd." Indeed we may hope so! For if not, there would be no point in this story at all, depending as it does essentially on the sense of the absurdity. Folk-lore origins (or guesses about them) are here quite beside the point. It is of little avail to consider totemism. For certainly, whatever customs or beliefs about frogs and wells lie behind this story, the frog-shape was and is preserved in the fairy-story[1] precisely because it was so queer and the marriage absurd, indeed abominable. Though, of course, in the versions which concern us, Gaelic, German, English,[2] there is in fact no wedding between a princess and a frog: the frog was an enchanted prince. And the point of the story lies not in thinking frogs possible mates, but in the necessity of keeping promises (even those with intolerable consequences) that, together with observing prohibitions, runs through all Fairyland. This is one of the notes of the horns of Elfland, and not a dim note.

And lastly there is the oldest and deepest desire, the Great Escape: the Escape from Death. Fairy-stories provide many examples and modes of this—which might be called the genuine *escapist*, or (I would say) *fugitive* spirit. But so do other stories (notably those of the scientific inspiration), and so do other studies. Fairy-stories are made by men not by fairies. The Human-stories of the elves are doubtless full of the Escape from Deathlessness. But our stories cannot be expected always to rise above

---

in agreement with what little is recorded concerning the thoughts of men of old on this subject, that this sense was once stronger. That fantasies which blended the human form with animal or vegetable forms, or gave human faculties to beasts, are ancient is, of course, no evidence for confusion at all. It is, if anything, evidence to the contrary. Fantasy does not blur the sharp outlines of the real world; for it depends on them. As far as our western, European, world is concerned, this "sense of separation" has in fact been attacked and weakened in modern times not by fantasy but by scientific theory. Not by stories of centaurs or werewolves or enchanted bears, but by the hypotheses (or dogmatic guesses) of scientific writers who classed Man not only as "an animal"—that correct classification is ancient—but as "only an animal." There has been a consequent distortion of sentiment. The natural love of men not wholly corrupt for beasts, and the human desire to "get inside the skin" of living things, has run riot. We now get men who love animals more than men; who pity sheep so much that they curse shepherds as wolves; who weep over a slain warhorse and vilify dead soldiers. It is now, not in the days when fairy-stories were begotten, that we get "an absence of the sense of separation."

1   Or group of similar stories.

2   *The Queen who sought drink from a certain Well and the Lorgann* [...]; *Der Froschkönig; The Maid and the Frog.*

our common level. They often do. Few lessons are taught more clearly in them than the burden of that kind of immortality, or rather endless serial living, to which the "fugitive" would fly. For the fairy-story is specially apt to teach such things, of old and still today. Death is the theme that most inspired George MacDonald.[1]

But the "consolation" of fairy-tales has another aspect than the imaginative satisfaction of ancient desires. Far more important is the Consolation of the Happy Ending. Almost I would venture to assert that all complete fairy-stories must have it. At least I would say that Tragedy is the true form of Drama, its highest function; but the opposite is true of Fairy-story. Since we do not appear to possess a word that expresses this opposite—I will call it *Eucatastrophe*. The *eucatastrophic* tale is the true form of fairy-tale, and its highest function.

The consolation of fairy-stories, the joy of the happy ending: or more correctly of the good catastrophe, the sudden joyous "turn" (for there is no true end to any fairy-tale):[2] this joy, which is one of the things which fairy-stories can produce supremely

---

1   [Scottish poet fantasy and fairy-tale writer (1824–1905).]

2   The verbal ending—usually held to be as typical of the end of fairy-stories as "once upon a time" is of the beginning—"and they lived happily ever after" is an artificial device. It does not deceive anybody. End-phrases of this kind are to be compared to the margins and frames of pictures, and are no more to be thought of as the real end of any particular fragment of the seamless Web of Story than the frame is of the visionary scene, or the casement of the Outer World. These phrases may be plain or elaborate, simple or extravagant, as artificial and as necessary as frames plain, or carved, or gilded. "And if they have not gone away they are there still." "My story is done—see there is a little mouse; anyone who catches it may make himself a fine fur cap of it." "And they lived happily ever after." "And when the wedding was over, they sent me home with little paper shoes on a causeway of pieces of glass."

Endings of this sort suit fairy-stories, because such tales have a greater sense and grasp of the endlessness of the World of Story than most modern "realistic" stories, already hemmed within the narrow confines of their own small time. A sharp cut in the endless tapestry is not unfittingly marked by a formula, even a grotesque or comic one. It was an irresistible development of modern illustration (so largely photographic) that borders should be abandoned and the "picture" end only with the paper. This method may be suitable for photographs; but it is altogether inappropriate for the pictures that illustrate or are inspired by fairy-stories. An enchanted forest requires a margin, even an elaborate border. To print it conterminous with the page, like a "shot" of the Rockies in *Picture Post*, as if it were indeed a "snap" of fairyland or a "sketch by our artist on the spot," is a folly and an abuse.

As for the beginnings of fairy-stories: one can scarcely improve on the formula *Once upon a time*. It has an immediate effect. This effect can be appreciated by reading, for instance, the fairy-story *The Terrible Head* in the *Blue Fairy Book*. It is Andrew Lang's own adaptation of the story of Perseus and the Gorgon. It begins "once upon a time," and it does not name any year or land or person. Now this treatment does something which could be called "turning mythology into fairy-story." I should prefer to say that it turns high fairy-story (for such is the Greek tale) into a particular form that is at present familiar in our land: a nursery or "old wives" form. Namelessness is not a virtue but an accident, and should not have been imitated; for vagueness in this regard is a debasement, a corruption due to forgetfulness and lack of skill. But not so, I think, the timelessness. That beginning is not poverty-stricken but significant. It produces at a stroke the sense of a great uncharted world of time.

well, is not essentially "escapist," nor "fugitive." In its fairy-tale—or otherworld—setting, it is a sudden and miraculous grace: never to be counted on to recur. It does not deny the existence of *dyscatastrophe*, of sorrow and failure: the possibility of these is necessary to the joy of deliverance; it denies (in the face of much evidence, if you will) universal final defeat and in so far is *evangelium*, giving a fleeting glimpse of Joy, Joy beyond the walls of the world, poignant as grief.

It is the mark of a good fairy-story, of the higher or more complete kind, that however wild its events, however fantastic or terrible the adventures, it can give to child or man that hears it, when the "turn" comes, a catch of the breath, a beat and lifting of the heart, near to (or indeed accompanied by) tears, as keen as that given by any form of literary art, and having a peculiar quality.

Even modern fairy-stories can produce this effect sometimes. It is not an easy thing to do; it depends on the whole story which is the setting of the turn, and yet it reflects a glory backwards. A tale that in any measure succeeds in this point has not wholly failed, whatever flaws it may possess, and whatever mixture or confusion of purpose. It happens even in Andrew Lang's own fairy-story, *Prince Prigio* (1889), unsatisfactory in many ways as that is. When "each knight came alive and lifted his sword and shouted 'long live Prince Prigio,'" the joy has a little of that strange mythical fairy-story quality, greater than the event described. It would have none in Lang's tale, if the event described were not a piece of more serious fairy-story "fantasy" than the main bulk of the story, which is in general more frivolous, having the half-mocking smile of the courtly, sophisticated *Conte*.[1] Far more powerful and poignant is the effect in a serious tale of Faërie.[2] In such stories when the sudden "turn" comes we get a piercing glimpse of joy, and heart's desire, that for a moment passes outside the frame, rends indeed the very web of story, and lets a gleam come through.

> *Seven long years I served for thee,*
> *The glassy hill I clamb for thee,*
> *The bluidy shirt I wrang for thee,*
> *And wilt thou not wauken and turn to me?*

> *He heard and turned to her.*[3]

---

1   This is characteristic of Lang's wavering balance. On the surface the story is a follower of the "courtly" French *conte* with a satirical twist, and of Thackeray's *Rose and the Ring* in particular—a kind which being superficial, even frivolous, by nature, does not produce or aim at producing anything so profound; but underneath lies the deeper spirit of the romantic Lang.

2   Of the kind which Lang called "traditional," and really preferred.

3   *The Black Bull of Norroway* [Scottish fairy tale, first published in 1842].

Epilogue

This "joy" which I have selected as the mark of the true fairy-story (or romance), or as the seal upon it, merits more consideration.

Probably every writer making a secondary world, a fantasy, every sub-creator, wishes in some measure to be a real maker, or hopes that he is drawing on reality: hopes that the peculiar quality of this secondary world (if not all the details)[1] are derived from Reality, or are flowing into it. If he indeed achieves a quality that can fairly be described by the dictionary definition: "inner consistency of reality," it is difficult to conceive how this can be, if the work does not in some way partake of reality. The peculiar quality of the "joy" in successful Fantasy can thus be explained as a sudden glimpse of the underlying reality or truth. It is not only a "consolation" for the sorrow of this world, but a satisfaction, and an answer to that question, "Is it true?" The answer to this question that I gave at first was (quite rightly): "If you have built your little world well, yes: it is true in that world." That is enough for the artist (or the artist part of the artist). But in the "eucatastrophe" we see in a brief vision that the answer may be greater—it may be a far-off gleam or echo of evangelium in the real world. The use of this word gives a hint of my epilogue. It is a serious and dangerous matter. It is presumptuous of me to touch upon such a theme; but if by grace what I say has in any respect any validity, it is, of course, only one facet of a truth incalculably rich: finite only because the capacity of Man for whom this was done is finite.

I would venture to say that approaching the Christian Story from this direction, it has long been my feeling (a joyous feeling) that God redeemed the corrupt making-creatures, men, in a way fitting to this aspect, as to others, of their strange nature. The Gospels contain a fairy-story, or a story of a larger kind which embraces all the essence of fairy-stories. They contain many marvels—peculiarly artistic,[2] beautiful, and moving: "mythical" in their perfect, self-contained significance; and among the marvels is the greatest and most complete conceivable eucatastrophe. But this story has entered History and the primary world; the desire and aspiration of sub-creation has been raised to the fulfillment of Creation. The Birth of Christ is the eucatastrophe of Man's history. The Resurrection is the eucatastrophe of the story of the Incarnation. This story begins and ends in joy. It has pre-eminently the "inner consistency of reality." There is no tale ever told that men would rather find was true, and none

---

1   For all the details may not be "true": it is seldom that the "inspiration" is so strong and lasting that it leavens all the lump, and does not leave much that is mere uninspired "invention."

2   The Art is here in the story itself rather than in the telling; for the Author of the story was not the evangelists.

which so many skeptical men have accepted as true on its own merits. For the Art of it has the supremely convincing tone of Primary Art, that is, of Creation. To reject it leads either to sadness or to wrath.

It is not difficult to imagine the peculiar excitement and joy that one would feel, if any specially beautiful fairy-story were found to be "primarily" true, its narrative to be history, without thereby necessarily losing the mythical or allegorical significance that it had possessed. It is not difficult, for one is not called upon to try and conceive anything of a quality unknown. The joy would have exactly the same quality, if not the same degree, as the joy which the "turn" in a fairy-story gives: such joy has the very taste of primary truth. (Otherwise its name would not be joy.) It looks forward (or backward: the direction in this regard is unimportant) to the Great Eucatastrophe. The Christian joy, the *Gloria*, is of the same kind; but it is pre-eminently (infinitely, if our capacity were not finite) high and joyous. But this story is supreme; and it is true. Art has been verified. God is the Lord, of angels, and of men—and of elves. Legend and History have met and fused.

But in God's kingdom the presence of the greatest does not depress the small. Redeemed Man is still man. Story, fantasy, still go on, and should go on. The Evangelium has not abrogated legends; it has hallowed them, especially the "happy ending." The Christian has still to work, with mind as well as body, to suffer, hope, and die; but he may now perceive that all his bents and faculties have a purpose, which can be redeemed. So great is the bounty with which he has been treated that he may now, perhaps, fairly dare to guess that in Fantasy he may actually assist in the effoliation and multiple enrichment of creation. All tales may come true; and yet, at the last, redeemed, they may be as like and as unlike the forms that we give them as Man, finally redeemed, will be like and unlike the fallen that we know.

THE FAIRY-TALE HERO:
THE IMAGE OF MAN IN THE FAIRY-TALE[1]

Max Lüthi

Is it mere chance that the principal characters we have encountered in our studies are more often female than male: Sleeping Beauty; the Greek princess who kneaded a husband for herself out of groats, sugar, and almonds; good little Anny in the story of the little earth-cow; Rapunzel; the riddle princesses; and the clever peasant girls? The only corresponding male figures we have seen in the European fairy tales are the dragon slayer and that clever poser of riddles, Petit-Jean. Is this preponderance of women typical? Does our sampling reflect the true situation? If we are asked just which fairy-tale figures are generally best known, we immediately think of Sleeping Beauty, Cinderella, Snow White, Little Red Riding Hood, Rapunzel, The Princess in Disguise, and Goldmarie in "Mother Hulda"—all female figures. In "Hansel and Gretel" and in "Brother and Sister," the girl also plays the leading role. We find ourselves nearly at a loss when called upon for the names of male protagonists: Iron Hans and Tom Thumb, perhaps; the Brave Little Tailor, Strong Hans, and Lucky Hans—but here we are already in the realm of the folk-tale jest. How can one explain this peculiar predominance of women and girls? All the names mentioned are taken from the Grimm brothers' collection. Despite the existence of innumerable other collections, this one today is, in German-speaking countries, almost the sole surviving source for the public at large of real contact with the fairy tale. Now the Grimm brothers' informants were predominantly women. And today children learn fairy tales mainly from their mothers, grandmothers, aunts, and female kindergarten and school teachers. Thus, it is natural that the principal figures are mostly women. Moreover, the child—whether boy or girl—is basically closer to the feminine than the masculine, living in the domain of the mother and female teachers and not yet that of the father and male teachers. The fairy tales which grownups remember are those of their childhood. Furthermore, our era, whose character, despite everything, is still determined by men, feels the strong and clear need for a complementary antipole. The woman is assigned a privileged position, not only by social custom; in art and literature, as well, she has occupied a central position since the time of the troubadours and the Mariology[2] of the late Middle Ages. In painting and in the novel, she has been the subject of persistent interest and loving concern.

---

1   From *Once Upon a Time: On the Nature of Fairy Tales*, trans. Lee Chadeayne and Paul Gottwald (New York: Frederick Ungar, 1970). All notes are editorial.

2   The study of the Virgin Mary.

Thus, it comes as no surprise that she also plays a significant role in the fairy tale—which for centuries was one of the most vital and indirectly influential art forms in Europe—the feminine component, that part of man closer to nature, had to come to the forefront to compensate for the technological and economic system created by the masculine spirit, which dominated the external world of reality.

However, that was a peculiarity of the era. Tellers of fairy tales were not always predominantly women, and not always was existence influenced so strongly by the masculine spirit that the antipole asserted itself with such conspicuous force in art. If we go beyond *Grimm's Fairy Tales* and leaf through the many volumes of the *Märchen der Weltliteratur* (Fairy Tales of World Literature), *Das Gesicht der Völker* (The Face of the Peoples), or Richard M. Dorson's *Folktales of the World*, we see that there are at least as many masculine as feminine protagonists, and that, in general, the masculine figures may even predominate, as they do in the myths. But one thing is quite clear: at the focal point in the fairy tale stands *man*. One cannot say this of the local legend and saint's legend: they portray the intrusion of another world upon our own existence; myths tell of gods; and among primitive peoples, animal stories predominate. The hero of the European fairy tale, however, is *man*. In the minds of the ancient Greeks, the earlier animal gods assumed human form. The humanism of the Greek classical period became a basic element of European culture. Thus, a connection no doubt exists between this European or Indo-European attribute and our fairy tales, which, in the main, concern not animals, as in the stories of primitive peoples, but men.

The European fairy tale draws a picture of man and shows him in his confrontation with the world. Since our children are interested in fairy tales in their most receptive years, and since even today almost all children have a considerable number of fairy tales which are told or read to them or which they read themselves, it is worthwhile to ask what sort of picture of man they find there. Can one say that the large number of fairy tales present a coherent picture? In a certain sense, yes. The fairy-tale hero, or heroine, to be sure, is sometimes a rollicking daredevil and sometimes a silent sufferer; at times a lazybones and at times a diligent helper; often sly and wily but just as often open and honest. At times he is a shrewd fellow, an undaunted solver of riddles, a brave fighter; at others, he is a stupid person or one who sits down and begins to cry every time he encounters difficulty. There are friendly and compassionate fairy-tale heroes, but others that are merciless and perfidious. To say nothing of the differences in social class: princess and Cinderella, prince and swineherd. Or must we perhaps say something about them? Are we not perplexed by something we see at just this point? Surprisingly, the difference in social class is often only apparent. The goose girl, in reality, is not at all one of the common folk but a princess forced into her lowly role by her servant girl. And the gardener boy with the mangy hair, whom the beautiful princess observes every morning, is, in reality, a prince who has tied an animal hide over his golden hair.

Thus, in the fairy tale, one and the same person can abruptly change from a mangy-headed youth into one with golden hair, and the despised Cinderella can suddenly turn into a dancer in a radiant gown at whom all gaze in wonder. The one considered to be stupid or loutish often turns out to be the wisest and cleverest of all. In addition, the real swineherd can unexpectedly become the princess's husband, and the poor girl can marry the prince or the king and thus be raised to royal status.

In the fairy tale, all things are possible, not just in the sense that all sorts of miracles occur, but in the sense just mentioned: the lowest can rise to the highest position, and those in the highest position—evil queens, princes, princesses, government ministers—can fall and be destroyed. It has therefore been said that fairy tales derive from the wishful thinking of poor people or those who have been unsuccessful or slighted. But such psychological and sociological interpretations are too limited. Wish dreams and wishful thinking play a part in fairy tales, just as they do in all human matters, and social tensions and yearnings also are reflected in them.

Yet these are only superficial aspects. Fairy-tale figures have an immediate appeal. The king, the princess, a dragon, a witch, gold, crystal, pitch, and ashes—these things are, for the human imagination, age-old symbols for what is high, noble, and pure or dangerous, bestial, and unfathomable; what is genuine and true, or what is sordid and false. The fairy tale often depicts how a penniless wretch becomes wealthy, a maid becomes queen, a disheveled man is changed into a youth with golden hair, or a toad, bear, ape, or dog is transformed into a beautiful maiden or handsome youth. Here, we feel at once the capacity for change of man in general. The focal point is not the rise of the servant to his position of master, not the esteem and recognition accorded the former outcast child; these are images for something more fundamental: man's deliverance from an inauthentic existence and his commencement of a true one. When the real princess lets herself be forced into the role of a goose girl while the lowly maid arrogates to herself the dominant position, this means that a false, ignoble side of the total personality gains control and suppresses that which is truly regal. When the prince marries the witch's ugly daughter instead of his bride-to-be, he has lost the way to his own soul and given himself up to a strange demon. The psychologist views things in this way, assuming that the fairy tale depicts processes within the mind. Although such specialized interpretations are often risky, it is evident that more is involved for both the author and his hearers than mere external action when the fairy tale tells how the hero conquers the dragon, marries the princess, and becomes king.

In general, one can say that the fairy tale depicts processes of development and maturation. Every man has within him an ideal image, and to be king, to wear a crown, is an image for the ascent to the highest attainable realms. And every man has within him his own secret kingdom. The visible kingdom, the figure of the princess and her bridegroom, are fascinating, influential, and oft-cited even in democratic societies because they have a symbolic force. To be king does not mean just to have power; in the modern world, kings and queens have been relieved of almost all their material power. One might say they have been freed of it and by this have acquired even greater symbolic appeal. To be a king is an image for complete self-realization; the crown and royal robe which play such a great role in the fairy tale make visible the splendor and brilliance of the great perfection achieved inwardly. They call to mind an analogous phenomenon in the saint's legend, the halo, which likewise renders visible the inward brilliance. When Goldmarie, after proving herself in the realm of Mother Hulda, is showered with gold, no one doubts that this is an image—one which reveals the girl's good soul. And when other fairy-tale heroines comb golden flowers out of their hair, or when a flower shoots out of the ground at their every step, we likewise immediately take it to be symbolic. Not only alchemists, but people generally feel gold to be a representative for a higher human and cosmic perfection. Kingship, like gold and the royal robe, has symbolic significance and power in the fairy tale. It may well be—as psychologists of the Jungian school assert—that the marriage with the animal bride or animal prince, the union of the king with the armless mute lost in the forest, and the wedding of the princess and the goatherd are images for the union of disparities in the human soul, for the awareness of a hitherto unrecognized spiritual strength, and for the maturation into a complete human personality. In any event, the fairy tale depicts over and over an upward development, the overcoming of mortal dangers and seemingly insoluble problems, the path toward marriage with the prince or princess, toward kingship or gold and jewels. The image of man portrayed in the fairy tale—or, rather, one aspect of this image—is that of one who has the capability to rise above himself, has within him the yearning for the highest things, and is also able to attain them. We can be sure that children, engrossed in the story as it is told to them, do not understand this in all its implications; but, what is more important, they can sense it. The child, at the fairy-tale age, is fascinated not by the upward social movement but by the overcoming of dangers and entry into the realm of glory, whether this is depicted as the realm of the sun and stars or as an earthly kingdom of unearthly splendor.

But the image of man as it appears in the fairy tale can be defined from yet another aspect upon closer examination. The fairy-tale hero is essentially a wanderer. Whereas the events in the local legend usually take place in the hometown or its vicinity, the fairy tale time and again sends its heroes out into the world. Sometimes the parents are too poor to be able to keep their children, at times the hero is forced away by a command or enticed away by a contest, or it may be merely that the hero decides to go out in search of adventure. In a Low German fairy tale, the father sends his two eldest sons out into the world as punishment, but does the same thing to his youngest son as a reward. Nothing shows more clearly that the fairy tale will use any excuse to make its hero a wanderer and lead him far away, often to the stars, to the bottom of the sea, to a region below the earth, or to a kingdom at the end of the world. The female protagonist is also frequently removed to a distant castle or abducted to that place by an animal-husband. This wandering, or soaring, over great distances conveys an impression of freedom and ease that is further strengthened by other characteristics in the fairy tale which also convey a feeling of freedom. Whereas in the local legends man is endowed from the very beginning with something stifling and unfree by stagnation in the ancestral village and dumbfounded gazing at the frightful phenomenon, the fairy-tale hero appears as a free-moving wanderer. In the local legend, man is an impassioned dreamer, a visionary; the fairy-tale hero, however, strides from place to place without much concern or astonishment. The other worldly beings which he encounters interest him only as helpers or opponents and do not inspire him with either curiosity, a thirst for knowledge, or a vague fear of the supernatural. The fairy tale depicts its heroes not as observing and fearful but as moving and active. In the local legend, man is embedded in the society of his village, not only that of the living, but also that of the dead. He is also rooted in the countryside or town in which he lives. The wild people in the forest and the mountains and the water sprites and poltergeists inhabit the general surroundings. The fairy-tale hero, however, breaks away from his home and goes out into the world. He is almost always alone; if there are two brothers, they separate at a certain crossroads and each experiences the decisive adventure alone. Frequently the fairy-tale hero does not return to his home town. When he sets forth to save a king's daughter or accomplish a difficult task, he usually does not know how he will accomplish his purpose. But along the way he meets a little old man, shares his bread with him, and gets from him the advice that will lead him to his goal. Or he meets a wild animal, pulls out a thorn that was hurting it, and thus gains the help of the thankful beast, whose abilities just suffice to solve his problem. In the local legend, people summon the priest or Capuchin[1] to help in conjuring spirits, but the fairy-tale hero enters strange lands all alone and there has the decisive confrontation. The priest or Capuchin is not only a member of the village community, everyone knows the source of his helping powers: the salvation of the Christian church, the grace of God. The helping animals and other supernatural beings in the fairy tale are, however, usually just as isolated as the fairy-tale hero himself. The latter takes their advice and magic gifts nonchalantly, uses them at the decisive moment, and then no longer thinks about them. He doesn't

---

1   Order of Catholic friars.

ponder over the mysterious forces or where his helpers have come from; everything he experiences seems natural to him and he is carried along by this help, which he has earned often without his knowledge. The fairy-tale hero quite frequently is the youngest son, an orphan, a despised Cinderella or poor goatherd, and this all contributes to making the hero appear isolated; the prince, princess, and king, as well, at the very pinnacle of society, are in their own way detached, absolute, and isolated.

Local legends and fairy tales, which have existed for centuries side by side among the common folk, complement one another. Local legends originate among the common people half spontaneously and half under the influence of simple traditions and ask, we might say, the anxious question, "What is man, what is the world?" Fairy tales certainly do not originate among simple folk but with great poets, perhaps the so-called "initiated," or religious, poets; and, in a sense, they provide an answer. In the local legend, one senses the anxiety of man, who, though apparently a part of the community of his fellow men, finds himself ultimately confronted with an uncanny world which he finds hard to comprehend and which threatens him with death. The fairy tale, however, presents its hero as one who, though not comprehending ultimate relationships, is led safely through the dangerous, unfamiliar world. The fairy-tale hero is gifted, in the literal sense of the word. Supernatural beings lavish their gifts on him and help him through battles and perils. In the fairy tale, too, the ungifted, the unblessed, appear. Usually, they are the older brothers or sisters of the hero or heroine. They are often deceitful, wicked, envious, coldhearted, or dissolute—though this is by no means always the case. It may be that they just don't come across any helping animal or little man; they are the unblessed. The hearer does not, however, identify with them, but with the hero, who makes his way through the world alone—and for just this reason is free and able to establish contact with essential things. Usually, it is his unconsciously correct behavior that gains him the help of the animal with the magic powers or some other supernatural creature. This behavior, however, need not be moral in the strict sense. The idler is also a favorite of the fairy tale; it may be that he is given the very thing he wants and needs most: that his every wish is fulfilled without his having to move a finger. In the fairy tale about the frog-king, the heroine who repeatedly tries to avoid keeping her promise and finally flings the irksome frog against the wall in order to kill it is neither kind, compassionate, nor even dutiful. But by flinging the frog against the wall, she has, without knowing it, fulfilled the secret conditions for the release of the enchanted prince who had been transformed into a frog.

The hero and heroine in the fairy tale do the right thing, they hit the right key; they are heaven's favorites. The local legend, provided it is not jesting in tone, usually portrays man as unblessed, unsuccessful, and as one who, despite his deep involvement in the community, must face life's ultimate questions alone and uncertain. The fairy tale sees man as one who is essentially isolated but who, for just this reason—because he is not rigidly committed, not tied down—can establish relationships with anything in the world. And the world of the fairy tale includes not just the earth, but the entire cosmos. In the local legend, man is seemingly integrated in the community, but inwardly, essentially, he is alone. The fairy-tale hero is seemingly isolated, but has the capacity for universal relationships. Certainly, we can say that both are true portrayals of man. The local legend expresses a basic human condition: although deeply entrenched in human institutions, man feels abandoned, cast into a threatening world which he can neither understand nor view as a whole. The fairy tale, however, which also knows of failure and depicts it in its secondary characters, shows in its heroes that, despite our ignorance of ultimate things, it is possible to find a secure place in the world. The fairy-tale hero also does not perceive the world as a whole, but he puts his trust in and is accepted by it. As if led by an invisible force and with the confidence of a sleepwalker, he follows the right course. He is isolated and at the same time in touch with all things. The fairy tale is a poetic vision of man and his relationship to the world, a vision that for centuries inspired the fairy tale's hearers with strength and confidence because they sensed the fundamental truth of this vision. Even though man may feel outcast and abandoned in the world, like one groping in the dark, is he not in the course of his life led from step to step and guided safely by a thousand aids? The fairy tale, however, not only inspires trust and confidence; it also provides a sharply defined image of man: isolated, yet capable of universal relationships. It is salutary that in our era, which has experienced the loss of individuality, nationalism, and impending nihilism, our children are presented with just such an image of man in the fairy tales they hear and absorb. This image is all the more effective for having proceeded naturally from the overall style of the fairy tale. The fairy-tale technique—the sharp lines, the two-dimensional, sublimating portrayal we have so often observed as well as the encapsulating of the individual episodes and motifs—this entire technique is isolating, and only for this reason can it interconnect all things so effortlessly. The image of man in the fairy tale, the figure of the hero, grows out of its overall style; this gives it a persuasive power which cannot fail to impress even the realistically minded listener.

Every type of fairy tale portrays events which can safely be interpreted as images for psychological or cosmic processes. Every single fairy tale has a particular message. A beautiful girl's eyes are cruelly torn out and then, one year and a day later, are replaced and can see seven times as clearly as before. Another fairy-tale heroine is locked up in a box by her wicked mother-in-law and hung in the chimney, where she remains without nourishment until her husband returns from the war; yet the smoked woman does not die of hunger—indeed, she emerges from her box younger and more beautiful. Such stories make the listener feel how suffering can purify and strengthen. In speaking of the wisdom in fairy tales, one is usually thinking of similar passages in particular fairy tales. Much more powerful, however, is the overall image of man and the world as portrayed in folk fairy tales generally. This image recurs in a large number of tales and makes a profound impression on the listener—formerly, illiterate grownups; today, children. Is this image in accord with our present-day view of life and the world?

Modern literature, narrative as well as dramatic, is characterized by a strange turning away from the heroic figure. This begins as far back as Naturalism, where the coachman or the cleaning woman takes the place of the tragic hero, the kings and noble ladies, and where the masses—the weavers, for example—can take the place of the individual. In the modern novel, interest centers on impersonal forces, subconscious powers, and processes transcending the individual. If an individual does become the center of attention, he is often an anti-hero, or, as he is sometimes called, the passive or negative hero. The stories of Franz Kafka, which influence so much of present-day literature, have been characterized as out-and-out anti-fairy tales. And yet they have much in common with fairy tales. Their figures, like those of the fairy tale, are not primarily individuals, personalities, characters, but simply figures: doers and receivers of the action. They are no more masters of their destiny than are the figures in the fairy tale. They move through a world which they do not understand but in which they are nevertheless involved. This they have in common with the figures of the fairy tale: they do not perceive their relationship to the world about them. Whereas Kafka's figures stand helpless and despairing amidst the confusion of relationships they do not understand, the fairy-tale hero is happy in his contacts. The fairy tale is the poetic expression of the confidence that we are secure in a world not destitute of sense, that we can adapt ourselves to it and act and live even if we cannot view or comprehend the world as a whole.

The preference of modern literature for the passive hero, the negative hero, is not without parallel in the fairy tale. The simpleton or dejected person who sits down on a stone and cries is not able to help himself, but help comes to him. The fairy tale, too, has a partiality for the negative hero: the insignificant, the neglected, the helpless. But he unexpectedly proves to be strong, noble, and blessed. The spirit of the folk fairy tale parallels that in modern literature to a degree, but then the listener is relieved of his feeling of emptiness and filled with confidence. The grownup, still under the influence of the Enlightenment and realism, quickly turns away from the fairy tale with a feeling of contempt. But in modern art, fascination with the fairy tale is everywhere evident. The turning away from descriptive realism, from the mere description of external reality in itself, implies an approach to the fairy tale. The same can be said of the fantastic mixtures of human, animal, vegetable, and mineral, which, like the fairy tale, bring all things into relationship with one another.

Modern architecture has a great preference for what is light, bright, and transparent; one often refers to the dematerialization in architecture, the sublimation of matter. The sublimation of all material things, however, is one of the basic characteristics of fairy-tale style. We find crystal-clear description combined with elusive, mysterious meaning in fairy tales, in modern lyric poetry, and in Ernst Jünger and Franz Kafka, who has said that true reality is always unrealistic. The modern Anglo-American writer W.H. Auden has said, "The sort of pleasure we get from folk fairy tales seems to me similar to that which we derive from [Stéphane] Mallarmé's poems or from abstract painting." We are not surprised at such a statement. The fairy tale is a basic form of literature, and of art in general. The ease and calm assurance with which it stylizes, sublimates, and abstracts makes it the quintessence of the poetic process, and art in the twentieth century has again been receptive to it. We no longer view it as mere entertainment for children and those of childlike disposition. The psychologist, the pedagogue, knows that the fairy tale is a fundamental building block and an outstanding aid in development for the child; the art theorist perceives in the fairy tale—in which reality and unreality, freedom and necessity, unite—an archetypal form of literature which helps lay the groundwork for all literature, for all art. We have attempted to show, in addition, that the fairy tale presents an image of man which follows almost automatically from its overall style. The fairy-tale style isolates and unites: its hero is thus isolated and, for this very reason, capable of entering into universal relationships. The style of the fairy tale and its image of man are of timeless validity and, at the same time, of specific significance in our age. Thus, we must hope that despite the one-sided rationalistic outlook of many grownups, it will not be neglected and forgotten by our children and by the arts.

THE STRUGGLE FOR MEANING[1]

Bruno Bettelheim

IF WE HOPE TO LIVE not just from moment to moment, but in true consciousness of our existence, then our greatest need and most difficult achievement is to find meaning in our lives. It is well known how many have lost the will to live, and have stopped trying, because such meaning has evaded them. An understanding of the meaning of one's life is not suddenly acquired at a particular age, not even when one

---

1 From *The Uses of Enchantment: The Meaning and Importance of Fairy Tales* (New York: Alfred Knopf, 1976). All notes are editorial.

has reached chronological maturity. On the contrary, gaining a secure understanding of what the meaning of one's life may or ought to be—this is what constitutes having attained psychological maturity. And this achievement is the end result of a long development: at each age we seek, and must be able to find, some modicum of meaning congruent with how our minds and understanding have already developed.

Contrary to the ancient myth, wisdom does not burst forth fully developed like Athena out of Zeus's head; it is built up, small step by small step, from most irrational beginnings. Only in adulthood can an intelligent understanding of the meaning of one's existence in this world be gained from one's experiences in it. Unfortunately, too many parents want their children's minds to function as their own do—as if mature understanding of ourselves and the world, and our ideas about the meaning of life, did not have to develop as slowly as our bodies and minds.

Today, as in times past, the most important and also the most difficult task in raising a child is helping him to find meaning in life. Many growth experiences are needed to achieve this. The child, as he develops, must learn step by step to understand himself better; with this he becomes more able to understand others and eventually can relate to them in ways which are mutually satisfying and meaningful.

To find deeper meaning, one must become able to transcend the narrow confines of a self-centered existence and believe that one will make a significant contribution to life—if not right now, then at some future time. This feeling is necessary if a person is to be satisfied with himself and with what he is doing. In order not to be at the mercy of the vagaries of life, one must develop one's inner resources, so that one's emotions, imagination, and intellect mutually support and enrich one another. Our positive feelings give us the strength to develop our rationality; only hope for the future can sustain us in the adversities we unavoidably encounter.

As an educator and therapist of severely disturbed children, my main task was to restore meaning to their lives. This work made it obvious to me that if children were reared so that life was meaningful to them, they would not need special help. I was confronted with the problem of deducing what experiences in a child's life are most suited to promote his ability to find meaning in his life, to endow life in general with more meaning. Regarding this task, nothing is more important than the impact of parents and others who take care of the child; second in importance is our cultural heritage, when transmitted to the child in the right manner. When children are young, it is literature that carries such information best.

Given this fact, I became deeply dissatisfied with much of the literature intended to develop the child's mind and personality, because it fails to stimulate and nurture those resources he needs most in order to cope with his difficult inner problems. The preprimers and primers from which he is taught to read in school are designed to teach the necessary skills, irrespective of meaning. The overwhelming bulk of the rest of so-called "children's literature" attempts to entertain or to inform, or both. But most of these books are so shallow in substance that little of significance can be gained from them. The acquisition of skills, including the ability to read, becomes devalued when what one has learned to read adds nothing of importance to one's life.

We all tend to assess the future merits of an activity on the basis of what it offers now. But this is especially true for the child, who, much more than the adult, lives in the present and, although he has anxieties about his future, has only the vaguest notions of what it may require or be like. The idea that learning to read may enable one later to enrich one's life is experienced as an empty promise when the stories the child listens to, or is reading at the moment, are vacuous. The worst feature of these children's books is that they cheat the child of what he ought to gain from the experience of literature: access to deeper meaning and that which is meaningful to him at his stage of development.

For a story truly to hold the child's attention, it must entertain him and arouse his curiosity. But to enrich his life, it must stimulate his imagination; help him to develop his intellect and to clarify his emotions; be attuned to his anxieties and aspirations; give full recognition to his difficulties, while at the same time suggesting solutions to the problems which perturb him. In short, it must at one and the same time relate to all aspects of his personality—and this without ever belittling but, on the contrary, giving full credence to the seriousness of the child's predicaments, while simultaneously promoting confidence in himself and in his future.

In all these and many other respects, of the entire "children's literature"—with rare exceptions—nothing can be as enriching and satisfying to child and adult alike as the folk fairy tale. True, on an overt level fairy tales teach little about the specific conditions of life in modern mass society; these tales were created long before it came into being. But more can be learned from them about the inner problems of human beings, and of the right solutions to their predicaments in any society, than from any other type of story within a child's comprehension. Since the child at every moment of his life is exposed to the society in which he lives, he will certainly learn to cope with its conditions, provided his inner resources permit him to do so.

Just because his life is often bewildering to him, the child needs even more to be given the chance to understand himself in this complex world with which he must learn to cope. To be able to do so, the child must be helped to make some coherent sense out of the turmoil of his feelings. He needs ideas on how to bring his inner house into order and on that basis be able to create order in his life. He needs—and this hardly requires emphasis at this moment in our history—a moral education which subtly, and by implication only, conveys to him the advantages of moral behavior, not through abstract ethical concepts but through that which seems tangibly right and therefore meaningful to him.

The child finds this kind of meaning through fairy tales. Like many other modern psychological insights, this was anticipated long ago by poets. The German poet [Friedrich] Schiller wrote: "Deeper meaning resides in the fairy tales told to me in my childhood than in the truth that is taught by life" (*The Piccolomini*, III, 4).

Through the centuries (if not millennia) during which, in their retelling, fairy tales became ever more refined, they came to convey at the same time overt and covert meanings—came to speak simultaneously to all levels of the human personality, communicating in a manner which reaches the uneducated mind of the child as well as that of the sophisticated adult. Applying the psychoanalytic model of the human personality, fairy tales carry important messages to the conscious, the preconscious, and the unconscious mind, on whatever level each is functioning at the time. By dealing with universal human problems, particularly those which preoccupy the child's mind, these stories speak to his budding ego and encourage its development, while at the same time relieving preconscious and unconscious pressures. As the stories unfold, they give conscious credence and body to id pressures and show ways to satisfy these that are in line with ego and super-ego requirements.

But my interest in fairy tales is not the result of such a technical analysis of their merits. It is, on the contrary, the consequence of asking myself why, in my experience, children—normal and abnormal alike, and at all levels of intelligence—find folk fairy tales more satisfying than all other children's stories.

The more I tried to understand why these stories are so successful at enriching the inner life of the child, the more I realized that these tales, in a much deeper sense than any other reading material, start where the child really is in his psychological and emotional being. They speak about his severe inner pressures in a way that the child unconsciously understands and—without belittling the most serious inner struggles which growing up entails—offer examples of both temporary and permanent solutions to pressing difficulties.

Fairy Tales and the Existential Predicament

In order to master the psychological problems of growing up—overcoming narcissistic disappointments, oedipal dilemmas, sibling rivalries; becoming able to relinquish childhood dependencies; gaining a feeling of selfhood and of self-worth, and a sense of moral obligation—a child needs to understand what is going on within his conscious self so that he can also cope with that which goes on in his unconscious. He can achieve this understanding, and with it the ability to cope, not through rational comprehension of the nature and content of his unconscious, but by becoming familiar with it through spinning out daydreams—ruminating, rearranging, and fantasizing about suitable story elements in response to unconscious pressures. By doing this, the child fits unconscious content into conscious fantasies, which then enable him to deal with that content. It is here that fairy tales have unequaled value, because they offer new dimensions to the child's imagination which would be impossible for him to discover as truly on his own. Even more important, the form and structure of fairy tales suggest images to the child by which he can structure his daydreams and with them give better direction to his life.

In child or adult, the unconscious is a powerful determinant of behavior. When the unconscious is repressed and its content denied entrance into awareness, then eventually the person's conscious mind will be partially overwhelmed by derivatives of these unconscious elements, or else he is forced to keep such rigid, compulsive control over them that his personality may become severely crippled. But when unconscious material *is* to some degree permitted to come to awareness and worked through in imagination, its potential for causing harm—to ourselves or others—is much reduced; some of its forces can then be made to serve positive purposes. However, the prevalent parental belief is that a child must be diverted from what troubles him most: his formless, nameless anxieties, and his chaotic, angry, and even violent fantasies. Many parents believe that only conscious reality or pleasant and wish-fulfilling images should be presented to the child—that he should be exposed only to the sunny side of things. But such one-sided fare nourishes the mind only in a one-sided way, and real life is not all sunny.

There is a widespread refusal to let children know that the source of much that goes wrong in life is due to our very own natures—the propensity of all men for acting aggressively, asocially, selfishly, out of anger and anxiety. Instead, we want our children to believe that, inherently, all men are good. But children know that *they* are not always good; and often, even when they are, they would prefer not to be. This contradicts what they are told by their parents, and therefore makes the child a monster in his own eyes.

The dominant culture wishes to pretend, particularly where children are concerned, that the dark side of man does not exist, and professes a belief in an optimistic meliorism.[1] Psychoanalysis itself is viewed as having the purpose of making life easy—but this is not what its founder intended. Psychoanalysis was created to enable man to accept the problematic nature of life without being defeated by it or giving in to escapism. Freud's prescription is that only by struggling courageously against what seem like overwhelming odds can man succeed in wringing meaning out of his existence.

---

1 A doctrine that the world can be made better by human effort.

This is exactly the message that fairy tales get across to the child in manifold form: that a struggle against severe difficulties in life is unavoidable, is an intrinsic part of human existence—but that if one does not shy away, but steadfastly meets unexpected and often unjust hardships, one masters all obstacles and at the end emerges victorious.

Modern stories written for young children mainly avoid these existential problems, although they are crucial issues for all of us. The child needs most particularly to be given suggestions in symbolic form about how he may deal with these issues and grow safely into maturity. "Safe" stories mention neither death nor aging, the limits to our existence, nor the wish for eternal life. The fairy tale, by contrast, confronts the child squarely with the basic human predicaments.

For example, many fairy stories begin with the death of a mother or father; in these tales the death of the parent creates the most agonizing problems, as it (or the fear of it) does in real life. Other stories tell about an aging parent who decides that the time has come to let the new generation take over. But before this can happen, the successor has to prove himself capable and worthy. The Brothers Grimm's story "The Three Feathers" begins: "There was once upon a time a king who had three sons…. When the king had become old and weak, and was thinking of his end, he did not know which of his sons should inherit the kingdom after him." In order to decide, the king sets all his sons a difficult task; the son who meets it best "shall be king after my death."

It is characteristic of fairy tales to state an existential dilemma briefly and pointedly. This permits the child to come to grips with the problem in its most essential form, where a more complex plot would confuse matters for him. The fairy tale simplifies all situations. Its figures are clearly drawn; and details, unless very important, are eliminated. All characters are typical rather than unique.

Contrary to what takes place in many modern children's stories, in fairy tales evil is as omnipresent as virtue. In practically every fairy tale good and evil are given body in the form of some figures and their actions, as good and evil are omnipresent in life and the propensities for both are present in every man. It is this duality which poses the moral problem and requires the struggle to solve it.

Evil is not without its attractions—symbolized by the mighty giant or dragon, the power of the witch, the cunning queen in "Snow White"—and often it is temporarily in the ascendancy. In many fairy tales a usurper succeeds for a time in seizing the place which rightfully belongs to the hero—as the wicked sisters do in "Cinderella." It is not that the evildoer is punished at the story's end which makes immersing oneself in fairy stories an experience in moral education, although this is part of it. In fairy tales, as in life, punishment or fear of it is only a limited deterrent to crime. The conviction that crime does not pay is a much more effective deterrent, and that is why in fairy tales the bad person always loses out. It is not the fact that virtue wins out at the end which promotes morality, but that the hero is most attractive to the child, who identifies with the hero in all his struggles. Because of this identification the child imagines that he suffers with the hero his trials and tribulations, and triumphs with him as virtue is victorious. The child makes such identifications all on his own, and the inner and outer struggles of the hero imprint morality on him.

The figures in fairy tales are not ambivalent—not good and bad at the same time, as we all are in reality. But since polarization dominates the child's mind, it also dominates fairy tales. A person is either good or bad, nothing in between. One brother is stupid, the other is clever. One sister is virtuous and industrious, the others are vile and lazy. One is beautiful, the others are ugly. One parent is all good, the other evil. The juxtaposition of opposite characters is not for the purpose of stressing right behavior, as would be true for cautionary tales. (There are some amoral fairy tales where goodness or badness, beauty or ugliness, play no role at all.) Presenting the polarities of character permits the child to comprehend easily the difference between the two, which he could not do as readily were the figures drawn more true to life, with all the complexities that characterize real people. Ambiguities must wait until a relatively firm personality has been established on the basis of positive identifications. Then the child has a basis for understanding that there are great differences between people and that therefore one has to make choices about who one wants to be. This basic decision, on which all later personality development will build, is facilitated by the polarizations of the fairy tale.

Furthermore, a child's choices are based, not so much on right versus wrong, as on who arouses his sympathy and who his antipathy. The more simple and straightforward a good character, the easier it is for a child to identify with it and to reject the bad other. The child identifies with the good hero not because of his goodness, but because the hero's condition makes a deep positive appeal to him. The question for the child is not "Do I want to be good?" but "Who do I want to be like?" The child decides this on the basis of projecting himself wholeheartedly into one character. If this fairy-tale figure is a very good person, then the child decides that he wants to be good, too.

Amoral fairy tales show no polarization or juxtaposition of good and bad persons; that is because these amoral stories serve an entirely different purpose. Such tales or type figures as "Puss in Boots," who arranges for the hero's success through trickery, and Jack, who steals the giant's treasure, build character not by promoting choices between good and bad, but by giving the child the hope that even the meekest can succeed in life. After all, what's the use of choosing to become a good person when one feels so insignificant that he fears he will never amount to anything? Morality is not the issue in these tales, but rather, assurance that one can succeed.

Whether one meets life with a belief in the possibility of mastering its difficulties or with the expectation of defeat is also a very important existential problem.

The deep inner conflicts originating in our primitive drives and our violent emotions are all denied in much of modern children's literature, and so the child is not helped in coping with them. But the child is subject to desperate feelings of loneliness and isolation, and he often experiences mortal anxiety. More often than not, he is unable to express these feelings in words, or he can do so only by indirection: fear of the dark, of some animal, anxiety about his body. Since it creates discomfort in a parent to recognize these emotions in his child, the parent tends to overlook them, or he belittles these spoken fears out of his own anxiety, believing this will cover over the child's fears.

The fairy tale, by contrast, takes these existential anxieties and dilemmas very seriously and addresses itself directly to them: the need to be loved and the fear that one is thought worthless; the love of life and the fear of death. Further, the fairy tale offers solutions in ways that the child can grasp on his level of understanding. For example, fairy tales pose the dilemma of wishing to live eternally by occasionally concluding: "If they have not died, they are still alive." The other ending—"And they lived happily ever after"—does not for a moment fool the child that eternal life is possible. But it does indicate that which alone can take the sting out of the narrow limits of our time on this earth: forming a truly satisfying bond to another. The tales teach that when one has done this, one has reached the ultimate in emotional security of existence and permanence of relation available to man; and this alone can dissipate the fear of death. If one has found true adult love, the fairy story also tells, one doesn't need to wish for eternal life. This is suggested by another ending found in fairy tales: "They lived for a long time afterward, happy and in pleasure."

An uninformed view of the fairy tale sees in this type of ending an unrealistic wish-fulfillment, missing completely the important message it conveys to the child. These tales tell him that by forming a true interpersonal relation, one escapes the separation anxiety which haunts him (and which sets the stage for many fairy tales, but is always resolved at the story's ending). Furthermore, the story tells, this ending is not made possible, as the child wishes and believes, by holding on to his mother eternally. If we try to escape separation anxiety and death anxiety by desperately keeping our grasp on our parents, we will only be cruelly forced out, like Hansel and Gretel.

Only by going out into the world can the fairy-tale hero (child) find himself there; and as he does, he will also find the other with whom he will be able to live happily ever after, that is, without ever again having to experience separation anxiety. The fairy tale is future-oriented and guides the child—in terms he can understand in both his conscious and his unconscious mind—to relinquish his infantile dependency wishes and achieve a more satisfying independent existence.

Today children no longer grow up within the security of an extended family or of a well-integrated community. Therefore, even more than at the times fairy tales were invented, it is important to provide the modern child with images of heroes who have to go out into the world all by themselves and who, although originally ignorant of the ultimate things, find secure places in the world by following their right way with deep inner confidence.

The fairy-tale hero proceeds for a time in isolation, as the modern child often feels isolated. The hero is helped by being in touch with primitive things—a tree, an animal, nature—as the child feels more in touch with those things than most adults do. The fate of these heroes convinces the child that, like them, he may feel outcast and abandoned in the world, groping in the dark, but, like them, in the course of his life he will be guided step by step, and given help when it is needed. Today, even more than in past times, the child needs the reassurance offered by the image of the isolated man who nevertheless is capable of achieving meaningful and rewarding relations with the world around him.

The Fairy Tale: A Unique Art Form

While it entertains the child, the fairy tale enlightens him about himself and fosters his personality development. It offers meaning on so many different levels, and enriches the child's existence in so many ways, that no one book can do justice to the multitude and diversity of the contributions such tales make to the child's life.

This book [*The Uses of Enchantment*] attempts to show how fairy stories represent in imaginative form what the process of healthy human development consists of and how the tales make such development attractive for the child to engage in. This growth process begins with the resistance against the parents and fear of growing up, and ends when youth has truly found itself, achieved psychological independence and moral maturity, and no longer views the other sex as threatening or demonic, but is able to relate positively to it. In short, this book explicates why fairy tales make such great and positive psychological contributions to the child's inner growth.

If this book had been devoted to only one or two tales, it would have been possible to show many more of their facets, although even then complete probing of their depths would not have been achieved; for this, each story has meanings on too many levels. Which story is most important to a particular child at a particular age depends entirely on his psychological stage of development and the problems which are most pressing to him at the moment. While in writing the book it seemed reasonable to concentrate on a fairy tale's central meanings, this has the shortcoming of neglecting other aspects which might be much more significant to some individual child because of problems he is struggling with at the time. This, then, is another necessary limitation of this presentation.

For example, in discussing "Hansel and Gretel," the child's striving to hold on to his parents even though the time has come for meeting the world on his own is stressed, as well as the need to transcend a primitive orality, symbolized by the children's infatuation with the gingerbread house. Thus, it would seem that this fairy tale has most to offer to the young child ready to make his first steps out into the world. It gives body to his anxieties and offers reassurance about these fears because even in their most exaggerated form—anxieties about being devoured—they prove unwarranted: the children are victorious in the end, and a most threatening enemy—the witch—is utterly defeated. Thus, a good case could be made that this story has its greatest appeal and value for the child at the age when fairy tales begin to exercise their beneficial impact, that is, around the age of four or five.

But separation anxiety—the fear of being deserted—and starvation fear, including oral greediness, are not restricted to a particular period of development. Such fears occur at all ages in the unconscious, and thus this tale also has meaning for, and provides encouragement to, much older children. As a matter of fact, the older person might find it considerably more difficult to admit consciously his fear of being deserted by his parents or to face his oral greed; and this is even more reason to let the fairy tale speak to his unconscious, give body to his unconscious anxieties, and relieve them, without this ever coming to conscious awareness.

Other features of the same story may offer much-needed reassurance and guidance to an older child. In early adolescence a girl had been fascinated by "Hansel and Gretel," and had derived great comfort from reading and rereading it, fantasizing about it. As a child, she had been dominated by a slightly older brother. He had, in a way, shown her the path, as Hansel did when he put down the pebbles which guided his sister and himself back home. As an adolescent, this girl continued to rely on her brother, and this feature of the story felt reassuring. But at the same time she also resented the brother's dominance. Without her being conscious of it at the time, her struggle for independence rotated around the figure of Hansel. The story told her unconscious that to follow Hansel's lead led her back, not forward, and it was also meaningful that although Hansel was the leader at the story's beginning, it was Gretel who in the end achieved freedom and independence for both, because it was she who defeated the witch. As an adult, this woman came to understand that the fairy tale had helped her greatly in throwing off her dependence on her brother, as it had convinced her that an early dependence on him need not interfere with her later ascendancy. Thus, a story which for one reason had been meaningful to her as a young child provided guidance for her at adolescence for a quite different reason.

The central motif of "Snow White" is the pubertal girl's surpassing in every way the evil stepmother who, out of jealousy, denies her an independent existence—symbolically represented by the stepmother's trying to see Snow White destroyed. The story's deepest meaning for one particular five-year-old, however, was far removed from these pubertal problems. Her mother was cold and distant, so much so that she felt lost. The story assured her that she need not despair: Snow White, betrayed by her stepmother, was saved by males—first the dwarfs and later the prince. This child, too, did not despair because of the mother's desertion but trusted that rescue would come from males. Confident that "Snow White" showed her the way, she turned to her father, who responded favorably; the fairy tale's happy ending made it possible for this girl to find a happy solution to the impasse in living into which her mother's lack of interest had projected her. Thus, a fairy tale can have as important a meaning to a five-year-old as to a thirteen-year-old, although the personal meanings they derive from it may be quite different.

In "Rapunzel" we learn that the enchantress locked Rapunzel into the tower when she reached the age of twelve. Thus, hers is likewise the story of a pubertal girl and of a jealous mother who tries to prevent her from gaining independence—a typical adolescent problem, which finds a happy solution when Rapunzel becomes united with her prince. But one five-year-old boy gained quite a different reassurance from this story. When he learned that his grandmother, who took care of him most of the day, would have to go to the hospital because of serious illness—his mother was working all day, and there was no father in the home—he asked to be read the story of Rapunzel. At this critical time in his life, two elements of the tale were important to him. First, there was the security from all dangers in which the substitute mother kept the child, an idea which greatly appealed to him at that moment. So what normally could be viewed as a representation of negative, selfish behavior was capable of having a most reassuring meaning under specific circumstances. And even more important to the boy was another central motif of the story: that Rapunzel found the means of escaping her predicament in her own body—the tresses on which the prince climbed up to her room in the tower. That one's body can provide a lifeline reassured him that, if necessary, he would similarly find in his own body the source of his security. This shows that a fairy tale—because it addresses itself in the most imaginative form to essential human problems and does so in an indirect way—can have much to offer to a little boy even if the story's heroine is an adolescent girl.

These examples may help to counteract any impression made by my concentration here on a story's main motifs, and demonstrate that fairy tales have great psychological meaning for children of all ages, both girls and boys, irrespective of the age and sex of the story's hero. Rich personal meaning is gained from fairy stories because they facilitate changes in identification as the child deals with different problems, one at a time. In the light of her earlier identification with a Gretel who was glad to be led by Hansel, the adolescent girl's later identification with a Gretel who overcame the witch made her growth toward independence more rewarding and secure. The little boy's first finding security in the idea of being kept within the safety of the tower permitted him later on to glory in the realization that a much more dependable security could be found in what his body had to offer him, by way of providing him with a lifeline.

As we cannot know at what age a particular fairy tale will be most important to a particular child, we cannot ourselves decide which of the many tales he should be told at any given time or why. This only the child can determine and reveal by the strength of feeling with which he reacts to what a tale evokes in his conscious and unconscious mind. Naturally a parent will begin by telling or reading to his child a tale the parent himself or herself cared for as a child, or cares for now. If the child does not take to the story, this means that its motifs or themes have failed to evoke a meaningful response at this moment in his life. Then it is best to tell him another fairy tale the next evening. Soon he will indicate that a certain story has become important to him by his immediate response to it, or by his asking to be told this story over and over again. If all goes well, the child's enthusiasm for this story will be contagious, and the story will become important to the parent too, if for no other reason than that it means so much to the child. Finally there will come the time when the child has gained all he can from the preferred story, or the problems which made him respond to it have been replaced by others which find better expression in some other tale. He may then temporarily lose interest in this story and enjoy some other one much more. In the telling of fairy stories it is always best to follow the child's lead.

Even if a parent should guess correctly why his child has become involved emotionally with a given tale, this is knowledge best kept to oneself. The young child's most important experiences and reactions are largely subconscious and should remain so until he reaches a much more mature age and understanding. It is always intrusive to interpret a person's unconscious thoughts, to make conscious what he wishes to keep preconscious, and this is especially true in the case of a child. Just as important for the child's well-being as feeling that his parent shares his emotions, through enjoying the same fairy tale, is the child's feeling that his inner thoughts are not known to his parent until he decides to reveal them. If the parent indicates that he knows them already, the child is prevented from making the most precious gift to his parent of sharing with him what until then was secret and private to the child. And since, in addition, a parent is so much more powerful than a child, his domination may appear limitless—and hence destructively overwhelming—if he seems able to read the child's secret thoughts, know his most hidden feelings, even before the child himself has begun to become aware of them.

Explaining to a child why a fairy tale is so captivating to him destroys, more-over, the story's enchantment, which depends to a considerable degree on the child's not quite knowing why he is delighted by it. And with the forfeiture of this power to enchant goes also a loss of the story's potential for helping the child struggle on his own and master all by himself the problem which has made the story meaningful to him in the first place. Adult interpretations, as correct as they may be, rob the child of the opportunity to feel that he, on his own, through repeated hearing and ruminating about the story, has coped successfully with a difficult situation. We grow, we find meaning in life and security in ourselves by having understood and solved personal problems on our own, not by having them explained to us by others.

Fairy-tale motifs are not neurotic symptoms, something one is better off under-standing rationally so that one can rid oneself of them. Such motifs are experienced as wondrous because the child feels understood and appreciated deep down in his feelings, hopes, and anxieties, without these all having to be dragged up and investi-gated in the harsh light of a rationality that is still beyond him. Fairy tales enrich the child's life and give it an enchanted quality just because he does not quite know how the stories have worked their wonder on him.

FAIRY TALES FROM A FOLKLORISTIC PERSPECTIVE[1]

Alan Dundes

THE FIRST THING TO SAY about fairy tales is that they are an oral form. Fairy tales, however one may choose ultimately to define them, are a subgenre of the more inclusive category of "folk tale," which exists primarily as a spoken traditional nar-rative. Once a fairy tale or any other type of folk tale, for that matter, is reduced to written language, one does not have a true fairy tale but instead only a pale and inadequate reflection of what was originally an oral performance complete with ra-conteur and audience. From this folkloristic perspective, one cannot possibly read fairy tales; one can only properly hear them told.

When one enters into the realm of written-down or transcribed fairy tales, one is involved with a separate order of reality. A vast chasm separates an oral tale with its subtle nuances entailing significant body movements, eye expression, pregnant

---

1   From *Fairy Tales and Society: Illusion, Allusion and Paradigm*, ed. Ruth Bottigheimer (Philadelphia, PA: U of Pennsylvania P, 1986). All notes are editorial.

pauses, and the like from the inevitably flat and fixed written record of what was once a live and often compelling storytelling event. To be sure, there are degrees of authenticity and accuracy with respect to the transcription of fairy tales. In modern times, armed with tape recorders or videotape equipment, a folklorist may be able to capture a live performance in the act, thereby preserving it for enjoyment and study by future audiences. But in the nineteenth century when the formal study of folklore began in Europe, collectors had to do the best they could to take down oral tales verbatim without such advances in technology. Many of them succeeded admirably, such as E. Tang Kristensen (1843–1929), a Danish folklorist who was one of the greatest collectors of fairy tales of all time. Others, including even the celebrated Grimm brothers, failed to live up to the ideal of recording oral tales as they were told. Instead, they altered the oral tales in a misguided effort to "improve" them. The Grimms, for instance, began to conflate different versions of the same tale, and they ended up producing what folklorists now call "composite" texts. A composite text, containing one motif from one version, another motif from another, and so on, exemplifies what folklorists term "fakelore." Fakelore refers to an item which the collector claims is genuine oral tradition but which has been doctored or in some cases entirely fabricated by the purported collector.

The point is that a composite fairy tale has never actually been told in precisely that form by a storyteller operating in the context of oral tradition. It typically appears for the very first time in print. And it is not just a matter of twentieth-century scholars trying to impose twentieth-century standards upon struggling nineteenth-century pioneering collectors. For the Grimms certainly knew better, and they are on record as adamantly opposing the literary reworking of folklore (as had been done in the famous folk song anthology of *Des Knaben Wunderhorn* [1805] which they severely criticized). They specifically called for the collection of fairy tales as they were told—in dialect. In the preface to the first volume of the *Kinder- und Hausmärchen* of 1812, the Grimms bothered to say that they had "endeavored to present these fairy tales as pure as possible…. No circumstance has been added, embellished or changed." Unfortunately, they were later unable or unwilling to adhere to these exemplary criteria. So the Grimms knew what they were doing when they combined different versions of a single folktale and presented it as one of the tales in their *Kinder- und Hausmärchen.*

What this means is that anyone truly interested in the unadulterated fairy tale must study oral texts or as accurate a transcription of oral texts as is humanly possible. The reality of far too much of what passes for fairy tale scholarship, including the majority of essays in this very volume [*Fairy Tales and Society*], is that such fairy tale texts are not considered. Instead, a strong, elitist literary bias prevails and it is the recast and reconstituted fairy tales which serve as the corpus for study.

When one analyzes fairy tales as rewritten by Charles Perrault or by the Grimm brothers, one is *not* analyzing fairy tales as they were told by traditional story-tellers. One is instead analyzing fairy tale plots as altered by men of letters, often with a nationalistic and romantic axe to grind. The aim was usually to present evidence of an ancient nationalistic patrimony in which the French or German literati could take pride. With such a laudable goal, it was deemed excusable to eliminate any crude or vulgar elements—How many bawdy folk tales does one find in the Grimm canon?—and to polish and refine the oral discourse of "rough" peasant dialects.

This does not mean that versions, composite or not, of tales published by Perrault and the Grimms cannot be studied. They have had an undeniably enormous impact upon popular culture and literature, but they should not be confused with the genu-ine article—the oral fairy tale.

There is another difficulty with the research carried out by deluded individuals who erroneously believe they are studying fairy tales when they limit themselves to the Grimm or Perrault versions of tales. Any true fairy tale, like all folklore, is char-acterized by the criteria of "multiple existence" and "variation." An item must exist in at least two versions in order to qualify as authentic folklore. Most items exist in hundreds of versions. Usually, no two versions of an oral fairy tale will be exactly word-for-word the same. That is what is meant by the criteria of multiple existence and variation. When one studies the Perrault or the Grimm text of a fairy tale, one is studying a single text. This may be appropriate for literary scholars who are wont to think in terms of unique, distinctive, individual texts written by a known author or poet. But it is totally inappropriate for the study of folklore wherein there is no such thing as *the* text. There are only texts.

Folklorists have been collecting fairy tales and other forms of folklore for the past several centuries. Not all these versions have been published. In fact, the majority of these tales remain in unpublished form scattered in folklore archives through-out the world. However, one can obtain these versions simply by applying to these archives. Folklorists have carried out extensive comparative studies of various fairy tales in which they have assiduously located and assembled as many as five hun-dred versions of a single tale type. Ever since the Finnish folklorist Antti Aarne pub-lished his *Verzeichnis der Märchen-typen* as Folklore Fellows Communication no. 3 in 1910, folklorists have had an index of folktales (including fairy tales). Twice revised by American folklorist Stith Thompson, in 1928 and again in 1961, *The Types of the Folktale: A Classification and Bibliography* is the standard reference for any serious student of Indo-European folktales. Thompson's revisions took account of the vari-ous local, regional, and national tale type indexes which appeared after Aarne's 1910 work. There are more than fifty or sixty national tale-type indexes in print, including several which are not referenced in the Aarne-Thompson 1961 index inasmuch as they were published after that date, for example, for Latvia, China, Korea, Madagascar, Friesland [i.e., Frisia, in northern Holland], and Norway.

The Aarne-Thompson tale-type index gives not only a general synopsis of each of some two thousand Indo-European tales but also some sense of how many versions are to be found in the various folklore archives. In addition, if there is a published article or monograph which contains numerous versions of a tale type, it is listed followed by an asterisk. If there has been a substantial, full-fledged comparative study of a particular tale, that bibliographical citation is marked by two asterisks. Thus, if one looked in the Aarne-Thompson tale-type index under tale type 425A, "The Monster (Animal) as Bridegroom (Cupid and Psyche)," one would in a matter of seconds discover no less than five double-asterisked monographs or articles devoted to this tale type. One would also learn that there are eighty-seven Danish versions, twenty-eight Hungarian versions, twenty-nine Rumanian versions, and others located in archives.

The gist of this is that if one is really interested in a particular fairy tale, one has the possibility of considering dozens upon dozens of versions of that tale. Whatever one's particular theoretical interest, the comparative data is essential. If one is concerned with identifying possible national traits in a particular version of a tale, one cannot do so without first ascertaining whether the traits in question are found in versions of the same tale told in other countries. If the same traits are to be found in twenty countries, it would be folly to assume that those traits were somehow typical of German or French culture exclusively.

The sad truth is that most studies of fairy tales are carried out in total ignorance of tale-type indexes (or the related tool, the six volume *Motif-Index of Folk Literature* which first appeared in 1932–36, and was revised in 1955–58). One can say categorically that it is always risky, methodologically speaking, *to limit one's analysis to one single version of a tale*. There is absolutely no need to restrict one's attention to a single version of a tale type when there are literally hundreds of versions of that same tale easily available. The fallacy of using but a single version of a fairy tale is compounded when that one version is a doctored, rewritten composite text, as occurs when one uses the Grimm version alone.

The abysmal lack of knowledge of folktale scholarship among academics in classics, comparative literature, and literature departments generally causes genuine concern among folklorists. Let one example stand for hundreds. Rhys Carpenter publishes a book, *Folk Tale, Fiction and Saga in the Homeric Epics* (Berkeley and Los Angeles: University of California Press, 1958), in which he discusses the story of the Cyclops with absolutely no mention of the fact that it is Aarne-Thompson tale type 1137, "The Ogre Blinded (Polyphemus)." It was in fact collected by the Grimms, and the Homeric version provides a useful *terminus ante quem*[1] for that tale. How can a scholar write a whole book about folk tales without any apparent knowledge of the tale-type index? (And what about the scholars who reviewed the manuscript for the university press involved?) Despite the existence of a tale-type index since 1910, most of the discussion of fairy tales occurs without the benefit of folkloristic tale typology.

It is hard to document the extent of the parochialism of the bulk of fairy-tale research. There are too few folklorists and too many amateurs. For example, one continues to find essays and books naïvely claiming to extrapolate German national or cultural traits from the Grimm tales. It is not that there could not be any useful data contained in the Grimm versions, it is rather that there are plenty of authentic versions of German fairy tales available which a would-be student of German culture could consult as a check. Psychiatrists writing about fairy tales commit the same error. They typically use only one version of a fairy tale, in most instances the Grimm version, and then they go on to generalize not just about German culture, but all European culture or even all humankind—on the basis of one single (rewritten) version of a fairy tale! This displays a certain arrogance, ethnocentrism, and ignorance.

There is another important question with respect to fairy tales. If one were to read through symposia and books devoted to the fairy tale [such as *Fairy Tales and Society*], one could easily come to the (false) conclusion that the fairy tale, strictly speaking, was a European form. Certainly, if one speaks only of Perrault and the Grimms, one is severely restricted—just to France and Germany, not even considering the fairy-tale traditions of Eastern Europe. But is the fairy tale a subgenre of folk tale limited in distribution to Europe or to the Indo-European (and Semitic) world? Are there fairy tales in Africa? in Polynesia? among North and South American Indians? If one defines fairy tales as consisting of Aarne-Thompson tale types 300 to 749, the so-called tales of magic—as opposed let us say to animal tales (Aarne-Thompson tale types 1–299) or numskull stories (AT 1200–1349) or cumulative (formula) tales (AT 2000–2199)—then one would have a relatively closed corpus. Vladimir Propp, for example, in his pioneering *Morphology of the Folktale*, first published in 1928, tried to define the structure of the "fairy tale," that is, Aarne-Thompson tale types 300–749. The Swedish folklore theorist C.W. von Sydow proposed the term *chimerate*, which included AT 300–749 *and* AT 850–879, which is perhaps a better sampling of the so-called European fairy tale.

The point is that these Aarne-Thompson tale types are *not* universal. They are basically Indo-European (plus Semitic, Chinese, and so on) tale types. "Cinderella," for example, AT 510A, although extremely widespread in the Indo-European world,

---

1 Latin, meaning "point before which."

is not found as an indigenous tale in North and South America, in Africa, or aboriginal Australia. In other words, more than half the peoples of the world do not have a version of "Cinderella" except as borrowed from Indo-European cultures. But they have their own tales. The question is: Are some of their tales fairy tales? Is the tale of Star-Husband which is found throughout native North America a "fairy tale"? An abundant scholarship has been devoted to this American Indian tale type, but the issue of whether or not it is a fairy tale has not been discussed.

The term *fairy tale* is actually a poor one anyway, for fairies rarely appear in fairy tales. The vast majority of stories with fairies in them are classified by folklorists as belonging to the legend genre, not folk tale. So since the term *fairy tale* is so inadequate, it is not clear that there is any advantage in forcing the folk tales of other peoples and cultures into such a Procrustean misnomer. Regardless of whether or not one wants to extend the notion of fairy tale to African and American Indian folk tales, the fact remains that *folk tale* as a folklore genre is a universal one—even if specific tale types do not demonstrate universal distribution. This emphasizes the unduly restrictive nature of treatments of folk tale which in effect ignore the rich folk-tale traditions of so much of the world.

Folklorists who choose to study the folk tales of non-Western cultures enjoy a distinct advantage. In Europe, the study of a particular tale is complicated by the fact that oral and written versions of that tale have existed side-by-side for more than a century. Sometimes the oral tradition influences the written/literary tradition; sometimes (less often) the written tradition influences the oral tradition. (Informants who mean to be helpful will often suppress their own traditional version of a tale, preferring instead to check with the standard literary version, for example, in the Grimm canon, and dutifully parrot the latter to the collector. Much evidence indicates that a number of the Grimms' "German" folk tales actually came from French literary sources—including Perrault.) In non-Western cultures, where literacy may still be relatively rare, storytellers may give oral versions untainted by literary rewritten texts. If one, therefore, is truly interested in studying folk tales, one would do well to consider investigating non-European tales. The study of the interrelationship of oral and printed texts is a legitimate and important one, but it is not the same as the study of a purely oral tradition.

Nowhere is the excessive bias of literary elitism more evident than in the consideration of so-called *Kunstmärchen* and children's book illustrations. The distinction between *Volksmärchen* and *Kunstmärchen* is intended to distinguish true folk tales from artistic or literary tales.[1] The latter are not and were never oral tales but instead are totally artistic imitations of the oral folk-tale genre. The "fairy tales" of Hans

---

1   *Volksmärchen*: folktale; *Kunstmärchen*: art-fairy tale, or literary fairy tale.

Christian Andersen, for example, are *Kunstmärchen*. He wrote them himself—he did not collect them from oral performances from informants. The very distinction between *Volksmärchen* and *Kunstmärchen* becomes virtually meaningless in an oral culture. In a culture which has no written language, there can be no *Kunstmärch-en*. So the distinction is once again an example of a strictly Europe-centric view of the folk tale. The same holds for children's book illustrations. While the content analysis of the various children's book illustrations of a tale like "Little Red Riding Hood" (AT 333) may be fascinating, it has little to do with the oral tale. There are no picture-book illustrations in an oral tale. Personally, I find children's book illustrations of fairy tales depressingly limiting and stultifying. Why should the audience see the dragon as one particular professional illustrator depicts it? Is not the human imagination far more powerful than anything a single book illustrator could possibly draw? In the oral-tale setting, each member of the audience is free to let his or her imagination create images without limit. So once again, children's book illustrations over and above the fact that versions of fairy tales rewritten for children are often heavily bowdlerized and simplified (in contrast to most societies where children are permitted to hear the same versions of the tales as told to adults) are a peculiar feature of European culture. One should be able to investigate the nature of fairy-tale book illustrations, but one should realize that one is dealing with a derivative, printed art-form, part of a literary and commercial tradition which is at least one full step removed from the original oral tale.

If one were to remove from this volume [*Fairy Tales and Society*] all the essays which treated literary fairy tales or which treated literary rewritten fairy tales such as by Perrault, the Grimms, or the ones in the *Thousand and One Nights*, or which were concerned with fairy tale children's book illustrations, one would have very little remaining. This is a pity insofar as the true fairy tale—even if one wished to restrict the subgenre to Europe or the Indo-European world—would essentially not be considered at all. The reader should be cautioned about this bias, especially since no doubt the majority of readers will, like the authors of the other essays, come from the ranks of students of literature, not folklore. The study of *Kunstmärchen* and liter-ary versions of fairy tales is a legitimate academic enterprise, but it is no substitute for and it ought not to be confused with the study of the oral fairy tale.

Finally, what is even more of an indictment of an overly literary bias in the stud-ies of fairy tale contained in this volume is the narrowness of theoretical approach. A host of alternative theories and methods exist with respect to the analysis of fairy tales, but very few of them are represented in this set of essays. Several essays are totally literal and historical, for example, looking for traces of old German law in the Grimm tales. Fairy tales, oral and literary, are essentially creatures of fantasy. They do not necessarily represent historical reality. The literal approach in folklore includes mythologists who lead expeditions to Mount Ararat searching for remains of Noah's ark or folk-tale scholars who go so far as to suggest that the dragons in fairy tales are primitive man's recollection of prehistoric pterodactyls! The attempt to extrapolate historical features of a culture from fairy tales is admittedly one approach, but it hardly exhausts the content analysis possibilities. Structural, ritual, Jungian, and Freudian interpretations of fairy tales are discussed [...], but none of these approaches is applied to any one tale.

The folkloristic approach to fairy tales begins with the oral tale—with literary versions being considered derivative and secondary. It includes a comparative treatment of any particular tale, using the resources of numerous publications and the holdings of folklore archives, as indicated in the standard tale-type indexes. Ideally, the folkloristic approach should incorporate a healthy, eclectic variety of theoretical orientations which would be more likely to reveal the richness of the fairy-tale genre, its symbolic nature, and its enduring fascination.

FEMINIST FAIRY-TALE SCHOLARSHIP[1]

Donald Haase

IN 1970 ALISON LURIE FUELED feminist scholarship on fairy tales by publishing "Fairy Tale Liberation" in the *New York Review of Books*. That article and its 1971 sequel, "Witches and Fairies," argued that folktales and fairy tales can advance the cause of women's liberation, because they depict strong females. Together, Lurie's two articles took the position that strong female characters could be found not only among the classic fairy tales but also among the much larger and more representative corpus of lesser-known tales. The presence of these competent, resourceful, and powerful female characters, Lurie concluded, ought to make fairy tales "one of the few sorts of classic children's literature of which a radical feminist would approve."[1]

Lurie's position provoked Marcia R. Lieberman, who in 1972 published a forceful rebuttal titled "'Some Day My Prince Will Come': Female Acculturation through the Fairy Tale." Lieberman was neither sympathetic to Lurie's main argument that fairy tales portrayed strong female characters nor receptive to her important qualification that liberating stories had been obscured by males who dominated the selection, editing, and publication of fairy tales. According to Lieberman, this latter argument was "beside the point" because as a feminist scholar she was specifically

---

1   From *Fairy Tales and Feminism: New Approaches* (Detroit: Wayne State UP, 2004).

concerned with the contemporary process of female acculturation: "Only the best-known stories, those that everyone has read or heard, indeed, those that Disney has popularized, have affected masses of children in our culture. Cinderella, the Sleeping Beauty, and Snow White are mythic figures who have replaced the old Greek and Norse gods, goddesses, and heroes for most children. The 'folk tales recorded in the field by scholars,' to which Ms. Lurie refers, or even Andrew Lang's later collections, are so relatively unknown that they cannot seriously be considered in a study of the meaning of fairy tales to women" (383–84).

In the catalytic exchange between Lurie and Lieberman during the early 1970s, we witness simultaneously the inchoate discourse of early feminist fairy-tale research and the advent of modern fairy-tale studies, with its emphases on the genre's sociopolitical and sociohistorical contexts. Already anticipated in their terms of debate are nascent questions and critical problems that over the next thirty years would constitute the agenda of much fairy-tale research. To come to grips with the arguments and evidence advanced by Lurie and Lieberman, gender-based scholarship would have to explore not simply the fairy tale's content but also the process of canonization and the institutional control of the classical fairy-tale collections. Questions about canonization and the male-dominated fairy-tale tradition would lead to the discovery and recovery of alternative fairy-tale narratives and to the identification of the woman's voice in fairy-tale production, from the earliest documented references to the present. The initial and rather simplistic debate over the effects of fairy tales on "the masses of children in our culture" and "the meaning of fairy tales to women" would require more detailed study of the relation between the process of socialization and the development of the classical fairy tale, as well as more convincingly documented studies of the fairy tale's reception by children and adults. Ultimately, there would be the development of an increasingly nuanced view of the relation between gender and fairy tale, a view that avoids insupportable generalizations about the genre as a whole and does justice to the complexity and diversity of the fairy-tale corpus and the responses it elicits.

So what began essentially as a debate over the value of fairy tales based on their representation of females would become a more multifaceted discussion of the genre's history and a more nuanced analysis of its production and reception, [...]. In this [...] essay, I want to identify significant developments in feminist fairy-tale scholarship in order to chart the progress that has been made, provide a context for the research presented in the essays that follow, and suggest some directions for further research.[2]

Gender and Socialization

Rooted in sociocultural critique and in the controversy "about what is biologically determined and what is learned" (Lieberman 394), early feminist criticism of fairy tales, as seen in the Lurie-Lieberman debate, was principally concerned with the genre's representation of females and the effects of these representations on the gender identity and behavior of children in particular. As Lieberman concluded, "We must consider the possibility that the classical attributes of 'femininity' found in these stories are in fact imprinted in children and reinforced by the stories themselves. Analyses of the influence of the most popular children's literature may give us an insight into some of the origins of psycho-sexual identity" (395). There was—and still is—widespread agreement with Lieberman's argument that fairy tales "have been made the repositories of the dreams, hopes, and fantasies of generations of girls" and that "millions of women must surely have formed their psycho-sexual self-concepts, and their ideas of what they could or could not accomplish, what sort of behavior would be rewarded, and of the nature of reward itself, in part from their favorite fairy tales" (385).

Throughout the 1970s these ideas were repeated in writings by American feminists, which did not always analyze fairy tales in depth but more frequently utilized them simply as evidence to demonstrate the sociocultural myths and mechanisms that oppress women.[3] In 1974, for example, Andrea Dworkin's *Woman Hating* echoed Lieberman's thesis by asserting that fairy tales shape our cultural values and understanding of gender roles by invariably depicting women as wicked, beautiful, and passive, while portraying men, in absolute contrast, as good, active, and heroic. Similarly, Susan Brownmiller, in the course of her book *Against Our Will: Men, Women and Rape* (1975), offered the tale of "Little Red Riding Hood" as a parable of rape and argued that fairy tales—particularly classic tales like "Cinderella," "Sleeping Beauty," and "Snow White"—train women to be rape victims (309–10). And in 1978 Mary Daly began the first chapter of *Gyn/Ecology: The Metaethics of Radical Feminism* by pointing to the fairy tale as a carrier of the toxic patriarchal myths that are used to deceive women: "The child who is fed tales such as *Snow White* is not told that the tale itself is a poisonous apple, and the Wicked Queen (her mother/teacher), having herself been drugged by the same deadly diet throughout her lifetime ..., is unaware of her venomous part in the patriarchal plot" (44).

By the end of the decade, both in scholarship and in books intended for mass-market distribution, these oversimplifications of the fairy tale's problematic relation to social values and the construction of gender identity gave way to somewhat more complex, or at least more ambivalent, approaches. In 1979 Karen E. Rowe reaffirmed the "significance of romantic tales in forming female attitudes toward the self, men, marriage and society." Moreover, Rowe emphasized in particular that the idealized romantic patterns in fairy tales were also evident in mass-market reading materials intended for adult women, including erotic, ladies,' and gothic fictions. The fairy tale's romantic paradigms could therefore be viewed as influential not simply in childhood but also in the lives of adult women, who "internalize romantic patterns from ancient tales" and "continue to tailor their aspirations and capabilities to conform with romantic paradigms" ("Feminism and Fairy Tales" 222).

However, Rowe also observed that ever since modern feminists had begun to expose and challenge society's "previous mores and those fairy tales which inculcate romantic ideals" (211), modern women had become increasingly conscious of the gap between romantic ideals and the reality that "all men are not princes" (222). Consequently, Rowe's work asserted that fairy tales "no longer provide[d] mythic validations of desirable female behavior ... [and had] lost their potency because of the widening gap between social practice and romantic idealization" (211). According to Rowe, the result for women was an ambiguity that left them in an unresolved tension between enacting cultural change and adhering to the deceptive ideals of the fairy tale, which still exerted an "awesome imaginative power over the female psyche" (218):

> Today women are caught in a dialectic between the cultural *status quo* and the evolving feminist movement, between a need to preserve values and yet to accommodate changing mores, between romantic fantasies and contemporary realities. The capacity of women to achieve equality and of culture to rejuvenate itself depends, I would suggest, upon the metamorphosis of these tensions into balances, of antagonisms into viable cooperations. But one question remains unresolved: do we have the courageous vision and energy to cultivate a newly fertile ground of psychic and cultural experience from which will grow fairy tales for human beings in the future? (223)

In Rowe's view, the fairy tale—perhaps precisely because of its "awesome imaginative power"—had a role to play in cultivating equality among men and women, but it would have to be a rejuvenated fairy tale fully divested of its idealized romantic fantasies.

Other feminists of the same era had specific ideas about how the fairy tale could be employed "to cultivate a newly fertile ground of psychic and cultural experience." In 1979 feminist literary scholar Carolyn G. Heilbrun proposed that "myth, tale, and tragedy must be transformed by bold acts of reinterpretation in order to enter the experience of the emerging female self" (150). Citing Rowe's essay, which she knew then as a 1978 working paper from the Radcliffe Institute, Heilbrun offered the Grimms' fairy tales as an example of cultural texts whose models of male self-hood could be adopted and reinterpreted by women in light of their own search for identity:

> One feels particularly the importance of not limiting the female imagination to female models. Bettelheim has shown how small boys can use the female model of helplessness in fairy tales to reduce their anxieties and unmention-able fears; similarly, young girls should be able to use male models to enhance their feelings of daring and adventure. To choose only the most obvious exam-ple, consider the many Grimm fairy tales employing the theme of the "three brothers." What if the girl could conceive of herself as the youngest of the three? Powerless, scorned, the one from whom least is expected, even by him-self, this third brother, because of virtues clearly "feminine"—animal-loving, kind, generous, affectionate, warm to the possibilities of affiliation—this third brother, again and again rejected, nonetheless persists to success with the help of his unlikely friends, and despite the enmity of what, in the person of the two older brothers, might be called the "male" establishment. (147)

Drawing on "The Golden Bird," "The Queen Bee," "The Three Feathers," "The Gold-en Goose," and "The Water of Life," Heilbrun suggested how the youngest brother's situation is actually "a paradigm of female experience in the male power structure that no woman with aspirations above that of sleeping princess will fail to recognize" (148). Identification with the male hero is possible, Heilbrun argued, once women recognize "that the structures [of the fairy tale] are human, not sexually dictated": "What woman must learn to assume is that she is not confined to the role of the princess; that the hero, who wakens Sleeping Beauty with a kiss, is that part of her-self that awakens conventional girlhood to the possibility of life and action" (150).

As if on cue and in the same year, Madonna Kolbenschlag published *Kiss Sleeping Beauty Good-Bye: Breaking the Spell of Feminine Myths and Models*. In an eclectic ap-proach that combined social concerns with psychology and religion, Kolbenschlag discussed fairy tales to expose the feminine myths of Western culture while reassert-ing the potential such stories have to awaken and liberate women. In other words, she took an approach that reconciled the cultural specificity of fairy tales as "parables of feminine socialization" (3) with the view that the same stories can call "women forth to an 'awakening' and to spiritual maturity" (4). As she notes in her intro-duction, "Much of what we live by and attribute to nature or destiny is, in reality, a pervasive cultural mythology. Because myths are no less powerful than nature and because they mirror as well as model our existence, I have introduced six familiar fairy tales as heuristic devices for interpreting the experience of women. These tales are parables of what women have become; and at the same time, prophecies of the spiritual metamorphosis to which they are called" (x).

Similarly, Colette Dowling's popular volume of 1981, *The Cinderella Complex: Women's Hidden Fear of Independence*, did not simply indict the fairy tale but instead suggested how women's psychological and social attitudes are mirrored in the stories. From this perspective, a critical understanding of the classical fairy tale as a mirror of the forces limiting women makes it possible to project alternative ways of constructing lives. This had been the goal, too, of Linda Chervin and Mary Neill's *The Woman's Tale: A Journal of Inner Exploration* (1980). By sharing the authors' personal reflections on fairy tales—such as "Rapunzel," "Hansel and Gretel," "Cinderella," "Little Red Riding Hood," "Sleeping Beauty," and "Snow White and Rose Red"—Chervin and Neill hoped to encourage women to reflect on their own responses to the stories and on their inner, or spiritual, journeys. In *Leaving My Father's House: A Journey to Conscious Femininity* (1992), feminist psychoanalyst Marion Woodman offered a Jungian interpretation of the Grimms' "All Fur" and the commentaries of her female patients to demonstrate how women could regain autonomy in a society dominated by men. Despite the diverse orientations of these works—which ranged from the literary to the psychological and sociological, to the philosophical and spiritual—they all encouraged a self-conscious, critical engagement with the classical tales as a means to liberate women to imagine and construct new identities.[4]

Folktale and Fairy-Tale Anthologies

Lurie, of course, had already advanced the idea that fairy tales could "prepare children for women's liberation" ("Fairy Tale Liberation" 42), and in 1978 Heather Lyons cautioned that critical feminist interpretations should be reconsidered, since one could identify extant tales that included strong heroines, stupid men, and the ambiguous treatment of otherwise stereotypical traits such as beauty.[5] These ideas lay behind new collections featuring lesser-known stories with unconventional heroines or better-known tales anthologized in such a way so as to foreground the strength of their female characters. These included Lurie's own collection, *Clever Gretchen and Other Forgotten Folktales* (1980), Rosemary Minard's *Womenfolk and Fairy Tales* (1975), and Ethel Johnston Phelps's two anthologies, *Tatterhood and Other Tales* (1978) and *The Maid of the North: Feminist Folk Tales from Around the World* (1981).

These early collections were followed over the next two decades by a second wave of fairy-tale collections emphasizing the breadth and diversity of women in fairy tales. As their titles and subtitles indicate, many of these foregrounded the cultural diversity of women's tales, including Sigrid Früh's *Europäische Frauenmärchen* (*European Fairy Tales about Women*, 2nd ed. 1996; 1st ed. 1985), Ines Köhler-Zülch and Christine Shojaei Kawan's *Schneewittchen hat viele Schwestern: Frauengestalten in europäischen Märchen* (*Snow White Has Many Sisters: Female Characters in European Fairy Tales*, 1988), Suzanne Barchers's *Wise Women: Folk and Fairy Tales from Around the World* (1990), Virginia Hamilton's *Her Stories: African American Folktales, Fairy Tales, and True Tales* (1995), A.B. Chinen's *Waking the World: Classic Tales of Women and the Heroic Feminine* (1996), and Kathleen Ragan's *Fearless Girls, Wise Women, and Beloved Sisters: Heroines in Folktales from Around the World* (1998). Despite the common attempt to revive and promote women-centered tales, the editors who collected (and in some cases retold) these tales do not present a uniform image or definition of the fairy-tale heroine. Interested in presenting a variety of European tale variants, folklorists Ines Köhler-Zülch and Christine Shojaei Kawan noted that folk narratives "offer a multicolored spectrum of female characters," who have every chance of being "sly," "lazy," "old," or "strong" (7).[6] Far more mythically inclined, Sigrid Früh, on the other hand, hoped to present "as broad as possible a spectrum of strong, active, and loving women" (195), so she privileged tales whose female characters could be classified under distinctly edifying rubrics: "saviors," "the helpful and faithful," "the clever and cunning," "warriors and rulers," and "the fates, the Great Mother, and goddesses." Kathleen Ragan, who gave priority to tales in which "main characters are female and ... worthy of emulation" (xxvi), differentiated her idea of the exemplary heroine from Angela Carter's, whose first collection Ragan described as being based on a "view of women in folktales that includes sexual exploits and victims as well as heroines" (437).

Angela Carter, of course, had no interest in presenting a one-dimensional view of women—let alone heroines without sexuality. Her first folktale collection, published in the United States as *The Old Wives' Fairy Tale Book* (1990), took pleasure in highlighting the heroine's multiple identities. "These stories have only one thing in common," wrote Carter in her introduction, "they all centre around a female protagonist; be she clever, or brave, or good, or silly, or cruel, or sinister, or awesomely unfortunate, she is centre stage, as large as life" (xiii). Moreover, Carter's two folktale collections aimed at reasserting precisely those dimensions of a woman's life—including sexuality—that male editors had suppressed. As Marina Warner explained in the introduction to Carter's second, posthumously published collection, *Strange Things Sometimes Still Happen: Fairy Tales from Around the World* (1992): "Angela Carter's partisan feeling for women, which burns in all her work, never led her to any conventional form of feminism; but she continues [in this collection] one of her original and effective strategies, snatching out of the jaws of misogyny itself, 'useful stories' for women.... [H]ere she turns topsy-turvy some cautionary folk tales and shakes out the fear and dislike of women they once expressed to create a new set of values, about strong, outspoken, zestful, sexual women who can't be kept down" (x).

Anthologies of literary fairy tales by and about women complemented these collections of folktales from the 1980s and 1990s. Some of these drew attention to historically neglected fairy tales penned by women.[7] Others assembled contemporary fairy tales authored by men and women engaged in the cultural debate over gender and sexual politics.[8] The most critically provocative of all these anthologies was *The Trials and Tribulations of Little Red Riding Hood*, published by Jack Zipes in 1983 (2nd ed. 1993). This anthology presented over thirty literary adaptations of "Little Red Riding Hood" in chronological order, thus encouraging an illuminating comparison of variants and a historical analysis of the tale's development. *Trials and Tribulations* contributed significantly to feminist fairy-tale scholarship not only in terms of the conclusions Zipes reached in his critical commentary but also in terms of the work's organization and methodology, which revealed just how vital the comparison of both oral and literary variants in sociohistorical contexts could be in understanding the fairy tale's relation to gender and socialization.[9] Zipes's introductory study of the story's history confirmed that "Little Red Riding Hood" not only reflects the civilizing process in Western societies but also has played a central role in that process by reinforcing the cultural ideology of the middle class. More specifically, he showed that the tale's many adaptations embody a cultural struggle over attitudes toward sexuality and sex roles and toward male and female power. Furthermore, by showing how Charles Perrault and the Brothers Grimm produced versions of the story that dramatically altered the oral folktale, erasing its positive references to sexuality and female power, Zipes exposed how the classical tale came to be "a male creation and projection" that "reflects men's fear of women's sexuality—and of their own as well" (80, 81).

Editing and the Female Image: Grimms' Fairy Tales

Demystifying the classical fairy tales as tools of socialization by exposing their male bias took a leap forward with research on the Grimms' *Kinder- und Hausmärchen*. The impetus originated in Germany in the 1970s, where ideological critics and left-wing pedagogues challenged sentimental views of the Grimms' stories by historicizing the tales and criticizing them for their role in promulgating repressive nineteenth-century bourgeois values.[10] At the same time, Heinz Rölleke began publishing his important philological-textual studies and fairy-tale editions that brilliantly illuminated the collecting and editing practices of the Brothers Grimm. In particular, his 1975 edition of the Grimms' tales in manuscript form—the so-called Ölenberg manuscript of 1810—permitted comparison of the brothers' original transcriptions with their published texts; and in a groundbreaking essay, also from 1975, he set the record straight on the nature of the Grimms' oral informants.[11] Specifically, Rölleke helped debunk the persistent myth that the brothers' tales were authentic transcriptions of the German folk tradition by demonstrating in convincing detail not only that the Grimms had relied heavily on literary sources and literate middle-class informants but also that they had undertaken significant editorial interventions in the texts they selected to publish.

It was not long before feminist-oriented Grimm scholars—especially in the United States—recognized the importance of these findings and built on them to show how the two brothers had revised tales so that they reflected or shaped the sociocultural values of their time. Jack Zipes led the way in 1979–1980 with his essay "Who's Afraid of the Brothers Grimm? Socialization and Politi[ci]zation through Fairy Tales." Zipes compared passages from different versions collected and edited by the Grimms to illustrate how they had altered tales to promote patriarchal bourgeois values as part of the socialization process. This research was integrated into Zipes's *Fairy Tales and the Art of Subversion*, which appeared in 1983 and discussed the Grimms' editing and appropriation of the oral tradition as part of a much larger social history of the fairy tale. In specific sociohistorical contexts Zipes demonstrated how the folktale had been appropriated and reappropriated by European and American writers as a special discourse on sociocultural values and how that fairytale discourse was intended to function in the socialization of children—especially in its modeling of gender-specific identity and behavior.

The pedagogical agenda and editorial history of the *Kinder- und Hausmärchen* were also the starting point for Maria Tatar's studies of male and female characters in the Grimms' tales. Published in the mid-1980s, these studies came together in *The Hard Facts of the Grimms' Fairy Tales*, which reexamined the perennial topics of sex and violence in fairy tales.[12] Stressing that the examination of "hard facts" like these "calls first for a long, hard look at the genesis and publishing history of *The Nursery and Household Tales*" (xxi), Tatar clarified how the ebb and flow of sex and violence in the collection relate to the Grimms' sociocultural attitudes and textual editing. But for Tatar, editorial history served only as a threshold to a broader study of sex and violence, one drawing productively on folklore, structuralism, and judiciously chosen concepts from psychoanalysis. Moreover, although Tatar illuminated the differences between male and female characters by organizing her interpretations of heroes and villains according to their gender, in the final analysis gender functioned primarily as a lens to view sex and violence. To be sure, Tatar certainly considered the construction of gender through the editorial process to be an indicator of how the classic fairy tale was appropriated to serve the purpose of socializing children. However, *The Hard Facts* and Tatar's later book *Off with Their Heads! Fairy Tales and the Culture of Childhood* remain ultimately concerned with what that process tells us not simply about male constructions of the female but about adult constructions of childhood as well.

The most detailed study of the effects of the editorial process on gender in the Grimms' fairy tales came in the pioneering research of Ruth B. Bottigheimer. In a series of articles from 1980 to 1985, Bottigheimer demonstrated how the Grimms' editorial interventions—including their apparently simple lexical revisions—weakened once-strong female characters, demonized female power, imposed a male perspective on stories voicing women's discontents, and rendered heroines powerless by depriving them of speech, all in accord with the social values of their time ("The Transformed Queen"; "Tale Spinners"; "Silenced Women"). Bottigheimer's research on the relation among gender, social values, and the Grimms' editing led to her important book of 1987, *Grimms' Bad Girls and Bold Boys: The Moral and Social Vision of the Tales*. Here she elucidated the Grimms' treatment of gender by closely analyzing the entire corpus of their tales in light of nineteenth-century social trends and the collection's editorial history.

It is important to note, however, that Bottigheimer did not simply replicate Zipes's conclusions or the widespread understanding that the Brothers Grimm had imposed bourgeois values on the folktale. To be sure, there were instances where she found that to be true. However, her attention to the Grimms' sources themselves convinced her that it was not their editorial revisions alone, or even primarily, that shaped the representations of women in their collection. She found among the brothers' stories, in fact, competing views of gender that were inherent in their sources, as well as "kindred values [that the collection] revived and incorporated from preceding centuries" (168). She made this case even more explicitly in her essay "From Gold to Guilt: The Forces Which Reshaped *Grimms' Tales*," where she took pains to distinguish her view from that of Marxist critics who claim that the Grimms transformed folktales by imposing bourgeois attitudes on the stories (she cites only Zipes). Instead, Bottigheimer argued that the image of women in the tales resulted in part from Wilhelm's increasing reliance on misogynistic folktales from the sixteenth and seventeenth centuries—not the magic tales of the Grimms' bourgeois informants. In other words, she claimed that it was the adopted voice of the folk, not the voice of the bourgeoisie, that spoke in such tales: "If ... isolation and silence for heroines creeps inexorably into *Grimms' Tales* ..., it is not from bourgeois experience, but is, instead, part and parcel of the restrictive values that emerge from the 'folk' versions of the tales.... It is the dictates of hard peasant and artisan life that produce domestic tyranny, female silence, and isolation in *Grimms' Tales*" ("From Gold to Guilt" 198).[13]

If the idealization of the folk and folk sources introduced "restrictive values" and negative images of women into the Grimms' collection, then the Romantic idealization of women and nature—effected through the Grimms' editing—introduced an opposite but equally restrictive stereotype. This is evident in what Renate Steinchen has referred to as the Grimms' "representation and polarization of two images of women" (293). Drawing on both sociocultural history and the publishing history of the Grimms' collection, Steinchen illustrated how repressive female models were idealized and elevated to mythic images for middle-class readers. Steinchen not only critiqued the myth of the idealized female storyteller that the brothers had presented in the preface to their collection, but she also compared their versions of "Snow White" from four different editions to analyze how Wilhelm Grimm had intervened in the story to shape idealized representations of men, women, nature, and romantic love, which were meant to serve as models for middle-class readers.

In emphasizing the Grimms' bipolar view of women, Steinchen's analysis of the brothers' "Snow White" parallels the influential interpretation offered by Sandra M. Gilbert and Susan Gubar in their book *The Madwoman in the Attic* (3–44). Without recourse to the tale's editorial history, Gilbert and Gubar stressed the conflict between the egotistically assertive stepmother and the angelically passive Snow White, and they interpreted this bipolar image of woman as a reflection of the self-destructive roles imposed by patriarchy, which reifies females as powerless aesthetic objects and subverts their creative powers.[14] Gilbert and Gubar's stimulating reading stands on its own, but that is precisely its weakness. Their interpretation lacks the contexts, both sociocultural and textual, that would justify their assertion that the voice of patriarchy is not only present in the story of "Snow White" but is also its controlling voice—the voice of the mirror that dominates each woman's sense of self. Steinchen's analysis, informed by both the textual and sociocultural history at work in the Grimms' tale, clearly demonstrates the shaping hand of patriarchy behind the representations of both the demonized queen and the idealized daughter, thereby providing a compelling sociohistorical basis for the speculative psychosocial interpretation presented by Gilbert and Gubar.

As in the early feminist treatises cited above, fairy tales are frequently considered out of context as exemplary texts that can be used to construct generalizations and theories. The studies by Zipes, Tatar, Bottigheimer, and Steinchen underline the need for feminist scholars to take both the textual and sociocultural contexts into account when generalizing or theorizing on the basis of fairy tales. Take, for example, Sandra Gilbert's article "Life's Empty Pack: Notes Towards a Literary Daughteronomy," in which she argues that the model of female maturation and duty in patriarchal society is based on father-daughter incest. She focuses principally on George Eliot, Edith Wharton, and Sigmund Freud, but she also introduces the Grimms' "All Fur" as a fairy tale that presents the paradigm of father-daughter incest in "its most essential psychic outline" (376).[15] However, Gilbert's close reading relies on a crucial line from the fairy tale that actually depends on a grammatical distinction that is significantly more ambiguous in German than it is in the English translation she uses, and this ambiguity bears directly on the question of incest that she is discussing.[16] Furthermore, a complete understanding of the incest theme in "All Fur" depends on knowledge of the tale's textual history and the alterations made by Wilhelm Grimm to render it more appropriate for his middle-class and juvenile audience.[17] Read in these contexts, "All Fur" becomes an even more credible and authoritative illustration of Gilbert's theory, which is otherwise founded on an essentializing psychological understanding of the story.

In his own essay on women in the Grimms' fairy tales, Heinz Rölleke advised feminist readers of these tales to avoid making generalized claims that were not based on rigorous studies of a tale's textual history ("Die Frau"). Rölleke's approach to the question of gender in the *Kinder- und Hausmärchen* takes into account the brothers' attitude toward women,[18] the sources of their tales, and the general representation of women in the collection, all of which tend to mitigate, according to Rölleke, the feminist critique of the stories. Like his other research on the textual provenance and sources of the Grimms' collection, Rölleke's essay on women helps to focus attention on the fact that females were among the most important of the brothers' informants and were the source for many of their important tales. Moreover, in identifying these female informants as largely young, educated women of the bourgeoisie, Rölleke helped to further demythologize the stereotype of the *Märchenfrau*.

Much later, in 1993, Maureen Thum followed Rölleke's lead by arguing that a discriminating analysis of the Grimms' stories in light of their informants gives us a much more complex view of female stereotypes in their collection. Thum argued that although tales contributed by Marie Hassenpflug, Dorothea Wild, and Friedrich Krause depict women with considerable differentiation, stories contributed by Dorothea Viehmann (the Grimms' ideal storyteller) portray positive female characters that resist the expected stereotype. Applying Mikhail Bakhtin's concept of "heteroglossia," Thum consequently confirmed the multiplicity of voices—including female voices—in the *Kinder- und Hausmärchen* and underlined, as had Bottigheimer earlier, the relative complexity of the Grimms' women.[19]

In terms of feminist fairy-tale scholarship, then, research based on the textual and editorial history of the Grimm brothers' tales has had far-reaching consequences. First, it laid bare the inscription of patriarchal values in the classic fairy tale, documented the appropriation of the genre by male editors and collectors, and sharpened our understanding of the complex editorial and cultural processes involved in the representation of women. Second, it confirmed the role of fairy tales in the process of socialization by showing how Wilhelm Grimm's representation of women helped construct a culturally specific model of gender identity. Finally, by renewing attention to the Grimms' female informants, it also identified the presence of female voices in the brothers' collection, revealed the diversity of those voices, and stimulated the search for narratives and characters that resisted the Grimm stereotype.[20]

Notes

1   Lurie, "Fairy Tale Liberation" 42. Lurie revised and reprinted this essay as "Folktale Liberation" in her 1990 book, *Don't Tell the Grown-Ups*. I am using the original essay from 1970.

2   Earlier discussions of feminist fairy-tale scholarship through approximately 1985 can be found in Stone, "Feminist Approaches," and in Zipes, *Don't Bet on the Prince* 1–36. See also McGlathery's brief discussions of feminist research on the Grimms' tales (*Grimms' Fairy Tales* 25–27, 51–53). A well-annotated bibliography of fairy-tale research and collections from the perspective of women's studies can be found in Helms. A good, up-to-date summary of feminism and fairy tales is provided by Jarvis, "Feminism." For a discussion of research on women and oral narrative in general, see Moser-Rath. DeGraff 's partially annotated bibliography, which includes only thirteen items, is very brief and selective. An incomplete and unsympathetic summary of feminist scholarship on the Grimms' tales is found in the generally unreliable and problematic study of the Brothers Grimm by Kamenetsky (279–87).

3   Early critiques from the 1970s sometimes invoked the even earlier observation of Simone de Beauvoir, who wrote in *The Second Sex*: "Woman is the Sleeping Beauty, Cinderella, Snow White, she who receives and submits. In song and story the young man is seen departing adventurously in search of a woman; he slays the dragon, he battles giants; she is locked in a tower, a palace, a garden, a cave, she is chained to a rock, a captive, sound asleep: she waits" (qtd. in Kolbenschlag 1). Kay Stone notes that early feminist works of the 1950s and 1960s—like those of de Beauvoir and Betty Friedan—viewed the fairy tale "uncritically ... as one of the many socializing forces that discouraged females from realizing their full human potential. Few writers from this period focused exclusively on the Märchen since it was only one of many sources of stereotyping. Thus critical descriptions tended to be vague and generalized" ("Feminist Approaches" 229). Christine Shojaei Kawan defends de Beauvoir against this depiction of her work and makes a strong case for viewing the French writer not just as an incidental precursor of feminist fairy-tale criticism but as an influential model, whose analysis of the fairy tale shaped the arguments of Lurie and Lieberman (see Shojaei Kawan 37–42).

4   Similarly, the men's movement, especially in its quasi-religious and religious manifestations, has given the fairy tale a role in defining and redefining manhood (Haase, "German Fairy Tales"). The most obvious example is, of course, Robert Bly's *Iron John*, which is roundly debunked by Zipes, "Spreading Myths."

5   In 1975 Kay Stone verified that more active heroines could be found in Anglo-American collections of folktales but that these collections were not as well known to readers as those of the Grimms (see Stone, "Romantic Heroines" and "Things").

6   Unless otherwise noted, translations of quotations and titles are mine throughout.

7   See Zipes, *Beauties* and *Victorian Fairy Tales*, and Auerbach and Knoepflmacher. These anthologies are part of the research that has been carried out to recover and make accessible the fairy tales of women writers.

8   See Zipes, *Don't Bet on the Prince* and *The Outspoken Princess and the Gentle Knight*. I am focusing this survey on feminist fairy-tale scholarship, not on fairy-tale revisions by feminist writers. For a bibliographic overview of primary literature up to 1986, see Zipes, *Don't Bet on the Prince* 11–33; see also Zipes, *Fairy Tale as Myth* 138–61, and "The Struggle."

9   Maria Tatar's 1999 anthology, *The Classic Fairy Tales*, also groups folktales and fairy tales together by type; and in her introductory essays to each tale type, Tatar undertakes comparisons that frequently draw attention to representations of women. Alan Dundes, of course, has argued persuasively that responsible

interpretations of fairy tales must take into account not simply a single text but the extant variants of that tale type: "It is never appropriate to analyze a folktale (or any other exemplar of a folklore genre) on the basis of a single text" ("Interpreting" 18). In his own study of "Little Red Riding Hood," Dundes reviews Zipes's analysis and notes: "The problem for the folklorist ... is that Zipes is really interested only in the particular impact of the Perrault and Grimm versions of AT 333 upon European society from the seventeenth century to the present" (40). Zipes responds to Dundes in the prologue to the second edition of *The Trials and Tribulations of Little Red Riding Hood* (1–15), where he faults Dundes for dehistoricizing the tale.

10 See, for example, Bürger, "Das Märchen und die Entwicklung," "Märchen und Sage," and "Die soziale Funktion"; and Gmelin. For attitudes toward the Grimms' tales in postwar Germany, see Zipes, "The Struggle" 167–74. On the ideological and textual reevaluation of the Grimms' work, in the 1970s and 1980s, see Haase, "Re-Viewing the Grimm Corpus" 127–29. See also the overview of Grimm scholarship in McGlathery, *Grimms' Fairy Tales*, especially 43–58.

11 See Rölleke, *Die älteste Märchensammlung* and "The 'Utterly Hessian' Fairy Tales by 'Old Marie.'" Rölleke's early essays on the editorial history of the Grimms' tales are collected in "*Nebeninschriften*" and "*Wo das Wünschen noch geholfen hat.*" His scholarly edition of the Grimms' seventh edition of 1857, *Kinder- und Hausmärchen: Ausgabe letzter Hand*, was also to become important upon its publication in 1980.

12 See Tatar, "Beauties vs. Beasts," "Born Yesterday," and "From Nags to Witches." All of these are revised and reprinted in Tatar's *Hard Facts*.

13 For an excellent discussion of the relative merits of the research published by Zipes, Tatar, and Bottigheimer, see Blackwell, "The Many Names of Rumpelstiltskin."

14 Employing an eclectic and rather confusing array of approaches, Ingrid Spörk's *Studien zu ausgewählten Märchen der Brüder Grimm* also singled out the relationship between mother and daughter as a significant structure, leading Spörk to identify the "mother-märchen" as a fundamental type among the Grimms' classic tales. On mother-daughter relationships in the Grimms' tales, see also Barzilai; Liebs; Lundell, *Fairy Tale Mothers*. Cristina Bacchilega offers an excellent reading of gender in the Snow White tale, especially in light of previous scholarship and literary adaptations by Angela Carter and Robert Coover ("The Framing of 'Snow White'").

15 See also Hirsch.

16 The line in question occurs after the daughter has fled from home to avoid her father's incestuous plan and arrives in a great forest: "Da trug es sich zu, daß der König, dem dieser Wald gehörte, darin jagte" (Rölleke, *Kinder- und Hausmärchen* 1: 352). A significant ambiguity arises from the fact that the German clause "dem dieser Wald gehörte" ("to whom this forest belonged") can be taken as either a restrictive or nonrestrictive clause, leaving a question as to whether the king mentioned here, who later marries All Fur, is another king or, in fact, her father. English translators must decide on one of the two mutually exclusive options: either the restrictive clause implying a different king, as in the translation Gilbert uses, "Then it so happened that the King to whom this forest belonged, was hunting in it" (Hunt 328); or the nonrestrictive clause implying her father the king, "Then it so happened that the King, to whom this forest belonged, was hunting in it" (my revision of Hunt's translation).

17 On the editorial history of "All Fur," see Dollerup, Reventlow, and Hansen.

18 A very interesting and worthwhile German master's thesis by Susanne Ude-Koeller in 1985 investigates the changing image of the female in the Grimms' collection against the background of the brothers' lives and their relationship to women.

19 Without specifically approaching the tales from a feminist point of view, Lutz Röhrich also pointed to the diversity of feminine characters and character traits in the Grimms' collection.

20 See, for example, Hayley S. Thomas, who makes the case for a subversive female perspective in "The Worn-Out Dancing Shoes."

FROM TRADITIONAL TALES, FAIRY STORIES, AND CAUTIONARY TALES TO CONTROVERSIAL VISUAL TEXTS: DO WE NEED TO BE FEARFUL?[1]

Sandra L. Beckett

CONTROVERSIAL PICTUREBOOKS ARE GENERALLY INNOVATIVE and provocative works that defy current codes and conventions of the genre. Paradoxically, however, many unconventional and controversial picturebooks have their roots in the time-honoured tradition of folk and fairy tales, cautionary tales, and nursery rhymes. These may be present only in a very subtle manner, sometimes in reminiscences and allusions which go unnoticed by many readers. A large number of controversial picturebooks, however, draw heavily on traditional sources, often retelling or revisualizing the well-known stories. Although many adults consider the picturebooks to be unsuitable or threatening, they do not necessarily see the original works in the same light. These vigilant and perhaps overly protective adults may withhold picturebooks from a young audience while freely giving the same children access to the stories that inspire them, many of which contain grim, grisly, and gruesome details and events.

The traditional stories do not flinch from the hard, even sordid facts of life: child abandonment, infanticide, incest, rape, abuse, cannibalism, murder, necrophilia, and madness, among others. Yet most, if not all, of these subjects are considered taboo in children's literature. Is it the fact that fairy tales and cautionary tales purportedly contain moral lessons that make them more acceptable to the mediators of children's literature? The Grimms' *Kinder- und Hausmärchen* (*Children's and Household Tales*) claimed to be "a manual of manners" (quoted in Tatar, 2003: 19). The title of Charles Perrault's *Histoires ou contes du temps passé, avec moralités* (*Stories or Tales of Times Past, with Morals*) stresses the lessons expressed in rhyming *moralités* at the end of each tale. However, the events and lessons contained in fairy tales often seem to be anything but moral: children are imprisoned, seduced, and devoured; adults are guilty of violence, abuse, and murder. Even the most popular fairy tales contain shocking and terrifying events. Snow White is a victim of attempted murder, Hansel and Gretel of attempted cannibalism, and Little Thumbling and his brothers of child abandonment. A poor little match girl freezes to death in the street, Cinderella's cruel stepsisters have their eyes pecked out, and Snow White's step-mother dances in red-hot iron shoes until she drops dead. All these stories, despite their grim and

---

1   From *Challenging and Controversial Picturebooks: Creative and Critical Responses to Visual Texts*, ed. Janet Evans (London and New York: Routledge, 2015).

horrific themes, have been deemed appropriate fare for children. Although they are associated with an even younger child audience, nursery rhymes also present a range of unsavoury, downright macabre subjects. In her paintings for *Nursery Rhymes*, an anthology of twenty traditional tales, the Portuguese artist Paula Rego (2010) demonstrates clearly that these beloved works are actually colourful stories about madness, cruelty, and sex. "Ring around the Rosy" ("Ring a Ring o' Roses") is claimed to be about the deadly bubonic plague and "Mary, Mary, Quite Contrary" is purported to be about Bloody Mary and instruments of torture. Even without looking beyond the literal meaning of the words, "Hush-a-Bye, Baby" describes a baby and its cradle falling out of a tree. Yet these are the tales that are told to infants and toddlers.

Challenging Fairy Tales

Traditional folk and fairy tales were not originally intended for children, but were told to general audiences at a time when the concept of childhood as we understand it did not exist and very little distinction was made between children and adults. The collection and publication of these tales coincided with the "invention" of children's literature and they gradually passed into the children's library and the nursery. Today many authors, illustrators and publishers are trying to restore them to a crossover audience of children and adults, as I demonstrate in *Red Riding Hood for All Ages: A Fairy-Tale Icon in Cross-Cultural Contexts* (Beckett, 2008; see also Beckett, 2014). In its innovative series Libros para niños—children's books which are "¡NO SOLO para niños!" (NOT ONLY for children!)—the groundbreaking Spanish publisher Media Vaca published an illustrated collection of the Grimms' tales, titled *El señor Korbes y otros cuentos de Grimm* (*Mr. Korbes and Other Tales by the Brothers Grimm*, 2001). Winner of the Bologna Ragazzi Award in the fiction category in 2002, the unusual book was intended, according to the publisher's catalogue, "to frighten and delight both young and old." The suitability of fairy tales for children has nonetheless been questioned over the centuries, particularly in the Anglo-American world. There was much criticism of the early editions of the Grimms' tales as being totally inappropriate for children. In response, the brothers strove to alter the tales to make them more edifying for youngsters. However, the preface to the second edition warned that some parents might still find certain parts unsuitable for children (1980: 17). In their effort to appease readers, the Grimm brothers removed sexual innuendo and heightened the violence, in order to more firmly punish the evil characters.

The Grimm brothers' approach to making the material more acceptable for children might have been questioned in the anglophone world. The eighteenth-century author and educationalist Sarah Trimmer was opposed to fairy tales because "the terrific image" that tales such as *Cinderella* "present to the imagination, usually make deep impressions, and injure the tender minds of children, by exciting unreasonable and groundless fears" (quoted in Carpenter, 1985: 3). Similar anti-fairy-tale sentiment arose in America. As Jack Zipes points out, many Americans, suspicious of anything European, "considered fairy tales ... subversive ... and potentially dangerous for the health and sanity of children" (2001: 84). *The Wonderful Wizard of Oz* was the result of L. Frank Baum's desire to create a "modernized fairy tale" in which the "nightmares are left out," and claimed to have eliminated "all the horrible and blood-curdling incidents devised ... to point a fearsome moral to each tale" (Baum, 1900: n.p.). Even today, opposition to fairy tales persists. For Banned Books Week in the year of the 200th anniversary of the first publication of the Grimms' tales, Sherry Liberman of the New York Public Library reminds readers that *The Complete Grimms' Fairy Tales* was challenged by a committee of parents, teachers, and administrators twenty years earlier due to its "excessive violence." Half of the "10 controversial kids' books" listed in an April 2013 *MSN Living* article on books that have been challenged or banned in the United States are fairy tales. Using the statistics collected in Robert P. Doyle's *Banned Books: Challenging Our Freedom to Read* (2010), the article cites Andersen's "The Little Mermaid" (for "pornographic" pictures of bare-breasted mermaids), the Grimms' "Little Red Riding Hood" (for violence and the presence of alcohol), and "Snow White" (for graphic violence). According to the *MSN Living* article, "sexually explicit content" tops the list of reasons why children's books are banned, followed by "offensive language" and "violence" (Pfeuffer, 2013). To a certain extent, fairy tales and controversial picturebooks, both of which constitute a form of crossover literature, share a similar fate in the world of children's books, at least in some countries.

Some fairy tales tend to be excluded from the children's canon and provoke controversy when they are reintroduced. The dark tale "The Juniper Tree," in which a mother kills her son and cooks him for supper, provided the title of the fairy-tale anthology *My Mother She Killed Me, My Father He Ate Me: Forty New Fairy Tales*, edited by Kate Bernheimer. When the anthology came out, "there was a controversial discussion online in which a bookstore browser—who admitted to not reading the book—accused [the editor] of seeking, through fairy tales, to 'glamorize cannibalism' for an unsuspecting generation of very young readers" (Bernheimer, n.d.). Maurice Sendak, one of the world's best-known children's illustrators, chose Grimms' "The Juniper Tree" as the title story of his 1973 collection, which includes some of the lesser-known and grimmer of the Grimms' tales. Fairy tales that are accepted fare for children in one country may not be in another. Perrault's version of "Little Red Riding Hood," which ends with the little girl being devoured, is not normally the subject of children's editions in English-speaking countries. This is explained not only by the tragic ending, but by what Bruno Bettelheim calls the "direct

Figure 1: *La Barbe Bleue* by Charles Perrault and Jean Claverie (1991).

and obvious seduction" (1975: 169). In Perrault's tale (1697), which warns girls to beware of charming, two-legged wolves, the little girl undresses and climbs into bed with the wolf, who tells her that his strong arms are for embracing her better. It is not surprising that Britain and America, among other Western countries, favoured the German "Rotkäppchen," in which the Grimms had eliminated Perrault's sexual innuendo and added a happy ending that mitigated the violence, or at least its consequences. "Bluebeard" and "Donkeyskin" are seldom illustrated for children in the Anglo-American world, but Perrault's versions of these tales are bedtime stories for French children from an early age. One of France's most popular author-illustrators, Jean Claverie, published *La Barbe Bleue* (1991) for very young readers, which contains a very gruesome illustration of the dead wives in various states of decomposition (Figure 1).

The book's success is indicated by the fact that it appeared subsequently in Gallimard Jeunesse's popular Folio Cadet series for children eight to ten years of age.

Figure 2: *Ma Peau d'Âne* by Anne Ikhlef and Alain Gauthier (2002).

A few years later, another French illustrator, Sibylle Delacroix (2000), offered an only slightly less grisly depiction of the bodies in Bluebeard's chamber of horrors. The tale has also been illustrated in Italy in a striking picturebook by Chiara Carrer (2007), whose illustration of the same scene is perhaps less disturbing because only the women's legs are visible. Adult mediators did not seem to be particularly concerned about the graphic violence in these books for young children, but it is difficult to imagine them being published for the same audience in North America. Even in France, some illustrated editions of the more violent Perrault tales have raised eyebrows and provoked discussion of appropriate target audience. In *Ma Peau d'Âne* (*My Donkeyskin*, 2002), the author Anne Ikhlef and the illustrator Alain Gauthier offer an intimate, sensual retelling of Perrault's tale about incest (Figure 2).

Although the sexual innuendo in the illustrations is more subtle than in their earlier picturebook retelling of "Little Red Riding Hood," this book was published by Seuil Jeunesse for readers from nine years of age, rather than six. For the most part, critics agree that it is more appropriate for older children and adults. In the eyes of some French reviewers, it is the esoteric nature of the text and images rather than the sexual content that makes this picturebook unsuitable for young children.

Broaching Dark and Difficult Subjects in Fairy-Tale Picturebooks

Fairy tales and nursery rhymes do provide a filter that allows authors and illustrators to broach more difficult subjects in picturebooks for young children. Many adults seem to find so-called "adult" subjects, particularly sexuality and violence, more acceptable in recastings of classic fairy tales. This is the case for Claude Clément and Isabelle Forestier's *Un petit chaperon rouge* (*A Little Red Riding Hood*, 2000), which uses the tale—"a story about pedophilia" according to the illustrator (letter, 5 October 2003)—to tackle the subject of sexual abuse in a picturebook published by Grasset & Fasquelle for readers four years of age and older. When illustrating canonical fairy tales, illustrators may get away with more unconventional artwork, although this is not always the case. Even a rather traditional visual rendition of a classic tale can encounter opposition. The illustrated edition of the Grimms' *Little Red Riding Hood* (1983) by Caldecott medallist Trina Schart Hyman was pulled from a first-grade recommended reading list by a California school district for its depiction of the fairy-tale heroine taking a bottle of wine to her grandmother.

Some picturebook editions of popular fairy tales have raised a great deal more controversy than Hyman's. One such picturebook is Sarah Moon's interpretation of Perrault's *Little Red Riding Hood*, published, in 1983, by the Creative Company, one of the most innovative American children's publishers. The French-born fashion photographer casts a child model, Morgan, in the role of an urban Little Red Riding Hood. The sober black-and-white photographs used to document the sinister events involving a young, flesh-and-blood girl explain the book's powerful, shocking effect on viewers (see Beckett, 2002: 49–53). In a dark, deserted street, a young schoolgirl is illuminated by the glaring headlights of the large car of a predatory, unseen driver. The wolf remains an invisible, menacing presence as the little girl begins to undress (Figure 3).

Moon's final, disturbing image depicting only white, rumpled bedclothes confronts the reader with the sexuality and violence inherent in Perrault's tale. Awarded the Premio Grafico at the Bologna Children's Book Fair in 1984, Moon's daring portrayal of child abuse in a children's book met not only with critical praise, but also with scandalized condemnation. An Italian reader felt the jury "mistook a very refined book for adult voyeurs for a children's book" and an American reviewer and social worker thought that the Bologna Book Fair prize sticker should be accompanied by a red "HANDLE WITH CARE" stamp since the book can frighten even adults (Garrett, 1993: 9). Moon's book did not meet with the same controversy in France, where it was published by Grasset Jeunesse for five years of age and up (1983). From an early age, young French readers are exposed to what Zipes calls the "seduction scene" (1993: 355) in Gustave Doré's famous and influential nineteenth-century

Figure 3: *Little Red Riding Hood* by Charles Perrault and Sarah Moon (1983).

engraving of the encounter scene (1861). Doré's even more troubling engraving of the bed scene presents an intimate tête-à-tête of the bonneted wolf and a little girl whose long, curly hair falls seductively over her shoulders and whose chubby bare arm pulls the sheet to her bosom. The Italian illustrator Beni Montresor reworks both of these Doré engravings in a rendition of Perrault's version of *Little Red Riding Hood* published in New York in 1991. The provocative bed scene, which is featured on the cover, is followed by a second disturbing illustration, in which the little girl's head has almost completely disappeared inside the wolf's jaws. The picturebook by the 1965 Caldecott medallist was not without controversy. One reviewer suggests that Montresor's darkly disturbing and violent interpretation of the classic tale is probably "more suited to adults searching into the deeper psychological meaning of fairy tales" (Robinson, 1991: 92).

In 1988, just five years after Moon's controversial, award-winning book, Roberto Innocenti depicted a similar, troubling encounter of a young schoolgirl and a dark, dangerous, urban wolf driving, not a car, but a motorcycle.

The preliminary work, which the illustrator kindly allowed me to reproduce in *Red Riding Hood for All Ages* (Figure 4), was unfortunately lost before he began work on *The Girl in Red* (Innocenti, 2012), released in 2012 by the Creative Company, who had published both Moon's *Little Red Riding Hood* (1983) and Innocenti's *Rose Blanche* (1985) in the 1980s. Innocenti admitted to me at the Bologna Book Fair

[414]

Figure 4: Preliminary work on "Little Red Riding Hood" by Roberto Innocenti (1988).

in 2013 that he preferred the original image, which had a decidedly darker tone than those in the book. Perhaps *The Girl in Red* would have caused more controversy had its illustrator retained the darker atmosphere of the earlier work, which is more reminiscent of his *Rose Blanche*. His first portrait of the girl in red running along a stone wall covered with graffiti bears more than a striking resemblance to Moon's Little Red Riding Hood running along a brick wall. The presence of bystanders in Innocenti's image does little to mitigate the sense of menace and dread, as they remain indifferent to the little girl's plight in a hostile cityscape.

It would be interesting to know how the adults who restricted the Grimms' "Snow White" to students with parental permission at some public school libraries in the United States because of its graphic violence—a hunter kills a wild boar and a wicked witch orders Snow White's heart torn out—would react to Ana Juan's *Snowhite*, published in Spain in 2001. Like Moon, Juan interprets the fairy tale entirely in black and white in order to create the "mysterious and troubling" ambiance she sought (email, 30 April 2014). In a hostile, dark world, the familiar characters either "lose their 'goodness' and become abusers," as in the case of the prince and the seven dwarfs (Figure 5), or become silent witnesses who look the other way.

As in Wim Hofman's disturbing psychological retelling of the same tale, *Zwart als inkt is het verhaal van Sneeuwwitje en de zeven dwergen* (*Black as Ink Is the Tale of*

Figure 5: *Snowhite* by Ana Juan (2001).

Snow White and the Seven Dwarfs, 1998), in which Snow White contemplates sui-
cide, Juan's tragic ending brings us full circle at the end. Neither Hofman's nor Juan's
young protagonist is able to escape the inexorable cycle of evil that dictates her fate.
Marketed for young adults and adults, Juan's cruel, sordid tale of narcissism, prosti-
tution, drugs, and abuse is a far cry from the sweet tone of the Disney movie that she
had loved as a child (email, 28 April 2014), and that, according to Jack Zipes (2001),
changed the negative attitude toward fairy tales in the United States.

The images of Susanne Janssen's *Rotkäppchen*, published by Carl Hanser in 2001,
restore some of the sexuality to the Grimms' version of "Little Red Riding Hood."
It is not so much the grotesqueness of the figures or the distorted perspective that
disturbs adult readers, but rather the sexual innuendo that re-enters the familiar tale.
Janssen focuses on faces and they tell a rather different story from the text. Setting
out under her mother's somewhat disapproving stare, the little girl with the saucy
red hat and seductive pink lips seems to cast a flirtatious gaze at the wolf who lolls
lasciviously on its back (Figure 6).

After her encounter with the wolf, the young girl herself is sprawled across the
doublespread and on her face is a look, not of fear, but of ecstasy. In the bedroom,
the intimate close-up of her face that fills the picture frame portrays a dreamy gaze,

Figure 6: *Rotkäppchen* by Jacob and Wilhelm Grimm and Susanne Janssen (2001).

shaped eyebrows that arch speculatively, and a sensual, lipstick-smeared mouth. The German critic Mattenklott Gundel finds it "hard to imagine the book in the hands of small children" pointing to "a precarious eroticisation of the pictorial narrative." In his view, Janssen's picturebook belongs "to the category of those books whose blurb points out from the outset that they are not suitable for children, but rather more so for adults interested in art" (Gundel, 2002: 38). Janssen has drawn a very different tale from the Brothers Grimm's "fairy tale for little children," according to the reviewer, who feels it might be different if she had included humour or irony to distance readers, as did Yvan Pommaux in *John Chatterton détective* (1993), winner of the Deutscher Jugendliteraturpreis (German Youth Literature Award) in 1995.

Pommaux's popular picturebook retelling of "Little Red Riding Hood" nonetheless has a sinister undercurrent, as it depicts a psychopathic wolf art-collector who abducts the heroine and holds her for ransom to obtain a coveted wolf painting for his art collection (Figure 7).

The eponymous black cat detective follows a trail of red items of clothing—ominous signs perhaps of the young victim's struggle with her abductor—through dark and deserted parks, streets, and alleys to the wolf's powerful, black car. However, the comic book style, humour, and happy ending of Pommaux's whodunnit mitigate the seriousness of the subject matter in this award-winning picturebook appreciated by

Figure 7: *John Chatterton détective* by Yvan Pommaux (1993).

adults and children alike. Even fairy-tale retellings in a playful, light-hearted mode can, however, be controversial. Fam Ekman (1985) adopted a humorous approach to the Grimms' version of "Little Red Riding Hood" in *Rødhatten og Ulven* (*Red Hat and the Wolf*), in which a sexy she-wolf in high heels and a low-cut red dress attempts to seduce a naïve country boy. The Norwegian public is quite accustomed to Ekman's sophisticated, challenging picturebooks, which are avidly collected by adults, so the picture book did not meet with any controversy until it was adapted as a television film. According to the author, the film was never aired due to the provocative scene in which Red Hat stares into the décolleté of the seductive saleswoman wolf in the café, a scene deemed inappropriate for children (Figure 8).

It is important to remember, however, that this occurred in the 1980s. The Scandinavian countries are much more tolerant toward sexual content in children's works than most other countries.

An increasing number of contemporary retellings of fairy tales in picturebook format adopt a darker, more ambiguous atmosphere and restore some of the sexuality and violence of the earlier sources. The majority of these books, however, have been published in non-English-speaking markets. Both the text and the images of *Rood Rood Roodkapje* (*Red Red Little Red Hood*), by the Dutch author Edward van de Vendel and the Belgian illustrator Isabelle Vandenabeele, received

Figure 8: *Rødhatten og Ulven* by Fam Ekman (1985).

awards when the picturebook was published in 2003 by the innovative Belgian publisher De Eenhoorn. The strikingly dramatic woodcuts create a dark, unsettling atmosphere, which becomes decidedly more troubling toward the end of the story. Vandenabeele portrays a composed little girl wielding a large, blood-drenched axe, as blood fills her grandmother's doorway and flows out into a pool on the ground beside her (Figure 9).

The final, ambiguous spread depicts the little girl standing in a blood-red room staring at the black wolf skin on the floor as she dreams of doing red things. More than a decade earlier, one of France's most successful children's publishing houses, L'École des loisirs, published *Mina je t'aime* (*Mina, I love you*), a picture-book by the French author Patricia Joiret and the Belgian illustrator Xavier Bruyère (1991). While there is nothing in *Mina je t'aime* that blatantly transgresses taboos, there is an underlying current of sensuality and a disturbing sense of menace. Joiret and Bruyère portray Little Red Riding Hood as a predatory seductress (she lures three young boys to her she-wolf grandmother) in a picturebook targeted at very young children. One particularly sensual portrait, inspired by Titian's *Venus of Urbino*, shows Carmina lounging on a divan in a sexy red mini-dress and red tights, her long, loose, red hair flowing erotically over her shoulder and a seductive smile on her red lips. Although it shocked my class of Canadian university students, there is no trace

[419]

Figure 9: *Rood Rood Roodkapje* by Edward van de Vendel and Isabelle Vandenabeele (2003).

of any controversy in France over this picturebook, which seems to be widely used by teachers with children aged nine to eleven. Despite its apparent success in France and the fact that it was released by a major publishing house, *Mina je t'aime* has not been translated (except for an adult audience in a scholarly anthology of retellings I published in 2014, titled *Revisioning Red Riding Hood around the World: An Anthology of International Retellings*).

One retelling of "Little Red Riding Hood" that did spark discussion of its appropriateness for young readers in France was *Mon Chaperon Rouge* (*My Red Riding Hood*, 1998) by Anne lkhlef and Alain Gauthier (Figure 10). Seuil Jeunesse released it for ages six years of age and up, but some critics consider it to be a sophisticated picturebook primarily for adolescents and adults. This is not due only to the sensuality and eroticism of both the text and illustrations, however, but also to the textual layering and sophisticated images. Adult readers may have difficulty with this picturebook because it is inspired by Ikhlef's earlier, rather provocative film, *La vraie histoire du Chaperon rouge* (*The Real Story of Red Riding Hood*), which was presented at the Cannes Film Festival in 1985. The five-year-old actress Justine Bayard is nude in the intimate bed scene, as she lovingly caresses the wolf, in the guise of the French actor Didier Sandre. In fact, the picturebook is less disturbing than the film, since the prepubescent heroine portrayed by Gauthier appears much older than the young actress who plays Little Red Riding Hood. *Mon Chaperon Rouge* nonetheless remains a daring picturebook which, like the film, presents an erotic, nocturnal version of the tale inspired largely from oral versions, notably the gruesome tale "The Story of Grandmother," with its

Figure 10: *Mon Chaperon Rouge* by Anne Ikhlef and Alain Gauthier (1998).

cannibalistic scene and ritualistic striptease. Ikhlef uses what Angela Carter calls "the latent content of those traditional tales," a content that is "violently sexual," but, unlike the British author, she does so in a children's picturebook (Goldsworthy, 1985: 10). The sexual content is perhaps made more palatable in this picturebook targeted at children by the fact that Ikhlef embeds in the poetic text other popular forms from children's culture, such as nursery rhymes, counting rhymes, riddles, and songs, although some of these also have grisly overtones. The author reworks a counting rhyme to retell the story of the cannibal repast (see Beckett, 2008: 89). Ikhlef's picturebook (1998) retains the lengthy, ritualistic striptease of "The Story of Grandmother," in which the little girl asks in turn what to do with her apron, bodice, stockings, and skirt, and the wolf tells her each time to throw the article in the fire, as she won't be needing it anymore. Gauthier's illustrations turn the scene into an erotic spectacle in which readers become complicit spectators, peering voyeuristically over the man-wolf's shoulder. A red curtain is pulled back to reveal the little girl, smiling enigmatically at the wolf (and readers) as she shrugs one shoulder out of her red dress. The more risqué version of the dramatic dialogue from the popular tradition receives a strikingly provocative treatment by Gauthier. The intimate picture of a naked Little Red Riding Hood lying on top of the wolf is once again framed by red bed curtains, as if readers/viewers were watching a love scene being enacted at the theatre.

Figure 11: *Les Contes de Perrault* (*The Fairy Tales of Perrault*) by Charles Perrault and Gustave Doré (1861).

The Figure of the Ogre in Picturebooks

The ogre is a common figure in folk and fairy tales, from where it made its way into children's literature. For many children today, the word "ogre" is likely to evoke the grotesque, harmless figure of Shrek. In the francophone world, however, the terrifying images that Doré created for Perrault's *Le Petit Poucet* (*Little Thumbling*) are still engraved on the collective unconscious of young and old alike (Figure 11).

The Swiss picturebook artist Béatrice Poncelet (2003) incorporates Doré's frightening images into *Les Cubes* (*The Blocks*), a challenging picturebook about dementia. The dominant image on the book's cover is a fragment of the fearsome face of Doré's ogre in the process of cutting his own daughters' throat. Superposed over his face is a children's block that depicts the fragment of his hand on the hilt of the knife. Poncelet adds colour to Doré's images, which makes them even more nightmarish, as it highlights the blood. Fragments of this gruesome scene reappear on blocks throughout the book with more frequency than other, less disturbing childhood images. Three blocks with fragments of Doré's engraving are positioned in the centre of one doublespread so as to reconstruct the most horrific part of the image (Figure 12).

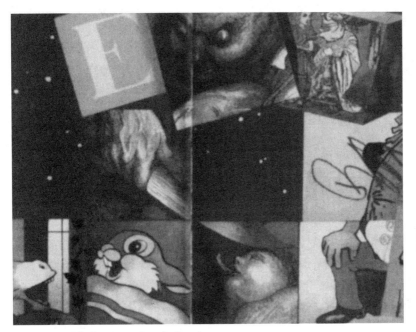

Figure 12: *Les Cubes* by Béatrice Poncelet (2003).

Midway through the story, the block bearing the ogre's face is isolated and en-larged to fill an entire page. Poncelet defends her inclusion of these images—essen-tial images of our cultural heritage—in her picturebooks. A child reader unfamiliar with Doré's work still "sees clearly that it is an ogre, and an ogre is scary, so why not show it (wink, also small homage) since it's part of our culture" (Poncelet, 2005: 60). Doré's ogre also finds his way into her picturebook *Chez elle ou chez elle* (*At Her Place or at Her Place*) (1997). A unique ogre is the eponymous protagonist of *L'Ogresse en pleurs* (*The Ogress in Tears*) by the French author Valérie Dayre and the Hans Chris-tian Andersen Award winner Wolf Erlbruch (1996). They use the filter of fairy tale to present the ultimate form of parental violence against a child, that of cannibalism. In Dayre's tale of "a woman so evil that she dreamed of eating a child," the sinister, grotesque ogress prowls an eerie, surreal landscape looking for a child to eat until finally she returns home and devours her own child (Figure 13).

Erlbruch's decision not to represent the horrific cannibalistic scene was not in-tended to protect young readers, but rather to highlight the horror and violence, which is witnessed by a circus monkey. The animal's yellow eyes almost pop out of his head, his mouth is open wide in a terrified scream, and he beats his drum fre-netically. The truncated German title *Die Menschenfresserin* (*The Ogress*) eliminates the sentimentality of the French title, which refers to the ogress's fate as she roams

Figure 13: *L'Ogresse en pleurs* by Valérie Dayre and Wolf Erlbruch (1996).

the countryside at the end of the story, now seeking a child to love, not to eat. The picturebook shocks many non-French-speaking readers, perhaps in part because the wordplay in French reduces some of the anguish (the expression "à croquer" or "to eat" has the figurative meaning of "to look good enough to eat"). In an article titled "How Much Cruelty Can a Children's Picturebook Stand?" Horst Künnemann (2005) points out that admiring critics who added the picturebook to their collection "would not read it to their own children." While Erlbruch's phenomenally successful illustrations for *Vom kleinen Maulwurf, der wissen wollte, wer ihm auf den Kopf gemacht hat* (*The Story of the Little Mole Who Knew It Was None of His Business*), by Werner Holzwarth (1989), sold well over a million copies, the German edition of *L'ogresse en pleurs*, with its darker title, was printed in only 15,000 copies. Needless to say, the picturebook has not been translated into English.

The Heritage of Traditional Tales

It is not surprising that controversial picturebooks are often inspired by traditional tales, cautionary tales, and nursery rhymes. Many contemporary picturebook artists turn to fairy tales as models of what children's literature should be. These genres have been popular with both children and adults for centuries. The French publisher

Figure 14: *Vous oubliez votre cheval* by Christian Bruel and Pierre Wachs (1986).

Christian Bruel acknowledged in 1981 that there is a connection between the traditional tale and the controversial picturebooks of his experimental publishing house
Le Sourire qui mord (The Smile That Bites) (Bruel 1985). Concerned by the fact that
many children's books ignore complete chunks of the reality experienced by children, the publishing house was founded with the intention of eliminating the stereotypes and taboos in children's literature. Its complex, crossover picturebooks deal
with difficult themes, notably sensuality and violence, in a manner that is particularly disturbing for adults. The wordless picturebook *Vous oubliez votre cheval* (*You Are
Forgetting Your Horse*), conceived by Bruel and illustrated by Pierre Wachs (1986),
is one of several enigmatic picturebooks in the groundbreaking series Grands pe-
tits livres (Large Little Books) that contain important allusions to fairy tales. The
doublespreads that refer to "Goldilocks" and "The Frog Prince" are perplexing and

unsettling, but the one devoted to "Little Red Riding Hood" is entirely unnerving. Opposite the black-and-white illustration depicting the inside of the grandmother's empty living room, where a bear trap has been set, is a colour illustration showing the bedroom, where a large, realistic wolf stands in the doorway, holding in its jaws a red slipper that evokes the absent, devoured grandmother (Figure 14).

It is not the violence done to the old lady that disturbs adult readers, however, but rather the implied sensuality. Obligingly bringing the grandmother's slippers, the wolf fixes his yellow gaze on Little Red Riding Hood, but viewers see only two vulnerable-looking bare legs and feet that bleed suggestively off the page, conjuring up images of a naked heroine. The ambiguous illustrations, which leave readers to determine if Little Red Riding Hood is the victim or the complicit partner of the wolf, are far more disturbing for adults than children. While adults will immediately interpret these multilayered, enigmatic pictures in the light of "Little Red Riding Hood," children may simply be fascinated by their strange and sometimes playful details.

Like fairy tales, nursery rhymes have inspired some rather controversial picturebooks. Maurice Sendak chose two nursery rhymes as the text of his picturebook *We Are All in the Dumps with Jack and Guy* (1993), an origin clearly indicated in the subtitle "Two Nursery Rhymes with Pictures." It is the pictures and the added text, not the original nursery rhymes that are a source of alarm for adults. Cleverly combining two little known and unrelated nursery rhymes, Sendak interprets them, with a great deal of social commentary, in the context of serious contemporary problems and issues that are introduced in newspaper headlines and articles. Although the illustrations are not necessarily frightening, they remind readers of horrific things in the real world: poverty, war, crime, pollution, famine, inflation, AIDS, unemployment, and so forth. A number of critics feel *We Are All in the Dumps* is not a picturebook for children. In a review for *School Library Journal*, Kay E. Vandergrift says that "adults may question presenting serious topics to children in this imaginative form," but she points out that its subject matter is part of children's experience: "Lucky children have seen homelessness, and worse, only on TV; the unlucky have lived it." Categorizing *We Are All in the Dumps* as a picturebook for four years of age and up, the reviewer concludes: "In this beautiful, passionately concerned book, Sendak creates visual poetry, rich in symbolism, that goes to the heart of such matters better than any earnest description" (Vandergrift, 1993: 119). Jane Doonan rightly points out that "*Dumps* shares with certain other modern picture books a quality that was formerly the preserve of folk and fairy tales: an open address" (1994: 166). For decades, Sendak's books have challenged established ideas about what children's literature is and should be, in an attempt to revolutionize the picturebook genre by introducing dark, contentious themes.

From Classic Cautionary Tales to Challenging Picturebooks

In addition to cautionary tales from the fairy-tale tradition, contemporary picture-book artists borrow from classic cautionary stories, in which cruel fates are purport-edly offered for children's edification. The most influential of these works is Heinrich Hoffman's popular collection of moral tales, *Der Struwwelpeter*, a German classic that has often been criticized for its violence. The cruelty is, of course, mitigated by hu-mour, as indicated by the original title, *Lustige Geschichten und drollige Bilder mit 15 schön kolorierten Tafeln für Kinder von 3–6 Jahren* (*Funny Stories and Whimsical Pictures with 15 Beautifully Coloured Panels for Children Aged 3 to 6* [1845]). In these nightmarish stories with their implausible and absurd morals, a thumb-sucking boy has his thumbs cut off with giant scissors, a girl is burned to death playing with matches, and a child who refuses to eat his soup wastes away and dies. Another German classic in the same vein, published in 1865, is Wilhelm Busch's *Max und Moritz* (English trans. *Mac and Murray*), in which the boys' pranks end with them being ground to bits and devoured by a miller's ducks, to no one's regret. The Anglo-French author Hillaire Belloc paro-dies nineteenth-century cautionary tales in his humorous work *Cautionary Tales for Children: Designed for the Admonition of Children between the Ages of Eight and Fourteen Years* (1907), illustrated by Basil Temple Blackwood (B.T.B.) and later by Edward Go-rey. The tongue-in-cheek poems recount the stories of "Jim, who ran away from his nurse, and was eaten by a lion," "Matilda, who told lies and was burnt to death," and "Henry King: Who chewed bits of string, and was early cut off in dreadful agonies."

Images from both of the German works find their way into *Chez elle ou chez elle* and Poncelet attributes this influence to the German side of her Swiss culture. Pon-celet is often accused of elitism and creating picturebooks for adults, but she insists that they are intended for children as much as adults. She feels that many children's books continue to address children in the same manner they did at the beginning of the twentieth century, that is, "avoiding truly confronting them with existence" (2005: 60). The French publisher François Ruy-Vidal, who collaborated with the controversial American publisher Harlin Quist, had made the same accusation in the 1960s. Quist and Ruy-Vidal both wanted to abolish the taboos in children's litera-ture and break down the boundaries that separated it from adult literature. In 1972, they published an adaptation of Hoffman's work, *Pierre l'ébouriffé: Histoires pas très drôles, d'un passé toujours présent* (*Dishevelled Peter: Not Very Funny Stories of a Past Still Present*), adapted by Ruy-Vidal and illustrated by Claude Lapointe. Unlike the majority of the Quist and Ruy-Vidal collaborations, *Pierre l'ébouriffé* did not appear in the United States. Although Quist's daring books gleaned critical acclaim, their European look and controversial content prevented their commercial success in the United States and to this day they remain unique in American children's publishing.

From Fear to Pleasure: Picturebooks as an Introduction to Life

Assumptions about children's limited ability to deal with certain topics have often restricted their literary experiences and deprived them of fictional opportunities to explore dark, disturbing, and painful subjects that nonetheless touch them personally and constitute part of their life experience. This is particularly true in the case of the picturebook genre (see Beckett, 2012). The Danish author Oscar K laments the attempt to keep "an often harsh reality out of children's books" and wonders "for whose sake—children or adults?" (2008: 46). He and his wife Dorte Karrebæk, whose unconventional and provocative illustrations brought a new look to Danish children's literature, contend that to take children seriously is to present them with raw and undiluted reality. As we have seen, there is a particular reluctance to portray those harsh realities in the picturebooks of the Anglo-American world. In his article "Creation of a Picture Book," the English children's author and illustrator Edward Ardizzone acknowledges that we tend to "shelter [the child] too much from the harder facts of life," and expresses his belief that subjects like poverty and death, "if handled poetically, can surely all be introduced without hurt." Books for children are, in his view, "an introduction to the life that lie ahead of them," so he feels that picturebook artists are not "playing fair" if "no hint of the hard world comes into these books." In support of his argument, Ardizzone points to fairy tales, like those of Andersen, and to nursery rhymes, which consist of "the very stuff of life itself" (1980: 293). Sendak attributes the appeal of the Grimms' tales with young and old alike to the fact that they are about "the pure essence of life—incest, murder, insane mothers, love, sex ..." (quoted in Lanes, 1980: 206). Many contemporary picturebook artists agree that it is their duty to tell young children some terrible truths even if this causes horror and distress.

Dark subjects can also cause immense pleasure, as a number of critics remind us. Maria Tatar states: "Children love fairy tales precisely because they speak the language of pain, suffering, loss, and torture with a candor they often do not encounter in real life." She admits being "hooked by the terror" as a child, explaining: "And I read voraciously, in the same way that I was also mesmerized by the images of people suffering from terrible diseases in the pages of *JAMA*, the professional medical journal that piled up over the years in my parents' bedroom" (quoted in Liberman, 2013). In *No Go the Bogeyman* (2000), Marina Warner has shown the pleasure both adults and children derive from the fantastic terrors used in tales, nursery rhymes, and cradle songs to allay real ones. A reviewer for *V&A Magazine* reported his ten-year-old child's reaction to Rego's collection of *Nursery Rhymes*: "Really, really scary Daddy ... But in a good way." In her work, Rego focuses on the fears and obsessions of childhood, conscious that those fears remain with us as adults. Should these fears not be faced while we are still children? Rego describes the cathartic nature of frightening images in the following manner: "If you put frightening things into a picture, then they can't harm you. In fact, you end becoming quite fond of them" (email from Sue Hopper on behalf of Paula Rego, 5 June 2014).

Some of the most celebrated picturebook artists, including Maurice Sendak, Tomi Ungerer, and Wolf Erlbruch, continue in the tradition of folk and fairy tales. Sendak was largely responsible for reintroducing subjects from the dark, disturbing side of childhood into picturebooks with *Where the Wild Things Are*, published in 1963. Since the 1960s, picturebooks have made great strides in freeing themselves from the rigid moral codes and taboos that long governed children's literature. They now deal with a wide range of topics that are often quite contentious and very far from the standard fare of children's books. However, the fact remains that we are still discussing "controversial" picturebooks. "The gulf between childhood and adulthood" that was demonstrated by the very different response of adult and child readers to *Where the Wild Things Are*, according to its author, still seems to exist more than fifty years later. Sendak describes the dual response to the picturebook in the following words: "Adults find the book fearful; however, they misinterpret childhood. Children find the book silly, fun to read, and fun to look at" (1995: 142–43). Of course, not all the picturebooks examined here will be "silly" and "fun" for young readers. And they will probably all be more frightening or alarming for adults than *Where the Wild Things Are*. In his essay "On Fairy-Stories," J.R.R. Tolkien contends that fairy stories provide moral or emotional consolation through their happy ending, which he terms a *"eucatastrophe"* (1964: 68). Perhaps it is the absence of this "eucatastrophe" in many contemporary picturebooks inspired by traditional tales that accounts, at least in part, for their controversial status. Künnemann describes the horrifying events in *L'Ogresse en pleurs* as "an existential catastrophe" and "a drama of cosmic proportions" (2005: 17, 16). However, does that mean that children cannot comprehend and appreciate the appalling and tragic events? As Sendak maintains, picturebook artists understand that "children know a lot more than people give them credit for" and "are willing to deal with many dubious subjects that grownups think they shouldn't know about" (Sendak, 1988: 192). In an article devoted to "inappropriate picturebooks for young readers," Carole Scott points out quite rightly that "their authors must view their texts as appropriate, providing an introduction to our world rather than constructing a cocoon for children to shelter from it ... as artists, they shy away from presenting 'inappropriate' works that are not truthful to the reality they perceive" (2005: 12).

Like Oscar K, Sendak insists that the "anxiety" over such books comes not from children, but "from adults who feel that the book has to conform to some set ritual of ideas about childhood" (1988: 193). Adult mediators who try to keep controversial picturebooks out of the hands of young readers feel that they are protecting children. Sendak, on the other hand, sees children's authors and illustrators as the only ones who attempt to "protect [children] from life." "All we're trying to do in a serious work is to tell them about life," he claims (Sendak, 1988: 193). Acknowledging that *We Are All in the Dumps* is a "potent, evocative book," Vandergrift contends that Sendak "respects children's ability to deal with powerful and potentially controversial issues and ideas." Such controversial picturebooks engender "discussion, speculation, and a variety of interpretations" (Vandergrift, 1993: 119), and therefore offer adults an opportunity to broach very difficult subjects with children. Scott insists on the role of the adult mediator and "the filter of adult interpretation" in children's reception of works that "may seem shocking or inappropriate for young children" (2005: 12). Picturebook artists who understand the importance of exploring the nightmare side of child experience also recognize the importance of presenting potentially disturbing images and ideas in a manner that is appropriate for their young readers.

Maybe we don't need to be fearful after all!

References

Ardizzone, E. (1980) Creation of a Picture Book in Egoff, S., Stubbs, G.T. & Ashley, L.F. (eds) *Only Connect: Readings on Children's Literature*, 2nd edn. New York: Oxford University Press, pp. 289–298.

Beckett, S. (2002) *Recycling Red Riding Hood*. London: Routledge.

Beckett, S. (2008) *Red Riding Hood for All Ages: A Fairy-Tale Icon in Cross-Cultural Contexts*. Detroit, MI: Wayne State University Press.

Beckett, S. (2012) *Crossover Picturebooks: A Genre for All Ages*. London: Routledge.

Beckett, S. (2014) *Revisioning Red Riding Hood around the World: An Anthology of International Retellings*. Detroit, MI: Wayne State University Press.

Bernheimer, K. (n.d.) The Strange, Beautiful, Subterranean Power of Fairy Tales. *The Center for Fiction*, http://centerforfiction.org/why-fairy-tales-matter#sthash.JoHpMKkY.dpuf (accessed 27 April 2014).

Bettelheim, B. (1975) *The Uses of Enchantment: The Meaning and Importance of Fairy Tales*. New York: Random House.

Bruel, C. (1985) Christian Bruel: conforter l'intime des enfants, interview, in Épin, B. *Les livres de vos enfants, parlons-en!* Paris: Éditions Messidor/La Farandole, pp. 150–151.

Carpenter, H. (1985) *Secret Gardens: The Golden Age of Children's Literature*. London: George Allen & Unwin.

Doonan, J. (1994) Into the Dangerous World: We Are All in the Dumps with Jack and Guy by Maurice Sendak, *Signal*, 75: 155–171.

Doyle, R.P. (2010) *Banned Books: Challenging Our Freedom to Read*. Chicago, IL: American Library Association.

Garrett, J. (1993) "With Murderous Ending, Shocking, Menacing ...": Sarah Moon's Little Red Riding Hood 10 Years After, *Bookbird*, 31(3): 8–9.

Goldsworthy, K. (1985) Angela Carter, *Meanjin*, 44(1): 10.

Gundel, M. (2002) Leg dich zu mir, Rotkäppchen, *Frankfurter Allgemeine*, 5 January, 24, 38.

K.O. [O. Dalgaard] (2008) It's Not the Fact That It Is Said—In Fact It's Just the Way You Say It, *Danish Literary Magazine* (Autumn): 46–48.

Künnemann, H. (2005) How Much Cruelty Can a Children's Picturebook Stand? The Case of Wolf Erlbruch's *Die Menschenfresserin, Bookbird*, 43(1): 14–19.

Lanes, S. (1980) *The Art of Maurice Sendak*. New York: Harry N. Abrams, Inc.

Liberman, S. (2013) Banned Books Week: The Complete Grimms' Fairy Tales, *New York Public Library*, 27 September. www.nypl.org/blog/2013/09/27/banned-books-week-grimms-fairy-tales (accessed 2 April 2014).

Pfeuffer, C. (2013) 10 Controversial Kids' Books, *MSN Living*, 2 April. http://living.msn.com/family-parenting/the-family-room-blog-post?post=65efcc07-75a5-468b-9532-47806b8be4bl (accessed 5 April 2014).

Poncelet, B. (2005) À bâtons très très rompus ..., *La lettre de l'enfance et de l'adolescence*, 3(61): 57–62.

Rego, P. *Famousquotes.com*. www.famousquotes.com/search/fact/141 (accessed 30 April 2014).

Robinson, L. (1991) Review of *Little Red Riding Hood*, by Charles Perrault, illus. by Beni Montresor, *The Horn Book Guide* (July–December): 92.

Scott, C. (2005) A Challenge to Innocence: "Inappropriate Picturebooks for Young Readers," *Bookbird*, 3(1): 5–13.

Sendak, M. (1998) *Caldecott and Co.: Notes on Books and Pictures*, New York: Farrar, Straus and Giroux.

Sendak, M. (1995) Maurice Sendak, in Hopkins, L.B. (ed.) *Pauses: Autobiographical Reflections of 101 Creators of Children's Books*. New York: HarperCollins, pp. 142–143.

Tatar, M. (2003) *The Hard Facts of the Grimms' Fairy Tales*, 2nd edn. Princeton, NJ: Princeton University Press.

Tolkien, J.R.R. (1964) On Fairy-Stories, in *Tree and Leaf*. London: George Allen & Unwin, pp. 3–83.

Vandergrift, K.E. (1993) Review of Maurice Sendak's *We Are All in the Dumps with Jack and Guy, School Library Journal*, 39(10): 119.

Warner, M. (2000) *No Go the Bogeyman: Scaring, Lulling and Making Mock*. London: Vintage.

Zipes, J. (1993) *The Trials and Tribulations of Little Red Riding Hood: Versions of the Tale in Sociocultural Context*, 2nd edn. New York: Routledge.

Zipes, J. (2001) *Sticks and Stones: The Troublesome Success of Children's Literature from Slovenly Peter to Harry Potter*. New York: Routledge.

Children's Literature

Baum, L.F., illus. Denslow, W.W. (1900) Introduction. *The Wonderful Wizard of Oz*. Chicago, IL: George M. Hill.

Belloc, H., illus. Temple Blackwood, B. (1907) *Cautionary Tales for Children: Designed for the Admonition of Children between the Ages of Eight and Fourteen Years*. London: Eveleigh Nash.

Bruel, C., illus. Wachs, P. (1986) *Vous oubliez votre cheval*. Paris: Le Sourire qui mord.

Busch, W. (1990) *Max und Moritz: eine Bubengeschichte in sieben streichen*. Bindlach: Loewe Verlag.

Carrer, C. (2007) *Barbablù*. Rome: Editore Donzelli.

Clement, C., illus. Forestier, I. (2000) *Un petit chaperon rouge*. Paris: Grasset & Fasquelle.

Dayre, V., illus. Erlbruch, W. (1996) *L'ogresse en pleurs*. Toulouse: Milan.

Ekman, F. (1985) *Rødhatten og Ulven*. Oslo: Cappelen.

Grimm, W. & J., Segal, L. & Sendak, M. (1973) *The Juniper Tree and Other Tales from Grimm*, 2 vols. New York: Farrar, Straus and Giroux.

Grimm, W. & J. (1980) *Kinder- und Hausmärchen Band 1*, Märchen no 1–86. Stuttgart: Philipp Reclam.

Grimm, W. & J., illus. Hyman, T.S. (1983) *Little Red Riding Hood*. New York: Holiday House.

Grimm, W. & J., illus. Dumas, O. (2001) *El señor Korbes y otros cuentos de Grimm*. Valencia: Media Vaca.

Grimm, W. & J., illus. Janssen, S. (2001) *Rotkäppchen*. Munich: Carl Hanser Verlag.

Hoffman, H. (1845) *Lustige Geschichten und drollige Bilder*. Frankfurt am Main: Literarische Anstalt (J. Rütten).

Hoffman, H., adap. Ruy-Vidal, F., illus. Lapointe, C. (1972) *Pierre l'ébouriffé: Histoires pas très drôles, d'un passé toujours présent*. Boissy-St-Léger: F. Ruy-Vidal and Harlin Quist.

Hofman, W. (1998) *Zwart als inkt is het verhaal van Sneeuwwitje en de zeven dwergen*. Amsterdam: Querido.

Holzwarth, W., illus. Erlbruch, W. (1989) *Vom kleinen Maulwurf der wissen wollte, wer ihm auf den Kopf gemacht hat*. Wuppertal: Peter Hammer Verlag.

Ikhlef, A., illus. Gauthier, A. (1998). *Mon Chaperon Rouge*. Paris: Seuil Jeunesse.

Ikhlef, A., illus. Gauthier, A. (2002) *Ma Peau d'Âne*. Paris: Seuil Jeunesse.

Innocenti, R. (1985) *Rose Blanche*. Story and illus. Innocenti, R., text Innocenti, R. & Gallaz, C., trans. Creative Education. Mankato, MN: Creative Education.

Innocenti, R. (2012) *The Girl in Red*. Story and illus. Innocenti, R., text Frisch, A. Mankato, MN: Creative Editions.

Joiret, P., illus. Bruyère, X. (1991) *Mina je t'aime*. Paris: L'École des loisirs.

Juan, A. (2001) *Snowhite*. Onil: Edicions de Ponent.

Perrault, C. (1697) *Histoires ou contes du temps passé avec moralités*. Paris: Claude Barbin.

Perrault, C., illus. Doré, G. (1861) *Les Contes de Perrault*. Paris: Pierre-Jules Hetzel.

Perrault, C., illus. Moon, S. (1983) *Little Red Riding Hood*. Mankato, MN: Creative Education.

Perrault, C., illus. Claverie, J. (1991) *La Barbe Bleu*. Paris: Albin Michel.

Perrault, C., illus. Montresor, B. (1991) *Little Red Riding Hood*. New York: Doubleday.

Perrault, C., illus. Delacroix, S. (2000) *La Barbe Bleue*. Tournai: Casterman.

Pommaux, Y. (1993) *John Chatterton, détective*. Paris: L'École des loisirs.

Poncelet, B. (1997) *Chez elle ou chez elle*. Paris: Seuil Jeunesse.

Poncelet, B. (2003) *Les Cubes*. Paris: Seuil Jeunesse.

Rego, P. (2010) *Nursery Rhymes*. London: Thames & Hudson.

Sendak, M. (1963) *Where the Wild Things Are*. New York: Harper & Row.

Sendak, M. (1993) *We Are All in the Dumps with Jack and Guy*. New York: HarperCollins.

Van de Vendel, E., illus. Vandenabeele, I. (2003) *Rood Rood Roodkapje*. Wielsbeke: Uitgeverij De Eenhoorn.

DID THEY LIVE HAPPILY EVER AFTER? REWRITING FAIRY TALES FOR A CONTEMPORARY AUDIENCE[1]

Laura Tosi

A long time ago, people used to tell magical stories of wonder and enchantment. Those stories were called Fairy Tales.

  * Those stories are not in this book. The stories in this book are almost Fairy Tales. But not quite. The stories in this book are Fairly Stupid Tales. [...] In fact, you should definitely go read the stories now, because the rest of this

---

1 From *Hearts of Lightness: The Magic of Children's Literature* (Venice: Universita Ca'Foscari Di Venezia, 2001). All notes are Tosi's unless in brackets.

introduction just goes on and on and doesn't really say anything. [...] So stop now. I mean it. Quit reading. Turn the page. If you read this last sentence, it won't tell you anything. (Scieszka 1992)

WE HAVE OBVIOUSLY TRAVELLED A long way from the familiar "Once upon a time" opening: a promiscuous anarchic genre which digests high and low elements, the fairy tale has undergone a process of textual and social alteration in the course of the centuries.[1]

The fairy tale, relying on various forms of cultural transmission and ever-changing ideological configuration for its very existence, has pride of place in the system of children's literature. Like many children's genres, it is characterized by a much higher degree of intertextuality than general literature. The term "intertextuality," still relatively recent, may not yet have reached a definitive formulation (see Kristeva 1970; Genette 1982; Worton 1990; Clayton and Rothstein 1991. Among Italian contributors see Polacco 1998 and Bernardelli 2000), but in its extended sense, it is an essential term, defining the intersection of texts or cultural and ideological discourses (see Segre 1984) within the literature system: as Stephens (1992) has put it succinctly: "intertextuality is concerned with how meaning is produced at points of interaction" (16). No text exists in isolation from other texts or from social and historical contexts (see Lotman 1980). The initiating and socializing function of children's literature, concerned, among other things, with transmitting the cultural inheritance of values, experiences, and prohibitions, makes it necessary to address an audience whose decoding must rely on the reader's recognition of familiar genres and narratives—hence the value of retelling as a strategy to activate the implied child reader's often partial competency and this reader's aesthetic pleasure of recognition and appreciation. Fairy tales in particular—possibly the first examples of poetic form we confront in life—as part of contemporary (even consumer) culture, are constantly refashioned, restructured, and defamiliarized in modern times, so that they resemble, as Marina Warner says,

[...] an archeological site that has been plundered by tomb robbers, who have turned the strata upside down and inside out and thrown it all back again in any old order. Evidence of conditions from past social and economic arrangements co-exist in the tale with the narrator's innovations: Angela Carter's Beauty is lost to the Beast at cards, a modern variation on the ancient memory,

---

1   By "fairy tales" I mean canonical fairy tales of the Western tradition which have always been called by that name even if they do not feature fairy or fairy-tale characters. I am aware of the looseness of the term, which overlaps with very similar genres, like the folk tale, the wonder tale, legends etc.

locked into the plot of Beauty and the Beast, that daughters were given in marriage by their fathers without being consulted on the matter. (Warner 1994: xix)

The scholar and common reader alike need a high threshold for tolerance as far as reinterpretation is concerned, since even a hasty overview of the rise of the literary fairy tale in Europe reveals further evidence of its hybridity and intertextual nature. As we are often reminded, the fairy tale was not even a genre meant primarily for children. By incorporating oral traditions into a highly literary and aristocratic discourse, the fairy tale dictated and celebrated the standards of *civilité* in the French salons of the seventeenth century (in Italy a century earlier, literary fairy tales circulated in the vernacular for an educated audience of upper-class men and women). As Zipes (1983) has written, challenging the assumption that the best fairy tales are universal and timeless:

The shape of the fairy tale discourse, of the configuration within the tales, was molded and bound by the European civilizing process which was undergoing profound changes in the sixteenth, seventeenth and eighteenth centuries. The profundity of the literary fairy tale for children, its magic, its appeal, is marked by these changes, for it is one of the cornerstones of our bourgeois heritage. As such, it both revolutionized the institution of literature at that time while abiding by its rules. (10, and see Zipes 1999)

Literary appropriation of oral folk tales also characterizes the Grimms' enterprise of collecting traditional folk tales of German origin (see Kamenetsky 1992), which, in translation, had a powerful influence on further developments of the genre. One of the most common misconceptions about the brothers Grimm's method regards their informants: far from being illiterate peasants, as has often been claimed, the Grimms' storytellers belonged to a cultivated middle class which might have been familiar with written, literary versions of folk tales. Any scholar who handles fairy tales (as the Grimms were perfectly aware) must necessarily abandon the idea of a faithful, "original" tale (for example, the myth of an "Ur-Little Red Riding Hood") and take the plunge in the wide sea of folklore variants in different countries or centuries, with diverse historical perspectives and ideological conformations. In our own time, the younger generation is probably best acquainted with the Disney versions of *Snow White* and *Cinderella*, only loosely based on the Perrault and Grimms plots and characterization, with much simplification and reinforcement of stereotypes of female passivity (see Zipes 1979 and Stone 1975). The wholesale exploitation of fairy tale and folklore material by the mass media has only recently been studied by critics and provides one of the latest additions to the abundant and heterogeneous body of criticism on the fairy tale.

As a transitional genre, intended for children and adults alike, the fairy tale has been made the object of several critical approaches. These range from the anthropological (for example, in studies of comparative mythologies and recurrent and cross-cultural folktale themes) to the psychoanalytic, of which Bettelheim's (1977) interpretation of the Grimms' tales as significant instruments in helping the process of maturation in a child is probably the best-known, to the formalistic and structuralist methods of classifying folktales in catalogues, or examining individual structural components as functions (see Propp 1928/1968 and Bremond 1977). When we analyze folk or fairy tales from the vantage point of children's literature, then, it is inevitable that we should use an integrated cross-cultural, interdisciplinary approach. In the last few decades, Jack Zipes has focussed critical attention on the social function of fairy tales, thus providing the basis for an ideological critique of dominant cultural patterns in fairy tales, previously perceived as natural, but "which appear to have been preserved because they reinforce male hegemony in the civilization process" (Zipes 1986: 9). Many contemporary rewritings of fairy tales tend to challenge the conservative norms of social behaviour and the implications of gender roles in fairy tales. Feminist critics and writers have collaborated in the critical exposure of fairy tales as narratives voicing, in the main, patriarchal values, both by providing critical readings which investigate the social construction of gender and by rewriting traditional fairy tales in order to produce non-sexist adult and children's versions.

However, the compulsion to retell or rewrite fairy tales in order to subvert historically inscribed ideological meanings should not be considered exclusively a contemporary practice. One only needs to recall the extraordinary flowering of the fairy tale in Victorian England, a flowering which succeeded the well-documented English resistance to fairy tales in the eighteenth century, born out of a combination of Puritan disapproval and a rationalist distrust of the imagination. Fairy tales, as carriers of reformist ideas and social criticism, not only provided Dickens and Wilde, for example, with a symbolic and imaginative form for their protest against the growing alienation of an increasingly industrialized society, they also questioned stereotypical gender roles and patterns (Zipes 1987 and 1999). Tales like MacDonald's *The Light Princess* (1893), a parody of "Sleeping Beauty," or Mary De Morgan's *A Toy Princess* (1877), the story of an unconventional princess who is rejected by her court in favour of a more docile toy replica, anticipate feminist issues and concerns in their depiction of strong heroines who refuse to conform to the passive female ideal of the age. In Edith Nesbit's *The Last of the Dragons* (1925/1975), for example, the traditional pattern of "prince rescues princess" is satirically reversed. Though familiar with endless tales where princesses, tied to a pole, patiently wait for a prince

[435]

to rescue them from the dragon ("such tales are always told in royal nurseries at twilight, so the Princess knew what she had to expect"), the heroine objects to this:

"All the princes I know are such very silly little boys," she told her father. "Why must I be rescued by a prince?"

"It's always done, my dear," said the King, taking his crown off and putting it on the grass, for they were alone in the garden, and even kings must unbend sometimes. [...]

"Father, darling, couldn't we tie up one of the silly little princes for the dragon to look at—and then I could go and kill the dragon and rescue the prince? I fence much better than any of the princes we know."

"What an unladylike idea!" said the King, and put his crown on again, for he saw the Prime Minister coming with a basket of new-laid bills for him to sign.

"Dismiss the thought, my child. I rescued your mother from a dragon, and you don't want to set yourself up above her, I should hope?"

"But this is the last dragon. It is different from all other dragons." (10)

In the end the strong, fencing princess and the pale weak prince "with a head full of mathematics and philosophy" (10) come to an agreement ("he could refuse her nothing," 12) about the way to handle the dragon, who is easily tamed by the princess and becomes a valuable asset to the court as a sort of scaly aeroplane employed to fly children around the kingdom or to the seaside in summer.

The impact of these protofeminist precedents in fairy-tale tradition should not be underestimated: Jay Williams's "The Practical Princess" and "Petronella" (1978) follow a very similar pattern in their depiction of a brave and assertive princess. Williams's ideal audience includes teenagers and adults; in the second half of the twentieth century the fairy tale, once again crossing the boundary between children's and adult literature, was appropriated by postmodernist and feminist writers like Angela Carter, Anne Sexton and Margaret Atwood, as a powerful discourse for the representation of gender (see Bacchilega 1997). Fairy tales have also served as structuring devices for both canonical novels (see the *Cinderella* and the *Beauty and the Beast* subtexts in *Jane Eyre*) and for popular romance. Rewritings both for children and adults assume the reader's knowledge of the original tales, thus encouraging the reader to take note of the formal changes which have led to an ideological reorientation of the tales.

In this essay I intend to give a survey (albeit incomplete and partial, given the ever-growing number of fairy-tale adaptations in the English language) of rewriting practices and techniques, although, as mentioned earlier, it is impossible to trace an archetypal "first telling" or version of a particular fairy tale, nor can the critic expect to fix a fairy tale "hypotext." Genette (1982), in his *Palimpsestes*, defines a hypertextual relationship as "toute relation unissant un texte B (que j'appellerai *hypertexte*) à un texte antérieur A (que j'appellerai, bien sûr, *hypotexte*) sur lequel il se greffe d'une manière qui n'est pas celle du commentaire" (11–12).[1] With reference to fairy tales, Genette's concept of the hypotext as a single and identifiable entity needs to be enlarged and renamed as "hypotextual class," which would include all those versions of a single fairy tale that have combined to create the reader's cultural and diegetic construct of that traditional tale in the canon (the hypotextual class of the *Cinderella* tales, for example). Ironically, the constant restructuring and rewriting of fairy tales' hypotextual classes, in order to adapt them to the new social and moral requirements of contemporary audiences, has had the effect of preserving and encoding traditional fairy tales within the canon so that they are still widely read, alongside more challenging and subversive versions (see Tatar 1992).

In an attempt to classify different practices of fairy-tale adaptations, so as to make this abundant and heterogeneous material easier to analyse, I have chosen to discuss three types of fairy-tale rewritings which I have called: a) "morally correct" rewritings; b) postmodernist/metafictional rewritings; c) feminist rewritings. There are several overlappings in the three groups: many adaptations could be grouped indifferently under more than one category as to their ideological orientation and often share formal changes (changes of setting, place and time, focalization—Genette's "transpositions diégétiques,"[2] 341). In the first group, however, I shall discuss primarily rewritings which aim at exposing the presence of an ambiguous morality or a moral gap in the hypotextual class, by superimposing a new ethics of justice and human compassion on traditional tales which reward, for example, acquisitive behaviour. The second group includes tales which emphasise their fictional and conventional status, which leads to a more or less good-natured critique of ideological assumptions about the culture of the child. The third group is probably the most widely studied and includes fairy-tale adaptations which, by breaking established diegetic patterns, like "Princess marries prince," subvert accepted notions of female cultural identity.

Discussions about the ethics or justice of traditional fairy tales are not a recent phenomenon: one only needs to think of the political-ideological appropriation of the Grimms' tales in the Nazi era (Kamenetsky 1992).

---

1 ["Any relationship uniting a text B (which I will call hypertext) with an earlier text A (which I will call, naturally, hypotext), in which the later text is grafted on the earlier text in a manner that isn't that of a commentary."]

2 [Diegetic transpositions: i.e., rewritten narratives.]

Even to the naïve reader it is painfully (or enjoyably) clear that the youngest brother often gets his fortune by chance rather than merit, that valiant little tailors are rewarded for deceit, and that the Giant's seven daughters do not really deserve to die at their father's hand. Many scholarly explanations of fairy or folk-tale ethics have been provided, from the analysis of the Grimms' own moral outlook to the discussion of the peculiar kind of knowledge about life that fairy tales were meant to instil: the value of resourcefulness and risk-taking rather than of traditional morality, and the importance of perseverance. Contemporary retellings have challenged the value system of some traditional fairy tales, which, contrary to popular belief, do not always reward good characters and punish evil ones.

This redressing of the moral balance can be effected by means of a change in the narrating voice and the point of view. In the traditional story "Jack and the Beanstalk," the young boy Jack comes into possession of magic beans which allow him to climb a beanstalk and reach the giant's house. He is fed by the giant's wife who takes pity on the starved boy each time he visits their house. As we all remember, Jack first steals the giant's gold, then the magic hen who lays golden eggs, and ultimately the giant's golden harp.[1] By chopping away at the beanstalk on his way home so that the giant falls to the ground on his head, Jack secures for his mother and himself a wealthy future, with the giant's gold, hen, and harp.

Alvin Granowsky's *Giants Have Feelings, Too* (1996) exposes the ambiguous morality of the tale, which sets greed as the rewarded virtue, by having the giant's wife retell the story:

I am sure that the rest of you people living down below are very nice. But that boy, Jack, is something else. After I was so kind to him, he stole from us, and he hurt my husband. All because we are giants! That's no reason to take our treasures or to make my husband fall on his head. See what you think. (3)

The giant couple is reframed as good-natured and middle class, with grown-up children, with savings which are a necessity for their old age, and with an innocent love of food, Mrs. Giant being apparently an exceptional cook:

Then Herbert came in singing "Fe! Fi! Fo! Fum! My wife's cooking is Yum! Yum!

---

1   In the English version of the tale, the giant is the villain of the piece. One only needs to remember his
     "Fe fi fo Fum
     I smell the blood of an Englishman
     Be he alive or be he dead
     I'll grind his bones to make my bread."

Yum! Be it baked or be it fried, we finish each meal with her tasty pies!" (13)

The reaction to Jack's treachery is a common-sense open-hearted discussion between husband and wife:

"Oh, dear," Herbert said. "We can only hope that the boy's mother will find out what he has done. Surely, she will make him return our things. Maybe she will even return them herself."

"You're right, Herbert," I said. "When his mother brings back our gold and our hen, I'll be here to thank her." (18)

Jack, as we all know, only comes back to collect the giant's last treasure, the golden harp:

"Stop! You're stealing!" Herbert yelled as he ran after Jack. "Don't you know it's wrong to steal?" (22)

The moral at the end of the tale turns into a direct appeal to the reader for sympathy:

He had no right to take what was ours or to hurt my husband. Giants have feelings, you know. You wouldn't hurt a giant's feelings, would you? (25)

One interesting aspect of this retelling is that both stories are contained in the same book with a "flip me over" system so that the reader can access both versions of the story at the same time (the series is called "Another Point of View") and question, rather than take passively for granted, Jack's real motives for his actions.

Garowsky's adaptations seem very serious when compared with Dahl's inventive and highly irreverent retellings in *Revolting Rhymes* (1982/1984) and *Rhyme Stew* (1989). His version of the story of *Goldilocks and the Three Bears*, in *Revolting Rhymes*, addresses the issue of Goldilocks' infraction of the basic rules of polite behaviour (i.e., entering a home without an invitation, touching other people's things, breaking an item of furniture in someone else's house) which parental figures teach children in order to ease their assimilation into the adult community. The socializing and cautionary function of fairy tales is generally dependent on the transmission of a code of social behaviour and norms from an older voice of experience to a younger audience badly in need of moral and social guidance.

Goldilocks is called in the course of the story "little toad," "little louse," "a delinquent little tot," "a brazen little crook"—graphic and comic expressions which, rather than celebrating the cuteness of the little blonde girl, convey adult horror at the misbehaved, unrestrained child's invasion of one's personal space. One interesting aspect of this retelling is that Dahl is clearly playing with the figure of his ideal reader—not so much the house-proud bourgeois wife who takes pride in "one small children's dining-chair, Elizabethan, very rare" smashed by Goldilocks, as the irreverent and playful reader, to whom he addresses one of his characteristic sadistic endings. In this version Big Bear advises Baby Bear to go upstairs and eat his porridge: "But as it is inside mademoiselle, you'll have to eat her up as well" (39).

Among the various kinds of correspondence that the Ahlbergs' *The Jolly Postman* (1986) delivers to fairy-tale characters, there is a repentant letter by Goldilocks, addressed to Mr. and Mrs. Bear, Three Bears Cottage, the Woods, which says:

Dear Mr and Mrs Bear and Baby Bear,

I am very sorry indeed that I cam into your house and ate Baby Bears porij. Mummy says I am a bad girl. I hardly eat any porij when she cooks it she says. Daddy says he will mend the little chair.

Love from
Goldilocks

In one of the next tableaux, among the several fairy-tale characters with whom Goldilocks is celebrating her birthday (a little pig, Humpty Dumpty, the magic goose, etc) Baby Bear has pride of place near the little girl, who has obviously been forgiven. The Ahlbergs' ingenious toy and picture book, which relies on the reader's knowledge of other children's texts, creates an appealing context for a genial twist in the morality of the tale. It is the heroine herself, in her own tentative and childish writing, who condemns her selfish behaviour and promises to mend her ways.

Not all the protagonists of fairy tales, when allowed to speak and give their side of the story, are as convincing or trustworthy. In Scieszka's *The True Story of the Three Little Pigs* (1989), Mr. Wolf's attempt to rehabilitate his good name is only partly convincing:

I'm the wolf. Alexander T. Wolf.
  You can call me Al.
  I don't know how this whole Big Bad Wolf thing got started, but it's all wrong.
  Maybe it's because of our diet.
  Hey, it's not my fault wolves eat cute little animals like bunnies and sheep

and pigs. That's just the way we are. If cheeseburgers were cute, folks would probably think you were Big and Bad, too.

A contemporary audience, due to environmental awareness, might be willing to concede that wolves eat little pigs as part of the nature food chain and not because they are intrinsically bad. Mr. Wolf's version of the story, however, lays the blame for the destruction of the pigs' houses on the wolf's bad cold and urge to sneeze while he was innocently asking to borrow a cup of sugar for his granny's birthday cake.

Another example of a fairy-tale retelling which, by giving voice to the traditional villain of the piece, attempts to justify his/her actions is Donna Jo Napoli's *The Magic Circle* (1983), marketed to a young adult audience. This prequel, in novel form, to *Hansel and Gretel*, explains the reason for the witch's cannibalistic drive. As the "Ugly One" unfolds the story of her past as a loving mother and blessed healer, the reader learns of the circumstances which led her to be claimed and possessed by devils. The description of her death, which she willingly brings about in order to disobey the demons' order to harm the children, is a tale of liberation and purification from evil.

"A site on which metanarratival and textual processes interact, either to reproduce or contest significance" (Stephen and McCallum 1998: 9), the retold fairy tale on the one hand can distance itself from conventional concepts of morality, perceived as unsuitable or outmoded guidelines for the child's social and moral development, on the other it may suggest a new ethics of compassion and respect for other people's culture and possessions, even extending it, in some cases, to canonically undeserving characters[1] whose motives and actions are defamiliarized in order to be re-encoded in a new system of beliefs.

A second group of fairy tale adaptations includes self-reflexive, often explicitly postmodernist, versions, where make-believe or illusionist conventions are exposed in order to highlight the hypercodification of fairy-tale conventions. In the case of *The Stinky Cheese Man and Other Fairly Stupid Tales*, which opened the present discussion, basic literary conventions are parodied so that the young reader is invited to reflect on what constitutes a book, and the rules that are normally followed by the author, the editor, the publisher etc. In Scieszka's book, essentially postmodernist in its critical and ironic revisiting and disruption of the cultural and literary pattern of the fairy tale, the table of contents falls and squashes all the characters of the first story of the collection ("Chicken Licken"), the dedication is upside down, the "lazy narrator" at some point disappears, leaving a blank page, the little red hen is never

---

1 For example, in Robert Coover's retelling of Snow White for an adult audience, "The Dead Queen" (1973), the prince feels sorry for the harsh punishment which is meted out for Snow White's stepmother as he tries, in vain, to kiss her back to life.

given the opportunity to tell her story and the various narratives are constantly interrupted by arguments between the narrator and the characters:

> "Now it's time for the best story in the book—my story. Because Once Upon a Time I traded our last cow for three magic beans and … hey, Giant. What are you doing down here? You're wrecking my whole story."
>
> "I DON'T LIKE THAT STORY," said the Giant.
>
> "YOU ALWAYS TRICK ME."
>
> "That's the best part," said Jack.
>
> "FEE FI FUM FORY I HAVE MADE MY OWN STORY."
>
> "Great rhyme, Giant […] But there's no room for it. So why don't you climb back up the beanstalk. I'll be up in a few minutes to steal your gold and your singing harp."
>
> "I'LL GRIND YOUR BONES TO MAKE MY BREAD."
>
> "[…] And there's another little thing that's been bugging me. Could you please stop talking in uppercase letters? It really messes up the page."

In such a context of textual and narrative instability a number of fairy-tale retellings are defined by parodic hyperrealism and comic dismissal of the magic and romantic element. "The Really Ugly Duckling" grows up to be just a really ugly duck instead of a beautiful swan; the frog lies to the princess about being a handsome prince under a spell ("'I was just kidding,' said the frog. He jumped back into the pond and the princess wiped the frog slime off her lips. The End"); the Prince, in order to make sure of marrying the girl of his dreams, places a bowling ball under the one hundred mattresses.

"Cinderrumpelstiltskin" in Scieszka's collection furnishes an example of fairy-tale conflation, or, as the Italian educationalist and children's writer Gianni Rodari would call it, a fairy-tale salad, "una insalata di favole" (Rodari 1973/1997: 72): Cinderella, expecting the customary visit of her fairy godmother to provide her with a dress, glass slippers and a coach to go to the ball, sends Rumpelstiltskin (a character from another Grimms' tale who knows how to spin gold) away ("I am not supposed to talk to strangers," she says), consequently missing the opportunity to become rich ("Please don't cry," he said, "I can help you spin straw into gold." "I don't think that will do me much good […] If you don't have a dress, it doesn't really matter"). Scieszka's Cinderella, who obviously intends to be faithful to the traditional version, is not rewarded at the end (the ironic subtitle to the tale is "The girl who really blew it").

Fairy-tale salads, based on the comic coexistence of heterogeneous fairy-tale plots and character types, create playful conflations of traditional fairy tales which are easily recognized by the implied child reader who brings his/her knowledge of the character's familiar traits to bear on the new version. These highly intertextual and metafictional versions work within conventions, casting well-known fairy characters in different settings and story lines or, by contrast, combining two or more plots with the same protagonist. An example of the latter kind of procedure is the conflation of *Red Riding Hood* with *The Three Little Pigs*, both based on the powerful and murderous figure of the wolf. In Dahl's *Revolting Rhymes* (1982/1984) Pig number 3, who has built his house of bricks, but is made nervous by the wolf's huffing and puffing, phones Little Red Riding Hood for help. Having already shot a wolf in her own story earlier in the collection, the resourceful girl can now boast a "lovely furry wolfskin coat," but the ending has an unexpected twist, as the pig makes the mistake of trusting Miss Riding Hood. At the end of the story, not only can she boast of two wolfskin coats, "But when she goes from place to place, / She has a PIGSKIN TRAVELLING CASE" (47).

Similarly, in the already quoted Ahlbergs' Postman book, the wolf receives a letter from a law-firm representing the interests of both Little Red Riding Hood and the Three Little Pigs:

Dear Mr. Wolf

We are writing to you on behalf of our client, Miss Riding-Hood, concerning her grandma. Miss Hood tells us that you are presently occupying her grandma's cottage and wearing her grandma's clothes without this lady's permission. [...] On a separate matter, we must inform you that Messrs. Three Little Pigs Ltd. are now firmly resolved to sue for damages [...]

Yours sincerely,
Harold Meeney, solicitor

Even in fairy tales which do not deviate from a recognizable story line, characters often show an unusual degree of knowledge of fairy-tale conventions and of their own fictional status. Their awareness of the conventionality of stock situations and the outcome of their expected choices may lead them to question and change the task or the role they are assigned in the story. In Jane Yolen's *Sleeping Ugly* (1997), Prince Jojo, who, "being the kind of young man who read fairy tales, [...] knew just what to do" (49), decides to devote special consideration to the issue of kissing and thus awakening the three ladies who lie asleep in the cottage, covered in spiderwebs. The most striking woman is the beautiful, albeit cruel, princess, protagonist of many fairy tales: "But Jojo knew that kind of princess. He had three cousins just like her. Pretty on the outside. Ugly within" (59). Prince Jojo decides to let the beautiful sleeping princess lie, so that she is later used as conversation piece or coat hanger, and kisses (and marries) instead plain Jane, blessed with a kindly disposition, with whom he will attain marital bliss if not social elevation or riches.

Fairy-tale characters who are not well informed regarding fairy-tale conventions are often at a disadvantage in contemporary retellings. In Drew Lamm's *The Prog Frince. A Mixed-Up Tale* (1999), the only chance for the heroine to break the spell, as the reader discovers only at the end of the story, is to learn "The Frog Prince" and behave accordingly towards the talking frog. A sensible girl, Jane dismisses tales of the imagination as untrue:

> "Do you read fairy tales?," interrupted the frog, "like the Frog Prince?"
> "No," said Jane. "They don't make sense. And they're not true."
> "What do you dream about?" he asked.
> "I don't," said Jane.
> "What do you do?"
> "I go to school," she said, glaring at the frog.
> "Unfortunate," croaked the frog, and he leapt off Jane's hand.

Only when she is ready to sit and listen to *The Frog Prince* and therefore begins to grow fond of the frog, does she recover her lost memory and identity as Jaylee, the prince's lover of base descent whom he had to forsake:

> Jaylee blinked. The spell was broken. In front of Jaylee stood the prince.
> He smiled.
> "I thought the princess had to kiss the frog," said Jaylee.
> "You're not a princess. You had to miss me."
> "Magnificent," said Jaylee. "I'd rather kiss you now, when you are not so green."

In this story the need for familiarity with fairy stories if one is to fulfil one's destiny (even if in a slightly different manner than that suggested in the canonical story) is constantly reasserted.

The comic retelling of *Snow White* in the "Happily Ever Laughter" series (Thaler 1997) has "Schmoe White and the Seven Dorfs" forming a pop group in which Schmoe will play the part of lead singer by virtue of her role in the fairy story:

> "We'll call ourselves 'Schmoe White and the Seven Dorfs,'" said Schmoe.
> "Why do you get top billing?" asked Grouchy.
> "Because if it weren't for me, you wouldn't be in this story," replied Schmoe.

Similarly, in Margaret Atwood's "Unpopular Gals" (1994), the character's self-consciousness as the narrative pivot of the folk tale emerges as the female villain is given a voice:

> The thing about those good daughters is, they're so good. Obedient and passive. Sniveling, I might add. No get-up-and-go. What would become of them if it weren't for me? Nothing, that's what. All they'd ever do is the housework, which seems to feature largely in these stories. They'd marry some peasant, have seventeen kids, and get 'A Dutiful Wife' engraved on their tombstones, if any. Big deal. […] You can wipe your feet on me, twist my motives around all if you like, you can dump millstones on my head and drown me in the river, but you can't get me out of the story. I'm the plot, babe, and don't you ever forget it. (11–12. See also Gilbert and Gubar's analysis of "Snow White" in *The Madwoman in the Attic* 1979: 38–39)

A strong narratorial voice (especially when it is intradiegetic) in fairy-tale adaptations (whether directed to an adult or a child reader) obviously implies that the story is a fictional construct which needs to be told (and retold) in order to exist, and relies on a number of diegetic, linguistic, as well as cultural and moral rules in order to be recognizable as such. In metafictional rewritings for children, a form of detachment and the surprise following defamiliarization are encouraged, rather than emphatic alignment with the characters. Adaptations of traditional fairy tales continue to awake the child reader's sense of wonder and humour through the introduction of new narrative incidents, and highly recognizable characters who, by reflecting on their fictional status, engage in playful alliance with the child reader—the aesthetic pleasure of recognition should not be underestimated.

It is to be noted, however, that child readers do not always tolerate retellings or modifications of their favourite stories. Within contemporary retellings, experiments of juxtaposing traditional fairy plot-types with unconventional patterns may serve to dramatize the child's resistance to letting go the stereotypes of the hypotextual class. The adaptation can turn into a hilarious battleground between orthodoxy and innovation, as in Storr's *Little Polly Riding Hood* (1953/1993). In this version the wolf is unable to assimilate the refashioning of the story of which he is a central character:

> "Good afternoon, Polly," said the wolf. "Where are you going, may I ask?"
>
> "Certainly," said Polly. "I am going to see my grandma."
>
> "I thought so!" said the wolf, looking very much pleased. "I've been reading about a girl who went to visit her grandmother and it's a very good story."

"Little Red Riding Hood?" suggested Polly.

"That's it!" cried the wolf. "I read it out loud to myself as a bedtime story. I did enjoy it. The wolf eats up the grandmother, and Little Red Riding Hood. It's almost the only story where the wolf really gets anything to eat," he added sadly.

"But in my book he doesn't get Red Riding Hood," said Polly. "Her father comes in just in time to save her."

"Oh, he doesn't in my book!" said the wolf. "I expect mine is the true story, and yours is just invented. [...] Where does your grandmother live, Polly Riding Hood?"

"Over the other side of town," answered Polly.

The wolf frowned.

"It ought to be 'Through the Wood,'" he said. "But perhaps town will do. How do you get there, Polly Riding Hood?"

"First I take a train and then I take a bus," said Polly.

The wolf stamped his foot.

"No, no, no, no!" he shouted. "That's all wrong. You can't say that. You've got to say, 'By the path winding through the trees,' or something like that. You can't go by trains and buses and things. It isn't fair. [...] it won't work, [...] You just can't say that!" (234–35)

The wolf's unwillingness to adapt to the new story, his blind adherence to the traditional configuration of Little Red Riding Hood, and his refusal to accept major changes in society (like modern means of transport), as well as a more active and assertive version of the tale, will lead him to frustration and defeat. The wolf may thus come to embody the young reader's anxiety about unfamiliar retellings of fairy tales, which pose a threat to his/her conventional assumptions and expectations about gender roles and social behaviour.

There is no need to expatiate on the fact that, as educators and psychotherapists have demonstrated, fairy tales do influence the way children conceive the world in terms of power relations, patterns of behaviour, and gender roles.

The third group of fairy-tale adaptations for children that I shall be examining shortly addresses precisely the issue of presenting a non-sexist vision of the world in fairy tales. As Zipes (1986) has remarked: "the political purpose and design of most of the tales are clear: the narratives are symbolical representations of the author's critique of the patriarchal status quo and their desire to change the current socialization process" (xi–xii). In feminist rewritings of canonical fairy tales a tendency to retell princess stories which dispense with marriage-dominated plots and the traditional equation between beauty and goodness can be detected. In both adult and children's modern revisions of princess stories, plots and patterns as well as characterization are subverted and deconstructed in order to reshape female cultural identity into that of an independent, liberated, and self-confident heroine. A new generation of smart princesses can oppose tyrannical or stereotyped role models by assuming active roles or considering alternative options for their self-definition as females: in A. Thompert's *The Clever Princess* (1977), self-fulfilment can be achieved through active involvement in ruling one's kingdom rather than by getting married.

Rewriting *Sleeping Beauty*, the tale that features the most emblematic example of female passivity, can turn into a positive attempt to acculturate women to new rewarding social roles as well as pointing out the value of overcoming ignorance and of intelligent initiative (see Lieberman 1972/1986). Katherine Paterson's *The Wide-Awake Princess* (2000) is given a very precious gift by her judicious fairy godmother, that of being wide-awake all her waking hours in a sleeping world (that is, in a world where greedy and indifferent nobles live in luxury). Throughout the story the value of seeing for oneself (the poverty and unhappiness of the people, for example), the value of being able to assess a situation, and the value of working to spread awareness are constantly reaffirmed. Only by keeping her eyes open while mixing with the people of the kingdom can Princess Miranda form a plan to help her people and regain her rightful place as a queen—a strikingly different model for female behaviour from that of submissive sleeping beauty waiting for a brave prince to kiss and wake her (on *Sleeping Beauty* as a literary model for female passivity, see Kolbenschlag 1979).

Cultural autonomy, and a sense of compassion and sisterhood for other girls who embody more conventional prototypes of female passivity, are emphasized in Harriet Hennan's *The Forest Princess* (1974), a rewriting of Rapunzel, where the lonely heroine is free to climb up and down the tower by a ladder. After having rescued a prince, she learns of gender differences and spends many happy hours with him. In the neutral setting of the forest they are free to exchange experiences and share the knowledge of the world. Back in the prince's court, however, rigid gender rules are assigned. What is considered praiseworthy in males (reading books, riding horses) is rejected in females, who are forbidden to read and must be suffocated in tight and uncomfortable clothes all day. When the forest princess questions the unfairness of the situation, the Prince defends the status quo:

> "There are so many people here and so many rules. Tell me, prince, why is it that only boys are taught to read in your land?"
>
> His smile turned into a frown.
>
> "That is the way it has always been."
>
> "But you taught me to read."

"That was in the forest. Things are different here."

"They don't have to be different. I could teach the girls what you taught me."

The prince stood up abruptly.

"Why can't you accept things the way they are?"

As things turn out, because of her outrageous requests, the Princess is forced to leave the castle:

> But if you go to the land of the golden castle today, you will find the boys and girls playing together, reading books together, and riding horses together. For you and I both know that a fairy tale isn't a fairy tale unless everyone lives happily ever after.

The female desire to conform to a pattern of desirability that posits beauty and passivity as the virtues required for marriage is presented as a dilemma in Desy's *The Princess Who Stood on Her Own Two Feet* (1982/1986). The protagonist, in order to subscribe to the prince's patriarchal view of femininity ("haven't you ever heard that women should be seen and not heard?" 42), pretends to be struck mute, as earlier she had feigned not to be able to walk due to a riding accident (the prince seems unable to get over the fact that the princess is much taller than he is). It is through a painful experience of loss that the princess arrives at a new understanding of her self-worth, which results in her meeting a wiser, if shorter, suitor for her hand. Desy's princess story, like *The Forest Princess* and *The Wide-Awake Princess*, is aimed at an audience of older children and can therefore explore gender issues in relative depth, but even in some picture books for younger children there is an awareness of sexual stereotyping. In Mike Thaler's *Hanzel and Pretzel* (1997), for example, Pretzel is much more assertive and resourceful than the original Gretel (who, in the Grimms' story, displays a worrying tendency to burst into tears at very inappropriate moments). In fact, it is a rejuvenated, frightened Hanzel who constantly cries and is jokingly reassured by his cool-tempered sister:

> "Hanzel looked out through the bars and began to cry.
> 'Look on the bright side,' joked Pretzel.
> 'At least we're not lost anymore.'"

The happy ending is brought about, as in the Grimms' tale, by efficient Pretzel who, after having thrown the witch into a cauldron, flies her brother home on the witch's broom without losing her sense of humour and love for puns.

Babette Cole's *Princess Smartypants* (1986/1996) and *Prince Cinders* (1993) comically reverse fairy-tale plots and culturally determined sexual stereotypes, keeping the text to a minimum and letting pictures convey most of the information regarding the characters. Princess Smartypants, for example, is pictured wearing denim dungarees, and watching horse races with her pet dragons, or brushing her pet giant crocodile with dishevelled hair like a common stable girl. It is only fair that such an informal and sporty princess should not automatically fall in love with smug Prince Swashbuckle who drives a posh sportscar, wears a multi-medalled uniform and flaunts a Clark Gable-type moustache. The end reaffirms the princess's independence and rejects the picture of the narcissistic macho man as the patronizing hero of the piece.

If we agree with the assumption that gender has a cultural character, we should not underestimate the impact of fairy-tale characters or circumstances in the formation of psycho-sexual concepts of the female or male self. The device of the change of sex in *Prince Cinders* is in itself a statement about the nature of male personality when this is culturally determined as a combination of physical strength, lack of sensitive feelings, and contempt for more vulnerable males. Prince Cinders' three hairy brothers, who belong to the same category as Prince Swashbuckle, spend their time at the palace disco with their princess girlfriends while Prince Cinders is left behind to clean up their mess: Cole's highly communicative pictures show the princes' rooms scattered with empty beer cans, football and bodybuilding magazines, and cigarette ends. Cinders' wish to be "big and hairy" like his brothers exposes the dominant cultural paradigm of masculinity (based on aggressive and insensitive behaviour) as ridiculous and old-fashioned: when the inexperienced fairy godmother, a teenage school-girl in her grey uniform and tie, performs the necessary magic, he will be turned into a big hairy monkey. After the customary happy ending with the marriage to Princess Prettypenny (who believes Cinders to have scared off the big hairy monster at midnight) the hairy brothers are suitably punished by being turned into house fairies, "and they flitted around the palace doing the housework for ever and ever."

By ridiculing stereotypical and outmoded notions of masculinity and having the fairy fulfil his desires to the letter (for in fairy tales one must really be careful what to wish for), Babette Cole's retelling ironically deconstructs a traditional paradigm of male identity, in order to stress the value of individuality and self-esteem. Even though some ambiguity as to gender roles remains, as Prince Cinders is cast in the conventional role of rescuer, this is one of the few adaptations which addresses the issue of male acculturation into traditional social roles. In retellings which challenge stereotypical sexual and social roles, fairy-tale discourse becomes emancipatory and innovative, rather than a reinforcement of patriarchal culture.

Fairy stories are "elastic": they evolve revealing a process of organic reshaping around a set of core elements in response to historical and cultural influences (see Hearne 1988). Fairy-tale hypotextual classes have survived many adaptations and will outlast many more. The central issue is that, by revitalizing canonical fairy-tale values and conventions, to which they add layers of non-conventional meanings, creative retellings liberate the imaginative and subversive potential of fairy tales in contemporary child culture.

References

Ahlberg, J. and A. (1986) *The Jolly Postman or Other People's Letters*. Harmondsworth: Penguin.

Atwood, M. (1994) *Bones and Murder*. London: Virago.

Bacchilega, C. (1997) *Postmodernist Fairy Tales. Gender and Narrative Strategies*. Philadelphia: University of Pennsylvania Press.

Bernardelli, A. (2000) *Intertestualita*. Bari: La Nuova Italia.

Bettelheim, B. (1977) *The Uses of Enchantment: The Meaning and Importance of Fairy Tales*. New York: Random House.

Bremond, C. (1977) "The Morphology of the French Fairy Tale: The Ethical Model." In Janson, H. and Segal, D. (eds.) *Patterns in Oral Literature*. Paris, The Hague: Mouton, 50–76.

Clayton, J. and Rothstein, E. (eds.) (1991) *Influence and Intertextuality in Literary History*. Madison: The University of Wisconsin Press.

Cole, B. (1986/1996) *Princess Smartypants*. Harmondsworth: Penguin.

Cole, B. (1993) *Prince Cinders*. Hayes, Middlesex: Magi Publications.

Coover, R. (1973) "The Dead Queen." *Quarterly Review of Literature* XVIII, 3–4; 304–13.

Dahl, R. (1982/1984) *Revolting Rhymes*. Harmondsworth: Penguin.

Desy, J. (1982) "The Princess Who Stood on Her Own Two Feet." in Zipes, J. (ed.) (1986) *Don't Bet on the Prince: Contemporary Feminist Fairy Tales in North America and England*. New York: Routledge, 39–47.

Genette, G. (1982) *Palimpsestes. La litterature au second degré*. Paris: Editions du Seuil.

Gilbert. S.A. and Gubar, S. (1979) *The Madwoman in the Attic: The Woman Writer and the Nineteenth-Century Imagination*. New Haven: Yale University Press.

Granowsky, A. (1996) *Giants Have Feelings, Too*. Austin: Steck-Vaughn.

Hearne, B. (1988) "Beauty and the Beast: Visions and Revisions of an Old Tale: 1950–1985." *The Lion and the Unicorn* 12.2: 74–109.

Herman, H. (1974) *The Forest Princess*. Berkeley: Rainbow Press.

Kamenetsky, C. (1992) *The Brothers Grimm and Their Critics: Folktales and the Quest for Meaning*. Athens: Ohio University Press.

Kolbenschlag, M. (1979) *Kiss Sleeping Beauty Good-bye: Breaking the Spell of Feminine Myths and Models*. San Francisco: Harper and Row.

Kristeva, J. (1970) *Le texte du roman: Approche semiologique d'une structure discoursive transformationelle*. The Hague, Paris: Mouton.

Lieberman, M.K. (1972) "'Some Day My Prince Will Come': Female Acculturation through the Fairy Tale." In Zipes, J. (ed.) (1986) *Don't Bet on the Prince: Contemporary Feminist Fairy Tales in North America and England*. New York: Routledge, 185–200.

Lotman, J. (1980) *Testo e Contesto. Semiotica dell'arte e della cultura*. Roma-Bari: Laterza.

Napoli, D.J. (1993) *The Magic Circle*. Harmondsworth: Penguin.

Nesbit, E. (1925/1975) *The Last of the Dragons and Some Others*. Harmondsworth: Penguin.

Paterson, K. (2000) *The Wide-Awake Princess*. New York: Clarion Press.

Polacco, M. (1998) *Intertestualita*. Bari: Laterza.

Propp, V. (1928/1968) *Morphology of the Folktale*. Austin: Texas University Press.

Rodari, G. (1973/1997) *Grammatica della fantasia: Introduzione all'arte di inventare storie*. Torino: Einaudi.

Scieszka, J. (1989) *The True Story of the Three Little Pigs*. Harmondsworth: Penguin.

Scieszka, J. (1992) *The Stinky Cheese Man and Other Fairly Stupid Tales*. New York: Viking.

Segre, C. (1984) "Intertestualita e interdiscorsivita nel romanzo e nella poesia." In *Teatro e romanzo*. Torino: Einaudi, 103–08.

Stephens, J. (1992) *Language and Ideology in Children's Fiction*. London and New York: Longman.

Stephens, J. and McCallum, R. (1998) *Retelling Stories, Framing Culture: Traditional Story and Metanarratives in Children's Literature*. New York and London: Garland.

Stone, K. (1975) "Things Walt Disney Never Told Us." In Farrer, C.R. (ed.) *Women and Folklore*. Austin: University of Texas Press, 42–50.

Storr, K. (1955) "Little Polly Riding Hood." In Zipes, J. (ed.) (1993) *The Trials and Tribulations of Little Red Riding Hood*. New York and London: Routledge, 234–38.

Tatar, M. (1992) *Off With Their Heads: Fairy Tales and the Culture of Childhood*. Princeton: Princeton University Press.

Thaler, M. (1997) *Schmoe White and the Seven Dorfs*. New York: Scholastic.

Thaler, M. (1997) *Hanzel and Pretzel*. New York: Scholastic.

Warner, M. (1994) *From the Beast to the Blonde: On Fairy Tales and Their Tellers*. London: Chatto and Windus.

Williams, J. (1978) *The Practical Princess and Other Liberating Fairy Tales*. London: The Bodley Head.

Worton, M. and Still, J. (1990) *Intertextuality: Theories and Practices*. Manchester: Manchester University Press.

Yolen, J. (1981/1997) *Sleeping Ugly*. New York: Putnam and Grosset.

Zipes, J. (1979) "The Instrumentalization of Fantasy: Fairy Tales, the Culture Industry, and Mass Media." In *Breaking the Magic Spell: Radical Theories of Folk and Fairy Tales*. Austin: University of Texas Press, 93–128.

Zipes, J. (1983) *Fairy Tales and the Art of Subversion: The Classic Genre for Children and the Process of Civilization*. New York: Routledge.

Zipes, J. (1986) *Don't Bet on the Prince: Contemporary Feminist Fairy Tales in North America and England*. New York: Routledge.

Zipes, J. (ed.) (1987) *Victorian Fairy Tales*. New York and London: Methuen.

Zipes, J. (1999) *When Dreams Come True: Classic Fairy Tales and Their Tradition*. London: Routledge.

DISNEY REVISITED, OR, JIMINY CRICKET, IT'S MUSTY DOWN HERE![1]

Betsy Hearne

I call him to account for his debasement of the traditional literature of childhood, in films and in the books he publishes:

He shows scant respect for the integrity of the original creations of authors,
manipulating and vulgarizing everything for his own ends.

His treatment of folklore is without regard for its anthropological, spiritual, or psychological truths. Every story is sacrificed to the "gimmick" ... of
animation....

Not content with the films, he fixes these mutilated versions in books
which are cut to a fraction of their original forms, illustrates them with garish pictures, in which every prince looks like a badly drawn portrait of Cary
Grant, every princess a sex symbol.

GUESS WHO FRANCES CLARKE SAYERS was talking about in 1965? This letter
she published in the Los Angeles *Times* was printed as part of a longer article in *The
Horn Book* (December 1965), and Walt Disney survived her attack by only one year.
He died December 15, 1966. Three decades later, the single subject that will ensure
debate among glazed undergraduates and exhausted graduate students of children's
literature is criticism of a Walt Disney production. I have learned to muffle my salvos
lest Disney devotees drop the course completely, but even so, one fan was close to
tears when she exclaimed, "Can't you leave the poor man alone? He's dead!" This
particular class presented me with a parting shot of three plastic figurines from the
Disney Studios' *Beauty and the Beast*—plus the paperback spin-off.

Do Sayers's assertions of 1965 need an update? She was a sharp critic, preceding by a decade and more the landmark commentary of scholarly theorists, from
Kay Stone ("Things Walt Disney Never Told Us," 1975) to Jack Zipes ("Breaking
the Disney Spell," 1993). Disney is continuously under attack by critics of both
academia and the popular press for messing up revered literature—witness the
recently skewered *Hunchback of Notre Dame*. And Disney films are more wildly popular than ever. Is this cultural schizophrenia? The pro-Disney crowds at
theaters and video stores speak in cash. The anti-Disney crowds speak in print.
What's happening here? And what could anyone add, besides micro-analytic
details, to Sayers's articulate assessment of the structural, tonal, stylistic, and

---

1   From *Horn Book Magazine*, March/April 1997.

didactic alterations with which Disney and company have "revised" traditional and/or classical stories?

Perhaps we can add just a bit of perspective. Disney's films changed within the forty-three years between his first Hollywood partnership with brother Roy in 1923, the year they released a short cartoon called *Alice's Wonderland*, and his last hands-on production, *The Jungle Book*, in 1966 (released posthumously in 1967). Disney films have changed between 1966 and 1996, too, and throughout both periods, the socio-economic and aesthetic context for Disney films has been changed by almost a century of events. To the audiences of the 1920s, Disney was entertainment. To the audiences of the 1960s, Disney was an icon. To the audiences of the 1990s, Disney is myth. In the absence of a permanent electrical blackout, the Disney Olympus is centrally mapped as a pinnacle in the kingdom of childhood. With just these few words, an image may have sprung to mind of the glowing castle with myriad spires thrusting phallically toward the heavens and triangulated banners waving over all.

Well, now that we're here, let's look over the landscape. Obviously, the concept of fairy-tale revision wasn't born with Disney in Chicago, Illinois, on December 5, 1901 (the same year *Peter Rabbit* was published, speaking of landmarks). In 1697 Charles Perrault refined some lusty old tales passed on by his children's nanny. In 1812 Wilhelm and Jacob Grimm made a real hit with the stories they collected from folk and family (more family than folk, as it turns out) and then revised, sometimes radically, over the next several editions of *Kinder- und Hausmärchen*. From 1889 to 1910 Andrew Lang stamped folk and fairy tales with his own style to the tune of ringing commercial success in a twelve-volume series starting with the *Blue Fairy Book* and proceeding through Red, Green, Yellow, Violet, and all the way to Lilac (multi-color literature was only a few letters short of multi-cultural, but the time wasn't ripe yet). Perrault, the Grimms, and Lang all addressed adults as much or more than children: Perrault and Lang with a wink-wink-nod-nod, and the Grimms with an agenda of glorifying—according to their lights—a cultural heritage. Is Disney the missing twentieth-century link in a chain of clever men who borrowed stories (often from anonymous women) and broadcast them via the latest mass medium? Whatever his critics say, Disney is even more of a cultural fact now than when he was alive. Thirty years worth of successful films produced by the studio that bears his name have extended his lifetime work beyond a mortal frame.

Now, of course, Perrault, Grimm, and Lang are, if not household words, at least uncontested cultural touchstones. And yet, in earlier chapters of high culture versus popular culture, they too had their share of detractors. It may come as no surprise that the folklore we so venerate today was once viewed as common and vulgar by the educated elite of the eighteenth and nineteenth centuries (most notably the moralistic Sarah Trimmer and Mrs. Sherwood). Will the newly created field of "Disney

Studies" legitimize animated versions during the last quarter of the twentieth century in the same way that "Folklore Studies" legitimized printed versions in the last quarter of the nineteenth century? Are the changes "frozen" into film from the print tradition any more deleterious than the changes "frozen" into print from the oral tradition?

Sayers's attitude was that "folklore is a universal form, a great symbolic literature which represents the folk. It is something that came from the masses, not something that is put over on the masses .... Disney is basically interested in the market." Now, the market part is certainly still true. The Disney home videos I bought to review for this article included a snowfall of glossy pamphlets advertising The Cinderella Vacation Package, Tropicana orange juice and Pillsbury products and Cheerios (there must be a connection), and, of course, lots of Disney products in print, CD-ROM, and video format: "Play with Pocahontas, Sing-Along with Pooh, Roar with Simba, and Soar with Aladdin." Favorite films are released for only a few months on the home video market and then held off the market for several years ("Sleeping Beauty is in moratorium," announced the video salesman solemnly), just to ensure ongoing consumer appetite; it's a long-term strategy that works well to create a rush on any newly released golden oldie that won't be around long. This is not to mention the myriad toy, clothing, and other products that sell because of Disney characters' copyrighted graphic motifs. Of course, in a marketplace society any product has to make money—remember that the nineteenth-century folklorist Andrew Lang was not immune to the profits from his best-selling fairy-tale series—but the sheer sophistication and international dominance of the Disney commercial machine guarantee that a Disney version of a fairy tale or classic will be THE authorized version for millions and millions of young viewers all over the world. Do we criticize Disney simply because he is so successful in shaping so many children's imaginations into one mold? In that case, shouldn't we be criticizing the capitalist/mass media system itself (the cause) rather than its cultural freight trains (the symptom)?

Probably. But in any effort to countermand the Disneyfication of storylore, dissenting parents, teachers, and librarians are often frustrated by the film company's monolithic global influence. How many children (and adults) can we reach with alternative fairy-tale variants or with classics whose originals become sausage in Disney's grinder? As he said to one of his "story men" assigned to work on The Jungle Book, "The first thing I want you to do is not to read it," adding later, "You can get all bogged down with these stories."

Remarks like this confirm every dissenter's objections to Disneyvision. Does this sound as curmudgeonly as Sayers's earlier remarks? Yes, but ... let's add some perspective to the rude facts, and here's where Sayers's assertions about the folk seem more questionable than her assertions about the films: "Folklore

CRITICISM

is a universal form, a great symbolic literature which represents the folk." Okay, but the folk keep changing; and although folklore is universal, the folk are not a universal unit. Further, she says of folklore: "It is something that came from the masses, not something that is put over on the masses"—as opposed to Disneylore, obviously, but that leads us to a conundrum. Disney *does* come from the masses as well as being put over on the masses, which we'll discuss further in a minute. Disney films represent the same chicken-and-egg syndrome as do the Barbie dolls his heroines so closely resemble. Our society exalts the impossible body form that Barbie represents, witness Playboy bunnies and Hollywood stars who have come closest to resembling her. Clearly, Mattel didn't originate that exalted body. But the dolls do perpetuate the exaltation through advertisement propaganda and mass distribution. Of course, there's also the little-studied question of what children do with those dolls. My kids cut off all their Barbies' hair and contorted the plastic bodies into what might benevolently be called positions of advanced yoga, but we'll try to stick to theory for a little longer and set aside the question of whether or not pernicious corporations are influencing every little girl to grow up wanting to look just like her Barbie doll (or a bald guru).

Although there's no question that private commerce manipulates public will, public will also shapes private commerce, and both are shaped by social forces that influence the creation of and response to Disney's films. Dare we look at Disneylore as a grassroots movement, as electronic myth driven by social need as well as commercial greed, as formulae of exaggerated effects à la American tall tales? As even, perhaps, a form of parody, which his wry 1922 Laugh-o-Gram films of Little Red Riding Hood, Jack and the Beanstalk, Cinderella, and others so clearly were? Indeed, Disney's *Hunchback of Notre Dame*—based on a book that never, of course, was intended for children—takes parody to dizzying heights. Why is Jon Scieszka and Lane Smith's *The Stinky Cheese Man and Other Fairly Stupid Tales* or *The True Story of the Three Little Pigs*—along with a recent multitude of revisionist fairy tales—considered cleverly entertaining by so many children's book literati while Disney revisions, also cleverly entertaining, are deeply suspect? Why is it okay for feminists (of which I am one) to update passive heroines into active roles, or for socially sensitive library-storytellers (ditto) to omit elements of violence, racism, and other unacceptables from their story hours, and not for Disney to make changes, too? Do we really want to go graphic with heroes who trick their adversaries into eating a boiled relative, one of Brer Rabbit's escapades that somehow got left out of Disney's *Song of the South*? Can you just see animated blood dripping from the toes and shoes of Cinderella's sisters, per the Grimms' version, or two adorable little pigeons plucking out the sisters' eyes at Cinderella's wedding, one eye from each sister going into the church, and one eye from each sister coming back out? The folks at Disney want to make zippy productions and make everybody happy and make money, not hemorrhage all over the audience.

But also, you are qualified to ask, does every single story that Disney commandeers have to get so *cute* (except for the sensationally villainous scenes), no matter the tone of its ancestors? That charming little fellow we know as Jiminy Cricket, Pinocchio's conscience and commentator in Disney's film, was just an anonymous bug that got squashed in the beginning of Collodi's book. (Let me thank University of Illinois graduate student Bill Michtom for ranting and raving about this point.) Collodi's Pinocchio does bad stuff because he doesn't have a conscience; in Disney's version, he does bad stuff because of influence from villains. In other words, it's a lot easier to blame outer forces than inner forces, to see the evil in others rather than in ourselves or those with whom we identify. Is it the dark side, our own shadows, from which Disney protects the twentieth century? Are the children of today, who have never experienced a Depression or a World War, especially susceptible to a diet unbalanced toward the sprightly side with dancing teacups, singing seafood, twittering birds, and nose-twitching bunnies? Do there have to be quite so *many* animal helpers? That crowd of small mammals in *Snow White* seems on perpetual verge of stampede.

What are the real offenses Disney commits, aesthetically (distracting story gimmicks, hyperactive graphic images) and socially (violence, gender and ethnic stereotypes)? Certainly no one, not even Sayers, has objected to Disney originals such as Mickey Mouse, Donald Duck, *Lady and the Tramp*, and Roger Rabbit, for instance, or the various realistic nature/family dramas. What draws fire are the re-visions, the abandonment of past traditions for current values, which Disney reflects with unnerving accuracy. His first full-length feature, *Snow White and the Seven Dwarfs* (1937), embroidered basic fairy-tale formula with Hollywood romance, slapstick humor, and a Utopian alternative to the harsh competition engendered by the Depression (witness the cooperative work ethic of the seven miners and of the heroine's menagerie of housecleaners, an aspect that Terri Wright has explored in "Romancing the Tale: Walt Disney's Adaptation of the Grimms' 'Snow White'").

Some fifty years later, *Beauty and the Beast* has again emphasized romance and humor, but the Depression is long gone, and Disney films have long since entered the conservative mode adopted by Disney himself after World War II. Here we see cut-throat competition for Beauty's love in context of a violent society including a brutish suitor, a bloodthirsty mob, and a demonic insane-asylum director. While the household appliances are friendly, the Beast has acquired a vile temper, and even the animals have turned nasty, with a pack of wolves attacking Beauty, her father, and the Beast himself. The wolves' villainous role is particularly ironic because one of the earlier story's basic motifs was the transformational power of animal and human nature in balance.

Structurally, we've lost Beauty as hero: she who instigated the action by asking for a rose no longer asks for a rose; she who almost killed the Beast with her lack of perception but instead saved him by developing perception becomes an observer of two guys fighting over a girl. May the best man win. He does, but the woman has lost in the process. It's not enough to pay lip service to women's intelligence by propping a book up in front of a gorgeous female or showing her disdain for a macho suitor, when she's been denuded of her real power. Doesn't all this reflect an ongoing condition in our own society? Some of us don't like what we see here because we are seeing what's happening to us. Common television shows are full of it, but to watch a world-class artist like Disney glamorizing it is harder to take. On the other hand, in criticizing Disney, do we want to echo those who blame authors for producing books that reflect social problems we've created ourselves?

Without getting bogged down in a textual analysis based on scores of quotations from books and film scripts, we see over and over that Disney and company have given society not only what it will pay for, but also what it wants. The 1950 hit *Cinderella* spends as much time on Lucifer the cat chasing Gus and the other mice as it does on the main characters. Even Cinderella's return from the ball turns into a chase scene, not just the prince following her down a flight of stairs, but a wild pursuit of the king's horsemen thundering after her carriage. This device for escalating suspense is common to most of the animated features. Disney films have turned the folklore journey into a chase. What's added? Speed and competition, both key characteristics of our society. All you have to do is look at stories mythologized on television and you'll know how much our culture reverberates to chase scenes. Journeys of westward expansion turn into cowboy and Indian chase scenes; stories of crime and punishment turn into cops-and-robbers chase scenes. *Beauty and the Beast*, a television series that started with some tonal adherence to the main characters' slow-paced journeys of development, ended as a chase between Beast and the villain who stole his son (Beauty is murdered after giving birth). Disney's *Beauty and the Beast* is full of chase scenes instead of the journeys between castle and home that characterized Beauty's earlier journey of maturation.

The truth of it is that Disney's films relate less to their folkloric or literary predecessors than to their contemporary audience. While not all Disney's films have been equally popular, their reception does not depend on fidelity to any original. *Pinocchio*, *Peter Pan*, and *The Little Mermaid*, all of which veered wildly from Collodi's and Barrie's and Andersen's stories, were blockbusters. *Alice in Wonderland*, which veered wildly from Carroll's work, was a bust. The remake of *101 Dalmatians* stirred up some negative response not because it changed Dodie Smith's book, but because it changed the "original" film version! Success seems to depend on a film's fulfilling the Disney formula of visual and musical entertainment (a formula defined, circularly, by public response) and on fitting into the self-referential world established by the Disney canon.

This process begins with the very selection of the story itself. *The Little Mermaid* is the kind of persecuted female that Hans Christian Andersen loved to persecute even further (see also "The Red Shoes," "The Little Match Girl," etc.) and that Disney loved to rescue, sort of. Where are the swashbuckling heroines like Mollie Whuppie? Well, she's maybe a little too active, switching necklaces in the dark of night to trick her giant host into smashing the skulls of his own three daughters instead of Mollie and her sisters, whom he has planned to cook the next day. Tit for tat, you may say, but it would make a tough scene for the two-year-olds who swarm with their caretakers to the theater or sit propped before their electronic babysitters. A point here: the viewing crowd has gotten younger and younger over the century we're discussing, and the venues more intimate. What stranger can you trust in your children's bedroom but a film-maker whose sales figures depend on innocence and socially acceptable villainy? Murderous stepmothers seem to be okay; murderous fathers wouldn't be. Interesting, hunh? The Grimms, by the way, modulated their version of "Hansel and Gretel" through several editions to blame the children's abandonment first on the mother and father, then on the stepmother and father, then mostly on the stepmother.

Disney's modifications originate from accurate readings of our culture. He got the address right. This is where we live. We who criticize Disney have seen the enemy, and he is us. We are mistaken to speak as a voice removed from the rest of the population, as eighteenth- and nineteenth-century educators did in criticizing fairy tales and fiction, or to condemn artists as gulling the rest of the population. Disney belongs to us and we belong to him. What he does to fairy tales and classics is, in a sense, our own shadow. We don't have to like it and we don't have to keep quiet about it, but we do have to understand our own society and the lore it generates. The alternative is critical mustification. Popular culture and art are a vital dynamic. The past is always renegotiating with the present to become the future, and that requires the fresh air of our awareness.

"Beauty and the Beast" is a story I have loved all my life and studied for twenty years. Do I like what the Disney film has done to it? No, with qualifications. The scenes where the film-makers risk focusing on two characters' slowly maturing transformation—on the dance floor, for instance—are moving, and the animated art is rich. However, the violation of profound elements and the frenetic pace bother me in the film just as they bother me in everyday life. Does my opinion matter? Yes, but there are better ways to express it than boycotting the film or keeping it from my kids. They live here, too. They need to know what's going on, just as I do. We've watched and discussed it together; they cheer while I rant and rave. Disney is fun, they remind me. Our society craves fun, I remind them—but isn't there something else to life? Sure, Mom.

So, can we have fun and still challenge what's fun? Can we aim our criticism not at censuring/censoring an artistic reality, but at changing the self, family, and society that inspires and supports it? Sure we can, kids.

Obviously, all parents should follow their instincts about whether or not—and at what age—to expose their children to Disneyed stories. However, we may be mistaken to overestimate the changes Disney makes and underestimate the changes we can make. In one of my favorite anecdotes, from the ChildLit Listserv, Megan L. Isaac describes

> a four-year-old who after months of pleading was finally given Beauty and the Beast dolls that were then being promoted as merchandising tie-ins for the film. (Previously her parents had resisted purchasing a Barbie, so they were loath to give in to this similar model of female perfection.) Anyway, as the adults chatted, she sat on the floor blissfully playing with her two new dolls and creating a dialogue between them. A rough paraphrase follows:
> Beast: Come on, Beauty, you have to come live in my castle.
> Beauty: No, I don't want to.
> Beast: You have to. I say so.
> Beauty: No I don't. You're not my boss. I'm going to put you in the zoo.

Here's to the film-makers of the future!

TECHNO-MAGIC: CINEMA AND FAIRY TALE[1]

Marina Warner

FROM THE EARLIEST EXPERIMENTS BY George Meliès in Paris in the 1890s to the present day dominion of Disney Productions and Pixar, fairy tales have been told in the cinema. The concept of illusion carries two distinct, profound, and contradictory meanings in the medium of film: first, the film itself is an illusion, and, bar a few initiates screaming at the appearance of a moving train in the medium's earliest viewings, everyone in the cinema knows they are being stunned by wonders wrought by science. All appearances in the cinema are conjured by shadow play and artifice, and

---

1   From *Once Upon a Time: A Short History of Fairy Tale* (Oxford: Oxford UP, 2014). All notes are editorial.

technologies ever more skilled at illusion: CGI produces living breathing simula-cra—of velociraptors (*Jurassic Park*), elvish castles (*Lord of the Rings*), soaring bi-onic monsters (*Avatar*), grotesque and terrifying monsters (the *Alien* series), while the modern Rapunzel wields her mane like a lasso and a whip, or deploys it to make a footbridge. Such visualizations are designed to stun us, and they succeed: so much is being done for us by animators and filmmakers, there is no room for personal imaginings. The wicked queen in *Snow White* (1937) has become imprinted, and she keeps those exact features when we return to the story; Ariel, Disney's flame-haired Little Mermaid, has eclipsed her wispy and poignant predecessors, conjured chiefly by the words of Andersen's story.

A counterpoised form of illusion, however, now flourishes rampantly at the core of fairytale films, and has become central to the realization on screen of the stories, especially in entertainment which aims at a crossover or child audience. Contemporary commercial cinema has continued the Victorian shift from irre-sponsible amusement to responsible instruction, and kept faith with fairy tales' protest against existing injustices. Many current family films posit spirited, hope-ful alternatives (in *Shrek* Princess Fiona is podgy, liverish, ugly, and delightful; in *Tangled*, Rapunzel is a super heroine, brainy and brawny; in the hugely suc-cessful Disney film *Frozen* (2013), inspired by *The Snow Queen*, the younger sister Anna overcomes ice storms, avalanches, and eternal winter to save Elsa, her elder). Screenwriters display iconoclastic verve, but they are working from the premise that screen illusions have power to become fact. "Wishing on a star" is the ideol-ogy of the dream factory, and has given rise to indignant critique, that fairy tales peddle empty consumerism and wishful thinking. The writer Terri Windling, who specializes in the genre of teen fantasy, deplores the once prevailing tendency towards positive thinking and sunny success:

> The fairy tale journey may look like an outward trek across plains and moun-tains, through castles and forests, but the actual movement is inward, into the lands of the soul. The dark path of the fairytale forest lies in the shadows of our imagination, the depths of our unconscious. To travel to the wood, to face its dangers, is to emerge transformed by this experience. Particularly for children whose world does not resemble the simplified world of television sit-coms ... this ability to travel inward, to face fear and transform it, is a skill they will use all their lives. We do children—and ourselves—a grave disservice by censor-ing the old tales, glossing over the darker passages and ambiguities ...

Fairy tale and film enjoy a profound affinity because the cinema animates phe-nomena, no matter how inert; made of light and motion, its illusions match the enchanted animism of fairy tale: animals speak, carpets fly, objects move and act of their own accord. One of the darker forerunners of Mozart's flute is an uncanny instrument that plays in several ballads and stories: a bone that bears witness to a murder. In the Grimms' tale, "The Singing Bone," the shepherd who finds it doesn't react in terror and run, but thinks to himself, "What a strange little horn, singing of its own accord like that. I must take it to the king." The bone sings out the truth of what happened, and the whole skeleton of the victim is dug up, and his murderer— his elder brother and rival in love—is unmasked, sewn into a sack, and drowned.

This version is less than two pages long: a tiny, supersaturated solution of the Grimms: grotesque and macabre detail, uncanny dynamics of life-in-death, moral piety, and rough justice. But the story also presents a vivid metaphor for film itself: singing bones. (It's therefore apt, if a little eerie, that the celluloid from which film stock was first made was itself composed of rendered-down bones.)

Early animators' choice of themes reveals how they responded to a deeply laid sympathy between their medium of film and the uncanny vitality of inert things. Lotte Reiniger, the writer-director of the first full-length animated feature (*The Adventures of Prince Achmed*), made dazzling 'shadow puppet' cartoons inspired by the fairy tales of Grimm, Andersen, and Wilhelm Hauff; she continued making films for over a thirty-year period, first in her native Berlin and later in London, for children's television. Her *Cinderella* (1922) is a comic—and grisly—masterpiece.

Early Disney films, made by the man himself, reflect traditional fables' personification of animals—mice and ducks and cats and foxes; in this century, by contrast, things come to life, no matter how inert they are: computerization observes no boundaries to generating lifelike, kinetic, cybernetic, and virtual reality.

Utopian Dreams/Wishful Thinking

By far the most striking development in the alliance of fairy tale and cinema as vehicles in family entertainment has been the rise of political sensitivity, and resulting tinkering with stories to show awareness of gender, power relations, and ethnic representation. Both the cultural-historical and psychoanalytical approaches to fairy tale have sharpened producers' awareness of social engineering. Whereas Reiniger could show a jolly frolic in a harem, and Prince Achmed carousing with lascivious Josephine Baker-style houris, the writer and director of *Snow White and the Huntsman* (2012) could not even end the story with a marriage—to the prince or to the pauper. This Snow White (Kristen Stewart of the *Twilight* series) has to remain a lone heroine, a role model for the independent woman—at times in full armour. The rules of genre, which require some resolution to the story, were flouted in the interests of exemplary gender moulding.

Interestingly, the first experiments in character building through cinematic enchantments took place under socialist or communist regimes. The masters of Soviet Russia and the communist bloc demanded that artists and writers celebrate heroic workers, agricultural quotas, and the brotherhood of man; stray into dream and fantasy and you were dangerously flirting with a degenerate bourgeois aesthetic—veering close to the decadence of surrealism or the moral vacuity of subjective feeling. Many went to the Gulag for such personal flights of fancy.

But retelling fairy tales for a *child* audience could offer cover for alternative messages, and turn the official political programme for the arts topsy-turvy: tractors disappeared and flying carpets took over; golden fish swam into view and blue unicorns with long gold eyelashes pranced on the screen. Miracles happened that were not the result of five-year plans. From the Soviet Union, to Czechoslovakia and Yugoslavia (as they were then called), the Grimms' founding principle—that fairy tale expressed the people and the nation—provided a rationale for dusting off traditional stories from all over the empire. Polishing them up for family viewing created a picture of joyous unity in diversity.

In the days when [Soviet dictator Joseph] Stalin [1878–1953] wanted everyone to be happy in the vast empire, fairy tales were collected, published (often in beautiful illustrated editions), and performed to forge community spirit. From Belgrade to Vladivostok, the Black Sea to the Arctic Ocean, ethnic stories were told, sung, acted—often in local national dress—to deepen the sense of belonging. Plots were fixed to give uplift: the brave little tailor rejects the princess in favour of the gardener's daughter; the greedybags treasure-hoarder is destroyed.

One of the most successful early fairytale films in colour, *The Singing Ringing Tree*, was made in 1957 in East Germany by the state-controlled studios, the DEFA. The story mashes many elements from favourite tales—several animal helpers, a wicked dwarf, a stuck-up princess, and a plucky, lowborn hero. Their struggles are epic, involving dark perils and terrifying trials. The tree itself reverberates with powerful magic, as in "The Juniper Tree." But these elements are slanted through the lens of East German politics: the proud, spoiled princess learns to love the people, makes common cause with the forces of righteousness, and leads a revolution against the dwarf.

Arguments did however flare up in East Germany around the use of fantasy and *The Singing Ringing Tree* in particular, and they sound very familiar. Why was the story about a princess at all? Why did it show her realizing the error of her arrogant ways? Surely this colluded reprehensibly with outdated notions of reform and *noblesse oblige*? What about the happy ending when the princess and the pauper marry? Cries of 'bourgeois' and 'revanchist!'[1] echoed round the bureaux of the censors.

---

1 Someone who wishes to reverse territorial losses caused by war.

The series was pulled, mothballed and forgotten—its makers were embarrassed to recall it when later asked by enthusiastic fans. But in 1962, the BBC bought the film—and sparked unforgettable thrills in a generation of British children, and continued enthusiasm among film buffs.

The East German case is highly illuminating of present tensions around the telling of fairy tales. On the one hand, the general consensus now agrees with [Charles] Dickens, [J.R.R.] Tolkien, [Bruno] Bettelheim, and [Terri] Windling, who, for different reasons, have declared that sweetening the tales is tantamount to vandalism. But at the same time, changes to the corpus are constantly being made in the light of current opinion—muting and muffling this bit or that—without any official censors needing to be brought in.

The kind of political wishful thinking that emanated from the old Soviet bloc resembles what is called PC or political correctness, which is often scorned, and perhaps applied to extremes. Yet it depends on recognizing that what we discover in books or other media when we are young imprints us—stories communicate values, like myths, and shape our understanding of the world.

One of the consequences has been the rise of self-censorship—by publishers, producers, scriptwriters, and editors, most especially when children are in view. Behind every book for young people and every global product of family entertainment, the hum of boardroom discussion about the politics of the work can be heard. Every scriptwriter and director takes up a passive Cinderella and turns her into a champion freedom fighter, or transforms Jack the Giant Killer into Robin Hood, in order to put across an approved code of conduct—the values that will win approval and ratings. The big film industry ("Hollywood") keeps straining to produce a fairytale heroine for the age of the female CEO, but its efforts fall foul of audiences and are still arousing fierce attacks from children's experts in every field.

One consequence of twenty-first-century social and political sensitivities has been a clear split in some cases between material for children and adults, similar to the division between top-shelf and eye-level magazines on a news stand or the two sides of the 9 p.m. watershed in television broadcasting. Many fairytale re-visionings now require Parental Guidance; several are classified Adults Only.

Current fairy tales on stage and screen reveal an acute malaise about sexual, rather than social, programming of the female, and the genre continues ever more intensively to wrestle with the notorious question Freud put long ago, "What do women want?" The singer Tori Amos, for example, adapted a Victorian fairy tale, *The Light Princess* (2013), about a girl who has lost her gravity—she has to be tethered to prevent her floating up and away and she can't do anything but laugh. George MacDonald wrote the original tale in 1867; he was a Christian allegorist, a friend of Lewis Carroll's, and encouraged and influenced the *Alice* books. Tori Amos's vision,

FOLK AND FAIRY TALES

by contrast, is sparked by the dominant, psychological concern today with young girls' troubles and unfocused desires, the search for numbness and nullity that leads to binge drinking, passing out, self-harm, even death.

The popularity of different fairy tales beats with an irregular pulse: recurrent favourites are "Snow White" and "Sleeping Beauty," with "Bluebeard" coming close behind. The idea that women must stop sleepwalking through life has its origins in feminist anger against the Sleeping Beauty ideal (think of *The Stepford Wives*), but the concern is spiking (Disney's *Maleficent* (2014) stars Angelina Jolie in the title role as the thirteenth fairy; the brilliantly inventive choreographer Matthew Bourne has turned Sleeping Beauty's prince into a vampire, who wakes her with a bite ... the fairy tale seen through *Twilight*). *Blancanieves* (2012), made in Spain, is an exhilarating, inspired reinvention of "Snow White," set among the flamenco dancers, bullfighters, and travelling circus folk of Andalusia. Directed and written by the Catalan director Pablo Berger, it is shot in expressionist chiaroscuro, and gorgeously controlled, with a play of shimmer and glare on mirrors, crystal, eyes, and lips in the stark sunlight of the bullring and the deep shadows of interiors, castles, caravans.

No compunction about depicting evil restrains the storyteller here: the wicked stepmother is a nurse who sees her chance when the gored hero of the bullring is admitted to her hospital, his wife dies in childbirth, and he is left paralysed; nothing is spared to show us her cruelty, vanity, greed—no plot lines are added to excuse her, in contrast to the Hollywood vehicles, for which scriptwriters are made to come up with back stories of trauma to soften her evil. Maribel Verdú, the actress playing the wicked queen, has an uncanny face that changes, with a twitch of her lips, from glorious serene diva to predatory fury, and she gives Berger's dominatrix a marvellous, witty energy, on the verge of parody, but always remaining too threatening to allow the release of laughter.

Like many current fairytale films, this one is not for children, but uses the famous children's story to think about what can happen to innocence. *Blancanieves* adopts the full awareness of adults, and shows us openly what adults are capable of in the fulfilment of desire—especially perverse desire.

The film is a tragedy, for this Snow White falls asleep forever and, as in [Franz] Kafka's "The Hunger Artist" [1922], she is exhibited in her glass coffin as part of a travelling fair, alongside a hairy girl, a fat lady, and a starveling. It's another form of Buñuel-style erotic fetishism, and the dwarf who loves her tends her with powder and paint; the film closes on a single tear leaking out of the corner of her eye.

The most disquieting treatment of the story is however a self-identified feminist film, Julia Leigh's *Sleeping Beauty* (2011), which exemplifies the dark turn fairy tales have taken, especially in the vision of women creators. A luminous, angelically beautiful student answers a job advert and is initiated into a specialist brothel, willingly becoming the drugged object of clients' fantasies. Like Carter's essay *The Sadeian Woman*, this version raises questions about women's complicity and self-possession, and about pornography as the norm of sexual exchange in our society, not an aberration.

Recognizing the dark heart of fairy tales has informed some stunning original works: *Pan's Labyrinth* (2006), directed and written by Guillermo del Toro, condenses many myths into his story, about the goddess Persephone abducted into the underworld, for example. The film opens with a direct allusion to the "Cottingley fairies," when two little girls persuaded [Arthur] Conan Doyle and other eminent Victorians that they had seen—and successfully photographed—tiny sprites dancing and sunbathing at the bottom of their garden, and it then unfolds into a searing tale of initiation in the gloomy forest, brilliantly weaving the actual historical reality of Spain under Franco into the fabric of magic and faery.

Many of the most widespread and powerful expressions of fairy tale today feature women—old and young—at their heart. Whether the creators are male (*Tangled*, for example, has a male screenwriter and director), or female (*Maleficent* is written by Linda Woolverton, also the screenwriter on Disney's *Beauty and the Beast*), readers and viewers, regardless of their gender, are drawn into the unfolding drama about a passionate female protagonist. Although Hollywood keeps trying to bring appealing young men into the picture (*Snow White and the Huntsman* struggled to make the male lead hunky *and* sensitive), Harry Potter stands pretty much alone among heroes, and J.K. Rowling's series is too baggy and epic to be called a fairy tale.

Twenty-first century films, such as *Sleeping Beauty* and *Blancanieves*, have broken with the chief defining principle of fairy tales that they should end happily. Fairy tales lift the spirits and spark a ray of hope for the future when they bring defeat and even death to the perpetrators of harm, to the vicious tyrants and greedy ogres and to the architects of family hell, cruel fathers and wicked queens. The darkness of contemporary retellings threatens to grow so deep it throws a shadow over the happy ending itself. But sometimes this gloom does not altogether destroy the sense that an alternative world has been created where goodness can brighten us, lighten us.

[465]

THE END OF FAIRY TALES? HOW SHREK AND FRIENDS HAVE CHANGED CHILDREN'S STORIES[1]

James Poniewozik

ONCE UPON A TIME, IN a land near near by, there were fairy tales. Brave princes slew dragons and saved fair damsels. Princesses and scullery maids waited for brave knights and true love. The good were pretty, the evil ugly, the morals absolute. And lo, it was good. If you liked that sort of thing.

Then a hideous green monster appeared and threw the realm into chaos. Handsome princes were mocked, damsels saved themselves, and ogres and dragons were shown to be decent folks once you got to know them.

And lo, it was even better—particularly for the movie industry. The first two *Shrek* movies, which upended every fairy-tale cliché they could get their meaty chartreuse paws on, grossed more than $700 million in the U.S. alone; there's little reason to believe that *Shrek the Third* won't fill its hungry Scottish maw with hundreds of millions more after it is released May 18 [2007].

Shrek consciously rebelled against the sentimental Disney hegemony of fairy-tale movies. But today the outlaw is king: parodying fairy tales has become the default mode of telling them. 2005's *Hoodwinked!* reimagined Little Red Riding Hood as a crime Rashomon, while this year's *Happily N'Ever After* sent up Cinderella. Broadway smash *Wicked* posits that the Wicked Witch of the West was misunderstood. This fall Disney (*et tu*, Mickey?) releases *Enchanted*, in which a princess (Amy Adams) is magically banished by an evil queen to modern New York City, where she must fend for herself, parodying her princess foremothers as she goes. (*Snow White's* Whistle While You Work scene is re-enacted with vermin and roaches.)

All this has been a welcome change from generations of hokey fairy tales with stultifying lessons: Be nice and wait for your prince; be obedient and don't stray off the path; bad people are just plain evil and ugly and deserve no mercy. But palace revolutions can have their own excesses. Are the rules of fairy-tale snark becoming as rigid as the ones they overthrew? Are we losing a sense of wonder along with all the illusions?

Shrek didn't remake fairy tales single-handed; it captured, and monetized, a long-simmering cultural trend. TV's *Fractured Fairy Tales* parodied Grimm classics, as have movies like *The Princess Bride* and *Ever After* and the books on which *Shrek* and *Wicked* were based. And highbrow postmodern and feminist writers, such as Donald Barthelme and Angela Carter, Robert Coover and Margaret Atwood, used the raw

---

1   From *Time Magazine*, 10 May 2007.

material of fairy stories to subvert traditions of storytelling that were as ingrained in us as breathing or to critique social messages that their readers had been fed along with their strained peas.

But those parodies had a dominant fairy-tale tradition to rebel against. The strange side effect of today's meta-stories is that kids get exposed to the parodies before, or instead of, the originals. My two sons (ages 2 and 5) love *The Three Pigs*, a storybook by David Wiesner in which the pigs escape the big bad wolf by physically fleeing their story (they fold a page into a paper airplane to fly off in). It's a gorgeous, fanciful book. It's also a kind of recursive meta-fiction that I didn't encounter before reading John Barth in college. Someday the kids will read the original tale and wonder why the stupid straw-house pig doesn't just hop onto the next bookshelf. Likewise, *Shrek* reimagines Puss in Boots as a Latin tomcat—but what kid today even reads "Puss in Boots" in the original?

This is the new world of fairy tales: parodied, ironized, meta-fictionalized, politically adjusted and pop-culture saturated. (Yes, the original stories are still out there, but they don't have the same marketing force behind them: the Happy Meals, action figures, books, games and other ancillary-revenue projects.) All of which appeals to the grownups who chaperone the movie trips and endure the repeated DVD viewings. Old-school fairy tales, after all, are boring to us, not the kids. The *Shrek* movies have a nigh-scientific formula for the ratio of fart jokes to ask-your-mother jokes; *Shrek the Third* includes a visit to a fairy-tale high school where there's a Just Say Nay rally and a stoner-sounding kid stumbles out of a coach trailed by a cloud of "frankincense and myrrh" smoke. More broadly, each movie gives Shrek and Fiona an adult challenge: in the first, to find love and see beyond appearances; in *Shrek 2*, to meet the in-laws; in *Shrek the Third*, to take on adult responsibility and parenthood (Shrek has to find a new heir to the throne of Far Far Away, or he will have to succeed the king).

Then there are the messages aimed at kids. What parent today wants to raise an entitled prince or a helpless damsel? Seeing Snow White turn from cream puff into kick-ass fury in *Shrek the Third*—launching an army of bluebirds and bunnies at the bad guys to the tune of Led Zeppelin's "Immigrant Song"—is more than a brilliant sight gag. It's a relief to parents of girls, with Disney's princess legacy in their rearview mirrors and Bratz dolls and Britney up ahead. It goes hand in hand with a vast genre of empowered-princess books (*Princess Smartypants*, *The Princess Knight*) for parents who'd rather their daughters dream of soccer balls than royal balls. As for the boys? Jocks have a rough time of it (a handsome prince is the villain of *Shrek the Third* and the buffoon in *Happily N'Ever After*), supplanted by gangly emo types—fairyland Adam Brodys. "Charming" is redefined rather than repealed—Justin Timberlake voices *Third*'s cute-boy hero Arthur—but at least that's some progress.

Tweaking fairy tales also allows moviemakers to tell stories about themselves without boring us. The *Shrek* movies are full of inside jokes (the kingdom of Far Far Away is essentially Beverly Hills; the first villain was widely seen as a stand-in for then Disney chief Michael Eisner). Fairy-tale parodies are safe rebellions, spoofing formulas and feel-good endings while still providing the ride into the sunset that pays the bills. In *Happily N'Ever After*, a wizard runs a "Department of Fairy-tale-land Security," seeing to it that each story—Rapunzel, Rumpelstiltskin, etc.—hews to the book. His bored apprentice Mambo articulates the strategy of his movie and its peers: "I just wish we could mix it up a little. Make it a little edgier! Then let 'em have their happy ending."

Sound like a formula to you? What these stories are reacting against is not so much fairy tales in general as the specific, saccharine Disney kind, which sanitized the far-darker originals. (As did *Shrek*, by the way. In the William Steig book, the ogre is way more brutal, scary and ... ogreish.) But the puncturing of the Disney style is in danger of becoming a cliché itself. The pattern—set up, then puncture, set up, then puncture—is so relentless that it inoculates the audience against being spellbound, training them to wait for the other shoe to drop whenever they see a moment of sentiment or magic. Every detail argues against seeing fairyland as something special, like the constant disposable-culture gags in *Shrek*, in which characters shop in chain stores like Versarchery and Ye Olde Foot Locker.

I feel like a traitor to my fellow parents for even saying this. These movies are made in part for me: a socially progressive, irony-friendly Gen Xer with rug rats. I thought *Hoodwinked!* and most of the *Shrek* series were hilarious, and God knows I don't want to go back to the days of suffering with my kids through a long, slow pour of Uncle Walt's wholesome syrup. But even if you ultimately reject their messages, old-school fairy tales are part of our cultural vocabulary. There's something a little sad about kids growing up in a culture where their fairy tales come pre-satirized, the skepticism, critique and revision having been done for them by the mama birds of Hollywood. Isn't irony supposed to derive from having something to rebel against? Isn't there a value in learning, for yourself, that life doesn't play out as simply as it does in fairy tales? Is there room for an original, nonparodic fairy story that's earnest without being cloying, that's enlightened without saying wonder is for suckers?

In fact, the strongest moments in *Shrek the Third* come when it steps back from the frantic pop-culture name dropping of *Shrek 2* and you realize that its Grimm parodies have become fleshed-out characters in their own right. In August, Paramount releases *Stardust*, an adaptation of a Neil Gaiman novel about a nerdy nineteenth-century lad who ventures from England to a magical land to retrieve a fallen star. The live-action movie covers many of the same themes as the ubiquitous cartoon parodies—be yourself, don't trust appearances, women can be heroic too. But it creates its own fantastic settings (a seedy witches' bazaar, a sky pirate's dirigible ship). There's a kind of surprise and unembarrassed majesty that come from minting original characters and imagery rather than simply riffing on our cartoon patrimony. In the end, that's how you make magic.

SELECT BIBLIOGRAPHY

Anthologies/Collections

Nineteenth Century and Earlier

Afanas'ev, Aleksandr, comp. *Russian Fairy Tales*. Trans. Norbert Guterman. New York: Pantheon, 1945.

Andersen, Hans Christian. *The Complete Fairy Tales and Stories*. Trans. Erik Haugaard. New York: Anchor, 1983.

Asbjørnsen, Peter, and Jorgen Moe, comps. *Norwegian Folktales*. Trans. Pat Shaw, Carl Norman. New York: Pantheon, 1982.

Basile, Giambattista. *Giambattista Basile's The Tale of Tales, or Entertainment for Little Ones*. Trans. Nancy Canepa. Detroit: Wayne State UP, 2016.

Calvino, Italo, comp. *Italian Folktales*. Trans. George Martin. New York: Pantheon, 1980.

Delarue, Paul, comp. *Borzoi Book of French Folk Tales*. Trans. Austin E. Fife. New York: Knopf, 1956.

Gonzenbach, Laura, ed. *Beautiful Angiola: The Lost Sicilian Folk and Fairy Tales of Laura Gonzenbach*. Trans. Jack Zipes. New York: Routledge, 2003.

Grimm, Jacob, and Wilhelm Grimm. *Grimms' Tales for Young and Old: The Complete Stories*. Trans. Ralph Manheim. Garden City, NY: Anchor P, 1977.

―――. *The Original Folk and Fairy Tales of the Brothers Grimm: The Complete First Edition*. Trans. Jack Zipes. Princeton, NJ; Oxford: Princeton UP, 2014.

Hearn, Michael P., comp. *The Victorian Fairy Tale Book*. New York: Pantheon, 1988.

Jacobs, Joseph, comp. *English Fairy Tales*. 1890; repr. New York: Dover, 1967.

Lang, Andrew, comp. *The Blue Fairy Book*. 1889; repr. New York: Dover, 1974. [series]

Mather, Powys, trans. *The Book of the Thousand Nights and One Night*. 4 vols. 2nd ed. London: Routledge and Kegan Paul, 1964.

Perrault, Charles. *Little Red Riding Hood, Cinderella, and Other Classic Fairy Tales of Charles Perrault*. Trans. Angela Carter. New York: Penguin, 2008.

Pitrè, Giuseppe. *The Collected Sicilian Folk and Fairy Tales of Giuseppe Pitré*. 2 vols. Trans. Joseph Russo and Jack Zipes. New York: Routledge, 2009.

Straparola, Giovanni Francesco. *The Facetious Nights of Straparola*. 4 vols. Trans. W.G. Waters. London: Society of Bibliophiles, 1901.

von Schönwerth, Franz Xaver. *The Turnip Princess and Other Newly Discovered Fairy Tales*. Trans. Maria Tatar. New York: Penguin, 2015.

Zipes, Jack D., comp. *Beauties, Beasts and Enchantment: Classic French Fairy Tales.* New York: North American Library, 1989.

_____ , ed. *The Complete Fairy Tales of Oscar Wilde.* New York: Signet, 1990.

_____ , comp. *The Great Fairy Tale Tradition: From Straparola and Basile to the Brothers Grimm.* New York: Norton, 2000.

Twentieth Century and Later

Bernheimer, Kate, ed. *My Mother She Killed Me, My Father He Ate Me: Forty New Fairy Tales.* New York: Penguin, 2010.

Block, Francesca Lia. *The Rose and the Beast: Fairy Tales Retold.* New York: Joanna Cotler Books, 2000.

Carter, Angela. *Angela Carter's Book of Fairy Tales.* Boston: Little, Brown, 2005.

_____ . *The Bloody Chamber and Other Stories.* London: Gollancz, 1979.

Datlow, Ellen, and Terri Windling, eds. *Snow White, Blood Red.* New York: Morrow/Avon, 1993. [series]

Donoghue, Emma. *Kissing the Witch: Old Tales in New Skins.* New York: HarperCollins, 1997.

Lee, Tanith. *Red as Blood, or Tales of the Sisters Grimmer.* New York: Daw, 1983.

Maitland, Sara. *The Book of Spells.* London: Michael Joseph, 1987.

Thompson, Jean. *The Witch and Other Tales Re-Told.* New York: Plume, 2014.

Critical/General

Ashliman, D.L. *Folk and Fairy Tales: A Handbook.* Westport, CT: Greenwood P, 2004.

Bacchilega, Cristina. *Fairy Tales Transformed? Twenty-First-Century Adaptations and the Politics of Wonder.* Detroit, MI: Wayne State UP, 2013.

_____ . *Postmodern Fairy Tales: Gender and Narrative Strategies.* Philadelphia: U of Pennsylvania P, 1997.

Beckett, Sandra. *Recycling Red Riding Hood.* New York: Routledge, 2002.

Blank, Trevor J., ed. *Folklore and the Internet: Vernacular Expression in a Digital World.* Logan: Utah State UP, 2009.

Bobby, Susan Redington, and Kate Bernheimer, eds. *Fairy Tales Reimagined: Essays on New Retellings.* Jefferson, NC: McFarland, 2009.

Bottigheimer, Ruth B., ed. *Fairy Tales and Society: Illusion, Allusion, and Paradigm.* Philadelphia: U of Pennsylvania P, 1986.

_____ . *Fairy Tales: A New History.* Albany: SUNY P, 2009.

Canepa, Nancy, ed. *Out of the Woods: The Origins of the Literary Fairy Tale in Italy and France.* Detroit: Wayne State UP, 1997.

Dundes, Alan, ed. *Cinderella: A Casebook.* Madison: U of Wisconsin P, 1988

_____ . *Little Red Riding Hood: A Casebook.* Madison: U of Wisconsin P, 1989.

Jones, Steven Swann. *The Fairy Tale: The Magic Mirror of Imagination.* New York: Twayne, 1995.

Joosen, Vanessa. *Critical and Creative Perspectives on Fairy Tales: An Intertextual Dialogue between Fairy-Tale Scholarship and Postmodern Retellings.* Detroit: Wayne State UP, 2011.

Lüthi, Max. *The European Folktale: Form and Nature.* Trans. John D. Niles. Bloomington: Indiana UP, 1982.

_____ . *The Fairy Tale as Art Form and Portrait of Man.* Trans. Jon Erickson. Bloomington: Indiana UP, 1984.

_____ . *Once Upon a Time: On the Nature of Fairy Tales.* Trans. Lee Chadeayne and Paul Gottwald. New York: Frederick Ungar, 1970.

Orenstein, Catherine. *Little Red Riding Hood Uncloaked: Sex, Morality, and the Evolution of a Fairy Tale*. New York: Basic Books, 2002.

Rohrich, Lutz. *Folktales and Reality*. Trans. Peter Tokofsky. Bloomington: Indiana UP, 1991.

Sumpter, Caroline. *The Victorian Press and the Fairy Tale*. Basingstoke; New York: Palgrave Macmillan, 2008.

Tatar, Maria M. *The Cambridge Companion to Fairy Tales*. Cambridge: Cambridge UP, 2015.

_____. *Off with Their Heads!: Fairy Tales and the Culture of Childhood*. Princeton, NJ: Princeton UP, 1992.

Teverson, Andrew. *Fairy Tale*. London: Routledge, 2013.

Tolkien, J.R.R. *Tree and Leaf*. Boston: Houghton Mifflin, 1965.

Warner, Marina. *From the Beast to the Blonde*. London: Chatto and Windus, 1994.

_____. *Once Upon a Time: A Short History of Fairy Tale*. Oxford: Oxford UP, 2014.

Zipes, Jack D. *Breaking the Magic Spell: Radical Theories of Folk and Fairy Tales*. 2nd ed. Lexington: UP of Kentucky, 2002.

_____. *Fairy Tale as Myth: Myth as Fairy Tale*. Lexington: UP of Kentucky, 1994.

_____. *Fairy Tales and the Art of Subversion: The Classic Genre for Children and the Process of Civilization*. 2nd ed. New York: Routledge, 2006.

_____. *The Irresistible Fairy Tale: The Cultural and Social History of a Genre*. Princeton, NJ: Princeton UP, 2012.

_____, comp. *The Oxford Companion to Fairy Tales: The Western Fairy Tale Tradition from Medieval to Modern*. Oxford: Oxford UP, 2000.

_____, ed. *The Trials and Tribulations of Little Red Riding Hood*. 2nd ed. New York: Routledge, 1993.

_____. *When Dreams Came True: Classical Fairy Tales and Their Tradition*. 2nd ed. New York: Routledge, 2007.

Brothers Grimm

Bottigheimer, Ruth B. *Grimms' Bad Girls and Bold Boys: The Moral and Social Vision of the Tales*. New Haven, CT: Yale UP, 1987.

Ellis, John M. *One Fairy Story Too Many: The Brothers Grimm and Their Tales*. Chicago: U of Chicago P, 1983.

Haase, Donald, ed. *The Reception of Grimms' Fairy Tales: Responses, Reactions, Revisions*. Detroit: Wayne State UP, 1993.

Joosen, Vanessa, ed. *Grimm's Tales around the Globe: The Dynamics of Their International Reception*. Detroit: Wayne State UP, 2014.

Murphy, G. Ronald. *The Owl, the Raven, and the Dove: The Religious Meaning of the Grimms' Magic Fairy Tales*. Oxford: Oxford UP, 2000.

Paradiz, Valerie. *Clever Maids: The Secret History of the Grimm Fairy Tales*. New York: Basic Books, 2005.

Tatar, Maria. *The Hard Facts of the Grimms' Fairy Tales*. Rev. ed. Princeton, NJ: Princeton UP, 2003.

Turner, Kay, and Pauline Greenhill, eds. *Transgressive Tales: Queering the Grimms*. Detroit: Wayne State UP, 2012.

Zipes, Jack D. *The Brothers Grimm: From Enchanted Forests to the Modern World*. 2nd ed. New York: Palgrave Macmillan, 2003.

_____. *Grimm Legacies: The Magic Spell of the Grimms' Folk and Fairy Tales*. Princeton, NJ; Oxford: Princeton UP, 2015.

Perrault and the French

Darnton, Robert. *The Great Cat Massacre and Other Episodes in French Cultural History*. New York: Basic Books, 1984.

Hearne, Betsy G. *Beauty and the Beast: Visions and Revisions of an Old Tale*. Chicago: U of Chicago P, 1989.

Jones, Christine. *Mother Goose Refigured: A Critical Translation of Charles Perrault's Fairy Tales*. Detroit: Wayne State UP, 2016.

Seifert, Lewis. *Fairy Tales, Sexuality, and Gender in France, 1690–1715: Nostalgic Utopias*. New York: Cambridge UP, 1996.

Tatar, Maria. *Secrets beyond the Door: The Story of Bluebeard and His Wives*. Princeton, NJ: Princeton UP, 2006.

Andersen

Bloom, Harold. *Hans Christian Andersen*. Philadelphia: Chelsea House, 2005.

Bredsdorff, Elias. *Hans Christian Andersen*. New York: Charles Scribner's Sons, 1975.

Zipes, Jack D. *Hans Christian Andersen: The Misunderstood Storyteller*. New York: Routledge, 2005.

Psychological

Bettelheim, Bruno. *The Uses of Enchantment: The Meaning and Importance of Fairy Tales*. New York: Alfred Knopf, 1976.

Cashdan, Sheldon. *The Witch Must Die: How Fairy Tales Shape Our Lives*. New York: HarperCollins, 2000.

Schanoes, Veronica. *Fairy Tales, Myth and Psychoanalytic Theory*. London: Routledge, 2014.

Anthropological/Folkloric/Linguistic

Aarne, Antti, and Stith Thompson. *The Types of the Folktale: A Classification and Bibliography*. Helsinki: FF Communications #184, 1961.

Degh, Linda. *Folklore and the Mass Media*. Bloomington: Indiana UP, 1994.

Dorson, Richard. *Folklore*. Bloomington: Indiana UP, 1972.

Dundes, Allan, ed. *Analytic Essays in Folklore*. The Hague: Mouton, 1975.

Gilet, Peter. *Vladimir Propp and the Universal Folktale: Recommissioning an Old Paradigm—Story as Initiation*. New York: P. Lang, 1998.

Propp, Vladimir. *The Morphology of the Folktale*. Austin: U of Texas P, 1968.

Rebel, Hermann. *When Women Held the Dragon's Tongue and Other Essays in Historical Anthropology*. New York; Oxford: Berghahn Books, 2010.

Thompson, Stith. *The Folktale*. New York: Holt, Reinhart, and Winston, 1946.

Feminist

Gould, Joan. *Spinning Straw into Gold: What Fairy Tales Reveal about the Transformations in a Woman's Life.* New York: Random House, 2006.

Haase, Donald, ed. *Fairy Tales and Feminism: New Approaches.* Detroit: Wayne State UP, 2004.

Harries, Elizabeth Wanning. *Twice Upon a Time: Women Writers and the History of the Fairy Tale.* Princeton, NJ: Princeton UP, 2001.

Kolbenschlag, Madonna. *Kiss Sleeping Beauty Goodbye.* Garden City, NY: Doubleday, 1979.

Zipes, Jack D., comp. *Don't Bet on the Prince: Contemporary Feminist Fairy Tales in North America and England.* New York: Methuen, 1986.

Images: Illustration, Film, and Television

Bell, Elizabeth, Lynda Haas, and Laura Sells, eds. *From Mouse to Mermaid: The Politics of Film, Gender, and Culture.* Bloomington: Indiana UP, 1995.

Evans, Janet, ed. *Challenging and Controversial Picturebooks.* London: Routledge, 2015.

Greenhill, Pauline, and Jill Terry Rudy, eds. *Channeling Wonder: Fairy Tales on Television.* Detroit: Wayne State UP, 2014.

Greenhill, Pauline, and Sidney Eve Matrix, eds. *Fairy Tale Films: Visions of Ambiguity.* Logan: Utah State UP, 2010.

Holliss, Richard, and Brian Sibley. *Walt Disney's "Snow White and the Seven Dwarfs" and the Making of the Classic Film.* New York: Simon and Schuster, 1987.

Meyer, Susan E. *A Treasury of the Great Children's Book Illustrators.* New York: Harry Abrams, 1987.

Nodelman, Perry. *Words about Pictures: The Narrative Art of Children's Picture Books.* Athens: U of Georgia P, 1988.

Schickel, Richard. *The Disney Version: The Life, Times, Art, and Commerce of Walt Disney.* New York: Simon and Schuster, 1985.

Zipes, Jack D., *The Enchanted Screen: The Unknown History of Fairy-Tale Films.* New York: Routledge, 2011.

_____, Pauline Greenhill, and Kendra Magnus-Johnston, eds. *Fairy-Tale Films beyond Disney: International Perspectives.* New York: Routledge, 2016.

Journals

Below are listed the major journals in which numerous articles on folk and fairy tales may be found.

Canadian Children's Literature (*CanCL*)
Children's Literature (*CL*)
Children's Literature Association Quarterly (*ChLAQ*)
Children's Literature in Education (*CLE*)
Fairy Tale Review
Horn Book
The Lion and the Unicorn (*LU*)
Marvels & Tales
Signal

Websites

These three websites provide a wealth of tales and reference materials.

www.pitt.edu/~dash/folklinks.html
www.pitt.edu/~dash/folktexts.html
www.surlalunefairytales.com

SOURCES

Afanas'ev, Aleksandr. "Vasilisa the Beautiful" from *Russian Fairy Tales*, translated by Norbert Guterman and illustrated by Alexander Alexeieff. Copyright © 1945 by Pantheon Books, copyright renewed 1973 by Penguin Random House LLC. Used by permission of Pantheon Books, an imprint of the Knopf Doubleday Publishing Group, a division of Penguin Random House LLC. All rights reserved. Any third party use of this material, outside of this publication, is prohibited. Interested parties must apply directly to Penguin Random House LLC for permission.

Andersen, Hans Christian. "The Ugly Duckling," "The Little Mermaid," and "The Emperor's New Clothes," from *The Complete Fairy Tales and Stories*, translated by Erik Haugaard. Copyright © 1974 by Eric Christian Haugaard. Used by permission of Random House Children's Books, a division of Penguin Random House LLC. All rights reserved. Any third party use of this material, outside of this publication, is prohibited. Interested parties must apply directly to Penguin Random House LLC for permission.

Beckett, Sandra. "From Traditional Tales, Fairy Stories, and Cautionary Tales to Controversial Visual Texts: Do We Need to Be Fearful?" Chapter 3 of *Challenging and Controversial Picturebooks: Creative and Critical Responses to Visual Texts*, edited by Janet Evans. Copyright © 2015 J. Evans. London & New York: Routledge. Reproduced with the permission of Taylor & Francis Books, UK.

Bettelheim, Bruno. Excerpts from "Introduction: The Struggle for Meaning," in *The Uses of Enchantment*. Copyright © 1975, 1976 by Bruno Bettelheim. Used by permission of Vintage Books, an imprint of the Knopf Doubleday Publishing Group, a division of Penguin Random House LLC. All rights reserved. Any third party use of this material, outside of this publication, is prohibited. Interested parties must apply directly to Penguin Random House LLC for permission.

Htin Aung, Maung. "The Frog Maiden," from *Burmese Folk-Tales*. Reproduced with the permission of Oxford University Press India; copyright © Oxford University Press 1948.

Lee, Tanith. "When the Clock Strikes," from *Red as Blood or Tales from the Sisters Grimmer*. New York: Daw Books, 1983. Reprinted with the permission of the Estate of Tanith Lee.

Lester, Julius. "The Death of Brer Wolf," from *The Tales of Uncle Remus: The Adventures of Brer Rabbit*. Text copyright © 1987 by Julius Lester. Used by permission of Dial Books for Young Readers, an imprint of Penguin Young Readers Group, a division of Penguin Random House LLC. All rights reserved. Any third party use of this material, outside of this publication, is prohibited. Interested parties must apply directly to Penguin Random House LLC for permission.

Lüthi, Max. "The Image of Man in the Fairy Tale," from *Once Upon a Time: On the Nature of Fairy Tales*, translated by Lee Chadeayne and Paul Gottwald. Frederick Ungar Publishing Co., 1970; Indiana University Press, 1979. Reprinted with the permission of the Estate of Lee Chadeayne in honor of his lifelong passion for languages.

Macmillan, Cyrus. "The Indian Cinderella," from *Canadian Wonder Tales*. London: The Bodley Head, 1918.

Maitland, Sara. "The Wicked Stepmother's Lament," from *A Book of Spells*. London: Michael Joseph, 1987.

McKissack, Patricia C. *Flossie and the Fox*. Text copyright © 1986 by Patricia C. McKissack. Reprinted with the permission of Dial Books for Young Readers, an imprint of Penguin Young Readers Group, a division of Penguin Random House LLC. All rights reserved. Any third party use of this material, outside of this publication, is prohibited. Interested parties must apply directly to Penguin Random House LLC for permission.

McPhail, David. "Little Red Riding Hood," from *Little Red Riding Hood: Favorite Tales from David McPhail*. Scholastic Inc./Cartwheel Books. Copyright © 1995 by David McPhail. Reprinted with permission.

The Merseyside Fairy Story Collective. "Snow White," first published in *Spare Rib* 51, 1976. Subsequently published in *Don't Bet on the Prince: Contemporary Feminist Fairy*

Tales in North America and England. Methuen Inc., and Gower Publishing, 1987; Routledge, Taylor & Francis Group, 2012.

Mitchison, Naomi. "The Fourth Pig," from *The Fourth Pig.* Princeton, NJ: Princeton University Press, 2014. Reprinted with the permission of Princeton University Press via Copyright Clearance Center, Inc.

Poniewozik, James. "The End of Fairy Tales? How Shrek and Friends Have Changed Children's Stories," from *Time Magazine,* May 10, 2007. Copyright © 2007 Time Inc. All rights reserved. Reprinted from TIME and published with the permission of Time Inc. Reproduction in any manner in any language in whole or in part without written permission is prohibited.

Sherlock, Philip Manderson. "From Tiger to Anansi," from *Anansi, The Spiderman: Jamaican Folk Tales.* Macmillan Caribbean, 1956. Reprinted with the permission of Hilary Sherlock.

Tolkien, J.R.R. "Children," from *On Fairy-Stories,* edited by Verlyn Flieger and Douglas A. Anderson. HarperCollins, 2008. Originally published in *Essays Presented to Charles Williams,* edited by C.S. Lewis. Oxford University Press, 1947. Copyright © 1947 by J.R.R. Tolkien. Reprinted in Canada with the permission of HarperCollins Publishers Ltd. "Children," from *The Monsters and the Critics and Other Essays.* Copyright © 1983 by Frank Richard Williamson and Christopher Reuel Tolkien as Executors of the Estate of J.R.R. Tolkien. Reprinted in the United States with the permission of Houghton Mifflin Harcourt Publishing Company. All rights reserved.

Tosi, Laura. "Did They Live Happily Ever After? Rewriting Fairy Tales for a Contemporary Audience," from *Children's Literature: Critical Concepts in Literary and Cultural Studies,* edited by Peter Hunt. Copyright © 2006, Routledge. Reprinted with the permission of Taylor & Francis Books UK.

Waddell, Helen. "The Woman of the Sea," from *The Princess Splendour and Other Stories.* Harmondsworth: Puffin, 1972.

Warner, Marina. "Techno-Magic & Utopian Dreams/Wishful Thinking," Chapter 9 of *Once Upon a Time: A Short History of Fairy Tale.* Oxford: Oxford University Press, 2014. Reprinted with the permission of Oxford University Press.

Illustrations

"From Traditional Tales, Fairy Stories, and Cautionary Tales to Controversial Visual Texts: Do We Need to Be Fearful?," Sandra L. Beckett:

Figure 1: Claverie, Jean. *La Barbe Bleue* by Charles Perrault and Jean Claverie. Paris: Albin Michel, 1991. Reprinted with the permission of Jean Claverie.

Figure 2: Gauthier, Alain. *Ma Peau d'Âne* by Anne Ikhlef and Alain Gauthier. Paris: Seuil Jeunesse, 2002.

Figure 3: Moon, Sarah. "Little Red Riding Hood and the Car," from *Little Red Riding Hood* by Charles Perrault and Sarah Moon. Mankato, MN: The Creative Company, 1983. Illustrations copyright © 1983 Sarah Moon. Reprinted with permission.

Figure 4: Innocenti, Roberto. "Outside, the forest is big," from *Little Red Riding Hood*, preliminary work for *The Girl in Red* by Aaron Frisch. Mankato, MN: Creative Editions, 2012. Illustrations copyright © 2012 Roberto Innocenti. Reprinted with permission.

Figure 5: Juan, Ana. *Snowhite*. Copyright © 2011, Ana Juan. Reprinted with permission.

Figure 6: Janssen, Susanne. *Rotkäppchen* by Jacob and Wilhelm Grimm and Susanne Janssen. Munich: Carl Hanser Verlag, 2001. Reprinted with the permission of Susanne Janssen.

Figure 7: Pommaux, Yvan. *John Chatterton détective*, by Yvan Pommaux. Paris: l'école des loisirs, 1994. Reprinted with the permission of l'école des loisirs.

Figure 8: Ekman, Fam. *Rødhatten og Ulven*. Oslo: Cappelen, 1985. Reprinted with the permission of Fam Ekman.

Figure 9: Vandenabeele, Isabelle. *Rood Rood Roodkapje*, by Edward van de Vendel and Isabelle Vandenabeele. Wielsbeke: Uitgeverij De Eenhoorn, 2003.

Figure 10: Gauthier, Alain. *Mon Chaperon Rouge*, by Anne Ikhlef and Alain Gauthier. Paris: Seuil Jeunesse, 1998.

Figure 11: Doré, Gustave. *Les Contes de Perrault* (*The Fairy Tales of Perrault*), by Charles Perrault and Gustave Doré. Paris: Pierre-Jules Hetzel, 1861.

Figure 12: Poncelet, Béatrice. *Les Cubes*. Paris: Seuil Jeunesse, 2003. Reprinted with the permission of Béatrice Poncelet.

Figure 13: Erlbruch, Wolf. *L'Ogresse en pleurs*, by Valérie Dayre and Wolf Erlbruch. Toulouse: Milan, 1996. Copyright © 1996 by Éditions Milan.

Figure 14: Wachs, Pierre. *Vous oubliez votre cheval*, by Christian Bruel and Pierre Wachs. Paris: Le Sourire qui mord, 1986.

Colour insert:

Figure 16: Barrett, Alan. *Beauty and the Beast* by Philippa Pearce. Longman Young Books, Longman Group, London, 1972; Prentice Hall Press, UK, 1972.

Figure 8: Browne, Anthony. *Hansel and Gretel*, copyright © 1981 by Anthony Browne. Reproduced with the permission of the publisher, Candlewick Press, Somerville, MA.

Figure 11: Dietrich, Sean. Illustration from *Hansel and Gretel: The Graphic Novel*, illustrated by Sean Dietrich. Copyright © 2008 by Capstone. All rights reserved.

Figure 20: Egnéus, Daniel. "The Wolf ran straight to Grandmother's house and knocked at the door," from *Little Red Riding Hood* by The Brothers Grimm and illustrated by Daniel Egnéus. Illustrations copyright © 2011 by Daniel Egnéus. Reprinted with the permission of HarperCollins Publishers.

Figure 18: Eidrigevičius, Stasys. *Puss in Boots*, from Charles Perrault's *Puss in Boots: A Fairy Tale*, translated by Naomi Lewis. Copyright © 1990 by NordSüd Verlag AG, Zurich/Switzerland.

Figure 6: Foreman, Michael. "Opening a Pathway to Briar Rose," in *Brothers Grimm Folk Tales*, published by Templar Publishing, 2012. Illustration copyright © 1978 Michael Foreman.

Figure 7: Hyman, Trina Schart. "The Sleeping Beauty," copyright © 1977 by Trina Schart Hyman. Reprinted with the permission of Little Brown Books for Young Readers. All rights reserved.

Figure 4: Innocenti, Roberto. "Outside, the forest is big," from *The Girl in Red* by Aaron Frisch. Mankato, MN: Creative Editions, 2012. Illustrations copyright © 2012 Roberto Innocenti. Reprinted with permission.

Figure 10: Janssen, Susanne. *Hansel und Gretel*. Edition Etre for Hinstorff Verlag GmbH, Rostock, 2007. Reprinted with the permission of Susanne Janssen.

Figure 14: Juan, Ana. *Snowhite*. Copyright © 2001, Ana Juan. Reprinted with permission.

Figure 5: Levert, Mireille. "Little Red Riding Hood Meets the Wolf," from *Little Red Riding Hood*. Toronto: Groundwood Books, 1995. Reprinted with the permission of Mireille Levert.

Figure 3: Moon, Sarah. "Little Red Riding Hood and the Car," from *Little Red Riding Hood* by Charles Perrault and Sarah Moon. Mankato, MN: The Creative Company, 1983. Illustrations copyright © 1983 Sarah Moon. Reprinted with permission.

Figure 17: Moser, Barry. *Beauty and the Beast* by Nancy Willard. San Diego: Harcourt Brace Jovanovich, 1992. Reprinted with the permission of Barry Moser.

Figure 13: Phelan, Matt. *Snow White*. Copyright © 2016 by Matt Phelan. Reproduced with the permission of the publisher, Candlewick Press, Somerville, MA.

Figure 22: Roberts, David. *Rapunzel*. Pavilion Children's Books, 2003. Reprinted with the permission of Pavilion Books Company Ltd.

Figure 9: Ross, Tony. "Hansel and Gretel," Andersen Press, 1989. Reprinted with the permission of Andersen Press, Ltd.

Figure 23: Scieszka, Jon. Excerpt from "Giant Story" from *The Stinky Cheese Man and Other Fairly Stupid Tales,* illustrated by Lane Smith. Text copyright © 1992 by Jon Scieszka; illustrations copyright © 1992 by Lane Smith. Used by permission of Viking Children's Books, an imprint of Penguin Young Readers Group, a division of Penguin Random House LLC. All rights reserved. Any third party use of this material, outside of this publication, is prohibited. Interested parties must apply directly to Penguin Random House LLC for permission.

Figure 12: Tyler, Joe and Ralph Tedesco. "Hansel and Gretel" from *Grimm Fairy Tales* (Volume 1, 4th edition). Reprinted with the permission of Zenescope Entertainment.

Figure 24: Willingham, Bill. "As sorry as I am ..." Page 15 of *Fables: Legends in Exile,* Volume 1, 2012, copyright © DC Comics. Written by Bill Willingham and illustrated by Lan Medina. Courtesy of DC Comics.

Figure 21: Zelinsky, Paul O. *Rumpelstiltskin,* retold and illustrated by Paul O. Zelinsky. Copyright © 1986 by Paul O. Zelinsky. Reprinted with the permission of Dutton Children's Books, an imprint of Penguin Young Readers Group, a division of Penguin Random House LLC. All rights reserved. Any third party use of this material, outside of this publication, is prohibited. Interested parties must apply directly to Penguin Random House LLC for permission.

The publisher has made every attempt to locate all copyright holders of the material published in this book, and would be grateful for information that would allow correction of any errors or omissions in subsequent editions of the work.

From the Publisher

A name never says it all, but the word "Broadview" expresses a good deal of the philosophy behind our company. We are open to a broad range of academic approaches and political viewpoints. We pay attention to the broad impact book publishing and book printing has in the wider world; for some years now we have used 100% recycled paper for most titles. Our publishing program is internationally oriented and broad-ranging. Our individual titles often appeal to a broad readership too; many are of interest as much to general readers as to academics and students.

Founded in 1985, Broadview remains a fully independent company owned by its shareholders—not an imprint or subsidiary of a larger multinational.

For the most accurate information on our books (including information on pricing, editions, and formats) please visit our website at **www.broadviewpress.com**. Our print books and ebooks are also available for sale on our site.

broadview press
www.broadviewpress.com

The interior of this book is printed on 30% recycled paper.